D1204824

CARD REMOVED

DATE			

92657

HB
171
.M527
Metzler, Lloyd
Appleton.
Collected papers

3 6289 0004 16344

Harvard Economic Studies / Volume 140

Portions of this volume were awarded the David A. Wells Prize for the
year 1944-45. The book is published from the income of the
David A. Wells fund.

The studies in this series are published under the direction of the
Department of Economics of Harvard University. The Department does
not assume responsibility for the views expressed.

Lloyd A. Metzler

Collected Papers
Lloyd A. Metzler

Harvard University Press
Cambridge, Massachusetts
1973

Contents

IV. Mathematical Economics and Statistics

Foreword

What makes a scholar's papers collectable? They should be scientifically important. They should reveal the action of a distinctive intellect applying itself to a series of interrelated problems. They should present lucid expositions of difficult problems that will attract generations of students (and their teachers). Lloyd Metzler's works pass each test with flying colors. It is a pleasure to bring between two covers nearly all of his scientific papers, including four not previously published.

The appearance of this volume in the Harvard Economic Studies merits a word of explanation. Metzler's doctoral thesis, "Interregional Income Generation," was accepted by Harvard University in 1942 and awarded the Wells Prize for the year 1944–45. Under the terms of the prize, it is formally handed over to its recipient only on delivery of a manuscript publishable in the Harvard Economic Studies. Over the years various Wells Prize manuscripts have dropped from sight on their way to the Studies, either because they were published in other forms or media, or because the task of making necessary revisions failed to assert successful claim on the author's time. Two of the three chapters of Metzler's thesis appeared as journal articles: the first in *Econometrica* as "Underemployment Equilibrium in International Trade" (Chapter 10 of this volume), the second as "The Transfer Problem Reconsidered" in the *Journal of Political Economy* (Chapter 2 below). Thus the prize essay now appears in print, vastly enriched by the company of Metzler's later papers, all of which have been lightly edited for consistency.

Around the time the thesis was written, a good deal of research was under way on international aspects of the Keynesian model. Metzler's study, along with Fritz Machlup's *International Trade and the National Income Multiplier*,[1] published a year later, worked out the essential properties of the foreign-trade multiplier in a two-country model. (Metzler's research on multiple markets was a later development.) The opening chapter of Metzler's thesis (Chapter 10 below) investigated the comparative statics and stability properties of a two-country world with Keynesian internal conditions. Although offering a less extensive series of comparative-statics cases than Machlup's

1. Philadelphia, Blakiston, 1943.

volume, it went much farther in considering the stability properties of the model. The results of Metzler's investigation of stability were also summarized in his review of Machlup's book.[2] A similar compact review of this discussion appears in Chapter 3 below.

The second chapter of Metzler's thesis approached the classic "transfer problem" in the context of a Keynesian two-country model. He was able to show that, when the two economies are stable in isolation, a capital transfer will always be undereffected, leaving a residual deficit in the paying country's balance of payments. This result has largely survived subsequent examinations of the question by other scholars.[3] It now appears to be agreed that the existence of a positive marginal propensity to save precludes the requiting of a transfer through income effects, at least if the transfer affects spending (on home goods and imports) in the same way as any other change in income. This justifies the contrast that Metzler drew between the Keynesian case and the classical model, in which the requiting of a transfer depends on whether or not the sum of the two countries' marginal propensities to import exceed unity, so the transfer may or may not be requited.

A general implication of Keynesian economics for the analysis of the transfer problem, brought out in Metzler's dissertation, is that there is no reason to expect spending in the two countries to be altered by just the amount of the transfer. It then becomes clear that adjustment to the transfer will depend on public policy affecting this financing. Two of Metzler's papers, not previously published, extend Keynesian transfer analysis to important special cases. "Flexible Exchange Rates, the Transfer Problem, and the Balanced-Budget Theorem" (Chapter 4) explores the case in which taxes are increased in the paying country and subsidies in the receiving country by the full amount of the transfer. The flexible exchange rate adjusts in response to the transfer, raising the exports and reducing the imports of the paying country. Metzler shows that these effects will leave national factor incomes unchanged in the paying and receiving countries, but will raise output in the paying country and reduce it in the receiving country by the amount of the transfer. This paper stands as one of the few examinations that have been made of capital transfers

---

2. *Review of Economic Statistics,* 27 (February 1945), 39–45.
3. For example, that of Harry G. Johnson, "The Transfer Problem and Exchange Stability," *Journal of Political Economy,* 64 (June 1956), 212–225, reprinted in *International Trade and Economic Growth* (London, George Allen and Unwin, 1958), Chap. 7.

under conditions of exchange-rate flexibility.[4] In "Imported Raw Materials, the Transfer Problem, and the Concepts of Income" (Chapter 3), Metzler considers the consequence for adjustment to capital transfers of the dependence of imports on the level of national output as well as income. Although it has been feared that this factor would in general make the underrequiting of a transfer more likely, he shows that no such presumption can be drawn.

The extensive final chapter of Metzler's thesis, which had not been published, dealt with financial equilibrium in the context of international capital transfers, augmenting the Keynesian income-equilibrium conditions that underlie the basic analysis of the foreign-trade multiplier with the requirement of equilibrium in the market for securities. It is not difficult to see here the genesis of his famous paper "Wealth, Saving, and the Rate of Interest" (Chapter 12 of this volume). The same factors are considered in Chapter 8, "The Process of International Adjustment under Conditions of Full Employment: A Keynesian View," read before the Econometric Society in 1960 but not published until 1968.

Metzler's later work in international economics touched upon a number of topics. One of these was the joint influence of tariffs on the terms of trade and the distribution of income, explored in two papers published in 1949 (Chapters 6 and 7). The famous Stolper-Samuelson theorem holds that a tariff tends to redistribute income by raising the real wage of the country's "scarce" factor or production used extensively in its import-competing industry. Metzler's contribution was to show that a tariff can cause sufficient improvement in the country's terms of trade to prevent this redistribution or cause it to run in the opposite direction. The country's terms of trade can improve enough that the relative *domestic* price of its import-competing good falls rather than rises, reversing the income-redistribution predicted by the Stolper-Samuelson theorem. This result survived a recent unsuccessful challenge.[5]

Metzler's contributions have also done much to advance the theory of monetary adjustments in the international economy. His 1949

4. Cf. R. G. Penner, "The Inflow of Long-term Capital and the Canadian Business Cycle, 1950–1960," *Canadian Journal of Economics and Political Science*, 28 (November 1962), 527–542; and J. G. Melvin, "Capital Flows and Employment under Flexible Exchange Rates," *Canadian Journal of Economics*, 1 (May 1968), 318–333.

5. B. Södersten and K. Vind, "Tariffs and Trade in General Equilibrium," *American Economic Review*, 58 (June 1968), 394–408; and R. W. Jones, "Comment," *American Economic Review*, 59 (June 1969), 418–424.

survey of international-trade theory (Chapter 1), a lamppost providing both support and illumination to a generation of graduate students, helped to popularize what is often known as the Robinson-Metzler condition of stability in the foreign-exchange market. Derived originally under partial-equilibrium assumptions, it has been recently suggested to hold in general equilibrium under certain assumptions.[6] In collaboration with Svend Laursen he investigated the link between the terms of trade and the level of saving in real terms, "Flexible Exchange Rates and the Theory of Employment" (Chapter 11). Their paper advanced this connection as a challenge to the argument that flexible exchange rates would insulate the level of domestic employment from disturbances emanating from the current-account balance. In this context, later discussion relegated the effect to the limbo of an empirically insignificant curiosity. The connection proved to be a theoretically intriguing one, however, and has preoccupied a generation of model-builders seeking to explore the full price- and income-effects of devaluation.

Chapter 8, "The Process of International Adjustment under Conditions of Full Employment: A Keynesian View," comprises a recent addition to the literature on interest-sensitive international capital flows in the process of international adjustment. It is one of the few to develop, at a simple level, the implications of such movements in a closed two-country model of the world economy. Its importance lies in showing, in a world of flexible money prices and fixed exchange rates, the relative roles of changes in money-price levels and the trade balance, on the one hand, and interest rates and the balance of capital movements, on the other, in responding to international disturbances.

Metzler's only empirically oriented paper to appear in this volume is "Exchange Rates and the International Monetary Fund" (Chapter 5), prepared in 1947 for the Board of Governors of the Federal Reserve System. It offered a sophisticated but practical discussion of the problems of applying the purchasing-power-parity hypothesis in setting exchange rates for the postwar period. Later studies seem to vindicate his faith in the usefulness of this tool,[7] and his comments on the relation between the over- or under-valuation of a currency and aspects of domestic and international balance anticipate some developments in

6. T. Negishi, "Approaches to the Analysis of Devaluation," *International Economic Review*, 9 (June 1968), 218–227.

7. See Leland B. Yeager, "A Rehabilitation of Purchasing-Power Parity," *Journal of Political Economy*, 66 (December 1958), 516–530.

the theory of macroeconomic policy during the subsequent decade. His discussion of the International Monetary Fund's decision to accept initial exchange rates that might lie far from their equilibrium levels correctly anticipated several difficulties that later plagued the "Bretton Woods system."

Metzler's papers on money, interest, and prices (Part II of this volume) concentrate on asset stocks and asset valuations in financial adjustment. "Wealth, Saving, and the Rate of Interest" (Chapter 12) addressed itself to the controversy over the neutrality of money by arguing that whether or not a change in the money supply alters the rate of interest and relative prices depends on whether "inside" or "outside" money creation is involved. He made use of the Pigou Effect to argue that an open-market purchase of securities, reducing financial assets below the desired level, will cause the interest rate to be bid down and increase the levels of both saving and investment. This paper led to an extensive discussion in the literature. Chapter 13 ("The Structure of Taxes, Open-Market Operations, and the Rate of Interest") deals with one line of criticism. An open-market purchase of securities reduces real wealth, it was suggested, but only because the central bank absorbs the yield of the securities it has purchased. To produce a "pure" open-market expansion of the money supply, one must suppose that taxes are reduced by the amount of this yield, in which case capitalization will simply put the same real wealth back into other hands. Metzler agrees theoretically with this criticism, but points out that only a minority of taxes in the American fiscal system are subject to capitalization.

His study of "The Rate of Interest and the Marginal Product of Capital" (Chapter 14) noted that the addition of one particular bundle of capital goods to the economy's endowment will in general alter the quasi-rents and capitalized values of other equipment in the economy. Gains in this form, he suggested, create a gap between the rate of interest received by the owners and the addition to the capital stock and the social marginal product of capital, encompassing as well the changes in quasi-rents elsewhere in the system. In a correction to this paper, however, he recognized that these changes in quasi-rents do not impose any distortion on the terms of trade between present and future consumption. This paper can perhaps best be viewed as a forerunner of the later concept of pecuniary externalities,[8] the market's

8. Tibor Scitovszky, "Two Concepts of External Economies," *Journal of Political Economy*, 62 (April 1954), 143–151.

signals of the changes in the marginal productivity of resources here and there in the economy resulting from a change in the resources committed to any one particular activity.

The papers on business cycles and economic fluctuations, Part III of this volume, contributed significantly to an undestanding of how changes in the underlying conditions of equilibrium may cause fluctuations in income as the economy adapts to such changes. Metzler's endogenous mechanism producing fluctuations results from the lag of output behind sales and the adjustment of production aiming to reach certain desired inventory levels. The 1941 article on "The Nature and Stability of Inventory Cycles" (Chapter 15) laid the groundwork for much subsequent investigation of inventory fluctuations. This paper examines the stability conditions of models combining an output-sales lag with a series of assumptions about desired inventory levels and expected sales. Metzler showed that if businessmen expect sales in the current period to equal those of the previous period, and if they try to produce enough to maintain inventories at some constant level, the reaction of income to an initial disturbance will carry it to a new stable equilibrium. If a constant level of inventories is sought and changes in sales are expected to be some multiple of past changes in sales, however, important restrictions are placed on the conditions of stability. Variation of desired inventories with expected sales, through an inventory accelerator, can impose severe limitations on the stability of the system.

In Chapter 16, a previously unpublished paper, Metzler considers the effects of introducing a process of partial adjustment over a series of periods to desired levels of inventory and output. A small coefficient of partial adjustment to desired inventory levels may convert an unstable sequence into a stable one. On the other hand, with partial adjustment of both output for sale and output for inventories, an unstable sequence cannot be converted into a stable one. Chapter 17 analyzes the effects of various values of the marginal propensity to consume, the inventory accelerator, and the coefficient of expectations on the length of the cycle as measured in production planning periods. Metzler shows that the length of the cycle varies positively with the marginal propensity to consume and the inventory accelerator, and negatively with the coefficient of expectations.

In "Three Lags in the Circular Flow of Income" (Chapter 18) Metzler argued that available data indicated the consumption-income lag was probably three months or less and the output-sales lag considerably longer. He suggested that the theory of endogenous cyclical mechanisms should therefore give more attention to the output-sales lag. In Chapter 19 Metzler urged that cyclical theories stressing unstable cumulative processes with turning points accounted for by limiting factors should give way to theories explaining turning points as inherent in the structure of the economic system. He believed that any change in underlying equilibrium conditions probably produces damped oscillations as income approaches the new equilibrium.

All but the final paper of Part IV represent a unified contribution to a problem that was later to become fundamental in a variety of fields: (*a*) of course, the multiple-sector multiplier analysis of the Keynes-Metzler type, as cultivated later by Chipman, Goodwin, and Johnson; (*b*) the so-called Metzler-Mosak-Hicks gross-substitute models, developed later by such theorists as Arrow-Hurwicz and many others; and (*c*) input-output matrices of the Leontief-Metzler-Frobenius-Minkowski type, employed later by the many writers on input-output and diagonal dominance (Sraffa, Dorfman-Samuelson-Solow, McKenzie, and many others). These nonnegative matrices, *a*, and their associated matrices, *I-a*, arise also in the statistical theory of Markov-Frechet transitional probabilities, and their elegant simplicities have been explored and extended by Solow, Morishima, and many others. Their simplicities are comparable only to that of symmetric positive definite matrices encountered in minimization theory, and Metzler early recognized that he could unify the comparative-statical stability analysis of Hicks with the dynamic stability analysis of Samuelson if it were stipulated that stability should hold regardless of the relative speeds of adjustments in the various markets.

The final paper is interesting because, before the breakthrough in simultaneous-equation estimation associated with the names of Haavelmo, Koopmans, Fisher, and other contemporaries of Frisch, Metzler had ingeniously provided a theorem about identification.

We are grateful to the various holders of the copyrights on Metzler's published papers for their kind permission to reprint them here. We hope that this collection will serve both to honor the influence that Metzler's writings have already wielded and to bring their power and clarity afresh to new generations of students and scholars.

> Alice Bourneuf, Evsey D. Domar, Paul A. Samuelson
> Richard E. Caves, Chairman
> Harvard Economic Studies

Part I | The Theory of International Trade

1 | The Theory of International Trade

The period between the First and Second World Wars was one of extraordinary and perhaps unprecedented developments in the field of international trade. The gold standard, which had been abandoned during the First World War, was never reestablished on a firm basis, and exchange rates of many countries underwent substantial fluctuations. The Great Depression of the thirties, which sharply reduced the level of output and employment in many countries, had a drastic effect upon international trade. Neither the timing nor the severity of the depression was uniform between countries, and the consequence was a serious lack of balance in the international payments and receipts of many countries. Partly to offset these discrepancies and partly to guard the dwindling markets for goods, country after country imposed additional barriers to international commerce.

Even after the general economic recovery of the late thirties had begun, the trade restrictions and special trading arrangements were for the most part retained. The Second World War was of course the occasion for much more comprehensive and complete governmental controls of international trade, but even if the war had not occurred we should have inherited an enormously complex system of trade regulations as our legacy from the unstable thirties. During the war years, it became increasingly apparent that such a complicated system would not automatically revert to a system of unregulated multilateral trade, and that any attempt to restore the old system would require constant

---

Reprinted from *A Survey of Contemporary Economics*, ed. Howard S. Ellis (Philadelphia, Blakiston, 1949), pp. 210–254. Copyright Richard D. Irwin, Inc., 1949.

international supervision and cooperation. This was the genesis of such organizations as the International Monetary Fund, the International Bank for Reconstruction and Development, and the proposed International Trade Organization. Whether these agencies will succeed in their avowed purpose of assisting in the establishment of a stable and relatively free international economic order remains to be seen. The difficulties encountered in postwar recovery and the general trend toward state intervention in economic activity have seriously complicated the problems of the new organizations.

In any event, it is not the purpose of this paper to discuss the future prospects for international trade or the future development of commercial policy. Nor do I intend to describe further the interesting history of international trade during the interwar years. This empirical inquiry has already been performed in a number of admirable studies, and it seems neither necessary nor useful to summarize the work of these able economists.[1] This paper is primarily a review or a summary of recent changes in the theory of international trade. The empirical developments are mentioned largely because of the profound influence which they have had upon economic theory. If the interwar period was a period of disturbed conditions in international trade, it was also a period of rapid change in the theory of international economics. The changes were so numerous, in fact, that it is quite impossible to summarize all of them. Nevertheless, it seems to me that the most significant of the recent developments can be classified under four main heads as follows: (*a*) the balance of payments and the theory of employment; (*b*) fluctuating exchange rates; (*c*) price theory and international trade; (*d*) the theory of tariffs. Although the discussion below is by no means exhaustive, an attempt has been made to evaluate the principal contributions in each of these four branches of international economics.

The Balance of Payments and the Theory of Employment

The revolution in economic theory which occurred in the 1930s had a profound influence upon almost all branches of economics, and

1. Perhaps the most interesting of these empirical studies are Seymour E. Harris, *Exchange Depreciation* (Cambridge, Mass., Harvard University Press, 1936); Margaret S. Gordon, *Barriers to World Trade* (New York, Macmillan, 1941); Howard S. Ellis, *Exchange Controls in Central Europe* (Cambridge, Mass., Harvard University Press, 1941); U.S. Dept. of Commerce, *The United States in the World Economy* (Washington, D.C., Government Printing Office, 1942); and League of Nations, *International Currency Experience: Lessons of the Interwar Period* (Geneva, 1944).

this was no less true of international trade than of other specialized fields. Since the new approach to economics was primarily a reconsideration of traditional ideas regarding money, interest rates, and prices, it was natural that the most important changes in international economics should have been in the monetary aspects of the subject. The revolution actually extended considerably beyond the monetary theory, however, as a later discussion of commercial policy will show.

Prior to the publication of Keynes's *General Theory*, the monetary theory of international trade had been one of the most widely accepted of economic doctrines. For more than a century and a half, English economists and others in the English tradition had believed that the monetary system operates in such a way that a country's balance of payments tends automatically toward a state of equilibrium. If one country had a deficit in its balance of payments with another, for example, it was recognized that part of its payments abroad would have to be made in gold, and it was believed that the gold movement would bring about certain price changes which eventually would restore an even balance of payments. As a result of the increased supply of money in the surplus country, and the reduced supply in the deficit country, prices and costs would rise in the former and fall in the latter. The deficit country would then become a relatively cheap market in which to buy goods, and its exports would rise while its imports declined. This process would continue, according to the classical view, until a balance between payments and receipts was again established.[2] The classical explanation of the balancing process was eventually modified to consider the influence of interest rate on capital movements, to allow for a fractional reserve banking system, to recognize the similarity between gold movements and changes in foreign balances, and in other respects as well, but in substance the theory remained essentially as it was originally developed by the early English economists.

The important feature of the classical mechanism, for the purpose of the present review, is the central role which it attributes to the monetary system. The classical theory contains an explicit acceptance of the Quantity Theory of Money as well as an implied assumption that output and employment are unaffected by international monetary disturbances.[3]

2. See, for example, John Stuart Mill, *Principles of Political Economy*, Ashley ed. (London, Longmans, 1909), bk. 3, chap. 21, sec. 4.

3. See James W. Angell, *The Theory of International Prices* (Cambridge, Mass., Harvard University Press, 1926), chaps. 3–6.

In other words, the classical doctrine assumes that an increase or decrease in the quantity of money leads to an increase or decrease in the aggregate money demand for goods and services, and that a change in money demand affects prices and costs rather than output and employment. The Keynesian revolution cast doubt upon both of these crucial assumptions. Say's Law of Markets, which had been the bulwark of both the Quantity Theory of Money and the classical theory of the balance of payments, was rejected, and the possibility of general overproduction or general unemployment was finally acknowledged. In the course of this revolution, the monetary system, regarded as a director of economic activity, was relegated to a somewhat secondary position, and economists increasingly emphasized the effects of saving and spending habits upon the circular flow of income.

After the foundations of the classical theory had crumbled, it was only a short time until a new explanation of the balancing process in international trade emerged. Although the new theory of the balance of payments was a direct outgrowth of the *General Theory*, Keynes himself had little to do with it; the first contributions were made by Joan Robinson[4] and R. F. Harrod.[5] Some of the practical as well as the theoretical implications of the new doctrine were later investigated by Haberler,[6] Salant,[7] Kindleberger,[8] Metzler,[9] Machlup,[10] and others. The essence of the new theory is that an external event which increases a country's exports will also increase imports *even without price changes*, since the change in exports affects the level of output and hence the demand for all foods. In other words, movements of output and employment play much the same role in the new doctrine that price movements played in the old. Before a detailed discussion of the relation of employment to the balance of payments, however, a brief account should be given of a number of empirical studies of the adjustment process which were published during the interwar years; for these

---

4. *Essays in the Theory of Employment* (New York, Macmillan, 1937), pt. 3, chap. 1.

5. *International Economics*, ed. 2 (London, Nisbet, 1939), chap. 5.

6. Gottfried Haberler, *Prosperity and Depression* (Geneva, League of Nations, 1940), chap. 12.

7. William A. Salant, "Foreign Trade Policy in the Business Cycle," *Public Policy*, ed. C. J. Friedrich and E. S. Mason, 2 (1941), 208–231.

8. Charles P. Kindleberger, "International Monetary Stabilization," in *Postwar Economic Problems*, ed. S. E. Harris (New York, McGraw-Hill, 1943), pp. 375–395.

9. Lloyd A. Metzler, "Underemployment Equilibrium in International Trade." This article appears as Chapter 10 of the present volume.

10. Fritz Machlup, *International Trade and the National Income Multiplier* (Philadelphia, Blakiston, 1943), passim.

studies, although carried out along classical lines, had a profound effect upon later developments in international trade theory.

Empirical Studies and the Classical Theory

At the suggestion of Taussig, several economists made detailed investigations of the balancing process under conditions of both fixed and fluctuating exchange rates.[11] In each of these studies a period of time was selected during which a particular country's balance of payments had been subjected to a disturbing influence, and the manner in which the balance of payments had adjusted itself to this disturbance was then examined. The general conclusion of most of the empirical investigations was that the balancing process had occurred largely as envisaged in the classical theory; that is, the price movements and gold movements had agreed with classical expectations. Taussig himself later made additional studies which gave further support to this view.[12] At the same time, however, some of the evidence which Taussig accumulated led him to doubt the adequacy of the classical theory. It was not that the balance of trade and the level of prices failed to conform to disturbing influences in the manner envisaged by the classical theory. Quite the contrary, they appeared to conform too well and too quickly. When Great Britain increased her capital exports, for example Taussig observed that the British balance on current account adjusted itself with amazing rapidity to the new capital position, even though both gold movements and changes in prices appeared to be relatively small.

The actual merchandise movements seem to have been adjusted to the shifting balance of payments with surprising exactness and speed. The process which our theory contemplates—the initial flow of specie when there is a burst of loans; the fall in prices in the lending country, rise in the borrowing country, the eventual increased movement of merchandise out of one and into the other—all this can hardly be expected to take place smoothly and quickly. Yet no signs of disturbance are to be observed such as the theoretic analysis previses.[13]

---

11. The best known of these studies are J. H. Williams, *Argentine International Trade under Inconvertible Paper Money, 1880–1900* (Cambridge, Mass., Harvard University Press, 1920); Jacob Viner, *Canada's Balance of International Indebtedness, 1900–1913* (Cambridge, Mass., Harvard University Press, 1924); and Harry D. White, *The French International Accounts, 1880–1913* (Cambridge, Mass., Harvard University Press, 1933).

12. F. W. Taussig, *International Trade* (New York, Macmillan, 1927), chaps. 20–25.

13. *Ibid.*, p. 239.

The smoothness and speed with which many countries' balances of payments seemed to adapt themselves to changing circumstances in the years before the First World War led Taussig to surmise that the classical theory might be an incomplete explanation of the adjusting mechanism. "It must be confessed," he said, "that here we have phenomena not fully understood. In part our information is insufficient; in part our understanding of other connected topics is also inadequate."[14] Even before the theory of employment had been developed, historical studies thus indicated that the balancing of international payments and receipts might be attributable to econimic forces not considered in the classical theory. Despite his misgivings, Taussig never abandoned the classical theory, for he could find no other explanation of the balancing process.

Meanwhile, other empirical studies were being made along entirely different lines, and these cast further doubt on the effectiveness of the price adjustments envisaged by the classical doctrine. The interwar period was a period in which extensive studies were made of the elasticity of demand for individual products, and the studies showed, almost without exception, that quantities sold were much less responsive to changes in prices than had formerly been suspected.[15] The elasticities proved in most cases to be less than unity, and in some instances they were so small as to be almost negligible. Studies of demand elasticities for imports as a whole were not made until a later date, but when they were made they confirmed the supposition which the earlier studies of individual commodities had raised, that the physical volume of imports might not be responsible to changes in prices. Hinshaw,[16] for example, estimated an elasticity of demand for imports in the United States of about 0.5, while a study of British imports[17] showed a price elasticity of approximately 0.64.

If these elasticities are representative of price elasticities in general, it is apparent that the operation of the classical mechanism is even more difficult to explain than Taussig had supposed. Not only did the trade

14. *Ibid.*

15. The pioneer work in this field was of course that of H. L. Moore and Henry Schultz. See particularly the latter's book, *The Theory and Measurement of Demand* (Chicago, University of Chicago Press, 1937).

16. Randall Hinshaw, "American Prosperity and the British Balance-of-Payments Problem," *Review of Economic Statistics*, 27 (February 1945), 4.

17. Tse-Chun Chang, "The British Demand for Imports in the Inter-War Period," *Economic Journal*, 56 (June 1946), 197.

balances move with surprising rapidity, but they moved in the expected direction despite the fact that the physical volume of imports is normally responsive only in a slight degree to changes in relative prices. In order to attribute the observed adjustments to changes in relative prices, it would in many instances be necessary to assume that demand elasticities are much higher than those which have actually been measured.

Income and the Balance of Payments

Although the empirical evidence accumulated during the interwar period has clearly indicated the need for a reconsideration of the balance-of-payments mechanism, no substantial revisions of the accepted theory were made until Keynes published his *General Theory*. Thereafter the missing link in the classical theory became almost self-evident: the rapid adjustment of a country's balance of payments which Taussig had observed, and which seemed to occur without the assistance of price changes or changes in central bank policy, was found to be largely the result of induced movements of income and employment. Suppose, for example, that country A increases its imports from B, and a deficit thus arises in A's balance of payments. The deficit may initially be financed by gold shipments or by a movement of short-term balances, but regardless of the method of financing, a more or less automatic mechanism will soon offset at least part of the initial disturbance. Income and employment will expand in the export industries of B; the demand for home goods will therefore rise in that country, and the expansion will spread from the export industries to the entire economy. As output and employment increase, country B will increase its imports from A thereby offsetting a part, or perhaps all, of the initial rise of exports to A.

This, in brief outline, is the revised theory of the balance of payments which grew out of the theory of employment. Although the new theory, in complete form, was first presented by Mrs. Robinson and by Harrod in works previously cited, its main features can be found as early as 1936 in a remarkable article by Paish.[18]

Perhaps the most important single feature of the new concept is its comparative independence of banking policy. The cumulative movements of output and employment which account for a large part of the

---

18. F. W. Paish, "Banking Policy and the Balance of International Payments," *Economica*, 3 (November 1936), 404–422.

adjustment of the balance of payments will normally be influenced only to a small extent by central bank action; to a much greater extent such income movements are a direct consequence of changes in the demand for goods and services. In the preceding illustration, for instance, if the initial surplus in country B were offset by a gold inflow into that country, the central bank might attempt to neutralize or sterilize the gold. In other words, the banking authorities might prevent the gold inflow from increasing either the reserve ratios of the banks or the amount of money in circulation. This they could easily do by selling securities. Unless domestic investment were highly sensitive to a change in interest rates, however, such action would not stop the rise of employment which was initiated in the export trades, and the adjusting process would accordingly proceed as before.

The divorcing of the modern balancing mechanism from bank policy explains why a balancing tendency between foreign payments and receipts is sometimes apparent even when banks at home and abroad are carrying out neutralizing operations. Bank policy, apart from its influence on capital movements, can affect the balance of payments only through the circular flow of income, and the relation of bank policy to the circular flow is at best tenuous and uncertain. In the words of P. B. Whale, "Since gold movements (or more generally, changes in reserves) and discount rate adjustments are displaced from their central position in the process of international price adjustment, the question of 'observing the rules of the game,' as this is ordinarily understood, loses much of its importance."[19] In short, a central bank which attempts to stabilize by offsetting rising exports with a sale of securities is not really interfering much with the "natural" balancing mechanism. But neither is it achieving much stability.

Antecedents of the Modern Theory

In the foregoing account of the balancing mechanism, the adjustment of international payments and receipts through changes in real income and employment has been referred to repeatedly as the "new" or "revised" or "modern" theory. Although this theory undoubtedly contains significant elements of innovation which justify calling it a new or modern theory, it also has, like other scientific innovations, important

19. P. B. Whale, "The Working of the Pre-War Gold Standard," *Economica*, 4 (February 1937), 31; see also League of Nations, *International Currency Experience* (reference 1), chap. 4.

antecedents. Indeed, after the publication of Viner's comprehensive studies,[20] it is now clear that even many of the English economists who are commonly regarded as members of the classical school subscribed to a theory of adjustment which differed considerably from the classical theory, and had much in common with the modern view. Ricardo, for example, believed that some disturbances to the international balance, such as an increase of agricultural imports resulted from a crop failure at home, could be rectified without gold movements and corresponding price changes.

Although his reasoning on this point was somewhat obscure, Wheatley, as Viner shows,[21] gave an account of the same type of adjustment which indicated clearly how the international accounts *might* be balanced without gold movements and price changes. Wheatley argued that if England increased her agricultural imports because of a crop failure, this in itself would increase the incomes of exporters to England, and that the ability of such exporters to purchase English goods would therefore be greater than before, even without price changes. To some extent, in other words, the balance of payments tended to adjust itself by means of changes in purchasing power at home and abroad.

A similar view was presented later (1840) by Longfield,[22] and still later (1889) by Bastable,[23] who applied this purchasing-power theory to the disturbance resulting from the payment of a loan. Bastable argued that a payment from country A to country B would automatically increase the purchasing power of the receiving country and reduce the purchasing power of the paying country. Imports of A would therefore fall while imports of B would rise, even without price changes, and Bastable believed that the paying country could thereby achieve an export surplus equal to the annual payments, without gold movements. During the interwar period, ideas similar to Bastable's appeared in the well-known theory of Ohlin[24] and other Scandinavian economists that reparations and similar transfers can be carried out by means of shifts in purchasing power, and that no price movements need occur.

All of these purchasing-power arguments sound surprisingly like the

20. Jacob Viner, *Studies in the Theory of International Trade* (New York, Harper and Bros., 1937), esp. chaps. 6 and 7.

21. *Ibid.*, pp. 295–297.

22. *Ibid.*, p. 297.

23. *Ibid.*, pp. 302–303.

24. Bertil Ohlin, "Transfer Difficulties, Real and Imagined," *Economic Journal*, 39 (June 1929), 172–178.

theory discussed earlier in the present review. What, then, is the justification for calling the adjustment through changes in income a new or modern theory? Wherein does it differ from the theories of Wheatley Ricardo, Bastable, Ohlin, and others? The difference, in my opinion, is primarily that the earlier expositions lacked a theory of employment or income, and were therefore unable to explain just how far the adjusting process could go. Some of the earlier explanations were vague and ambiguous as to the extent of income movements, while the later ones were frequently erroneous. There was a strong tendency in the later discussions, for example, to cling to the assumption that full employment prevails at all times, and to assume, therefore, that in the case of a money transfer, purchasing power is increased in the receiving country and reduced in the paying by exactly the amount of the transfer. In the words of Iversen, "the total amount of buying power in the two countries together is unchanged; only its distribution between them is changed."[25]

In the light of the modern theory of employment, it is obvious that this doctrine of the conservation of purchasing power, which was an integral part of a number of the pre-Keynesian discussions, cannot be supported. When secondary as well as primary changes in income have been taken into account, it is clear that something more than a mere shift in purchasing power has occurred; in addition there may be a net change in output and employment both at home and abroad. It is the ability to set limits to these changes in purchasing power, or at any rate to determine the conditions on which the changes depend, which distinguishes the new theory from the older shifts-of-purchasing-power doctrine. From this point of view, the theory of Bastable and Ohlin is a stepping stone to the new theory, but is not in itself a complete explanation of how balances of payments are affected by changes in income.

Limits to the Adjusting Process

If the modern theory establishes more definite limits than its predecessors to the balancing influence of income movements, what are these limits? In particular, is the theory of employment a complete explanation of the balancing process or is it only a partial explanation? In

---

25. Carl Iversen, *Aspects of the Theory of International Capital Movements* (Copenhagen, Lewin and Munksgaard, 1936), p. 232.

order to give complete answers to these questions, it would be necessary to consider the components of national income in considerable detail. The following remarks will therefore be limited to a summary of general conclusions and to a statement of the opinions of a number of economists.

The balancing process is closely related to what might be called "the fundamental income identity for an open economy." This identity states simply that, for any individual country, savings are the sum of two components: (a) net domestic investment; (b) the balance of payments on current account. Although this is an identity, being simply a definition of savings over any past accounting period, it may also be regarded as a condition of equilibrium, provided all the components are interpreted as intended savings, intended investment, and the like. Let us see how the income identity can be applied to our earlier discussion of the balance of payments between countries A and B, when this balance is disturbed by an increased demand in A for the products of B.

Consider the situation in B, the country which initially has an increase in exports. Since income rises in B, we may take it for granted that savings, interpreted in the *intended* sense, will also rise. From the savings-investment relation it follows that the sum of domestic investment plus the balance on current account must also be higher than before. Thus, net domestic investment must be higher than in the initial position, or the balance on current account must be more favorable to B, or some combination of these two must occur. Which outcome is most likely? In the earlier discussions of the balancing process by Mrs. Robinson and R. F. Harrod, there was a tendency to take the level of investment as given, and to consider only the influence of saving and consumption in the balance of payments. Under these assumptions, the balancing process is obviously incomplete. Unless domestic investment increases in B, for example, savings can remain above the previous level only to the extent that the balance on current account remains more favorable to that country. The induced rise of income in B will thus offset a part, but not all, of that country's surplus on current account.

Later discussions modified this view somewhat by showing that investment, in the short run at any rate, may depend upon the level of income, and that induced cumulative movements of income may accordingly be large enough to offset a balance-of-payments disturbance completely.[26] While some differences of opinion still exist concerning the role of induced investment, the conclusion of most economists seems to be that, except under unusual conditions, the adjustment of a country's balance of payments by means of income movements is likely to be incomplete.

Past and Future

Like the classical theory of the balance of payments, the theory which has emerged in the last ten years envisages a more or less automatic balancing mechanism. Unlike the classical theory, however, the new explanation, as we have seen, normally accounts for only a part of the adjustment and thus constitutes a theory of disequilibrium as well as a theory of equilibrium. Moreover, the cumulative movement of income at home and abroad which is the essence of the modern theory will not occur unless the disturbing influence affects the circular flow of income as well as the balance of payments. The adjustment of a country's balance of payments to speculative capital transfers or other disturbances which have no *direct* effect upon the circular flow of income is thus likely to be slow and insignificant. On the other hand, if the initial disturbance is an increase or decrease of direct investments abroad or any other event which alters the flow of income, the secondary adaptation of the balance of payments to the new conditions will probably be substantial. In this respect, as in others, the new theory differs from the classical, for the adjustment envisaged by the classical theory was much the same regardless of the nature of the initial disturbance.

Perhaps the most important difference, however, is in the nature of the adjustment itself. In the modern view, a country with a deficit in its balance of payments is likely to eliminate this deficit, in part at least, through a low level of income and employment. The conflict between domestic stability and international equilibrium, which has long been a familiar part of classical monetary theory, is thus shown to be much more important than had formerly been supposed. In an unstable world, the choice confronting an individual country is not merely between

---

26. See, for example, Metzler, "Underemployment Equilibrium" (reference 9); League of Nations, *International Currency Experience* (reference 1), chap. 4, sec. 5; and Ragnar Nurkse, "Domestic and International Equilibrium," in *The New Economics*, ed. S. E. Harris (New York, Alfred A. Knopf, 1947), chap. 21.

price stability and international equilibrium, as envisaged by the classical theory, but between stability of employment and international equilibrium. In recent years there has been a growing recognition of this conflict and the difficulties of resolving it. The necessity for international cooperation to ensure a balanced and stable rate of economic growth throughout the world has thus become increasingly apparent.

It cannot be said that much has yet been accomplished in reaching this objective. Nevertheless, a tremendous change is evident almost everywhere in the attitude of individual countries toward control of the rate of economic activity. If international planning for stability is not yet popular, many countries at least are making plans of their own for stabilizing their economies and using their resources fully. It remains to be seen how successful the new programs will be, once the prolonged period of transition from war to peace has passed. It is my own judgment, however, that most of them, while perhaps not eliminating all fluctuations of economic activity, probably will eliminate the large movements of employment which we associate with major business cycles. If so, the conditions under which international trade is carried on in the future will be entirely different from the conditions of the interwar period, and probably somewhat different also from the conditions before the First World War. Fluctuations of demand arising from movements of income will be relatively small, and resources will be largely employed, as postulated by the classical theory of the balance of payments. This means, among other things, that induced movements of output and employment, such as those which have explained a part of the balancing of international accounts in the past, will probably not be permitted in the future. We have thus reached the somewhat paradoxical result that the more successful Keynesian remedies prove to be in solving problems of domestic stability, the less need we shall have for Keynesian economics in describing international affairs.[27]

What, then, will be the mechanism of adjustment in the future? If induced changes in employment are prevented or greatly reduced, virtually the only method of balancing international accounts without resort to direct controls will be through changes in the terms of trade,

27. It is perhaps unfair to describe the modern theory of adjustment of the balance of payments as "Keynesian economics," since Keynes himself had little to do with it. The new theory is Keynesian only in the sense that it is a direct outgrowth of the theory of employment.

in other words, through the price system. This does not mean, however, that the classical mechanism of price adjustments will experience a renaissance, for countries which adopt policies to stabilize output will no doubt be equally interested in stabilizing the general level of prices and costs. It is therefore not to be expected that general price movements will supplant movements of output as regulators of the balance of payments. Although the classical theory, in the strict sense, will thus be as outmoded as the modern theory, the method of adjustment which finally evolves will probably be more nearly akin to the classical mechanism than to the modern. Even without general price and cost changes, the essential means of adjustment contemplated by the classical theory—a change in the terms of trade—can be accomplished through changes in exchange rates, and if the present trend toward widespread state control of trade is to be halted the international monetary system will have to move increasingly toward such an arrangement. Indeed in a world of high and stable employment, movements of exchange rates are virtually the only more or less automatic means of influencing international trade without resorting to direct controls. For this reason it seems appropriate to review, in the section which follows, the developments during the interwar period in the theory of fluctuating exchange rates.

Fluctuating Exchange Rates

Economic Events and Economic Theory

During the First World War, the gold standard was suspended throughout the world, and although most countries eventually returned either to the gold standard or to the gold exchange standard after the war had ended, the resumption of gold payments was a long and protracted process. Throughout most of the decade of the twenties there were accordingly substantial fluctuations in the external values of many currencies. Moreover, the process of stabilization had hardly been completed when a large part of the world once more abandoned the gold standard as a consequence of the Great Depression in the early thirties. Later, during one period in the middle thirties, currency values were relatively stable without a formal return to the gold standard, but this stability was again disrupted, this time by the United

States depression of 1937–38 and by the abnormal capital movements which preceded the outbreak of the Second World War. The interwar period was thus a period of fluctuating exchange rates; only a few years during the entire period were characterized by exchange-rate stability.[28]

It was natural, under such conditions that economists should have devoted considerable attention to the effects of exchange fluctuations and that permanent contributions should have been made, in consequence, to this particular branch of the theory of international trade. The theoretical development, however did not proceed at a uniform rate throughout the interwar years. The underlying causes of exchange fluctuations in the twenties were quite different from the causes of the later exchange movements, and the theories developed in the two periods also were different. Movements of exchange rates in the early twenties were largely an aftermath of the war. Postwar inflation had brought about marked disparities in the internal price levels of different countries, and the exchange-rate movements of this period were principally a reflection of these price movements. Indeed, inflation and the resulting price differences played such a dominant part in the determination of exchange rates during this period that a distorted theory of exchange rates enjoyed wide popularity. This was the theory of purchasing-power parity, which attributed changes in exchange rates entirely to relative movements of internal purchasing power.[29] Even at the height of its popularity, however, the parity theory was a target of severe criticism, and eventually it was almost completely discredited as an explanation of exchange rates.[30] There is no need, in a review such as this, to discuss the criticisms in detail. The inability of the parity theory to allow for shifts in international demand, for capital movements, for technological changes, or for any other events altering the terms of trade soon made it apparent that the theory was not a *general* explanation of exchange rates, but was applicable only

28. One of the best descriptions of exchange-rate movements during the interwar period as a whole is in chap. 5 of the League of Nations study cited in reference 1. For an excellent account of the exchange situation in the early thirties, see Harris, *The New Economics* (reference 26), *passim*.

29. See Gustav Cassel, *Money and Foreign Exchange after 1914* (New York, Macmillan, 1922), pp. 137–186.

30. One of the definitive accounts is that of C. Bresciani-Turroni, "The Purchasing Power Parity Doctrine," *L'Egypte Contemporaine*, 25 (May 1934), 433–464.

under special conditions.[31] There were also other criticisms of a more technical nature, such as the difficulty of selecting an appropriate index of prices or costs, but these need not concern us here.

The movement away from the parity theory was accelerated in the early thirties, when the Great Depression forced most countries off the gold standard once more, and when exchange rates were subjected to influences which clearly could not be explained by price movements alone.[32] The balance-of-payments difficulties of the depression years were principally attributable to the fact that the depression did not affect the demand for all countries' exports uniformly. Although induced movements of real income tended, to some extent, to redress the balance, as described in the preceding section, these income movements did not effect a complete adjustment.

From the point of view of economic analysis, one of the most important results of the experience with fluctuating exchange rates during the thirties was a profound skepticism concerning the effectiveness of exchange-rate adjustments in rectifying a balance-of-payments discrepancy. This skepticism was partly a consequence of certain special conditions of the thirties which are not likely to be repeated in the future, but it was also a consequence, as we shall see, of more fundamental difficulties with the balance-of-payments mechanism. Consider first the special conditions of the thirties.

The adjustment of exchange rates in the thirties was complicated both by large-scale speculative capital movements, which added to the instability of exchange rates, and by competitive devaluation, which reduced the effectiveness of depreciation for the deficit countries. Although these complications created serious doubts regarding the benefits of flexible exchange rates, neither of them presents an insurmountable obstacle to a flexible exchange system. Moreover, there are good reasons for supposing that such disturbing events, in the future, will be entirely prevented or at any rate greatly reduced. Under the Articles of Agreement of the International Monetary Fund the member

---

31. Cf. Viner, *Theory of International Trade* (reference 20), pp. 379–387. In my opinion, the criticism of the parity doctrine went too far, and the theory was rejected even for situations in which it was valid. During the twenties, for example, disparities in price movements between countries were clearly the most important influences on exchange rates, and purchasing-power parity was therefore a useful doctrine. See Lloyd A. Metzler, "Exchange Rates and the International Monetary Fund," which appears as Chapter 5 of the present volume.

32. See Harris, *The New Economics* (reference 26), *passim*, esp. chap. 4.

countries have committed themselves, in effect, to submit the question of exchange-rate adjustments to international collaboration. Changes in the par value of a currency are to be made only when necessary to correct a fundamental disequilibrium,[33] and this presumably means that a member of the Fund will not be able to devalue its currency unless it has a persistent deficit in its balance of payments.[34]

If devaluation is limited to deficit countries, the degree of such devaluation will likewise be limited largely to the amounts needed to restore equilibrium, and will not be affected, to the extent that it has been in the past, by speculative capital transfers. During the war, and even before, comprehensive exchange controls were adopted throughout the world, and up to the present time most of these controls have been retained. While controls of foreign exchange received on current account will eventually be removed under the Fund agreement, there is no commitment to remove controls of capital movements, and it is generally believed that such capital controls will continue in force. Indeed, under certain conditions the Fund itself may require a member country to adopt controls of capital exports.[35] It will be impossible, of course, to control or prevent every undesirable capital transfer, since some transfers can be disguised as export transactions. Nevertheless, the bootleg transfers which manage to evade control will clearly be much smaller and less disruptive than were the speculative capital transactions of the thirties.

The Stability of Exchange Markets

Although some of the most troublesome features of the fluctuating exchange rates during the thirties can thus probably be prevented in the future, one fundamental problem remains to be discussed before concluding that exchange-rate adjustments are an effective way of balancing international payments and receipts. Even in the absence of

---

33. Articles of Agreement of the International Monetary Fund, article IV.

34. See Ragnar Nurkse, *Conditions of International Monetary Equilibrium*, Princeton University, Essays in International Finance, 4 (Princeton, N. J., International Finance Section, 1945); see also Gottfried Haberler, "Currency Depreciation and the International Monetary Fund," *Review of Economic Statistics*, 26 (November 1944), 178–181; and Alvin H. Hansen, "A Brief Note on 'Fundamental Disequilibrium,'" *Review of Economic Statistics*, 26 (November 1944), 182–184.

35. Article VI, sec. 1(a) of the Articles of Agreement provides that "a member may not make net use of the Fund's resources to meet a large or sustained outflow of capital, and the Fund may request a member to exercise controls to prevent such use of the resources of the Fund."

speculative transactions there is some doubt as to whether currency depreciation, in the short run at least, can eliminate or reduce a deficit in a country's balance of payments. Exchange-rate movements affect the principal items in a country's balance of payments—exports and imports—primarily by altering the ratio of domestic to foreign prices, and if elasticities of demand are small, such relative price movements may be ineffective or may even affect the balance of payments adversely. In other words, the questions which were asked in an earlier section concerning the operation of the classical gold-standard mechanism under conditions of inelastic demand must be asked again with regard to fluctuating exchange rates.

In classical and neoclassical economics the possibility of exchange fluctuations having a perverse effect was seldom if ever discussed, but during the interwar period the question assumed increasing importance. Empirical investigations, on the one hand, revealed that price elasticities of demand were much smaller than had usually been assumed; and on the other hand, the experience of certain countries with depreciation, particularly producers of primary products, led these countries to doubt the effectiveness of this method of increasing the value of exports. The possibility that flexible exchange rates might be inherently unstable, a fall in the price of a currency increasing rather than reducing that country's deficit, was thus widely discussed, and an important contribution to the theory of exchange stability was gradually developed. Before considering the part played by individual economists in this development, however, let us look briefly at the present status of the theory itself.

Stability of market exchange rates, like the stability of any price system requires that a fall in the price of a particular currency shall reduce the excess supply of that country's currency on the foreign-exchange markets, or that a rise in price shall reduce excess demand. A theory of exchange stability, based upon this principle, was developed during the interwar years, but the theory remains in a relatively elementary state. It is customary, and indeed necessary in the incomplete state of our knowledge, to discuss the effects of depreciation for the simplified case of two countries trading in only two commodities. Even with this simplification the theory of exchange stability, as it was worked out during the interwar period, remains somewhat complicated. Since most of the basic conclusions are simple, however, it seems better to state these conclusions in the form of a few categorical remarks than to present the cumbersome algebra. In what follows, the terms "exports" and "imports" will be understood to include all of the items in a country's foreign receipts and payments on current account.

If the demand for both exports and imports is inelastic, depreciation normally reduces a country's foreign-exchange receipts as well as its disbursements. The physical volume of exports is increased, of course, but the increase in volume does not compensate for the decline in foreign price, and the foreign-exchange value of exports accordingly declines. With respect to imports, both the physical volume and the foreign price decline to some extent, and depreciation thus reduces expenditures of foreign currency no matter how small the elasticity of import demand may be. The final effect upon a country's balance of payments therefore depends upon the magnitude of the decline in the foreign value of exports compared with the decline in the value of imports. The balance of payments will not be improved unless the value of imports falls more than the value of exports. While it is conceivable that this may occur even when the demand for both exports and imports is inelastic, it is not likely to occur if such elasticities are exceedingly small.

Most economists who have considered the problem of exchange stability have presented what might be called an "elasticity of the balance of payments." Consider only two countries, Y_1 and Y_2, and let η_1 and η_2 be the elasticities of demand for imports in the two countries. Similarly, let e_1 and e_2 be the elasticities of supply of exports. If the discrepancy between exports and imports is small, relative to the total value of foreign trade, it can easily be shown that a devaluation of the currency of either country in the proportion K will bring about a change, positive or negative, in that country's balance of payments on current account, which has the following value, relative to the value of exports:

$$K\left\{\frac{\eta_1\eta_2(1 + e_1 + e_2) + e_1e_2(\eta_1 + \eta_2 - 1)}{(\eta_1 + e_2)(\eta_2 + e_1)}\right\}.$$

The foreign-exchange market is obviously unstable unless the expression in brackets is positive, for exchange stability requires that depreciation must increase a country's net supply of foreign exchange. If the supply schedules of exports are positively sloped while the demand schedules for imports are negative, all of the elasticities of supply and demand in the above expression will be positive.[36] From this it follows that the elasticity of the trade balance cannot be negative unless $\eta_1 + \eta_2 - 1$ is negative and large. A sufficient condition for stability is this that the sum of the two demand elasticities shall be greater than unity. Even if this sum is smaller than unity, the elasticity of the trade balance may still be positive if the supply elasticities e_1 and e_2 are sufficiently small.

Since stability depends upon supply elasticities as well as demand elasticities, it may be useful to consider two limiting cases. First, if exports are produced under constant supply prices, as they are for many manufactured products, both e_1 and e_2 are infinite, and the elasticity of the balance of payment becomes $\eta_1 + \eta_2 - 1$. The minimum requirement for stability in this case is thus that the sum of the two demand elasticities shall exceed unity. At the other extreme, where the supply of exports is completely inelastic, as it is in short run for certain agricultural products, the elasticity of the balance of payments is always positive and has a value of unity, regardless of the demand elasticities. Under such conditions, depreciation always improves a country's balance of payments no matter how inelastic the demands for imports may be.

The foregoing conclusions are the principal technical results of the interwar discussion of exchange stability. When we attempt to apply these results to actual problems and to form a judgment as to the effects of exchange-rate movements, we are confronted, unfortunately, with a serious lack of empirical evidence. Almost no information is available concerning supply elasticities, and estimates of demand elasticities are available for only a few countries. Nevertheless, such information as we do have indicates rather small demand elasticities—estimates of 0.5 for the United States and 0.64 for the United Kingdom have already been mentioned. If such elasticities are typical, we are forced to conclude, I believe, that fluctuations of exchange rates are not likely, in the short run at least, to bring about an appreciable improvement in a country's balance of payments. But perhaps this is too pessimistic. It is no doubt true that the demand for imports is frequently inelastic, but in the short run the same is true of the supply of exports, particularly of agricultural exports, and the theory of exchange stability discussed above has shown that inelastic export supplies may conceivably

---

36. Demand elasticities are here defined, in the Marshallian manner, as $-dx/dp \cdot P/x$, whereas supply elasticities are defined as $dx/dp \cdot P/x$ without the change in sign.

compensate for the unfavorable effects of inelastic demand. Even if the reaction of the balance of payments is favorable to the depreciating country, however, it is likely to be small in magnitude. If the demand for imports is highly inelastic, as it normally is in the short run, the elasticity of the balance of payments will likewise be inelastic, unless the supply of exports is completely unresponsive to changes in price. A small change in the balance of payments, relative to the value of exports, may therefore require a very large proportionate change in exchange rates.

If we consider the problem over a longer period of time, the prospects for exchange depreciation are more promising. In the short run the demand for imports is inelastic primarily because both producers and consumers cannot rapidly adapt their purchasing habits or methods of production to a change in relative prices. In the long run, however, the possibilities of substitution between domestic and foreign products or raw materials is considerably greater. It seems probable, therefore, that the long-run elasticity of demand for imports in most countries is larger than the statistical evidence, based upon short-run conditions, would indicate. If a country with a balance-of-payments deficit depreciates its currency, a considerable improvement in its balance of payments may eventually occur, even though the immediate effects are small. During the interwar years, the long-run influences were for the most part nullified by competitive devaluation; hardly any of the deficit countries had an opportunity to test the effects of cheaper currency over a protracted period of time. The interwar experience therefore gave a somewhat distorted view of the effects of depreciation.

History of the Stability Discussion

The foregoing account of exchange fluctuations and the balance of payments has been presented without any reference to the economists who were responsible for this line of thought. Actually, the conditions of exchange stability discussed above were discovered independently during the interwar period by three different economists. So far as I am aware, the correct conditions of exchange stability appeared first in the *Economic Journal* of 1920, in a brief and unfortunately neglected note by C. F. Bickerdike.[37] At the time the note was published, the pound sterling was an inconvertible currency. Currency controls which had been

37. "The Instability of Foreign Exchange," *Economic Journal*, 30 (March 1920), 118–122.

introduced during the war were removed in the early part of 1919, and as a result the dollar price of the pound sterling declined sharply, from $4.76 in February of that year to $3.81 in December. A large part of this depreciation was attributable to the abnormal British demand for imports at the end of the war, and to the discrepancy which had developed during the war between the British and American price levels.[38] Nevertheless, the violence of the decline in the price of sterling led to a considerable amount of discussion in the United Kingdom as to whether free exchange markets for inconvertible currencies were not inherently unstable. In other words, the British began to doubt that currency depreciation would reduce the deficit in their balance of payments, and suspected, on the contrary, that such depreciation might only make the situation worse.

Bickerdike's note was, to my knowledge, the first scientific expression of these doubts. Bickerdike derived a formula for the relation between depreciation and the balance of payments which was essentially the same as the one given above, and he then gave a pessimistic interpretation to his results:

With the prospect of inconvertible paper money in many countries for a considerable time, it is important to recognize that a high degree of instability of exchange rates is almost inevitable, and is not solely due to the continual increase of such money to which Governments have been obliged to resort. The question may be looked at from the point of view of very short periods, such as day to day, or rather short periods, such as a year, or over considerable periods of years. In each case a consideration of the circumstances leads to the conclusion that a high degree of instability is to be expected with inconvertible paper currencies.[39]

Bickerdike pointed out, as we have shown above, that in the short run the foreign and domestic elasticities of demand are likely to be small, and that modest balance-of-payments deficits may therefore produce violent changes in exchange rates. It is perhaps arguable, in this regard, that he did not attach sufficient importance to the stabilizing influence of inelastic short-run export supply. In any event, his work was largely forgotten after the postwar period of exchange fluctuations had ended, and the subject was not revived again until the thirties.

38. In 1919, the British wholesale price index stood at 242 (1913 = 100), compared with an index of 206 for the United States (League of Nations, *Statistical Yearbook*).
39. Bickerdike, "Instability of Foreign Exchange" (reference 37), p. 118.

The second presentation of the theory of exchange stability was in Mrs. Robinson's well-known essay on the foreign exchanges, published in 1937 at the end of another period of fluctuating exchange rates.[40] Although Mrs. Robinson's method of presentation was somewhat different, her analytical results were the same as Bickerdike's, and she reached similar conclusions. She placed more emphasis than had Bickerdike, however, on the stabilizing effects of low supply elasticities. She pointed out, for example, that the inelasticity of the Australian wool supply was an important factor in the benefit which that country derived from depreciation in 1931.

The third treatment of the subject of exchange stability was by A. J. Brown.[41] Except for a complication introduced by the presence of imported materials in exports,[42] Brown's analytical results were the same as those of Bickerdike and Mrs. Robinson. His interpretation of the results, however, was more optimistic. He argued, in particular, that the foreign elasticity of demand for British exports is likely to be high, since Britain is competing with other countries in these foreign markets, and depreciation would enable her to take customers away from her rivals. This is a question of considerable importance for the theory of exchange rates, and it is a question which, in my judgment, has not been satisfactorily answered. It is frequently said, by analogy with the theory of perfect competition, that a country which is small, or a country whose exports constitute a small part of the world market, can improve its balance of payments by means of depreciation, since the demand for this single country's products will normally be highly elastic.[43] From this it is then sometimes concluded that discussions of exchange stability which consider only two countries involve a pessimistic bias, and that if a world economy consisting of many countries were taken into account the probability of exchange stability would be appreciably greater.

Graham raised the same point in a slightly different way in two articles in the *Quarterly Journal of Economics*.[44] Although he did not state whether

40. Robinson, *Theory of Employment* (reference 4), pp. 188–201.
41. "Trade Balances and Exchange Stability," *Oxford Economic Papers*, 6 (April 1942), 57–76.
42. His treatment of raw materials contained an error. He argued that a high proportion of foreign raw materials in exports is a stabilizing factor. Although space does not permit a demonstration here, it can be shown that this is incorrect, and that the contrary is true.
43. See, for example, *The New Economics* (reference 26), pp. 62–66.
44. Frank D. Graham, "The Theory of International Values Re-examined," *Quarterly Journal of Economics*, 38 (November 1923), 54–86; and "The Theory of International Values," *Quarterly Journal of Economics*, 46 (August 1932), 581–616.

he was considering a system of flexible exchange rates or the classical gold-standard mechanism, his argument is applicable to either case, since he dealt with the barter or reciprocal-demand diagrams of neo-classical economics. He argued that the classical analysis in terms of two commodities and two countries exaggerated the instability of the terms of trade. With a wide variety of exports, or with several countries participating in trade, Graham believed that the terms of trade, or the exchange rates, would be confined within rather narrow limits, through the substitution of the products of one country for those of another. In his own words, "any alteration in the rate of interchange will affect the margin of comparative advantage of some country in the production of some one of the commodities concerned, will bring that country in as an exporter where formerly it was an importer, or as an importer where formerly it was an exporter, according as the terms of trade move one way or the other."[45]

While these substitution effects on the supply side undoubtedly exert a stabilizing influence, it seems to me that Graham has overstated his case. The mere existence of a large number of trading countries or a large number of commodities will not stabilize the exchange markets unless there is a wide variation in cost conditions among the different countries. In other words, competition, by itself, is no guarantee of stability. Suppose, for example, that three countries, B, C, and D, were in close competition in the import market of A. The world demand for the products of any one of these countries would then be highly elastic; if B depreciated, for instance, she could thereby increase her exports to A at the expense of C and D. But this would involve a deterioration in the balances of payments of C and D which, in turn, would normally lead to exchange adjustments in these latter countries, and when all such secondary adjustments have been taken into account it is by no means clear that the initial depreciation by B would have reduced the deficit in that country's balance of payments. In order that substitution between products shall stabilize the exchange markets, it is not only necessary that B, C, and D shall be in close competition in A, but also that A shall be in close competition with at least one of these countries in the markets of a third country.

Graham was well aware of this fact, but he believed that the type of "linked" competition which he postulated in his numerical examples

45. Graham, "International Values Re-examined" (reference 44), p. 86.

was fairly common in the actual world. In other words, he felt that a number of countries would always change from exporters to importers of particular commodities with slight movements in the terms of trade. With the world divided as it has been in the past between exporters of raw materials and exporters of manufactures, Graham's supposition of continuous variation seems to me too optimistic. Indeed, our experience during the Great Depression has shown that enormous deterioration can occur in the terms of trade of an agricultural country without materially altering the character of that country's exports or imports. The substitution effects which Graham discusses are thus slow to occur and frequently do not take place rapidly enough to offset the adverse effects of low elasticities of demand.[46] In the short run therefore, and perhaps even over periods of time as long as five to ten years, low elasticities of demand may be a serious source of instability in foreign-exchange markets, even with a large number of countries competing in world markets.

Adjustment of Exchange Rates in the Future

Both the interwar experience with fluctuating exchange rates and the theory of exchange stability which emerged during the interwar years have clearly shown that adjustments of exchange rates are not likely, in the short run, to be an efficient or effective means of eliminating a deficit or a surplus from a country's balance of payments. If the demand for imports is inelastic, as it appears to be in many countries, currency depreciation may have an insignificant or even a perverse effect upon a country's balance of payments. Considering the low price elasticities which have been found in most empirical studies of demand, it seems probable that depreciation, in the short run, cannot improve a country's trade balance unless the inelastic demand for imports is matched by a correspondingly inelastic supply of exports. Even in this case the elasticity of the trade balance will probably be small, and a substantial movement of exchange rates may therefore be required to eliminate rather modest deficits. In other words, over comparatively short periods of time, movements of exchange rates are not an efficient means of allocating resources between foreign and domestic use.

This fact became increasingly apparent in both theory and practice during the interwar years, and it has now been explicitly recognized in

---

46. In his second article, Graham recognized this possibility and conceded that the classical reciprocal demand equations, for the short run, might have considerable validity.

the plans and institutions which have been developed for international trade in the future. Under the Articles of Agreement of the International Monetary Fund, exchange rates are stabilized, and exchange adjustments are to be made only occasionally in response to a fundamental disequilibrium in a country's balance of payments. In the short run, deficits are to be met by the use of foreign balances or, under the proposed International Trade Organization,[47] by the direct control of imports. While this procedure is clearly more realistic than some of the earlier proposals for a flexible exchange system, there is a danger that in recognizing the limitations of exchange adjustments we shall overlook their benefits. In the long run, when time has been allowed for the substitution of one method of production for another, and when consumers have had an opportunity to adjust their spending to a change in relative prices at home and abroad, demand elasticities for imports will obviously be considerably greater than the elasticities computed for the interwar period. Movements of exchange rates are therefore likely to have a significant ultimate effect upon a country's balance of payments even though the immediate effects are small. The problem which confronts us today is how to preserve the long-run position of exchange adjustments while frankly recognizing the short-run limitations. To solve this problem, we must prevent the direct controls, which may be necessary in the short run, from becoming frozen into a permanent system of trade regulations.

Price Theory and International Trade

Among economists, the interwar period will no doubt be remembered most vividly as the period of the Great Depression and the closely related revolution in the theory of employment. Even without the Keynesian revolution, however, the period would have been one of extraordinary growth in economics, particularly in the field of general price theory; several important discoveries were made, during the interwar years, in such diverse subjects as the theory of consumer's choice, the theory of production, and the theory of monopoly and competition. Since price theory, or the theory of value, has always been intimately associated with international economics, it was not surprising that many

---

47. Havana Charter for an International Trade Organization, United Nations Conference on Trade and Employment, held at Havana, Cuba, November 21, 1947 to March 24, 1948. Final Act and Related Documents (Havana, 1948), articles 13, 14, 15, and 23.

of the innovations in price theory were eventually applied to the special problems of international trade. The classical theory of the international price system was thus somewhat modified and modernized. Despite these modifications, however, many of the conclusions which the English economists had reached with more antiquated equipment remained essentially unchanged. Because of space limitations, it is impossible to consider all of the recent changes in the theory of international prices. The following discussion is therefore limited to the innovations in three broad fields: the theory of demand, the theory of income distribution, and the theory of general equilibrium.

The Theory of Demand and the Gains from International Trade

The theory of demand, or the theory of consumer's choice, enters into international economics primarily in the discussion of the gains from international trade. In the classical theory, the benefit which a country derived from specialization and trade was measured by the difference between the international rate of exchange of commodities and the rate which would have prevailed in the absence of international trade.[48] In other words, the gain from trade was an objective quantity, indicating the saving in resources from specializing and trading rather than producing all commodities at home. One of Mill's great achievements, of course, was to show how the gain from trade, thus measured, is determined by conditions of demand both at home and abroad.[49] Although Mill did not go beyond this conception, and did not attempt to relate his demand schedules to underlying utilities, he was nevertheless able to reach conclusions with respect to commercial policy which require very little modification even today.

It remained for Marshall to apply the utility concept to international demand, and to measure the gain from trade by means of his well-known theory of producer's and consumer's surpluses.[50] This refinement, however, was not revolutionary, for Marshall's conclusions tended, in the main, to confirm those of Mill. Subsequent developments with regard to demand theory consisted principally in discarding the concept of measurable utility and substituting ratios of marginal utilities. With this

48. See David Ricardo, *Principles of Political Economy and Taxation*, Gonner ed. (London, Bell, 1891), chap. 7.
49. John Stuart Mill, *Essays on Some Unsettled Questions of Political Economy*, ed. 3 (London, Longmans, 1877), pp. 1–21.
50. Alfred Marshall, *Money, Credit, and Commerce* (London, Macmillan, 1923), appendix J.

innovation, attempts to measure the total gains from trade by means of Marshall's consumer's and producer's surpluses were discarded, but once more the fundamental principles remained largely intact. Prior to the interwar period, the principal modifications of the classical concept of "gains from trade" thus consisted primarily in changes in the theory of demand. On the side of production, the labor theory of value, although largely discredited in general price theory, continued to be employed in the theory of international trade.[51]

Although Bastable had earlier altered the classical theory of production to some extent by introducing diminishing returns into his theory of international trade,[52] perhaps the principal innovation in this regard was made by Haberler, who employed a production substitution curve to indicate the possible combinations of quantities of two goods which could be produced with given quantities of the factors of production. This curve was defined in such a way that its slope at any given point represented the ratio of the marginal costs of the two products.[53] Haberler then demonstrated that the gains from international trade could be indicated, if not measured, by means of his production substitution curves. Leontief later made this idea more precise by combining the production substitution curve with a system of indifference curves.[54]

The principal advantages of the new approach, as Haberler pointed out, were, first, that it dispensed with the labor cost or real cost theory of value and, second, that it enabled one to consider a number of different factors of production simultaneously. Viner, however, argued that these advantages were illusory, and that the substitution curve concealed a number of important problems. In particular, he attacked the assumption of a fixed quantity of factors of production which is implied in the substitution curve. He insisted that the substitution curve could not be accepted as a fixed curve, determined by technological conditions, because the amount of each of the factors of production was not fixed but depended upon its price. The latter, in turn, was influenced by

51. See, for example, F. Y. Edgeworth, *Papers Relating to Political Economy* (London, Macmillan for Royal Economic Society, 1925), vol. 2, pp. 42–45; also Taussig, *International Trade* (reference 12), pt. 1.

52. C. F. Bastable, *The Theory of International Trade*, ed. 4 (London, Macmillan, 1903), pp. 29–30.

53. Gottfried Haberler, *The Theory of International Trade* (London, William Hodge, 1936), pp. 175–182.

54. W. W. Leontief, "The Use of Indifference Curves in the Analysis of Foreign Trade," *Quarterly Journal of Economics*, 47 (May 1933), 493–503.

international trade.[55] In short, Viner argued that if the supply of the factors of production can be varied, the "real cost" of supplying such services must be taken into account along with the utility of commodities, in measuring the gains from trade. A similar objection was raised with regard to the use of indifference curves, but this is an older argument and is perhaps a less distinctive contribution of Viner than his discussion of real costs. The essence of the argument is that indifference curves for a country as a whole depend not only upon the amounts of the commodities but upon their distribution between different individuals, and since international trade affects the distribution of income it also produces a shift in the community indifference curves.

Considering these logical flaws in the theory of international trade, it is natural to inquire what remains of the concept of gains from international trade. If the assumption of fixed quantities of resources is rejected, and if it is impossible to derive meaningful indifference curves for a country as a whole, in what sense can we say that international trade contributes to welfare? Answers to these questions were given in 1939 by Samuelson, who demonstrated that even without the restrictive classical and neoclassical assumptions international trade involves a potential, if not an actual, economic gain to all participating countries.[56] Samuelson's argument consisted essentially in proving that, if trade is opened between countries, each country, if it chooses to do so, can obtain more of every commodity while performing less of every productive service. Although no objective measure can be given for the total gain in this case, it is nevertheless clear that an increase of the quantity of every commodity and a decrease in the amount of every type of work performed represents an improvement of welfare. In this sense, international trade involves a gain for all countries. Samuelson was careful to point out that his demonstration did not imply that completely unrestricted trade is the optimum position for all countries. His argument, on the contrary, was restricted to the proposition that some degree of trade, *however restricted or unrestricted it may be*, is necessarily better for all countries than no trade at all.[57] The modern conception of the gains from trade thus provides no answer to the problem of free trade vs

55. Viner, *Theory of International Trade* (reference 20), pp. 516–526.
56. Paul A. Samuelson, "The Gains from International Trade," *Canadian Journal of Economics and Political Science*, 5 (May 1939), 195–205.
57. In a reflective and perhaps nostalgic mood, an economist once remarked that the argument over whether some trade is necessarily better than no trade at all reminded him of a favorite cliché of his college days: "Prohibition is better than no liquor at all."

protection. It simply shows that protection, if carried to the point where all trade is eliminated, will reduce welfare, compared with any intermediate position.

International Trade and the Distribution of Income

We have argued above that new developments in price theory have refined but have not fundamentally altered the classical concept of the gains from international trade. In one respect, however, the application of innovations in price theory to the special problems of international trade has been more revolutionary. Although the classical theory gave a good explanation of the gains which international trade brings to a country as a whole, the traditional theory was never able to explain adequately how these gains are distributed between different factors of production or between different industrial groups. In other words, the classical theory could not explain the relation of international trade to the distribution of income. The clarification of this relation during the interwar period was therefore a major achievement in international economics.

It can hardly be said that the classical economists were entirely unaware of the influence which foreign trade can exert upon the distribution of a country's income. The later development of the classical theory itself was to a considerable extent an outgrowth of the controversy in England over the Corn Laws, and one of the principal issues in this controversy was the conflict of interests between owners of agricultural land and industrialists. With the help of the Ricardian theory of rent, the English economists of the nineteenth century were able to show clearly that tariff reductions in a country (such as England) importing agricultural products could reduce the landowners' share of the national income.[58] But despite their insight into this particular problem, they never succeeded in integrating their international economics with a general theory of distribution. This is hardly surprising, for until Clark, Marshall, Wicksteed, and others had generalized the Ricardian law of diminishing returns into a law of variable proportions for all factors of production, no completely general theory of distribution was available.[59] Even after the theory of distribution had been discovered there was a considerable lag in applying it to international problems, and the theory

58. Mill, *Principles of Political Economy* (reference 2), bk. 5, chap. 4, sec. 5.
59. George J. Stigler, *Production and Distribution Theories* (New York, Macmillan, 1941), *passim*, esp. chap. 1.

of distribution did not become a systematic part of international economics until the interwar period of the present century.[60]

The pioneer work was a Swedish essay of 1919 by Heckscher.[61] Because of language difficulties, this essay was generally neglected by English and American economists, but it is now recognized as one of the first contributions to an important development in international economics. Heckscher's contribution consists essentially in explaining the flow of international trade in terms of the relative scarcity or abundance of different factors of production. The classical economists had explained the flow of trade by means of their law of comparative advantage, but the fact of comparative advantage itself had been accepted more or less without explanation. By using the generalized theory of production—the doctrine of marginal productivity—Heckscher was able to show that in many instances the advantage which a country enjoys in the production of a particular commodity is attributable to a large supply, relative to other countries, of the factor or factors of production which are most important in that commodity. In other words, if country A has more land per laborer than country B, rents, relative to wages, will be lower in the former country than in the latter. Country A will therefore have a comparative advantage in wheat and other products requiring much land and little labor, while country B has a comparative advantage in manufactures.

Although this proposition may now seem self-evident, it nevertheless represented a major improvement in the theory of international trade, for it opened the door to a systematic treatment of the relation between international trade and the distribution of income within a single country. Thus, by demonstrating how international trade increases the demand for the factors of production which a country has in relative abundance, while reducing the demand for its relatively scarce factors, Heckscher also showed that international trade has a tendency to equalize the *relative* returns to land, labor, and capital, throughout the world.

60. In his *Theory of International Trade* (Dublin, Hodges, Figgis, 1887), C. F. Bastable had included a chapter on "The Influence of Foreign Trade on the Internal Distribution of Wealth," but his discussion did not go much beyond that of the classical economists. See also Simon N. Patten, *The Economic Basis of Protection* (Philadelphia, Lippincott, 1890), chap. 5.

61. Eli F. Heckscher, "The Effect of Foreign Trade on the Distribution of Income," *Ekonomisk Tidskrift*, 2 (1919), 1–32. For an English version of Heckscher's paper, see American Economic Association, *Readings in the Theory of International Trade* (Philadelphia, Blakiston, 1949), chap. 13.

The full significance of this conclusion will become apparent in our later discussion of the theory of tariffs.

Heckscher's analysis concerning the relation of comparative advantage to relative quantities of the factors of production, and his conclusion that international trade has an equalizing tendency upon relative factor prices, later became the basis for the well-known treatise of Ohlin.[62] Ohlin modified and refined the Heckscher theories in several respects. Among other things, he considered the possibility that a change in relative factor prices, brought about by international trade, might eventually alter the available supply of some of these factors.[63] He also took account of the complications which arise when more than two factors of production are considered, and when relations of complementarity exist among some of the factors.[64] Apart from such complications, however, Ohlin's conclusions were in substantial agreement with those of Heckscher.

General Equilibrium

To complete our discussion of price theory and international trade, a word should be said about two studies in the field of general equilibrium. The classical theory, in its rigorous form, dealt only with the problem of two countries trading in two commodities, and subsequent revisions or refinements of the classical theory have seldom gone beyond this simple framework. Even the work of Ohlin, which is sometimes considered as a more general approach, is best understood in the classical context; that is, the Heckscher-Ohlin conclusion can be most clearly stated and most rigorously demonstrated if the theoretical scheme is limited to two countries, two commodities, and two factors of production. The only rigorous attempts, so far as I am aware, to develop a completely general approach to international economics, are the studies by Yntema[65] and Mosak.[66] Yntema's work appeared in 1932, and the work of Mosak, which he regards as a sequel to Yntema's book, was published twelve years later.

Except for their greater degree of generality, both of these books

62. Bertil Ohlin, *Interregional and International Trade* (Cambridge, Mass., Harvard University Press, 1933).

63. *Ibid.*, chap. 7.

64. *Ibid.*, pp. 97–99.

65. Theodore O. Yntema, *A Mathematical Reformulation of the General Theory of International Trade* (Chicago, University of Chicago Press, 1932).

66. Jacob L. Mosak, *General-Equilibrium Theory in International Trade*, Cowles Commission Monograph No. 7 (Bloomington, Ind., Principia Press, 1944).

adopted a distinctly classical point of view, and in the main their conclusions confirmed the classical reasoning. Like the classical economists, Yntema and Mosak were interested primarily in the effects of international disturbances, such as tariffs and indemnity payments, upon relative prices at home and abroad. Apart from a final chapter in Mosak's book, little attention was paid in either book to the influence of international trade on the level of output. In at least one respect, however, both books have gone considerably beyond the classical theory; both authors have shown that a study of dynamic economics, of stable and unstable market systems, can be extremely useful in the field of international trade, particularly in complex problems involving a large number of countries and a large number of commodities.

Yntema's study of dynamic problems was necessarily elementary, since he was writing at a time when little was known about the stability of market systems. Nevertheless, he carried the discussion of stable and unstable international markets beyond the pioneer stage at which Marshall had left it,[67] and in Chapter 5 of his book he adopted a method that was surprisingly similar to the dynamic approach which Hicks later presented in *Value and Capital*. He argued, for example, that a money payment from country B to country A would normally increase money prices and costs in the latter and reduce them in the former, essentially through the operation of the quantity theory of money. In studying the static equations of supply and demand, he therefore suggested that any shapes of these functions, such as extremely inelastic demands, which indicated that a money payment would *reduce* prices in the receiving country and raise them in the paying country could be rejected as fundamentally unstable.[68] Here, in a book published in 1932, is the germ of the Hicksian concept of imperfect stability. Elementary and incomplete as it was, Yntema's conception of the relation between dynamics and statics was nevertheless prophetic of the work to be done later in the field of general price theory.

Mosak began his study of general equilibrium where Yntema had ended, and in several respects he advanced the theory of international trade beyond the stage at which Yntema had left it. Perhaps most important, Mosak took account of the effects of shifts in purchasing power, such as those associated with indemnity payments, on the demand for

---

67. Cf. Marshall, *Money, Credit, and Commerce* (reference 50), appendix J.
68. Yntema, *A Mathematical Reformulation* (reference 65), p. 80.

internationally traded goods. Yntema had neglected such income effects, and in this respect his system was even more classical than that of many of the classical economists. Except for Chapter 9 of his book, Mosak dealt with a system in which incomes were entirely expended on commodities, either foreign or domestic. For this reason, the "balance-of-payments problem," as such, did not enter explicitly into most of his work; equality between supply and demand in all commodity markets in Mosak's system, implies equilibrium in the foreign-exchange markets. He made a sweeping application of Hicks's concepts of perfect and imperfect stability to the special problems of international trade, but his conclusions in this regard are vitiated to some extent by the fact that the Hicks conditions are not true stability conditions except under special circumstances.[69]

It is extremely difficult, in a review such as this, to evaluate the position or importance of the two general-equilibrium studies in the body of international econommics as a whole. Unlike the classical theory, the more general approaches to international economics have not had a profound influence upon economic policy. To some extent this is probably attributable to their complexity—to the fact that the general solutions admit many different possible consequences of a given policy. To some extent also, it may be result of the fact that the more general theories have not, on the whole, revealed any serious flaws in the classical position. Both Yntema and Mosak discuss the classical theories as special cases of their more general theories, and their results tend largely to confirm the classical reasoning.[70]

The Theory of Tariffs

The preceding account of the relations between price theory and international economics has considered only the logical development of the theory, and no attempt has been made to relate this development to problems of economic policy. For this reason, the discussion above probably has an unrealistic and abstract quality which belies the true nature of the classical tradition. In the actual course of its growth, the accepted theory of international trade was intimately connected with

69. See Paul A. Samuelson, "The Stability of Equilibrium: Comparative Statics and Dynamics," *Econometrica*, 9 (April 1941), 97–120; and Lloyd A. Metzler, "Stability of Multiple Markets: The Hicks Conditions," which appears as Chapter 20 of the present volume.

70. Yntema, *A Mathematical Reformulation* (reference 65), pp. 80–87; and Mosak, *General-Equilibrium Theory* (reference 66), chap. 4.

highly controversial questions of policy. Indeed, almost all of the major contributions to the theory of international trade were a direct outgrowth of practical economic issues. During the nineteenth century, foreign-trade policy was for the most part synonymous with tariff policy, and the theory of tariffs accordingly occupies a prominent place in the classical economics. Even during the interwar period of the twentieth century, when other methods of trade control such as import quotas, exchange controls, and the like were widely adopted, tariffs continued to occupy an important place in the commercial policies of many countries. It seems appropriate, therefore, to conclude this review with a brief discussion of some recent changes in the theory of tariffs.

The tariff literature is perhaps as voluminous as that of any branch of applied economics, but fortunately it will not be necessary to make a detailed study of all the books, articles, and pamphlets dealing with this subject. Much of the writing about tariffs is concerned with problems of politics, ethics, or administration, and all of these questions, however important they may be, are outside the scope of the present review. With regard to the purely economic issues, recent developments in the theory of tariffs may be grouped under there main heads: (*a*) tariffs and the terms of trade; (*b*) tariffs and the distribution of income; (*c*) commercial policy and the revival of mercantilism. Each of these will be considered in turn.

Tariffs and the Terms of Trade

Events of the interwar period led to a notable revival of interest in tariffs regarded as bargaining weapons. The reciprocal Trade Agreements program in the United States, the new tariff policy of the United Kingdom, and tariff increases in other countries all emphasized once more the monopolistic character of tariff restrictions, and the effects of tariffs on the terms of trade. A number of economists dealt with these problems, but perhaps the outstanding contributions were those of Samuelson,[71] Kaldor,[72] Benham,[73] and Scitovszky.[74] The outcome of the discussion was to demonstrate anew the shaky foundation of some of the

---

71. Paul A. Samuelson, "Welfare Economics and International Trade," *American Economic Review*, 28 (June 1938), 261–266.

72. Nicholas Kaldor, "A Note on Tariffs and the Terms of Trade," *Economica*, 7 (November 1940), 377–380.

73. Frederic Benham, "The Terms of Trade," *Economica*, 7 (November 1940), 360–376.

74. Tibor Scitovszky, "A Reconsideration of the Theory of Tariffs," *Review of Economic Studies*, 9 (Summer 1942), 89–110.

arguments for free trade. Samuelson, for example, pointed out that tariffs or other trade restrictions, if they improve the terms of trade and increase the welfare of the country imposing them, will do so by worsening the position of some other country. Since the gains of one country cannot be measured against the losses to another, there is no presumption that trade restrictions always reduce welfare for the world as a whole.

Scitovszky carried this point of view further by showing that a tariff in one country increases the probability that retaliation will prove profitable to other countries. He thus developed a theory of tariff retaliation which depicted each country as raising tariffs in a rational manner in order to secure for itself a more favorable position in world markets. Although each country separately might gain, in Scitovszky's view, by a moderate increase in tariffs, the effect of all countries following the same policy would be to reduce the welfare of each of them. In the end, therefore, Scitovszky believed tariff retaliation would lead either to bilateral barter deals or to some form of tariff bargaining. Since each country may have a rational interest in higher tariffs, quite apart from the pressure of special groups within the country, Scitovszky emphasized that a free-trade system, like a cartel, has a natural tendency to disintegrate, and must be enforced by some kind of international convention.

The general effect of the work by Samuelson, Scitovszky, and others was to call attention to the similarity between the theory of tariffs and the theory of monopoly. An individual country, under certain conditions, can gain by limiting trade with other countries, just as a monopolist can gain by restricting the supply of the monopolized product. The rational argument against tariffs is not, as free-traders sometimes suppose, that tariffs harm all countries, but that, like monopoly restrictions, they impose a loss on some countries which is greater than the gain to the country imposing them. In modern terminology, we would say, following Lerner, that tariffs result in an inefficient allocation of resources, since the price ratios between commodities differ from one country to another.[75]

Tariffs and the Terms of Trade: The Classical View

What relation does this recent work have to the general literature on the theory of tariffs? Perhaps most important, the new contributions to

---

75. Abba P. Lerner, *The Economics of Control* (New York, Macmillan, 1944), pp. 356–362.

tariff theory correct a misconception which has long been common among advocates of free trade. In popular discussions, and even among some professional economists, the classical theory of comparative advantage has frequently been presented as a proof that all countries gain, individually, by a policy of unrestricted commerce. When the monopolistic character of tariffs and other impediments to trade is considered, however, it is obvious that this popular view is incorrect. Tariffs do not always involve a decline in the welfare of all countries, but may involve a loss in some countries and a gain in others. The importance of this misconception regarding tariffs, and the tendency to disregard the influence of tariffs on the terms of trade, are well illustrated by the following quotations from a report on tariffs prepared in 1930 by a distinguished committee of British economists:

As a matter of history, the assertion that the advantages of Free Trade depend upon its being mutual, has always been made by people who were attacking Free Trade. It has never been made by any of the principal advocates of Free Trade. For this there is a simple reason. It represents complete misunderstanding of the nature of international trade and the working of tariffs.

International trade is never free of all obstacles. The argument of the Free Traders has been directed to making the obstacles as few as possible. The gain through removing one obstacle depends in no way at all upon the removal of all the other obstacles or any of them.

. . . For other countries to tax our exports to them is an injury to us and an obstacle to trade. For us to tax their exports to us is not a correction of that injury; it is just a separate additional obstacle to trade.[76]

In the light of recent tariff discussions, statements such as these obviously need to be made more cautiously and with more reservations. As a practical matter it may well be true that actual tariffs have been so high as to inflict injury upon all parties, but there is no presumption, from the law of comparative advantage, that this will always be true. The arguments for retaliation are stronger than the literature on free trade would lead one to suppose.

Although the recent contributions to the theory of tariffs have made an important correction in free-trade arguments such as those above, it would be a mistake to suppose that the modern view represents a pronounced divergence from the classical theory. The English economists of

76. Sir William Beveridge *et al.*, *Tariffs: The Case Examined* (London, Longmans, 1931), pp. 108–110.

the nineteenth century, while they did not perhaps give the point sufficient emphasis, were fully aware of the favorable effects which a tariff may have upon a country's terms of trade.[77] Indeed, one of the primary purposes of Mill's profound work in international trade was to show how tariffs and other obstacles to trade affect the ratio of interchange between exports and imports. As Taussig has shown,[78] Mill probably drew too sharp a distinction between revenue duties and protective duties, but with regard to revenue duties he, Mill, never had any misconceptions about the benefits which a single country could derive, at the expense of its neighbors, from imposing such duties. The following quotation, if any is necessary, should make this obvious: "A country cannot be expected to renounce the power of taxing foreigners, unless foreigners will in return practice toward itself [sic] the same forbearance. The only mode in which a country can save itself from being a loser by the duties imposed by other countries on its commodities, is to impose corresponding duties on theirs."[79]

Marshall,[80] Edgeworth,[81] and Taussig[82] were likewise untouched by the error of the free-traders. All of these economists recognized the possible gains which a country may achieve by means of tariffs. Marshall, however, felt that as a practical matter the terms-of-trade argument for tariffs was not of great importance. In the first place, he doubted whether any single country in the modern industrial world was of sufficient importance to have an appreciable effect on the terms of trade. Second, his observations, particularly in the United States, led him to the conclusion that the pressure of special interests usually forces tariff rates far above the optimal level, so that the country imposing such tariffs, as well as the rest of the world, is likely to lose.[83]

Space limitations forbid any further elaboration of this theme. The point to be emphasized is the continuity between the classical theory and the recent discussions of the relation of tariff to the gains from trade. By

77. See Marian C. Samuelson, "The Australian Case for Protection Reexamined," *Quarterly Journal of Economics*, 54 (November 1939), 147–148.

78. Taussig, *International Trade* (reference 12), p. 146.

79. Mill, *Unsettled Questions of Political Economy* (reference 49), p. 29.

80. Marshall, *Money, Credit, and Commerce* (reference 50), appendix J and chaps. 8–10.

81. Edgeworth, *Political Economy* (reference 51), vol. 2, sec. 4.

82. Taussig, *International Trade* (reference 12), chap. 13.

83. It is interesting to note the similar remark of Edgeworth (reference 51, vol. 2, p. 18) on this point: "protection might procure economic advantage in certain cases, if there was a Government wise enough to discriminate those cases, and strong enough to confine itself to them; but this condition is very unlikely to be fulfilled."

utilizing modern price theory, contemporary economists have given a more precise statement of the possible gains and losses from tariffs, and they have indicated, perhaps more accurately than before, the limits to a rational tariff policy; but they have not altered the fundamental principles as developed by Mill, Marshall, Edgeworth, and Taussig. Further elaboration was needed, not because the classical view was incorrect, but because it was not given sufficient emphasis and, as a consequence, was later misinterpreted by advocates of free trade.

Tariffs and the Distribution of Income

The preceding discussion has been concerned primarily with the effects of tariffs on the distribution of world income between countries. An equally important problem, and one which was never satisfactorily solved by the classical economists, concerns the effects of tariffs upon the distribution of income within a single country. Even though a country has no monopolistic position in world markets and cannot gain a larger share of the world's income by restricting trade, it may nevertheless be true that a particular class or group within the country would be benefited by a tariff. This question of income distribution has been a central issue in almost all tariff controversies. In the United States, it took the form of an assertion that tariffs on manufactures protect or raise the real wages of workers. In the United Kingdom the issue appeared in the familiar conflict between landlords and manufacturers over the effects of the Corn Laws on agricultural rents and real wages.

More recently, the question arose again in a report on the Australian tariff which was prepared in 1929 by a distinguished group of Australian economists.[84] The outstanding feature of this report was that it gave qualified support to the tariff as a permanent part of Australia's commercial policy. Although the terms-of-trade argument played some part in the conclusion of the Australian economists, their principal reason for favoring protection was the belief that tariffs maintained a better distribution of income between landlords and workers than would otherwise have been possible. A tariff reduction, according to the report, would reduce the Australian output of manufactured goods and increase the output of the principal export goods, wool and wheat. And since wages are normally a much greater proportion of the value of manufactures

---

84. J. B. Brigden et al., The Australian Tariff: An Economic Enquiry, a report prepared for the Commonwealth Government (Melbourne, Melbourne University Press, 1929).

than of the value of agricultural products, the effects of this shift in the composition of Australian production would be to increase the demand for land and reduce the demand for labor. Workers would accordingly receive a smaller proportion of the national income than under protection, even if labor were perfectly mobile between agriculture and industry.[85]

The Australian report, as well as the tariff controversies in the United States, the United Kingdom, and other countries, have all emphasized the influence of tariffs on the distribution of income. In this particular branch of economic policy, however, economic theory until recently has had little to contribute. As noted earlier, the classical economists, with their oversimplified theory of production, were unable to cope with the problem.[86] They realized, of course, that protection benefits the producers of particular commodities, and that factors of production which are specific to these protected industries will likewise gain from tariffs. But if labor and capital are mobile, and the standard wage rate tends to equality in all industries, the traditional theory of international economics cannot show how tariffs affect the distribution of income between such broad categories as "labor," "capital," and "land." In the absence of a theory of production which recognized the substitution of one factor for another, there was a tendency to assume that the reward of each of the factors depended upon the productivity of the entire economy, and to conclude that foreign trade, which increases the effectiveness of the economy as a whole, must also increase the rewards to each of the factors separately.[87]

Although widely held, this view was by no means universal even among followers of the classical tradition. As early as 1906, for example, Pigou had pointed out that a tariff increases the output of one industry A at the expense of another industry B, and that if one factor of production plays a more important part in A than B, the change in the composition of the national income will increase the proportion of the total

---

85. Thus on p. 5 the report states: "The tariff has had the effect of pooling the national income to a greater extent than would have been practicable if assistance to industry were derived solely through the more obvious method of taxation. Employment has been subsidized at the expense of land values, enabling the standard of living to be maintained with a rapidly increasing population."

86. This is perhaps a slight exaggeration, for the classical economists had a great deal to say about the effects of the Corn Laws on agricultural rents. See, for example, three letters of Colonel Robert Torrens to the Marquis of Chandos (London, 1839).

87. See, for instance, F. W. Taussig, "How the Tariff Affects Wages," in his *Free Trade, the Tariff, and Reciprocity* (New York, Macmillan, 1920), p. 59.

product accruing to that factor. Moreover, even if the tariff reduces the national real income as a whole, Pigou argued that the absolute position of the favored factor might be improved. "The increase per cent in the share of the dividend obtained by the favored factor might exceed the shrinkage per cent of the dividend itself."[88] Viner and Ohlin later expressed similar views, although the latter regarded it as unlikely that the *absolute* as well as the *relative* returns to the favored factor would be increased by protection.[89]

Thus during the interwar years there seems to have been agreement that tariffs tend to increase the relative share of the national income accruing to certain factors of production, but there were doubts as to whether the *absolute* returns to the favored factors are also increased. If protection went so far as to reduce real income as a whole, it was believed that the absolute returns to the favored factors might conceivably be reduced even though their relative share in total income was increased. In other words, economists were still uncertain about the effects of protection upon the real income of certain factors, even though they were agreed that such protection would probably increase the *proportion* of the national income accruing to the favored factors of production.

Much of this uncertainty was eliminated in 1941 in a paper by Stolper and Samuelson which presented a remarkable application of the Heckscher-Ohlin system to the special problem of tariffs.[90] The paper demonstrated that, regardless of its effects on the term of trade and real income as a whole, protection, unless followed by retaliation, always increases the real return as well as the relative share in the total product of the factor of production which is relatively most important in the protected industries.

Suppose, for example, that a country has two industries, clothing and food, and two factors of production, labor and capital. Suppose further that labor is more important in the production of clothing than in the food industry, and that the country is an importer of clothing. A tariff on clothing will then increase production in that industry and shift both capital and labor from agriculture to manufacturing. According to the Stolper-Samuelson argument, this shift of resources will necessarily

88. A. C. Pigou, *Protective and Preferential Import Duties* (London, Macmillan, 1906), pp. 58–59.

89. Viner, *Theory of International Trade* (reference 20), pp. 533–534; and Ohlin, *Interregional and International Trade* (reference 62), p. 44.

90. Wolfgang F. Stolper and Paul A. Samuelson, "Protection and Real Wages," *Review of Economic Studies*, 9 (November 1941), 58–73.

reduce the proportion of labor to capital in both industries. In other words, the food industry, where a comparatively small amount of labor is employed, cannot supply enough labor to maintain the old labor-capital ratio in the clothing industry without creating a disparity between the marginal productivities, and consequently the wage rates, in the two industries. Now if the ratio of labor to capital is reduced in both industries, it follows from the law of variable proportions that the marginal product of labor, and hence the real wage rate, must be higher than before, regardless of whether real wages are measured in terms of the protected commodity, clothing, or the unsheltered commodity, food. Thus if protection increases the money price of clothing, it must increase the money wage rate even more. The real return to the second factor, capital, is *reduced*, compared with the free-trade position, for the shift in the composition of output brought about by the tariff makes capital a more abundant factor in both industries. And since the quantities of the factors are assumed to be unaffected by the tariff, it is clear that the tariff has increased the relative as well as the absolute returns to labor, and has reduced both the relative and absolute returns to capital. This conclusion, which Stolper and Samuelson reached in their paper, does not depend upon any monopolistic or other restrictions to the movement of factors of production. On the contrary, it assumes that labor and capital receive the same return in all industries. Neither does the result depend upon a gain in real income for the country as a whole, such as that which might arise from a favorable movement in the terms of trade. Even when protection leaves the external prices of exports and imports unchanged, and when the national real income as a whole is accordingly reduced, it remains true that the real income of the factor most important in the protected industries is increased by the tariff.

When we attempt to make practical applications of the Stolper-Samuelson tariff argument, a number of complications arise. Perhaps the most important of these is the large number of factors of production. The conclusion summarized above concerning the effects of tariffs on the distribution of income can be rigorously proved only for the simplified case of two factors of production; when more than two factors are involved, the terms "relatively scarce factors" and "relatively abundant factors" lose some of their precise meaning. Moreover, if some of the factors are complementary it is no longer possible to say that the marginal product of a particular factor depends exclusively upon its amount, relative to some other factor. Despite this complication, however, it seems reasonable, as Stolper and Samuelson have suggested, to propose a number of tentative conclusions. In the United States during the early nineteenth century, for example, our comparative advantage in agriculture was clearly governed by the large amount of land per worker. Under these circumstances, the tariffs which were imposed upon manufactured imports may well have improved the standard of living of the working class as a whole, since labor is a more important factor in manufactures than in agriculture. The same argument is applicable to the present position of Australia. In other words, the Stolper-Samuelson theorem provides a scientific foundation for the conclusion of the Australian committee that the tariff has helped to maintain the living standard of the working class.

Recent discussions of tariffs and the distribution of income thus give limited support to the "pauper labor" argument for tariffs. We would no doubt agree today with Taussig that "no economist of standing would maintain that a protective tariff is the one decisive factor in making a country's rate of wages high," but it is doubtful whether we would also agree that "no economist . . . would sanction the pauper-labor argument for tariffs." On the other hand, as Viner has pointed out, the favorable effect on the distribution of income from the point of view of one factor of production is not, ipso facto, a valid argument for tariffs from the point of view of the country as a whole. If repercussions on the terms of trade can be neglected, tariffs always reduce the total quantity of commodities available to the country as a whole, and the gain to one factor of production is therefore more than offset by losses to others.[91]

Commercial Policy and the Revival of Mercantilism

Having touched upon two aspects of the theory of tariffs, it seems appropriate to conclude this section with a few remarks concerning commercial policy as a whole. Although this subject is much broader than the theory of tariffs, the tariff question has been at the center of so many of the historical conflicts in commercial policy that it seems best to consider the broader subject here.

The basic conflicts in the field of commercial policy are well illustrated by the familiar differences of opinion between the mercantilists and the classical economists. To the mercantilists, the primary functions of foreign trade were to provide an outlet for a country's surplus produc-

91. Viner, *Theory of International Trade* (reference 20), pp. 533–534.

tion and to acquire a large stock of the monetary metals.[92] In order to achieve these ends, they advocated tariffs, export subsidies, and other measures designed to assure a country a steady and substantial export surplus. The classical system of economic theory was developed, in part, as a refutation of these mercantilist doctrines, and although the classical theory has been misinterpreted and misused by the advocates of free trade, it remains nevertheless as a bulwark against protectionism and other commercial restrictions. The fundamental tenet of the classical theory was that the purpose of all economic activity is not to find markets for surplus production or to increase mercantile profits but to satisfy human wants. Foreign trade, like other economic activity, was to be evaluated according to its contribution to this want-satisfying function. The classical economists accepted Say's Law and therefore believed that general overproduction was impossible. From this it followed that the primary problem in economics was not how to find employment for unused capital, labor, and land, but how to use these resources in the most effective manner.

In the field of international trade, this meant a shift in emphasis from exports to imports. The usefulness of exports was to be judged not by their contribution to output and employment but by the value of the imports obtained in exchange. To the mercantilist argument that export subsidies were desirable because they created an outlet for surplus production, the classical economists replied that no such outlet was needed, and that an increase of exports, in itself, meant a smaller amount of goods available for domestic consumption.[93] In other words, exports were considered to be desirable only if the additional imports which could thereby be obtained were worth more to consumers than the home consumption which had to be sacrificed. From this it followed that an export surplus, financed by imports of the precious metals, was not a desirable long-run policy, since monetary stocks of metal have no intrinsic ability to satisfy wants. It would be better, according to the classical view, to export only enough to pay for imports and to use the additional resources to produce for home consumption. In any event, the classical system envisaged an automatic tendency toward a balancing of exports and imports through the effects of gold movements on the level of prices. Attempts to maintain an export surplus were therefore regarded as self-defeating: tariffs and other impediments to trade, instead of increasing

92. See Angell, *Theory of International Prices* (reference 3), chap. 2.
93. See Mill, *Principles of Political Economy* (reference 2), bk. 5. chap. 10, sec. 1.

employment at home, would simply transfer resources from export industries to domestic-goods industries, thereby reducing the effectiveness of labor and other factors in satisfying wants.

Among economists in England, this classical system rapidly supplanted the mercantilist doctrines, and it was by far the most widely accepted system throughout the nineteenth century. Among businessmen and statesmen, on the other hand, the mercantilist doctrines continued to have much influence. Time and again, the argument that tariffs increase employment appeared in popular discussions, and just as regularly these arguments were refuted—sometimes impatiently—by economists.[94] Apart from the appeal to special interests which is no doubt the dominant factor in almost all tariff legislation, the genuine economic reasons for the persistence of the mercantilist arguments did not become apparent until the decade of the nineteen-thirties when the Keynesian revolution led to a reconsideration of the classical position. It was Keynes himself who pointed out the grain of truth in the mercantilist system, and except for the fact that this review is supposed to cover the whole field of international economics it would perhaps be best simply to refer the reader to Keynes's discussion.[95] The classical argument against an export surplus as a permanent policy stands or falls with the acceptance or rejection of the idea that the economic system tends automatically toward a state of full employment, and since Keynes had rejected this idea he was bound to reject also the idea that encouragement of exports through subsidies or reduction of imports through tariffs will have no influence on employment. If a country starts from a position in which it has unemployed resources, it is no longer true, as the classical economists assumed, that an increase of exports means a reduction of goods available for domestic consumption. On the contrary, if we consider the repercussions of higher income earned in the export trades on the demand for goods and services, it is probably that an increase of exports means also an increased demand for and an increased output of domestic goods. An export surplus financed by an inflow of gold may therefore be a direct cause of increased income and a higher standard of living in the exporting country. Thus the mercantilists may have been justified, in certain circumstances, when they advocated an

94. For example, F. W. Taussig's 1904 presidential address before the American Economic Association, reprinted in his *Free Trade, the Tariff, and Reciprocity* (reference 87), p. 29.
95. J. M. Keynes, *General Theory of Employment, Interest, and Money* (New York, Harcourt, Brace, 1936), chap. 23.

export surplus as an outlet for excess production. The theoretical foundations of the classical view, as Keynes shows, were weaker than had been suspected.

One problem still remains, however: How can the promotion of an export surplus as a permanent policy be reconciled with the classical argument that imports tend automatically to balance exports? If a country reduces its imports by means of tariffs, will not the increased employment in the protected industries soon be offset by a corresponding reduction of exports? In order to answer these questions, we must refer again to what was said earlier concerning the balancing mechanism. It must be conceded that the imposition of a tariff or the granting of a subsidy *will* set up a balancing process, although the mechanism is somewhat different from that envisaged by the classical economists. If the initial disturbance is a tariff, imports will eventually rise, despite the tariff, as a result of higher income and employment at home, while exports will decline as a result of lower income abroad. It was argued at the beginning of this article, however, that this balancing process is likely to be incomplete. The modern theory of the balance of payments thus suggests that a country may have an export surplus over a considerable period of time without any pronounced automatic tendency toward a complete equalization of exports and imports.

A large export surplus cannot be maintained indefinitely, however, for eventually the rest of the world will be drained of all its monetary gold. Even before this occurs, other countries will probably be provoked to retaliation, particularly if unemployment prevails in the rest of the world. The most any individual country can hope to do is to maintain an export surplus which will ensure it a reasonable proportion of the world's new production of gold. If this policy succeeds, and retaliation is avoided, the export surplus, as Keynes shows, is doubly beneficial to the exporting country. On the one hand, it increases income and employment directly, and on the other hand, the increase of gold stocks, by reducing the rate of interest, tends to increase domestic investment. Both of these favorable effects would have been denied by the classical economists, who saw no need for a stimulation of employment and who had a somewhat exaggerated idea of the effectiveness of the balancing process.

While all of this clearly indicates that the economic grounds for mercantilism were stronger than economists have generally recognized, the revival of the theory of mercantilism is not necessarily a reason for its advocacy as a practical policy. On questions of policy, the primary problem, of course, is the reconciling of divergent national interests. The classical economists minimized this problem, for they believed that, within limits, national self-interest coincides with the welfare of the world economy as a whole. The revival of mercantilism demonstrates, unfortunately, that such harmony of interests cannot be taken for granted. The practical conduct of international trade is thus much more a problem of negotiation and compromise than the classical economists believed. If unemployment prevails through the world, as it did in the decade of the thirties, a mercantilist policy clearly benefits some countries at the expense of others. And this easily leads to retaliation which deprives all countries of the benefits of international specialization without increasing employment in any of them. But on these political questions, I can perhaps not do better than to quote a passage from Keynes's discussion of mercantilism:

There are strong presumptions of a general character against trade restrictions unless they can be justified on special grounds. The advantages of the international division of labour are real and substantial, even though the classical school greatly overstressed them. The fact that the advantage which our own country gains from a favourable balance is liable to involve an equal disadvantage to some other country (a point to which the mercantilists were fully alive) means not only that great moderation is necessary, so that a country secures for itself no larger a share of the stock of precious metals than is fair and reasonable, but also that an immoderate policy may lead to a senseless international competition for a favourable balance which injures all alike. And finally, a policy of trade restrictions is a treacherous instrument even for the attainment of its ostensible object, since private interest, administrative incompetence, and the intrinsic difficulty of the task may divert it into producing results directly opposite to those intended.[96]

Conclusions

The review presented above of international economics during the interwar years has covered a wide variety of subjects. In the monetary part of the field, it has attempted to describe recent developments in the theory of the balance of payments under conditions of both fixed and flexible exchange rates. And in the so-called "pure" theory of international trade it has presented an account of the adaptation of new discoveries in price theory to the special problems of international trade.

96. *Ibid.*, pp. 338–339.

Finally, the recent changes in the theory of international trade have been related to selected problems in tariff policy.

Considering the diversity of subjects discussed, we should perhaps inquire, in conclusion, whether the recent innovations and discoveries in all the various branches of international economics have anything in common. Is there, for example, any unifying principle or any basic philosophy which unites the modern theories of the balance of payments with the revised theory of tariffs? Or has each of the new discoveries in each of the separate branches been a more or less isolated phenomenon? A cursory glance at the preceding pages may suggest that the latter has been true. I believe, however, that a more careful study will convince the reader that the new theories have not been as disconnected and isolated as seems at first to be the case. The connecting idea, however, is essentially negative.

Historically, the interwar period will probably be remembered as a period of retreat from the price system, when all sorts of temporary or provisional measures were adopted to regulate economic activity. The market mechanism had broken down and no one seemed to know quite why or just what to do about it. This was perhaps even more true of the international mechanism than of domestic markets, and to a very great extent the theoretical developments reflected the empirical. Where the classical economists had discussed the broad operation of the price system, twentieth-century economists described the exceptions and qualifications, or the special circumstances in which the international price mechanism would not work. Thus, for example, the balance-of-payments mechanism under the gold standard was found to be less effective and more disruptive than the classical economists had believed. And even with flexible exchange rates, it was realized during the interwar years that a balancing of foreign receipts and expenditures cannot be taken for granted. Doubts concerning the price system were by no means limited to the monetary aspects of international economics. In the field of price theory, too, there was a movement away from traditional ideas. Increasing emphasis was placed upon the fact that an unimpeded working of the free market system is not necessarily in the interest of each individual country. The classical conception of a harmony of interest between countries, which even the classical theory did not entirely support, was called further in question. Much importance—perhaps too much—was attached to the benefits which individual countries could derive by the regulation of exports and imports.

Part of this general retreat from the price system in international economic theory was no doubt beneficial, for it contributed to a more realistic appraisal of international trade than we had inherited from the classical economists. It seems likely, however, that the pendulum has now swung too far in the anticlassical direction. The interwar years give a distorted picture of the normal working of an international market system—indeed, it is more of a caricature than a picture—and economic theory has shared in this distortion. If in the past we have expected the price system to accomplish too much, there is a danger that in the future we shall expect it to do less than it is capable of doing.

Our major error in the past, and the error which contributed perhaps more than anything else to discrediting of the price system, consisted in expecting the price mechanism to solve the problem of economic stability. On this point we were immensely enlightened during the interwar years, and it is now generally recognized that economic stability requires constant supervision and planning. To the extent that the world succeeds in solving the problem of stability by measures supplementary to the price system, the equally important problem of the allocation of resources, both domestic and international, might reasonably be left to the market mechanism. In the absence of severe depressions, there is reason to believe that the balances of payments of most countries could be kept in reasonable equilibrium by means of moderate adjustments in exchange rates. The trade restrictions and trade controls which grew so rapidly in the interwar years would therefore be unnecessary. Moreover, in a stable and expanding world economy, individual countries would have less incentive to adopt trade controls in order to safeguard their domestic markets. World economic stability would thus greatly reduce the force of the two most important incentives for controlling international trade in the past. Whether this would be sufficient to counteract the present trend toward increasing state intervention can hardly be foretold. But at any rate it is clear that our hopes for a revival of the market mechanism, however weak they may be, are greatly dependent upon a world stability which must be achieved, for the most part, by conscious planning and direction.

2 | The Transfer Problem Reconsidered

The analysis of capital movements has been characterized in recent years by increasing complexity. Few economists today would defend the adequacy of the orthodox theory of price-level adjustments induced by gold movements; and yet the theories which have been substituted for this simple doctrine are so eclectic as to allow for almost any conceivable type of reaction. We are told, for example, that a transfer of purchasing power from one country to another may move the terms of trade in favor of either country[1] or, again, that real income in the receiving country may either increase or decrease as a result of the transfer.[2] In short, an element of truth is found in almost every theory.

Unfortunately, discussion has been confined largely to special cases in which the possibility of a particular reaction is demonstrated. Hence, although it is known that a capital transfer may produce a great variety of results, very little may be said with precision about the conditions necessary for the occurrence of a particular set of reactions. This unsatisfactory state of affairs will no doubt continue until a manageable general-equilibrium theory of capital transfers has been developed. Such a theory must be sufficiently simple, on the one hand, that properties of

1. Carl Iversen, *Aspects of the Theory of International Capital Movements* (Copenhagen, Lewin and Munksgaard, 1936), *passim*.
2. W. W. Leontief, "Note on the Pure Theory of Capital Transfer," in *Explorations in Economics: Notes and Essays Contributed in Honor of F. W. Taussig* (New York, McGraw-Hill, 1936), p. 88.

the system may be examined and sufficiently complex, on the other hand, to include the relevant factors of adjustment.[3]

Equilibrating factors usually considered are changes in relative price levels, modifications of resource distribution, movements of interest and exchange rates, and changes in sectional price levels. Of these, the first two have undoubtedly received the greatest amount of attention. It is now generally recognized that shifts of monetary purchasing power may change not only prices and factor allocations but also levels of total employment and hence real incomes. A completely general theory must include these output adjustments, as well as the types of change enumerated above. The difficulties of such a general analysis are so formidable, however, that I have attempted the more modest task of isolating the influence of real-income adjustments alone.[4]

To discuss this problem I have set up a simplified model of trade between two countries, in which changes of prices, interest rates, and exchange rates are impossible. The assumptions of unemployment, rigid monetary wage structures, competitive industries, and constant returns are sufficient to ensure that changes of monetary demand will affect levels of output rather than prices. Monetary assumptions necessary to isolate real-income effects are (a) the maintenance of constant interest rates in both countries and (b) the maintenance of fixed exchange rates. With the fixed-exchange-rate assumption, the currency unit of either country may be used as a unit of measure in both. Henceforth, all figures of income, consumption, and so forth will be given in the currency of the paying country.

Under the simplified conditions set forth above, total income in each country will be determined by the amount of net investment and the character of consumption functions. The definition of income is the usual one of consumption *plus* net investment. But net investment now comprises two parts: (a) the net increase of producer's goods (and stocks), which I shall call "domestic investment," and (b) the increase

3. Most general equilibrium theories satisfy the second criterion but not the first; see, for example, Bertil Ohlin, *Interregional and International Trade* (Cambridge, Mass., Harvard University Press, 1933), appendix I, pp. 553–562.

4. Although my conclusions are strictly applicable only to economies conforming to a rather rigid set of assumptions, I believe that much can be said to justify the real-income approach. In the first place, a partial analysis may considerably improve one's intuition and make "guessing" about the general problem more intelligent. Second, the results even for this simple case are so numerous as to defy broad generalization. Finally, impediments to movements of prices and monetary costs frequently make it extremely useful to know whether real-income adjustments alone can create for a debtor country the required export surplus.

(decrease) of indebtedness abroad, arising from a favorable (unfavorable) trade balance. This second item of investment is simply the difference between exports and imports. Since total consumption for a given country consists of its consumption of domestic goods *plus* its imports, it follows that income may be measured by the sum of consumption of domestic goods, domestic investment, and exports.[5]

We may assume that initially the system is in equilibrium in the sense that any difference between exports and imports of one of the two countries is made up by private-capital movements. Suppose that an international transfer of 10 units disturbs this equilibrium. The mechanics of the monetary transfer will not be discussed. I shall assume either that foreign balances of the paying country are drawn upon or that gold is shipped or that banks of the receiving country extend loans to those of the paying country, the proceeds of which are used to make payment. In any case, as long as interest rates and exchange rates are not altered, the effects of the transfer upon incomes are independent of these financial arrangements.[6]

The income effects depend entirely upon the fiscal policies of the two countries. Thus, if budgets are exactly balanced in both countries, the transfer will increase monetary income in the receiving country and reduce it in the paying country, regardless of whether the banking systems respond with a movement of gold or with a shift of international balances. It is dangerous to assume, however, that purchasing power will always expand (initially) in the receiving country and contract in the paying country by exactly the amount of the transfer. The government of the receiving country, for example, may simply build up a surplus with the transfer sums. In this case the only income adjustment is that attributable to disinvestment (taxation) in the paying country. Likewise, the debtor country may pay from the proceeds of a bond issue, in which case the sole income adjustment arises from public spending in the receiving country. Thus there are three cases to consider: (*a*) a transfer accompanied by government disinvestment in the

5. I have introduced here the simplifying assumption that imports in both countries are for consumption purposes. If the period of time considered is sufficiently long, so that investment is independent of the level of output, my simplification will not alter the final outcome.

6. Invariance of exchange and interest rates implies a flexibility of bank policy which probably does not exist among any of the modern banking systems. I have assumed that gold movements and movements of international balances leave lending terms of the central banks unchanged, not because I regard this as a realistic assumption but because I wish to isolate the influence of real-income adjustments alone.

paying country and government investment in the receiving country; (b) a transfer accompanied by government disinvestment in the paying country but no government investment in the receiving country; (c) a transfer accompanied by government investment in the receiving country but no government disinvestment in the paying country.

These original changes of monetary incomes should not be confused with secondary movements of consumption and investment, in subsequent periods, induced by the initial purchasing-power shift. I shall refer hereafter to the initial change as a "direct" or "primary" income effect to distinguish it from "induced" or "secondary" changes. Solution of the transfer problem, for my simple model, reduces to analysis of the manner in which secondary effects alter incomes and the balance of trade of the two trading countries. Such secondary changes will obviously vary according to the time sequence of income receipt and expenditure; consequently, it is necessary to specify a dynamic system. For this purpose I shall assume, throughout, a lag of one period in the consumption of income behind its receipt. Likewise, I shall assume that induced private investment in a given period depends upon income of the previous period. With this dynamic system in mind, interpretation of Tables 1, 2, and 3, where the analysis is set forth, is a simple matter.

Each of the tables is divided into three parts. In Case a the transfer is assumed to affect income directly in both countries; that is, money incomes are expanded in the receiving country and contracted in the paying country by exactly the amount of the transfer. In Case b, on the other hand, contraction in the paying country is the only direct effect of the transfer; the government of the receiving country is assumed not to pay out the proceeds to its citizens. Finally, in Case c of each table direct income effects are limited to public spending in the receiving country; the debtor government is assumed to make payment either from an accumulated surplus or from the proceeds of a loan.

Since the construction of all the tables is the same, it will suffice to explain one of them. Consider the first line of Table 1. In the first period the income of the paying country is reduced by 10 and that of the receiving country increased by the same amount. These changes react upon consumption and investment of subsequent periods in the manner indicated. A marginal propensity to consume domestic goods of 0.2 in the debtor country means that consumption of these goods in the second period is 2 units less than it would have been in the

Table 1. Transfer effects when both countries are stable in isolation (international transfer = 10 units) *

Case	Changes in paying country				Changes in receiving country			
	Consumption of domestic goods (1)	Consumption of foreign goods (2)	Investment (3)	Income (4)	Consumption of domestic goods (5)	Consumption of foreign goods (6)	Investment (7)	Income (8)
a. Transfer affects income directly in both countries	—	—	− 10.0	− 10.0	—	—	10.0	10.0
	− 2.0	− 2.0	− 1.0	− 2.0	3.0	1.0	1.0	2.0
	− 0.4	− 0.4	− 0.2	− 0.4	0.6	0.2	0.2	0.4
	− .08	− .08	− .04	− .08	.12	.04	.04	.08
	− .016	− .016	− .008	− .016	.024	.008	.008	.016
	− .0032	− .0032	− .0016	− .0032	.0048	.0016	.0016	.0032
	.	.	.	.	.	.	.	.
	.	.	.	.	.	.	.	.
	.	.	.	.	.	.	.	.
	− 2.500	− 2.5000	− 11.2500	− 12.5000	3.7500	1.2500	11.2500	12.5000

b. Transfer affects income directly in paying country

—	—	—	—	—	—	—	—
-2.0	-2.0	-10.0	-10.0	-0.6	-0.2	-0.2	-2
-0.6	-0.6	-1.0	-3.0	-.42	-.14	-.14	-1.4
-.22	-.22	-0.3	-1.1	-.234	-.078	-.078	-0.78
-.094	-.094	-.11	-0.47	-.1218	-.0406	-.0406	-.406
-.0438	-.0438	-.047	-.219				-.2062
		-.0219	-.1063				
. . .	. . .	. . .	. . .	. . .	. . .	. . .	. . .
-3.000	-3.000	-11.5000	-15.0000	-1.500	-0.500	-0.500	-5.000

c. Transfer affects income directly in receiving country

—	—	—	—	—	—	—	—
0.2	0.2	0.1	1.0	3.0	1.0	10.0	10.0
.14	.14	.07	0.7	1.2	0.4	1.0	4.0
.078	.078	.039	.39	.54	.18	0.4	1.8
.0406	.0406	.0203	.203	.258	.086	.18	0.86
			.1031	.1266	.0422	.086	.422
						.0422	.2094
. . .	. . .	. . .	. . .	. . .	. . .	. . .	. . .
0.500	0.500	0.250	2.500	5.250	1.750	11.750	17.500

* The following values are assumed for the three cases (paying country given first in each instance, then receiving country): marginal propensity to consume domestic goods, 0.2 and 0.3; marginal propensity to consume foreign goods, 0.2 and 0.1; and marginal propensity to invest, 0.1 and 0.1.

absence of the transfer. Likewise, imports are 2 less and domestic investment 1 less, since marginal propensities to consume foreign goods and to invest are 0.2 and 0.1, respectively. Similar considerations explain the deviations of consumption and investment from equilibrium levels (in the second period) in the receiving country.

It was shown above that income in each country may be expressed as the sum of consumption of domestic goods, exports, and domestic investment. Deviations of income from equilibrium may therefore be obtained by addition of the deviations of these three items. Thus the quantity -2 in the income column of the paying country (for the second period) is found by adding the items in line 2, columns 1, 3, and 6, while the excess income of the receiving country for this same period represents an addition of the items in line 2, columns 2, 5, and 7. Changes of income in the second period then react upon consumption and investment of the third period and so on. In this manner the time sequence of income and trade adjustments following a single transfer may be computed for as many periods as desired. The systems outlined in the tables are all stable, so that, in the absence of further payments, incomes of the two countries return eventually to their original positions.

Discussions of the transfer mechanism usually distinguish between two problems: (a) analysis of time sequences (such as those discussed above) which follow a single payment and (b) comparison of the old equilibrium with the one which eventually prevails when transfer payments are regular. The distinction is the familiar one between dynamic analysis and comparative statics.

The behavior of dynamic adjustments is obvious from the tables, but it is perhaps less obvious that the same tables may be used to compare a new equilibrium with an old one. For the cumulative effect upon income (let us say) in the nth period after regular payments are begun is simply the sum of the first n terms in our income columns. That is, the total effect of the n regular payments is the sum of the effects of single payments made $n - 1, n - 2, \ldots, 2, 1, 0$ periods previously. But the effect (in the nth period) of a payment made $n - 1$ periods previously is given by line n, while the effect of a payment made $n - 2$ periods previously is given by line $n - 1$, and so on. Hence the sum of the first n lines represents the total influence (in the nth period) of all previous payments. The process of addition may be continued indefinitely, but eventually the sums will approach limits. When this point is reached, we say that a new equilibrium has been established. Displacements of the new equilibrium from the old are then measured by the column totals.[7] In other words the totals may be interpreted alternatively as the sums of income adjustments in all periods to a single payment or as the eventual displacement of equilibrium which will result from a series of regular payments.

The upper part of Table 1 shows that, with a periodic payment of 10 units affecting income directly in both countries, the new equilibrium level of income is 12.5 less in the paying country and 12.5 greater in the receiving country than without the transfer.[8] Collection of the transfer sums has depressed the level of output in the debtor country, while spending of the same sums has stimulated output of the creditor. These changes, in turn, have reduced imports of the paying country by 2.5 per period and have increased her exports by 1.25 per period. Income adjustments induced by the shift of purchasing power have thus made available 3.75 units of foreign exchange per period— an amount obviously inadequate to make the entire payment.

When the direct effects of the transfer are limited to its collection in the paying country (Table 1, Case b), real income of each country is reduced, that of the paying country by taxation and that of the receiving country by lower exports to the paying country. Thus both exports and imports of the debtor country decline. But her imports decline more than her exports so that 2.5 units of foreign exchange per period are freed for making the actual transfer.

Finally, Case c of Table 1 shows that, if the transfer affects income directly in the receiving country, but not in the paying country, real incomes of both countries rise. The higher income of the former is attributable to public spending induced by the transfer, that of the latter to greater exports to the receiving country. Both exports and imports of the paying country are increased, and again foreign exchange is freed for making the actual payment, since exports rise more than imports. Once again, however, the foreign exchange set free is inadequate to make the entire transfer.

It appears from Table 1 that adjustments of real income brought about by a transfer of purchasing power are capable of creating a part, but not all, of the necessary export surplus for the paying country

7. Totals given in the tables are not the actual ones but the limits which the sums in each column approach (see the appendix to this chapter).
8. It is only an accident of the particular numerical example chosen that reduction of income in the paying country is exactly equal to the rise of income in the receiving country.

Table 2. Transfer effects when the receiving country is unstable in isolation (international transfer = 10 units)*

Case	Changes in paying country				Changes in receiving country			
	Consumption of domestic goods (1)	Consumption of foreign goods (2)	Investment (3)	Income (4)	Consumption of domestic goods (5)	Consumption of foreign goods (6)	Investment (7)	Income (8)
a. Transfer affects income directly in both countries	—	—	−10.0	−10.0	—	—	10.0	10.0
	−1.0	−1.0	−1.0	6.0	1.0	8.0	3.0	3.0
	0.6	0.6	0.6	3.6	0.3	2.4	0.9	1.8
	.36	.36	.36	2.16	.18	1.44	.54	1.08
	.216	.216	.216	1.296	.108	0.864	.324	0.648
	.1296	.1296	.1296	0.7776	.0648	.5184	.1944	.3888
	.	.	.	.	.	.	.	.
	.	.	.	.	.	.	.	.
	0.500	0.500	−9.500	5.000	1.750	14.000	15.250	17.500
b. Transfer affects income directly in paying country	—	—	−10.0	−10.0	—	—	—	—
	−1.0	−1.0	−1.0	−2.0	—	—	—	−1.0
	−0.2	−0.2	−0.2	−1.2	−0.1	−0.8	−0.3	−0.6
	−.12	−.12	−.12	−0.72	−.06	−.48	−.18	−.36
	−.072	−.072	−.072	−.432	−.036	−.288	−.108	−.216
	−.0432	−.0432	−.0432	−.2592	−.0216	−.1728	−.0648	−.1296
	.	.	.	.	.	.	.	.
	.	.	.	.	.	.	.	.
	−1.500	−1.500	−11.500	−15.000	−0.250	−2.000	−0.750	−2.500

c. Transfer affects income directly in receiving country	—	—	—	—	—	—	10.0	10.0
	0.8	0.8	0.8	8.0	1.0	8.0	3.0	4.0
	.48	.48	.48	4.8	0.4	3.2	1.2	2.4
	.288	.288	.288	2.88	.24	1.92	0.72	1.44
	.1728	.1728	.1728	1.728	.144	1.152	.432	0.864
				1.0368	.0864	0.6912	.2592	.5184
	⋯	⋯	⋯	⋯	⋯	⋯	⋯	⋯
	2.000	2.000	2.000	20.000	2.000	16.000	16.000	20.000

* The following values are assumed for the three cases (paying country given first in each instance, then receiving country): marginal propensity to consume domestic goods, 0.1 and 0.1; marginal propensity to consume foreign goods, 0.1 and 0.8; and marginal propensity to invest, 0.1 and 0.3.

and that the surplus will be greater if both countries allow incomes to be affected directly than if only one does so. A glance at Tables 2 and 3, where the same problem is worked out for different marginal propensities to consume and invest, shows, however, that the results obtained in Table 1 are not general.

Consider Case *a* of Table 2. Despite government disinvestment in the debtor country, income has risen there, as well as in the creditor country. Increased exports to the receiving country have exerted a more important influence on the income of the debtor country than has reduced consumption arising from collection of the transfer sum. Hence both her exports and her imports have increased. But exports have risen much more than imports, and the foreign exchange set free in this manner is more than sufficient to make the actual transfer.

Case *b* of Table 2 presents a situation entirely analogous to the Keynes dilemma over German reparations. Contraction in the paying country being the only direct income effect, real income naturally declines in both countries. As a consequence, both exports and imports of the debtor country are reduced. Her exports, however, decline more than her imports. In other words, taxation has moved the balance of trade against the paying country—a result quite contrary to usual expectations. No amount of contraction in the debtor country will, in this case, create an export surplus. It follows that the transfer imposes an impossible burden upon the paying country unless the receiving country will cooperate in expanding her citizens' money incomes.

On the other hand, if direct income effects are limited to expansion in the receiving country (Case *c*, Table 2), the real-income adjustment is sufficient in this case to make the actual transfer. As in Table 1, Case *c*, income rises in both countries, and higher incomes increase both exports and imports of the paying country. But unlike Table 1, Case *c*, the rise of exports in the present case is sufficiently greater than the rise of imports to move the trade balance in favor of the paying country by an amount greater than the transfer.

It is clear from Table 2 that, for the propensities to consume and invest there postulated, the cooperation of the receiving country is absolutely essential; contraction in the paying country only makes matters worse. But if monetary income in the receiving country expands by the amount of the transfer, it makes no difference whether or not the paying country's income is reduced in its collection, for in any case the change of the trade balance arising from expansion in the receiving country will be sufficient to make the actual transfer.

A third set of possible results is given in Table 3. Contraction of purchasing power in the paying country and its expansion in the receiving country (Case *a*) serve here to reduce real incomes in both countries. The lower income of the former is attributable to the transfer collection; the latter's income is reduced because the secondary effects of reduced exports to the paying country are more important than the original expansion of purchasing power. Imports of the debtor country decline more than her exports, and the shift of the trade balance is greater than the amount of the transfer. With both countries cooperating, therefore, the income adjustments alone are adequate, but neither party gains, since incomes of both are reduced. Likewise, when the paying country contracts income in collection of the transfer sum, but the receiving country does not expand (Case *b*), incomes of both countries are again reduced, and once more the reduction of the debtor's imports is sufficiently greater than the reduction of her exports to make the transfer possible with no further adjustments. But again the transfer is detrimental to both countries. Finally, expansion in the receiving country unaccompanied by contraction in the paying country (Table 3, Case *c*), while increasing incomes in both, moves the balance of trade in a direction unfavorable to the debtor through an increase of her imports (4.000) which exceeds the increase of her exports (3.500). In this case no part of the actual transfer may be completed through income adjustments of the creditor country.

In discussing Table 2 it was noted that the transfer could not be completed through income adjustments without cooperation of the receiving country and that contraction in the paying country only aggravated the situation. Table 3 represents, in some respects, the converse of Table 2. For now it appears that income adjustments will not suffice unless the paying country is willing to contract income in collection of the transfer sum and that expansion in the receiving country makes the balance of trade unfavorable to the debtor.

Study of our three tables reveals that purchasing-power shifts incident to an international transfer may either increase real income of the receiving country while decreasing that of the paying country (Table 1, Case *a*), or increase real income of both countries (Table 2, Case *a*), or decrease real income of both countries (Table 3, Case *a*). The tables also show that the trade balance may move in favor of the paying country by more than the transfer or by less than the transfer, or that

Table 3. Transfer effects when the paying country is unstable in isolation (international transfer = 10 units)*

	Changes in paying country				Changes in receiving country			
	Consumption of domestic goods (1)	Consumption of foreign goods (2)	Investment (3)	Income (4)	Consumption of domestic goods (5)	Consumption of foreign goods (6)	Investment (7)	Income (8)
a. Transfer affects income directly in both countries	—	—	−10.0	−10.0	—	—	10.0	10.0
	−1.0	−8.0	−2.0	−1.0	1.0	2.0	1.0	−6.0
	−0.1	−0.8	−0.2	−1.5	−0.6	−1.2	0.6	−2.0
	−.15	−1.20	−.30	−0.85	−.20	−0.40	−.20	−1.6
	−.085	−0.680	−.170	−.575	−.160	−.320	−.160	−1.000
	−.575	−.4600	−.1150	−.3725	−.1000	−.2000	−.1000	−.6600
	. . .	. . .	. . .	. . .	. . .	. . .	. . .	. . .
	−1.500	−12.000	−13.000	−15.000	−0.250	−0.500	9.750	−2.500
b. Transfer affects income directly in paying country	—	—	−10.0	−10.0	—	—	—	—
	−1.0	−8.0	−2.0	−3.0	—	—	—	−8.0
	−0.3	−2.4	−0.6	−2.5	−0.8	−1.6	0.8	−4.0
	−.25	−2.00	−.50	−1.55	−.40	−0.80	.40	−2.80
	−.155	−1.240	−.310	−1.025	−.280	−.560	.280	−1.800
	−.1025	−0.8200	−.2050	−0.6675	−.1800	−.3600	.1800	−1.1800
	. . .	. . .	. . .	. . .	. . .	. . .	. . .	. . .
	−2.000	−16.000	−14.000	−20.000	−2.000	−4.000	−2.000	−20.000

	0.500	4.000	1.000	5.000	1.750	3.500	11.750	17.500
c. Transfer affects income directly in receiving country	—	—	—	—	—	—	10.0	10.0
	—	—	—	2.0	1.0	2.0	1.0	2.0
	0.2	1.6	0.4	1.0	0.2	0.4	0.2	2.0
	.1	0.8	.2	0.3	.2	.4	.2	1.2
	.07	.56	.14	.45	.12	.24	.12	0.80
	.045	.360	.090	.295	.080	.160	.080	.520
	. . .	. . .	. . .	. . .	. . .	. . .	. . .	. . .

* The following values are assumed for the three cases (paying country given first in each instance, then receiving country): marginal propensity to consume domestic goods, 0.1 and 0.1; marginal propensity to consume foreign goods, 0.8 and 0.2; and marginal propensity to invest, 0.2 and 0.1.

it may even move against the paying country. The diversity of results may appear to preclude the possibility of useful generalization. If, by alteration of marginal propensities to consume and invest, such pronounced differences as those noted are obtained, it is not difficult to believe that still other types of solution might be obtained with other propensities to consume and invest. Fortunately, this is not the case. It may be shown that, for the dynamic system postulated, the three tables are typical of the only solutions which are consistent with stable equilibrium. Hence, if we can summarize the tables, our answers will be general.

It is desirable, first, to note the essential differences between the tables. I have selected marginal propensities to consume and invest in such a way that certain stability conditions are fulfilled. Suppose for a moment that the entire consumption function of each country refers to domestic goods only and that each country is isolated. Call the sum of the marginal propensity to consume domestic goods and the former marginal propensity to consume imports the "marginal aggregate propensity to consume." It is easily shown that an isolated country is in stable equilibrium (in the sense that, after small displacements, the variables of the system tend to return to their old equilibrium positions) if the marginal aggregate propensity to consume *plus* the marginal propensity to invest is less than unity. If, for example, spendable income is increased by 10 in a country whose marginal aggregate propensity to consume is 0.5 and whose marginal propensity to invest is 0.1, the income of the next period will be $5 + 1 = 6$ higher than otherwise, because of the induced comsumption and investment. Likewise, income of the second period after the spending program will be $3 + 0.6 = 3.6$ higher than without the spending, because of the consumption and private investment induced by higher income of the previous period. Thus the sequence of differences between the equilibrium level of total income and the actual level will be a convergent series of the form 10, 6, 3.6, 2.16, 1.296, and so forth. On the other hand, if the marginal aggregate propensity to consume is 0.8 with a marginal propensity to invest of 0.5, the same reasoning as above shows that a spending program will set in motion a series of increasing differences between the actual and equilibrium levels of income. No tendency exists, in this case, for a return to the old equilibrium position.

In summarizing the tables, I shall say that a country is stable in isolation if the marginal aggregate propensity to consume *plus* the marginal propensity to invest is less than unity; otherwise it is unstable in isolation. The three tables may now be distinguished readily according to our stability condition. In Table 1 both countries are stable in isolation; in Table 2 the paying country is stable in isolation while the receiving country is unstable; finally, in Table 3 the receiving country is stable in isolation while the paying country is unstable. Although in Tables 2 and 3 one of the two countries is always unstable in isolation, the world economies in each case are nonetheless stable because of the low propensities to consume and invest of the stable country. The obvious fourth case—of two countries which are both unstable in isolation—is excluded because it is inconsistent with stability of the world economy.

A brief summary of our results may facilitate examination of the tables. Regular transfers affecting income directly in both countries (Case *a* of all three tables) will modify the system as follows:

(1) When both countries are stable in isolation, income will fall in the paying country and rise in the receiving country. The decline of imports and the rise of exports of the paying country will create a surplus of exchange which is inadequate to make the actual transfer; hence some further restriction in the paying country or expansion in the receiving country will be necessary.

(2) When the paying country is stable in isolation while the receiving country is unstable, total income will rise in both countries. The exports of the paying country will rise by more than her imports, and the favorable change in her balance of trade will be larger than the amount of the transfer.

(3) Conversely, if the paying country is unstable in isolation while the receiving country is stable, total income will fall in both countries. Imports of the paying country will fall by more than her exports, and again the favorable change in the trade balance will be greater than the amount of the transfer.

If the paying country permits the transfer to reduce income directly while the receiving country uses it to accumulate a government surplus, we may expect the following:

(1) Total income will fall in both countries regardless of stability conditions.

(2) In the normal case—in which both countries are stable in isolation—imports of the paying country will decline more than her

exports, but the surplus of bills thus created will not be sufficient for the entire transfer.

(3) With the paying country stable in isolation and the receiving country unstable, the decline of exports of the paying country will be greater than the decline of her imports. In other words, collection of the transfer sum by the paying country will turn the balance of trade against her and make payment more difficult than before. In this case no amount of income reduction in the paying country will create a surplus of bills of exchange.

(4) In the converse case—in which the paying country is unstable in isolation while the receiving country is stable—imports of the former will decline more rapidly than exports, and the surplus of bills will be greater than the amount of the transfer.

The following changes will occur if the transfer affects income directly in the receiving country only:

(1) Total income will rise in both countries, regardless of stability conditions.

(2) If both countries are stable in isolation, the rise of exports in the paying country will exceed the rise of imports, but the exchange surplus will be smaller than the amount of the transfer.

(3) An exchange surplus will likewise be created when the receiving country is unstable in isolation while the paying country is stable. Moreover, the excess of the rise in exports over the rise in imports will, in this case, be larger than the amount of the transfer.

(4) On the other hand, if the paying country is unstable in isolation and the receiving country is stable, the rise of imports of the paying country will exceed the increase of her exports. Thus direct expansion of income in the receiving country will serve only to aggravate the situation.

The multiplicity of results summarized above may seem, at first glance, rather bewildering. Even with a system as simple as the one with which I have dealt, no very broad generalizations may be demonstrated. Nevertheless, we are now beyond the stage of analysis in which literally "anything may happen," for it is possible to state precisely the conditions necessary to bring about a particular result. The conclusions, moreover, are not so complex as they first appear. Their systematic character may be examined most readily in Table 4 where, for purposes of comparison, I have tabulated them according to stability conditions and direct income effects.

Table 4. Summary of transfer results

Condition	Income affected directly in both countries	Income affected directly in paying country only	Income affected directly in receiving country only
Both countries stable in isolation	1. Income falls in paying country, rises in receiving country	1. Income falls in both countries	1. Income rises in both countries
	2. Trade balance moves in favor of paying country by less than amount of transfer	2. Trade balance moves in favor of paying country by less than amount of transfer	2. Trade balance moves in favor of paying country by less than amount of transfer
Paying country stable in isolation, receiving country unstable	1. Income rises in both countries	1. Income falls in both countries	1. Income rises in both countries
	2. Trade balance moves in favor of paying country by more than amount of transfer	2. Trade balance moves against paying country	2. Trade balance moves in favor of paying country by more than amount of transfer
Paying country unstable in isolation, receiving country stable	1. Income falls in both countries	1. Income falls in both countries	1. Income rises in both countries
	2. Trade balance moves in favor of paying country by more than amount of transfer	2. Trade balance moves in favor of paying country by more than amount of transfer	2. Trade balance moves against paying country

We are now in a position to evaluate the importance of real-income adjustments, induced by shifts of purchasing power, in creating a favorable change in the trade balance of the paying country. It is clear that such adjustments will not produce a sufficient surplus unless (a) one of the two countries is unstable in isolation and (b) the unstable country permits the transfer to affect its income directly. Empirical evidence is inadequate to determine how often such a situation may be encountered.

Most investigations of consuming and importing habits have revealed marginal aggregate propensities to consume considerably less than unity. It seems likely, therefore, that few countries will have marginal propensities to consume and invest large enough to place them in the unstable class. In other words the "normal" case—of stability in both countries—appears to be the most probable one. If this is true, real-income movements induced by shifts of purchasing power may be expected to create only a part of the surplus required for capital transfers.

Appendix

The propositions set forth above may easily be verified analytically. Let $y = u_1(y) + v(y) + u_2'(y')$ represent income of the debtor country, where $u_1(y)$ is her consumption of domestic goods, $v(y)$ her domestic investment, and $u_2'(y')$ her exports, assumed to depend upon income of the creditor country. Likewise, income of the creditor country may be represented by $y' = u_1'(y') + v'(y') + u_2(y)$. The balance of trade of the paying country is then given by $b = u_2'(y') - u_2(y)$. The three equations of our static system are sufficient to determine the three unknowns y, y', and b:

$$y = u_1(y) + v(y) + u_2'(y') - \theta - \tau,$$

(A1) $$y' = u_1'(y') + v'(y') + u_2(y) + \theta' + \tau,$$

$$b = u_2'(y') - u_2(y).$$

Parameters θ, θ', and τ of Eqs. (A1) represent, respectively, transfers which affect income directly in the paying country only, transfers which affect income directly in the receiving country only, and transfers which affect income directly in both countries. By differentiating Eqs. (A1) partially with respect to these parameters it may be shown that

$$\frac{\partial b}{\partial \theta} = \frac{u_{2y}(1 - v'_{y'} - u'_{y'})}{\Delta} \equiv 1 - \frac{(1 - v_y - u_y)(1 - v'_{y'} - u'_{y'})}{\Delta},$$

(A2) $$\frac{\partial b}{\partial \theta'} = \frac{u'_{2y'}(1 - v_y - u_y)}{\Delta} \equiv 1 - \frac{(1 - v_y - u_{1y})(1 - v'_{y'} - u'_{y'})}{\Delta},$$

$$\frac{\partial b}{\partial \tau} = \frac{u_{2y}(1 - v'_{y'} - u'_{y'}) + u'_{2y'}(1 - v_y - u_y)}{\Delta}$$

$$\equiv 1 - \frac{(1 - v_y - u_y)(1 - v'_{y'} - u'_{y'})}{\Delta},$$

where

$$\Delta \equiv (u_{1y} + v_{1y} - 1)(u'_{1y'} + v'_{y'} - 1) - u_{2y}u'_{2y'},$$

$$u_y \equiv u_{1y} + u_{2y},$$

and

$$u'_{y'} \equiv u'_{1y'} + u'_{2y'}.$$

Letter subscripts, of course, indicate differentiation. "Income effects," obtained in the same process of differentiation, are given by Eqs. (A3).

$$\text{(A3)} \qquad
\begin{aligned}
\frac{\partial y}{\partial \theta} &= -\frac{(1 - v'_{y'} - u'_{1y'})}{\Delta}, & \frac{\partial y'}{\partial \theta} &= -\frac{u_{2y}}{\Delta}, \\[2mm]
\frac{\partial y}{\partial \theta'} &= \frac{u'_{2y'}}{\Delta}, & \frac{\partial y'}{\partial \theta'} &= \frac{1 - v_y - u_{1y}}{\Delta}, \\[2mm]
\frac{\partial y}{\partial \tau} &= -\frac{(1 - v'_{y'} - u'_{y'})}{\Delta}, & \frac{\partial y'}{\partial \tau} &= \frac{1 - v_y - u_y}{\Delta}.
\end{aligned}$$

I have shown elsewhere that, for the dynamic system postulated, stability of the world economy requires that Δ be positive and that both $u_{1y} + v_y$ and $u'_{1y'} + v'_{y'}$ be less than unity.[9] Further, the paying country is stable or unstable in isolation according as $u_y + v_y$ is less than or greater than unity, while the receiving country is stable or unstable in isolation according as $u'_{y'} + v'_{y'}$ is less than or greater than unity. With these restrictions in mind, all the conclusions of Table 4 may be established from Eqs. (A2) and (A3).

9. The proof is obtained from solution of a set of difference equations, of which the system of equations (A1) in the appendix is a limiting case. See Lloyd A. Metzler, "Underemployment Equilibrium in International Trade," which appears as Chapter 10 of the present volume.

3 | Imported Raw Materials, the Transfer Problem, and the Concepts of Income

The analysis of income transfers presented in the preceding chapter assumed that both the paying country and the receiving were self-sufficient economies, so that all imports were either for business expenditure (investment) or for personal expenditure; imports of raw materials to be worked into final products were left out of the picture. Subsequently, a more sophisticated system, in which output required the importation of raw materials, was developed by Professor Meade,[1] and the results of Meade's work, in a somewhat modified form, were applied to the transfer problem by my colleague, Harry Johnson.[2]

Superficially, the sophisticated version seemed to differ from the earlier and more elementary version which I had developed. The concepts of income used in the two theories were different, however, and the results accordingly were difficult to compare. In this chapter, I propose to examine the two versions with similar definitions of income. Specifically, I shall demonstrate that the elementary theory for economies self-sufficient in raw materials, with which I initially studied the

Revised version of a lecture delivered before the student-faculty seminar, Massachusetts Institute of Technology, December 11, 1963. Not previously published.

1. James E. Meade, "National Income, National Expenditure, and the Balance of Payments," *Economic Journal*, 58 (December 1948), 483–505, and 59 (March 1949), 17–39. See also Meade's *The Theory of International Economic Policy*, vol. 1: *The Balance of Payments* (London, Oxford University Press, 1951), chap. 7.

2. In a lecture delivered at the University of Chicago. Johnson's most important contribution to the transfer problem employs the same assumption concerning production as mine—namely, that both countries are self-sufficient. See Harry G. Johnson, "The Transfer Problem and Exchange Stability," *Journal of Political Economy*, 64 (June 1956), 212–225, reprinted in *International Trade and Economic Growth* (London, George Allen and Unwin, 1958), chap. 7.

transfer process, leads to results which are identical to those developed by Meade and Johnson for an interdependent system. In short, the existence of imported raw materials does not in any essential way alter the conclusions of Chapter 2.

In order to establish this result, I shall begin with a simplified version of the elementary theory presented in the preceding chapter. The simplifications are based largely upon the work of Meade.[3] In my initial study of the transfer problem, I assumed that domestic expenditure consisted in personal expenditure plus net investment. In accordance with Meade's procedure, I shall combine these two elements into a single expenditure function. In addition, I shall also alter the concept of domesticity, again to make it comparable to Meade's.

In Chapter 2, I considered domestic expenditure to be the expenditure of a country's residents upon its own goods. In this chapter, domestic expenditure will be defined as expenditure of a country's residents upon all goods, regardless of whether these goods are produced at home or abroad. This definition has certain obvious advantages, both from a statistical and from an analytical point of view. Statistically it allows one to concentrate upon the relation between income and expenditure, without considering whether such expenditure is upon home goods or imports. When interpreted in this way, domestic expenditure is readily available from budget studies and from studies of investment; and the overcounting which results from including imports in domestic expenditure can be corrected, simply by subtracting such imports from the total. Analytically, the alternative definition of domestic expenditure greatly simplifies the matrix of the system for a two-country economy. This will become apparent, I believe, when I present below a version of the elementary theory based upon Meade's concept of domestic expenditure.

The Elementary Theory for Self-Sufficient Economies

I hope the reader will forgive me if I change the notation slightly from my original scheme. Upon rereading my initial study of income transfers in Chapter 2, I find the notation used there exceedingly confusing, to say the least.

Consider two countries A and B, trading with each other, and suppose that A makes an annual reparation payment or income transfer

3. "National Income" (reference 1), p. 491.

to B, the payment being an amount τ. Let the currency units be chosen in such a way that one unit of A-currency is equal to one unit of B-currency. The income transfer, in money terms, will then be the same for B as for A.

Before proceeding further, we must make a distinction between two types of income which arise whenever a transfer is considered. An income transfer is essentially a redistribution of income between one country and another. This means that, after the transfer takes place, income accruing to the factors of production will differ systematically from the value of income produced by the economy. In this chapter the value of income produced will be called "national output," while the income accruing to the factors of production, after allowing for the transfer, will be called "factor income."

Suppose now that the government of each country passes on the full effects of the transfer, in the form of increased taxes in A and increased subsidies, or reduced taxes, in B. For the paying country, factor income then falls short of the national output by the amount of the transfer; and for the receiving country, factor income exceeds national output, again by the amount of the transfer.

Let y_a and y_b represent factor income in A and B, respectively; and let $\hat{y}_a$ and $\hat{y}_b$ represent national output. Recalling that A is the paying country and B the receiving, we have:[4]

$$y_a = \hat{y}_a - \tau, \text{ or } \hat{y}_a = y_a + \tau$$

(1)

and

$$y_b = \hat{y}_b + \tau, \text{ or } \hat{y}_b = y_b - \tau .$$

My first study of income transfers adopted factor income as the appropriate definition. Meade, on the other hand, carried out his analysis in terms of national output. I intend to show later that for self-sufficient economies, it makes no difference which definition of income is used. But if output requires the importation of raw materials, the situation is quite different. In this case the demand for finished goods depends upon factor income, whereas the demand for imported raw materials depends upon the level of economic activity or national output; and in computing the state of a country's foreign payments and receipts, we must include both finished goods and raw materials in the accounts.

---

4. For these relationships to hold exactly, national output must be defined as net of capital accumulation.

In the analysis which follows, I shall describe the transfer process in terms of factor incomes and self-sufficient economies. Let $S_a(y_a)$ represent domestic expenditure of country A, expressed as a function of factor income y_a. The term $S_a(y_a)$ includes business expenditure as well as personal expenditure, expenditure on imports as well as expenditure on home-produced goods. Let $m_a(y_a)$ represent imports of country A, again expressed as a function of factor income in A. The terms $S_b(y_b)$ and $m_b(y_b)$ are analogous functions for country B. Bearing in mind that one country's imports are the other country's exports, and assuming that the full effects of the transfer are transmitted to the factors of production—through increased taxes in the paying country and increased subsidies in the receiving—we may describe factor income in each of the two countries, and the balance of payments of country A, by the following equations:

$$y_a = S_a(y_a) + m_b(y_b) - m_a(y_a) - \tau,$$

(2) $$y_b = S_b(y_b) + m_a(y_a) - m_b(y_b) + \tau,$$

and $$B_a = m_b(y_b) - m_a(y_a) - \tau.$$

Equations (2) are the basic equations of my initial theory of income transfers, adjusted to Meade's definition of domestic expenditure. In principle, these equations could be solved to express y_a, y_b, and B_a as explicit functions of the transfer τ. The explicit functions could then be differentiated to see how a change in τ alters our three variables y_a, y_b, and B_a. In practice, however, such a procedure is impossible, for we do not know the exact form of $S_a(y_a)$, $S_b(y_b)$, $m_a(y_a)$, or $m_b(y_b)$. We must therefore differentiate (2) implicitly with respect to τ, and solve the equations for $dy_a/d\tau$, $dy_b/d\tau$, and $dB_a/d\tau$. When this is done, it will be found that

$$\frac{dy_a}{d\tau} = \frac{-(1 - S_b')}{\Delta},$$

(3) $$\frac{dy_b}{d\tau} = \frac{(1 - S_a')}{\Delta},$$

and $$\frac{dB_a}{d\tau} = \frac{-(1 - S_a')(1 - S_b')}{\Delta},$$

where Δ is the Jacobian determinant,

$$(4) \qquad \Delta = \begin{vmatrix} 1 - S_a' + m_a' & -m_b' \\ -m_a' & 1 - S_b' + m_b' \end{vmatrix}.$$

Two alternative expansions of Δ are[5]

$$(5) \qquad \Delta = (1 - S_a' + m_a')(1 - S_b' + m_b') - m_a'm_b'$$

and

$$(6) \qquad \Delta = m_b'(1 - S_a') + m_a'(1 - S_b') + (1 - S_a')(1 - S_b').$$

The terms S_a' and m_a' are the marginal propensities to spend and to import for country A, while S_b' and m_b' are analogous functions for country B. As long as S_a' and S_b' both are less than unity, Eq. (6) shows that all of the terms of Δ are positive and Δ must therefore be positive. Conversely, if S_a' and S_b' are both greater than unity, Eq. (5) shows that Δ must be negative. The sign of Δ is therefore indeterminate. Fortunately, it is possible, by setting up a dynamic system and using Samuelson's well-known "correspondence principle,"[6] to show that the system cannot be stable unless Δ is positive.[7] This is done in the appendix to this chapter. I leave it to the reader to prove, from (5) and (6) above, that the following combinations of S_a' and S_b' are consistent with a positive Δ and a stable, two-country economy:

$$S_a' < 1, \; S_b' < 1,$$

$$S_a' < 1, \; S_b' = 1,$$

$$(7) \qquad S_a' = 1, \; S_b' < 1,$$

$$S_a' > 1, \; S_b' < 1,$$

and

$$S_a' < 1, \; S_b' > 1.$$

If $S_a' > 1$, I shall say that country A is a "spendthrift country"; its marginal increment in spending exceeds its marginal increment in factor income. If $S_a' < 1$ the country will be called a "frugal country";

5. The first expansion, in Eq. (5), is the one I used in the preceding chapter. The second expansion, in Eq. (6), is attributable to my colleague, Harry Johnson.

6. Paul A. Samuelson, *Foundations of Economic Analysis* (Cambridge, Mass., Harvard University Press, 1947), chap. 9. For a more complete description of the correspondence principle see the appendix to this chapter.

7. The condition of stability is necessary, but not sufficient. See the appendix.

the marginal increment of spending is here less than the marginal increment of income. Finally, if $S_a' = 1$, country A will be called a "borderline spender"; in this situation, the marginal increase in spending is exactly equal to the marginal increase of income. Needless to say, a similar terminology applies to B.

From Eqs. (3) above, one can see how an income transfer affects the factor income of A, the factor income of B, and the balance of payments of country A, excluding capital movements but allowing for the influence of the transfer itself. Table 1 gives the direction of change of each

Table 1. Influence of an income transfer upon y_a, y_b, and B_a for all stable combinations of S_a' and S_b'

Variable	$S_a'<1, S_b'<1$	$S_a'<1, S_b'=1$	$S_a'=1, S_b'<1$	$S_a'>1, S_b'<1$	$S_a'<1, S_b'>1$
$\dfrac{dy_a}{d\tau}$	$-$	0	$-$	$-$	$+$
$\dfrac{dy_b}{d\tau}$	$+$	$+$	0	$-$	$+$
$\dfrac{dB_a}{d\tau}$	$-$	0	0	$+$	$+$

of these variables for all combinations of S_a' and S_b' consistent with stability of our two-country economy.

The possibilities depicted in Table 1 are numerous, but I shall attempt to summarize them in a few points:

(1) The adjustment of country A's balance of payments to the transfer may be incomplete ($dB_a/d\tau$ negative), exactly complete ($dB_a/d\tau = 0$), or overcomplete ($dB_a/d\tau$ positive).

(2) In the normal case, where S_a' and S_b' are both less than unity as in the first column of the table, the adjustment is incomplete in spite of the fact that both countries contribute to improving A's balance of trade; the paying country's imports are reduced as a result of contracting income in that country, while her exports are increased as a consequence of expanding income in the receiving country. Nevertheless, the declining imports and rising exports create an export surplus less than the amount of the transfer.

(3) The balance-of-payments adjustment is exact whenever one of the two countries is a borderline spender. If A is the borderline spender, the adjustment takes place entirely through a reduction of income and

imports in that country; the receiving country's income remains constant and her imports from the paying country are therefore unchanged. Conversely, if B is the borderline spender, the adjustment takes place entirely through an increase in A's exports to B, while income in A remains unchanged. Thus, in the cases where the transfer creates an exact adjustment, it does so in spite of the fact that the adjustment is one-sided.

(4) The balance-of-payments adjustment will be overcomplete whenever one of the countries is a spendthrift country. Again, it makes no difference, so far as the payments adjustment is concerned, whether the spendthrift country is A or B. If A is the spendthrift country, the transfer leads to a general contraction of factor incomes in both countries. As a consequence, exports and imports of country A both decline. But the reduction of imports is so much larger than the reduction of exports that country A has a favorable balance of payments despite the adverse effects of her transfer payment and declining exports. If B is the spendthrift country, the transfer leads to a general expansion, so that exports and imports of A both rise. Again, the increase of exports is so large relative to the increase of imports that country A has a favorable balance of payments, despite her rising imports and transfer obligations.

(5) In all cases in which the adjustment is exact or overcomplete, the transfer takes place entirely through changes of income in the spendthrift country. The frugal country makes no contribution to the adjustment process; indeed its contribution may even be negative.

(6) The marginal propensities to import, which played such an important role in the orthodox theory, have disappeared entirely from the picture. As far as the *direction* of change of any variable is concerned, as distinguished from its *magnitude*, the final results do not depend at all upon the import functions. The outcome is governed, instead, by the internal relations between income and expenditure in each of the two countries. This fact reflects the close relation of my analysis to Professor Alexander's income-absorption approach.[8] In examining the effects of devaluation upon a country's balance of payments, Alexander found it necessary to change his emphasis from the traditional elasticities of supply and demand to the internal relations between income and absorption. Likewise in examining the influence of an

8. S. S. Alexander, "The Effects of a Devaluation on a Trade Balance," *International Monetary Fund Staff Papers*, 2 (April 1952), 263–278.

income transfer upon the paying country's balance of payments, I have found myself drawn ineluctably away from the orthodox marginal propensities to import, and toward the internal relations between income and expenditure.

(7) Finally, a few words should be said about the movements of factor incomes y_a and y_b revealed in Table 1. The orthodox theory envisaged a decline of purchasing power in the paying country and a rise in the receiving. The term "purchasing power," I believe, may be regarded as equivalent to factor income in my terminology. A glance at Table 1 shows that factor income behaves according to the orthodox theory in only one situation, namely, when both A and B are frugal countries as in the first column. Otherwise, factor income may remain unchanged in A and rise in B, as in the second column; fall in A and remain unchanged in B, as in the third column; fall in both countries, as in the fourth column; or rise in both, as in the fifth column. The orthodox theory did not recognize such a wide variety of possibilities, principally because it concentrated upon the *primary* movement of income associated with the transfer and did not consider the *secondary* repercussions. As I have shown, the combination of primary and secondary changes produces some rather unpredictable results. Thus a transfer of money income between one country and another may put both countries into a state of depression or lead to a general expansion of factor incomes in each. But whatever happens to factor incomes, it is obvious from Eqs. (3) and Table 1 that the transfer process depends entirely upon the internal relations between income and expenditure and not at all upon the external marginal propensities to import. I regard the change of emphasis from external conditions to internal ones as the principal contribution of my initial examination of the transfer problem.

The Transfer Process between Interdependent Economies

As I have mentioned earlier, whenever imported raw materials are taken into account, the distinction between factor income and national output is a matter of considerable importance. Factor income is a measure of economic welfare, and in this capacity it governs the demand for finished goods, including both imports and domestic expenditure. National output, on the other hand, is a measure of economic activity or employment, and in this respect it determines the demand for imported raw materials.

Now we have seen that an income transfer creates a systematic discrepancy between factor income and national output. Since the balance of payments includes both raw materials and finished goods, it is evident that the existence of imported raw materials in the production function must complicate the import function to a considerable extent. Indeed, a case can be made that the transfer process between interdependent economies is more sluggish than that between self-sufficient economies. Consider, for example, the borderline situation where either S_a' or S_b' is equal to unity. My analysis of the transfer process between self-sufficient economies suggests that, under these conditions, the adjustment process is exact; primary and secondary movements of factor incomes create an export surplus for the paying country precisely equal to the transfer payment. On the other hand, if output requires the importation of raw materials, the balance-of-payments adjustment may be incomplete, so that the paying country has a deficit in its balance of payments even when one country or the other is a borderline spender.

The reason for this discrepancy is that the transfer itself creates an adverse movement in the demand for raw materials. In country A, for example, the demand for imports of raw materials rises, while in B the demand for such imports from A declines. The paying country therefore begins with a deficit in raw-materials trade, which must be offset by a corresponding surplus of trade in finished goods. In order to achieve a balance on trade as a whole, the paying country must accordingly have a surplus in the only thing it can produce, namely, finished goods measured at value added in manufacture, or factor cost.

Upon first examination of this reasoning, I was inclined to accept it at face value. But later it occurred to me that the very element which makes the process of adjustment more difficult, that is, the adverse movement in the demand for raw materials, is also the source of a greater shift in purchasing power. Thus the decline of raw-material imports in country B augments the initial, negative effect of the transfer payment in country A, while the rise of raw-material imports in A likewise augments the initial, positive effect of the transfer receipt in B. On balance, the larger autonomous decline in A's factor income, and the larger autonomous rise in B's, exactly offset the adverse movement in the demand for raw materials, leaving a final result which, at the margin is identical to my initial theory for self-sufficient economies. In short, the presence of imported raw materials does not, in any essential respects, alter the conclusions I have drawn from my elementary theory in Chapter 2.

At this juncture the argument will be clarified, I believe, by introducing a rectangular diagram. Figure 1 shows, for both country A and

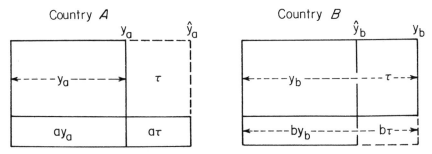

Figure 1

country B, the interrelations between factor income, national output, the transfer τ, and imported raw materials. National output is measured at value added by manufacture, or factor cost, and not at market prices. Since the transfer is in money terms and is the same for both countries, it follows that, in order to express the transfer in real terms, units of output must be chosen so as to make value added by manufacture, or factor cost, the same for A as for B. This can be done without any loss of generality.

Factor income at factor cost is measured by the top part of the diagrams, while the raw-materials content is measured by the lower portion. I have said above that the presence of imported raw materials creates an adverse movement in the demand for such materials, relative to factor income; the demand for imported materials rises in the paying country and falls in the receiving. From Fig. 1 it should be clear why this is true. Consider, for example, the situation in country A. Between y_a (factor income) and $\hat{y}_a$ (national output), there is an area of output which yields no income. Within this region, the income that would normally be earned in production is taxed away in financing the transfer payment. Conversely, in country B there is an area of income between $\hat{y}_b$ and y_b which requires no output. Within this region, factor income has been augmented, not by increased production, but simply by the additional subsidies associated with the transfer receipt.

The reader will recall that the demand for imported raw materials depends upon national output, $\hat{y}_a$ or $\hat{y}_b$, and not upon factor income, y_a

or y_b. In country A, for example, the region $\hat{y}_a - y_a$, although it earns no income, still requires the importation of raw materials simply because it represents a region of output; from the diagram, the additional demand for raw materials is $a\tau$. Thus if the transfer is analyzed in terms of factor income, the demand for such materials will not be ay_a, but $ay_a + a\tau$. Conversely, in country B, the demand for imported raw materials will not be by_b but $by_b - b\tau$.

I have now shown that, in terms of factor incomes, a transfer induces a systematic increase in the paying country's demand for raw materials and a systematic decrease in the receiving country's demand for such materials. It follows that, as of given factor incomes, the debtor country is faced with a less favorable balance on raw-materials account, the deterioration of its balance being $(a + b)\tau$. In order to achieve balance on both finished goods and raw-materials accounts, the movements of factor incomes must therefore be sufficient to create a surplus on finished goods. I presume that this is the basis for the argument that the adjustment process is more difficult for interdependent economies than for self-sufficient ones.

But such an argument neglects an important point: although the income movements have a greater job to perform, because of the adverse movement in the debtor country's raw-materials account, the forces which induce the adverse movement also augment the autonomous decline of factor income in the paying country and the autonomous rise of such income in the receiving. At the margin, the adverse movement on raw-materials trade is exactly offset by the more favorable movement in factor incomes, leaving a result which is identical to the conclusions of my original theory.

In order to demonstrate this proposition, I shall adopt a definition of expenditure which is as comprehensive as possible and make the necessary corrections at a later stage. First, both domestic expenditure and imports will be evaluated at market price rather than factor cost; and second, domestic expenditure, as before, will include expenditure on goods produced abroad as well as expenditure on home goods. Starting then with national output at market price, we must make three adjustments to reduce this gross concept to factor income at factor cost: first, imports of finished goods must be subtracted from the total, as in the preceding section; second, the value of imported raw materials must be subtracted in order to reduce the measurement of income components from market price to value added by manufacture, or factor cost; and finally, the transfer τ must be subtracted in A and added in B in order to convert all figures into factor incomes rather than national outputs.

Let y_a, as before, be the factor income of country A, evaluated at factor cost in A. This y_a is equivalent to the money income actually received by the country's residents, after allowing for the transfer. Let y_b represent the same concept for country B. Finally, let $S_a(y_a)$, $m_a(y_a)$, $S_b(y_b)$, and $m_b(y_b)$ represent the domestic expenditure and import functions, respectively. All functions are defined at market prices and depend upon factor income for the relevant country.

We may begin by deriving the income equation for the paying country, A. The expression

$$(8) \qquad S_a(y_a) + m_b(y_b) - m_a(y_a)$$

for a self-sufficient economy represents national output at market prices. In an interdependent system, however, the demand for a country's exports comprises two parts. The first is the value of B's imports of finished goods from A, represented by the term, $m_b(y_b)$ in (8). The second is the value of raw materials which B imports from A. As we have seen in Fig. 1, these imported raw materials have a value of $b\hat{y}_b$, or $by_b - b\tau$, an expression which does not appear at all in (8). Suppose then that we add A's exports of raw materials to her exports of finished goods. We obtain another expression, as follows:

$$(9) \qquad S_a(y_a) + m_b(y_b) - m_a(y_a) + by_b - b\tau.$$

In (9) we have a representation for country A's national output at market price. (There is no notation for this particular type of income and we shall need none, since (9) is merely an intermediate stage in the derivation of factor income at factor cost.) If we subtract the value of imported raw materials from (9), the resulting equation represents national output at factor cost. We have seen above that the import content for country A is $a\hat{y}_a$, or $ay_a + a\tau$. Subtracting this amount from (9), and using the term $\hat{y}_a$ to denote national output at factor cost, we have

$$(10) \qquad \hat{y}_a = S_a(y_a) + m_b(y_b) - m_a(y_a) + by_b - b\tau - ay_a - a\tau.$$

Finally, in order to derive factor income at factor cost it is necessary to subtract τ from the right-hand expression in Eq. (10). When this is done and the terms involving τ are combined, we find

(11) $\quad y_a = S_a(y_a) + m_b(y_b) - m_a(y_a) + by_b - ay_a - (1 + a + b)\tau.$

By a similar process, it is possible to show that the equation for factor income at factor cost in country B is

(12) $\quad y_b = S_b(y_b) + m_a(y_a) - m_b(y_b) + ay_a - by_b + (1 + a + b)\tau.$

The equation for the balance of payments of country A is obtained directly from Eq. (11), without adjustment:

(13) $\quad B_a = m_b(y_b) - m_a(y_a) + by_b - ay_a - (1 + a + b)\tau.$

Combining (11), (12), and (13), we have three equations in the three unknowns y_a, y_b, and B_a, thus:

$$y_a = S_a(y_a) + m_b(y_b) - m_a(y_a) + by_b - ay_a - (1 + a + b)\tau,$$

(14) $\quad y_b = S_b(y_b) + m_a(y_a) - m_b(y_b) + ay_a - by_b + (1 + a + b)\tau,$

and $\quad B_a = m_b(y_b) - m_a(y_a) + by_b - ay_a - (1 + a + b)\tau.$

Equations (14) are the analogues, for interdependent economies, of my original model for self-sufficient economies. Although they appear to be quite complicated, their solution is exceedingly simple, owing to the fact that several terms vanish. Before attempting a solution, I should like to call attention to a number of interesting features of these equations. Largely, these are conditions of consistency, but they are also conditions which simplify the solution of Eqs. (14). First, the balance of payments of B is the negative of the balance of payments of A, as it should be in a two-country economy; if B has a surplus in her balance of payments, A has a deficit *of exactly the same amount*. To put the matter another way, one may say that every foreign payment in A is matched by an equal foreign receipt in B; this result is a consequence of the comprehensive definition I have given to the expenditure functions, a definition which always requires a negative correction. Second, under an interdependent system, the power of the transfer to create an autonomous shift in demand is considerably augmented. Thus, a transfer of τ creates an autonomous reduction of demand in country A amounting to $(1 + a + b)\tau$, and an equal autonomous increase of demand in country B. The augmentation of demand does not mean, however, that the process of adjustment proceeds more smoothly. Looking at the equation for B_a in (14), we see that the deficit to which the income movements must adjust is augmented by the same amount. In terms of factor income at factor cost, the deficit toward which the system must be adapted is not $-\tau$ but $-(1 + a + b)\tau$. As I have said above, the income movements have a bigger job to do, but at the same time the stimulus to do this job is greater. This confirms my earlier conjecture that the adverse movement in the demand for raw materials would be exactly offset by larger shifts in purchasing power.

Finally, a word should be said about the distinction between finished goods and raw materials. Consider, for example, the trade between the United States and Bolivia. Bolivia has a large supply of tin deposits and is accordingly an exporter of tin concentrates to the United States. At the same time she needs mining machinery to extract the deposits, and this machinery she imports from the United States. The United States, on the other hand, has a shortage of minerals, and must therefore import tin concentrates to be used in the production of machinery. Now, from the point of view of Bolivia, tin concentrates are obviously a final product and machinery is the imported material required for its production. Conversely, from the point of view of the United States, machinery is a final product and tin concentrates are the raw materials required for its production.

From this example, it is obvious that the distinction between raw materials and final products is a rather ambivalent one, shifting about as it does between one point of view and another. Nevertheless, I believe my equations, although perhaps unduly rigid, are still flexible enough to allow for this change in viewpoint. In the second of Eqs. (14), for example, raw-materials imports for country B are set at $b\hat{y}_b = by_b - b\tau$, and this amount is subtracted from the total in order to measure y_b at factor cost. In the first of these equations, however, B's imports of raw materials are regarded as A's exports of final products and accordingly added to the expression for income in A. Likewise, imports of raw materials by A are recorded as exports of final products by B. The situation described in Eqs. (14) is thus entirely analogous to the trade between the United States and Bolivia.

This concludes what I have to say about the transfer process between interdependent economies. I turn now to a solution of the basic system. Differentiating (14) with respect to τ and solving the linear equations for $dy_a/d\tau$, $dy_b/d\tau$, and $dB_a/d\tau$, we find:

$$\frac{dy_a}{d\tau} = \frac{-(1 + a + b)(1 - S_b')}{D},$$

(15)

$$\frac{dy_b}{d\tau} = \frac{(1 + a + b)(1 - S_a')}{D},$$

and

$$\frac{dB_a}{d\tau} = \frac{-(1 + a + b)(1 - S_a')(1 - S_b')}{D}.$$

D in (15) is again the Jacobian determinant,

$$(16) \quad D = \begin{vmatrix} (1 - S_a' + m_a' + a) & -(m_b' + b) \\ -(m_a' + a) & (1 - S_b' + m_b' + b) \end{vmatrix},$$

and again the condition of stability is that D be positive.

Comparing Eqs. (15) with Eqs. (3) for self-sufficient economies, one finds that the numerators are identical, except for the positive constant $(1 + a + b)$. Again the marginal propensities to import have been replaced by the internal relations between income and expenditure. And again the condition for exact adjustment is that one of the two countries be a borderline spender. Indeed, if a table were prepared from Eqs. (15), similar to Table 1 from Eqs. (3), the signs would be precisely the same for the new table as for Table 1. At a cursory glance, the reader might be tempted to say that movements of factor incomes would be larger for the interdependent system than for the self-sufficient one, since the positive term $(1 + a + b)$ appears in the equations for y_a and y_b in (15) but not in similar equations in (3). Such a conjecture would be incorrect, however, for the Jacobian determinant in (15) differs from that in (3). Nevertheless, on purely intuitive grounds, it seems probable that the existence of imported raw materials would, in some degree, magnify the income adjustments in both countries. This will necessarily be true, for example, in the normal case if S_a' and S_b' are not only less than one but also equal to each other.

To summarize, the existence of imported raw materials increases the initial deficit to which the system must adjust, on the one hand, and thereby makes the process of income adjustment more difficult. The initial deficit is not $-\tau$, but $-(1 + a + b)\tau$. On the other hand, while the primary deficit is larger, so is the primary reduction of purchasing power in A and the primary increase in B. Moreover, the shift in purchasing power is augmented in both countries to the same extent that the deficit is augmented, that is, by a factor $(1 + a + b)$. The larger reduction of purchasing power in A, and the larger increase in B, are exactly canceled by the larger deficit to which the income movements must adjust, leaving a net result which does not differ essentially from my elementary theory for self-sufficient economies.

A careful reader of the preceding argument will no doubt see that it contains a restrictive implicit assumption, namely, that the raw-materials content of national output is the same for the debtor country as for the creditor; in the notation employed above this says that $a = b$. Paradoxically, a less careful reader may have considerable difficulty in seeing that such an assumption enters the analysis at all. The resolution of this paradox lies in the definition of the expenditure function: domestic expenditure is the expenditure of a country's residents upon all finished goods, including expenditure on home-produced goods as well as on imports. Such expenditure is measured at market price and, in the present context, market price means cost of production, including the cost of imported materials as well as the cost of finished goods. This implies that, unless the import content of production is the same for country A as for country B, the expenditure function for any given country will necessarily exhibit a discontinuity as the spenders shift their outlays from home goods to imports. The assumption that $S_a(y_a)$ and $S_b(y_b)$ are continuous functions of y_a and y_b thus implies that $a = b$ or that the import content of production is the same for country A as for country B.

I have no doubt that the preceding discussion of income transfers could be modified by assuming that the raw-materials content of output differs between country A and country B; algebraically, this implies $a \neq b$. I feel certain, moreover, that such an assumption would not alter the conclusions of my initial examination in any essential respects. A procedure of this sort, however, would require the introduction of input-output analysis, and would thus complicate the problem to a considerable degree. In any event, the analysis presented above shows that the introduction of imported raw materials produces no *systematic* bias in the conclusions of my initial study.

Before I conclude this chapter, however, there is some unfinished business to which I must attend. In the first section, I suggested that for self-sufficient economies it is a matter of indifference whether the study of income transfers is carried out in terms of factor income or national output; properly interpreted, both concepts of income lead to the same conclusions. Now I propose to demonstrate this proposition.

Self-Sufficient Economies and the Concepts of Income

National output, to repeat, is the value of a country's total output, without making allowance for the fact that some of this output may be redistributed from one country to another through the transfer. Factor income, on the other hand, is the income accruing to a country's residents after allowing for the transfer payment in country A and the transfer receipt in country B. Thus in the debtor country, factor income falls short of national output, while in the creditor country, factor income exceeds national output; in both cases, the discrepancy is exactly equal to the transfer τ.

A general agreement prevails, I believe, that the expenditure functions, $S_a(y_a)$ and $S_b(y_b)$, depend upon factor income and not national output. The same is true for the import functions, $m_a(y_a)$ and $m_b(y_b)$, in the self-sufficient economy. It follows that if Eqs. (2) are to be described in terms of national output, a correction must always be made to bring one concept in line with the other. Moreover, in the equations defining national output, the transfer τ may be omitted entirely, for national output is a gross concept, independent of the distributive effects of the transfer. In short, national output equals domestic expenditure *plus* exports *less* imports for either country. Thus, in the notation I have used, the system of equations in terms of national output is as follows:

$$\hat{y}_a = S_a(\hat{y}_a - \tau) + m_b(\hat{y}_b + \tau) - m_a(\hat{y}_a - \tau),$$

(17)
$$\hat{y}_b = S_b(\hat{y}_b + \tau) + m_a(\hat{y}_a - \tau) - m_b(\hat{y}_b + \tau),$$

and
$$B_a = m_b(\hat{y}_b + \tau) - m_a(\hat{y}_a - \tau) - \tau.$$

These can be transformed into my initial equations (2), in terms of factor income, by the most elementary algebraic operations. First, subtract τ from both sides of the first equation in (17); second, add τ to both sides of the second equation; and, finally, substitute y_a for $\hat{y}_a - \tau$ and y_b for $\hat{y}_b + \tau$. This makes clear that the assumptions implied in the factor-income equations (2) are identical to those implied in the national-output equation (17).

Once more, it must be noted that Eqs. (17) are valid only for self-sufficient economies. Since the transfer τ appears explicitly in all of the expenditure and import functions, one may readily determine that the marginal propensity to spend or to import, as a function of the transfer, is assumed to be the same as the marginal propensity to spend or to import, as a function of income from production. This means that the taxes imposed in country A do not affect either $S_a(y_a)$ or $m_a(y_a)$. Similar statements are valid, of course, for country B. In my factor-income system of Eqs. (2), the transfer τ does not appear explicitly in any of the functions $S_a(y_a)$, $m_a(y_a)$, $S_b(y_b)$, or $m_b(y_b)$. Hence it is natural to assume that the marginal propensity to spend or to import, as a function of the transfer, is zero for both countries. And second, the transfer τ in Eqs. (2) appears at the end of the equations for y_a and y_b, only as $-\tau$ and $+\tau$, respectively. Again, it is natural, from the implicit system, to assume that $-\tau$ and $+\tau$ are part of the domestic-expenditure functions and that the marginal propensity to spend, relative to the transfer, is unity in both countries. A glance at Eqs. (17), where the transfer enters explicitly, shows that neither of these premises is correct.

Since, for self-sufficient economies, the effects of an income transfer may be examined either in terms of factor income or in terms of national output, the definition of income would seem to be a matter of taste. Another consideration, however, argues strongly in favor of factor income as the appropriate concept. This consideration is the relative simplicity of the two systems. Analysis in terms of factor income turns out to be much more direct and simple than analysis in terms of national output. In the factor-income equations (2), for example, the parameter τ appears only three times. By contrast, in the national-output equations (17), τ appears no less than nine times. From this point of view factor income is thus the "natural" concept to use in the study of income transfers. Anyone who doubts this statement is invited to differentiate both (17) and (2) with respect to τ, and to solve the resulting equations.

As a corollary to the results I have achieved thus far, it is interesting to compare my initial theory for self-sufficient economies with the ingenious theory set forth by my colleague, Harry Johnson.[9] The two theories ought to be comparable, for Johnson considers self-sufficient economies, as I have done in Chapter 2. And yet his final results, superficially at any rate, appear to be quite different and considerably more complex than mine. The increased complexity arises from two sources. First, the transfer problem is examined from the point of view of national output. Second, the analysis is further complicated by the introduction of a system more general than the one in Chapter 2, that allows the marginal propensities to spend domestically and to import,

---

9. "The Transfer Problem and Exchange Stability" (reference 2), sec. 2.

as functions of the transfer, to differ from similar propensities to spend and to import, as functions of national output. As a consequence, his model contains eight propensities, or first derivatives, whereas my model contains only four. In the remainder of this chapter, I propose to show that, if the premises with respect to marginal propensities to spend and to import are the same, Johnson's complex model is identical to my more simple one, provided both models are expressed in the same concept of income.

Let us begin then with a brief resume of Johnson's model. I use his notation (the differences are minor and need no explanation) but change his equations by defining domestic expenditure as expenditure of a country's residents upon all goods, regardless of whether produced at home or abroad. This, of course, requires that we deduct imports from the income equations for both countries, and Johnson's system becomes:

$$Y_a = I_a + S_a Y_a + M_b + m_b Y_b - M_a - m_a Y_a,$$

(18) $$Y_b = I_b + S_b Y_b + M_a + m_a Y_a - M_b - m_b Y_b,$$

and $$B_a = M_b + m_b Y_b - M_a - m_a Y_a - \tau.$$

Johnson does not indicate explicitly what concept of income he employs, but it is clear from the equations for Y_a and Y_b that he is actually dealing with national output. Otherwise the transfer would appear in both equations.

In order to transform the model (18) into something resembling (17), one must first of all substitute for the autonomous shifts of domestic and foreign expenditure, I_a, I_b, M_a, and M_b, functions involving the transfer τ explicitly. Johnson assumes that the marginal propensities to spend and to import, as functions of the transfer, differ from similar propensities, as functions of national output. Thus we have:

(19)
$$I_a = -S_a' \tau, \qquad I_b = S_b' \tau,$$
$$M_a = -m_a' \tau, \quad \text{and} \quad M_b = m_b' \tau.$$

In (19), the marginal propensities to spend and to import have been written with primes to indicate that the spending and import functions, relative to the transfer, are allowed to differ from corresponding functions, relative to national output. Johnson's model is accordingly less restrictive and more general than mine.

In principle, a good case can be made for Johnson's more general approach. If someone gave me ten dollars, for example, I have no doubt that I would spend it in a different way than if the ten dollars had been earned by increased activity. Conversely, if I were forced to give ten dollars to another person, there are good reasons to suppose that I would reduce my spending in a different way than if the reduction of my income had come from decreased activity or employment. Thus, the more general approach is obviously superior, in principle, to the restricted approach of my initial theory. In practical application, however, the superiority is not so clear. In the first place, there are virtually no criteria to determine, a priori, how one propensity differs from another. And in the second place, given this ambiguity, the final results turn out to be equally ambiguous. Thus Johnson's equation for the effect of the transfer on the balance of payments of country A is

$$(20) \qquad B_a \tau = \left\{ m_a' + m_b' - \frac{m_a'}{s_a} s_a' - \frac{m_b'}{s_b} s_b' - 1 \right\} \frac{s_a s_b}{\Delta} \tau.$$

In Eq. (20), $s_a = 1 - S_a$, $s_a' = 1 - S_a'$, and so on, while Δ has the same value as previously and is necessarily positive as a condition of stability.

From Eq. (20), it is clear that nothing can be inferred about the movement of country A's balance of payments unless something is known about the relative values of the primed and unprimed propensities. This ambiguity is the price that must be paid for generalizing the system. Under the circumstances, we are faced with the choice of considering a restrictive model, which yields a definite result, or a more general one, which yields an ambiguous result. The choice, I suppose, is largely a question of taste. As for myself, I have always preferred the former to the latter. It is on these grounds that I defend my initial position; a general model producing an ambiguous result is, in my judgment, a step backward toward the days of Walras, when counting of equations and variables was believed to constitute a solution to the problem.

But more than this can be said in favor of my original system. In making a separate distinction between marginal propensities to spend and to import, according to the source of income changes, Johnson is implicitly considering the results of a compound change, consisting first of the effects of the transfer itself, and second of the effects of an internal redistribution of income within both countries. It would indeed be a contribution to economics if we could discover the effects of such compound parameters. But obviously we cannot do this. Given the complexity of the problem, even for a two-country economy, the most reasonable procedure would seem to be to isolate the influence of the transfer alone, and to abstract from the influence of redistributions of income in both countries.

If this is done, I would stress that Johnson's system (18), which is in terms of national output, becomes equivalent to Eqs. (17). Moreover, I have shown that (17) bears a one-to-one correspondence to my model expressed in terms of factor income. The premises described by Eqs. (18) and (19) are precisely the ones I used in my initial study (Chapter 2). The identity between Johnson's approach and mine includes more than the balance-of-payments equation; it is valid for incomes as well, provided the concept of income is the same in both cases. Johnson reaches the conclusion that his income movements differ from mine, but I believe I have shown that such an interpretation is unwarranted.

At the time of this writing, my contribution to the theory of income transfers is only a few years short of its silver anniversary. It is worthwhile, I believe, to ask how the theory has withstood the test of time. To suppose that no changes are required, after such a lapse of time, would be foolish if not arrogant. When I first began my examination of the transfer problem, I had no clear idea of the distinction between factor income and national output, which has played such a dominant role in this chapter. Nor did I understand the significance of imported raw materials. Indeed, my first examination of income transfers contained only an elementary concept of income and was based upon a two-country model in which both countries were self-sufficient in production. It was Meade and Johnson who first called my attention to the complexities which arise when output requires the importation of raw materials and to the necessity of distinguishing between one type of income and another. For this increase in the sophistication of my elementary theory, I am greatly indebted to both of these distinguished economists.

Appendix

In the text of this chapter I asserted without proof that both Δ, for the self-sufficient system, and D, for the interdependent one, must be positive as conditions of stability. As the reader will recall, Δ and D are Jacobian determinants having the following notations first, for the self-sufficient system, we have

(A1)
$$\Delta = \begin{vmatrix} (1 - S_a' + m'_a) & - m_b' \\ - m_a' & (1 - S_b' + m_b') \end{vmatrix};$$

and, second, for the interdependent system, D is

(A2)
$$D = \begin{vmatrix} (1 - S_a' + m'_a + a) & (- m_b' + b) \\ - (m_a' + a) & (1 - S_b' + m_b' + b) \end{vmatrix}.$$

In this appendix, I propose to give rigorous proofs for both of the propositions stated in Chapter 3, namely, that Δ and D must be positive to assure the stability of either the self-sufficient economy or the interdependent one. I shall begin with the self-sufficient system, which adopts the premise of my initial contribution to the theory of income transfers.

Stability of a Self-Sufficient System

The static equilibrium for a two-country economy, in which country A makes an income transfer of τ currency units to country B, has been represented by the following system of equations:

$$y_a = S_a(y_a) + m_b(y_b) - m_a(y_a) - \tau,$$

(A3)
$$y_b = S_b(y_b) + m_a(y_a) - m_b(y_b) + \tau,$$

and
$$B_a = m_b(y_b) - m_a(y_a) - \tau.$$

Equations (A3) are static equations. They show how a given transfer alters the equilibrium income in country A, the equilibrium income in country B, and the balance of payments, excluding capital movements, of country A. But they give no information whatever as to how the system, once disturbed, tends to approach its new equilibrium, or whether it converges toward any equilibrium at all. Dynamic stability depends upon neither the nature of the autonomous disturbances nor the character of the static equations, but only upon the explicit system of dynamic equations. If the system is stable for an income transfer, it will also be stable for a general expansion of demand in one of the two countries, provided the autonomous disturbances are small. Likewise, if the system is *unstable* for an income transfer, it will be unstable for an expansion of demand, again on the premise that the autonomous disturbances are small. In short, stability depends only upon the homogeneous part of a system of dynamic equations, and not at all upon the particular solution. On this account, the system may be considerably simplified by assuming that the transfer τ, initially has a value of zero. With τ put equal to zero, Eqs. (A3) become homogeneous in y_a, y_b, and B_a; furthermore, the discrepancy between factor income and national output, which played such an important part in the preceding discussion, disappears from the picture. Thus $\hat{y}_a = y_a$ and $\hat{y}_b = y_b$; as a result, national output and factor income may be treated synonymously. To complete the analysis of stability, one must first specify an explicit dynamic system, a point which many distinguished economists have neglected. Moreover, if we are to evaluate the sign of Δ from an examination of dynamic stability, the dynamic system must be equivalent to or, in Samuelson's terms, must correspond to, the static equations (A3), with $\tau = 0$. "Equivalence" or "correspondence" in this sense means that, when the dynamic system has come to rest so that $\hat{y}_a$ and $\hat{y}_b$ are equal to zero, the resulting equations are identical to the static equations.

Let us begin then with the following premises: Suppose that, whenever the demand for aggregate output exceeds actual output in either country, producers in that country expand output. Suppose further that whenever the demand for aggregate output falls short of actual output, producers contract output. And let the speed of adjustment in each case be proportional to the discrepancy between demand and output. Finally, suppose that the balance of payments of country A, excluding capital transfers, is merely a definitional equation, expressing this balance as an instantaneous function, without lag, of exports *minus* imports. These premises may be incorporated in the following system of differential equations:

$$\dot{y}_a = [S_a(y_a) + m_b(y_b) - m_a(y_a) - y_a],$$

(A4) $$\dot{y}_b = [S_b(y_b) + m_a(y_a) - m_b(y_b) - y_b],$$

and $$B_a = m_b(y_b) - m_a(y_a).$$

If the ρ-matrix for the differential equations (A4) is represented by $\phi(\rho)$, we have

(A5)
$$\phi(\rho) = \begin{bmatrix} \rho & 0 & 0 \\ 0 & \rho & 0 \\ 0 & 0 & 0 \end{bmatrix}.$$

Let $-A$ represent the general matrix, with the coefficients of y_a, y_b, and B_a combined, and all expressions reduced to linear form, thus:

(A6)
$$-A = \begin{bmatrix} (S_a' - m_a' - 1) & m_b' & 0 \\ m_a' & (S_b' - m_b' - 1) & 0 \\ -m_a' & m_b' & -1 \end{bmatrix}.$$

From (A6) it follows that

$$(A7) \qquad A = \begin{bmatrix} (1 - S_a' + m_a') & -m_b' & 0 \\ -m_a' & (1 - S_b' + m_b') & 0 \\ m_a' & -m_b' & 1 \end{bmatrix}.$$

Finally, from (A5) and (A7), the characteristic equation of our differential system is

$$(A8) \qquad |\phi(\rho) + A| = \begin{vmatrix} \rho + (1 - S_a + m_a') & -m_b' & 0 \\ -m_a' & \rho + (1 - S_b' + m_b') & 0 \\ m_a' & -m_b' & 1 \end{vmatrix} = 0.$$

The determinant in (A8) is readily reduced to a second-degree determinant by expanding along the third column. This procedure yields a much simplified equation,

$$(A9) \qquad |\phi(\rho) + A| = \begin{vmatrix} \rho + (1 - S_a' + m_a') & -m_b' \\ -m_a' & \rho + (1 - S_b' + m_b') \end{vmatrix} = 0.$$

By expanding the second-degree determinantal equation (A9) about its principal diagonal, we find:

$$(A10) \qquad \rho^2 + [(1 - S_a' + m_a') + (1 - S_b' + m_b')]\rho + \Delta = 0.$$

In Eq. (A10) the expression Δ has the same notation as in the text and in (A1).

Well-known Routh-Hurwitz conditions for stability, or dampened characteristic roots, are that both coefficients in this quadratic be positive. Thus, $\Delta > 0$ is necessary. Even if one of the saving coefficients, S_a' or S_b', were to exceed unity, provided that the middle coefficient added up to a positive number and $\Delta > 0$, we would be assured of dynamic stability.

I have now completed the proof that a positive Δ is necessary, but not sufficient, for stability of a transfer—or any other autonomous disturbance—between two self-sufficient economies. I turn next to the stability of an interdependent system, where output requires the importation of raw materials in each country.

Stability of an Interdependent System

I have shown in the text of this chapter that an income transfer amounting to τ between two interdependent countries, A and B, may be represented by the following system of equations:

$$y_a = S_a(y_a) + m_b(y_b) - m_a(y_a) + by_b - ay_a - (1 + a + b)\tau,$$

(A11) $y_b = S_b(y_b) + m_a(y_a) - m_b(y_b) + ay_a - by_b + (1 + a + b)\tau,$

and $B_a = m_b(y_b) - m_a(y_a) + by_b - ay_a - (1 + a + b)\tau.$

Starting with (A11), I wish to show that a positive D is essential for stability, where D is the determinant,

$$
(A12) \qquad D = \begin{vmatrix} (1 - S_a' + m_a' + a) & -(m_b' + b) \\ -(m_a' + a) & (1 - S_b' + m_b' + b) \end{vmatrix}.
$$

The proof is quite similar to that given in the preceding section for a self-sufficient system. Note that Eqs. (A3) and (A11) are both of the same form, in that $m_a(y_a) + ay_a$ is the same kind of monotone function in y_a as $m_a(y_a)$ itself is; the same is true of a comparison involving $m_b(y_b) + by_b$ and $m_b(y_b)$. So no separate proof is needed, once we note that D involves the denominator of our new functions in exactly the same way that Δ involves the denominator of the old function.

Summarizing the results of this appendix, one may say that it gives a rigorous proof that the self-sufficient system, as well as the interdependent one, cannot be stable unless their respective Jacobian determinants, Δ and D, are each positive.

4 | Flexible Exchange Rates, the Transfer Problem, and the Balanced-Budget Theorem

The purpose of this paper is to demonstrate the close analogy between the transfer process and the balanced-budget theorem, on the assumption that the transfer takes place between two countries linked to each other through a flexible exchange-rate system. In the course of the argument, I hope to show that an income transfer, rather than creating a fall of purchasing power in the paying country and a rise in the receiving country, actually has no effect whatever upon the incomes of the factors of production in either country. This means that the concept of a shift in purchasing power, which played a significant role in the famous controversy between Lord Keynes and Professor Ohlin concerning the feasibility of German reparations after World War I, need not be taken into account. Indeed, the effects of the transfer may be examined on the basis of given schedules of demand for imports in both countries. All this is true on the assumption that the governments of both countries follow balanced-budget policies and thereby pass on to the income earners the full effects of the transfer in the form of increased taxes in the paying country and increased subsidies in the receiving country. It also assumes an efficient free-market exchange rate so that the paying country has neither a surplus nor a deficit in its balance of payments.

To be sure, the balanced-budget assumption will not always be consistent with internal price stability, for the analysis below shows that the

Revised version of a lecture delivered before the International Economic Relations Seminar, Harvard University, December 12, 1963, and the graduate students' seminar at Purdue University, February 3, 1964. Not previously published.

95

rate of economic activity, or national output, tends to rise in the paying country and to fall in the receiving country in spite of the fact that factor incomes remain unchanged in both countries. The price effects thus depend upon the supply schedules for goods and services in both countries. If general unemployment prevails and output is produced at constant cost, the changes in national output may have no serious consequences upon prices and costs. In this case, a balanced-budget policy is consistent with domestic price stability. On the other hand, if output is rather rigidly fixed or is produced under conditions of increasing costs, prices can be stabilized, in the face of an income transfer, only by monetary or fiscal measures which maintain the demand for goods and services at a constant level.

For simplicity, I shall assume that the stabilizing measures are changes in taxes or subsidies. To maintain a constant demand for output, both countries must then overbalance their budgets: in the paying country, where output rises, taxes must be increased by more than the payment; and in the receiving country, where output falls, *subsidies* must be increased by more than the receipts. In short, the paying country must have a budget surplus, while the receiving country must have a deficit. Moreover, the smaller the marginal propensity to spend in each country, the larger will be the size of the surplus in the former and the deficit in the latter.

In describing the transfer process under flexible exchanges, I shall proceed as follows. The first section will briefly describe the balanced-budget theorem for an isolated economy, including the two concepts of income needed for an understanding of this theorem. Then I shall demonstrate how the balanced-budget theorem can be applied to a reparation payment or other income transfer between countries, assuming that output can rise or fall at constant cost so that the combination of balanced budgets and flexible exchanges produces both price stability and equilibrium in the balance of payments. The third section will be devoted to a situation where the supply of output is produced at increasing cost; to stabilize internal costs, it is necessary in this situation to keep the demand for output at a constant level. In the fourth section, the controversy between Lord Keynes and Professor Ohlin will be discussed in the light of conclusions reached in the preceding sections. I shall attempt to reconcile these divergent views by showing that Keynes's view is valid when output is produced at constant cost, while Ohlin's view is valid when output is produced at increasing cost. The paper will conclude with a few remarks about the monetary policies required to make real equilibrium consistent with monetary equilibrium. At the same time, I shall demonstrate that exchange flexibility is not essential to the argument but is merely a way of ensuring equilibrium in each country's balance of payments.

The Balanced-Budget Theorem for an Isolated Economy

The essence of the balanced-budget theorem, of course, is that a uniform increase of both taxes and expenditures increases the amount of economic activity or employment while leaving income after taxes unchanged. From this statement it should be evident that two concepts of income are needed to describe the effects of a balanced-budget expansion; and later it will be clear that these two concepts have perfect counterparts in the case of an income transfer between countries.

The first of these is income after taxes, or "factor income" as I shall call it. Factor income resembles closely the concept of "personal income" which the Department of Commerce uses in its numerous studies of spending and saving. It is significant because it governs the demand for goods and services, including the demand for both domestic goods and imports. The second concept is the level of economic activity, or "national output" in my terminology. The counterpart of national output in the Department of Commerce statistics is "gross national product" less depreciation of capital. National output is important because it measures the expansion or contraction of economic activity in contrast to the income earned by such activity; if anyone wished to stabilize employment, for example, he would stabilize national output rather than factor income.[1]

I shall begin with a highly simplified version of the circular flow of output or income and of the role which government plays in such output or income. Suppose, for example, that the government's tax receipts and expenditures are balanced at a level of zero so that national output is determined entirely by personal and business expenditures. Let y

1. Whether national output should be measured net or gross of capital depreciation is a question I have not answered here. If it is to be used as a measure of employment, gross national product is of course the appropriate measure. But if factor income and output are to be related to government expenditures and receipts, the problem is greatly simplified by considering national output net of capital depreciation. This is the procedure I have followed. A reservation should accordingly be made to the statement in the text that national output measures the expansion or contraction of economic activity.

represent factor income and $\hat{y}$ national output. And let $S(y)$ represent the spending function of both income earners and businessmen, that is, personal expenditure *plus* business investment, with the stability assumption that $0 < S' < 1$. (Many readers will object, no doubt, that to neglect the rate of interest as a determinant of investment is a greater oversimplification, if not a complete distortion. Under some conditions, this would clearly be true. But for the particular problem of income transfers under flexible exchanges that I am discussing here, the balance of payments is in equilibrium, adjustment takes place without a flow of money, and, except for movements in the terms of trade, the rate of interest may reasonably be given a secondary position.)

Under the initial assumption of no government expenditures and no taxes, factor income y is equal to national output $\hat{y}$. Suppose that we begin with factor income. In the notation outlined above, factor income is determined by the following equation:

(1) $$y = S(y).$$

Suppose now that the government enters upon a balanced-budget expansion program, increasing its expenditures by an amount θ and taxing its residents by the same amount. As soon as taxes and expenditures rise, a systematic discrepancy is created between factor income y and national output $\hat{y}$. Specifically:

(2) $$y = \hat{y} - \theta, \text{ or } \hat{y} = y + \theta.$$

I assume that the expenditure function S continues to depend upon factor income y rather than national output $\hat{y}$. Nevertheless, it is convenient to express this function in such a way that national output becomes an explicit variable in the argument, thus: $S = S(\hat{y} - \theta)$. The demand for national output, after the expansion occurs, consists of private and business expenditures, $S(\hat{y} - \theta)$, *plus* government expenditures θ. If output is adjusted so that it is equal to total demand, we therefore have:

(3) $$\hat{y} = S(\hat{y} - \theta) + \theta.$$

Differentiating Eq. (3) implicitly with respect to θ and collecting coefficients of $d\hat{y}/d\theta$, we find:

(4) $$(1 - S') \frac{d\hat{y}}{d\theta} = (1 - S'),$$

where S' is the marginal propensity to spend out of factor income. From Eq. (4) it is evident[2] that

$$(5) \qquad \frac{d\hat{y}}{d\theta} = \frac{(1 - S')}{(1 - S')} = 1.$$

Equation (5) says that national output rises as much as government expenditures. Moreover, since $y = \hat{y} - \theta$, we have

$$(6) \qquad \frac{dy}{d\theta} = \frac{d\hat{y}}{d\theta} - 1 = 1 - 1 = 0.$$

Thus factor income remains constant while national output rises to the full extent of the balanced-budget expenditures. The increased taxes are paid, not through a reduction of income, but rather through an expansion of economic activity which earns additional income; despite the rise of output or employment, factor income remains unchanged because the additional earnings are taxed away.

The effects of a balanced-budget *contraction* are exactly opposite to those of a balanced-budget expansion; factor income again remains unchanged, but national output or employment *falls* instead of rising as in the expansion case. This proposition can be established simply by changing the sign of θ in Eq. (3) above. Obviously, a balanced-budget contraction means that government expenditures are reduced while subsidies are increased by the same amount. Factor income thus rises, relative to national output, because of the increased subsidies. The relation between factor income and national output, after the contraction, may be expressed as follows:

$$(7) \qquad y = \hat{y} + \theta, \text{ or } \hat{y} = y - \theta.$$

Assuming, as before, that personal and business expenditures depend upon factor income y and not upon national output $\hat{y}$, we have from (3) the following equation for a country undertaking a balanced-budget contraction:

$$(8) \qquad \hat{y} = S(\hat{y} + \theta) - \theta.$$

A minor problem arises here in the treatment of government expenditures, for it appears that such expenditures are negative. What meaning can be attached to negative government expenditures? The problem could have been avoided by starting with some initial, positive level $\bar{\theta}$

---

2. Obviously, the system is indeterminate unless $S' < 1$.

of expenditures and assuming that this level is reduced by an amount $\theta(<\bar{\theta})$. For the uses to which I expect to apply the balanced-budget theorem, however, even this small degree of complication is unnecessary; the government's contribution to expenditures, in the transfer case, is an indirect one, arising through the influence of the transfer upon the balance of trade; this indirect influence may well be negative. Consider, for example, the position of the receiving country. Under a flexible-exchange system, an inflow of transfer funds must be balanced by an import surplus of the same amount, and the import surplus is equivalent, as far as national output is concerned, to indirect, negative government expenditures.

Once again, differentiating (8) with respect to θ and collecting coefficients of $d\hat{y}/d\theta$, we find

$$(9) \qquad \frac{d\hat{y}}{d\theta}(1 - S') = (S' - 1),$$

from which it follows that

$$(10) \qquad \frac{d\hat{y}}{d\theta} = -1.$$

Equation (10) says that national output falls as government expenditures are reduced in a balanced-budget contraction; and the reduced output is exactly equal to the reduced expenditures.

Since $y = \hat{y} + \theta$, we have the following equation for the movement of factor income:

$$(11) \qquad \frac{dy}{d\theta} = \frac{d\hat{y}}{d\theta} + 1 = -1 + 1 = 0.$$

Factor income remains unchanged despite the reduction of output or employment; reduced earnings from lower employment are exactly offset by increased subsidies.

These basic and well-understood ideas concerning the effects of a balanced-budget expansion or contraction will now be applied to the transfer problem. I shall begin with the situation where unemployment exists and output is produced at constant cost. It is perhaps worth noting that under these conditions the paying country is put in the position of a country undertaking a balanced-budget expansion, while the receiving country occupies the position of a country undertaking a balanced-budget contraction.

The Transfer Process with Elastic Supply

Consider two countries, A and B, and suppose that A makes an annual income transfer to B, the transfer being equal to τ currency units of the receiving country B. Suppose that the two countries have a flexible exchange rate, and that π is the price of B's currency in terms of A's. Let y_a and y_b represent the factor incomes of A and B, respectively, while $\hat{y}_a$ and $\hat{y}_b$ are the corresponding national outputs. The currency units will be chosen in such a way that $\pi = 1$ before the transfer begins.

Whenever a flexible exchange rate is introduced, two difficulties immediately arise: first, the measure of real income is ambiguous, since the prices of foreign goods differ from those of domestic goods; and, second, even if a measure of income were derived, the relation of domestic expenditures to income would remain uncertain, because any movement in the rate of exchange involves a rise or fall in the real income associated with a given level of employment and no statistical studies have been made for this type of expenditure function.

In an earlier paper, written with Svend Laursen, my collaborator and I suggested that, given a fixed money income and a fixed domestic price level, currency depreciation is likely to reduce the amount of saving because it raises the prices of imports and thereby reduces the real value of a given money income.[3] To this suggestion, there were a number of objections. Professor White objected that Duesenberry's study of the consumption function had shown the long-run ratio of saving to real income to be constant, regardless of the level of real income.[4] Professor Haberler commented that the exchange influence, if any, was likely to be of second order of smalls.[5] My colleague, Harry Johnson, expressed the opinion I have suggested above—namely, that no evidence is available to decide the question since a decline in real income resulting from higher import prices at constant output is essentially different from a decline resulting from lower output at constant import prices.[6]

3. Svend Laursen and Lloyd A. Metzler, "Flexible Exchange Rates and The Theory of Employment." This article appears as Chapter 11 of the present volume.

4. W. H. White, "The Employment-Insulating Advantages of Flexible Exchanges: A Comment on Professors Laursen and Metzler," *Review of Economics and Statistics*, 36 (May 1954), 225–228.

5. Gottfried Haberler, personal conversation with the author.

6. This argument was developed by Johnson in a lecture before the student-faculty seminar at the University of Chicago. In his publication of this lecture it seemed to me that he accepted the view of White; see Harry G. Johnson, *International Trade and Economic Growth* (London, George Allen and Unwin, 1958), p. 187n.

In view of all these objections, I shall assume hereafter that the expenditure function, in money terms, is a function of factor income alone and is independent of the terms of trade. Except when the average propensity to save is constant, such a function can easily be shown to be inconsistent with rational behavior; but, alas, I cannot satisfy everyone! In any event, part of this paper deals with a situation where such a problem does not arise. In a fixed-exchange system, the central question of income transfers is whether a given transfer will alter demand so that the paying country has an export surplus equal to its transfer, and a balance-of-payments equilibrium can be achieved with no movements in money and prices. By contrast, in a flexible-exchange system, the balance of payments is *always* in equilibrium, since the exchange rate is adjusted to make it so. Overadjustment or underadjustment in such a system is reflected, not by a surplus or deficit in the balance of payments, but by what happens to the exchange rate. If the price of foreign currencies rises in the paying country, for example, this signifies underadjustment; conversely, a fall signifies overadjustment. Only when the exchange rate remains constant after the system has adjusted itself to the transfer can we say that the adjustment is complete. Complete adjustment, however, is precisely the condition I wish to examine; and under such a condition there will be no movements in import prices and no ambiguity about the expenditure function.

Returning now to our transfer problem we may recall that A is obligated to pay an amount τ to B, the sum being designated in terms of the currency of B. The currency units of the two countries were initially determined so that the price of B's currency was unity; but in the short run there will be an interim price π, probably greater than unity, the exact amount depending upon the elasticities of demand for imports in both countries. This means that A must pay to B an income transfer equal to $\pi\tau$, measured in its own currency. And if A follows a policy of balancing its budget, taxes to the full extent of the transfer, or $\pi\tau$, must be levied upon its residents. Domestic expenditures will then be a function, $S_a(\hat{y}_a - \pi\tau)$, of domestic output *less* taxes, or factor income.

Since we are now dealing with open economies, new definitions are needed for factor income and national output, in both the paying country and the receiving. In each country, the demand for output is *equal* to domestic expenditures *plus* exports. And, if we follow Meade's procedure of including in domestic expenditures the expenditures of residents on foreign goods as well as on home-produced goods, we must subtract out the total of these imports which really do not constitute a demand for home goods at all.[7] The definition of national output then becomes: national output *equals* domestic expenditures *plus* exports *less* imports.

For the paying country, the exchange rate has adjusted itself to the point π where the export surplus, in domestic currency, is equal to the transfer payment $\pi\tau$. In the notation I have used above, national output for country A may therefore be represented by the following equation:

$$\hat{y}_a = S_a(\bar{y}_a - \pi\tau) + \pi\tau.$$

The analogy between the position of the paying country and that of an isolated country undertaking a balanced-budget expansion is obvious from a comparison of Eqs. (12) and (3). It is hardly necessary to show that national output and factor income behave as follows:

(13)
$$\frac{d\hat{y}_a}{d(\pi\tau)} = 1,$$

and
$$\frac{dy_a}{d(\pi\tau)} = \frac{d}{d\pi\tau}(\hat{y}_a - \pi\tau) = 1 - 1 = 0.$$

In words, Eq. (13) says that national output or employment in the paying country rises by the amount of the transfer payment while factor income remains unchanged; the residents of country A pay for the transfer by increased activity and not by reduction of income.

Consider now what happens in the receiving country. In B, the amount of the transfer is τ, regardless of the exchange rate, since it is payable in terms of B currency. On the assumption that country B balances its budget, receipt of the transfer will be accompanied by an increase in subsidies; as a consequence, factor income will exceed output by the amount of the transfer. Moreover, when the market for foreign exchange is in balance, receipt of the transfer must carry with it an import surplus of the same amount. Thus the national output equation for country B is

(14)
$$\hat{y}_b = S_b(\bar{y}_b + \tau) - \tau.$$

Equation (14) will be recognized as the equation for a country carrying

---

7. See James E. Meade, "National Income, National Expenditure, and the Balance of Payments," *Economic Journal*, 58 (December 1948), 485.

out a balanced-budget contraction. From our earlier discussion we know that such a contraction reduces national output or economic activity while leaving factor income unchanged.

We are now in a position to summarize the consequences of an income transfer from A to B, under the premises of flexible exchanges and constant costs: first, output after taxes, or factor income, remains constant in both countries; and second, economic activity, or national output, rises in the paying country and falls in the receiving, the change in each country being exactly equal to the payment or receipt, measured in domestic currency. At first glance, these conclusions seem paradoxical, for we have seen that factor income remains unchanged in both countries, even though the full effects of the transfer are transmitted to income earners in the form of higher taxes in the paying country and higher subsidies in the receiving. In the paying country, for example, factor income remains constant in spite of the fact that taxes are increased by the full extent of the transfer; and, in the receiving country, factor income remains constant in spite of the fact that subsidies are increased, again by the full extent of the transfer.

The resolution of this paradox is to be found in the interrelation between taxes, subsidies, and the balance of trade. In the paying country, for example, taxes are increased by the amount of the transfer, and this initially reduces the factor income associated with a given level of output. Eventually, however, the debtor country acquires an export surplus, which increases factor income and national output concomitantly; under the premise of flexible exchange rates, the export surplus is exactly equal to the amount of the transfer payment. Thus, in country A an increase in taxes, which reduces factor income, is exactly offset by an export surplus, which augments both factor income and national output. On balance, therefore, the transfer payment leaves the returns of income earners unchanged while increasing the rate of economic activity, or national output, by the exact amount of the transfer.

In the creditor country, an increase in subsidies is exactly offset by an *import* surplus of the same amount; the former increases factor income at a given level of output while the latter reduces *both* factor income and national income. The net effect of the transfer in the receiving country is accordingly a constant factor income and a falling rate of economic activity or national output.

Thus far I have assumed that national output rises or falls with no appreciable consequences upon the level of domestic costs; that is, I have assumed a state of constant cost for the output of both countries. To complete my examination of income transfers, I propose next to consider a situation in which output is produced at rising costs; external balance will be maintained, as before, through the operation of a flexible exchange rate. But a rise or fall of internal costs, under increasing supply price, can be prevented only if the debtor and creditor countries take measures to stabilize national output. As I have pointed out before, this means that both countries must abandon their balanced-budget policies. The debtor country must increase its taxes by more than its transfer payment, while the creditor country must increase its subsidies by more than its receipt.

The Transfer Process, Internal Balance, Taxes, and Subsidies

Let θ_a and θ_b represent the taxes in the paying country and the subsidies in the receiving country, respectively. Suppose that these taxes and subsidies are determined in each country so as to stabilize output in each. The stabilized outputs may be represented by $\bar{y}_a$ and $\bar{y}_b$ for each of the two countries. Factor income will then be $\bar{y}_a - \theta_a$ in A, and $\bar{y}_b + \theta_b$ in B. Equations for national output in both countries will then be given by Eqs. (15) below.

$$(15) \qquad \bar{y}_a = S_a(\bar{y}_a - \theta_a) + \pi\tau \qquad \text{and} \qquad \bar{y}_b = S_b(\bar{y}_b + \theta_b) - \tau.$$

Implicit differentiation of the first equation with respect to $\pi\tau$, and of the second with respect to τ, yields.

$$(16) \qquad \frac{d\theta_a}{d\pi\tau} = \frac{1}{S_a'} \qquad \text{and} \qquad \frac{d\theta_b}{d\tau} = \frac{1}{S_b'}.$$

As long as S_a' and S_b' are less than unity, Eqs. (16) show that the increased taxes in A and the increased subsidies in B, required for internal stability, are larger than the monetary transfer in each country. Moreover, the smaller the marginal propensity to spend in the given country, the larger the budget surplus in A and the corresponding deficit in B. Since national output remains unchanged in both countries, factor income falls in A by the amount of increased taxes and rises in B by the amount of increased subsidies. Thus under the premise of over-balanced budgets in both countries, the income transfer *does* create a shift of purchasing power which may conceivably give A an export surplus equal to the transfer, even with no movement of exchange rates. Indeed, as long as the marginal propensity to spend is less than unity in each country, the fall of factor income in A, and the rise in B, will both be larger than the domestic-currency equivalent of the transfer in each country.

In country A, for example, factor income falls by an amount $\pi\tau/S_a'$, compared to an income payment of $\pi\tau$; and in B, factor income *rises* by τ/S_b', compared to an income *receipt* of τ. Such changes in factor incomes clearly imply a fall in the demand for imports in the paying country and a rise in such demand in the receiving country.

What are the conditions under which the shift of purchasing power will produce a complete adjustment of A's balance of payments with no changes in the exchange rate? In order to answer this question we must set $\pi = 1$. The balance of payments of country A, in either A-currency or B-currency, then becomes:

$$(17) \qquad B_a = m_b\left(\bar{y}_b + \frac{\tau}{S_b'}\right) - m_b\left(\bar{y}_b - \frac{\tau}{S_a'}\right) - \tau.$$

Differentiating Eq. (17) with respect to τ, and equating the differential to zero, we find that the condition for complete adjustment, on the assumption that taxes and subsidies in both countries are established so as to maintain national output at a constant level, may be expressed as follows:[8]

$$(18) \qquad \frac{dB_a}{d\tau} = \frac{m_a'}{S_a'} + \frac{m_b'}{S_b'} - 1 = 0.$$

With overbalanced budgets and constant output, Eq. (18) shows that the paying country's balance of trade may adjust itself quite easily to the transfer; as I have mentioned above, the possibility of a complete adjustment is greater, the smaller are the marginal propensities to spend, S_a' and S_b', in A and B, respectively. The reason for this is that, with low propensities to spend, higher taxes in the paying country and higher subsidies in the receiving country must be imposed in order to prevent potential inflation in the former and potential deflation in the latter. As consequence of these higher taxes and subsidies,

---

8. These equations bear a family resemblance to similar ones derived by Harry G. Johnson for a transfer process in which the financing of the transfer was not expected to leave spending functions unchanged. See particularly his *International Trade and Economic Growth* (reference 6), p. 179.

the size of the transfer is augmented from the point of view of income earners. In short, factor income falls by more than the transfer in the paying country and rises more in the receiving. The demand for imports therefore falls more in the paying country and rises more in the receiving country than it would under a balanced budget situation.

The Keynes-Ohlin Controversy

The conclusions obtained thus far throw an interesting light on the well-known controversy between Lord Keynes and Professor Ohlin concerning the feasibility of German reparations following World War I. I should like to present a documented version of this dispute, but space limitations do not permit it. Although most of the controversy occurred in a single volume (1929) of the *Economic Journal*,[9] it has nevertheless developed into a sort of legend, with little reference to what these distinguished economists actually said.

According to the legend, Keynes is supposed to have examined the transfer process on the assumption that the demand for imports is fixed in both countries. Ohlin, on the other hand, is now widely regarded as the originator of the doctrine of a shift in purchasing power. This view postulates that the transfer reduces factor income in the paying country and thereby diminishes the demand for imports. In the receiving country, on the other hand, factor income is increased and the demand for imports from the paying country rises. Thus, even without a change in prices or exchange rates, the paying country automatically acquires an export surplus which may conceivably be as large as her transfer.

The legend regarding Ohlin's work, but for which Ohlin himself was not directly responsible, may be described roughly as follows:

9. A list, in chronological order, of the contributions of Keynes and Ohlin, together with an article by Jacques Rueff, whose criticism of Keynes started the controversy anew, is presented below:

(*a*) J. M. Keynes, "The German Transfer Problem," *Economic Journal*, 39 (March 1929), 1–7.

(*b*) B. Ohlin, "The Reparation Problem: A Discussion. I. Transfer Difficulties, Real and Imagined," *Economic Journal*, 39 (June 1929), 172–178.

(*c*) J. M. Keynes, "The Reparation Problem: A Discussion. II. A Rejoinder," *ibid.*, 179–182.

(*d*) J. Rueff, "Mr. Keynes' Views on the Transfer Problem. I. A Criticism," *Economic Journal*, 39 (September 1929), 388–399.

(*e*) B. Ohlin, "Mr. Keynes' Views on the Transfer Problem. II. A Rejoinder," *ibid.*, pp. 400–404.

(*f*) J. M. Keynes, "Views on the Transfer Problem. III. A Reply," *ibid.*, pp. 404–408.

national output remains unchanged in both countries; if both countries balance their budgets, factor income falls in the paying country by the exact amount of the transfer and rises in the receiving country by the same amount. In the notation used here, factor incomes in countries A and B, respectively, are

$$(19) \qquad y_a = \bar{y}_a - \pi\tau \quad \text{and} \quad y_b = \bar{y}_b + \tau.$$

If we assume that the adjustment is complete, $\pi = 1$ and Eqs. (19) become

$$(20) \qquad y_a = \bar{y}_a - \tau \quad \text{and} \quad y_b = \bar{y}_b + \tau.$$

The balance of payments of country A is therefore

$$(21) \qquad B_a = m_b(\bar{y}_b + \tau) - m_a(\bar{y}_a - \tau) - \tau.$$

Differentiating B_a with respect to τ, and setting the differential equal to zero, we obtain for the condition of complete adjustment:

$$(22) \qquad \frac{dB_a}{d\tau} = m_b' + m_a' - 1 = 0,$$

where m_b' and m_a' are the marginal propensities to import of countries B and A, respectively. Thus the condition of complete adjustment is that the sum of the marginal propensities to import of the two countries be equal to unity, or that the average propensity to import be 1/2. This theory of income transfers became so widely accepted after 1929 that I shall refer to it as the "orthodox" theory.[10]

The orthodox theory, in the form I have expressed it, involves an inconsistency, at least under the premise of flexible exchange rates. The fact that factor income falls in A by the amount of the transfer and rises in B by the same amount while national output is constant in both countries implies that the two countries are following balanced-budget policies; and if S_a' and S_b' are both less than unity, one can readily demonstrate that such policies are inconsistent with a constant national output.

10. Professor Jacob Viner traces what I have called the orthodox theory back to the classical economists of the nineteenth century and even earlier. See his masterful work, *Studies in the Theory of International Trade* (New York, Harper and Bros., 1937), chap. 6. On p. 180 of *International Trade and Economic Growth* (reference 6), Johnson refers to the theory as the "classical" theory. I prefer, however, to reserve the term "classical" for the works of early nineteenth-century economists such as David Ricardo and John Stuart Mill.

In country A, for example, taxes $\pi\tau$ will reduce the demand for goods and services by $S_a'\pi\tau$ while the ensuing export surplus will increase demand by the greater amount $\pi\tau$. Thus national output inevitably rises. Conversely, in country B an increase of subsidies in the amount of τ increases domestic demand by $S_b'\tau$ while the induced import surplus reduces demand to the full extent of the transfer τ. Under the assumed conditions, the transfer therefore has a deflationary influence on national output in B. The premise that factor income falls by the amount of the transfer in A and rises by the same amount in B is thus inconsistent with the premise that national output is constant in both countries.

One exception to this rule exists. Specifically, if Say's Law of Markets prevails in both countries, so that S_a' and S_b' are both equal to unity, the orthodox theory will be valid. Under these circumstances the amount of taxes needed to stabilize output in the paying country will be exactly equal to the domestic-currency value of the transfer payment shown by Eqs. (16) above. Conversely, the subsidies required for stabilized output in the receiving country will be equal to the transfer receipt, again from (16). Finally, Eq. (18) for complete adjustment reduces to

$$(23) \qquad\qquad m_b' + m_a' - 1 = 0,$$

which is the orthodox theory.

From this point of view Ohlin may be regarded as the originator of a theory of income transfers intermediate between the classical theory and the Keynesian. The orthodox theory is classical to the extent that it assumes full employment and implies Say's Law.[11] It is Keynesian to the extent that it allows for shifts in purchasing power. This fact loses much of its significance, however, for if Say's Law applies, in one or more countries, the market for foreign exchange is in neutral equilibrium in both countries.

Summary and Conclusions

The analysis above has shown that the notion of a shift in purchasing power cannot always be taken for granted. Specifically, when two countries are linked to each other through a flexible exchange rate, the

---

11. An excellent numerical example of the orthodox theory, implicitly adopting Say's Law, may be found in James E. Meade, *The Theory of International Economic Policy*, vol. 1: *The Balance of Payments* (London, Oxford University Press, 1951), pp. 90–91.

returns to factors of production remain unchanged in both countries while economic activity rises in the paying country and falls in the receiving country. A potential inflation thus arises in the debtor country and a potential deflation in the creditor, contrary to the usual expectations.

The arguments above tend, on the whole, to support Keynes in his controversy with Ohlin. They show, at any rate, that there are some conditions under which a reparation payment will have no effects upon factor income in either country. We have seen that this paradoxical result arises from a neglect of the interactions between taxes or subsidies and the balance of payments. Is there evidence that Keynes recognized the significance of these interactions? I have gone through the literature and one quotation hints at an intuitive grasp, but the relation is vague and imprecise. I quote from Keynes's rejoinder to Ohlin's criticism:

Let us assume (what was not far off the truth a short time ago) that Germany is borrowing £200,000,000 a year and paying £125,000,000 in reparations. Let us then suppose that her foreign borrowing drops to £100,000,000 and her reparation payments to £50,000,000; i.e., she succeeds in improving her trade balance, borrowing and reparations apart, by £25,000,000. Now it is true that we have increased "buying power" for £25,000,000 (not £100,000,000) in the world outside Germany. But this will have been exactly used up in paying for the £25,000,000 additional goods exported (net) from Germany, which have improved sufficiently to make her reparations payments possible. Professor Ohlin has to maintain that the "increased buying power" is more than £25,000,000, and—if his repercussion is to be important—appreciably more.[12]

Taking a sympathetic view of this quotation, we may assume that borrowing is equivalent to an income receipt—a point which Keynes initially denied. In this case, Germany is the net recipient of transfers amounting to £75,000,000 (£200,000,000 borrowing *less* £125,000,000 reparations). Subsequently, her receipts are reduced to £50,000,000 (£100,000,000 borrowing *less* £50,000,000 reparations). And Keynes assumes that the German balance of trade improves by an equivalent amount. Looking at the rest of the world as a paying country, then, we may say that net payments are reduced by £25,000,000 while the balance of trade is reduced by the same amount. The reduction in net

12. Keynes, reference 9(c).

payments increases factor income by £25,000,000 even though national output remains unchanged. The reduction in the balance of trade, however, reduces both factor income and economic activity by an equivalent amount. On balance, therefore, factor income remains unchanged while output falls by £25,000,000.

The missing link in this argument is that Keynes does not specify exactly how the balance of trade is adjusted to the change in the income transfer. Such an adjustment would, of course, be automatic in a flexible-exchange system. But again, paradoxically, Keynes rejected flexible exchange rates as a means of adjustment on the grounds that such a system might invoke the transfer protection clauses of the Dawes plan! On the whole then, it seems that while Keynes had a glimmer of the relations between an income transfer and the balance of trade, which would justify his neglect of shifts in purchasing power, his knowledge of these relations was decidedly limited.

5 | Exchange Rates and the International Monetary Fund[1]

The International Monetary Fund, conceived at Bretton Woods in 1944, commenced operations on March 1, 1947, after having negotiated with member countries an initial pattern of international exchange rates. These negotiations, which proceeded within an agreed framework laid down in the Fund's Articles of Agreement, represented a marked advance over previous attempts at securing coordinated action in the international monetary field. It is the purpose of this paper to assess the results of this new procedure in the highly important and complex field of exchange relations.

Methods of Setting Exchange Rates

Exchange Rates after the First World War

A major factor in the international economic disturbances and frictions which followed the First World War was the unbalanced condition of exchange rates. During the war years and in the period immediately following the war, most currencies were divorced from

Reprinted from Lloyd A. Metzler, Robert Triffin, and Gottfried Haberler, *International Monetary Policies*, Postwar Economic Studies, No. 7 (Washington, D.C., Board of Governors of the Federal Reserve System, 1947), 1–45.

1. A number of people assisted in preparing this paper. Florence Jaffy of the Division of Research and Statistics of the Board of Governors of the Federal Reserve System compiled the parity estimates. Leila N. Small of the Institute for International Studies at Yale University lent helpful assistance throughout the preparation of the paper. The final manuscript was read and criticized by Walter R. Gardner of the International Monetary Fund and J. Burke Knapp, Assistant Director of the Division of Research and Statistics of the Board of Governors. The author wishes to thank all of these people without implicating any of them.

gold, and since exchange controls had to a considerable extent been abandoned at the close of the war, exchange rates were subject to substantial fluctuations. These exchange fluctuations created opportunities for speculative capital movements which frequently tended further to upset the balance. As a result, in many countries the actual exchange rates differed widely from those which would have provided a balanced condition between the supply and demand for foreign exchange.

When the important trading nations finally stabilized their exchange rates by returning to the gold standard, no systematic attempt was made to remove the discrepancies which had developed. Instead, each individual country simply resumed the purchase and sale of gold at a price which was determined, for the most part, by unilateral action. Too much attention was paid in this process to the superficial aspects of the gold standard, such as the commitment of each country to redeem its currency in gold, and too little attention was paid to the more fundamental fact that the gold standard is a means of establishing or stabilizing the relative values of different currencies in international trade.

The results of the unilateral and haphazard return to the gold standard after the war are well known and need not be repeated in detail here.[2] It is now generally recognized that the relative values at which a number of currencies were stabilized failed to reflect the movements of prices and other economic disturbances which had been brought about by war.

Perhaps the most conspicuous of these discrepancies was the overvaluation of the pound sterling. When the United Kingdom made the pound sterling convertible in 1925, the prewar rate of exchange between the pound and the dollar—approximately $4.87—was reestablished. Since prices and costs had increased more in the United Kingdom than in the United States, and since a number of the most important British export trades, such as coal and textiles, were meeting increased competition from other sources, the prewar value of the pound was no longer appropriate. A lower price for the pound, in other words, would have contributed to equalizing Britain's supply of foreign exchange with her demand.

---

2. See League of Nations, *International Currency Experience: Lessons of the Interwar Period* (Geneva, 1944), chap. 1.

In the long run, the effects of overvaluation of the pound might have been offset by a vigorous attack upon the cost structure through rationalization and modernization of British industries. But this is a time-consuming process which could not solve the immediate problems confronting the British exporters at the time Britain returned to the gold standard. In any event, the rationalizing and modernizing of industry did not proceed rapidly enough to avoid a serious depression during the twenties in the British export trades.

The difficulties confronting the United Kingdom as a result of the initial stabilization of the pound were subsequently aggravated by the stabilization of the French franc at a price which, from some points of view, appeared to be too low. In the case of the French franc, the problem of returning to the gold standard was complicated by speculative capital movements. Prices and costs had increased so much both during the war and in the postwar years that a return to the old parities between the franc and other currencies was clearly out of the question. The external value of the franc of course declined as prices increased within the country. Moreover, since the period of postwar inflation in France was also a period in which large holdings of money assets were being transferred from Paris to London and other financial centers, the depreciation of the franc was considerably greater than the relative decline in its purchasing power. Between November 1918 and July 1926 the price of the franc in American currency declined from 18.37 cents to 2.47 cents. Later, when internal financial conditions in France had improved, a repatriation of French capital occurred, and the franc accordingly increased in value. When the French currency was finally stabilized in 1926 and 1927, however, the price of the franc in terms of either dollars or pounds sterling was somewhat low relative to its purchasing power in France. Thus France became a cheap market in which to buy, while the United Kingdom became a relatively expensive market.

Similar mistakes were made in other countries, but their effects upon world trade and finance were less important than the effects of the return to the gold standard in France and the United Kingdom. All of this is well known and would not need to be repeated here except for the bearing which it has on the problem of exchange rates in the present period of readjustment. As a result of the planless manner in which exchange rates were stabilized after the First World War, the balances of payments of many countries were subjected to continuous stresses and strains throughout most of the decade of the twenties and in the early thirties. While some of these disturbances were an inevitable consequence of the war many of them could have been avoided by a more systematic approach to the problem of postwar exchange rates.

Exchange Rates after the Second World War

The plan evolved at Bretton Woods for setting initial exchange rates, and for subsequent adjustments in exchange rates through the International Monetary Fund, offers a striking contrast to the stabilization of currencies after the First World War. Whether the contrast in final results will be as striking as the contrast in method of approach, however, depends almost entirely upon how the new international monetary organization is administered, and upon the cooperation which the Fund receives from member countries.

Unlike the unilateral and uncoordinated stabilization of currencies during the twenties, the plan set out in the Articles of Agreement of the Fund created an opportunity for establishing relative exchange rates by mutual agreement among the members of the Fund. The Fund agreement provided that unless either the Fund or the member country concerned objected, the initial exchange rate at which the Fund commenced operations in a particular currency should be the rate prevailing sixty days before the Agreement went into effect. If either the member country concerned or the Fund regarded the rate prevailing on that date as unsatisfactory, however, a different rate was to be established by agreement between the member and the Fund. The feature of this procedure which distinguishes it from the stabilizing procedure adopted after the First World War is the explicit recognition of the fact that exchange rates, or gold parities, are a matter of international interest and cannot be determined satisfactorily by unilateral action.

In September 1946, Mr. Camille Gutt, Managing Director of the Fund, issued a call to all member countries for information concerning their exchange rates, and after an extended period of study and discussion, announcement was made in December 1946 of the initial exchange rates at which the Fund would begin operations. The purpose of the present paper is to discuss some of the problems which were involved in this setting of exchange rates, and to describe the approach of the Fund to solving these problems.

The rates finally agreed upon were, in every case, the rates existing at the time the Fund made its call for information. In other words, no changes were made in the existing pattern of exchange rates when the Fund commenced operations. This does not mean, however, that the Fund regards all of the present exchange rates as long-run rates, or that it does not contemplate changes in some of these rates in the future. In their first report, published in September 1946 before the initial rates were agreed upon, the Executive Directors of the Fund made a statement on this question which is so important that it is worth quoting at some length.

We recognize that in some cases the initial par values that are established may later be found incompatible with the maintenance of a balanced international payments position at a high level of domestic economic activity. Because the entire world is in need of goods, some countries may maintain foreign exchange values for their currencies which are not for the time being a great handicap to the sale of their exports, but which prove to be too high when production is revived all over the world and the immediate shortage of import goods is in large part met. Such countries may later find difficulty in selling sufficient exports to pay for their needed imports. When this occurs, the Fund will be faced with new problems of adjustment and *will have to recognize the unusual circumstances under which the initial par values were determined.* . . .[3]

Parts of this statement of policy were later repeated in the Fund's announcement of initial exchange rates. It is evident from the statement that the Fund has foreseen from the outset that it might be desirable or necessary to postpone the downward adjustment of some exchange rates. Reasons for this postponement will be discussed in a later section of this paper.

Movements of Currency Values since 1937

General Survey

How do the initial exchange rates announced by the Fund compare with rates existing before the Second World War? To give a partial answer to this question, initial rates for twenty of the member countries are presented in Table 1. Average exchange rates during a prewar "base" period are also shown. For most countries, the period selected as a prewar base was the nine-month period October 1936 to June

3. *First Annual Report of the Executive Directors of the International Monetary Fund* (Washington, D.C., 1946), p. 12. Italics added.

Table 1. Initial exchange rates announced by the International Monetary Fund compared with prewar exchange rates for selected countries (in cents per unit of foreign currency)

Country	Initial rate announced by Fund	Rate in base period October 1936-June 1937[1]
Belgium	2.28	3.37
Canada	100.00	100.04
Chile	3.23	5.17
Colombia	57.14	57.06
Costa Rica	17.81	16.26[2]
Cuba	100.00	99.92[3]
Czechoslovakia	2.00	3.51
Denmark	20.84	21.91
Egypt	413.30	503.23
France	0.84	2.88[4]
India	30.23	37.07
Iran	3.10	6.07
Mexico	20.60	27.75
Netherlands	37.70	54.55
Norway	20.15	24.66
Peru	15.38	25.07[5]
Turkey	35.71	80.00
Union of South Africa	403.00	485.70
United Kingdom	403.00	490.81
Venezuela	29.85	26.53[5]

[1] Unless otherwise indicated.
[2] 1936 annual average.
[3] July-December 1937 average.
[4] 1938 average.
[5] 1936–37 average.
SOURCES: *Federal Reserve Bulletin, Foreign Commerce Weekly,* and Schedule of Exchange Rates issued by the International Monetary Fund.

1937. This period was selected because it was relatively close to the war years but at the same time reasonably free of war influences. If an earlier period had been used, difficulties would have arisen from the wave of currency devaluations which occurred in the early thirties and mid-thirties. If a later period had been used, on the other hand, complications would have been introduced both by the American depression of 1937–38 and by the effects which the imminence of war had upon foreign-exchange markets.

The base period selected is one of relative exchange stability which followed the Tripartite Agreement between the United States, the United Kingdom, and France. The exchange rates prevailing in this base period are assumed, in later sections of the present paper, to be more or less normal prewar rates, but it is probable that in the unstable international economic situation which prevailed before the war no single period can be regarded as a completely normal or balanced period. The base period exchange rates must therefore be accepted with reservations.

With the exceptions of Colombia, Costa Rica, Cuba, and Venezuela, the exchange rates at which the Fund commenced operations, when expressed in American currency, are all lower than the rates in the prewar base period. The extent of depreciation varies from 71 percent in the case of the French franc to only 5 percent in the case of the Danish krone. What were the causes of these changes in currency values and how were they related to war and postwar economic conditions? In order to answer these questions, it will be necessary to con-

Table 2. Exchange rates of selected nonmember countries and of member countries for which no official Fund rates have been announced (in cents per unit of foreign currency)

Country	Rate in December 1946[1]	Rate in base period October 1936–June 1937[1]
Nonmember countries:		
Argentina	29.77	32.72
Australia*	321.07	391.08
New Zealand	322.36	394.01
Sweden	27.82	25.30
Switzerland	23.36	22.90
Member countries for which rates have not been announced:		
Brazil	5.41	6.17
Greece	0.02	0.90
Italy	0.26[2]	5.26[3]
Poland	1.00	18.90
Uruguay	56.27	79.47[4]

[1] Unless otherwise indicated.
[2] February 1947.
[3] 1937 average.
[4] 1936–37 average.
* Admitted to membership on August 5, 1947, after this analysis had been completed.
SOURCES: *Federal Reserve Bulletin* and *Foreign Commerce Weekly*.

sider not only the exchange rates which have been announced by the Fund, but also the present exchange rates or certain member countries for which no rates have yet been determined, as well as the rates of a number of nonmember countries. Information concerning such rates in both the base period and the month of December 1946 is presented in Table 2.

In comparing the present pattern of exchange rates with the pattern prevailing in the base period, we shall find it convenient to divide all countries into three groups: (*a*) the countries occupied by the German army; (*b*) the countries in the British Commonwealth of Nations, and other countries such as Sweden and Argentina which followed a policy before the war of stabilizing the values of their currencies in terms of the pound sterling; (*c*) the Latin American countries, exclusive of Argentina. Although this classification is not exhaustive, a consideration of these three broad groups will nevertheless serve to indicate the main developments in the movement of exchange rates since 1937.

The Countries Occupied by Germany

Among other countries included in the tables, Belgium, Czechoslovakia, Denmark, France, the Netherlands, and Norway were occupied by the Germans and their currencies were cut off from the dollar and sterling markets during most of the war years. In several instances, the postwar exchange rates of these countries therefore represented a more or less complete break with the past. When the period of occupation came to an end, there were no customary or accepted rates which could be used as a guide to the new dollar and sterling rates for these currencies. Each country had to decide for itself, perhaps in consultation with other members of the United Nations, what its exchange rate would be. As a result of German expenditures in the occupied countries, prices and costs in most of them had risen during the war more than they rose in the United States or the United Kingdom, and largely for this reason the rates at which the former occupied countries began doing business in dollars and pounds sterling were usually well below the war rates.

The movement of dollar exchange rates in these countries since 1937 is shown in Fig. 1, which reveals a sharp contrast between postwar and prewar rates both with respect to the level of such rates and with respect to exchange movements. In the period from 1938 to the time of invasion, the dollar rates in most of these countries were subject to

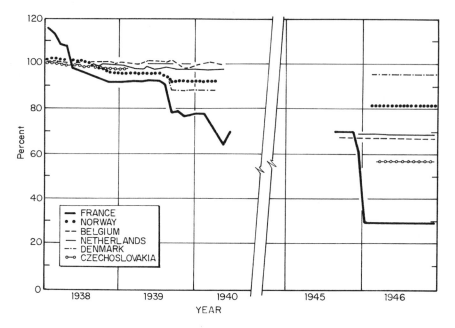

Figure 1. Dollar prices of currencies of formerly occupied countries (as percentage of average prices, October 1936 to June 1937)

moderate fluctuations, the general tendency being downward. In the period since the occupation came to an end, on the other hand, fluctuations in exchange rates have been confined within narrow limits by means of general exchange controls. The preinvasion depreciation in Norway, Denmark, the Netherlands, and France is attributable partly to capital flights and a general fear psychology, and partly to the depreciation of the pound sterling, which will be discussed later.

The Prewar Sterling Area

Index numbers of dollar exchange rates for the United Kingdom and Canada, and for two non-British countries formerly in the sterling area, are shown in Fig. 2, which covers the period 1938 through 1946. As in the case of the occupied countries, the inflexible exchange rates of the early postwar period are in sharp contrast to the exchange fluctuations of the years prior to 1940.

The most striking feature of exchange movements in the prewar sterling area is the general depreciation which occurred between

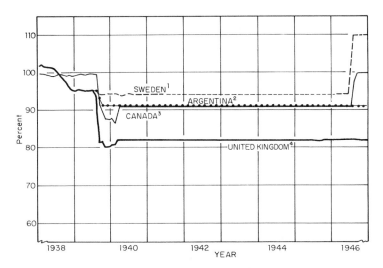

Figure 2. Dollar prices of selected currencies in prewar sterling area and Canada (as percentage of average prices, October 1936 to June 1937)

1. No rates were certified between June 14, 1941, and Feb. 5, 1946. During this period the official Stockholm selling rate was 4.20 kronor to the dollar (23.8095 cents per krona), as indicated by the thin broken line.

2. Official rate.

3. Beginning March 1940, official rate.

4. From March 1940 through June 1945, official rate.

June 1938 and September 1939. Since the other members of the sterling area had stabilized their currencies relative to the pound sterling in the period prior to 1938, the depreciation in the sterling area during the immediate prewar period may be considered largely in terms of the British currency.

Many reasons have been given for the depreciation of the pound. As with the countries occupied by Germany, the flight of capital was undoubtedly a contributing factor. It seems probable also that in the face of this capital movement the British authorities may have decided to relax the efforts at stabilization which they had been making through their Exchange Equalization Account. No doubt the depression in the United States was also partly responsible for the depreciation of sterling. In any event, the pound sterling depreciated steadily in terms of dollars throughout the second half of 1938. With the outbreak of war in September 1939, extensive exchange controls were introduced and the pound sterling was sharply depreciated by the control authorities from more than $4.60 to $4.03. During the early period of exchange control, a free market in pounds sterling developed at rates considerably below the official rate, but by the end of 1940 the free rate was approximately the same as the official rate, and both the free rate and the official remained stabilized throughout the war years. After the war, the single rate of $4.03 was maintained and was accepted as the initial rate for the United Kingdom by the International Monetary Fund.

The prewar changes in the value of the currencies of other British countries were almost identical with the changes in the pound sterling. With the exception of Canada, these countries continued to maintain stability of their currencies relative to the pound sterling, and the dollar prices of their currencies therefore declined with the fall in the price of sterling. The Canadian dollar, however, remained close to parity with the U.S. dollar until the United Kingdom depreciated its currency sharply at the outbreak of war. Canada then followed part way by depreciating its currency about 10 percent relative to the American dollar. Between June 1938 and March 1940, the decline in dollar prices of the currencies of Australia, India, New Zealand, the Union of South Africa, and the United Kingdom was approximately 18.5 percent, whereas the decline in the price of the Canadian currency in the same period (based upon the official rate in 1940) was less than 10 percent. As in the case of the pound sterling, the depreciated rates were subsequently maintained throughout the war years by means of exchange controls. Except for the Canadian dollar, which was appreciated to its former parity with the American dollar during 1946, the fixed rates established during the war were also maintained after the end of the war, and for India and South Africa they are the official rates of the Monetary Fund.

The non-British members of the sterling area, including Argentina and Scandinavian countries, also permitted their currencies to depreciate during 1938, in conformance with the price of the pound sterling, but when war began and the pound sterling was rapidly depreciated, these countries followed only to a limited extent and the overall depreciation of their currencies between June 1938 and 1940 was therefore somewhat smaller than the depreciation of the pound. The exchange rates of two of these countries, Denmark and Norway, have been discussed above in connection with the occupied countries. The other two countries, as Fig. 2 indicates, both had dollar rates at the end of the war which were substantially the same as the rates prevailing in 1940. In the case of Argentina, a slight appreciation occurred in the special export rate in 1944, but the official rate remained unchanged, and since the end of the war no alterations have been made in the dollar price of the Argentine peso. In the case of Sweden, the dollar price of the krona was adjusted upward in 1946 by more than 15 percent, and this adjusted rate is the one which is currently being used.

The Latin American Countries

Movements of Latin American exchange rates are extremely difficult to describe because of the multiple currency systems which prevail in many of these countries. When the Argentine rate was discussed above in connection with the sterling area, movements of the official rate alone were analyzed and the multiplicity of rates was disregarded. This is a somewhat dangerous procedure, for Argentina, like many other countries of South and Central America, has a number of different rates, the particular rate in any given instance depending upon the use to which the foreign exchange is to be put or upon the source from which it is derived.

There is no need at this point to give a detailed description of the multiple-exchange system. Its origin, for the most part, was in the Great Depression of the thirties, when the rapid and pronounced decline in raw material and agricultural prices created serious balance-of-payments problems for the Latin American exporters of such products. For a number of reasons, many of these countries felt that outright exchange depreciation would not improve their balances of payments. Depreciation would have made it possible to reduce the foreign-exchange prices of their exports while maintaining the domestic prices received by producers, but since their exports consisted largely of products for which the demand was relatively unresponsive to changes in prices, it was widely believed that price concessions would reduce rather than increase the amount of foreign exchange accruing to the Latin American countries. If a 10-percent reduction in the price of coffee, for example, would have resulted in an increase of Brazilian exports of only 5 percent, the amount of foreign exchange derived from coffee sales would obviously have been smaller after the price reduction than before. This situation was regarded as typical of many Latin American exports, and a reduction in foreign prices, made possible by currency depreciation, was therefore not considered to be a solution to the shortage of foreign exchange.

The situation was further complicated in many countries by the fact that substantial amounts of foreign exchange were required by governments to make payments on foreign debts denominated in foreign currencies. Currency depreciation in such cases would not have reduced the demand for foreign exchange but would merely have increased the price which the Latin American countries had to pay in their own currencies to service their foreign obligations. While this budgetary problem was essentially an internal one, there is nevertheless considerable evidence that it played an important part in the decision of some countries to adopt measures other than currency depreciation when confronted with deficits in their balances of payments.

In the end, the balance-of-payments problems during the depression were temporarily solved, or postponed, by a widespread adoption of exchange controls. Foreign exchange acquired by exporters had to be sold to a central authority at fixed prices, and importers in turn purchased their needed exchange at rates prescribed by the central authority. Having become monopolists in their foreign-exchange markets, the governments of many of the Latin American countries found it profitable or desirable to set up schedules of varying rates for the purchase and sale of foreign currencies.

Although the details of these multiple-exchange systems differed considerably from one country to another, certain features were nevertheless common to almost all of them. Preferential treatment was accorded, in the first place, to governmental agencies which needed exchange to service their foreign obligations. Dollar or sterling exchange was usually made available or acquired for this purpose, at the lowest price in the schedule of rates. Favorable prices were also provided for importers of commodities which were regarded as necessities, with correspondingly more expensive rates established for luxury imports. A similar schedule of rates usually prevailed in the purchase of foreign exchange from exporters. High prices were paid for foreign exchange arising from the export of products which the government wished to encourage, and somewhat lower prices were paid for exchange arising from other exports. Thus, in effect, the Latin American governments frequently depreciated their currencies for some purposes such as luxury imports and certain classes of exports, but left the rates at the old levels for other purposes, such as government debt service and the import of certain necessary items.

In all this maze of rates it is not feasible to give a brief description of what happened to the external value of a country's currency in the period between 1938 and 1946. The best that can be done, in many

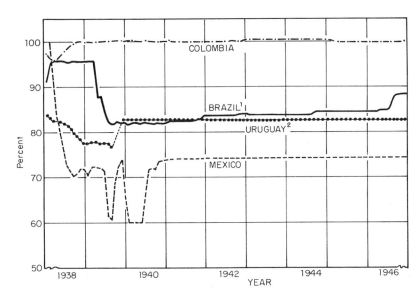

Figure 3. Dollar prices of selected currencies in Latin America (as percentage of average prices, October 1936 to June 1937)

1. Beginning April 1939, free rate.

2. Beginning January 1939, controlled rate. No quotations September 1 through November 28, 1939.

instances, is to select one or two rates which seem to be most representative and to describe the movements of these rates. In following this course, however, it is well to remember that for many of the Latin American countries no single exchange rate can possibly represent a complete picture of exchange developments.

Movements of some of the more important exchange rates for a selected group of Latin American countries are shown in Fig. 3. It is apparent that the prewar exchange movements for the Latin American countries were much less uniform than the movements of sterling-area currencies. While the general tendency in 1938 and 1939 was a downward adjustment relative to the dollar, there were exceptions to the tendency, as the line for Colombia indicates. Some Latin American currencies, such as the Uruguayan and Argentine pesos, were clearly influenced by the depreciation of sterling, but the timing of the downward movement in others is quite out of line with the depreciation of the British currency. This suggests that other influences, such as the American depression of 1937 and 1938, may have been responsible for some of the immediate prewar depreciation in the Latin American currencies.

Like the European exchange rates, the Latin American rates have been rigidly controlled both during the war years and in the postwar period. This means, in general, that any depreciation of present dollar prices of these currencies compared with the dollar rates in the base period October 1936 to June 1937 is attributable to the depreciation which occurred prior to 1941, and cannot be directly ascribed to changes in prices and costs which occurred during the war.

Summary of Exchange-Rate Movements

The description presented above of exchange-rate adjustments since 1937 naturally shows a considerable diversity among countries. Despite this diversity, however, certain more or less general tendencies stand out both in the countries which are members of the Fund and in nonmember countries. Since these general tendencies are important in the discussion of postwar exchange rates, a brief summary may be given here.

For a period of slightly less than one year after the stabilization agreement was made between the United States, the United Kingdom, and France in 1936, fluctuations in exchange rates remained within relatively narrow limits. Except for certain Latin American countries and countries in Eastern Europe, exchange controls were not widespread at this time, and exchange-rate fluctuations were controlled largely by indirect means such as equalization accounts. Since equalization accounts or stabilization funds are known to be relatively ineffective against a pronounced and persistent discrepancy between the supply and demand for foreign exchange, it seems likely that the stability of exchange rates in this period was indicative of a generally balanced condition in the foreign exchange markets. This is one of the reasons why the period from October 1936 to June 1937 was chosen as a base period for the comparison of prewar and postwar exchange rates.

Beginning in the middle of 1937, the French franc slowly depreciated in terms of dollars, and this movement was followed, in the middle of 1938, by a gradual but persistent depreciation of the pound sterling. The threat of war and the resulting capital flights, as well as the depression in the United States, were no doubt contributing factors in the depreciation of both the franc and the pound. After the outbreak of war, the pound sterling was sharply depreciated to $4.03 (official rate). In France, the movement was similar; the franc depreciated at irregular intervals until it had reached a level of approximately 2 cents at the time of the German invasion.

It was pointed out above that the depreciation of the pound sterling, and to a lesser extent the depreciation of the French franc, had far-reaching effects on other exchange rates. Although not all of the currencies of South and Central America shared in the movement, there was a general tendency for these currencies, like the European currencies, to fall in value relative to the dollar during the period between 1938 and 1940. The period between 1938 and 1940 was thus a period of fluctuating exchange rates, the general tendency being a reduction in currency values relative to the dollar. In most countries, these currency fluctuations were finally stopped after the outbreak of war by the introduction of exchange controls, and thereafter the pattern of exchange rates was relatively stable throughout the war years.

Stability of exchange rates did not end with the end of the war. For the most part, the exchange controls which were devised in the early war years have been continued in operation, and exchange fluctuations have been confined within relatively narrow limits. Except for the Swedish krona and the Canadian dollar, which were appreciated by official action in 1946, the present pattern of exchange rates in the sterling countries is substantially the same as the pattern prevailing in 1940. Similarly, among the countries of Latin America, present dollar exchange rates are broadly the same as the rates prevailing in 1940 or 1941, and the stability which is characteristic of postwar rates in other countries also characterizes the Latin American rates. This means that the rates announced by the International Monetary Fund have made allowance for war-induced changes in international economic conditions only to the extent that the 1940 rates anticipated wartime economic developments.

In the countries occupied by the German army, postwar exchange rates are in most instances considerably different from the 1940 rates. A different set of rates was inevitable, since the wartime rise in prices was considerably greater in these countries than in most other nations. It seems doubtful, however, that the rates established represented the results of any careful and deliberate study of changes in economic conditions brought about by the war. The speed with which the new rates had to be set up precluded such studies, and in any event there were so many uncertainties regarding the economic future that political factors and considerations of expediency inevitably played a dominant part.

This, in brief, is the evolution of present exchange rates for a selected group of countries. A general description of exchange-rate movements has been given because it was believed that such a background would be helpful in discussing the appropriateness of present rates. In any comparison of present rates with prewar rates it is useful to know how the rates got where they are from the prewar level. This, indeed, is an essential part of a judgment as to the appropriateness of existing rates. It would obviously be impossible, within the limits of a paper such as this, to indicate how each individual rate is likely to affect the future course of world trade. An attempt is made below, however, to suggest certain probable consequences of the present exchange-rate pattern as a whole.

Exchange Rates and Prices

The Purchasing-Power-Parity Theory

One of the factors which must be taken into account in any discussion of present currency values is the general rise in prices and costs which was brought about by the war. Appendix Table A1 demonstrates the situation in the United States. Even in countries where price controls were maintained throughout the war years, the inflationary effects of large government purchases of goods and services could not be entirely avoided. If these price increases had been uniform throughout all countries, no particular difficulties would have arisen insofar as foreign trade is concerned. A casual glance at a few statistics, however, will convince the reader of the enormous disparity which has developed between the price changes in one country and those in another (see Appendix Table A2). In France, for example, wholesale prices have increased about 700 percent above the prewar level, compared with increases of 200 percent in Czechoslovakia, 185 percent in Mexico, and 45 percent in Australia.[4] In view of these discrepancies, it is obvious that relative changes in the internal purchasing power of different currencies will have substantial effects on the course of international trade unless they are offset by corresponding changes in exchange rates.

After the First World War, the discrepancies between movements of price levels in different countries were equally great, and since exchange

4. These figures, taken from Appendix Table A2, represent a comparison of prewar prices prevailing at the end of 1946.

rates in many countries were uncontrolled, these changes in relative purchasing power exerted a considerable influence on exchange rates. Indeed, the changes in prices and costs were so striking by comparison with other economic changes that there was a tendency to explain the observed movement of exchange rates entirely in terms of changes in relative purchasing power. This was the doctrine of purchasing-power parity which enjoyed a considerable popularity among economists in the 1920s. The theory of purchasing-power parity, in its simplest form, may be illustrated by means of a numerical example.

Suppose that in some initial period, when international payments are in a balanced condition, the exchange rate between the dollar and the pound sterling is $4.50 = £1. And suppose that as a result of a war, prices and costs in the United States increase uniformly to a level just twice their former level, while prices and costs in the United Kingdom rise to three times their former level; in other words, the index of prices in the United States increases to 200 while the index in the United Kingdom increases to 300. According to the purchasing-power-parity doctrine, the internal purchasing power of the dollar at the close of the war is one-half its former level, and the internal purchasing power of the pound is one-third its former level. Hence, it is argued, in order to preserve balanced trade relations between the two countries, the price of the pound, in terms of dollars, must drop to two-thirds of the old price, or to $3 = £1. More generally, the so-called parity exchange rate is equal to the price of the pound in the base year, in terms of dollars, multiplied by the ratio of the price index in the United States to the price index in the United Kingdom.

The virtue of the parity rate is that it preserves the earlier real exchange ratio between the goods and services of one country and the goods and services of another. To see why this is true, suppose in the above example that an American product X before the war sold for $1.50, while a British product Y sold for £1. At the old exchange rate, American purchasers of Y would have had to pay $4.50 per unit, and the price per unit in the United States would thus have been three times the price of a unit of the American product X. We may assume now that as a result of the war inflation the cost of production and the price of each commodity, in the currency of the selling country, rises according to the general price rise. In other words, the selling price of X, the American product, is doubled while the price of Y, the British product, is tripled; the new price of X is $3.00, and the new price of Y is £3. At the parity exchange rate of $3 = £1, the American price of the British product is thus $9. Once again, therefore, the unit price of the British product, in dollars, is three times the unit price of the American product.

Since the relative price of British goods, compared with the price of American goods, is the same after the inflation as before, the general rise in prices will not affect the import of British goods; unless tastes or conditions of production and trade have changed, the physical volume of British imports will be the same as in the prewar situation, and only the monetary units in which these imports are measured will have changed. Likewise, in the United Kingdom the sterling price of United States goods, relative to the price of British goods, will remain the same as before the inflation, and a presumption exists that the physical volume of British imports will be unchanged.

Criticisms of Purchasing-Power Parity

While adoption of the parity rate is desirable in the solution of some problems, it may be quite undesirable in the solution of others, for in some circumstances it may be necessary to change the real terms of trade between countries in order to restore a balanced condition in international trade. If this is true, the so-called "equilibrium" rate of exchange will differ from the parity rate. Suppose, for example, that the base period chosen for the calculation of a parity rate in the numerical example above had been a period in which the United States had a deficit in its balance of payments. Other things being equal, the parity rate between the dollar and the pound, by perpetuating the real terms of exchange between British and American goods, will likewise perpetuate the deficit. Only the money units in which the deficit is measured will have changed. In order to restore a balanced condition, exports of the United States must be encouraged, and imports reduced, by means of a depreciation in the value of the dollar below the parity rate. Thus if the base period is one of disequilibrium, the parity rate, after the price rise has taken place, will not be the same as the rate which will establish equilibrium in a country's balance of payments.[5]

Other factors will also create a disparity between the parity rate and the equilibrium rate. Consider, for example, the effects of capital movements. Suppose that in the prewar base period there were no capital

5. On all of these criticisms of parity calculations, see Gottfried Haberler, "The Choice of Exchange Rates after the War," *American Economic Review*, 35 (June 1945), 311–315.

movements, and that after the rise in prices has taken place the United States expects to make extensive loans to the United Kingdom. Assuming that the base period was one of balanced trade without capital movements, the parity rate will also establish a balanced condition, in the absence of capital movements, after the price rise has taken place. But if the United States is to make large foreign loans an export surplus can and should be allowed to develop in the United States balance of trade, and in order to bring about such an export surplus, the exchange rate for the dollar must be depreciated below the parity rate. Accordingly, we find once more a difference between the parity rate and the equilibrium rate. Changes in tastes or in methods of production will create a similar difference between the two rates. If, because of such changes, the American demand for British goods has increased during the time interval between the base period and the period of comparison, the parity rate, by reestablishing the earlier ratio of exchange between British and American goods, will lead to a deficit in the United States balance even though the initial period was one of equilibrium. In order to make the supply of foreign exchange equal to the demand, the value of the dollar in this case must again be depreciated below the purchasing-power-parity rate.

Movements of output and employment are also important in judging the validity of parity calculation, for these movements bring with them substantial changes in the demand for imports. In times of comparative economic stability, the effects of changes in employment upon the equilibrium level of exchange rates can perhaps be neglected, but in a period such as the prewar decade of the thirties, when movements of output and employment were the dominant feature of economic activity, large discrepancies may develop between the parity exchange rates and the rates which would restore equilibrium in a country's balance of payments.

To see why this is true, suppose that international trade is initially in equilibrium, and that the level of output in a single country is increased while output in other countries remains unchanged. As a result of the higher output in the expanding country, the demand for imports rises; a greater volume of imported materials is required to produce the higher level of output and, at the same time, consumers with higher incomes increase their purchases of foreign commodities. The expanding country is faced with a deficit in its balance of payments which will normally lead to a depreciation of its currency even if there are no changes in sellers' prices either at home or abroad. In other words, a relative expansion of output in one country alters the equilibrium exchange rate in a way which does not correspond to the movement of prices; in extreme examples the equilibrium exchange rate can be altered with no changes in prices at all.

The foregoing criticisms of purchasing-power parity have all considered the most favorable case for the parity theory in which prices and costs rise or fall uniformly within any given country. Although this implied assumption may be justified, to a considerable extent, in periods of hyperinflation, the practical application of the parity doctrine is usually complicated by differences in the degree of price rise or fall within each country. When some prices or costs rise more rapidly than others within the same country, no simple comparison between price movements in different countries can be made. The best that can be done is to use an average or index number of price changes, and if the discrepancies in price movements between different commodities in the same country are large, such an index number at best is only a rough indication of the change in the value of the monetary unit. Moreover, since several types of price index numbers are usually available, the calculation of parity rates is not a simple procedure, but involves a considerable element of judgment as to what prices and costs are important for a country's balance of payments.

Considering this element of judgment, it is not surprising that the selection of an appropriate price index has been one of the most controversial topics concerning purchasing power parity. Indeed, in some cases the difficulty of selecting an index has been the most important single cause for the disrepute into which the parity theory has fallen. It has been said, on the one hand, that the prices of commodities which do not enter into international trade are irrelevant, since these prices at most have only an indirect influence on a country's balance of payments. And on the other hand, it has been argued that international prices, or the prices of goods which enter into international trade, cannot be used because these prices necessarily adjust themselves to changes in exchange rates. In other words, it has been argued that prices for commodities which have a world market, such as many agricultural products and raw materials, necessarily adjust themselves within a given country to any change in that country's exchange rate.

To clarify this point, suppose that Canada is an exporter of such a product, Z, to the United Kingdom. If the exchange rate between

Canada and the United Kingdom is $4 = £1, and if the British price of Z is one-fourth pound per unit, the Canadian price will necessarily be $1.00, since Canada is an exporter of Z and its price is governed by the world price. Now suppose the exchange rate is altered to $5 = £1. If the British price of Z were to remain unchanged, the price in Canadian currency would rise to $1.25, and the relative change in the price of Z between the two countries would conform exactly to the change in the exchange rate. Since this type of behavior is characteristic of many commodities which are sold in competitive international markets, it has been said that the prices of internationally traded goods cannot be used in parity calculations. To include such prices, it is said, imparts a bias in the parity calculations which tends to justify the existing exchange rate, whatever it may be. If prices of domestic goods cannot be used in the calculations because they are irrelevant, and if prices of international goods cannot be used because they always adjust themselves to movements of exchange rates, it must seem, as it did to some economists, that the theory of parity has little substance and must be replaced by other methods of judging exchange rates.

One proposed solution of the price dilemma is a substitution of data on unit costs of production for price data. In other words, it has been suggested that parity rates might be computed from indexes of costs rather than price indexes. If adequate information concerning costs were available, this would no doubt be a useful approach, for the cost figures would be free, to a considerable extent, of some of the most glaring logical problems which beset the use of price indexes. Unlike some price comparisons, it could hardly be said that parity calculations based upon costs of internationally traded goods would inevitably justify existing exchange rates, for costs of production do not adjust themselves as quickly or as completely to a change in exchange rates as do the prices of some international goods.

Although cost comparisons would obviously be preferable to price comparisons in some respects, it is clear that the use of cost data in the parity calculations could also present some new difficulties. If costs of production for a given product vary between different firms, for example, which firms' costs are to be included in the index of general costs? And if the costs for a particular firm vary according to the level of output, at what level of output should the parity calculations be made? These questions will be recognized as the same difficult questions as those which arose in connection with the tariff to equalize costs of production at home and abroad, and the answers are no less difficult to find now than they were with regard to the tariff.

The selection of cost data for parity calculations, like the selection of price index numbers, involves a more or less arbitrary judgment, and the resulting parity rates are thus to be regarded as rough approximations to the effects of monetary inflation or currency values, and not as final answers to the problem of exchange rates.

Perhaps the principal advantage of cost comparisons over price comparisons is that costs are likely to represent more or less permanent changes in monetary values, whereas prices may reflect the transitory effects of inflation. At the close of a period of general inflation, it is possible that prices may have increased considerably more than wage rates and other costs. In this event a short recession may cause a significant reduction in prices without a corresponding reduction in costs. In many instances the permanent effects of inflation on the value of a currency will accordingly be measured more accurately by cost changes than by price movements.

Despite the obvious advantage of cost comparisons, it has been impossible to make such comparisons in the present study. Accurate and comprehensive data of unit costs of production are seldom published even in countries with as much economic data as the United States and the United Kingdom, and in other countries having less advanced statistical services cost information is virtually nonexistent. Changes in wage rates, the most important element of unit costs, might be substituted for the unavailable unit cost figures, but here again the investigation is confronted with a lack of data, for general indexes of wages are much less common than are general price indexes. In our consideration of the effects of war inflation on relative currency values, it has therefore been necessary to employ only price data, even though a comparison of wage changes or changes in other costs of production would have been a useful supplement.

Parity Rates in Peace and in War

The arguments against purchasing-power parity appeared to be so overwhelming during the interwar period that many economists abandoned the theory entirely. It is a curious fact, nevertheless, that despite its abandonment in principle the theory continues to be widely used in practice as a means of judging the pattern of postwar exchange rates. What are the reasons for this divergence between theory and practice? Why is the purchasing-power-parity doctrine generally discredited and at the same time widely employed? The explanation of this inconsistency, I believe, is in the fact that the parity theory is not a *general* theory of exchange rates, and that it has been applied in the past to conditions for which it was not intended. The parity doctrine was used primarily for the purpose of explaining the movements of exchange rates after the First World War, and as a theory of postwar exchange rates it retains much validity notwithstanding the arguments against it. The theory was discredited not because it was unimportant or irrelevant in the explanation of exchange rates after the war, but because attempts were later made to use it in the explanation of exchange rates under more normal conditions for which it was not appropriate.

The factors which should be taken into account in setting exchange rates after a period of war-induced inflation are obviously quite different from those which affect exchange rates under more normal conditions. In particular, wartime movements in prices and costs are unusually large, and the discrepancies in price movements between different countries are likewise large. Examples of these discrepancies, taken from wholesale price statistics, were presented at the beginning of the present discussion of prices and exchange rates. Equally great discrepancies appeared during the war in retail prices. Although retail price movements did not always agree with wholesale price movements in any particular country, the order of magnitude of the two types of price change was in most instances roughly comparable, and the changes in prices, whether measured by one index or the other, were so large and so different between one country and another that they immediately impress the observer as one of the most important influences on relative currency values.

Perhaps even more important than the amplitude of the price and cost movements is the fact that such movements, in times of war, tend to be more or less independent of changes in output and employment. Indeed, the really large price changes do not occur until output has approached the limits of a country's capacity. In contrast to these war developments, price and cost changes in normal years of peace are smaller and much more closely related to rising and falling output and employment. The disturbances in a country's balance of payments during nonwar periods are therefore largely attributable to factors other than price change, and parity calculations have a correspondingly small significance.

This was particularly true during the thirties when international payments throughout the world were disrupted by large and divergent movements of output and employment as well as by large and rapidly changing capital movements. Under these circumstances it is not surprising that a method of estimating equilibrium exchange rates which was reasonably satisfactory for conditions of war and postwar inflation should have been quite inapplicable to the depressed and unstable conditions of the early thirties. It is unfortunate, however, that the inappropriateness of the parity doctrine to the conditions of the thirties should have led to a complete condemnation of purchasing-power parity under all conditions. Despite the limitations of parity calculations, it ought to be recognized that a comparison of price movements in different countries, in times of war inflation, provides much useful information regarding exchange rates and international equilibrium. In other words, war-induced movements of prices and costs should be recognized as an independent influence on the flow of foreign payments and receipts.

Parity Rates Based upon Wholesale and Retail Prices

Without any denial of the relevance of other forces, Table 3 indicates roughly to what extent the exchange rates announced by the International Monetary Fund have made allowance for war-induced changes in prices. For nineteen of the member countries, purchasing-power-parity rates have been computed using the period from October 1936 through June 1937 as a base. The parity rate for a given country is the rate which would make the present purchasing power of that country's currency the same, relative to the purchasing power of the dollar, as it was in the base period. Reasons for the choice of the base period used here have been discussed earlier in connection with the prewar movement of exchange rates. Most of the parity rates have been computed as of November or December 1946, but in any event the date for which each rate was computed is indicated in the table. Since prices seldom moved in an entirely uniform manner within a single country, parity rates have been computed for two types of average prices, a wholesale price index and a cost-of-living or retail price index.

The table shows a rather persistent tendency for the rates announced by the Fund to exceed the parity rates. Of the nineteen countries whose

Table 3. Parity exchange rates compared with rates announced by the International Monetary Fund[1] (in cents per unit of foreign currency)

| Member country | Parity rates | | Rates announced by the Fund |
	Wholesale price parity	Cost-of-living parity	
Belgium	—	(12/46) 1.52	2.28
Canada	(11/46) 120.33	(11/46) 118.45	100.00
Chile	(11/46) 3.19	(11/46) 2.35	3.23
Colombia	—	(10/46) 39.39	57.14
Costa Rica	(11/46) 17.28	(11/46) 11.38	17.81
Cuba	—	(10/46) 72.17	100.00
Czechoslovakia	(11/46) 1.90	(11/46) 1.54	2.00
Denmark	(11/46) 18.54	(9/46) 19.34	20.84
Egypt	(7/46) 246.27	(7/46) 251.93	413.30
France	(11/46) 0.63	(9/46) 0.53	0.84
India	(8/46) 16.69	(11/46) 21.21	30.23
Iran	(5/46) 1.54	(5/46) 1.07	3.10
Mexico	(11/46) 15.89	(11/46) 11.63	20.60
Netherlands	(10/46) 34.16	(9/46) 42.11	37.70
Norway	(11/46) 22.80	(11/46) 21.59	20.15
Peru	(11/46) 15.58	(11/46) 17.40	15.38
Turkey	(9/46) 29.50	(9/46) 35.23	35.71
Union of South Africa	(9/46) 425.24	(9/46) 500.27	403.00
United Kingdom	(11/46) 467.59	(11/46) 549.46	403.00

[1] Sources of price data are given in Appendix Table A2, sources of exchange rates in preceding tables. The base period used in calculating these parity rates is the same as the base period for which prewar exchange rates are given in the earlier tables. Figures in parentheses indicate the month and year for which the parity rate was computed.

rates are included, nine—Belgium, Colombia, Costa Rica, Cuba, Egypt, France, India, Iran, and Mexico—have official exchange rates which appear to be well above the parity rates, regardless of whether such parity rates are measured in wholesale or retail prices. In only three cases—Canada, the Union of South Africa, and the United Kingdom—are the rates announced by the Fund substantially lower than the parity rates for the end of 1946.

The fact, shown by the table, that official rates announced by the Fund exceed parity rates for a considerable number of countries does not mean, of course, that the currencies of the countries involved are necessarily overvalued by the Fund. The question of whether any particular rate is too high or too low in terms of dollars is an extremely involved one which cannot possibly be answered in an overall survey of postwar exchange rates such as the present paper. In order to make an exact estimate of the exchange rates which would be consistent with a balanced position in international trade, it would be necessary to consider all of the changes in tastes, techniques, real income, and capital movements mentioned above, in addition to the changes in prices. In other words, the parity calculations are only a first approximation which indicates to what extent present exchange rates have made allowance for the war-induced changes in the domestic purchasing power of various currencies. Nevertheless, the fact that the parity rates tend to fall short of the rates announced by the Fund is, in my opinion, a general indication that present exchange rates of a number of countries are somewhat higher than the rates which will ultimately be consistent with a balanced state of international payments.

The tendency for present exchange rates to exceed parity rates is also apparent in countries which are not members of the Fund, as well as in member countries for which no exchange rates have been announced. Table 4 presents parity rates and actual rates as of December 1946 for five nonmember countries and for five member countries whose official rates have not been agreed upon. Since the general picture presented by this table is much the same as that depicted in Table 3, it will not be necessary to comment in detail. It may be useful, however, in concluding the presentation of parity rates, to make a few remarks concerning the general pattern of rates in both member and nonmember countries. Insofar as possible, rates will be considered within broad economic or geographic groups of countries.

The only group of countries for which parity rates are consistently higher than actual rates are the United Kingdom and the British dominions of Canada, Australia, New Zealand, and South Africa. In all of these countries, price controls were effective during the war and to a considerable extent have subsequently been maintained. Up to the present time, war and postwar inflation have thus been largely avoided, and at present exchange rates the purchasing power of the currencies of these countries has increased, relative to the purchasing power of the dollar. The position of these countries is discussed further in a later section. Parity rates for the Western European countries, except for the Netherlands, are to a greater or smaller extent below the actual dollar

Table 4. Parity exchange rates compared with rates in December 1946 for nonmember countries and for member countries for which rates have not been announced[1] (in cents per unit of foreign currency)

Country	Parity rates		Rates in December 1946
	Wholesale price parity	Cost-of-living parity	
Nonmember countries:			
Argentina	(11/46) 24.66	—	29.77
Australia*	(11/46) 440.51	(9/46) 424.97	321.07
New Zealand	(10/46) 395.27	—	322.36
Sweden	(11/46) 24.66	(9/46) 24.11	27.82
Switzerland	(11/46) 18.77	(11/46) 21.86	23.36
Member countries for which rates have not been announced:			
Brazil	—	(11/46) 3.87	5.41
Greece	—	(10/46) 0.0083	0.02
Italy	(11/46) 0.14	(9/46) 0.26	0.26
Poland	—	(10/46) 0.23	1.00
Uruguay	—	(9/46) 74.94	56.27

[1] Sources are the same as in preceding tables. The base period is the same as in the tables of exchange rates. Figures in parentheses indicate the month and year for which the parity rate was computed.

* Admitted to membership on August 5, 1947, after this analysis had been completed.

exchange rates. Among the Scandinavian countries, the parity rates for Denmark and Sweden are below present rates, while the parity rate for Norway is slightly above the actual rate. In any event, the discrepancies between parity rates and actual rates for the Scandinavian countries are not large.

Egypt, India, and Iran all have parity rates which are well below the actual rates. The parity rate of the Egyptian pound, for example, is approximately $2.50, compared with an actual rate of $4.13. Likewise, with respect to India, the parity rate for the rupee is between 17 and 21 cents, compared with an actual rate of approximately 30 cents. Although these figures indicate a substantial change in comparative purchasing power, the reader is warned against placing too much reliance upon any particular figure. The price index numbers for these countries are at best rough approximations, and more comprehensive indexes might deviate considerably from the ones used in the parity calculations. Moreover, in nonindustrial countries such as these, the cost structure is much more flexible than in countries like the United States and the United Kingdom. If a decline in prices eventually sets in, price indexes for these countries may therefore decline quite rapidly. It would accordingly be a mistake to assume that the war-induced inflation of prices and costs is as permanent in countries such as Egypt and India as it will probably be in the United States and the United Kingdom.

The same consideration applies, to a considerable extent, to prices and to costs in Latin America. As the two tables show, the Latin parity rates are, with a few exceptions, somewhat below the actual rates. This does not necessarily mean, however, that the Latin American countries will experience difficulties in exporting at existing rates, for the cost structure is relatively flexible in many of these countries and may adjust itself rather rapidly in a period of general deflation.

Multilateral and Bilateral Comparisons

The foregoing description of exchange rates and of the relation of such rates to parity rates has been devoted exclusively to a comparison of individual currencies with the U.S. dollar. Nothing has been said about such additional problems as the relation of the French franc to the pound sterling, or the relation of the Scandinavian currencies to those of France, Belgium, and the Netherlands. A bilateral comparison of individual currencies with the dollar, such as the comparison above, is obviously important, since the foreign trade and foreign financial transactions between the United States and other countries will continue to be a substantial part of world trade and finance, particularly in the immediate future. A complete description of exchange rates and prices, on the other hand, must consider not only such bilateral relations but also the multilateral character of all currency values and prices.

In Belgium, for example, the relation of the French franc to the Belgian franc is normally more important than the relation of these two currencies to the dollar. Similarly in Denmark, the sterling-krone ratio is more significant than the dollar-krone ratio. These "cross rates" should therefore be considered as well as the dollar rates.

Unfortunately, a completely multilateral assessment of exchange rates is confronted at the outset with tremendous technical difficulties. It is possible to consider the balance of payments of a particular country with the rest of the world, and to say that with the existing cross rates of exchange in the rest of the world the present value of the particular currency appears to be too high or too low. But what if these cross rates are altered by a change in the value of some other country's currency? How will this affect the judgment that the particular country's currency is overvalued or undervalued relative to the rest of the world? To the professional reader it will be apparent that the problem posed here is really a problem of simultaneous equations, and a complete solution cannot be obtained in any other way. For present purposes, therefore, the multilateral comparison must necessarily be limited to a few rather general observations.

It may be noted at the outset that *so far as price effects are concerned* there is no need to make a multilateral comparison in addition to the bilateral study of parity rates, for the parity rates of all currencies in relation to a particular currency will establish cross rates which are also parity rates for the currencies concerned.

To clarify this point, let us consider a numerical example. Suppose that in a base period the price of the pound sterling in dollars is $4.50, while the price of the French franc is $0.05. The cross rate between the franc and the pound will then be 90 francs to the pound. Suppose now that at the end of a period of inflation, representative price index numbers in the three countries, with the base period as 100, are as follows: United States, 150; United Kingdom, 300; France, 600. The parity rates for the pound and the franc, relative to the dollar, are then $2.25 and $0.0125 respectively. This implies a cross rate between the pound and the franc of 180 francs to the pound, which is also the parity rate of the franc relative to the pound. Thus, as far as price comparisons are concerned, parity calculations and multilateral comparisons come to the same thing. Multilateral comparisons must be made only when we are considering the complications introduced by capital movements, changes in methods of production, and other nonprice influences on a country's balance of payments, or when we wish to study the effects of maintaining exchange rates which in some instances do not agree with the parity rates.

The significance of multilateral comparisons is readily apparent in some of the regional problems which were suggested above. We have seen that, as far as prices alone are concerned, the present value of the pound sterling relative to the dollar appears to be somewhat low, while the prices of the Scandinavian currencies are not far from the dollar parity rates. If we assume that no change is made in the value of the pound relative to the dollar, this means that the Scandinavian currencies will be expensive relative to sterling. Unless Danish exports of agricultural products are subsidized, these exports to the United Kingdom may accordingly be expensive compared with other prices in the United Kingdom. Thus if the dollar price of the pound remains unchanged, it may be necessary at some point to change the dollar prices of the Scandinavian currencies, even though they are at present not far from the dollar parities.

Similar arguments apply to other cross rates such as that between France and Belgium. Although both the French franc and the Belgian franc appear to be expensive in terms of dollars, the degree of overvaluation is about the same in both cases; the Belgian dollar parity rate, based on retail prices, is 67 percent of the actual rate, while the French parity is 63 percent of the actual rate. In export markets where the two countries are in competition, overvaluation relative to the dollar is thus less significant than it would have been had the degree of overvaluation differed between the two countries, and Belgium's decision concerning any future adjustment of the external value of its currency will be greatly influenced by the policy adopted concerning the French franc.

Other examples of cross relationships could be given, but for present purposes the ones above should suffice to indicate the complicated character of the multilateral system of exchange rates. Every rate is related to every other rate, and changes in one will inevitably have repercussions upon many others.

The Policy of the International Monetary Fund

Alternatives Which Faced the Fund

When initial exchange rates were under discussion during the last quarter of 1946, the Fund and the member countries were faced with two alternative courses of action. First, they could have attempted to determine the pattern of exchange rates which would be consistent with a long-run balance in international payments and receipts, and these rates could then have been adopted as the initial rates with which the Fund began operations. This course of action would probably have required substantial changes in some exchange rates, but if the original calculations were carefully done there might have been a reasonable expectation that subsequent changes in rates would be relatively small.

The second alternative was to accept more or less the existing pattern of exchange rates with the expectation that adjustments would be made later when more normal conditions returned. In other words, the adjustment of exchange rates to the new economic conditions brought about by the war could be postponed until a later date.

In fact, the Fund adopted the second alternative. Although Mr. Gutt, in requesting information from the member countries relative to their exchange rates, had announced that the Fund must solve its most difficult problem—the agreement on initial exchange rates—before it commenced operations, in the end a decision was made, in effect, to postpone the solution of the problem by accepting the present pattern of exchange rates. The member countries requested that the rates at which they had stabilized their currencies after the war be used as official rates by the Fund, and after considerable discussion this was agreed to in the case of all the countries for which rates were announced. As noted earlier, however, it was frankly recognized at the time the initial rates were announced that adjustments would probably be necessary later. The foregoing discussion of parity rates lends support to this view, for it indicates that unless unforeseen changes in prices and costs occur, the currencies of a considerable number of countries will probably prove to be too high, when normal conditions have returned, to preserve a balance between foreign payments and receipts.

Reasons for Accepting Current Rates

Why were the existing rates accepted as initial rates by the Fund despite the fact that some of them were known to be out of line with current prices and costs? And what will be the consequences of this action on the flow of international trade? Perhaps the most important reason for beginning operations with existing rates is that the member countries themselves were anxious to keep their present rates, and that most of them had good economic reasons for wanting to do so. It is an interesting fact that many countries today want to keep the value of their currencies as high as possible, despite wartime increases in prices and costs, whereas in the prewar decade these same countries, in many instances, were rivals in a general move to depreciate their currencies. Although this reversal in attitude may seem strange at first sight, it is easily explained in terms of the difference between the primary economic problems of the thirties and those of the present day. In the thirties, the overriding economic problem in almost all countries was deflation, inadequate demand, and unemployment. Most countries were extremely anxious to increase the demand for their products, including the foreign demand, and one means of increasing foreign demand was to depreciate the currency. Once this process was started, it led to depreciation of other currencies in retaliation or selfprotection, and thus we witnessed a wave of competitive currency depreciation.

The situation today offers a sharp contrast with conditions in the thirties, and the currency policies followed by individual countries are accordingly different. The problem today is how to avoid a *rise* in prices rather than how to avoid a price decline. A considerable part of the world's productive capacity has been destroyed or worn out and at the same time the demand for goods in general has reached an unprecedented height as the combined result of accumulated war shortages and accumulated purchasing power. The primary problem today is how to produce enough to satisfy the present demand, whereas the problem of the thirties was how to find markets for the goods which could be produced. In view of this contrast in economic conditions, it is not surprising that the foreign financial policies of many countries are strikingly different from their policies during the thirties. Although many countries recognize that their current exchange rates in terms of dollars and pounds sterling are probably too high relative to present prices and costs most of these countries are extremely reluctant to depreciate at the present time.

This reluctance to depreciate is in part attributable to a fear that depreciation would aggravate inflationary developments. Just as currency depreciation in the thirties helped individual countries to avoid a fall in domestic prices and incomes by creating a foreign demand for their goods, so today the maintenance of high currency values helps many of these same countries to retard inflation by keeping down the domestic prices of their imports. Despite present inflationary pressures, many countries have finally succeeded in achieving a precarious price stability and an equally precarious balance between prices and costs by means of price controls, wage controls, and rationing. Although these controls in many instances are neither as comprehensive nor as strictly enforced as war controls, they have frequently accomplished the purpose of preventing or retarding a further spiral of increased prices and increased costs. The distaste for currency depreciation is in many instances attributable to a fear that depreciation, by increasing the domestic prices of imports, will disturb the precarious balance and lead to additional increases in both prices and wages. If a country's domestic prices for imported goods rise as a result of depreciation, this means in many cases a substantial increase in the cost of living, and an increase in living costs may easily lead to demands for wage increases which will start the entire inflationary process anew. Considering this possibility, it is easy to understand why many countries, and particularly those countries whose economies were badly damaged by war, are reluctant to depreciate their currencies at the present time.

Apart from its effect on the cost of living, currency depreciation in the near future might have serious inflationary consequences simply as a result of its psychological effects. This is particularly true of the European countries in which inflation after the First World War was accompanied by a rapid currency depreciation. The people in many of these countries have an exaggerated idea of the relation between depreciation and the internal value of a currency and tend in some cases to regard depreciation and inflation as synonymous. Depreciation in these countries, under present circumstances, might therefore lead to a wave of spending which would further aggravate the tendency of prices to rise. It would be assuming a considerable responsibility to insist, in the face of these conditions, that an immediate adjustment should be made in the exchange rates of the countries whose currencies seem from a long-run point of view to be overvalued.

Apart from the dangers of further inflation, there are a number of other convincing arguments against making an immediate adjustment in exchange rates. Most countries whose currencies appear to be too expensive in relation to their domestic prices are also countries which will be borrowing heavily from the dollar area during the next three or four years. In other words, the normal condition for these countries during the transition years will be an import surplus, the excess of imports to be paid for out of dollar loans from such agencies as the Export-Import Bank and the International Bank for Reconstruction and Development. Thus even if such countries had no import controls and their exchange rates were immediately adjusted to a level where their foreign receipts, including loans, were equal to their foreign payments, the presence of the import surplus financed by loans would mean that the currency values of the borrowing countries could be somewhat higher during the borrowing period, relative to prices, than the prewar equilibrium rates. To put the matter another way, the equilibrium rates for the borrowing countries during the transition period will be above the parity rates.

How much significance should be attached to this point is difficult to estimate. For some countries exchange rates are probably so high, relative to prices, that the present rates are above equilibrium rates even if allowance is made for borrowing from abroad. In cases where the parity rate indicates only a slight overvaluation relative to prices, on the other hand, the present exchange rates may not be far out of line.

Another reason for maintaining present exchange rates during the transition years is the condition of the export industries. In many countries whose currencies appear to be overvalued, exports are limited not by market conditions but by inability to produce. As long as this is the case, a depreciation of the currency will not enable the depreciating country to increase its receipts of foreign exchange. It is true, of course, that depreciation will enable a country to reduce its export prices, in terms of foreign currency, while maintaining or even increasing the prices which domestic producers receive in their own currency, but if the physical volume of exports cannot be increased because of limits to productive capacity the reduction in foreign prices will.not increase the foreign exchange available to the exporting country. On the contrary, depreciation in this case will *reduce* the amount of foreign exchange received in the depreciating country and thereby worsen the country's balance of payments.

In addition to the reasons mentioned above, it seems likely that the decision of the Fund to begin operations with existing exchange rates was influenced to a considerable extent by the great uncertainty concerning the future course of world trade. Although comparisons of price changes with changes in exchange rates establish a presumption that many currencies today are too expensive relative to the dollar for a long-run balanced world economy, it would be a mistake to assume that the parity rates themselves are necessarily the proper rates. Many changes in basic economic conditions have occurred during the war and these changes will inevitably affect the terms on which goods will be exchanged in the future. For this reason, it is not sufficient simply to adjust exchange rates to the observed price movements. In addition, an allowance must be made for the increased or decreased ability of some countries to export, and for changes in the demand for imports.

Unfortunately, adjustments of this type are extremely difficult to make. How, for example, will the decline of Germany and Japan in world trade affect the trade balances of other countries? What effect will the rebuilding of the devastated countries have on their ability to produce and to export? At the present time it is obviously impossible to give precise, quantitative answers to questions such as these. The network of world trade is so complex that it is extremely difficult to trace the consequence of Germany's decline or the rebuilding of the French and British economies through all of their ramifications. This uncertainty adds weight to the decision of the Fund to postpone exchange adjustments, for only actual experience can tell us which countries are likely to have deficits and which to have surpluses as a result of the war-induced changes in conditions of production and consumption.

With regard to the course of prices in different countries, uncertainties are almost equally great. It has been said, on the one hand, that prices and costs in countries which now have overvalued currencies will probably fall as normal production is resumed and the accumulated war losses are replaced. On the other hand, the continuing inflationary pressures in some countries may raise prices above present levels. Probably even more important as far as price comparisons are concerned is the fact that the index numbers upon which these comparisons are based are limited for the most part to official prices and make only slight allowance for the higher black-market prices. As output is increased and accumulated demands are satisfied, some of these black-market prices will clearly tend to fall. At the same time, however, it seems highly probable that official prices will tend to rise, since the current cost structure almost certainly reflects in part the high level of black-market prices. Taking all of these possibilities into account, I feel it is doubtful that a significant part of the disparities between current prices and exchange rates will be corrected by a fall in prices in the countries with overvalued currencies.

Several of the reasons discussed above for postponing action on exchange adjustments were explicitly recognized by the Fund. The announcement of initial rates which was made on December 18, 1946, contained the following statement:

The Fund realizes that at the present exchange rates there are substantial disparities in price and wage levels among a number of countries. In present circumstances, however, such disparities do not have the same significance as in normal times. For practically all countries, exports are being limited mainly by difficulties of production or transport, and the wide gaps which exist in some countries between the cost of needed imports and the proceeds of exports would not be appreciably narrowed by changes in their currency parities. In addition, many countries have just begun to recover from the disruption of war, and efforts to restore the productivity of their economies may be expected gradually to bring their cost structures into line with those of other countries. Furthermore, for many countries now concerned with combating inflation there is a danger that a change in the exchange rate would aggravate internal tendencies toward inflation.

From this statement it is apparent that the Fund placed considerable weight on the numerous reasons for postponing adjustments. Even if the Fund had wanted to change some of the present rates, however, there is some doubt as to whether it would have been able to establish its authority to require such changes under the present abnormal conditions. Article XX of the Articles of Agreement of the Fund stipulates that the par value of a currency communicated to the Fund by a member shall be the initial value for the purpose of the Fund's operations unless, " (i) the member notifies the Fund that it regards the par value as unsatisfactory, or (ii) the Fund notifies the member that in its opinion the par value cannot be maintained *without causing recourse to the Fund on the part of that member or others on a scale prejudicial to the Fund and to members.*"[6] From this part of the Agreement, it appears that the Fund has only rather limited authority in the setting of initial rates. The member country itself can apparently object to the communicated par value for any reason whatsoever, whereas the Fund can object only if it feels that the communicated par value would cause undue recourse to the Fund.

The difficulty about this criterion is that a number of war-ravaged countries, *whatever exchange rate they adopt,* may be expected to have a deficit in their balance of payments over the next year or so of a size necessitating their making full use of their annual drawing rights on the Fund and yet of such an apparently transitory character as to justify use of the Fund's resources. In the case of such countries, the scale of recourse to the Fund will not be dependent, in the initial period, upon the level of the exchange rate. Of course the Fund might fear that if the existing rate were maintained over a period of years, these drafts upon the Fund might become chronic. But in view of the uncertainties concerning long-range predictions of balance-of-payment developments, the Fund would find it difficult to offer convincing substantiation for such fears. Even if it could, the country concerned might well respond

6. Article XX, sec. 4(b). Italics added.

that the time for adjustment would arrive only later when the scale of its recourse to the Fund actually came to depend upon its exchange-rate policy. It is not known to what extent this limitation on the Fund influenced the decision concerning initial rates, but it may have played some part.

Dangers of Postponing Action

Unless radical readjustments of prices occur in some countries, it seems apparent from the preceding discussion that the initial exchange rates at which the Fund has commenced operations are in a substantial number of cases too high for a long-run balanced state of trade. This is not necessarily an indication that an immediate adjustment should be made, for we have seen that there are strong arguments for postponing the adjustment and continuing during the transition period with existing rates. At the same time, however, it is well to recognize that maintaining exchange rates which are too high in relation to prices may involve certain dangers for the future of a liberal foreign economic program.[7]

The principal danger is that once a country has adjusted its trade controls to an overvalued currency the country may later be reluctant to relax these controls and depreciate its currency to a level compatible with balanced international payments. Apart from the question of national prestige, an overvalued currency may be tempting to some countries even after the period of reconstruction has ended and the threat of inflation has subsided. Rightly or wrongly, there is a tendency to associate a high-priced currency with low prices for imports relative to the prices received for exports. In other words, it is widely believed that an appreciated currency means favorable terms of trade. Whether this is always true or not is beside the point. For present purposes, it is sufficient that many people believe it is true, and that some countries may therefore desire to maintain overvalued currencies more or less permanently, and to preserve balance in their international payments by means of trade controls or other barriers to trade. In other words, if exchange rates are set for a considerable period of time in a pattern which is not consistent with balanced international payments, there is a danger that balance will nevertheless be achieved by means of various

7. A substantial number of the advantages and disadvantages of an immediate adjustment of exchange rates were listed by Professor Haberler in the article previously cited. In contrast to the present paper, however, Haberler concluded that undervaluation of European currencies was preferable to the present rather general overvaluation.

direct controls, and that the pressure for a readjustment of rates arising from loss of external reserves will accordingly be negligible.

A second danger of the present exchange pattern is that it may freeze a system of export subsidies more or less permanently into many economic systems. In some countries, exchange rates are so high relative to prices that it seems doubtful whether many industries in these countries will be able to resume their prewar normal export trade without substantial subsidies. Like import controls, these export subsidies may come to be regarded as a permanent feature of international trade, If so, the cost of postponing adjustments of exchange rates will be a permanent distortion of the price system.

Whether the dangers of postponing action are real or only apparent depends to some extent upon the success or failure of current efforts to establish an International Trade Organization. Under the draft charter of this proposed organization, the member countries would agree to a code of trade practices calling for a general reduction of trade barriers and export subsidies. The charter recognizes that quantitative import controls may be needed, in some instances, to preserve equilibrium in a country's balance of payments; but if equilibrium continues to require import restrictions it is anticipated that other measures, such as an adjustment of exchange rates or of prices and costs, will be undertaken. Tariffs and export subsidies are presumably not to be considered, under the organization's charter, as means of adjusting the balance of payments either temporarily or in the long run. Thus if the charter is accepted by a large number of countries there will be less danger that the present pattern of rather abnormal exchange rates will become permanent than would otherwise be the case. Although these rates might be compensated or offset for a considerable period of time by export subsidies and direct import controls, the International Trade Organization would presumably exert strong influence on the member countries to reduce their controls and subsidies, and to adjust their exchange rates to a level compatible with balanced international payments and receipts. Whether the International Trade Organization comes into existence or not, however, it seems to me doubtful that the arguments in favor of an immediate adjustment of exchange rates are sufficiently convincing to offset the serious disadvantages of such action.

The " Undervalued " Currencies

In discussing the probable consequences of the acceptance by the Fund of existing exchange rates, we have considered thus far only the countries whose currencies appear to be too expensive relative to the dollar. This indeed is the problem which has received most attention in current discussions, and it is no doubt the most important problem from a practical point of view. Nevertheless, as noted earlier, the table of parity rates for members of the Fund shows that a few of the present rates are below the parity rates, relative to the dollar. In other words, for a few countries depreciation of the currency in terms of dollars, relative to the prewar situation, was greater than the relative rise in prices. In order to complete the description of present exchange rates, we ought to consider briefly the position of these undervalued currencies.

The countries whose currencies seem to be undervalued in terms of dollars are the United Kingdom and the following members of the British Commonwealth of Nations: Australia, Canada, New Zealand, and the Union of South Africa. Although Australia[8] and New Zealand are not yet members of the Fund, their present exchange rates will nevertheless be considered along with the other British currencies. Whether measured in wholesale or in retail prices, the parity rates for all of these countries are above the actual rates. For convenient reference, the ratio of parity rates to actual rates in all five countries is given in Table 5 for the end of 1946.

Table 5. Ratio of parity rates to actual rates for selected British currencies at the end of 1946 (ratios computed with reference to U.S. dollar)

Country	In wholesale prices	In retail prices
Australia	1.37	1.32
Canada	1.20	1.18
New Zealand	1.23	—
Union of South Africa	1.06	1.24
United Kingdom	1.16	1.36

The extent of undervaluation, measured by prices, varies from 6 percent to 37 percent, with an average of perhaps 20 percent. The actual numbers are not as important, however, as the general direction, for we have seen that it is impossible to give a precise interpretation to the parity calculations.

The undervaluation of British currencies shown by these figures is to

8. Australia was admitted to membership on August 5, 1947, after this analysis had been completed.

a large extent attributable to the price inflation which has taken place in the United States since price controls were abandoned in the middle of 1946. In August of that year, parity calculations comparable to those included in the present paper were made, and at that time the currency rates for the British countries, except for India and Egypt, appeared to correspond roughly with parity rates. Subsequently, however, both retail and wholesale prices increased much more rapidly in the United States than in the British countries.

A few examples will indicate the disparity in price movements. Between June and December 1946, the index of wholesale prices in the United States increased 25 percent, whereas the British wholesale price index increased by only 4 percent. During the same period, retail prices in the United States increased by 15 percent, compared with an increase of 2.4 percent in Canada and virtually no change in the United Kingdom. As a result of these changes, the British currencies, including the Canadian dollar, now appear to be low-priced in relation to the movement of prices in general.

If this is true, why did the countries of the British Commonwealth not request an appreciation of their currencies, relative to the dollar, when initial exchange rates for the Fund were being considered? A complete answer to this question would be beyond the scope of the present paper, since it would require a detailed investigation of economic conditions in each of the countries concerned. It will suffice at this point to indicate a number of broad considerations bearing on the question.

Unlike many other countries, the British countries whose currencies appear to be undervalued do not have an acute problem of inflation. It is true, of course, that most of them have a substantial amount of accumulated demand and a corresponding amount of liquid purchasing power, but this development, which would otherwise be inflationary, has not been permitted to have any appreciable effect upon prices, since wartime controls have been carried over into the period of reconstruction. The situation is accordingly less precarious in these countries than in many others, and there is less danger that a price rise in a particular group of commodities such as imports will set off an inflationary spiral of prices and costs. This means that countries such as the United Kingdom and Australia do not have to rely on low prices of imports as a means of preventing inflation at home. In other words, their domestic controls are so strong that it is not necessary, or at least not imperative, to use their exchange rates as instruments of domestic policy. It may be presumed that this is one reason why the British countries did not insist upon more expensive currencies, relative to the dollar.

Another factor in the decision, no doubt, was the feeling that the price situation in the United States is only temporary, and that prices here will eventually fall. Also, price indexes used for the United Kingdom probably overstated somewhat the degree of undervaluation of the pound sterling, since the cost of living index, at any rate, was known to be relatively insensitive to the war-induced rise of prices. The complaint was frequently heard in the United Kingdom that the British authorities had stabilized the cost-of-living index but not the cost of living. This fact, together with the belief that prices in the United States may fall to some extent from their present high level, means that the price comparison is not so valid an indication of the equilibrium rate for the pound sterling as would otherwise be the case. The British apparently do not wish to appreciate now and be confronted later with the necessity of reducing the price of their currency as the result of a decline in American prices.

Apart from the price factors, additional reasons for not appreciating the pound may be found in the state of Britain's balance of payments. The British international position is well known and it will not be necessary to review it in detail here. Liquidation of British overseas assets as well as the great increase in her overseas liabilities which occurred during the war will make it necessary for the United Kingdom to export a larger volume of goods in order to pay for a given volume of imports than was the case in the prewar years. Adjustment to this new situation will of course be postponed by the loans which the United Kingdom has received from the United States and Canada, but eventually it is highly probable that a rate of exchange for the pound lower than the parity rate will be needed in order to increase Britain's exports relative to her imports. In the present state of general world shortage of goods, the British could no doubt sell as much abroad as they are now selling even if they increased their foreign prices. This means that appreciation of the pound might, in the immediate future, increase Britain's receipts from exports. At a later date, however, when world markets become more competitive, it is almost certain that British exports would be affected adversely if the pound had been appreciated.

In its current export drive, the United Kingdom is apparently taking the long view, being willing to forego some temporary gains for the benefit of a more lasting position in the world's export markets.

Moreover, in view of the key importance of the sterling-dollar rate in the world rate structure, the British may have been very hesitant to upset their existing relationship; they may also have had some feeling that the American public would find it difficult to reconcile an upward revaluation in the pound sterling with continued British requests for American financial support.

The Canadian situation is somewhat different from that of the United Kingdom. In the United Kingdom, as we have seen, there might be a short-run advantage to an appreciation of the pound, but over a longer period, when borrowing from other countries will have ceased, it is doubtful whether a value of the pound as high as the parity rate could be maintained. In Canada, on the other hand, an upward adjustment of the currency value might be appropriate as a long-run measure but in the immediate future there are pressing reasons for retaining the present rate, even though it is low relative to the war-induced movement of prices. The Canadians have committed themselves to make postwar loans of approximately 2 billion dollars, and Canadian exports must therefore be considerably greater than imports, in the near future, in order to preserve a balanced state of international payments. Canada is already beginning to feel the effects of this situation in a deficit with the United States, and there is little prospect that the Canadian authorities will want to raise the value of their currency.

With regard to the other countries—Australia, New Zealand, and South Africa—little need be added. As in the past, they will probably wish to maintain a stable relation between their currencies and the pound sterling. As far as relative prices are concerned, there is no reason why this should not be possible. In the long run, however, the fact that they have reduced their indebtedness to the United Kingdom will mean that their exports will be smaller relative to imports than in the past. In other words, they will no longer need an export surplus to make service payments on their foreign debts, and on this account a long-run appreciation of their currencies, relative to the pound and the dollar, might reasonably be expected.

Conclusions

A contrast was drawn at the beginning of this paper between the manner of setting exchange rates after the First World War and the procedure provided through the International Monetary Fund for establishing such rates after the Second World War. The uncoordinated, almost anarchistic establishment of relative currency values through unilateral return to the gold standard after the First World War was compared with the deliberations contemplated under the Articles of Agreement of the Fund.

From the discussion of present exchange rates, however, and from the action of the Fund in announcing these rates as initial rates for the Fund's operations, it should be apparent that the contrast, at the present time, is more in the *mechanism* for setting rates than in the actual results. It was a considerable achievement, even though a belated one, to have recognized in the Fund Agreement that gold parities of different currencies are important primarily because they govern relative currency values in international trade. It was an achievement also to have obtained an explicit statement of the importance of multilateral negotiations in establishing gold parities and relative currency values. It can hardly be said, however, that progress in exchange rate policy has gone much beyond these statements of principle, for we have seen that the exchange rates announced by the Fund involve, to some extent, discrepancies similar to those which disturbed world trade after the First World War. Many currencies appear to be too expensive, relative to prices, while a few are too cheap.

This is not to say that the Fund made a mistake in deciding to begin operations with the rates at which the member countries had pegged their exchanges. There are many convincing reasons, as noted above, for postponing action in the adjustment of exchange rates, particularly in the adjustment of rates which at the present time appear to be too high. Inflationary pressures are still strong and persistent in many of the countries having currencies which are expensive relative to prices, and depreciation at this time would intensify these inflationary tendencies by increasing the domestic prices of imports. Depreciation, moreover, would not increase the foreign exchange available to such countries from the sale of exports, for under present market conditions the limitation on exports is usually inability of export industries to produce rather than inability to sell, and depreciation would do little, in the short run at least, to increase a country's capacity to produce for export.

Another reason for maintaining rates which in some cases appear to be too high is that the countries with apparent overvaluation in their currencies are, generally speaking, countries which will be borrowing heavily in the next few years. Such borrowing countries will not expect to secure an even balance of payments on current account in the near future. They will expect, instead, to have an excess of imports of goods and services over exports, and the exchange rate appropriate to this situation, even if no direct controls were maintained, would be a rate somewhat above the parity rate. For the borrowing countries, apparent overvaluation relative to prices is thus not necessarily an indication that a downward adjustment is desirable.

In addition to all these considerations, a probable further factor in the Fund's decision to accept existing exchange rates as initial rates is the large amount of uncertainty regarding the future development of world trade. The future is uncertain with respect to both the pattern of trade and the pattern of prices. The Second World War was much more destructive than the first, and as a result it is almost impossible to say at this time which countries will have a comparative advantage in particular commodities when the period of reconstruction has ended. Two countries, Germany and Japan, have been almost completely eliminated from world markets and it is not known to what extent their trade will revive or what effect their diminished importance will have on the trade of other countries. In any event, many uncertainties remain both with respect to changes in the pattern of trade and with respect to future price movements, and these uncertainties make it almost impossible to establish a pattern of long-run exchange rates immediately even if it were desirable on other grounds to do so.

It was probably for all of the reasons given above that the Fund decided to postpone the adjustment of exchange rates. The real test of the new mechanism for setting exchange rates will not come until more normal conditions return. In the meantime, the fact that some exchange rates are out of line will not necessarily have serious financial consequences since both trade and payments will be rather strictly controlled during the reconstruction years. Eventually, however, when inflationary pressures have subsided, when individual economies have been restored to a high productive capacity, and when the ability to export has been increased, many countries will be in a position to remove import controls and exchange controls, to reduce export subsidies, and to adjust the values of their currencies downward, in consultation with the Fund. When this time comes, and not before, the value of the Fund arrangements for adjusting exchange rates will be given a genuine trial.

Appendix Table A1. U.S. wholesale price and cost-of-living indexes (October 1936 to June 1937 = 100)

Month in 1946	Wholesale price index	Cost-of-living index
March	127.2	128.7
April	128.7	129.3
May	129.7	130.1
June	131.9	131.7
July	145.2	139.3
August	150.8	142.0
September	154.9	144.2
October	156.7	146.6
November	163.1	149.9
December	164.6	151.9

SOURCES: Converted to given base from Bureau of Labor Statistics index.

Appendix Table A2. Price indexes used in parity calculations (base period October 1936 to June 1937 unless otherwise indicated)

Country	Wholesale price index		Cost-of-living index	
	Date for which computed	Value of index	Date for which computed	Value of index
Argentina	November 1946	216.4	—	—
Australia	November 1946	144.8	September 1946	132.7
Belgium	—	—	December 1946	336.7
Brazil	—	—	November 1946	237.3
Canada	November 1946	135.6	November 1946	126.6
Chile	November 1946	264.5	November 1946	330.1
Colombia	—	—	October 1946	212.8[1]
Costa Rica	November 1946	211.5[2]	November 1946	210.5[2]
Cuba	—	—	October 1946	235.8[3]
Czechoslovakia	November 1946	302.0	November 1946	340.8
Denmark	November 1946	192.7	September 1946	163.4
Egypt	July 1946	296.7	July 1946	278.3
France	November 1946	808.3[4]	September 1946	787.0[4]
Greece	—	—	October 1946	15,834.2
India	August 1946	335.0	November 1946	262.0

Appendix Table A2.—*continued*

Country	Wholesale price index		Cost-of-living index	
	Date for which computed	*Value of index*	*Date for which computed*	*Value of index*
Iran	May 1946	512.3	May 1946	753.7[5]
Italy	November 1946	5,884.5[6]	November 1946	3,344.0[7]
Mexico	November 1946	284.8	November 1946	357.8
Netherlands	October 1946	250.2	September 1946	186.8
New Zealand	October 1946	156.2	—	—
Norway	November 1946	176.4	November 1946	171.2
Peru	November 1946	262.5	November 1946	216.0
Poland	—	—	October 1946	11,900.0
Sweden	November 1946	167.3	September 1946	151.3
Switzerland	November 1946	199.0	November 1946	157.0
Turkey	September 1946	392.9	September 1946	329.0[4]
Union of South Africa	September 1946	165.5	September 1946	140.0
United Kingdom	November 1946	17.1.2	November 1946	133.9
Uruguay	—	—	September 1946	157.9[8]
Venezuela	August 1946	155.6	—	—

[1] February 1937 base period.
[2] 1936 base period.
[3] July to December 1937 base period; food prices only.
[4] 1938 base period.
[5] March 1936 to March 1937 base period.
[6] 1937 base period. Index includes black-market prices on rationed goods.
[7] 1937 base period; food prices only.
[8] 1936–37 base period.

Sources: United Nations statistical bulletins, government publications of Cuba, Poland France, and China; consular reports. Recent cost-of-living figures for Belgium, Greece, France, and Poland were obtained from consular reports or government publications, and converted to the 1936–37 base period by the use of earlier indexes as given by the League of Nations. In other cases, continuous series were available.

6 | Tariffs, the Terms of Trade, and the Distribution of National Income

The classical concept of the gains from international trade was essentially a concept of increased productivity. The gains from trade, in the classical view, consisted in an increased output of all goods and services, made possible through specialization and exchange. In other words, the classical "law of comparative advantage" demonstrated that, with a given amount of productive resources in every country, it was possible, by an interchange of goods, for all countries to consume more of all commodities. In addition to its description of the potential gains from trade, the classical theory, from the time of John Stuart Mill, also gave an excellent account of how these gains are actually divided among different countries. Stated more broadly, the theory of reciprocal demand, which was added to the classical doctrine by Mill, indicated how international exchange affects the distribution of world income among countries.[1]

With its strong emphasis upon productivity and upon the division of the gains from trade between different countries, however, the classical doctrine, as well as the subsequent theoretical work of neoclassical economists, seriously neglected the closely related problem of how international trade affects the division of income within each country among

Reprinted from *Journal of Political Economy*, 57 (February 1949), 1–29. Copyright University of Chicago, 1949.

1. John Stuart Mill, *Essays on Some Unsettled Questions of Political Economy*, ed. 1 (London, J. W. Parker, 1844), essay 1.

the various factors of production.[2] The classical theory and its neo-classical refinements could show well enough how a country, considered as a unit, tends to benefit from specialization and trade; but these doctrines had very little to say about how the gains of real income within each country are divided among labor, capital, and land.[3]

The division of the gains from trade among the different factors of production or, what amounts to substantially the same thing, the influence of international trade upon the distribution of national income is a subject which has received an adequate theoretical treatment only in comparatively recent times. The pioneer works in this branch of international economics were, of course, the studies which E. F. Heckscher[4] and B. Ohlin[5] made during the years between the two world wars. It is a curious fact that, just as the classical discussion of the terms of trade had neglected or left unsolved the related problem of the distribution of income, so the more recent contributions to the study of income distribution have neglected the complications arising out of changes in the terms of trade. Indeed, at the very beginning of his article Heckscher asserted that a discussion of the gains from trade has no relevance to the problem of income distribution. "No attention is paid," he said, "to the advantages one particular country may achieve, by means of protection, in altering the relation between supply and demand of a certain commodity and thereby wholly or partly letting the 'foreigner pay the duty'; since this problem has been discussed so widely, and since it is not relevant in the present connection, it seems unnecessary to discuss it here."[6] In the historical development of the theory of international

2. In view of the fact that the marginal-productivity theory of distribution did not appear until late in the nineteenth century and in view, further, of the generally recognized opinion that even the present theory of distribution has many deficiencies, it is perhaps not surprising that the influence of international trade upon the distribution of income was inadequately discussed by the classical economists. But even with due allowances for the backward state of distribution theory, the lag in development of this aspect of international trade was surprisingly long.

3. Although the question of income distribution arose early in the nineteenth century in the English controversy over the Corn Laws, the results of the controversy in this respect were inconclusive and had no permanent influence on the theory of international trade. Cf., however, C. F. Bastable, *The Theory of International Trade* (London, Macmillan, 1903), chap. 6.

4. "The Effect of Foreign Trade on the Distribution of Income," American Economic Association, *Readings in the Theory of International Trade* (Philadelphia, Blakiston, 1949), chap. 13.

5. *Interregional and International Trade* (Cambridge, Mass., Harvard University Press, 1933), chap. 2 and *passim*.

6. Heckscher, "The Effect of Foreign Trade" (reference 4), p. 274.

trade, questions of income distribution have thus been rather sharply separated from questions of productivity and of gains or losses to a country as a whole.

In view of this distinct cleavage in the purely theoretical aspects of international trade, it is not surprising that the practical application of economic theory to the particular problem of tariffs has suffered from a similar lack of integration. On the one hand, the concept of reciprocal demand has been employed to demonstrate how tariffs may improve a country's terms of trade—that is, reduce the prices it pays for its imports relative to the prices it receives for its exports—but little attempt has been made to employ this same concept in showing how the resulting increase of real income is divided among the different factors of production. Indeed, there has at times been a tendency in the classical theory to deny that tariffs exert any influence at all upon the distribution of national income.[7] On the other hand, when a theory of the influence of international trade upon the distribution of income was finally developed, this theory was based in part, as the preceding quotation from Heckscher demonstrates, upon the assumption that the influence of tariffs upon the terms of trade can be neglected. Despite this historical separation of two important aspects of tariff theory, it is easily shown that changes in a country's terms of trade are closely related in a number of ways to changes in the distribution of its national income. It is the purpose of the present paper to show some of the relations between these two distinct and heretofore largely independent branches of tariff theory. Since Heckscher's work is basic to the later studies of tariffs and income distribution, it seems advisable to present a brief summary of his principal conclusions.

Heckscher began his discussion, as did the classical economists, with the assertion that trade between countries depends upon the law of comparative advantage, that is, upon the fact that the ratio of the cost of production of two commodities is different in one country from the corresponding cost ratio in another. Unlike the classical economists,

---

7. The following statement by Taussig illustrates the point: "The general proposition that a high rate of wages is a result of high productiveness of industry is simple and undeniable. . . . Beyond doubt there remain questions which are more difficult. Just how and through what channel or mechanism does high productivity lead to the high wages? And what determines the share of the total product, be that great or small, which shall go to the laborer, the employer, the owner of capital, the owner of land? But these questions, the most important and perhaps the most complex in the field of economics, *lie quite outside the tariff controversy.*" Quoted from *Free Trade, the Tariff, and Reciprocity* (New York, Macmillan, 1920), p. 54. Italics added.

however, Heckscher placed great emphasis upon the way in which the supplies of various factors of production affect comparative costs. He argued, in particular, that comparative costs in one country differ from those in another primarily because the relative degree of scarcity of some factors of production differs between countries and because different commodities require varying proportions of the factors of production.[8]

Suppose, for example, that one country, A, has a large amount of land per worker as compared with another country, B. The ratio of rent to wage rates will then be lower in A than in B, since land in the former country will be used to the point where its marginal product is relatively small. Consider now the comparative costs in the two countries of producing two products, wheat and textiles. Since wheat requires a larger amount of land per worker than textiles do, the money cost of producing a unit of wheat, relative to the cost of producing a unit of textiles, will be lower in A than in B. In other words, A will have a comparative advantage in wheat, the product requiring relatively large amounts of its abundant factor, while B will have a comparative advantage in textiles.

It is a simple step from these basic propositions concerning comparative advantage to the final conclusions of Heckscher with respect to the distribution of income. Suppose that A and B are initially isolated and self-sufficient but that trade is finally opened up between the two countries. A, the low-rent country, will then export wheat, and B, where rents are comparatively high and wages low, will export textiles. This exchange of goods has a definite and predictable influence upon the demand for land and labor in the two countries. In each country the demand for factors of production is increased in the export industry and reduced in the industry competing with imports; but, as Heckscher pointed out, the proportions in which the factors of production are required in the export industry are not exactly the same as the proportions in which they are released by the industry competing with imports. In the present illustration the expansion of the wheat industry in A requires, at prevailing wages and rents, a small number of workers per acre of land, while the contraction of the textile industry, under the pressure of competitition from abroad, releases a relatively larger number of workers and only a small amount of land. The shift of resources from textiles to

8. Heckscher, "The Effect of Foreign Trade" (reference 4), p. 279.

wheat thus increases the relative scarcity of land in A, the country which initially had a comparatively large supply of that factor. Wages per unit of labor accordingly fall in A, relative to rent per unit of land. In other words, the shift in production which was brought about by international trade has given land, the relatively abundant factor in A, a larger share of the total product.

An analogous argument could easily be presented—and, indeed, has been presented both by Heckscher and later by Ohlin—to show that in B, where land is relatively scarce and labor abundant, international trade increases wage rates relative to rents. The central feature of the Heckscher-Ohlin analysis is thus the proposition that international trade, by increasing the demand for each country's abundant factors, tends to equalize the relative returns to the factors of production in different countries.[9]

With this brief introduction, we may now examine the relation of the Heckscher-Ohlin theory to the tariff problem. In view of the tendency of international trade to equalize relative factor returns among different countries, it might seem that the owners of a factor of production which is relatively scarce in a given country would have a strong interest in restricting international trade; for by so doing they could preserve the relative scarcity which might otherwise be threatened by competition

9. Whether international trade achieves a *complete* or only a *partial* equalization of relative and absolute factor returns in different countries has been a controversial issue. Heckscher, working with a simple model in which the coefficients of production were fixed, argued that the equalization would be complete in both an absolute and a relative sense. Thus, on p. 287 of reference 4, he said: "With fixed supplies of the factors of production and the same technique of production in all countries, we have seen that the final effect of international trade, with unimportant reservations, is the equalization of the *relative* prices of the factors of production. We must next inquire whether the equalization will be *absolute* as well as *relative*, i.e., whether rent, wages and interest for the same qualities of the factors of production will amount to the same real return in all countries. This proposition has not thus far been demonstrated, but it is an inescapable consequence of trade."

If the coefficients of production were variable, on the other hand, Heckscher believed that substitutions of one factor for another would lead to different techniques of production and hence to differences in relative and absolute factor returns between countries (*ibid.*, p. 288). It was this latter conclusion, rather than the former one, which was subsequently adopted and elaborated by Ohlin (reference 5, pp. 37–39) and which became more or less the generally accepted view.

Paul A. Samuelson, however, in a recent study prepared independently of Heckscher's work ("International Trade and the Equalization of Factor Prices," *Economic Journal*, 58 [June 1948], 163–184), has shown that the equalization of relative and absolute returns may be complete even when account is taken of factor substitutions. In other words, Heckscher's first conclusion—that is, the conclusion that equalization is *complete*—is applicable even to the case of variable coefficients of production. This suggests that the theory of international trade might have been advanced considerably, in the English-speaking world at any rate, by an earlier translation of Heckscher's pioneer article.

from abroad. In a country with an abundant supply of land and a limited supply of labor, for example, the working class might well benefit by tariffs on manufactured goods. Superficially at least, the Heckscher-Ohlin analysis lends support to the pauper-labor argument for tariffs.

Against this view, it may be objected that the conclusions with regard to the influence of trade upon the distribution of national income take account only of the *relative* position of a particular factor of production and make no allowance for the fact that the *absolute* return of the scarce factor may deteriorate even when its relative position improves. Tariffs interfere with the allocation of resources, and if the real income of an entire nation is thus reduced by protective duties, it may be small compensation to the scarce factor that it now obtains a larger share of the reduced total. Fifty percent of a national income of 75 is clearly worse[10] than 40 percent of a national income of 100.

But this possibility of a divergence in the movements of *real* and *relative* returns need not detain us further; for Stolper and Samuelson, in a study which forms a sequel to the works of Heckscher and Ohlin, have shown that the real return and the relative return of a particular factor of production are likely to move in the same direction.[11] In other words, if a tariff increases the share of the national income accruing to the working class, it will also improve the workers' standard of living, and conversely. According to the Stolper-Samuelson argument, a country with a comparatively small labor supply could thus increase its real wage rate by means of protection, even though national income as a whole were thereby diminished. To use a common expression, the workers would get not merely a larger share of a smaller pie but a share which was larger, in absolute magnitude, than their previous smaller share of a larger pie. The detrimental effects of the tariff would be shifted entirely onto the country's "abundant" factors of production.

These results follow directly from two assumptions. The first is that a tariff causes factors of production to be shifted from export industries to industries competing with imports. If labor, as before, is taken to be the country's relatively scarce and high-cost factor of production, it follows from the Heckscher-Ohlin conclusions that the export industries will be those requiring a comparatively small amount of labor in relation to

10. Unless conspicuous consumption and social standing are more important than the absolute standard of living.

11. Wolfgang F. Stolper and Paul A. Samuelson, "Protection and Real Wages," *Review of Economic Studies*, 9 (November 1941), 58–73.

other factors, while the industries competing with imports will require a large proportion of labor to other factors. In the absence of changes in factor prices, the shift of resources brought about by a tariff accordingly leads to a scarcity of labor and an excess supply of land and other factors. Wage rates rise relative to rents, and in all industries a substitution of land for labor occurs.

This brings us to the second fundamental assumption, namely, that the marginal physical productivity of a given factor in any industry depends exclusively upon the proportion of that factor to the other factors of production. More explicitly, it is assumed that the marginal product of a factor declines as the ratio of that factor to others in a particular industry is increased. Stolper and Samuelson show that, when wages rise relative to rents, the resulting substitution of land for labor causes the ratio of labor to land to decline in all industries. To put the matter another way, the surplus of land and scarcity of labor arising from the shift of resources from exports to industries competing with imports can be eliminated only if there is a reduction, in all industries, in the ratio of labor to land. But if this occurs, then according to our second assumption, the marginal product of labor must have increased in all industries, compared with the former position of equilibrium. If competitive conditions prevail or if the degree of monopoly is about the same in one industry as in another, it follows that the real wage rate must have increased, regardless of whether this real return is measured in export goods or in the commodities of the industries competing with imports.

Although this conclusion concerning the influence of tariffs upon real wages represented a definite improvement in the theory of tariffs, a number of questions still remained unanswered. Like the earlier works on the subject, the study by Stolper and Samuelson made no allowance for changes in the terms of trade. The rigid separation between the classical theory of the gains from trade and the modern theory of the distribution of income has thus continued to exist even in the most recent contribution to the subject.

This naturally raises the question of whether modifications in the existing theory of tariffs are required if changes in the terms of trade and in the distribution of income are considered simultaneously. The classical theory of the gains from trade demonstrated that, under certain conditions of international demand, a country could increase the external purchasing power of its exports by means of tariffs on imports and that, if this favorable movement in its terms of trade were sufficiently large, the real income of the country imposing the tariff might be increased despite the unfavorable effects of the tariff upon the allocation of resources. Now, since Stolper and Samuelson assumed that a country's external terms of trade were unaffected by a tariff, they were actually considering the least favorable case possible with respect to the real income of the country imposing the duty; the tariff, in the Stolper-Samuelson argument, interfered with the allocation of resources without bringing about any offsetting favorable movement in the terms of trade. Real income of the country as a whole was therefore unambiguously reduced by the import duty.

Let us consider, for a moment, a more favorable case. Suppose that a particular country's exports and imports are important influences on world markets and that a tariff reduces the external prices of imports, relative to the prices of exports, to such an extent that real income for the country as a whole is clearly increased. How does this alter the conclusions summarized above concerning real and relative wage rates? If we assume, as before, that the country has a scarcity of labor and therefore imports commodities requiring a large amount of labor, it might appear at first glance that the tariff would increase real wages, perhaps to a considerable extent; for, if the real as well as the relative returns of labor are increased by a tariff even when the duty reduces real income of the country as a whole (the Stolper-Samuelson case), it might seem that the rise in real wages would be even greater if real income as a whole were increased. To return to our previous analogy, it would surely seem better for labor to receive a larger share of an increasing pie than to receive a larger share of a diminishing pie.

Although this argument seems plausible, it is actually misleading, for the improvement in terms of trade affects not only real income as a whole but also the degree of scarcity of the so-called "scarce" factors. Paradoxical as it may seem, when changes in the terms of trade are taken into consideration, tariffs or other impediments to imports do not always preserve or increase the scarcity of the scarce factors of production. Under some conditions of international demand, the industries competing with imports and the scarce factors of production, which are usually required in large amounts in such industries, may benefit from free trade and suffer from protection.

The precise conditions of international demand required to bring about such an unexpected result are described in the next section of this paper. The argument is presented by means of the familiar Mill-Marshall schedules of reciprocal demand.[12]

Whether a tariff injures or benefits a country's scarce factors of production depends largely upon how it affects the output of exports and of commodities competing with imports. If output expands in the industries competing with imports and contracts in the export industries, the increased demand for scarce factors of production in the expanding industries will normally exceed the supplies made available in the contracting export industries; and, as Stolper and Samuelson have shown, the real returns as well as the relative shares of the scarce factors in the national income will thus be increased.

In a large part of the nontechnical literature dealing with tariffs, and even in some of the technical literature, a shift of this sort is normally taken for granted; indeed, it is frequently regarded almost as a truism that tariffs injure export industries and benefit industries competing with imports. Nevertheless, when both primary and secondary price changes are taken into consideration, this is by no means a self-evident proposition. To be sure, the tariff itself is the cause of a direct increase in the domestic prices of imports over and above world prices, and this constitutes an immediate benefit to the industries competing with imports. But, on the other hand, the tariff is also the cause of a series of events which tend to reduce world prices of the country's imports relative to the prices of its exports—that is, to improve the terms of trade—and this secondary reduction of world prices of imports relative to exports may more than offset the initial primary increase.

Now it is reasonable to suppose that resources will not be permanently shifted from the export industries to the industries competing with imports unless the net effect of all primary and secondary price changes is an increase in the domestic prices of imports (including tariffs) relative to the domestic prices of exports. Whether a tariff increases or reduces the real and relative returns of the scarce factors, therefore, depends upon the magnitude of the favorable movement in the terms of trade, compared with the size of the tariff. If the former is greater than the

12. The reader will recognize that in adopting this method I have not added anything essentially new to the well-known classical technique. My purpose, rather, is to apply this technique to a problem which was seldom discussed and never strongly emphasized in the classical literature. In doing this, I have made particular use of the classical theory in the form in which it was expounded by Abba P. Lerner in "The Symmetry between Import and Export Taxes," *Economica*, 3 (August 1936), 306–313.

latter, the final effect of the tariff will be a reduction of the domestic prices of imports relative to the prices of exports, and resources will accordingly be shifted from industries competing with imports to the export industries. In other words, the industries producing commodities for export will expand, after tariffs are imposed, while industries competing with imports will contract, an outcome diametrically opposite to the usual expectation.

Suppose, for example, that the ratio of the world prices of a country's imports to the world prices of its exports is initially taken to be 1:1. Suppose now that a tariff of 50 percent ad valorem is placed upon all imports and that, as a result of the ensuing reduced demand for imports, the ratio, in world prices exclusive of tariffs, of import prices to export prices falls to 1:2. The domestic price ratio, which differs from the world price ratio by the amount of the tariff, will then be 1.5:2, compared with 1:1 before the tariff was imposed. The tariff has thus reduced the domestic prices of imports relative to the prices of exports, and a transfer of resources from the "protected" industries to the export industries may be anticipated. Under these circumstances the effects of the tariff upon the distribution of income are exactly opposite to the conclusions reached by Stolper and Samuelson; the scarce factor of production, that is, the factor relatively most important in the industries competing with imports, suffers both a relative decline in its share of the national income and an absolute decline in its real return. The most important factor of production in the export industries, on the other hand, enjoys both a relative and an absolute increase of income.

The magnitude of the favorable movement of the terms of trade which

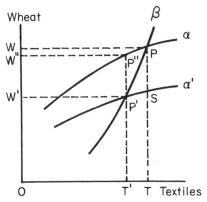

Figure 1

occurs when tariffs are imposed obviously depends upon conditions of international demand in a way that has been familiar to all economists at least since the time of Mill. It is therefore appropriate to state the argument in terms of the Mill-Marshall equations of reciprocal demand. As before, I shall assume that there are two countries—A and B—producing two commodities—wheat and textiles—and that, for the reasons discussed above, A has a comparative advantage in the production of wheat, while B has an advantage in textiles. In Fig. 1, the curves α and β represent the reciprocal demand schedules for the two countries, A and B, for imported textiles and wheat, respectively, under conditions of free trade.[13] Equilibrium is established at the point P, which implies that A imports an amount OT of textiles in exchange for OW of wheat.

Suppose now that A imposes an ad valorem duty of 50 percent upon imported textiles. If we neglect for a moment the effects of the spending of the proceeds of the tariff by the government of A, it is clear that the initial effect of the tariff is to reduce the demand schedule facing the exporters of textiles in B from α to α'. In other words, textile importers in A will now be willing to give to the exporters in B only TS units of wheat for OT of textiles; a money value equal to the additional amount, SP, which citizens of A formerly gave to B, now goes to the A government as a duty. This means that SP is 50 percent of TS or that TS is two-thirds of TP, and similarly for any other point, such as P', on the new demand schedule.

After the tariff has been imposed, the new equilibrium in terms of quantities actually traded is at P', at which point OW' units of wheat are exported by A and OT' units of textiles are imported. Unless β is a straight line from the origin, which implies that the demand in B for the exports of A is infinitely elastic, it is obvious from Fig. 1 that the tariff will improve the terms of trade of A. The fraction OT'/OW' is clearly larger than OT/OW, which means that A obtains more units of textiles for a given amount of wheat than was true under free trade. Or, to put the matter another way, the world price of textiles, exclusive of the tariff, has fallen, relative to the world price of wheat. The bargaining

13. In all the figures the reciprocal demand schedules are assumed to depend not only upon conditions of demand but also upon conditions of production. The elasticity of a given reciprocal demand schedule is thus a combined result of substitutions on the part of consumers and shifts of resources on the part of producers. See W. W. Leontief, "The Use of Indifference Curves in the Analysis of Foreign Trade," *Quarterly Journal of Economics*, 47 (May 1933), 493–503.

position of A, the country imposing the tariff, is thus improved. Such an improvement in A's terms of trade is, of course, completely explained by the classical theory of international trade and would not need to be considered further except for its influence upon the distribution of income.

In order to see how the tariff has affected the distribution of income in A, we must look at domestic prices rather than at world prices. This means that the tariff must be added to the world price of textiles. Measured in terms of their export commodity, the total outlay of the residents of A for imported textiles, including their outlay for the tariff, is not OW', in Fig. 1, but OW'', an amount 50 percent greater than OW'. In other words, in terms of value actually expended, the residents of A are giving up the equivalent of OW'' units of wheat for OT' units of textiles; the domestic ratio of exchange is therefore given by the fraction OT'/OW''. Now since OT'/OW'' is less than OT/OW in Fig. 1, it is obvious that, with the schedules of reciprocal demand there assumed, the tariff has caused the domestic price of textiles in A to rise, relative to the price of wheat; land and labor are therefore shifted from wheat to textile production; and the relative share of labor in the national income, as well as the real wage rate, is increased.

It is easily shown that this conclusion is valid for reciprocal demand schedules other than those depicted in Fig. 1, as long as the demand of B for the products of A is elastic. The foregoing argument may therefore be generalized as follows: If the world demand for a country's exports is elastic and if we neglect the effects of government expenditures on the demand for imports, (a) a tariff always increases the domestic prices of imports relative to the prices of exports; (b) the improvement in the terms of trade is not sufficient in this case to offset the tariff itself; (c) the protected industries become more profitable, relative to the export industries; (d) resources are shifted from the latter to the former; and (e) the real returns to the country's scarce factors of production, as well as these factors' share in the national income, are increased. The Stolper-Samuelson conclusion is thus valid, even when changes in the terms of trade are taken into account, as long as the demand for exports is elastic.

When the demand for exports is inelastic, the conclusions of the last paragraph must be reversed. This situation is depicted in Fig. 2, where the demand of B for the product of A is assumed to be inelastic at the equilibrium point P. In other words, in the neighborhood of P the residents of B are willing to give up decreasing amounts of textiles in exchange for an increasing amount of wheat. The notation is the same as

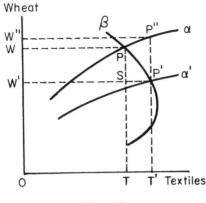

Figure 2

in Fig. 1. The original equilibrium is at P; but after the tariff is imposed, the point of balanced trade moves to P', at which point A gives up OW' units of wheat in exchange for OT' units of textiles. As before, the terms of trade move in favor of A. Indeed, in the present example a greater amount of textiles is obtained for a smaller amount of wheat, and the favorable movement in the terms of trade of A is now so great that the domestic price of textiles, including the tariff, is lower, relative to the price of wheat, than it was before the tariff was imposed. This is shown in Fig. 2 by the fact that OT'/OW'' is greater than OT/OW.

When the demand for a country's exports is inelastic, the foregoing argument shows that a tariff, far from protecting the industries competing with imports, may actually make these industries worse off than under free trade. In Fig. 2, for example, the tariff on textile imports into A reduces the domestic price of textiles, relative to the price of wheat, and leads to a shift of resources in A from the textile industry to the wheat industry. This result is, of course, well known from the classical and neoclassical theories of international trade; but, so far as I am aware, its implications for the distribution of income have never been fully discussed.

Figure 2 implies that, when the demand for a country's exports is inelastic, the scarce factors of production—those required in comparatively large amounts in the import industries—actually suffer both a relative and an absolute decline in income when tariffs are increased. Although it seems paradoxical, the scarce factors of production and the industries competing with imports, under the conditions of Fig. 2, actually achieve economic gains from free trade and suffer losses from protection. In other words, if labor is the scarce factor of production and the standard of living is therefore high, a country is not likely to be able, by means of tariffs, to protect its workers from the competition of "cheap foreign labor" unless the demand for its exports is elastic. Some of the implications of this conclusion for producers of primary products who are attempting to industrialize by means of tariffs are discussed in the next section of this paper.

Nothing has been said yet about how the government which imposes import duties disposes of the resultant revenue. In this respect the preceding discussion of Figs. 1 and 2 is deficient, for the manner in which the government revenues are spent will obviously influence the reciprocal demand schedule of the country introducing the tariffs. If the customs revenues are used in part to purchase imported goods, for example, the reciprocal demand schedule of A will not decline from α to α' but will lie somewhere between these two curves. In the classical discussion of this question two limiting examples were usually considered: the customs revenues were assumed to be spent either entirely upon the export goods of the taxing country or entirely upon imports.[14] The reader will no doubt have recognized that Figs. 1 and 2 belong to the first of these alternatives. No part of the tariff proceeds, in these two illustrations, is spent on imported goods; for if it were, the reciprocal demand schedule would not fall, as assumed in the figures, by the full amount of the tariff.

Moreover, it is easy to see that both diagrams implicitly assume the full proceeds of the tariffs to be spent on goods formerly exported from A. Thus at the new equilibrium point P', A exports OW' of wheat to T. The equilibrium point P', however, is stated in world prices, and this equilibrium corresponds to a domestic ratio of exchange in A, including tariffs, of OT' units of textiles for OW'' units of wheat. In other words, at the new domestic price ratio, exporters in A offer OW'' units of wheat, an amount which exceeds the purchases of wheat in B by $W'W''$. The supply of wheat is thus not equal to the demand unless this excess supply is purchased by the government of A. But the excess supply of wheat $W'W''$ is simply the amount of duties collected by the government of A, measured in the export product of that country. Figures 1 and 2 are thus implicitly based upon the assumption that the tariff imposing country uses the entire proceeds of the tariff to purchase goods from its own exporters.

14. See, for example, Alfred Marshall, *Money, Credit, and Commerce* (London, Macmillan, 1923), pp. 344–348.

Such an assumption is clearly unrealistic. It would be more reasonable to suppose that the purchasing power acquired through customs duties is divided in some manner between the purchase of domestic goods and the purchase of imports. Before we consider this intermediate case, however, it may be useful, following the Marshallian tradition, to go from the one extreme, at which customs revenues are used entirely in the purchase of the tariff-imposing country's export product, to the other extreme, at which the customs revenues are devoted entirely to the purchase of imports.

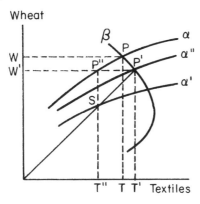

Figure 3

This second extreme case is represented by Fig. 3. As in the earlier diagrams, equilibrium is initially at P, with A giving up OW units of wheat in exchange for OT units of textiles. A tariff of 50 percent is imposed upon textile imports into A, but, unlike the earlier examples, the government collecting the duties is now assumed to spend the entire proceeds upon imported textiles. The additional demand for imports by the government accordingly prevents the demand schedule of A for the products of B from falling as far as it otherwise would have. In Fig. 3 the new demand schedule, including government demand for imports, is given by the line α'', whereas the private demand alone has fallen, as before, to the line α'.

The relations between the three demand schedules—α, α', and α''— may be illustrated by considering the point P'' on the old schedule α. This point indicates that, before the tariff was imposed, the traders in A would have been willing to give up OW' units of wheat for OT'' units of textiles. When the new tariff becomes effective, the private traders' demand schedule drops, as before, from α to α'. The vertical distance between α and α′ thus indicates the amount of the tariff, measured in wheat, corresponding to any given level of textile imports.

In Fig. 3, for example, the distance SP'' is 50 percent of $T''S$. Suppose, for purposes of illustration, that the world rate of exchange between wheat and textiles, exclusive of any tariffs, were given by the slope of the line OSP' drawn through the origin of Fig. 3. Consumers and traders in A would then purchase OT'' units of textiles, for which they would pay $T''S$ units of wheat to B and an additional SP'' units of wheat to their own customs officials. But the government of A is assumed, in the present example, to spend the entire tariff revenues on imported commodities, and this means that the amount SP'' must be exchanged for textiles at the world price ratio. At this given ratio, the government collecting the duties would accordingly acquire an amount of textiles equal to $P''P'$ in exchange for customs revenues which, measured in wheat, amount to SP''.

The final effect of the tariff on the demand schedule of A, including the government demand for imports as well as the private demand, is thus found to be a horizontal shift in the entire schedule, the relative extent of the shift being exactly equal to the rate of the tariff. The distance $P''P'$, in Fig. 3, for example, is 50 percent of the distance $W'P''$. The new demand schedule α″ might have been derived by more direct methods, but the preceding argument, I believe, shows more clearly than most others why α″ must lie between α and α′.[15]

With these preliminary remarks we may now return to the effects of the tariff on prices at home and abroad. As in the earlier examples, the tariff improves the terms of trade of the country imposing it, which means that the price of A's imports, exclusive of the tariff, declines relative to the price of that country's exports. This is shown in Fig. 3 by the fact that A now imports a larger amount of textiles (OT') in exchange for a smaller amount of wheat (OW'). These terms of trade, however, are measured in foreign prices and, as before, it is the domestic price ratio rather than the foreign price ratio which governs the distribution of income in the taxing country. The domestic price of textiles in A is higher than the foreign price by exactly the amount of the tariff; and when this is taken into account, it is clear from Fig. 3 that the final effect of the tariff, including both primary and secondary effects, is to raise the domestic price of textiles relative to the price of wheat. In other words,

15. If the demand of A for the product of B is inelastic, α′ will actually lie *above* the curve α— that is, under these circumstances a tariff will *increase* the demand of A for the products of B.

under the conditions assumed in Fig. 3, the direct influence of the tariff in raising the price of textiles in A is more important than is its indirect influence in improving that country's terms of trade.

As far as private traders and consumers are concerned, the domestic rate of exchange is given, as in the earlier examples, by the point P''. The private traders obtain OT'' units of textiles in exchange for OW' units of wheat. The remaining $T''T'$ units of textiles are in effect paid to the government of A as customs duties. Now since the demand schedule α'' was derived from the schedule α by a horizontal shift, it is apparent from the diagram that the point P'' on the old schedule must lie to the left of the original equilibrium point P. And, as in Fig. 1, unless the demand schedule of A has an infinite elasticity, the point P'' represents for that country a higher domestic price of textiles relative to the price of wheat than does the point P.

When the proceeds of a tariff are spent entirely on imports, as in Fig. 3, it is evident that the domestic price of imports rises in the country imposing the tariff, relative to the domestic price of exports, even though the foreign demand for the exported commodity is inelastic. The tariff accordingly leads, as in the earlier example depicted by Fig. 1, to a shift of resources from the export industry, wheat, to textiles, the industry competing with imports. Both the real income and the relative share in the national income of the scarce factor, labor, are thereby increased in the manner envisaged by Stolper and Samuelson.

In other words, when customs duties are employed entirely in the purchase of imports, no modifications are required in the Stolper-Samuelson conclusion that tariffs benefit the factors of production which are required in relatively large amounts in the industries competing with imports. And this is true regardless of the size of the elasticity of demand for a country's exports. If the foreign demand is extremely inelastic, the improvement in terms of trade will, of course, prevent import prices in the high-tariff country from rising by a large amount and will thereby mitigate to some extent the influence of the tariff on the distribution of income. But in any event the direction, if not the size, of the change in income distribution will be substantially as envisaged in the earlier work on the subject.

We have now illustrated the effects of a tariff with two extreme examples. In the first, the customs duties were assumed to be spent entirely upon the export goods of the taxing country, while in the second the duties were spent entirely in the purchase of imports. It remains only to consider the intermediate and more realistic case in which expenditure of the tariff revenues is divided in some manner between export goods and imports. Before we consider a geometric illustration of this intermediate case, however, a few general statements are needed concerning the relations between tax revenues and governmental expenditures.

The fiscal systems of most modern states are so complex that it is virtually impossible to associate any particular expenditure with a given type of revenue. What sense does it make, under such conditions, to assert that the proceeds of a tariff are spent in a certain manner on home goods and imports? How can any particular expenditure or group of expenditures be identified as a direct consequence of tariff revenues? Some economists have gone so far as to say that the problem is an impossible one and that the circular flow of income through the government accounts cannot be traced in such an exact manner. Although there is considerable substance to this argument, it seems to me that the conclusion to which it leads is unduly pessimistic. Without any attempt to find a direct link between every individual expenditure and every item of revenue, it may yet be possible to say that expenditures as a whole, including private expenditures as well as public, have been affected in a certain way by an increase or a decrease of tariffs.

For most purposes, including the present one, it is probably best to regard government expenditures as fixed and largely independent of the particular type of taxation employed to collect revenues. If the overall budgetary deficit or surplus is likewise the result of an independent decision, tariffs can then be envisaged as replacing or supplementing other forms of taxation. In other words, an increase in government revenues from customs duties can be associated directly with a decrease in some other form of taxation or can be considered as making unnecessary an increase in some other form of taxation.

When viewed in this way, the problem of tracing the effects of tariffs on the circular flow of income is largely shifted from the governmental to the private sphere of the economy. The question now is not how the tariff affects *government* expenditures on export and import goods but how the change in taxation affects *private* expenditures. The increase in customs revenues means that other forms of taxation (such as income taxes, for example) can be correspondingly reduced; and the added income thereby made available to the private sector of the economy will normally be spent in a certain way on imports and domestic goods.

Suppose, for example, that income earners on the average spend about 20 percent of their incomes on imported goods, including raw materials and semifinished goods as well as finished goods. A reduction of income taxes, made possible by increased customs duties, will then lead to an increase in expenditures on imports equal to roughly two-tenths of the customs duties. Although there is no immediate connection between the customs revenues themselves and the added expenditures on imports, we can nevertheless say that the latter were indirectly the result of the former. More generally, if the marginal propensity to import of the private sector of the economy is k, we can carry out our examination of the effects of the tariff *as though* a fraction k of all customs revenue were actually spent on imported goods; the remaining part of the re-mitted taxes, or a fraction $1 - k$ of customs duties, can then be regarded as spent, directly or indirectly, on the purchase of export goods.[16] The size of k will, of course, vary with the nature of the taxation system, but this is a refinement which cannot be discussed here.

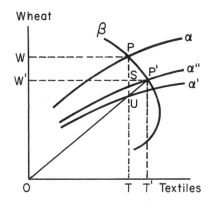

Figure 4

With these ideas in mind, consider now the situation in Fig. 4. As in the earlier diagrams, foreign trade is initially in equilibrium at the point P, with A exporting OW units of wheat and importing OT units of textiles; and once again this equilibrium is disturbed by a 50 percent tariff on textile imports. Unlike the previous illustration, however, the

16. The argument at this point is distinctly classical in that added income is assumed to be entirely spent, directly or indirectly, in the purchase either of home goods or of imports. There is, of course, no logical reason why a propensity to save could not be introduced along with the two propensities to spend; but this would raise a number of vexatious questions concerning the effects of tariffs upon employment which could not possibly be given adequate treatment within the limits of the present study.

proceeds of the tariff are now assumed to be divided in the proportions k and $1 - k$ between the purchase of imports and exports, respectively. It makes no fundamental difference in the geometric argument whether these proportions are determined directly by government purchases or indirectly through the reduction of other taxes.[17] Figure 4 has been drawn with such values for k, the marginal propensity of A to import, and η, the price elasticity of demand for A's exports, that the favorable movement in that country's terms of trade exactly offsets the direct effect of the tariff itself, leaving the domestic price ratio of the two commodities unchanged.

Before we discuss the relation between the marginal propensity to import and the price elasticity which is necessary to bring about this result, a word should be said about the three reciprocal demand schedules α, α', and α''. The line α', as in Fig. 3, represents the private demand for imports after the tariff is imposed, without any allowance for the expenditure, direct or indirect, of the customs revenues. Thus the distance UP is 50 percent of TU, and so forth. Now consider a world rate of exchange of the two commodities, exclusive of the tariff, represented by the slope of the diagonal OP'. If we neglect the effects of spending the duties, private traders and consumers in A, at this rate of exchange, would import OT of textiles and would export TU of wheat. The tariff received by the government, expressed in the exports of the taxing country, would then be UP. This amount would be returned to the residents of A in the form of reduced taxes, and part of the income so received would be used to augment the demand for imports. In the diagram the assumption is made that a proportion equal to US/UP of this added income is spent on imports; in other words, $k = US/UP$. At the given foreign price ratio, importers in A would thus obtain an additional amount of textiles equal to SP', or TT', which means that expenditure of the tariff revenues would have the effect of shifting the point U on the line α' over to the point P' on line α''.[18] A similar construction could be developed for any other point on α'.

17. This statement is an approximation which is strictly accurate only when the size of the tariff is small. If the tariff is substantial, the shift in demand will not be the same when the government spends the customs revenues as when they are spent by private traders. The difference is attributable to the fact that private traders pay duties on their added purchases from abroad, whereas the government does not. But this is a matter of detail which does not affect the substance of the argument, and it may accordingly be held over to a later paper.

18. This statement again ignores the fact that private traders pay duties on their added imports as well as on their original imports. If the tariff is small, however, these "duties on duties" will be insignificant compared with the duties on total imports.

After the tariff becomes effective, the new demand schedule of A facing the exporters of B, including indirect as well as direct effects on the tariff, is of course the line α''. The demand schedule of B for the products of A has not been altered, and the point of equilibrium between the two countries, in terms of quantities actually imported and exported, accordingly shifts from P to P' in Fig. 4. Where A formerly exported OW units of wheat and imported OT of textiles, she now exports a smaller quantity of wheat (OW') in exchange for a larger quantity of textiles (OT'). The gain to the taxing country, regarded as a unit, is obvious; the foreign price of textiles has fallen, relative to the foreign price of wheat, and this favorable movement in A's terms of trade is so great that the country obtains more textiles than before in exchange for a smaller amount of wheat.

And yet, if we look at the domestic price ratio in A, including the tariff, we find that this ratio is exactly the same as before the tariff became effective. To put the matter another way, the direct effect of the customs duty in raising the price of textiles in A, relative to the price of wheat, is exactly offset by its indirect effect through the change in world prices. The new foreign price ratio—that is, the ratio exclusive of the tariff—is shown in Fig. 4 by the line OP'. The domestic price ratio in A, which differs from the foreign ratio only by the tariff, will therefore be given by the slope of a line through the origin (not shown in the diagram) whose vertical distance from the OT axis is 50 percent above the vertical distance of a corresponding point on OP'. Since OP' cuts the schedule α' at U, a point which is directly below P, and since the original schedule α is 50 percent above α', it follows that the new domestic price ratio in A is represented by the original equilibrium point P. In other words, the relative prices actually paid and received by consumers and producers of the two goods in A are unaltered by the tariff.

Under these circumstances, it may at first seem paradoxical that the country imposing the tariff should alter the physical quantity of its exports and imports at all. Relative domestic prices remaining unchanged, producers of both textiles and wheat in A presumably continue to produce the same quantities of the two commodities as before. No shift in resources between the two industries takes place, and the distribution of income earned in production is therefore the same as before the tariff was imposed.

How does it happen then that A exports a smaller amount of wheat than in the original equilibrium and imports a larger amount of textiles? The answer to this question is to be found in the effects of the customs duties upon the circular flow of income. Since the revenues received from the tariff enable the government of A to reduce other taxes without disturbing its expenditures upon goods and services, income available to the factors of production increases, even though total output remains unchanged. And according to our original assumption, a fraction k of this increased income is devoted to imports, while $1 - k$ is spent on goods produced by the export trades. Thus both the rise in imports (TT') and the fall in exports ($W'W$) are indirect consequences of added purchases in A from the proceeds of the customs duties themselves. Indirectly, the customs proceeds are used both to purchase goods which would otherwise have been available for export and to increase the volume of imports. Here is perhaps the clearest case imaginable in which, to use a familiar expression from innumerable tariff controversies, "the foreigner pays the tax."

In Fig. 4 the reciprocal demand schedules of both countries and the marginal propensity of A to import have been drawn in such a way that a tariff on imports leaves all domestic price ratios in the taxing country unaltered. We must now see whether this result can be generalized. In other words, instead of considering a given tariff rate of 50 percent, we shall consider a general rate τ, and instead of assuming a particular set of reciprocal demand schedules and a given marginal propensity to import, we shall assume a general set of demand schedules and a general propensity to import. We may then inquire what relations must exist between all these functions in order that a tariff shall leave the taxing country's domestic price ratios unchanged.

It turns out that the answer to this question depends upon only two functions, the price elasticity of demand for imports abroad, that is, the price elasticity in B, and the marginal propensity of the taxing country, A, to import. The symbol η will be used to indicate the elasticity of demand for imports in B, while k, as before, will be used to indicate the marginal propensity of A to import. The precise relation between η and k which is required to bring about the situation depicted in Fig. 4 was first derived more than a decade ago by Lerner; but since Lerner's work was presented in a somewhat different context, it seems desirable to give a slightly modified version here.[19]

If relative prices in the taxing country are unaffected by the tariff, this means, as noted before, that the primary influence of the duty in raising the domestic price of imports in A is exactly offset by its secondary in-

19. Lerner, "Import and Export Taxes" (reference 12), pp. 310–311.

fluence upon world prices or upon the terms of trade. Suppose that this is actually true. In other words, suppose that the decline in the world price of textiles, relative to the world price of wheat, is just sufficient to offset the tariff in A. We now wish to know what conditions of demand and supply must prevail in order that this new world price ratio shall be an equilibrium ratio. In view of the fact that the reciprocal demand schedules represent both a demand for one commodity and a supply of another, it will be sufficient to consider either the supply and demand for textiles or the supply and demand for wheat. Equilibrium in the one market implies equilibrium in the other, and it is unnecessary to consider both. As a practical matter it is perhaps easiest to consider the supply and demand for textiles.

Since the domestic price ratio in A remains unchanged, that country's demand for textile imports is influenced only by the expenditure of the tariff proceeds. With a tariff rate of τ, customs duties as a percentage of the value of private imports will likewise be τ. By assumption, a proportion k of these duties is spent on imports. The relative increase in the demand for imports in A will therefore be $k\tau$. The question now is whether and under what circumstances this increased demand in A will be matched by an equivalent increase in supply from B. The demand in B for the exports of A is assumed to be inelastic; and when the world price of textiles declines, as it does when the tariff is imposed, B therefore offers an increased amount of textiles in exchange for a reduced quantity of wheat.

If we use the notation of Fig. 4, the relative increase in the supply of textile exports from B is TT'/OT. This in turn is approximately equal to $-\phi(W'W/OW)$, where ϕ is the elasticity of the reciprocal demand schedule β. But $W'W/OW$ represents the additional wheat consumption in A, relative to the previous level of exports, and this additional expenditure arises entirely from the proceeds of the tariff. An amount $k\tau$ was spent on imports, and the remainder, or $(1-k)\tau$, is accordingly spent on wheat formerly exported. The quantity $W'W/OW$ is then equal to $(1-k)\tau$, and the additional supply of textile exports from B may be expressed thus: $-\phi(1-k)\tau$. If this additional supply is to equal the additional demand, we must have[20]

(1) $$k\tau = -(1-k)\tau\phi, \quad \text{or}$$

(2) $$k = -(1-k)\phi.$$

20. The expression $(1-k)\tau\phi$ is positive because with an inelastic demand for imports in B, ϕ is negative.

This is one way of expressing the condition that must be met if a tariff is to leave the taxing country's internal prices unaltered. The term ϕ, however, represents the elasticity of the reciprocal demand schedule β, and it is frequently more useful to express the results, as Lerner has done, in terms of the elasticity of the ordinary money demand schedule. If η represents this latter elasticity, it is well known[21] that, subject to certain supply limitations, $\phi = 1 - 1/\eta$. Substituting this value of ϕ in Eq. (2), we have

$$(3) \qquad\qquad k = -(1-k)\left(1 - \frac{1}{\eta}\right),$$

which, after simplifying, becomes

$$(4) \qquad\qquad \eta = 1 - k.$$

In words, this says that if a tariff is to leave domestic price ratios and the distribution of income within the taxing country unaltered, the foreign elasticity of demand for that country's exports must be equal to the difference between unity and the marginal propensity to import of the country imposing the tariff. If a country has a marginal propensity to import of 0.25, for example, a tariff imposed by that country will not leave domestic price ratios unchanged unless the foreign elasticity of demand for its exports is 0.75. If the foreign elasticity is smaller than this, the tariff will cause the domestic prices of imports to fall relative to the domestic prices of exports. On the other hand, if the foreign elasticity is larger than 0.75, the tariff will increase domestic import prices relative to export prices.

The practical consequences of these results will be discussed in the next section; but before we proceed further it seems desirable to summarize the main argument of the present section. The conclusions are intimately related to the proposition developed by Stolper and Samuelson that any event, other than a change in technology, which leads to a shift in resources from one industry to another will increase both the real income and the relative share in total income of the factor

---

21. Let t equal the quantity of textiles that B is willing to export, and let w represent that country's demand for imported wheat. The elasticity ϕ of the reciprocal demand schedule is then $dt/dw \cdot w/t$. But the quantity t, from one point of view, is simply the total outlay of B for imports, w. In money terms, in other words, $t = pw$, where p is the import price of wheat. We may therefore write $\phi = d(pw)/dw \cdot w/pw$. Upon simplifying and carrying out the indicated differentiation, this becomes $\phi = 1 + dp/dw\,(w/p) = 1 - 1/\eta$, the elasticity η being defined now in the Marshallian sense.

required in relatively large amounts in the expanding industry. A corollary of this, of course, is the proposition that the factor of production required in relatively large amounts in the contracting industry will find both its real return and its relative share of the total income reduced.

The problem of how a tariff influences the distribution of income is therefore largely resolved into a discussion of the effects of the tariff in shifting resources from one industry to another. The shift in resources, in turn, depends upon how the tariff affects domestic prices; for it may be taken for granted that, if resources shift at all, they will move into industries the products of which have enjoyed relative price increases. The present section has therefore been devoted largely to a discussion of the influence of customs duties on domestic prices of both exports and imports.

We have found that a tariff has two effects which influence relative domestic prices in opposite directions. On the one hand, the tariff itself represents a direct increase in import prices, and on the other hand, the resulting reduction in the demand for imports depresses the foreign prices of these goods relative to corresponding prices for export goods. The net effect upon relative prices at home thus depends upon which of these forces is the stronger. By following a technique originally expounded by Lerner, we have shown that a tariff will not increase the relative domestic price of imports unless η, the foreign elasticity of demand for the country's exports, is greater than $1 - k$, where k is the marginal propensity to import.

Although the final conclusions with respect to prices have been presented in four diagrams, the first three are really special cases of the fourth. In Figs. 1 and 2, the proceeds of the tariff were assumed to be spent entirely on export goods and the marginal propensity to import was thus implicitly set at zero. Since the expression $1 - k$ then had a value of unity, it was found that the tariff would not increase the relative domestic price of imports unless the foreign elasticity of demand for the country's exports was greater than unity. In Fig. 3, on the other hand, the proceeds of the tariff were assumed to be spent entirely upon imports, and this was equivalent to assuming a marginal propensity to import of unity. The value of $1 - k$ for the special case represented by Fig. 3 was thus zero; and we found that a tariff always increased the relative domestic price of imports, no matter how small the foreign elasticity of demand for the country's exports. Now since $1 - k$ is in all circumstances less than unity, it is clear that if the foreign demand for a country's exports is elastic with respect to prices, a tariff will always increase domestic import prices relative to export prices. In all such cases the shift of resources will be toward industries competing with imports and away from the export industries. The factors of production used in relatively large amount in the protected industries will consequently gain, both absolutely and relatively, while the factors used in large amounts in the export trades will lose.

All of this is completely in accord with the Heckscher-Ohlin conclusions as well as with the work of Stolper and Samuelson. It is only when the foreign demand for a country's exports is inelastic that the earlier works on the subject require modification. When the foreign demand is sufficiently inelastic, a tariff, far from protecting industries competing with imports at the expense of the export trades, may actually benefit the latter at the expense of the former. If this happens, resources tend to be shifted from the "protected" industries to the export industries, and the factors of production which are used in relatively large amounts in the export industries enjoy both a relative and an absolute increase in real income.

The aspect of tariff theory which the preceding discussion outlines most sharply is the potential or actual conflict of interests that may arise between a country's relatively scarce factors of production and the remainder of the economy. The classical dictum that real wages and the returns to other factors of production depend upon productivity remains true in a general way, of course; but the preceding argument shows that this dictum cannot be applied to the particular problem of tariffs without numerous reservations and exceptions. It cannot be asserted, for instance, that tariffs necessarily reduce productivity and thereby lower the real incomes of all factors of production. In the first place—and this is an argument of which the classical economists were fully aware—tariffs, under favorable circumstances, may improve a country's terms of trade so much that real income for the country as a whole is thereby increased. But this is a familiar argument to which the present paper has made no particular contribution. The point to be emphasized is a second reservation, namely, that the returns to each of the factors of production does not necessarily move in the same direction as general productivity or real income of the economy as a whole. In other words, regardless of whether a high-tariff policy increases or diminishes real income for a country as a whole, such a policy is likely to affect some factors of production favorably and others adversely. This point of view, in fact, might be stated even more strongly: the real income of a country's scarce factors of production is not likely to be increased by a tariff unless world demand is such that the tariff clearly diminishes the country's total income; and, conversely, the scarce factors are not likely to be injured by a tariff unless the tariff benefits the rest of the economy.

To clarify these propositions, consider a country having a comparative scarcity of labor and importing commodities with a high labor content. Stolper and Samuelson have shown that, *if the terms of trade are not affected*, a tariff in such a country will probably increase both the real wage rate and the proportion of the national income accruing to the working class. Now if the terms of trade remain unchanged, this means that the tariff, while disrupting the allocation of resources and thereby tending to reduce real income for the country as a whole, has not succeeded in bringing to the economy the benefits of a more favorable bargaining position in world markets. In other words, when the terms of trade remain unaltered, a tariff causes an unambiguous reduction in a country's real income as a whole. This is precisely the condition, according to the Stolper-Samuelson argument, when a tariff increases the absolute and relative return to labor, the country's scarce factor of production. If I may return to an earlier metaphor, the scarce factor of production receives a larger piece of a smaller pie.

But what if the size of the pie is increased by the tariff? How does labor fare under these circumstances? An increase in real income for the economy as a whole is of course possible, provided that the tariff causes a sufficient improvement in the terms of trade to offset its interference with the allocation of resources. A substantial improvement in the terms of trade could take place, however, only if the foreign demand for the country's exports was inelastic; and in this event, as we have seen, there is a strong probability that the tariff, far from protecting the industries competing with imports, would actually injure these industries and lead to a transfer of resources from them to the export industries. This shift in resources would reduce the degree of scarcity of labor and thereby lead to a reduction in both its relative and its absolute return.

The conflict of interests emphasized by the preceding summary is in sharp contrast to the doctrine of a harmony of interests which occupied such a prominent place in the work of many nineteenth-century liberal economists. The preceding argument has shown that, with respect to problems of commercial policy, the economic interests of such broad groups as manual workers, landlords, and capitalists are not likely to coincide. A policy of reducing tariffs may therefore be the source of widespread political cleavages, quite apart from the pressure which is inevitably exerted by the industries immediately affected. This, of course, is no argument against reducing trade barriers. Rather, it is simply an indication that the political conflicts inherent in tariff reduction may have a much broader base than would be supposed from concentrating one's attention upon the protected industries alone.

The fact that the influence of tariffs on the distribution of income can be a matter of considerable economic and political significance is demonstrated, I believe, by a well-known report on the tariff in Australia, which was published in 1929.[22] This report, prepared by a committee of Australian economists at the request of the Australian prime minister, presented both the terms-of-trade argument and the distribution-of-income argument in favor of the Australian tariffs. The Australian economy is characterized by an abundant supply of land, relative to the supply of labor, and capital; and Australia therefore has a comparative advantage in agriculture, particularly in wheat and wool. The committee argued that if tariffs were reduced, Australian manufacturing would be retarded and resources would be diverted from manufacturing to agriculture. But since the world demand for agricultural products, especially for wheat, is decidedly inelastic, it was felt that an increase in Australian wheat exports would lead to a substantial reduction in world wheat prices. In short, the eventual effect of the tariff reduction would be a considerable deterioration in the Australian terms of trade.[23]

Much more important than the deterioration in terms of trade, however, was the effect which the committee expected a tariff reduction to have upon the distribution of income. In general, the labor component of most manufactured products is considerably greater than the labor component of agriculture. A shift of resources from manufacturing to agriculture would therefore lessen the relative scarcity of labor, thus reducing real wages and increasing rents. It was this adverse effect upon the distribution of income which the committee of Australian

22. J. B. Brigden *et al.*, *The Australian Tariff: An Economic Enquiry* (Melbourne, Melbourne University Press, 1929).
    23. *Ibid.*, p. 80.

economists regarded as the principal deterrent to a general tariff reduction.[24]

What can be said about the Australian point of view in the light of the discussion in our preceding section? In the abstract, a good case can be made both for the terms-of-trade argument and for the distribution-of-income argument in favor of tariffs. *But this is true only when each argument is considered separately.* When the two are presented together, the validity of one of the two arguments becomes doubtful. It may well be true that the world demand for Australian wheat is inelastic, as the committee implies, and that a tariff reduction might lead to serious deterioration of Australia's terms of trade. But if this is actually the case, then it is unlikely, as we have seen previously, that a tariff reduction would lead to a shift of resources from manufacturing to agriculture. When the Australian economy finally became adjusted to the tariff reduction, domestic prices of manufactured goods might actually be higher relative to agricultural prices than before the tariff was reduced. And, if this should happen, the reduction of tariffs would be the cause of a shift of resources *into* the protected industries, with a concomitant increase in the proportion of the national income accruing to workers. Paradoxical as it seems, the Australian manufacturing industries might be better " protected" and receive more encouragement under free trade than under a system of protective tariffs.[25]

This idea is not new. Quite the contrary, it is implicit in much of the nineteenth-century work on the theory of reciprocal demand. Nevertheless, it is an idea which would no doubt be received with great incredulity, not to say outright disbelief, by the average Australian businessman. How, he might ask, could he possibly benefit from a reduction of the tariff on his own manufactures? To some extent his disbelief is probably the result of an instinctive and well-founded

---

24. *Ibid.*, pt. 7.

25. This statement, as well as subsequent remarks concerning the foreign trade of the Latin American countries and the United States, requires one modification. The theoretical treatment in the previous section was based upon the assumption that the protective duty was a general duty applicable to all or virtually all types of imports. If this is not true, the final results will obviously differ somewhat from those presented there. It is intuitively evident, for example, that a tariff on a particular commodity constituting a small part of total imports will increase the domestic price of that commodity relative to the prices of exports, even though the foreign demand for the country's exports is quite inelastic; for in this case the adjustment of the terms of trade will occur largely through price changes among the duty-free imports. Whether the presence of nontaxed imports requires a substantial revision of my previous conclusions depends upon the ratio of duty-free imports to total imports. But this is a question which I shall discuss in a later paper.

distrust of what the economist calls the "process of adjustment"; for if Australia should attempt, after a substantial unilateral reduction of tariffs, to maintain her exchange at the old rates relative to other currencies, a new equilibrium in her balance of payments could be achieved only by a reduction in real income or by a general deflation of prices and costs. The businessman is rightfully suspicious of both of these "processes of adjustment."

If Australia were willing to alter the foreign value of her currency, on the other hand, the adjustment to the new situation might be achieved in a less painful manner. Even in this event, however, it seems doubtful whether producers in the protected industries would concede that a reduction in tariffs would benefit them; for most of them would probably be unwilling to carry through the argument to its logical conclusion. Of course, if a typical producer were asked whether he would prefer a 50 percent tariff with the pound sterling selling for 1.25 Australian pounds or no tariff with the pound sterling selling for 2.50 Australian pounds, he would probably immediately see the advantage to himself of the latter arrangement. And if the demand for Australia's exports is really inelastic, this is precisely the sort of choice with which the producer is confronted; for, as we have seen, when the foreign demand is inelastic, there is a strong probability that the indirect effects of the tariff on the terms of trade will more than offset the direct effects on domestic prices. Nevertheless, if tariffs were actually reduced in Australia and if the Australian pound began to depreciate as a consequence, it seems highly probable that many businessmen would complain of their losses from the tariff reduction without associating the tariff in any direct way with their gains from the depreciation of their currency.

This tendency to look only at immediate effects and to ignore secondary consequences is well illustrated by Australia's tariff experience after the first World War, recounted by A. H. Tocker in the *Economic Journal*.[26] Under the pressure of a balance-of-payments deficit, Australian tariffs were substantially increased in 1921. The higher customs duties, together with Australian borrowing in London and a generally improved world economic situation, brought about a marked improvement in the balance of payments; and the Australian banks began to accumulate sterling balances in London. At that time

26. "The Monetary Standards of New Zealand and Australia," *Economic Journal*, 34 (December 1924), 556–575.

Australia was on a sort of informal sterling-exchange standard, but with no legal commitment to maintain a fixed rate of exchange between the Australian pound and the pound sterling. The accumulation of sterling balances by the Australian banks in 1922 finally induced the banks to sell these balances at a discount, whereas in 1921 a slight premium on pounds sterling had prevailed. The decline in the Australian price of sterling was clearly a result, to some extent at least, of the higher tariffs; despite this obvious connection there were complaints, according to Tocker, that the banks were deliberately pursuing an independent foreign-exchange policy that was detrimental to Australian business interests. "The Australian," said Tocker, "who recently complained that the banks were using their big balances in London to nullify the effects of the tariff, and to attack the protected Australian industries, voiced an economic truth more profound than he knew, and one quite beyond the power of bankers to control."[27]

Although it was a comparatively small incident, the Australian experience illustrates a rather widespread tendency on the part of businessmen to take account only of the immediate or direct effects of tariffs and to ignore their secondary or indirect repercussions upon exchange rates and relative costs. This attitude largely explains, in my opinion, why protective tariffs frequently are strongly supported by the industries directly affected, even though it is widely recognized at the same time that the demand for a country's exports is quite unresponsive to changes in price. With their constant and unremitting attention required in the solution of immediate and pressing problems of production and sales, few businessmen have either the time or the inclination to trace the final consequences of tariffs through all their various ramifications; and the price that is paid for this "direct" approach is an exaggerated idea of the effectiveness of tariffs in protecting home industries.

The tendency to exaggerate the effectiveness of tariffs in raising or maintaining the incomes of a country's scarce factors of production is by no means limited to Australia. Quite the contrary, it is a tendency

27. *Ibid.*, p. 571. In citing these Australian experiences, I have no intention of casting a reflection upon the intelligence of any particular group. The so-called "direct" approach to international economics and the neglect of secondary repercussions are perhaps even more common in the United States. A typical example is the belief that in normal times export surpluses are desirable, while foreign loans are undesirable. This point of view is encountered with regrettable frequency in the halls of Congress as well as among Americans in othe walks of life.

which is perhaps even more pronounced in other countries, particularly in Latin America. Like Australia, the Latin American countries have a comparative advantage in the production of foodstuffs and raw materials. Their leading exports include such products of agriculture and the extractive industries as coffee, crude-petroleum, copper, sugar, cotton, nitrates, wheat, and meat.[28] Most of these exports are commodities for which the world demand is decidedly inelastic; and, since the Latin American countries in many instances provide a substantial proportion of the world's supply of such goods, it seems likely that the external demand for their exports as a whole may be quite inelastic even over considerable periods of time.

The Latin American foreign trade, which consists largely of exporting primary products, for which the world demand is inelastic, in exchange for manufactured goods, thus has marked similarities to the Australian foreign trade. And, like the Australians, the Latin Americans are dissatisfied with the distribution of national income which this type of trade engenders. Indeed, the problem of income distribution is probably a much more pressing one in many parts of Latin America than it is in Australia, for the Latin American people as a whole have not benefited, as have the Australians, from the scarcity of labor in relation to natural resources. In other words, the Latin American problem is not simply a problem of maintaining the standard of living in the face of a growing population but rather a problem of raising the standard of living as a whole.

Although Latin America's comparative advantage up to the present time has clearly been in the agricultural and extractive industries, the region as a whole has nevertheless had many areas of subsistence farming, in which the productivity of workers was extremely low; and one of the important economic purposes of the present move toward industrial development is to provide alternative and more useful employment for these low-productivity workers. Whether the current programs of industrialization will attain the various economic, political, and social goals which have been set for them is a question which cannot be discussed here. My purpose in mentioning the Latin American programs is simply to indicate their relation to the tariff problems analyzed in this paper. To a very considerable extent the governments

28. For an excellent summary of the pattern of Latin American trade see R. F. Behrendt, *Inter-American Economic Relations* (New York, Committee on International Policy, 1948), pp. 1–33.

of South and Central America have sought to encourage domestic manufacturing by means of tariffs on the importation of competing products; and, in view of what has been said above, it seems probable that this particular part of the program may contain a basic inconsistency.[29] If the demand for Latin America's exports as a whole is actually inelastic—and there is little reason to doubt this—the preceding discussion suggests strongly that tariffs may accomplish little either in protecting Latin American manufacturing or in increasing the share of the workers in national income.

This does not mean, of course, that the tariffs entail no economic benefits to the countries imposing them, but the benefits may be quite different from those originally contemplated. With the low price elasticity of demand for their products, the countries of Latin America are in a particularly good position to employ tariffs as a means of achieving more favorable terms of trade. A favorable movement in the Latin American terms of trade, however, means an increase in the prices received for exports relative to the prices paid for imports; and to the extent that such a shift occurs, part or all of the protection intended for domestic manufacturing is wiped out. In other words, since tariffs do not alter the basic techniques of production, any benefits which they confer upon one industry or one segment of the population are likely to be at the expense of another industry or another segment of the population. The Latin American tariffs cannot simultaneously benefit industry at the expense of agriculture and agriculture at the expense of industry; and although these tariffs are imposed upon manufactured goods, it is possible that, in the end, world conditions of demand may be such that the tariffs actually injure the industries which they are intended to protect. In the language of the foregoing discussion, the favorable movement in the terms of trade may more than offset the initial effects of the tariff in raising domestic prices of manufactured goods. Even if the conditions of demand are not so extreme, it remains true, in any event, that the degree of protection afforded by Latin American tariffs is much smaller than appears at first glance to be the case.

It should perhaps be emphasized that these remarks are by no means intended to imply that industrialization is a bad policy for

29. The extent to which the Latin American programs of industrial development depend upon tariff protection is indicated by a survey made by the United Nations: U.N. Department of Economic Affairs, *Economic Development in Selected Countries* (Lake Success, New York, 1947), pp. 1–150.

Latin America. This broader problem, involving as it does sociological and political as well as extremely complex economic questions, is entirely beyond the scope of the present paper. My purpose here is simply to indicate one of the limitations to a policy of industrialization by means of protective tariffs.

The foregoing remarks concerning the influence of tariffs on the industrial development of agricultural countries bear a close resemblance to a proposition stated more than a century ago by Friedrich List. Although List thought that protective duties on manufactures are a useful means of promoting industrial growth, it was by no means his view that such duties are appropriate under all circumstances and at all stages of economic development. He divided the economic growth of a country into four periods, and it was in only two of these periods that he regarded protective duties as beneficial to manufactures. "In the first period, agriculture is encouraged by the importation of manufactured articles; in the second, manufactures begin to increase at home, whilst the importation of foreign manufactures to some extent continues; in the third, home manufactures mainly supply domestic consumption and the internal markets; finally, in the fourth, we see the exportation upon a large scale of manufactured products, and the importation of raw materials and agricultural products."[30]

It was in the second and third of these periods that List thought protective duties would be effective in raising the level of industrial activity. With regard to countries in the first and fourth stages of development, free trade was preferred to protection. In other words, free trade was thought to be better than protection both for an undeveloped country specializing in agriculture and raw materials, and for a highly developed industrial nation. For the latter, tariffs on manufactures were considered unnecessary, since the industrial country had already achieved a strong competitive position in the world's markets for manufactured goods.[31] For the former, that is, for the completely undeveloped country, List thought that tariffs were likely to defeat their purpose.[32] It is in this respect that his conclusions are

30. Friedrich List, *National System of Political Economy*, trans. S. S. Lloyd (London, Longmans, Green, 1885).
31. *Ibid.*, chap. 4.
32. "The economical education of a country of inferior intelligence and culture, of one thinly populated, relatively to the extent and fertility of its territory, is effected most certainly by free trade, with more advanced, richer, and more industrious nations. Every commercial restriction in such a country aiming at the increase of manufactures, is premature, and will prove detrimental, not only to civilization in general, but the progress of the nation in particular" (*ibid.*, pp. 78–79).

similar to those given in the present paper, for it has been argued above that, in countries whose exports consist largely of primary products, tariffs will probably afford little if any encouragement to manufacturing.

The comparison must not be carried too far. Although List concluded, as I have above, that a policy of protection is a questionable method of increasing manufacturing output in an undeveloped country, his reasons for holding this view were not exactly the same as my own. According to List, a prosperous and powerful industrial nation must possess a well-developed commercial system in addition to its factories. And in the early stages of economic development List believed that free trade rather than protection would promote this prerequisite to industrialization. Commercial enterprises would be encouraged because free trade would increase the volume of commercial transactions. In this manner an undeveloped country, according to List, would achieve a certain degree of economic and cultural sophistication more quickly under free trade than under protection. But, once this position was reached and the country was ready to begin the development of manufacturing, List believed that further economic progress would be promoted by protective tariffs.[33]

It is somewhat ironical that, by employing the classical method of comparative statics, I have reached a conclusion which, in one respect at least, is in agreement with one of the most anticlassical economists of the nineteenth century. List's approach to the problem was highly dependent upon a dynamic theory of economic development and involved, in addition, a liberal admixture of political considerations. My own approach, by contrast, has been static in character and limited exclusively to economic arguments. But both the dynamic and the static approaches have led, in one respect, to the same conclusion. It is a moot question whether List, in advocating free trade for backward countries, could have had in mind some of the arguments advanced in the present paper concerning the elasticity of demand for raw materials and agricultural commodities. In view of his aversion to classical economics, however, such a possibility seems rather remote.

The arguments in favor of free trade for undeveloped countries, whether stated in List's terms or in the terms of the present paper, might be called "infant-country" arguments for free trade, just as the arguments for protection of undeveloped industries have generally been called "infant-industry" arguments for protection. And just as the

33. *Ibid.*, pp. 181–182.

latter, in practical application, frequently raise difficult questions concerning exactly what constitutes an infant industry, so the former also raise questions as to what constitutes an infant country.

In discussing the tariff history of the United States, for example, List assumed that by the early decades of the nineteenth century the United States had passed beyond the primitive and undeveloped stage in which free trade would have been beneficial. He believed in other words, that tariffs were helpful in promoting manufacturing in the United States throughout the early part of the nineteenth century.[34] In order to substantiate or refute this assertion from List's point of view, it would be necessary to make a detailed factual study of the state of American agriculture and commerce at the time. But if the question is approached from the point of view of the present paper, there is at least one circumstance which suggests that the actual degree of protection to American manufacturing may have been considerably less than intended and considerably less important in American economic development than List supposed.

Throughout the first half of the nineteenth century the United States was in a position, as far as foreign trade was concerned, quite like the position of Australia and the Latin American countries today. She was predominantly an exporter of raw materials and agricultural products and an importer of manufactured goods. Thus, in the period from 1820 until the outbreak of the Civil War, American exports of raw materials and unprocessed foodstuffs accounted for more than two-thirds of the total value of exports.[35] Moreover—and this is perhaps even more important—approximately three-fourths of these exports of primary products consisted of raw cotton, of which the United States at the time was by far the most important source of world supply. In view of the dominant position of the United States in the world cotton market and in view, further, of the dominance of cotton and other primary products in American exports as a whole, there is a strong probability that the demand for American exports during the first half of the nineteenth century was inelastic with respect to price. If this conjecture is correct, it follows from the analysis above that, considering both the primary and the secondary effects of the tariffs on domestic prices, the policy of protection to manufacture must have had a relatively small effect upon the rate of industrial growth

34. *Ibid.*, chap. 9.
35. These and subsequent figures on United States foreign trade have been computed from data in U.S. Department of Commerce, *Statistical Abstract of the United States.*

in the period before the Civil War. Indeed, the net effect of protection during this period may even have been slightly adverse to manufacturing as a whole.[36]

The conjecture that early American tariff policy probably exerted a comparatively minor influence upon the growth of domestic manufactures is in substantial agreement with the well-known conclusion which Taussig reached by a somewhat different method. After a detailed study of a number of protected industries, including the textile and iron and steel industries, Taussig concluded that their rate of expansion had not been substantially affected by the ebb and flow of protective measures. Thus, in discussing the period before 1860, he said in his *Tariff History of the United States:* "In the main, the changes in duties have had much less effect upon the protected industries than is generally supposed. Their growth has been steady and continuous, and seems to have been little stimulated by the high duties of 1842, and little checked by the more moderate duties of 1846 and 1857."[37]

In his *International Trade*, published thirty years later, Taussig recognized the special nature of United States exports during the first half of the nineteenth century—that is, the high proportion of raw materials and agricultural products for which the world's demand was comparatively rigid—but there is no evidence that this feature of American trade had anything to do with his original conclusion concerning the effects of protective duties.[38] His views regarding the early tariffs were largely derived from empirical observation, and when he later studied the history of protected industries during the years 1860 to 1930, he modified his earlier opinions somewhat.[39] In particular he cautiously advanced the view that the protective system may have contributed to the development of American manufactures.

At first glance, this later conclusion of Taussig's seems to contradict the argument of the present paper that exporters of raw materials and other primary products are not likely to find a general tariff system, short of completely prohibitive duties, an effective means of promoting industrial development. A further examination of the statistics of

---

36. This statement, like others in the present section, must be interpreted in a long-run sense. There is no intent to deny that during the period of adjustment a tariff on a particular product may afford the protected industry a substantial measure of protection.

37. F. W. Taussig, *The Tariff History of the United States*, ed. 4 (New York, Putnams, 1898), p. 152.

38. F. W. Taussig, *International Trade* (New York, Macmillan, 1928), p. 148.

39. See F. W. Taussig, *Some Aspects of the Tariff Question*, ed. 3 (Cambridge, Mass., Harvard University Press, 1931), *passim*.

United States exports, however, resolves at least a part of this apparent conflict. Although foodstuffs and raw materials, particularly raw cotton, continued throughout the nineteenth century to be important United States exports, these products with the passing of the years became considerably less significant, relative to total exports. At the close of the nineteenth century, for example, exports of primary products accounted for less than half of total exports, compared with a proportion of two-thirds in 1830.

The decline in the relative importance of primary exports was, of course, accompanied by a corresponding increase in the importance of manufactured exports. Thus during the second half of the nineteenth century, American exports were not dominated by primary products to the extent that had been true earlier. Increasingly the United States was becoming an exporter of a wide variety of manufactures as well as the staple raw materials and foodstuffs. It follows that, with regard to the second half of the nineteenth century at any rate, there is no conflict between the results of this paper and Taussig's conclusion that the tariff system provided a limited stimulus to manufactures; for the United States after the Civil War was rapidly developing beyond the simple stage of an agricultural exporter.[40] The character of American exports was changing sufficiently to reduce some of the earlier rigidity of foreign demand and, accordingly, to make tariffs more effective in increasing the domestic prices of the protected products.

In concluding this paper, a word should be said about the relation of the arguments presented here to the earlier work of Heckscher and Ohlin. As noted previously, the well-known view of both Heckscher and Ohlin is that international trade tends to equalize the relative returns to different factors of production among the trading countries. In other words, it is their view that trade increases the relative demand, and therefore the relative return, of the factor of production which is comparatively most abundant and comparatively cheapest in a particular country. In this manner wages tend to be raised, relative to the returns to other factors of production, in countries which have a large population in relation to their other resources. Superficially it might seem that any measure, such as a tariff reduction, which reduces the impediments to international trade, would have these same effects. In a country with a large supply of land, for example, it might be expected, following

40. A further factor in the increasing effectiveness of tariffs in protecting domestic industries was the lower proportion of dutiable imports to total imports.

the Heckscher-Ohlin argument, that a tariff reduction would increase rents and lower wages. But we have found that if the demand for a country's exports is inelastic, this result does not necessarily follow. Under some conditions with respect to international demand a reduction of tariffs may *increase* the demand for a country's scarce factors and *reduce* the demand for its abundant factors. How can this conclusion be reconciled with the view of Heckscher and Ohlin that international trade always increases the demand for a country's abundant factors?

Despite superficial differences, the conclusions reached in this paper are essentially consistent with those of Heckscher and Ohlin. The contradictory appearance of the conclusions is attributable entirely to a difference in the point of comparison. When Heckscher and Ohlin say that international trade increases the demand for a country's scarce factors, they mean that the demand is increased *compared with the demand in a state of complete isolation*. In other words, they are comparing free trade or restricted trade with a state of affairs in which there is no trade at all; and this is by no means the same as comparing trade under one tariff system with trade under smaller tariffs. My argument that an increase in customs duties may reduce the demand for a country's scarce factors of production was limited in its application to tariff changes within a range for which the foreign demand for the country's exports had a certain degree of inelasticity. In other words, the argument was valid only for movements along a limited part of the foreign reciprocal demand schedule.

In order to make the present analysis comparable to that of Heckscher and Ohlin, we should have to consider an increase in tariffs so large that all imports were eliminated. In short, all tariffs on all commodities would have to be completely prohibitive. From the nature of the reciprocal demand schedules, however, it is apparent that if tariffs were gradually increased to a level where they threatened to cut off all trade, the point of equilibrium would sooner or later move to a position where the foreign demand for the tariff-imposing country's exports was elastic. Thereafter, any further increases in tariffs would increase the demand for the country's scarce factors and reduce the demand for its abundant factors, in the manner envisaged by Heckscher and Ohlin. When the present technique is applied to changes in foreign trade as great as those envisaged by Heckscher and Ohlin, my conclusions are thus in agreement with theirs. An appearance of conflict arises only when one attempts to apply to the entire reciprocal demand schedule an argument which is applicable only to a segment of that schedule.

7 | Tariffs, International Demand, and Domestic Prices

The influence of tariffs on a country's domestic prices was discussed in the preceding paper,[1] and the argument was there presented that when tariffs are imposed, the prices that the residents of the country must pay for their imports, relative to the prices received for exports, are subject to two forces working in opposite directions. On the one hand, the tariffs themselves represent a direct increase in the prices of imports, relative to the prices of exports. But, on the other hand, the tariffs reduce the demand for imports, and unless the country imposing the duties is small, this reduction in demand is likely to reduce the world prices of such imports, relative to the prices of the country's exports.

Whether the one or the other of these two opposing influences will dominate depends upon conditions of international demand for the country's exports and upon the way in which the tariffs affect the demand for imports. If the world's demand for exports of the tariff-imposing country is elastic or if the tariffs do not reduce the demand for imports at home to any substantial degree, the movement of world prices is likely to be negligible. The final effect will therefore be an increase in the domestic prices of imports, including the tariffs, relative to the prices of the country's exports. But if the world demand for the tariff-imposing country's exports is inelastic and if the tariffs reduce

Reprinted from *Journal of Political Economy*, 57 (August 1949), 345–351. Copyright University of Chicago, 1949.

1. Lloyd A. Metzler, "Tariffs, the Terms of Trade, and the Distribution of National Income." This article appears as Chapter 6 of the present volume.

the demand for imports in the tariff-imposing country to a considerable extent, the fall in world prices of imports, relative to world prices of exports, may be so large that domestic prices of imports are relatively lower than before the tariffs were imposed, even after the tariffs are added to the world prices. Between these extremes, an intermediate case can be found in which the one force exactly offsets the other, leaving domestic price ratios unaltered in the country imposing the tariffs. Using the symbol η_2 to represent the elasticity of world demand for exports of the tariff-imposing country, and the symbol k to represent the proportion of tariff proceeds spent on imports, I demonstrated in my earlier paper that the condition for the occurrence of the intermediate case is simply that

$$(1) \qquad\qquad \eta_2 = 1 - k.$$

In words, the elasticity of foreign demand for the country's exports must be equal to the proportion of tariff proceeds *not* spent on imports. If the foreign elasticity of demand is greater than this, the tariffs will *increase* the domestic prices of imports, relative to the prices of exports; if the elasticity is smaller, the domestic prices of imports will be *reduced*, relative to exports.

Although Eq. (1) is probably sufficiently accurate for most purposes it actually is not an exact statement of the conditions under which the forces affecting domestic prices will cancel each other. Rather, it is an approximation in two respects. In the first place, it is based upon the implicit assumption that tariff rates are comparatively low. Second and perhaps more important, it does not distinguish between the situation in which the customs revenues are spent by the government and the situation in which such revenues are passed on to residents of the country through remission of other taxes. In other words, the statement in the earlier paper that a proportion k of customs revenues was spent on imports did not specify whether these expenditures were made by the government or by private traders. Under some conditions the distinction is important, for the total shift in international demand that occurs when tariffs are imposed sometimes varies considerably, depending upon whether the tariff proceeds are spent directly by the government or indirectly by individual traders.

The purpose of the present paper is to eliminate the approximations of my earlier paper and to derive exact equations to describe the condition that tariffs shall leave domestic price ratios unchanged.

I begin with some observations regarding the effects of tariffs on the demand for imports.

The change in the demand for imports that occurs when tariffs are imposed or increased may be divided into two parts, one negative and the other positive. In the first place, the physical quantity of goods that importers are willing to purchase out of given incomes and at given foreign prices will clearly be reduced by tariffs, with the extent of the reduction depending upon the price elasticity of demand. Second, against this negative influence must be set a positive influence: the customs revenues represent additional income either for the government or for individuals; and this additional income will probably be spent, in part, on imported goods. In other words, the customs revenues will either be spent directly by the government or they will be passed on to individuals through reduction of other taxes, and in either event the demand for imports as well as the demand for home goods will be increased.

Now if the proportion of government revenues customarily spent on imported goods is the same as the proportion of private income devoted to imports, it might seem to make no difference in the total demand for imports whether the government spends its customs revenues directly or whether these revenues are spent indirectly through the remission or reduction of taxes of private traders. If the government were to collect customs duties of $1,500,000, for example, what difference would it make in the total demand for imports whether, say, 20 percent of these revenues were expended by the government on foreign goods or whether the government augmented the incomes of private traders by $1,500,000 and these traders in turn spent 20 percent of their increased incomes on imports?

Although the two situations appear superficially to be the same, they are actually different, owing to the fact that private traders pay duties on their added imports, whereas the government does not. If the tariff were 50 percent, for example, and if the world price of imports, exclusive of the tariff, were $1.00 per unit, government expenditures of $300,000 (20 percent of customs duties) on imports would bring in 300,000 units. Private expenditures of the same amount, on the other hand, would bring in only 200,000 units, since the price to the private traders, including the tariff, would be $1.50 per unit. Thus, considering only the expenditure of a given amount of customs revenues, it appears from our numerical example that the demand for imports will be larger if the government spends the revenues directly than if private traders spend them indirectly.

Unlike government expenditures on imports, however, private expenditures tend to be cumulative, and the cumulative effects offset to some extent the retarding influence of the tariff. In the preceding illustration, for example, private expenditures of $300,000 on imports would create additional customs revenues of $100,000; and these, in turn would be remitted to the private traders for further expenditure, thereby creating still more customs revenues. It can easily be shown, however, that even after allowing for this cumulative increase in the demand for imports, the demand by private traders remains smaller than the corresponding government demand. In other words, if the proportion of income devoted to imports is the same for the government as for the individual, the secondary increase in the demand for imports arising from the tariff proceeds will always be larger when the government spends the revenues directly than when they are spent indirectly by private traders.[2]

In order to demonstrate this point, let m represent the total amount, exclusive of the tariff, that would be spent on imports if no allowance were made for the effects of spending the customs revenues. Assuming that the ad valorem tariff rate is τ, the total customs revenues arising from the initial expenditure m will then be τm. If k is the proportion of income devoted to imports (either by the government or by individuals), direct government expenditure of the tariff proceeds will increase the amount spent on imports by $k\tau m$. We wish to compare this amount $k\tau m$ with the additional amounts that would be spent by private traders if the customs duties were passed on to individuals. If the customs revenues were used to augment the incomes of individuals, the first additional private expenditure for imports would be $k\tau m$, which is the same as the government's additional expenditure in the preceding case. But, on the one hand, not all this expenditure would go to foreign producers, since a part would be paid back to the government as tariff; and,

2. Throughout this paper the assumption is made that the proportion of income spent on imports—k in our notation—is independent of the domestic ratio of import prices to domestic-goods prices. Except when the price elasticity of demand for imports is unity, this assumption of a constant k probably is inconsistent with the classical postulate of a homogeneous consumption function of degree zero. To allow for variations in k with changes in the price ratio would complicate the problem considerably without introducing any important new principles. For this reason, the assumption of a constant k has been adopted despite its possible inconsistency with the classical theory of consumers' choice.

on the other hand, the part paid as tariff would again be returned to the individuals, thereby leading to a further increase in imports. Each currency unit that the importers paid to foreign exporters would be accompanied by an amount τ paid to the government, and the ratio of the tariff proceeds to total expenditures including the tariff would accordingly be $\tau/(1 + \tau)$.

Of the additional amount $k\tau m$ spent on imports, an amount $k\tau m\tau/(1 + \tau)$ would be paid to the government, while an amount $k\tau m(1 + \tau)$ would be paid to the foreign exporters. The "secondary tariff receipts," $k\tau m\tau/(1 + \tau)$, would be returned to the private traders, and once more a proportion k of such additional income would be spent on imports. The secondary expenditure on imports would then be $k\tau mk\tau/(1 + \tau)$, of which $k^2\tau^3 m/(1 + \tau)^2$ would be paid to the government as tariff, while $k^2\tau^2 m/(1 + \tau)^2$ would be paid to foreign exporters. Continuing in the same way, we may show that the "tertiary" expenditure to foreign producers would be $k^3\tau^3 m/(1 + \tau)^3$, and so on for all subsequent expenditures. In other words, if the tariff proceeds were passed on to individuals, initial expenditure m on foreign goods would give rise to a series of subsequent expenditures, exclusive of the tariff, as follows:

$$(2) \qquad m\left\{\frac{\tau k}{1 + \tau} + \left(\frac{\tau k}{1 + \tau}\right)^2 + \left(\frac{\tau k}{1 + \tau}\right)^3 + \ldots\right\}.$$

Since $\tau k/(1 + \tau)$ is positive and less than unity, each term in this series is less than the preceding term, and the sum of an infinite series of such terms is

$$(3) \qquad m\left\{\frac{\tau k}{1 + (1 - k)\tau}\right\}.$$

Now as long as k is less than unity, the expression (3) is always less than $k\tau m$. But $k\tau m$ is the additional demand for imports that would arise if the tariff revenues were spent directly by the government. The preceding argument thus shows that, despite the cumulative effect of private expenditures, the total demand for imports is always less when the customs revenues are spent by individuals than when they are spent in a similar manner by the government.

Having considered the effects of tariffs on the demand for imports under two different hypotheses concerning the disposition of the tariff proceeds, we may now go on to ask how the duties under each hypothesis influence domestic prices in the tariff-imposing country. Consider first the case in which a proportion k of the customs revenues is spent directly by the government in the purchase of imports. Let the tariff-imposing country be called country A, and let the rest of the world be called country B. Let u_1 and u_2 represent the private demand for imports in country A and country B respectively, the demand in each case being measured in physical units. Suppose that each country's exports are produced and sold at constant money cost, and let the unit of exports be chosen in each country in such a manner that the price per unit, in the currency of the exporting country, is 1.00. Suppose further that the terms of trade between the two countries are adjusted by means of movements in exchange rates, and let π be the price of country B's currency in terms of country A's currency. An increase in π will then indicate a depreciation of country A's currency, while a decrease will indicate appreciation. Under these assumed conditions, the price per unit of imports in country A, exclusive of the tariff, is simply π, and if τ is the rate of duty, the price, including the duty, is $(1 + \tau)\pi$. Thus we have $u_1 = f_1\{(1 + \tau)\pi\}$ as the demand function for imports in country A. Likewise, in country B the price of imports is $1/\pi$, and if there is no tariff in B we have $u_2 = f_2\{1/\pi\}$.

Since the price of each country's exports is unity, when measured in its own currency, the private expenditure of the residents of country A for imported goods, measured in foreign currency, is u_1. Duties on this private expenditure, again in foreign currency, amount to τu_1, and a proportion k of this amount is spent on additional imports by the government that collects the duties. Total expenditures on imports by country A, in foreign currency therefore amount to $(1 + k\tau) f_1\{(1 + \tau)\pi\}$. The demand for imports in country B is $f_2\{1/\pi\}$, and the total value of these imports, in the currency of country B, is accordingly $(1/\pi)f_2\{1/\pi\}$. The condition that the value of each country's exports shall equal the value of its imports may thus be expressed, in the currency of B, as follows:

$$(4) \qquad (1 + k\tau)f_1\{(1 + \tau)\pi\} = \frac{1}{\pi}f_2\left(\frac{1}{\pi}\right).$$

Equation (4) indicates the relation which must hold between the exchange rate π and the tariff rate τ in order that international balance may be preserved. If τ is changed, the exchange rate must also be altered in an appropriate manner. To see how π changes with a change in τ, differentiate Eq. (4) with respect to τ, remembering that π is to be regarded as a function of τ. It will then be found that

$$(5) \qquad \frac{d\pi}{d\tau} = \frac{\pi}{(1+\tau)\Delta}\left\{\frac{k(1+\tau)}{1+k\tau} - \eta_1\right\},$$

where $\Delta = \eta_1 + \eta_2 - 1$ and where η_1 and η_2 are the ordinary elasticities of demand for imports in A and B respectively.

Equation (5) shows that when the demand for imports is elastic in the country imposing the tariff, an increase in tariff rates leads to an appreciation of the tariff-imposing country's currency, and vice versa.[3] This is the result that, in the absence of special circumstances, would normally be expected. The tariff reduces the demand for imports and thereby gives the tariff-imposing country a temporary surplus in its balance of payments; and the balance-of-payments surplus in turn leads to an appreciation of the currency. If the demand for imports is inelastic, however, and if the proportion of income spent on imports is large, $d\pi/d\tau$ of Eq. (5) may well be positive, which means that an increase in tariffs may *depreciate* rather than appreciate the country's currency.

Superficially, such an outcome appears somewhat paradoxical; the currency cannot depreciate unless the demand for imports is *increased*, and it is rather difficult, at first glance, to see how a tariff can increase the total demand for the goods upon which it is imposed. Upon closer examination of the problem, however, the paradox is easily resolved. When the tariff is increased, the demand for imported goods is subject to two influences which, as we have seen earlier, may work in opposite directions. On the one hand, the rise in the domestic prices of the commodities subject to duties causes the demand for such commodities to decline. And, on the other hand, the increase in tariff rates brings about a change in the government receipts from the customs, and the change in custom receipts in turn affects the demand, either public or private, for imported goods. Now if the demand for imports is inelastic, the reduction in demand resulting from a rise in the domestic prices of imports will be small. At the same time, the customs receipts will be *increased* by a rise in the tariff rates, and if the proportion of income spent on imports is high, the increase in demand for imports on account of the rise in customs receipts may well be larger than the reduction in demand

---

3. It is well known that stability of exchange rates requires that Δ be positive. See for example, Joan Robinson, *Essays in the Theory of Employment* (New York, Macmillan, 1937), p. 194.

on account of higher prices. Under such conditions, in other words, the net effect of an increase in duties may well be an increase in demand for imports with a corresponding depreciation of the currency.[4]

Our primary interest at present, however, is not in the movement of the exchange rate but in domestic prices in country A. Since under our assumptions the export price is always constant, the ratio of domestic prices of imports to prices of home goods will move as the import price, including the tariff, moves. Now the import price, including the tariff, is $(1 + \tau)\pi$; and, when the tariff rate is increased, one part of this expression, $(1 + \tau)$, grows larger while the other, π, normally declines. Differentiating $(1 + \tau)\pi$ with respect to τ, and substituting the value of $d\pi/d\tau$ given in Eq. (5), we find

(6)
$$\frac{d(1 + \tau)\pi}{d\tau} = \frac{\pi}{\Delta}\left\{ \frac{k(1 + \tau)}{1 + k\tau} + \eta_2 - 1 \right\}.$$

Since export prices remain constant, the condition that domestic price ratios of imports to exports shall remain unchanged when tariffs are increased is simply that import prices, including the tariff, shall remain constant; this implies

(7)
$$\eta_2 = 1 - k\left(\frac{1 + \tau}{1 + k\tau}\right).$$

If η_2 is larger than the amount indicated by Eq. (7), an increase in tariff rates will cause domestic prices of imports in country A to rise, relative to prices of exported goods. Conversely, if η_2 is smaller than the indicated quantity, higher tariffs will lead to a *decline* in domestic prices of imported goods, relative to prices of exports. If we compare (7) with the approximation used in my earlier paper—that is, with Eq. (1) of the present paper—it is evident that the approximation given by (1) overstates somewhat the demand elasticity that is required in order that the domestic ratio of import to export prices shall remain unaltered when tariffs are increased. In other words, if customs revenues are spent directly by the government, the foreign elasticity of demand may be smaller than $1 - k$, and yet, if it is not too much smaller, the added tariff may cause domestic prices of imports in the tariff-imposing country to rise, relative to the prices of exports.

4. It was once suggested to me by Professor Tibor Scitovszky that the Latin American countries may be in such a position, since a large proportion of their incomes is spent on foreign goods, the demand for which is relatively inelastic with respect to price.

Suppose, for example, that k, the proportion of government revenue spent on imports, were 0.4, while τ, the general tariff rate, were 0.5. According to the approximation given by (1), the foreign elasticity of demand would have to exceed 0.6, in order that the tariff should increase the domestic ratio of import to export prices ($1 - k = 0.6$ in this instance). According to the exact expression (7), however, import prices, including the tariff, would rise, relative to export prices, whenever the foreign elasticity exceeded 0.5 (for the figures given, $1 - k$ $[1 + \tau]/(1 + k\tau)] = 0.5$). Thus if the foreign elasticity of demand had any value between 0.5 and 0.6, the exact expression (7) would indicate that an increase in tariffs would raise the domestic ratio of import to export prices, while the approximation (1) would indicate the reverse. All of this, of course, is based upon the hypothesis that customs revenues are spent directly by the government of the tariff-imposing country.

Consider now the alternative hypothesis, that is, that the tariff proceeds are passed on to the private traders who spend a proportion k of their augmented incomes on imports. Let u_1, as before, represent the initial private demand for imports in country A before any allowance has been made for expenditure of the tariff proceeds. Let w_1 represent the total physical volume of imports, and let v_1 be the imports purchased from the tariff proceeds, so that $w_1 = u_1 + v_1$. The customs revenues, in the currency of country A, are then $\pi\tau w_1$, and the amount of these spent on imports is $k\pi\tau w_1$. Since the price of imports to the traders in A is $(1 + \tau)\pi$, the physical volume of imports purchased from the customs revenues, or v_1, is $w_1 k\tau/(1 + \tau)$. Thus we have $w_1 = u_1 + w_1 k\tau/(1 + \tau)$, from which it follows that

$$(8) \qquad w_1 = \left\{ \frac{1 + \tau}{1 + (1 - k)\tau} \right\} u_1.$$

As before, the value of exports of country A, measured in the currency of B, is $(1/\pi)f_2(1/\pi)$. The condition of equilibrium is therefore $w_1 = (1/\pi)f_2(1/\pi)$, or, in slightly different form,

$$(9) \qquad \left\{ \frac{1 + \tau}{1 + (1 - k)\tau} \right\} f_1\{(1 + \tau)\pi\} = \frac{1}{\pi} f_2 \left(\frac{1}{\pi} \right).$$

Differentiating as above with respect to τ and solving the resulting equation for $d\pi/d\tau$, we find

$$(10) \qquad \frac{d\pi}{d\tau} = \frac{\pi}{(1 + \tau)\Delta} \left\{ \frac{k}{1 + (1 - k)\tau} - \eta_1 \right\}.$$

From Eq. (10) it immediately follows that

(11)
$$\frac{d(1 + \tau)\pi}{d\tau} = \frac{\pi}{\Delta}\left\{\frac{k}{1 + (1 - k)\tau} + \eta_2 - 1\right\}.$$

In order for import prices in the tariff-imposing country to remain unchanged when the tariff is increased or decreased, the expression in braces in Eq. (11) must be zero, and this means that

(12)
$$\eta_2 = 1 - \frac{k}{1 + (1 - k)\tau}.$$

Once again we may compare the exact expression, given under our second hypothesis by Eq. (12), with the original approximation represented by Eq. (1). Since $k/[1 + (1 - k)\tau]$ is less than k, it is apparent that, when customs revenues are spent by individuals rather than by the collecting government, domestic prices of imports *may* decline, relative to prices of exports, even when the foreign elasticity of demand for imports exceeds $1 - k$. In other words, under the hypothesis of private expenditure of customs receipts the approximation (1) *understates* the elasticity required for a balancing of price movements. As in our previous case, the approximation and the exact expression are not equal unless either $k = 1$ or $\tau = 0$.

The preceding discussion has been presented in order to describe accurately the extent of the shifts in international demand that occur when tariffs are imposed and to analyze, with the aid of such shifts in demand, the conditions that must exist if tariffs are to leave the domestic ratio of import to export prices unaltered in the country imposing the duties. We have found that the demand for imports is larger when the tariff revenues are spent by the government collecting them than when such revenues are spent in a similar manner by individuals. The terms of trade therefore become more favorable to the tariff country in the latter case than in the former, and the chances are greater that domestic import prices, including the duties, will not rise relative to export prices.

It may be useful to recapitulate briefly the exact conditions which are necessary if domestic import prices are to remain unchanged, relative to export prices, and to compare these conditions with the approximate condition represented by Eq. (1). The approximate condition, it will be recalled, is

$$\eta_2 = 1 - k.$$

The exact condition, when customs revenues are spent by the government, is

$$\eta_2 = 1 - k \left(\frac{1 + \tau}{1 + k\tau}\right).$$

Finally, when the tariff proceeds are spent by private traders, the exact condition is

$$\eta_2 = 1 - k \left(\frac{1}{1 + (1 - k)\tau}\right).$$

Since $(1 + \tau)/(1 + k\tau)$ is greater than unity while $1/[1 + (1 - k)\tau]$ is less than unity, it is clear that the approximate condition for a balancing of forces is intermediate between the two exact conditions. In other words, if the customs duties are spent by the government, the approximate formula overstates the magnitude of the foreign demand elasticity that is required if domestic price ratios are to remain unchanged. On the other hand, if the customs duties are spent by private traders, the approximate formula gives too small a value for the relevant elasticity of demand. The three expressions are identical only if $k = 1$ or $\tau = 0$.

Considering the crudeness of most empirical estimates of demand elasticities, and considering the difficulties in defining schedules of reciprocal demand rigorously, the approximation represented by Eq. (1) is probably satisfactory for most practical purposes. Nevertheless, it seemed worthwhile to clear up some of the theoretical issues involved and to point out that the formula used in my earlier paper was not exact. At least, the derivation of exact formulas provides a measure of the magnitude of error committed in using the simpler approximation. And, at best, there may be instances, particularly in smaller countries, where the distinction between government and private transactions in international trade is highly significant and where, as a consequence, the exact formulas are much better than the approximate formula.

8 | The Process of International Adjustment under Conditions of Full Employment: A Keynesian View

Contemporary ideas about the way in which an even balance of payments is achieved have always been closely related to prevailing theories of money and prices. In the pre-Keynesian era, when the quantity theory of money was the accepted version, the balancing process was described largely in terms of movements in money and the level of prices. Later, under the influence of Lord Keynes's *General Theory of Employment, Interest, and Money*, these monetary variables were replaced by changes in the circular flow of income or by movements in the level of output and employment. To some extent the *General Theory* reflected a condition of deep depression and widely fluctuating output; it was therefore not applicable to the prosperous conditions which prevail today. Nevertheless, in modifying his concepts of monetary theory to allow for conditions of depression and fluctuating output, Keynes made a contribution to the traditional theory which will have a profound influence on the theory of international adjustment even when full employment prevails. Specifically, he introduced the concept of a monetary rate of interest which altered the foundation upon which the traditional quantity theory of money was based.

The purpose of this paper is to consider a situation where full employment prevails but where the Keynesian monetary rate of interest is also taken into account. I shall assume that prices are governed by the demand for goods and services compared with the supply, so that a rise

---

Delivered before the Econometric Society, December 1960; reprinted from American Economic Association, *Readings in International Economics*, ed. Richard E. Caves and Harry G. Johnson (Homewood, Ill., Richard D. Irwin, 1968), chap. 28. Copyright Richard D. Irwin, Inc., 1968.

of prices indicates an excess demand while a fall indicates an excess supply. Further, I shall assume that we are dealing with trade between two countries, an advanced country and an underdeveloped one. The characteristic of the advanced country, of course, is that it possesses a larger amount of capital per worker; the marginal return on investment therefore is smaller than in the underdeveloped country, while productivity and the rate of saving are higher. I shall assume that in both countries the level of demand is high enough so that at some point in the saving and investment schedules a rate of interest exists at which potential saving at full employment equals potential investment. Thus the two-country economy with which I shall be dealing represents a reconciliation of two monetary theories which a generation ago were the subject of lively controversy among economists: first, the traditional theory which recognized changes in the quantity of money and prices as the principal regulators of the system; and second, the Keynesian theory which emphasized movements of the circular flow of income as the determinants of a country's balance of payments.

Before elaborating further, however, let me say a word about the general consensus which has now developed concerning the relations between the monetary rate of Keynes and the traditional theory. In order to simplify the relationships as much as possible, I shall start with an economy which is isolated from the rest of the world. Consider, for example, Fig. 1. The left-hand side, Fig. 1a, represents potential saving

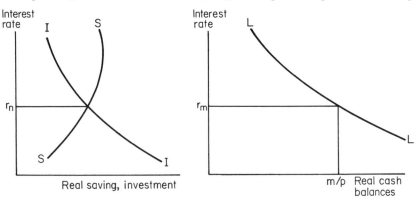

Figure 1a   Figure 1b

and net investment at a full-employment level of income. The vertical axis indicates the rate of interest on newly issued securities, while the horizontal axis depicts real investment and real saving. Looking at the matter from the point of view of newly issued securities, we may say that the saving line *SS* represents a demand for these securities. The investment line *II*, on the other hand, represents a supply of new securities issued by entrepreneurs to finance their planned investment. We may thus look upon the *SS* and *II* schedules from two points of view: from the point of view of the new-securities market, they depict the supply of and demand for such securities; and from the point of view of the goods-and-services market, the saving and investment schedules may be said to represent a condition where the total demand for such goods and services *equals* its full-employment capacity.

In contrast to Fig. 1a, Fig. 1b represents the *monetary* conditions of balance, or the market for existing securities. If r_n is the natural rate, or the rate which creates a balance between the *flow* of real saving and the flow of investment, r_m is the monetary rate, or the rate which satisfies the asset-owners with their existing *stocks* of securities and real cash balances. Thus at any point along *LL* of Fig. 1b, the asset-owners are holding real cash balances in a manner which gives them no incentive to shift from cash to securities or from securities to cash. These comparisons suggest the relation between a profit-and-loss statement and a balance sheet. Figure 1a describes the flow of income per unit of time and shows how this flow is distributed between saving and investment. Figure 1b, on the other hand, presents the ownership of assets and the distribution of such assets between securities and cash.

At the moment of time for which Fig. 1b represents the balance sheet, the amount of existing securities is a fixed quantity, governed by past investments. Moreover, the capitalized value of these security holdings is higher, the lower the rate of interest. We may assume, as Keynes does, that as the rate of interest falls, the asset-owner wishes to hold a larger ratio of real cash balances to securities. The higher degree of desired liquidity will be a result of three considerations. First, as the rate of interest falls, the opportunity cost of holding cash rather than securities becomes smaller; second, a fall in security yields (which means a rise in security prices) may eventually create an expectation that security prices will fall and their yields will therefore rise; and third, a fall in interest rates increases the capitalized value of existing securities.

But all of this is by now a well-accepted part of monetary theory. What I wish to concentrate upon is the relation between the monetary rate and the natural rate. Clearly, there can be no difference between the one and the other; for both types of securities, once issued, are the same. What happens, then, when the real value of cash balances together with the demand for these balances is such that the natural rate differs from the monetary? This situation is depicted in Fig. 2. The

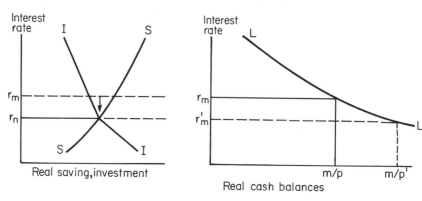

Figure 2a   Figure 2b

natural rate—the rate which balances the new-securities market—is r_n, which is lower than the monetary rate r_m. Under these conditions, both markets cannot be in equilibrium simultaneously. Whenever a discrepancy exists between the monetary rate and the natural rate, there is general agreement, I believe, that in the short run the prevailing rate will be dominated by monetary conditions, regardless of the discrepancies which may arise between saving and investment at the monetary rate. This conclusion is based upon the fact that the stock of assets which governs the monetary rate is normally large relative to the flow of saving and investment which determines the demand for goods and services and hence the movement of prices.

Consider, for example, an economy where the amount of saving represents approximately 10 percent of the national income per year. And suppose that the capital supply or the stock of capitalized wealth is four times the national income. This means that the market for existing securities will be roughly forty times the size of the flow of saving and investment. Moreover, we can make the predominance of existing securities as large as we please by reducing the period of time upon which the tentative figures given above were based. Thus, if we consider saving and investment on a semiannual basis, these variables will be only half what I have described, while the stocks of assets, which has no time dimension, will be the same as before; and if we consider saving and investment on a monthly basis, we can further reduce the significance of the market for goods and services, or that of the new-securities market.

Paradoxically, although the monetary rate determines the actual rate of interest in a very short period of time, over a larger period the monetary rate eventually adapts itself to the natural rate through changes in the price level which alter the real value of cash balances. Consider again the situation represented by Fig. 2. With a nominal quantity of money equal to m and a price level of p, the real value of cash balances m/p is such that the monetary rate r_m is larger than the natural rate r_n. Suppose now that the period of time is short enough so that the prevailing rate is governed by monetary conditions and therefore lies at r_m. This means that the demand created by a full-employment level of output falls short of productive capacity. In other words, a deflationary gap exists in the demand for goods and services, and the general level of prices, costs, and income accordingly tends to fall. If we assume that the nominal quantity of money remains fixed, the deflation will increase the real value of cash balances. Since the economy is now more liquid, the rate of interest which satisfies the asset-holders with their portfolios will have to fall. In short, the real value of cash balances in Fig. 2b increases from m/p to m/p', where p' represents the lower price index, and the monetary rate of interest accordingly falls.

This process of adaptation of the money rate to the natural rate must continue until r_m' is again equal to r_m, as indicated in Fig. 2b. For as long as the monetary rate is above the natural rate, a deflationary situation will continue to exist and the deflation, by increasing the real value of cash balances, will push the monetary rate of interest downward.

A careful examination of the foregoing argument will show that, under conditions of full employment, Keynes's *General Theory of Employment, Interest, and Money* does not differ substantially from his *Treatise on Money*. The pendulum has made a full swing and we are back where we started, despite liquidity preference. Keynes himself would no doubt have been the first to recognize this fact. In the preface to his *General Theory* he said:

The relation between this book and my *Treatise on Money*, which I published five years ago, is probably clearer to myself than it will be to others; and what in my own mind is a natural evolution in a line of thought which I have been pursuing for several years, may sometimes strike the reader as a confusing change of view. . . . This book . . . has evolved into what is primarily a study of the forces which determine changes in the scale of output as a whole; and, whilst it is found that money enters into the economic scheme in an essential and peculiar manner, technical monetary detail falls into the background.[1]

The fact that the monetary rate of interest eventually adapts itself to the natural rate under conditions of full employment enables us to simplify the theory of international adjustment to a great extent, for we can express the conditions of international balance entirely in terms of the saving and investment schedules. Since I am concerned here with the monetary process of adjustment, however, I shall introduce the demand for money at a later stage of the process. It will be found then that liquidity preference determines not the final position of equilibrium after our economy has been disturbed, but rather the amount of money flow required to create a condition where the natural rate and the monetary rate are equal under the new conditions. And the money flow in turn will determine the length of time during which the economy has a deficit or surplus in its balance of payments.

Apart from the condition of monetary equilibrium, there are three markets that I wish to describe: the market for goods and services, the market for foreign exchange, and the market for new securities. One can demonstrate, however, that if any two of these markets are in balance, the third market must also be in balance. Thus we need not consider all markets simultaneously but may choose any two that we please. I shall begin with the market for goods and services.

The components which comprise the demand for a country's output may be specified as follows:

Net output = domestic consumption
+ domestic investment + exports − imports.

The negative correction for imports is necessary because domestic consumption, domestic investment, and exports all contain items, such as imported raw materials, which do not represent a direct demand on the country's resources. Moreover, in defining domestic consumption and domestic investment, I have considered the total demand of residents, whether they purchase at home or abroad. In other words, the criterion of domesticity is the location of the spender, not the

1. J. M. Keynes, *The General Theory of Employment, Interest, and Money* (New York, Harcourt, Brace, 1936), pp. vi–vii.

location of the goods upon which his income was spent. To avoid double counting, a correction must be made for imports of finished goods, including the raw-material content of these imports, and for the imported raw materials contained in domestic expenditures and exports. But this correction obviously includes the total of all imports.

Transposing domestic consumption and domestic investment to the left-hand side of the above equation and changing signs, we have

Net output − domestic consumption
         − domestic investment = exports − imports.

Since net output minus domestic consumption is a measure of domestic saving, the foregoing equation may be written in the following form:

Saving − investment = exports − imports.

Thus if a country has an excess of saving over investment, at a given rate of interest, the resulting deflationary pressure can be eliminated, provided the country has an export surplus equal to its excess saving. Moreover, a market mechanism exists by which the country will eventually achieve the balance of trade needed to give her an equilibrium in the commodities market. Consider, for example, the schedules of saving and investment depicted in Fig. 3.

Suppose that the quantity of money in real terms is such that the prevailing rate of interest is at r_n, where saving and investment are equal.

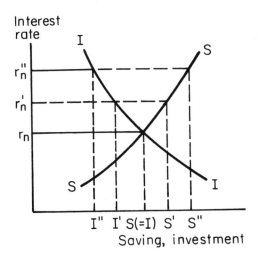

Figure 3

At this point the commodities market will not balance unless prices are at a level, relative to prices in the rest of the world, where the value of the country's exports is equal to the value of its imports. Suppose now that the quantity of money is reduced, and the rate of interest in the short run rises from r_n to r_n'. At the old prices the value of exports continues to be equal to the value of imports. Since saving now exceeds investment at the higher rate of interest, the result of the contraction in money and the rise of interest rates is a deficient demand for goods and services. Inventories therefore rise, and prices as well as costs tend to fall. As prices fall, the country becomes a cheaper place in which to purchase and the balance of trade improves. This process must continue until the country has an export surplus equal to the amount of its excess saving. Thus, in Fig. 3, if the rate of interest is r_n', the country's export surplus must be $S' - I'$. Continuing this line of reasoning, we may suppose that the rate of interest is further increased by a contraction of the money supply until it reaches the level of r_n''. At this higher rate an even larger export surplus will be required to create a balance in the goods-and-services market, for the excess of real saving over real investment will be larger at r_n'' than at r_n'. And again market forces will create the necessary export surplus through a movement of prices.

I have now shown that corresponding to any given rate of interest there exists a unique balance of trade at which the demand for a country's goods and services is equal to its productive capacity at full employment. I shall call this relationship a schedule of the "natural balance of trade." The method of deriving this schedule is indicated in Fig. 4. For any given rate of interest, the equilibrium balance of trade is represented in Fig. 4b as the balance which makes the difference between saving and investment equal to the difference between exports and imports. The schedule of the natural balance of trade will prove to be a valuable tool in describing the process of international adjustment. But before carrying the analysis further, I must ask the reader's indulgence while I examine the interdependence between the various markets in a trading country.

I have already described the market for goods and services. The market for newly issued securities must now be considered. Even if the banking system supplies the required degree of liquidity through open-market purchases, the excess demand for new domestic securities cannot be represented entirely as an excess of saving over investment. For quite apart from the demand for liquidity, a portion of current saving will be

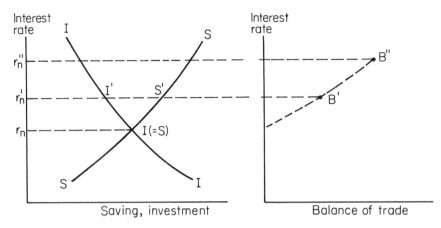

Figure 4a   Figure 4b

devoted to the purchase of foreign rather than domestic securities. This assumes, of course, that interest rates are higher in the foreign country than at home.

At this point, in order to make ideas explicit, I shall present a diagrammatic representation of the saving and investment relations between the two countries mentioned earlier, namely an advanced country with a large amount of capital per worker and an underdeveloped country with a small amount of capital per worker. Let the advanced country and the underdeveloped country be called country A and country U respectively. Schedules of saving and investment are given for each of these countries in Figs. 5a and b. If both countries were isolated, the natural rate of interest would be r_a in country A and r_u in country U. A presumption thus exists that the rate of return on securities will be higher in the underdeveloped country than in the advanced one.

Suppose now that we are describing the demand for and supply of new securities in the advanced country. Apart from liquidity considerations, the demand for new domestic securities will fall short of saving to the extent that a part of such saving is devoted to the purchase of U securities where the return is higher. Thus the net domestic demand for new securities in A will be saving *less* purchase of securities in U. A similar adjustment must of course be made for the fact that some investors in U will sell their securities in A and convert their A currency into U currency on the foreign-exchange market. But in order to simplify the problem I shall assume that the only element in capital movements

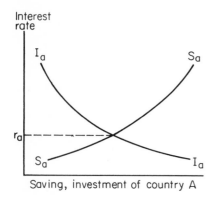

Saving, investment of country A

Figure 5a

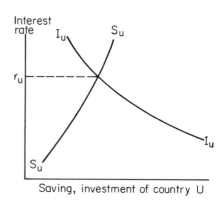

Saving, investment of country U

Figure 5b

is the purchase of foreign securities by A savers, which represents a capital outflow. The condition of balance in newly issued A securities will then be

$$\text{Saving} - \text{capital outflow} = \text{investment,}$$

or

$$\text{Saving} - \text{investment} = \text{capital outflow.}$$

With this relationship in mind, the interrelations among our three markets may now be discussed. Specifically, I wish to show that if the market for goods and services and the market for new domestic securities are in equilibrium, the market for foreign exchange must also be in balance. I shall begin with a tabulation which represents, on the left side, the type of market and, on the right side, the conditions of equilibrium for that market.

TYPE OF MARKET	CONDITIONS OF EQUILIBRIUM
(1) Goods and services	Saving – investment = exports – imports.
(2) New domestic securities	Saving – investment = capital outflow.

From (1) and (2) the export surplus and the capital outflow are both equal to the excess of saving over investment. Since two quantities equal to the same thing must be equal to each other, it follows that

$$\text{Exports} - \text{imports} = \text{capital outflow.}$$

But this condition is the condition for balance in the country's foreign-exchange market; the export surplus creates a supply of foreign exchange, while the capital outflow represents a demand. Thus a balance in the foreign-exchange market is achieved when the export surplus is equal to the capital outflow.

It follows that if both the new-securities market and the market for goods and services are in balance, the third market, or the market for foreign exchange, must also be in equilibrium. This is a special application of Walras's well-known proposition that in a general equilibrium involving n markets, if $n - 1$ of these markets are balanced, the nth market must also balance. And it is a slightly generalized treatment of Professor Alexander's conception of "income absorption," which states that currency devaluation will not be effective in improving a country's balance of payments unless it is accompanied by measures to reduce the demand for goods and services. All such ideas are derived from the basic tautology that a businessman's costs represent an income earner's revenue and are therefore closely linked to the notion of a circular flow of income.

Bearing in mind the interrelations among the various markets in an open economy, we can now consider the conditions of international balance between two countries as well as the process by which such an adjustment is achieved. As before, I shall describe a situation of trade between an advanced country and an underdeveloped one.

In depicting international trade between two countries, we come upon a minor complication which may as well be settled at once. The important consideration in explaining the state of a country's balance of trade was the absolute level of interest rates, which determines the saving-investment relation or the surplus available for export—assuming that prices are adjusted both at home and abroad so that the foreign demand absorbs the required surplus. But in considering the balance of payments as a whole, the capital inflow or outflow must be taken into account as well as the balance of trade; the awkwardness of putting capital movements into the balance of payments arises from the fact that they do not depend upon absolute interest rates, as the balance of trade does, but upon the *difference* of interest rates between the two countries. Thus savers in country A purchase securities in U because the rate of return is greater in U than in A. To avoid this difficulty, I shall define the schedule of the natural balance of payments in such a way that it can be expressed in terms of differences in interest rates between the two countries. A certain amount of information will be lost thereby, but this can easily be reclaimed at the end of the demonstration.

The basic ideas are presented in Fig. 6. Suppose we start with an

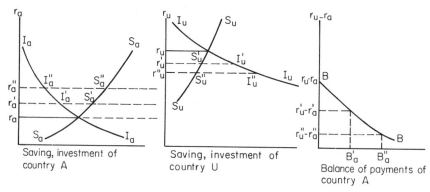

Figure 6a   Figure 6b   Figure 6c

interest rate of r_a in country A, where saving is equal to investment. At this rate, internal balance in A's goods-and-services market requires that exports *equal* imports; for, as we have seen, the excess of saving over investment must be equal to the excess of exports over imports. But if country A's balance of trade is zero, country U's balance of trade must likewise be zero, for in our two-country economy the exports of one country are imports of another; and if U's balance of trade is zero, her natural rate of interest must be r_u to preserve internal balance in the goods-and-services market, for r_u is the rate where saving is equal to investment. Thus, for a given interest rate r_a in A, there exists another rate r_u in U and a balance of trade between the two countries at which both trading countries will have a full-employment demand for goods and services.

Continuing in this direction, we may suppose that the prevailing rate of interest is increased from r_a to r_a'. At r_a' country A's saving exceeds her investment, and full-employment equilibrium in the goods-and-services market cannot exist until the resulting deflation increases that country's export surplus to the amount of her excess saving. Again, if A has an export surplus of $S_a' - I_a'$ (Fig. 6a), U will have an import surplus of the same amount (Fig. 6b). But if full-employment equilibrium is to exist in U's market, her import surplus must be offset by an excess of investment over saving exactly equal to the amount of her import surplus. Thus, for any given interest rate r_a' in A there is another, and lower, interest rate r_u' in U at which both countries have a state of full employment with an export surplus in A equal to $S_a' - I_a'$. In general, the higher the interest rate in A, the lower the interest rate in U;

"tight money" in the one country creates "easy money" in the other. Thus we have a pattern of interest rates in the two countries and a balance of trade between them which is consistent with full employment in both country A and country U.

This relationship is presented in Fig. 6c as the line BB. As before, I shall call the revised schedule BB, expressed in differentials, a schedule of the "natural balance of trade." Any point along BB involves an implicit price level between A and U; with given tastes, the price ratio required for full employment will be lower as the interest-rate differentials are narrowed. Moreover, the ordinary operation of the market mechanism will establish the natural balance of trade required for full employment. Since BB is expressed as a function of interest-rate differentials, it is necessary to show how the differentials can be translated into absolute interest rates. To avoid confusion I shall repeat Fig. 6 as Fig. 6' without the broken lines required to derive the BB schedule.

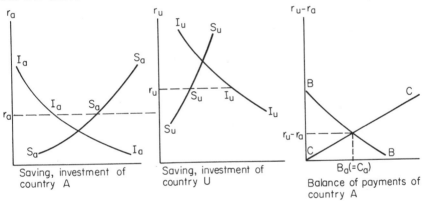

Figure 6'a   Figure 6'b   Figure 6'c

As far as country A's balance of payments is concerned, the conditions of equilibrium are represented in Fig. 6'c. Here we see that the advanced country has an export surplus of B_a, exactly offset by a capital outflow C_a of the same amount. (The capital outflow does not entirely equalize interest rates because some interest-rate differential is required to induce it.) The equality between a country's balance of trade and its capital outflow, as shown by Fig. 6'c, is achieved when the interest-rate differential is $r_u - r_a$. I propose to show how this difference in rates can be transformed into actual rates in the two countries. The key to such a transformation lies in the fact that at any point along the BB schedule the export surplus of A is equal to her excess of saving over investment. Thus in Figs. 6'a and c the absolute interest rate r_a is found at a point where $B = S_a - I_a$. And likewise, for country U the rate r_u is that at which the import surplus $-B$ is the (negative) difference between saving and investment. In the notation of Figs. 6'b and c, $-B = S_u - I_u$ or $B = I_u - S_u$.

To summarize the results of Fig. 6', we may say that international trade, combined with a capital outflow from A to U, has the effect of raising the natural rate in country A and lowering that rate in U, compared with the situation where the two countries are isolated. At the same time, since A has an export surplus after trade, her price level must be somewhat lower than it would have been if capital movements did not exist. Conversely, in country U the interest rate will be reduced by the existence of trade and capital movements, while the price level will be increased in order to give U the required import surplus, $-B$.

Suppose then that we start from the position of equilibrium represented by Fig. 6'. And suppose further that this equilibrium is disturbed by some event which gives the advanced country a potential deficit in its balance of payments. What is the process by which this deficit will eventually be eliminated, and how does the new equilibrium in the balance of payments compare with the old? Finally, what part does the monetary system—that is, the movement in the stock of real cash balances—play in the process of adjustment?

A complete answer to these questions must take account of two elements, interest rates and the balance of capital movements, and prices and the balance of trade. Thus the deficit country, if it is pledged to buy and sell foreign currencies at fixed rates, will find that the demand exceeds the supply so that its foreign currency reserves decline, together with a corresponding decline in the nominal quantity of money. And of course the surplus country will find its quantity of money increasing because the supply of foreign exchange exceeds the demand. Thus the monetary rate of interest, which governs the actual rate in the short run, will tend to rise in the deficit country and to fall in the surplus. The differences between interest rates will be narrowed, and any capital outflow which may have taken place will be discouraged. At the same time, the temporary rise in interest rates will have a deflationary effect on demand and prices will fall, with the result that the balance of trade will improve. The deficit will accordingly be altered partly by a movement of interest rates with a corresponding backflow of capital and partly by a change in prices which will improve the balance of trade in the deficit country.

The question that needs to be explored is whether most of the adjustment will take the form of interest-rate changes and a backflow of capital or whether changes in prices and an improvement in the deficit country's balance of trade will be the dominant factor in creating an even balance of payments. One might suppose that banking policy would have a considerable influence upon the nature of this adjustment. But it can be shown that if the banks wish to maintain equilibrium both externally and internally they have no choice as to how a given disturbance will ultimately affect their position. We have seen that in an isolated economy the banking system can affect neither the natural rate of interest nor the real value of cash balances; the same holds true in an open economy.

Before exploring this avenue further, however, I wish to emphasize that the nature of the adjustment process is determined largely by the type of initial disturbance. For some types of disturbance the balance of trade will do most if not all of the adjustment, while for others interest and capital flows will be more significant. I propose to consider two types of disturbances. The first of these is a change of tastes of such a nature that, with the given price structure, income earners in A prefer to buy a larger amount of U goods and a smaller amount of their own goods; in other words, the disturbance consists of a shift in demand from A goods to U goods. The second is an increased awareness of A citizens of the advantages of buying securities in U, or an increase in the amount of A's capital outflow corresponding to a given difference in interest rates between U and A.

The simpler of these disturbances is a change of tastes, and this is the one with which I shall begin. The initial effect of the increased desire of A income-earners to purchase goods from U will be to increase the amount of A's imports. If we start from a position where A's export surplus is just equal to her capital outflow, the initial effect of the shift in demand will be to reduce A's export surplus to a point where it is less than her given capital outflow. Country A, then, has a deficit in her balance of payments, and money flows from A to U. As a result of the changes in the quantity of money, the monetary rate, which governs the natural rate, tends to rise in A and to fall in U. This discourages the capital outflow from A to U and also creates a deflationary gap in A and an inflationary gap in U. The process continues until the potential deficit is ultimately eliminated.

Note, however,[2] that the type of disturbance I am here considering does not affect either the saving and investment schedules in A or U or the capital outflow from A to U. This means that in the new position of equilibrium the schedule of the natural balance of payments BB, as well as the schedule of capital outflows CC, will remain unchanged. As a consequence the amount of capital outflow, the rates of interest, and the balance of trade are the same as before. In other words, for the type of disturbance now being considered—that is, an increase in the desire of income earners in A to buy goods from U—the process of adjustment takes place entirely through a change in money and prices, and an adaptation of A's balance of trade to a fixed capital movement. In the final equilibrium, interest rates remain in their original positions. The rise of the interest rate in A is only temporary; it is the means by which the deflation needed to improve the balance of trade is brought about. Likewise, the temporary reduction in country U's interest rate is the method of achieving a rise in prices there.

The process of adjustment is presented in Fig. 7. Initially, country A's

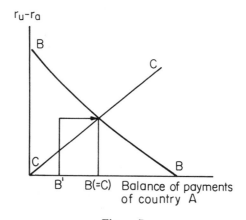

Figure 7

balance of payments is in equilibrium; an export surplus of B is offset

2. The adjustment in price levels involves a change in the terms of trade between A and U. I am thus assuming that changes in the terms of trade have no effect on the levels of real saving and investment occurring at any given rate of interest. For a discussion of this assumption, see the concluding remarks of this chapter and my "Flexible Exchange Rates and the Theory of Employment," which appears as Chapter 11 of the present volume.

by a capital outflow of the same amount. When her demand for imports from U rises, the value of imports also rises. As a result, the export surplus of country A falls (from B to B' in Fig. 7). The advanced country now has a deficit in her balance of payments; the supply of foreign exchange arising from her export surplus is no longer large enough to offset the capital outflow. As a result, both the quantity of money and foreign reserves decline in A and the monetary interest rate which governs the natural rate in the short run tends to rise. The rise in the interest rate, by increasing the excess of saving over investment, creates a deflationary gap which leads to a fall in prices and costs. As a consequence of the fall in prices, country A becomes a cheap place in which to buy and her export surplus expands. From Fig. 7 we see that the shift in demand leaves the BB schedule unchanged because it does not affect the saving and investment schedules in either country. Thus the difference in interest rates $r_u - r_q$, the balance of trade B, and the absolute rates r_u and r_a remain where they were before the change in demand created a deficit. In this case country A's deficit has obviously been eliminated, through changes in relative prices, by an adaptation in the balance of trade to a given level of capital outflows.

In the later stages of the adjustment, when the economic system begins to adapt itself to the deficit, something also happens to the monetary rate of interest. We saw before that in the long run the monetary rate adapts itself to the natural rate. Since the natural rate is unchanged, as shown in Fig. 7, the monetary rate must likewise remain unchanged. Given the demand for real cash balances, this means that the change in the price level needed to give A an export surplus of B (again in Fig. 7) must be proportionate to the loss of nominal balances attributable to the deficit. If prices fall by 15 percent, the nominal quantity of money must fall by the same amount. Conversely in country U, where lower interest rates create an inflationary situation, while a surplus in the balance of payments increases the nominal quantity of money, the monetary rate must again adapt itself to the unaltered natural rate. Given the demand for real cash balances, this means that the relative increase of prices must be proportionate to the relative increase in the nominal quantity of money. For the type of disturbance I have been considering, a reasonably good case could thus be made for the classical, quantity theory of money. In spite of saving and investment, liquidity preference, and all the rest, the system seems to behave rather like the traditional theory in which the balance of trade adjusts itself to fluctuations in capital movements through movements in the quantity of money and corresponding changes in prices.

The example is misleading, however, for a change in the demand for imports is only one of the possible disturbances which may create a deficit or surplus in a country's balance of payments; for other disturbances, the quantity theory does not fare so well.

Consider, for example, the case where country A's deficit is the result of an increase of capital outflow from A to U. If we start again from a position of international balance where country A's export surplus is offset by capital outflow, the increase in capital outflow will create a situation where A has a deficit in her balance of payments; the demand by A for U currency in order to purchase securities in that country will now exceed the supply of such currency arising from an export surplus. Money will flow from the deficit country, A, to the surplus country, U. The stock of money will accordingly fall in A and rise in U, and the monetary rate which governs the natural rate in the short run will rise in A and fall in U. As a consequence of these changes in interest rates country A, the deficit country, will have a deflationary gap, while U will experience inflationary pressures. Prices will therefore fall in A and rise in U, and the export surplus of A will increase.

Thus far the mechanism of adjustment to A's deficit seems quite like the first case where the disturbing element was an increased demand in A for the imports of U. In the early stages, at least, the deficit is reduced partly by a narrowing of interest rates and a backflow of capital, partly by a fall of prices in A relative to prices in U, and an increase in A's export surplus. When a final adjustment has been made, however, we can see from Fig. 8 that after the system has adapted itself to the increase in capital outflows, the rate of interest, rather than being a temporary force to get the required changes in prices in A and U, is a permanent part of the new adaptation. Interest rates remain higher in A even after the balance of payments has reached a new equilibrium and the flow of money has ceased. The higher interest rates are attributable to the fact that under the new conditions country A's balance of trade has increased from B to B'. In order to preserve balance in the internal demand for goods and services, A must have an increase in her excess of saving over investment, and this will occur automatically as a result of the operations of the market.

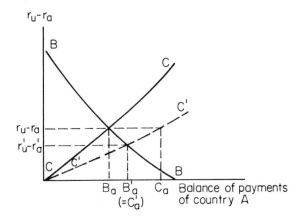

Figure 8

In elimination of the deficit, the importance of interest rates and capital movements, compared with price movements and the balance of trade, obviously depends upon the slope of the capital outflow schedule CC, relative to the slope of the BB schedule. In general, interest rates and capital movements will play a significant role if the CC schedule is relatively flat while the BB schedule is steep. Conversely, prices and the balance of trade will be the dominant influence if the BB schedule is flat while the CC schedule is steep. Figure 9a shows a situation in

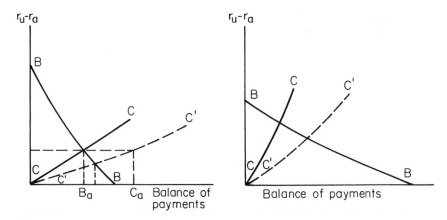

Figure 9a

Figure 9b

which most of the adjustment takes place through movements of interest rates, with the balance of trade playing a minor role. In Fig. 9b, on the other hand, the balance of trade and price levels adapt themselves to a relatively stable pattern of interest rates. But apart from these differences, the most important condition to note is that an increase of capital outflows entails a permanent alteration of interest rates. In A the interest rate rises; and, unlike the previous case, it remains higher even after a balance has been achieved. Likewise in country U the interest rate falls and continues to be somewhat lower even after the balance of payments between the two countries is again in equilibrium.

I turn now from the real aspects of the problem to a discussion of the monetary process of adjustment. We have seen that when the initial disturbance is an increased demand in A for the imports of U, the monetary adjustment is quite like the quantity theory of money. The quantity of money and the level of prices both fall in the deficit country A and rise in U. And the changes in the quantity of money are proportional to the price movements in both countries. Apart from movements in the terms of trade, the real value of cash balances thus remains unchanged in both countries.

When the initial disturbance is an increase of capital outflows from A to U, this conclusion no longer holds true. For the movement of capital outflows has altered the rate of interest in both countries, and the change in interest rates affects the demand for real cash balances. In country A, for example, the rate of interest rises and the demand for real cash balances falls. This means that if adjustment of the balance of payments in A calls for a 15-percent reduction in prices, the monetary rate will not be in line with the natural rate unless the nominal quantity of money has been reduced, through A's deficit, by something more than 15 percent. (The reduction in nominal balances might be 25 percent, for example.) Likewise, in country U the rate of interest falls and this means that the monetary rate will not be in line with the new natural rate unless the real value of cash balances has risen. In short, the nominal quantity of money must rise more than the level of prices has risen.

Thus the introduction of liquidity preference creates a certain inertia in the system. Prices do not react as readily to movements in the nominal quantity of money as they would in the classical system. Moreover, the higher the elasticity of demand for money with respect to the rate of interest, the higher the degree of inertia. To put the matter another way, we may say that as the elasticity of demand for real cash balances increases, the significance of money movements as a regulator of the system declines.

What determines the rise or fall in a country's nominal quantity of money? Obviously for a system of pegged exchange rates it is the surplus or deficit in its balance of trade *and the length of time required to eliminate this surplus or deficit.* In view of this fact it is clear that as liquidity preference becomes more elastic in both countries, the time interval of adjustment will become longer for the entire system. The situation is depicted in Figs. 10a and b for countries A and U respectively.

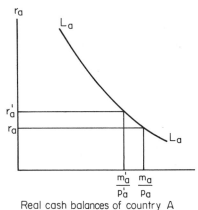

Real cash balances of country A

Figure 10a

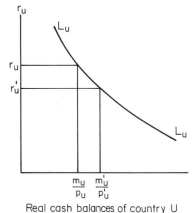

Real cash balances of country U

Figure 10b

When we were considering the relations between the monetary rate and the natural rate in an isolated state, we started with the supposition that the banking system stabilized the nominal quantity of money; in this system, fluctuations in the real value of cash balances resulted from movements in the level of prices. In an open economy, however, there are two influences which alter the real value of cash balances. In country A for example, the deficit reduces the nominal quantity of money, and the reduction in nominal balances must continue as long as the deficit exists. At the same time, the fall in prices induced by a rise of interest rates increases the real value of the lower nominal balances. If the real value of cash balances is to be reduced in A, in order to adapt the monetary rate to the higher natural rate, it is obvious that the deficit effect on nominal balances must overshadow the price effect on real balances. Conversely, in country U, the surplus in that country's balance of payments increases the nominal quantity of money, while the inflation arising from the fall of interest rates reduces the real value of this increased stock of money. And again, if the real value of cash balances is to rise, as it must to adjust the demand for real cash balances to the lower interest rate, the rise in nominal balances attributable to the surplus must be relatively larger than the fall in real value attributable to the inflation.

Referring again to Fig. 10b, we see that the absolute rate of interest in country U at the original position of equilibrium is r_u. The price level is p_u, determined by income-earners' tastes and the size of the equilibrium balance of trade. The quantity of money which makes the monetary rate equal to the prevailing rate is thus m_u, and the real value of cash balances is m_u/p_u. In the new position, after the increase of capital outflow has reduced the prevailing rate of interest to r_u', the real value of cash balances has increased to m_u'/p_u'. Thus the money inflow exceeds the rise of prices. In country A, on the other hand (see Fig. 10a), the real value of cash balances falls from m_a/p_a to m_a'/p_a'. And again this means that the reduction of nominal balances is greater than the reduction of prices.

At first glance one might suppose that the system, including the demand for money, is overdetermined. For p_u' and p_a' are governed by the condition that an equilibrium balance of payments be achieved. If the banking system is one in which no money is created except through deficits and surpluses in the balance of payments, the total quantity of money is restricted to the condition that $m_a' + m_u' = M$, where M represents the total quantity of nominal balances in the two-economy system. Thus it might seem that since m_a' and m_u' are restricted by bank policies, while p_a' and p_u' are governed by conditions of equilibrium in the balance of payments, it might be impossible to find an m_a'/p_a' for A and an m_u'/p_u' for U such that the monetary rate. of interest would be in line with the natural rate for both countries.

In reality, however, the possibility of having an overdetermined system does not arise. The prices p_a' and p_u' are not absolute prices but relative prices. And the absolute level at which each price settles will be determined by the size of M in the equation $m_a' + m_u' = M$. Nevertheless, an interesting question arises when the elasticity of liquidity preference differs between the two countries. In view of the fact that the position of equilibrium ultimately depends upon relative prices, or the terms of trade, rather than absolute prices, the question naturally arises as to whether most of the adjustment will take place in one country or the other.

One can demonstrate that, other things being equal, most of the price adjustment will fall upon the country which has the smaller elasticity of demand for real cash balances. Consider again, for example, the situation where the disturbance is an increase in capital outflows. And suppose, as in Fig. 10, that the natural rate of interest rises from r_a to r_a' in country A and falls from r_u to r_u' in country U. Suppose further that the demand for real cash balances is less elastic in U than in A. This situation is presented in Fig. 11.

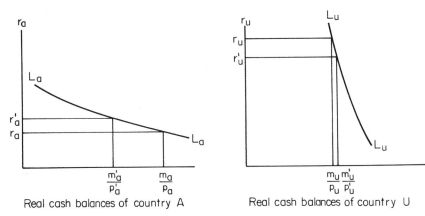

Real cash balances of country A Real cash balances of country U

Figure 11a   Figure 11b

As a result of the capital outflow from A to U, the prevailing rate of interest rises in A and falls in U. In A the rise is from r_a to r_a' in Fig. 11a; in U the fall is from r_u to r_u' in Fig. 11b. Because U's demand for real cash balances has a small elasticity with respect to the interest rate, a relatively small increase in cash balances is sufficient to align the monetary rate with the prevailing rate. In Fig. 11b the increase is from m_u/p_u to m_u'/p_u'. This means that the rise in nominal cash balances attributable to the surplus is only slightly larger than the rise in the price level attributable to the interest rate. On the other hand, in Fig. 11a the elasticity of A's liquidity preference schedule is high, and the reduction in real cash balances required to equalize the monetary rate with the prevailing higher rate r_a' is therefore significant.

Now the total decline in the nominal stock of money in A $(m_a - m_a')$ is exactly the same as the total rise in the nominal stock in U $(m_u - m_u')$. Since the change in real balances in U $(m_u'/p_u' - m_u/p_u)$ is considerably smaller than the decline in A's real balances $(m_a/p_a - m_a'/p_a')$, a presumption exists that the change in relative prices required to improve

A's balance of trade will consist largely in a rise in prices in U and a comparatively small decrease of prices in A. The degree of inertia of the adjustment process may thus be unevenly divided between the two countries because of differences in their elasticity of demand for liquidity. The fact that A has a relatively elastic demand for real cash balances enables her to put most of the adjustment process on the shoulders of U.

The time has come for a summation of the results of this paper. In a few words, what is the significance of introducing liquidity preference to the process of international adjustment? I believe that I have demonstrated a number of things. In the first place, when a final balance has been achieved, the real variables of the system—terms of trade, interest rates, and the like—are unaffected by the demand for money. It remains true that a country which has a deficit in its balance of payments will eliminate this deficit partly by a rise of interest rates, relative to interest rates in the rest of the world, which will lead to a capital backflow, and partly by an outflow of money, which will lead to a deflation at home, inflation abroad, and an improvement in the country's balance of trade. But all this is common knowledge, at least since Keynes's *Treatise on Money.* What changes have been made then by introducing liquidity preference?

In the first place, I have shown that a degree of inertia is added to the equilibrating process. A larger flow of money is required to achieve a new balance; moreover, the more elastic the liquidity preference, the higher the degree of inertia. And if we consider differences in elasticity of demand for real balances, the country with the larger elasticity is able to force a larger part of the necessary price movement onto the country with a relatively small elasticity of demand for money. The way in which relative prices are transformed into absolute prices thus depends in an important way upon the nature of the demand for money.

With respect to the real variables, I have shown that whether most of a deficit is eliminated through prices and the balance of trade or whether it is eliminated through interest rates and the balance of capital movements does not depend upon the external conditions of the demand for imports but upon the internal conditions of saving and investment. At this point the reader may ask why it has been possible to go so far without introducing the demand for imports at all. In answer to this question I would say that the elasticity of demand does not determine the degree to which the balance of trade expands to meet a given deficit; this depends, rather, upon internal conditions such as the slopes of the saving and investment schedules, relative to the slope of the capital outflow formation. The elasticities of demand for imports govern merely the changes in terms of trade needed to get the balance of trade required for equilibrium. In general, it can be said that as the elasticities of demand become smaller, the changes in relative prices needed to get a given balance of trade will be larger. Since the terms of trade were implicit throughout most of the paper, it was not necessary to introduce the demand for imports explicitly.

Nevertheless, with regard to these terms of trade the paper is by no means complete. A change in the terms of trade, for example, can alter the real value of a given capital outflow to the borrowing country without altering its value to the lending country. Likewise, a change in the terms of trade can alter the real value of cash balances without changing domestic prices. I cannot say with certainty how much the general conclusions would be modified if some of these terms-of-trade effects were taken into account, but I suspect the changes would not be of great importance. In any event, a few constructive criticisms along these lines should go far toward deciding whether Keynes's ideas have made a substantial contribution to the concept of monetary adjustment.

9 | Graham's Theory of International Values

The same rule which regulates the relative value of commodities in one country does not regulate the relative value of the commodities exchanged between two or more countries.

With this sentence, written in the chapter on foreign trade in his *Principles of Political Economy and Taxation*,[1] Ricardo introduced a doctrine which served for more than a century to distinguish the theory of prices in international trade from the theory of prices within a single country. According to the Ricardian view, which later became the accepted view among the great majority of English economists, relative prices within a single country are determined largely by costs of production. Capital and labor being mobile, there is a tendency for the returns to the factors of production to be the same in all segments of the economy; this means that when the demand for various commodities is altered, the supply of each product is adjusted to the state of demand, with only moderate changes in relative prices. In short, cost of production governs relative prices, while demand governs the allocation of labor and capital in the production of different commodities.

With respect to trade between countries, Ricardo argued that his simple cost-of-production theory of relative prices was not applicable.

Reprinted from *American Economic Review*, 40 (June 1950), 301–322. Copyright American Economic Association, 1950.

---

1. David Ricardo, *Principles of Political Economy and Taxation*, Everyman's Library ed. (London, Dent, 1911), p. 81.

Since labor and capital do not move freely from one country to another, there is no *necessary* tendency for the profits on capital to be the same in all countries. In other words, substantial differences can exist between wages and profits in one country and wages and profits elsewhere without bringing about a migration of labor and capital between countries. For this reason it is not meaningful, according to Ricardo, to say that relative prices in *international* trade are governed, as in domestic trade, by relative costs of production.[2]

Although Ricardo was aware that a cost-of-production theory was inadequate to explain prices in international trade, he was always somewhat vague as to how international prices or the terms of trade are actually determined.[3] It was John Stuart Mill who first saw that the pattern of international prices is governed, through the price-specie flow mechanism, by the intensities of demand in each country for the goods of other countries.[4] And it was Mill who explained how an increase in demand for foreign goods in one country tends to increase the prices of the goods which that country buys from abroad, relative to the prices of the country's exports. The introduction of demand schedules into the theory of international trade and the explanation of relative prices in terms of these demand schedules is generally regarded as one of Mill's most substantial contributions to economics. By showing that *international* values depend upon demand conditions, while *domestic* values depend upon costs, Mill supported Ricardo's thesis concerning the difference between the theory of international trade and the theory of trade within a single country.

The ideas originally developed by Mill were later considerably refined and presented in geometric form by Marshall,[5] but the basic principles of the so-called classical theory of international trade are all to be found in Mill's earlier work. Starting with a simple case of trade in two commodities between two countries, Mill demonstrated how the relative prices of the two commodities are governed by each country's demand—or "reciprocal demand" as he called it—for the export product of the other country. Many of the most important propositions in

2. *Ibid.*, pp. 82–83.
3. In his chapter on foreign trade, for example, he simply assumed an arbitrary division of the gains from trade without indicating how this division came about. *Ibid.*, p. 82.
4. John Stuart Mill, *Essays on Some Unsettled Questions of Political Economy* (London, J. W. Parker, 1844), written in 1829 and 1830, but not published until 1844, essay I.
5. Alfred Marshall, *The Pure Theory of Foreign Trade*, printed for private circulation in 1879. The substance of this paper was later published, with minor changes, as appendix J to his *Money, Credit, and Commerce* (London, Macmillan, 1923).

the theory of international values were proved by employing such demand schedules. Among these propositions, the following should perhaps be mentioned specifically, although others might also be mentioned. (a) The terms of trade between two commodities and two countries must necessarily lie between the relative costs of production in one country and the relative costs in the other, the final equilibrium being determined by intensities of demand in such a way that the country with the more intense demand for the export of the other enjoys a smaller part of the gains from trade. (b) As a corollary of (a), it follows that tariffs, by reducing a country's demand for imports, may bring about a favorable movement in the tariff-imposing country's terms of trade. (c) A duty on exports has substantially the same effects as a duty on imports, that is, it moves the terms of trade in favor of the country imposing the duty. (d) If each country's demand for imports is inelastic, an equilibrium of prices *may* be unstable in the sense that slight deviations from the equilibrium position will lead to even larger deviations.[6]

Although some of the preceding propositions were at times misunderstood, particularly by the advocates of free trade, the basic technique by which they were derived was a familiar and widely accepted technique throughout the second half of the nineteenth century. During the interwar years of the present century, however, the equations of reciprocal demand and many of the conclusions derived from them were seriously criticized by the late Professor Frank D. Graham. In two articles published almost a decade apart, Graham argued that the classical method of dealing with international problems as though international trade consisted in two countries trading in two commodities was an oversimplification which concealed the true nature of the balancing process and frequently led to incorrect conclusions concern-

---

6. Mill, who paid no attention to problems of market stability in his *Essays*, later became concerned (as a result of criticisms of his earlier work) about the possibility that his law of reciprocal demand might describe a state of neutral equilibrium; that is, he believed it possible "that several different rates of international value may all equally fulfill the conditions of this law" (*Principles of Political Economy* [New York, Appleton, 1893], reprinted from the fifth London ed., p. 154). He argued incorrectly that such a neutral equilibrium would exist if each country had a unitary elasticity of demand for imports, or in his own words, if "any given increase of cheapness produces an exactly proportional increase of consumption" (*ibid.*, p. 155). In a long and involved argument introduced at the end of the chapter on international values in the third edition of this work, Mill attempted without success to solve the problem arising from neutral equilibrium. The correct conditions of market stability were first derived by Marshall in chap. 2 of his *Pure Theory of Foreign Trade*; and later, in *Money, Credit, and Commerce* (p. 355), Marshall pointed out the error in Mill's earlier treatment of the subject.

ing the terms of trade.[7] He argued in particular that if all commodities are produced at constant costs in terms of "units of productive power" and if trade is of the complex sort in which several countries are dealing in several commodities, the adjusting process in response to a shift of international demand is not essentially different from the Ricardian adjusting process within a single country. Graham thus rejected the classical view that the theory of international values differs in fundamental respects from the theory of domestic values.

Graham's critique of the classical theory and his proposal for an alternative theory constituted, in my opinion, a major contribution to international economics. But neither the critique nor the alternative theory has succeeded in the twenty-six years since they were first published in bringing about general rejection of classical doctrines. To a considerable extent economists have continued, as before, to analyze international problems by means of the classical, two-country, two-commodity equations of reciprocal demand. The differences between Graham's theory and the classical theory have remained unresolved. It is therefore most fortunate that Graham published shortly before his death a new book, *The Theory of International Values*,[8] in which his fundamental ideas are restated, elaborated, and applied to a number of practical problems. My purpose in this paper is to attempt an evaluation of Graham's theory as it appears both in the book and in his earlier articles.

To anticipate the discussion below, it is my opinion that Graham's theory, despite its importance in international economics, does not really call for such a complete rejection of the classical theory as its author at times seemed to suggest. What is required instead is a considerable modification of our way of interpreting the classical equations of reciprocal demand as well as a reconsideration of the probable or likely form of such equations. If this does not represent exactly a revolution in the theory of international trade, it is nevertheless a substantial innovation, and perhaps one of the most important innovations since the classical theory was first presented.

The basic principle of Graham's theory may be stated quite simply. In a complex situation in which a considerable number of countries

7. Frank D. Graham, "The Theory of International Values Re-examined," *Quarterly Journal of Economics*, 38 (November 1923), 54–86; and "The Theory of International Values," *Quarterly Journal of Economics*, 46 (August 1932), 581–616.

8. Frank D. Graham, *The Theory of International Values* (Princeton, N.J., Princeton University Press, 1948).

carry on international trade in a considerable number of commodities, some of the commodities are almost certain to be marginal commodities in some of the countries; marginal in this sense means that at existing prices and costs one or more countries is in a zone of indifference as to whether a given commodity shall be imported or produced at home and possibly exported. If such marginal commodities exist, disturbances in the world balance of international payments can usually be offset by appropriate adjustments of output and no significant changes in the terms of trade will occur. It follows that, if the network of trade is sufficiently complex, the process of adjustment to a disturbance in international trade does not differ significantly from the process of adjustment in domestic trade.

Graham argued, in other words, that the classical distinction between the theory of international values and the theory of domestic values was largely redundant. He believed that international prices are for the most part determined by cost of production, just as in domestic trade, and that conditions of demand play only a minor role. In the first of his two articles he gave numerical examples of trade in three commodities among four countries, and in his book he considered a more complex situation in which ten countries carry on trade in ten commodities. Since the process of adjustment is virtually the same in all of the examples, however, Graham's theory may be illustrated by relatively simple models. I shall therefore present only two models; in the first of these, two countries are assumed to be trading in three commodities, while in the second, three countries are trading in two commodities.

Let France and England be the trading countries in the first example, and suppose that these two countries are trading in cloth, wheat, and machinery. Following Graham's procedure, I assume that the three commodities are produced at constant cost in both countries. Although Graham spoke of "units of productive power" and described the cost conditions in terms of such units, his theory in this respect does not differ fundamentally from the labor theory of value. I shall therefore assume that the unit of productive power in each country is a unit of labor, and that the productivity of one unit of labor in each country, over a given period of time, is as follows:

Country	Wheat	Cloth	Machinery
England	1	2	4
France	1	1	1

Under the assumed conditions of productivity England will clearly be an exporter of machinery, since English comparative productivity is higher in that commodity than in any other commodity. And for a similar reason, France will export wheat. With respect to cloth, however, the situation is indeterminate. Cloth, being an intermediate commodity in the scale of comparative productivity, may move in either direction depending upon the level of wages and costs in the two countries. Conceivably the two price levels may be such that the cost of producing cloth will be exactly the same in both countries. Assume that this is actually the case. Suppose, for example, that the wage rate is £1 in France and £2 in England.[9] The world price of machinery will then be £0.5, its cost of production in England, while the world price of wheat will be £1, which is the cost of wheat production in France. The price of cloth, finally, will be £1, and this is exactly equal to its cost of production in both countries. Cloth is thus a marginal commodity which may be exported by either country, the outcome depending upon conditions of demand.

Suppose now that the residents of each country spend half of their incomes on wheat, the remaining income being divided equally between cloth and machinery. In order to know what the demand for the three commodities will be under these conditions, we must make some assumption as to the size of the two countries' labor forces. Let the labor force of England consist in 300 labor units and that of France consist in 800 labor units. With the given wage rates, the national incomes in the two countries, at full employment, will then be as follows: England, £600; France, £800. At this level of incomes, the total expenditures on wheat of the two countries together will be £700 (half of £1400), and since France clearly has a comparative advantage in wheat, the entire production must come from that country; this means that French exports of wheat will amount to £300. Production of machinery, on the other hand, must take place entirely in England, and the total demand for machinery will be £350, of which £200 represents exports to France. Looking at the French exports of wheat and imports of machinery, we see that, in order to balance its international accounts, France must import cloth to the extent of £100. At an income level of £800, the domestic demand for cloth in France will be £200, so that

<hr />

9. In both examples exchange rates are assumed to be constant; prices and costs in France have accordingly been expressed in pounds sterling at the given exchange rate between the franc and the pound.

France must use £100 of resources in the production of cloth in addition to importing cloth from England. The English demand for cloth will be £150, and England must accordingly produce £250 of cloth in order to satisfy both her domestic and her foreign demand.[10] All of these interrelations are summarized in Table 1.

Table 1. Trade in three commodities between two countries (in pounds sterling)

Country	Wheat	Machinery	Cloth	Total
England				
Production	—	350	250	600
Consumption	300	150	150	600
Exports	—	200	100	300
Imports	300	—	—	300
France				
Production	700	—	100	800
Consumption	400	200	200	800
Exports	300	—	—	300
Imports	—	200	100	300

I assume now that the balanced state of trade between France and England is disturbed by an increase in demand for imports in France, and a corresponding decline in demand for domestic goods in that country. More exactly, I assume that after the change in tastes has taken place, the French spend half of their income on machinery and one-fourth on each of the other two commodities. This leads initially to a deficit in the French balance of payments, and according to the classical theory the resultant flow of gold from France to England should lower prices in the former country and raise prices in the latter, thereby moving the terms of trade against France and ultimately restoring equilibrium in the balance of payments. As Graham emphasized, however, such a shift in the terms of trade can hardly occur as long as France and England are both producing the intermediate commodity, cloth. Any slight increase in English prices and costs relative to French prices and costs would enable France to undersell English cloth producers in both countries, thereby greatly expanding French exports

10. Throughout his numerical examples Graham employed units of physical product rather than units of value. Units of value have been used in my own examples in order to show the relative importance of each commodity in a country's total output. Since all prices remain constant, the choice of units is purely a matter of convenience.

and reducing French imports. If this were to occur, the French deficit might well be converted into a surplus, and the flow of gold reversed. Following this line of thought, Graham would have said that the French deficit could be eliminated simply by a shift of production in the two countries, with no permanent gold movement in either direction and with no change in relative prices between the two countries.

In order to see what sort of shifts in production will be required, we may adopt the same type of argument employed in developing Table 1. As before, France will continue to supply wheat to both countries. But the French demand for wheat is now £200 rather than £400, and French wheat production must accordingly fall from £700 to £500. The English demand for wheat remaining unchanged, French wheat exports will continue at the former level of £300. French imports of machinery, on the other hand, will rise from £200 to £400. International trade in wheat and machinery thus gives the French a deficit of £100, and in order to balance its accounts, France must export cloth in the amount of this deficit. In other words, France must shift from an import of cloth in the amount of £100 to an export in the same amount, which means that the £200 of resources freed from the production of wheat must be employed in producing cloth. In England, the production of machinery must rise from £350 to £550 in order to satisfy the new French demand. This means that English cloth production must be reduced from £250 to £50, and that the English will accordingly have a demand for the £100 of cloth which France must export in order to balance its accounts. When we take account of all of these changes, the new table of production and trade is as shown in Table 2.

Table 2. Effect of shift of one country's demand toward imported goods, between two countries (in pounds sterling)

Country	Wheat	Machinery	Cloth	Total
England				
Production	—	550	50	600
Consumption	300	150	150	600
Exports	—	400	—	400
Imports	300	—	100	400
France				
Production	500	—	300	800
Consumption	200	400	200	800
Exports	300	—	100	400
Imports	—	400	—	400

At this point it may be useful to compare the adjustments of supply indicated in Table 2 with the adjustments that would have occurred had there been no impediments to the movement of resources. The initial disturbance, it will be recalled, was a shift in demand from wheat to machinery in France, the amount of the shift being £200 at prevailing prices. Now if France and England had been a single economic system, the ultimate effect of such a shift in demand would have been a movement of resources in the amount of £200 from the wheat industry to the machinery industry. Since France produces no machinery, however, and since labor is not free to move from France to England, such a direct shift of resources is clearly impossible. Nevertheless, a comparison of Table 2 with Table 1 reveals that the *net* effect of the shifts in resources which take place in both countries is equivalent to a direct movement of resources from wheat production to machinery production. In France, wheat production is reduced by £200 while cloth production is increased by the same amount. In England, cloth production is reduced by £200 while machinery production is increased by this amount. Considering both countries together, the changes in cloth production thus cancel each other, leaving only a *net* shift of output from wheat to machinery. The intermediate product, cloth, acts as a sort of buffer and through this intermediate product a shift in resources which would otherwise have been impossible is accomplished. The increased demand for imports in France creates, so to speak, an automatic increase in demand for French exports, with no change at all required in the terms of trade between the two countries.

The validity of this conclusion obviously depends upon the existence of an intermediate product which can be produced at the same cost in both countries. With only three commodities being produced, it would be sheer accident if the cost of production were exactly the same in both countries for the intermediate commodity. Graham argued, however, that if there is a large number of commodities, one or more of these is almost certain to be a marginal or intermediate commodity; and if this is the case, a disturbance in the balance of payments may be rectified in the manner indicated above, without a movement in the terms of trade.

If the number of commodities entering into international trade is small, it is still conceivable that one or more of them may be an intermediate commodity; but this is likely to be true only if the number of countries participating is large and if relative costs of production of the various commodities differ among the countries. Perhaps it would be better to say, in such an event, that the adjustment takes place through an intermediate country rather than through an intermediate commodity. An intermediate country is one whose domestic cost ratios for at least two of the commodities are about the same as international price ratios; such a country would have no incentives to specialization as far as these particular commodities are concerned, and would accordingly be indifferent as to importing one or the other of them or producing them both at home. The role of the intermediate country in Graham's theory may be illustrated by a second numerical example. Suppose there are three countries, England, France, and Hungary, trading in two commodities, cloth and wheat, and let the productivity of a unit of labor in each country be as follows:

Country	Cloth	Wheat
England	2	1
France	1	1
Hungary	0.5	1

From the productivity figures it is obvious that France is the intermediate country. England has the greatest comparative advantage in cloth and will therefore specialize in that commodity, while Hungary for a similar reason will specialize in wheat. France, on the other hand, may specialize in either commodity or in neither, depending upon the terms of trade between the two commodities and upon the state of international demand. Suppose that the wage rate is £2 in England and £1 in both France and Hungary. England will then specialize in cloth, since her cost of producing wheat will exceed the cost of producing wheat in the other two countries. Hungary will be unable to produce cloth on a competitive basis and will therefore specialize in wheat, while France, the intermediate country, will be able to produce either commodity at the same cost that it is exported from one of the other countries. The price of each commodity will of course be £1.

Suppose that the labor supply is 300 in England, 800 in France, and 400 in Hungary. At the prevailing wage rates, national incomes of the three countries will be as follows: England £600; France £800; Hungary £400.

We may assume now that each country spends half of its income on each commodity. Total money expenditures of all countries on cloth will then be £900. But since the English capacity, even under complete specialization, is only £600, cloth production of £300 will have to be undertaken in France. The world demand for wheat will likewise be £900; of this amount, £400 can be supplied by Hungary, leaving £500 of wheat to be produced by France. Production, consumption, and trade of the three countries will then be as shown in Table 3.

Table 3. Trade in three commodities among three countries (in pounds sterling)

Country	Wheat	Cloth	Total
England			
Production	—	600	600
Consumption	300	300	600
Exports	—	300	300
Imports	300	—	300
France			
Production	500	300	800
Consumption	400	400	800
Exports	100	—	100
Imports	—	100	100
Hungary			
Production	400	—	400
Consumption	200	200	400
Exports	200	—	200
Imports	—	200	200

With the given state of demand the intermediate country, France, thus imports a small amount of cloth and exports a small amount of wheat while producing both commodities for itself.

Suppose now that the English demand for wheat increases so much that the residents of England spend three-fourths of their incomes on that imported commodity. In other words, at the full-employment level of income, the English demand for imports rises from £300 to £450. Initially this increase in demand for imports leads to a deficit in the English balance of payments; and according to the classical theory the resultant outflow of gold from England to the other two countries should lower prices and costs in the deficit country while raising prices and costs in France and Hungary. In this manner the British deficit should be gradually eliminated through an adverse movement in the English terms of trade.

It is easily seen, however, that as long as France is producing both wheat and cloth at constant cost no such change in the terms of trade is possible. As soon as wheat rises in price in world markets, relative to the price of cloth, it immediately becomes profitable for France to shift resources from cloth to wheat. This increases the French demand for imported cloth and at the same time counteracts the initial movement of world prices. In other words, the increase in English demand for wheat is matched by an equivalent increase in the French supply of wheat and in the French demand for English cloth. The shift in supply from cloth to wheat in France means that any price changes which occur can be only temporary and that, as a consequence, the gold movements from England to the other two countries must eventually be returned. The new world demand for wheat, including the increased English demand, is £1050, and since Hungary can supply only £400 of this, the French output of wheat in the new equilibrium must be £650. Similarly, the world demand for cloth in the new position is £750, of which £600 will be supplied by England; the remaining £150 of cloth will, of course, be produced in France. A new equilibrium between world supply and world demand is thus established through shifts in French output without any permanent movements in prices and costs. The new equilibrium is shown in detail in Table 4.

Comparing Table 4 with Table 3, we see that the world supply of wheat at prevailing prices has increased from £900 to £1050, while the world supply of cloth has declined from £900 to £750. Considering the world economy as a unit, the adjustment to the new conditions of demand is thus seen to conform completely to the Ricardian theory of value within a single country, that is, supply has been determined by conditions of demand, while prices have been determined by the unchanged cost ratios. Our second numerical example, like the first, thus supports Graham's argument that the classical distinction between international-value theory and domestic-value theory is redundant. Once again the world supply has adjusted itself to a new world demand, despite the fact that resources cannot be moved from one country to another.

The difference between the two examples is that in the second example the adjustment of supply takes place entirely in the intermediate country, whereas in the first example the adjustment occurs in two

Table 4. Effect of shift of one country's demand toward imported goods, among three countries (in pounds sterling)

Country	Wheat	Cloth	Total
England			
Production	—	600	600
Consumption	450	150	600
Exports	—	450	450
Imports	450	—	450
France			
Production	650	150	800
Consumption	400	400	800
Exports	250	—	250
Imports	—	250	250
Hungary			
Production	400	—	400
Consumption	200	200	400
Exports	200	—	200
Imports	—	200	200

countries and is made possible through the presence of an intermediate commodity. In more complex situations in which there are a large number of both commodities and countries, the adjustment of supply may occur either through an intermediate commodity or through an intermediate country. But regardless of the particular adjustment, if either type of adjustment is possible a new equilibrium can be established, as Graham demonstrated, without a significant movement of the international price ratios.

Whether an adjustment of supply will be possible without a substantial change in international terms of trade obviously depends upon the existence of intermediate commodities or intermediate countries and upon the productive capacity with respect to such commodities or countries. In this regard Graham's method of presentation is somewhat lacking in generality; he demonstrated his thesis entirely by means of numerical examples, similar to the examples given above, and did not attempt to show that his conclusions are valid for all such examples. It is my own belief, however, that this lack of generality does not seriously impair the validity of Graham's case. He argued that intermediate commodities and intermediate countries are more likely to be present the more complex the network of trade.

To illustrate this point, he presented an example in which ten countries were trading in ten different commodities, and showed that in such a complex situation large shifts in world demand would exert a relatively small influence upon the international price ratios. Starting from an equilibrium position in which each country spent one-tenth of its income on each of the ten commodities, he assumed that the world demand changed in such a way that the demand for five of the commodities increased by 50 percent while the demand for the other five declined by the same percentage. He then demonstrated that, if constant costs prevailed, a new equilibrium would be established in which two of the commodities increased in price, relative to the others, by only 5 percent, while all other commodity price ratios remained unchanged.[11] He demonstrated also that other equally large shifts of international demand would have similarly small effects upon international price ratios. From such examples he concluded that "once a trade between many countries in many commodities has been established . . . the existing norm in the ratio of exchange is unlikely to be altered much, if at all, by any change in demand that would ordinarily occur."[12]

In evaluating Graham's theory, it is perhaps best to begin by asking how it is related to traditional economics. Do Graham's arguments really represent, as their author asserted in his book, a "complete refutation of classical doctrine," or is it better to say, as Graham said in the first of his earlier articles on the subject, that "the classical theory of international values seems . . . to be open to grave objections, objections which, while they do not subvert its foundations, nevertheless call for substantial modification of its conclusions"? In short, must the classical theory be replaced by a completely different theory, or is it capable of being modified to allow for Graham's major criticisms?

It is my opinion, as I have indicated earlier, that Graham's theory, when it is examined in the perspective of history, will be regarded as a modification, albeit an important modification, rather than a complete refutation of the classical doctrines. In other words, I believe that for the most part the classical theory can be reinterpreted so as to include

11. Graham, *Theory of International Values* (reference 8), chap. 7.
12. *Ibid.*, p. 135. At another point (pp. 112–113) he said, "the more complex the trade the greater will be the permutations in the number of producers on the margin of indifference between differing pairs, triads, or larger aggregations of products, and, once the general lines of trade have been established, the less likely, therefore, is any ordinary shift in demand to alter the normal ratio of exchange."

the process of adjustment envisaged in *The Theory of International Values*. This seems to me to be true for two reasons. First, the classical theory as it was expounded by Marshall already contained a considerable number of the elements of the process of adjustment which Graham later presented so lucidly. Second, and equally important, some of the contributions to the theory of international trade which were made by Graham's contemporaries were quite similar in substance to Graham's own contributions, even though in form they appeared to be different. For both of these reasons I believe that a synthesis of Graham's ideas and the classical doctrines will ultimately be possible.

There is no need to dwell at length on the elements of Graham's theory which were already contained in the classical doctrines. Viner has shown that, although the classical economists presented the rigorous part of their theory in terms of two countries trading in two commodities, they were by no means unaware of the modifications required for a more realistic theory involving many countries and many commodities.[13] And if they did not succeed as Graham did in developing a rigorous theory of complex trade, they were at any rate clear in a general way as to how an increase in the number of countries or commodities would affect their conclusions.

In comparing *The Theory of International Values* with the classical theory, the question naturally arises as to whether any of the complications introduced by Graham can be incorporated in the classical reciprocal demand schedules. Professor G. A. Elliott, in a most stimulating article, has given a partial answer to this question.[14] He has shown, in particular, that reciprocal demand schedules can be constructed for the two-country case even when the number of commodities in each country is large, provided that all commodities are produced under constant cost

13. Jacob Viner, *Studies in the Theory of International Trade* (New York, Harper and Bros., 1937), pp. 535–555. In this connection it is interesting to note that Ricardo, whose work antedated the theory of reciprocal demand, was aware that the presence of a large number of commodities in international trade would tend to stabilize the relative price levels of different countries. Thus, after discussing the effects of an innovation in one of two trading countries on gold movements and price levels, he said in the *Principles* (reference 1), p. 87: "To simplify the question, I have been supposing the trade between two countries to be confined to two commodities—to wine and cloth; but it is well known that many and various articles enter into the lists of exports and imports. By the abstraction of money from one country, and the accumulation of it in another, all commodities are affected in price, and consequently encouragement is given to the exportation of many more commodities besides money, which will therefore prevent so great an effect from taking place on the value of money in the two countries as might otherwise be expected."

14. G. A. Elliott, "The Theory of International Values," *Journal of Political Economy*, 58 (February 1950), 16–29.

conditions. More than this, Elliott has also shown that his technique for deriving a single demand schedule for all commodities is essentially the same as the technique proposed by Marshall.

It was for this purpose, in fact, that Marshall presented the concept of a representative bale. The term "representative bale" as used in this connection is unfortunate; it does not denote, as the name suggests and as Graham supposed, a sort of "typical" assortment of exports or imports.[15] Instead, it denotes simply the units of productive power embodied in each country's exports.[16] When this concept is employed in constructing reciprocal demand schedules, the "terms of trade" between the two countries are not measured by indexes of commodity prices but by the rate at which the units of productive power of one country exchange for those of the other country. If the output of various commodities is subject to increasing or decreasing returns, or if the proportions in which the factors of production are employed are variable, it is of course impossible to speak of homogeneous units of productive power embodied in exports and imports. But these complications were not present in the classical theory of international trade, which was based largely on a constant-labor-cost theory of value; nor are they present in Graham's theory, which is based on constant units of productive power.

In other words, if the average cost ratios among the various commodities are always the same regardless of how a country's resources are employed, it is possible to consider each commodity as the equivalent of a certain number of units of homogeneous productive power, and a reciprocal demand schedule can then be derived for many commodities, in the manner proposed by Marshall and Elliott, in terms of these homogeneous units. Such a demand schedule will have a "kink" at any point at which a country ceases to produce a given commodity and begins to import its entire supply of that commodity from abroad, and at any point at which the country begins to import something which it formerly produced entirely for itself. Some segments of the demand schedule, corresponding to terms of trade at which a country is both an importer and a domestic producer of a given commodity, will be infinitely elastic, while other segments will have a much lower elasticity. As Elliott shows, however, an increase in the number of commodities reduces the length of the alternating elastic and inelastic segments until

15. *Ibid.*, p. 5.
16. Marshall, *Money, Credit, and Commerce* (reference 5), p. 324.

the reciprocal demand schedule finally begins to look much like the classical, smooth curve.[17] A schedule derived in this manner is of course much more elastic than it would be if it were dependent upon demand conditions alone; but, on the other hand, it is less than infinitely elastic and accordingly leaves room for movements in the terms of trade as envisaged in the classical theory.

It thus seems apparent that, for the case of two countries trading in many commodities, Graham's theory and the classical theory have much in common. Whether this is also true for more complex cases in which the number of countries as well as the number of commodities is large seems to me doubtful. I suspect, in other words, that the reciprocal demand technique breaks down when the number of countries exceeds two. If so, Graham's theory still represents a substantial departure from the classical doctrines. In any event, what is important is not the particular technique employed, but the conclusions to which it leads; and in this regard Graham's contribution is his repeated emphasis on the fact that the process of adjustment is as much dependent upon conditions of supply as upon conditions of demand. If his emphasis on the conditions of supply seems at times to be too great, it constitutes at any rate a healthy antidote to the tendency so apparent in recent years to discuss many international problems entirely in terms of elasticities of demand.

Graham was by no means alone among his contemporaries in stressing the influence of supply conditions on the international terms of trade. During the interwar period there were at least two other lines of development in the theory of international trade, and while both of these were more heavily indebted to the classical doctrines than was Graham's theory, they both attached considerable importance to supply conditions as factors influencing the terms of trade. The first of these alternative lines of development was a partial-equilibrium approach which considered only one commodity at a time and was used primarily in discussing the incidence of particular tariffs. Although it appeared in several places, the partial-equilibrium approach was perhaps best explained by Haberler.[18] This approach expressed the demand for imports of a given commodity in a given country as a derived demand, in monetary terms. The demand at a given price was described as the difference between the total amount demanded at that

17. Elliott, "International Values" (reference 14), p. 25.
18. Gottfried Haberler, *The Theory of International Trade* (London, William Hodge, 1936), chap. 15.

price and the amount domestically produced. And from this it was apparent that the elasticity of *demand for imports* of a given commodity is normally greater than the elasticity of *total demand* for that commodity, since import elasticity is dependent upon the elasticity of domestic supply as well as upon conditions of demand.

The second line of development during the interwar years was more intimately related to the classical theory. It was largely the work of Lerner,[19] Haberler,[20] and Leontief,[21] and its central feature was the so-called "product-substitution curve." The product-substitution curve depicted the alternative combinations of two commodities, *A* and *B*, which could be produced within a given country with a given amount of resources. It was usually constructed on the assumption that *A* could be substituted for *B* only at increasing cost in terms of resources. This approach thus led to the conclusion that comparative advantage is a *relative* matter—relative, that is, to the pattern of production—and that complete specialization is unlikely even with perfect competition. Like Graham's theory, the product-substitution approach envisaged a situation in which a country is both an importer and a producer of a given commodity. And like Graham, the alternative theory emphasized that the elasticity of demand for imports is dependent upon the elasticity of substitution on the side of production as well as upon the overall elasticity of demand. Unlike the Graham theory, however, the product-substitution approach did not assume that the elasticity of substitution between products is infinite, and accordingly left room for greater movements in the terms of trade than those envisaged by Graham. In this respect it is more general than Graham's theory. In its practical application, however, the product-substitution approach has thus far been limited largely to the case of two commodities and two countries, and in this respect it is less general than Graham's approach.

In the briefest possible manner, I have attempted to show why I do not regard Graham's theory as a complete break with the traditional theory of international trade. His theory, rather, is one of several strands of thought, all emanating in one way or another from the classical theory, and all emphasizing to a greater extent than did Mill and Marshall the role of supply conditions in governing the terms of

19. Abba P. Lerner, "The Diagrammatical Representation of Cost Conditions in International Trade," *Economica*, 12 (August 1932), 346–356.

20. Haberler *International Trade* (reference 18), chap. 12.

21. W. W. Leontief, "The Use of Indifference Curves in the Analysis of Foreign Trade," *Quarterly Journal of Economics*, 47 (May 1933), 493–503.

international interchange. Graham no doubt stressed the rigidity of the terms of trade more than some of his contemporaries, but the difference in this respect was one of degree and not of principle. For this reason we may look forward, I hope, to a gradual fusing of Graham's doctrines with the traditional theory of international trade.

When he came to practical application of his basic ideas, Graham was on much more controversial ground. It is to these practical problems that I now turn.

Almost all of the proposals Graham made with respect to economic policy were derived from his fundamental concept that, in a complex trading situation, discrepancies between supply and demand for the products of any country can be eliminated by appropriate shifts in output without any substantial changes in the terms of trade. Consider, as a first example, his views concerning tariffs. The classical economists who inherited Mill's ideas believed that the *national* interests of any one country in international trade are to some extent opposed to the interests of other countries. Basing their case on the theory of reciprocal demand, these economists argued that a given country, by means of tariffs, can alter the term of trade in its own favor, thereby gaining an advantage at the expense of the rest of the world. Since such an opportunity for manipulating the terms of trade is presumably open to each country individually, it follows from the classical theory that free trade will not be the natural outcome, as some free-traders have supposed, of each country following its own self-interests. The classical theory suggests, to the contrary, that an unfettered and uncoordinated pursuit of national self-interests is more likely to culminate in a tariff war and in a process of international negotiation which has much in common with the market situation in oligopoly or bilateral monopoly.

With this classical theory of tariffs, Graham largely disagreed. Although he recognized that the countries producing certain primary products may be in a vulnerable position and may not be able to protect themselves against adverse movements in their terms of trade, he held the view that the opportunities for such deliberate manipulation of the terms of trade are extremely limited if not nonexistent. "In the world as it is," he said, "with many countries producing commodities in common, and with most or all commodities *somewhere* on the margin of producers' indifference as regards various other commodities, the chance of shifting the normal international ratio of exchange through the imposition of protective duties is always small."[22] If this is correct, it follows that tariffs or other trade restrictions can seldom be used as a rational means of promoting the interests of a country as a whole; rather, they will normally appear in their more familiar role of protecting one segment of a country's economy at the expense of other segments of the same economy.

Most economists will probably agree to a very considerable extent with Graham's arguments concerning tariffs. In the light of Graham's theory, it seems probable that the classical schedules of reciprocal demand *did* exaggerate somewhat the possibilities of manipulating the terms of trade by means of tariffs. Nevertheless, it is my own opinion that Graham did not attach sufficient importance to the possible magnitude of movements in the terms of trade between industrial countries and producers of primary products. He recognized, as noted above, that the countries which specialize in primary products do not have many alternative lines of production and are therefore vulnerable to trade obstructions imposed by the industrial countries. But is it not also true, to some extent at least, that the industrialized countries are vulnerable to tariffs imposed by the primary producers? There are many agricultural products and raw materials—coffee and other products of tropical regions are examples—for which there are few if any alternative sources of supply outside of the undeveloped countries which specialize in these products. Moreover, the demand of the industrial countries for such products is likely to be inelastic, and this means that tariffs imposed by the undeveloped countries will effect a noticeable improvement in the tariff-imposing countries' terms of trade.

Thus for certain problems of trade between industrial and nonindustrial countries the classical reciprocal demand schedules are useful tools; and the possibilities of large and sustained movements in the terms of trade between primary products and manufactures are greater, I believe, than Graham's theory would suggest. The network of world trade, although complex, is not yet sufficiently complex, in my judgment, to stabilize the price ratios between manufactured goods and primary products. Even with this reservation, it remains true that Graham's theory, by emphasizing a feature of the adjustment process which was not given sufficient attention in the classical theory, makes an important contribution to the analysis of trade barriers.

22. Graham, *Theory of International Values* (reference 8), p. 178.

Far more controversial than his views on tariffs are Graham's views and proposals concerning foreign-exchange markets, and particularly his views with respect to exchange rates. Since he believed that disturbances in the balance of international payments could be rectified without significant changes in relative prices, Graham paid virtually no attention to the possibilities of unstable exchange rates which might arise if the demand for various commodities were inelastic. At one point, for example, he said, "Whatever the evils that may arise from any adverse combination of elasticities of demand or supply, . . . they cannot be held accountable for a persistent lack of balance in the international accounts."[23] And at another point he characterized as "solemn nonsense" the view that depreciation of a country's currency may not improve that country's balance of payments.[24] In general, he was of the opinion that a deficit in a country's balance of payments is a purely monetary affair—in other words, it is an indication that the country's prices and money incomes are too high, relative to prices and incomes elsewhere.

In Graham's view, then, the appropriate remedy for a deficit is either a monetary contraction or a devaluation of the currency. Basing his arguments on his theory of international prices, he asserted that neither of these remedies for a deficit would have a significant effect upon a country's terms of trade, but would simply alter the ratio of international prices, *including both export and import prices*, to domestic prices. In the same vein, he insisted that the current dollar shortage is purely a matter of overvaluation of the deficit countries' currencies.[25]

Whether one agrees or disagrees with these conclusions with respect to foreign-exchange markets depends almost entirely, in my opinion, upon the length of time envisaged for the process of international adjustment. If interpreted as statements of long-run tendencies, most of Graham's conclusions would probably be accepted by virtually all

---

23. *Ibid.*, p. 303.
24. *Ibid.*, p. 297.
25. Thus, on p. 295 he said: "There is a perennial shortage of any valuable thing in the sense that not everyone can get all he wants of it on terms satisfactory to him. But in a free market there is, on the other hand, *never* a shortage of anything in the sense that the amount offered, at the price obtainable in such a market, falls short of the amount demanded at that price. It is, in fact, the function of (upward) price movements to eliminate any such shortage. The shortage of dollars, in the market sense, is explicable on precisely the same grounds as the shortage of any other economic good the price of which is kept below what a free market would establish. We should never forget that exchange rates are prices."

economists. If interpreted as arguments for free exchange rates as an immediate remedy for all balance-of-payments disturbances, on the other hand, the conclusions are highly questionable. For Graham's theory of international adjustment is entirely a long-run theory of adjustment, whereas most of the balance-of-payments problems, including the disturbances of the interwar period as well as the current dollar shortage, are essentially short-run problems. Any differences which may arise between Graham's policy recommendations and those of other economists are thus likely to center about the difficult question of what constitutes a "long run" or a "short run" for the purpose of international economics.

The long-run character of Graham's theory is apparent from even a casual examination of his numerical examples. In all of these examples, an extremely high degree of mobility of resources within a given country is always postulated. In some of the examples, for instance, a three-fold or four-fold increase in the output of particular industries and a corresponding reduction in the output of other industries may be required, within a given country, to restore international equilibrium. In other examples, a country's output of a particular commodity may be completely eliminated and an entirely new industry established to take the place of the eliminated product. It is true, of course, that Graham's examples are extreme cases, inasmuch as the shifts in international demand which he postulates are exceedingly large. Even after we make due allowance for this fact, however, it remains true that Graham's theory assumes a high degree of mobility of resources within each country. And it is perhaps unnecessary to say that a movement of capital and labor from one industry to another frequently requires a protracted period of time. Indeed, adjustments of this sort sometimes continue over several generations.

Graham was well aware that his theory is a long-run theory. He emphasized throughout his book that he was dealing with "normal" values and not with "market" values. Moreover, he explicitly recognized at several points in his argument that demand conditions play an important part in determining the terms of trade whenever factors of production are not completely mobile between one industry and another. The second of his two journal articles contains a statement on these problems which seems to me to be worth quoting at considerable length.

So far as short-run effects are concerned, . . . the neoclassical analysis is of great value. . . . In periods too short to permit of shifting of resources through the gradual process of decay of existing fixed capital and the growth of new forms thereof, in a word, too short to permit of a change in long-run conditions of supply, the character of demand schedules is, indeed, of predominating import. Where inelastic demand (or inelastic supply) schedules are involved, moreover, short-run changes in the terms of trade may be very violent. . . . Short-run phenomena, moreover, are sometimes affected but slowly by the forces making for long-run equilibrium. At the present time [1932], for instance, any transition toward the long-run equilibrium position appropriate to such disturbances as may have occurred in the years just prior to the outbreak of the depression is hindered by the prevailing uncertainty and by the fact that *all* goods now seem difficult of sale. In such circumstances "short-time" phenomena may dominate the situation for a rather lengthy period.[26]

If this careful and explicit distinction between long-run and short-run adjustments in international trade had been carried over into all parts of Graham's book, I should probably have had few, if any, occasions to disagree with the author's policy recommendations. But one has the feeling that in discussing such problems as exchange rates and dollar shortages Graham tended to lose sight of the essential difference, which he elsewhere indicated, between the short run and the long run. How else can his strong statements concerning the effectiveness of exchange-rate adjustments be explained? In other words, in his policy recommendations, Graham did not succeed in bridging the gap between a long-run theory and a short-run problem.

It would be most unfortunate if the confusion between the long run and the short run which characterizes the discussion of economic policy in *The Theory of International Values* should discredit the important contributions Graham has made to the pure theory of international trade. For, as a long-run theory of adjustment, Graham's doctrine emphasizes a point which, in the present world of exchange controls and other governmental controls, is in constant danger of being overlooked. In particular, Graham's theory of adjustment shows that, *with a reasonable degree of flexibility of prices and exchange rates*, there would be a strong underlying tendency toward international equilibrium. To put the matter another way, the international economic system has a high degree of long-run stability. If the factors of production are sufficiently mobile within each country, a state of international balance can ulti-

26. Graham, "Theory of International Values" (reference 7), p. 615.

mately be achieved without serious adverse movements in the terms of trade of the deficit countries.

Such long-run stability, however, is by no means inconsistent with substantial short-run fluctuations in the terms of trade; and it is the possibility of these short-run movements, aggravated by inelastic demand for imports in many countries, which makes some of our present problems so difficult to solve. Long-run stability, in other words, does not guarantee, as Graham's book frequently seems to imply, that a system of free-market exchange rates would be an effective and efficient system under present conditions. *Reasonable flexibility* of exchange rates is not synonymous with *freely fluctuating* rates, and the former may be desirable while the latter are not. There is considerable evidence, to be sure, that in attempting to alleviate their short-run problems many countries have adopted policies which stand in the way of the long-run adjustments envisaged by Graham. But what is required in this event is not a widespread adoption of long-run solutions and a complete neglect of the exigencies of the moment, but a reasonable compromise between long-term and short-term measures. The great merit of Graham's book is not that it presents a solution of both types of problem, but that it shows clearly the direction in which the long-term solutions are to be sought.

10 | Underemployment Equilibrium in International Trade

The current interest in variations of investment and consumption, while affecting almost all branches of economic analysis, has wrought more far-reaching changes in the theory of closed economies than in the analysis of international equilibrium. Discussions of trade between countries continue to emphasize movements of prices, interest rates, and the rate of exchange, whereas the modern analysis of national income relegates money prices, money wages, and the like to a secondary position.[1]

Good reasons for the difference in approach no doubt exist. The balance of payments, the level of commodity exports and imports,

Reprinted from *Econometrica*, 10 (April 1942), 97–112. Copyright Econometric Society, 1942. I am indebted to Professor Joseph A. Schumpeter not only for his criticism of this paper, but for suggestions regarding several related topics. I wish also to thank Professor Paul A. Samuelson, whose work on the stability of equilibrium has paved a way to the solution of many problems (such as this one) which would otherwise have remained intractable.

1. One may distinguish three broad groups of trade theories: (a) those which rely mainly upon price-level, interest-rate, and exchange-rate adjustments; (b) those which emphasize the influence of shifts in monetary purchasing power upon the distribution of resources, the balance of trade, and so on; and (c) those which consider the dependence of the level of real income upon the international situation. Examples of the first group may be found in the works of the early English economists, although Professor Viner has shown that the "classical" economists were not unmindful of purchasing power effects. See Jacob Viner, *Studies in the Theory of International Trade* (New York, Harper and Bros., 1937), pp. 290–311. Shifts of purchasing power receive much attention in Bertil Ohlin's *Interregional and International Trade* (Cambridge, Mass., Harvard University Press, 1933), chaps. 4, 18, 19, and 20. The work of R. F. Harrod provides perhaps the best example of the real-income approach. See his *International Economics* (London, Nisbet, 1933), chaps. 6 and 7, and *The Trade Cycle* (Oxford, Clarendon Press, 1936), pp. 145–158. My analysis is confined entirely to the third approach.

short-term capital movements, and similar factors may respond much more readily to changes in *relative* prices and interest rates than the variables of a closed economy respond to changes in *absolute* prices, money wages, and interest rates.

But frequently it becomes important to know whether there are equilibrating forces in international trade other than price adjustments,[2] and if so, how these other forces operate. For example, if two countries which are trading with each other have substantial amounts of unemployment, and if, because of minimum-wage laws, union restrictions, or custom, money wages are relatively inflexible, equilibrium of the balance of payments and the balance of trade cannot be obtained readily by adjustments of prices and money costs. If it is assumed, in addition, that the two countries are on gold standards with sufficient reserves so that central-bank policies are not affected by gold movements, then changes in the rate of interest and the exchange rate may be ruled out. The consistency of domestic changes with the maintenance of external equilibrium will then depend upon the way in which variations of investment and consumption in one country react upon investment and consumption in others. The effects of such changes are isolated, in the following analysis, by setting up a model of trade between two countries in which variations of prices, interest rates, and the rate of exchange are impossible.

Specifically, price and wage-rate changes are eliminated by assuming the existence of unemployed resources in each of the trading countries, with perfect competition, no economies or diseconomies of large-scale operation, and a perfectly elastic supply of the unemployed resources. I assume also that the central banks offer to borrow and lend at fixed interest rates (not necessarily the same in each country) so that no changes in either economy can react upon capital costs. Finally, it is possible to abstract from exchange-rate fluctuations by assuming that the central banks agree to buy and sell foreign balances at a fixed rate, replenishing such balances when necessary either by interbank loans or by gold movements. Alternatively, rates of interest might be introduced with the assumption that the central banks adjust differences in rates so as to equate the amount of foreign lending to the balance of trade. Such an assumption complicates the problem, however, and obscures the

---

2. The term "price adjustment" denotes, in the present context, any movement of monetary variables and is understood to include interest- and exchange-rate fluctuations.

investment-consumption relations which I wish to analyze. I shall therefore confine myself to the simpler model.

It is immaterial what unit of measurement of income, investment, and consumption is adopted, since prices, monetary costs, and effort per unit of output are constant in both countries. Suppose that the wage unit in one of the two countries is used as a unit of measure in both. The two economies may be designated Y and Y'; in what follows all letters with a prime (') affixed refer to functional relations in country Y', and all letters without the prime refer to country Y.

Income, as usual, is defined as the sum of consumption and investment. The consumption function for each country is divided between consumption of domestic goods and consumption of foreign goods, both depending upon income. Thus for country Y we may write $u = u_1(y) + u_2(y)$ where y represents total income, $u_1(y)$ consumption of domestic goods, $u_2(y)$ consumption of foreign goods, and u total consumption. Likewise, investment is divided between net increases in producers' goods and stocks by domestic manufacturers and increases in foreign claims arising out of favorable trade balances, as follows: $v = v(y) + u_2'(y') - u_2(y)$. In this last equation v denotes total investment, $v(y)$ domestic investment (assumed to depend upon the level of national income),[3] and $u_2'(y') - u_2(y)$ foreign investment (or disinvestment) arising out of a favorable (or unfavorable) trade balance;[4] $u_2'(y')$, of course, is the consumption by country Y' of goods produced in Y.

The complete system of equations for the two countries may be obtained by writing down a set for Y' similar to that for Y.

(1)
$$u = u_1(y) + u_2(y) + \beta + \mu,$$
$$v = v(y) + u_2'(y') - u_2(y) + \alpha - \gamma - \mu,$$
$$u' = u_1'(y') + u_2'(y'),$$
and
$$v' = v'(y') + u_2(y) - u_2'(y') + \gamma + \mu.$$

Since $y \equiv u + v$ and $y' \equiv u' + v'$, Eqs. (1) represent four equations in the four unknowns u, v, u', and v'. If certain stability conditions to be discussed below are satisfied, this fundamental system determines the

---

3. It is important not to confuse this income-investment relation with the acceleration principle. I follow Lange here in assuming that, in the short run, entrepreneurs' expectations, and hence rates of private investment, vary directly with changes of income. Such an interpretation is not inconsistent with the fact that private net investment over a longer period is independent of the level of economic activity.

4. A country may import, of course, for purposes of investment as well as for consumption. I have excluded this assumption from my model because the complexity occasioned by its addition does not change matters of principle.

equilibrium of investment and consumption in each country, and hence total incomes and the balance of trade. The parameters α, β, γ, and μ are inserted to represent changes which will be analyzed later.

Equations (1) represent a *static* scheme in the sense that the variables are not dated. Suppose the equilibrium values of this system are $u_o, v_o, y_o, u_o', v_o', y_o'$. If time sequences are assigned to the variables of (1), we no longer have a set of simultaneous equations with equilibrium values, but a set of difference equations defining time paths for all the variables of the system. Suppose that initially the variables have some values other than those obtained by the solution of Eqs. (1). I shall follow Frisch[5] and Samuelson[6] in defining the system as stable if, for initial values of the variables slightly different from the solutions of the static equations, the time paths tend to approach the equilibrium values $u_o, v_o, y_o, u_o', v_o', y_o'$. Thus stability depends not only upon the character of the static equations (1), but also upon the nature of the assumed dynamic system.

The dynamic system to be used henceforth is derived from the following assumptions. (*a*) Consumption of both foreign and domestic goods in period t depends upon income of the period $t - 1$. (*b*) Entrepreneurs' expectations of future profits, and hence the rates of present domestic investment, depend upon income of the previous period. The difference equations corresponding to the static system (1) are then given by:[7,8]

$$
\begin{aligned}
u(t) &= u_1[y(t-1)] + u_2[y(t-1)], \\
v(t) &= v[y(t-1)] + u_2'[y'(t-1)] - u_2[y(t-1)], \\
u'(t) &= u_1'[y'(t-1)] + u_2'[y'(t-1)],
\end{aligned}
$$

(2)

and $\qquad v'(t) = v'[y'(t-1)] + u_2[y(t-1)] - u_2'[y'(t-1)].$

5. Ragnar Frisch, "On the Notion of Equilibrium and Disequilibrium," *Review of Economic Studies*, 3 (February 1936), 100–105.

6. Paul A. Samuelson, *Foundations of Economic Analysis* (Cambridge, Mass., Harvard University Press, 1947), chap. 8.

7. The results obtained in the remainder of this paper may seem to be valid only for the assumptions of Eqs. (2). I have experimented, however, with two other systems. In the first of these a lag of one period in the expenditure of income behind its receipt is postulated, with investment in a given period dependent upon income of the same period. Income, in the second alternative system, is consumed (or saved) in the period in which it is received, while changes of investment lag one period behind changes of income. For the normal case in which the marginal aggregate propensity to consume and the marginal propensity to invest are both less than unity, the two alternative systems place substantially the same restrictions upon the character of the static scheme as Eqs. (2). The final conclusions therefore possess greater generality than the method of analysis suggests.

8. Parameters are omitted from Eqs. (2) because they do not alter the conditions of stability.

Since income of period t is equal to consumption plus investment of period t, we may also write:

(3) $\qquad y(t) = u_1[y(t-1)] + v[y(t-1)] + u_2'[y'(t-1)],$

and $\qquad y'(t) = u_1'[y'(t-1)] + v'[y'(t-1)] + u_2[y(t-1)].$

Explicit solutions of (3) for y and y' as functions of time should enable one to state the conditions which our consumption and investment functions must fulfill for stability of the world economy. A general solution is impossible, however, since the exact forms of $u(y)$, $u'(y')$, and so on are not known and even if known would probably be nonlinear. But if displacements from equilibrium are small, the functions of (3) may be expanded about y_o and y_o' and all except first-order terms neglected thus:[9]

(4)
$$y(t) - y_o = (u_{1y} + v_y)[y(t-1) - y_o] + u'_{2y'}[y'(t-1) - y_o'] + \ldots,$$
$$y'(t) - y_o' = (u'_{1y'} + v'_{y'})[y'(t-1) - y_o'] + u_{2y}[y(t-1) - y_o] + \ldots,$$

where the letter subscripts indicate differentiation evaluated at the equilibrium points y_o and y_o'. Equations (4) are linear difference equations with constant coefficients, whose solutions may readily be obtained. Before discussing the conditions of convergence, however, I wish to consider two other cases with stability conditions somewhat more simple than those of (4).

Suppose first that the economy Y is in complete isolation and let $u(y) \equiv u_1(y) + u_2(y)$ be the aggregate consumption function, now relating exclusively to domestic goods. The linear difference equation for this simple case is $y(t) - y_o = (u_y + v_y)[y(t-1) - y_o] + \ldots$. Its solution is $y(t) = y_o + [y(0) - y_o](u_y + v_y)^t$. where $y(0)$ is the initial value of income at time $t = 0$. In order that $y(t)$ shall converge to the value y_o it is necessary and sufficient that $u_y + v_y < 1$. In words, for a single economy to be in equilibrium in isolation, the marginal aggregate propensity to consume plus the marginal propensity to invest must be less than unity.

Next suppose that the economy Y is trading with the rest of the world, but that it is such a small part of the world economy that reactions of other countries to changes in Y's demand for foreign goods may be neglected. The exports of Y to the rest of the world, $u_2'(y')$, may then be taken as data. Again, the linear difference equation corresponding to (4) is $y(t) - y_o = (u_{1y} + v_y)[y(t-1) - y_o]$. The solution of this equation

9. Cf. Samuelson, *Foundations* (reference 6), pp. 200–226.

converges to the value y_0 provided $u_{1y} + v_y < 1$. Thus in order that an economy trading with the rest of the world be stable under conditions in which world reactions may be neglected, it is necessary that the marginal propensity to consume domestic goods plus the marginal propensity to invest be less than unity. The size of the marginal propensity to consume foreign goods and hence of the marginal aggregate propensity to consume is immaterial. If other factors remain the same, changes in the consumption of foreign-made goods will not affect income in Y, as may be seen from (3). Consequently, a very large marginal aggregate propensity to consume is compatible with perfect stability, provided only that the marginal propensity to consume domestic goods and the marginal propensity to invest domestically be sufficiently small.

In the usual case, however, the assumption that other things remain equal is not justified, since greater imports (in Y) will change the incomes of other countries and their demands for Y goods. Thus the more general case of trade between two countries with all reactions taken into account must be considered. The time paths of income in Y and Y', for small deviations from equilibrium, are given (as previously noted) by Eqs. (4), the solutions of which are

$$(5) \qquad\qquad y(t) = y_0 + A\rho_1{}^t + B\rho_2{}^t$$
$$\text{and} \qquad\qquad y'(t) = y_0' + C\rho_1{}^t + D\rho_2{}^t,$$

where ρ_1 and ρ_2 are roots of the quadratic equation

$$(6) \qquad \begin{vmatrix} (u_{1y} - v_y) - \rho & u'_{2y'} \\ u_{2y} & (u'_{1y'} + v'_{y'}) - \rho \end{vmatrix} = 0,$$

and where A, B, C, D are constants dependent upon the initial values of y and y'. It is clear from (5) that $y(t)$ will approach y_0 as t becomes large provided ρ_1 and ρ_2, the roots of (6), are less than unity. Necessary and sufficient conditions for this to be true are

$$(7) \quad u_{1y} + v_y + u'_{1y'} + v'_{y'} < 1 + (u_{1y} + v_y)(u'_{1y'} + v'_{y'}) - u_{2y}u'_{2y'} < 2.$$

The inequality $u_{1y} + v_y + u'_{1y'} + v'_{y'} < 2$ shows that at least one of the two countries must be in stable equilibrium without considering reactions of the other; that is, either $u_{1y} + v_y$ or $u'_{1y'} + v'_{y'}$ must be less than unity. Suppose this stable country is Y'. The first of the inequalities of (7) may then be written

$$(8) \qquad\qquad u_{1y} + v_y + \left(\frac{u'_{2y'}}{1 - u'_{1y'} - v'_{y'}} \right) u_{2y} < 1,$$

which shows that the other country must also be stable with reactions of the first ignored; in other words, that $u_{1y} + v_y$ must also be less than unity. Thus stability of the world economy with all reactions considered implies stability of each economy with the reactions of the other ignored.

Other implications of our general stability conditions are as follows:[10]

(1) If both countries are stable when isolated, the world economy will likewise be stable; that is, (7) will always be satisfied if $u'_{1y'} + u'_{2y'} + v'_{y'}$ and $u_{1y} + u_{2y} + v_y$ are both less than unity.

(2) If both countries are *unstable* when isolated, the world economy will likewise be unstable; that is, (7) will never be satisfied for two economies in both of which the marginal aggregate propensity to consume plus the marginal propensity to invest is greater than unity.

(3) One of the two countries *may* be unstable when isolated, provided marginal propensities of the other to consume and invest are sufficiently low. In other words, a country which would be unstable when left to itself may be perfectly stable in a two-economy world because of the dampening influence of low propensities in the other country.

A summary of the three cases examined above may facilitate further discussion. Briefly, I have considered the equilibrium of an economy in isolation, of a single economy dealing with a world whose level of economic activity was regarded as independent of the particular economy studied, and of two economies trading with each other, with due allowances for the reactions of each to changes within the other. The isolated economy was found to be stable if the marginal aggregate propensity to consume plus the marginal propensity to invest were less than unity. Stability of the single economy dealing with a world without reactions was shown to depend upon the sum of the marginal propensity to consume domestic goods and the marginal domestic propensity to invest being less than unity. Stability of the two-economy case is not so easily summarized. In general, one of the two must fulfill the conditions of stability for an isolated economy, both must fulfill the conditions of stability for a single economy dealing with the rest of the world, and the one which does not fulfill the conditions for stability of an isolated economy must have marginal propensities to consume and invest which are sufficiently small to satisfy inequality (8).

---

10. The proof is so simple in each case that I leave it to the reader.

The stability conditions developed above may now be used to determine some of the properties of the static system summarized in Eqs. (1). Suppose that shifts occur in the functional relations (1). The equilibrium values u_o, v_o, u_o', and v_o' of the old system will not in general satisfy the new equations. A time sequence of changes, depicted by (2), will ensue and eventually, if the system is stable, a new set of equilibrium values will be approached. It is my purpose to compare the new equilibrium with the one which prevailed before the changes in (1) occurred.

Equations (1) are symmetric. Consequently, it will suffice to consider the effects upon both countries of changes in either country alone. I shall assume that the changes occur in Y. Four types of variation will be analyzed. The parameter α of (1) may be interpreted alternatively as an increase in the marginal efficiency of capital or as an increase in public investment. Changes in the average propensity to consume domestic goods are represented by β, while γ is used to indicate a shift in consumption from domestic to foreign goods. Changes in the average propensity to consume foreign goods, accompanied by no change in the average propensity to consume domestic goods, are measured by μ. All movements in consumption and investment functions are uniform shifts, so that marginal propensities remain unchanged.

To analyze the effects of an increased marginal efficiency of capital[11] or an increase in public spending, we may differentiate Eqs. (1) with respect to α and solve the resulting simultaneous equations for $\partial u/\partial \alpha$, $\partial v/\partial \alpha$, $\partial u'/\partial \alpha$, and $\partial v'/\partial \alpha$ as follows:

(9)
$$\frac{\partial u}{\partial \alpha} = \frac{u_y(1 - v'_{y'} - u'_{1y'})}{\Delta}, \qquad \frac{\partial u'}{\partial \alpha} = \frac{u'_{y'} u_{2y}}{\Delta},$$

$$\frac{\partial v}{\partial \alpha} = \frac{(1 - u_y)(1 - v'_{y'} - u'_{1y'})}{\Delta}, \qquad \frac{\partial v'}{\partial \alpha} = \frac{(1 - u'_{1y'})u_{2y}}{\Delta},$$

and
$$\frac{\partial y}{\partial \alpha} = \frac{1 - v'_{y'} - u'_{1y'}}{\Delta}, \qquad \frac{\partial y'}{\partial \alpha} = \frac{u_{2y}}{\Delta},$$

where $\Delta \equiv (u_{1y} + v_y - 1)(u'_{1y} + v'_{y'} - 1) - u_{2y}u'_{2y'}$ and where u_y is the marginal aggregate propensity to consume in Y (that is, $u_y \equiv u_{1y} + u_{2y}$), with a similar interpretation of $u'_{y'}$.

---

11. Keynes devotes a section of his *Treatise on Money* (New York, Harcourt, Brace, 1930) to this problem (vol. 1, chap. 12, pt. 2). The adjustments he envisages are largely price changes, however, since he assumes a constant rate of utilization of the factors of production.

No general statement about the sign of Δ may be made. Indeed, it may even be zero, in which case the derivatives (9) do not exist. But if one may assume stability in the trade relations between the two countries—and an explanation of why a slight change does not increase or decrease the values of the variables at exponential rates is otherwise difficult—then the sign of Δ may be determined from our stability conditions. By means of a few transformations, the first of the inequalities of (7) may be reduced to $\Delta > 0$. In other words, stability of our two-economy world implies that the denominator of the expressions in (9) is positive. Evaluation of the numerators depends partially upon whether the economies are stable or unstable when isolated. Since both $u_{1y} + v_y$ and $u'_{1y'} + v'_{y'}$ must be less than unity, the only ambiguities are in the values of u_y and $u'_{y'}$, one of which *may* be greater than unity if the economy to which it refers is unstable in isolation.

Thus the following results are obtained:

(1) An increase in the marginal efficiency of capital or public spending in Y will increase consumption and income in both countries, provided only that the most general stability conditions (7) are satisfied.

(2) If the two countries would have been stable in isolation, then the increased marginal efficiency of capital or spending will increase investment in both countries. Otherwise, the direction of change of investment is indeterminate. From (8), however, it is easily shown that both u_y and $u'_{y'}$ cannot exceed unity. Hence total investment *must* increase in one of the two countries and it *may* increase in both.

There are striking similarities between the effects of an increase in the marginal efficiency of capital and the effects of an increased average propensity to consume domestic goods, accompanied by no change in the propensity to consume foreign goods. Again differentiating (1), this time with respect to β, and solving for the unknown derivatives, we find:

$$\frac{\partial u}{\partial \beta} = 1 + \frac{u_y(1 - v'_{y'} - u'_{1y'})}{\Delta}, \qquad\qquad \frac{\partial u'}{\partial \beta} = \frac{u'_{y'} u_{2y}}{\Delta},$$

$$(10) \quad \frac{\partial v}{\partial \beta} = -1 + \frac{(1 - u_y)(1 - v'_{y'} - u'_{1y'})}{\Delta}, \qquad \frac{\partial v'}{\partial \beta} = \frac{(1 - u'_{y'})u_{2y}}{\Delta},$$

$$\text{and} \quad \frac{\partial y}{\partial \beta} = \frac{1 - v'_{y'} - u'_{1y'}}{\Delta}, \qquad\qquad \frac{\partial y'}{\partial \beta} = \frac{u_{2y}}{\Delta}.$$

Comparison of (9) with (10) shows that an increase in the average propensity to consume domestic goods in Y affects income, consumption, and investment in Y' in exactly the same way that an increase in the marginal efficiency of capital in the former affects the situation in the latter. In the most general case, income and consumption in Y' will rise with the direction of change of investment remaining indeterminate. But if Y' is a country which would have been stable in isolation, then investment there will also increase. Again the results agree with what we might have expected intuitively. Increased propensity to consume domestic goods in Y means a higher level of income with a consequent rise in imports. And it is by means of these added imports that the income stimulus is transferred from one country to the other, for goods imported by Y are exported by Y'.

Investment in the country with altered consuming habits may either increase or decrease, but if it decreases (because of an unfavorable change in the trade balance) it cannot decrease by as much as consumption increases so that income must rise. The total change in such investment comprises two parts, the change of domestic investment and the change in the trade balance. Increased consumption of domestic goods induces a rise in domestic investment (v_y is positive) so that the first item is positive, but the trade balance may move in either direction. If it moves *against* the country with altered tastes (Y), it may counteract the influence of higher domestic investment. To discuss this possibility, let us write the second of Eqs. (10) as follows:

$$\frac{\partial v}{\partial \beta} = \frac{(1 - v'_{y'} - u'_{1y'})(v_y - u_{2y}) + u_{2y}u'_{2y'}}{\Delta}.$$

Thus if v_y exceeds u_{2y}, $\partial v/\partial \beta$ is clearly positive, regardless of special stability conditions. In words, if the marginal propensity to invest domestically exceeds the marginal propensity to consume foreign goods, unfavorable changes in Y's trade balance arising from a higher propensity to consume domestic goods cannot be as large as induced domestic investment. Hence total investment must rise. By another simple transformation of the second of Eqs. (10) it may be shown that $\partial v/\partial \beta$ is always positive if the passive country (Y') is unstable in isolation, regardless of the relation between marginal propensity to invest and marginal propensity to import in the country with altered tastes. This arises, as we shall see presently, from the fact that, with Y' unstable in isolation, higher demand in Y for her own goods moves the trade balance in favor of the latter country. Finally, if Y is the unstable country, and her marginal aggregate propensity to consume is greater than unity, it is clear from (10) that an increase in her propensity to consume domestic goods will reduce her total investment; in this case, the unfavorable change in the trade balance necessarily exceeds the rise of domestic investment.

The third parameter, γ, of Eqs. (1) represents a shift in consumption in country Y from domestic goods to foreign-made goods. The influence of this shift may be examined by differentiating (1) partially with respect to γ and solving once more for the unknown derivatives.

$$(11)\quad \frac{\partial u}{\partial \gamma} = \frac{-u_y(1 - v'_{y'} - u'_{y'})}{\Delta}, \qquad \frac{\partial u'}{\partial \gamma} = \frac{u'_{y'}(1 - v_y - u_y)}{\Delta},$$

$$\frac{\partial v}{\partial \gamma} = \frac{-(1 - u_y)(1 - v'_{y'} - u'_{y'})}{\Delta}, \qquad \frac{\partial v'}{\partial \gamma} = \frac{(1 - u'_{y'})(1 - v_y - u_y)}{\Delta},$$

$$\text{and}\quad \frac{\partial y}{\partial \gamma} = \frac{-(1 - v'_{y'} - u'_{y'})}{\Delta}, \qquad \frac{\partial y'}{\partial \gamma} = \frac{1 - v_y - u_y}{\Delta}.$$

Consider first the income effects. If both countries exhibit stability when isolated, the shift of consumption in Y from domestic to foreign-made goods will lower income there and raise it in Y'. This is the result which might have been expected; diminished foreign investment arising from increased imports reduces the total income of Y, while the additional exports from Y' serve to increase income of the latter country. But this "normal" case, as I shall call it, is by no means the only possible one.

Suppose that Y exhibits stability in isolation while Y' does not. Under such circumstances a shift in Y from domestic to foreign-made goods will *increase* income in both countries. The explanation of the paradoxical result is to be found in the secondary effects of higher income in Y'. Initially, of course, income of the country with changed tastes is reduced as a result of a lower propensity to consume domestic goods and reduced foreign investment. Income of the passive country (Y'), on the other hand, is stimulated by a rise of exports to Y. So far the results do not differ from the case of stability in both countries. If Y' is unstable in isolation, however, there are important repercussions to be considered. In this case her added exports may increase her income considerably—the multiplier effect is large. And eventually, if Y' is unstable in isolation, the secondary movement of goods from the country with changed tastes (Y) to the unstable country (Y') will be sufficient to counteract the depressing influence of the primary shift of consumption in the former country. Hence income rises in both countries.

If Y is an economy which would be unstable in isolation, while Y' is stable, the foregoing conclusion must be reversed; the shift in Y from domestic goods to foreign-made goods will then *reduce* income in both countries. The primary effect, as before, is an increase of income in the country the demand for whose goods has risen (Y') and a reduction of income in the country with altered tastes (Y). Because Y is an unstable country, however, her income movements ultimately dominate the situation. That is, the reduction of her income induces a secondary decline in exports of the passive country, and this decline of exports will then reduce income of the latter country despite the initial stimulus afforded by increased propensity abroad to consume Y' goods. Income therefore declines in both countries.

In explaining the behavior of income in response to a shift of consumption, I have discussed only the secondary changes in the unstable country. Needless to say, there are also secondary repercussions in the stable country. Analysis of such repercussions has been omitted not because their quantitative influence is small, but simply because conclusions regarding the final outcome of a particular domestic change always depend upon which country is unstable when isolated.

Both countries cannot be unstable in isolation, for then the two would be unstable also when dealing with each other. Hence a shift of consumption in Y from domestic goods to foreign goods must have one of three results:

(1) If both Y and Y' are stable in isolation (the normal case), income will diminish in Y and increase in Y'.

(2) If Y is stable in isolation but Y' is unstable, income will rise in both countries.

(3) If Y is unstable in isolation and Y' is stable, income will fall in both countries.

The shift in consumption to Y' goods cannot conceivably reduce income in Y' while increasing it in Y, since the conditions necessary to bring about this result contradict our stability hypothesis.

The influence of γ on total consumption and investment in the two countries may now be indicated briefly. Total consumption always moves in the same direction as income. Investment, on the other hand, moves directly or inversely with the movement of income in each country according as the marginal aggregate propensity to consume is less than or greater than unity. Since we know that the marginal aggregate propensity to consume cannot be greater than unity in both countries, it follows that investment *must* move in the same direction as income in either Y or Y' and *may* do so in both.

The fourth parameter to be considered (μ) represents an increase in consumption of foreign goods by Y, with no change in consumption of domestic goods. By the method outlined above it may be shown that

$$\frac{\partial u}{\partial \mu} = 1 + \frac{u_y u'_{2y'}}{\Delta}, \qquad \frac{\partial u'}{\partial \mu} = \frac{u'_{y'}(1 - v_y - u_{1y})}{\Delta},$$

$$(12) \quad \frac{\partial v}{\partial \mu} = -1 + \frac{(1 - u_y)u'_{2y'}}{\Delta}, \qquad \frac{\partial v'}{\partial \mu} = \frac{(1 - u'_{y'})(1 - v_y - u_{1y})}{\Delta},$$

$$\text{and} \quad \frac{\partial y}{\partial \mu} = \frac{u'_{2y'}}{\Delta}, \qquad \frac{\partial y'}{\partial \mu} = \frac{1 - v_y - u_{1y}}{\Delta}.$$

If the general stability postulates (7) are accepted, an increase in the average propensity of Y to consume Y' goods must increase total consumption and income in both countries. In the case of Y' this is obvious since the increased demand for Y' goods abroad has resulted in greater foreign investments. In the case of Y it means simply that the stimulating effect of a higher aggregate propensity to consume plus the secondary repercussions of higher income in Y' have exerted a more important influence on income of the former than the depressing consequences of increased imports. Once again, the change of investment in the two countries is indeterminate. If the marginal aggregate propensity to consume is less than unity in Y', investment there must increase; otherwise it will decline. Investment in Y will decline if the marginal aggregate propensity to consume is greater than unity there; otherwise the direction of change is difficult to determine.

The second of Eqs. (12), however, may be written as follows:

$$\frac{\partial v}{\partial \mu} = \frac{1}{\Delta}[v_y(1 - u'_{1y'} - v'_{y'}) - (1 - u_{1y})(1 - u'_{y'} - v'_{y'})].$$

This shows that investment must rise in the country with altered tastes (Y) whenever the passive country (Y') is unstable in isolation. The conclusion, as shown below, depends upon the fact that a higher propensity to consume foreign goods moves the balance of trade in favor of the country with altered tastes whenever the country with which it is dealing is unstable in isolation. Thus if Y' is unstable in isolation, both the foreign and domestic components of Y's investment change are positive.

The fundamental equations (1) represent an equilibrium system only in a restricted sense. Except in the special case in which the desire to lend abroad on the part of Y (assuming the trade balance to be favorable) plus the desire of Y' to repatriate funds is exactly equal to the trade balance, the equilibrium of (1) requires annual changes in the indebtedness of one banking system to the other. It is therefore important to know how the changes discussed above will affect the balance of trade. Let $b \equiv u_2'(y') - u_2(y) - \gamma - \mu$ represent this balance.[12] From Eqs. (9) through (12) it is then possible to determine how b changes with movements of $\alpha, \beta, \gamma, \mu$.

$$\frac{\partial b}{\partial \alpha} = \frac{\partial b}{\partial \beta} = \frac{-u_{2y}(1 - v'_{y'} - u'_{y'})}{\Delta},$$

(13)
$$\frac{\partial b}{\partial \gamma} = \frac{-(1 - v_y - u_y)(1 - v'_{y'} - u'_{y'})}{\Delta},$$

and
$$\frac{\partial b}{\partial \mu} = \frac{-(1 - v_y - u_{1y})(1 - v'_{y'} - u'_{y'})}{\Delta}.$$

Public spending and increases in the average propensity to consume domestic goods affect the balance of trade in exactly the same way, as might have been expected, since these changes were found to affect incomes in the same way. If Y' is a country which would be stable in isolation, public spending and a higher average propensity to consume domestic goods in Y will move the balance of trade in a direction unfavorable to the expanding country and, other things remaining the same, will reduce the balance of Y banks abroad. But if, on the other hand, Y' would be unstable when isolated, then the balance of trade will move in favor of Y. The sequence of events in this case is roughly as follows: (a) imports of the expanding country increase because of greater income arising either from domestic investment or from an increased propensity to consume domestic goods; (b) higher exports of the passive country (Y' in the present instance) exert a stimulating influence on that country's income, with a consequent increase in her

12. It is perhaps needless to say that b represents the trade balance *from the point of view of the country with altered tastes* (that is, Y).

demand for goods of the country initiating the change, and (c) if Y' is unstable in isolation, the induced rise of her imports will exceed the rise of her exports occasioned by the initial change in Y. In other words, domestic expansion will lead to a drain on foreign balances only if the country with which the expanding country deals is stable in isolation.

We have seen above that a shift in the propensity to consume from domestic to foreign goods (γ) may (a) decrease income in the country whose tastes have changed, while increasing income of the other country, or (b) increase income in both countries, or (c) reduce income in both. The three possibilities correspond respectively to the three situations in which (a) both countries are stable in isolation, (b) the passive country is unstable in isolation, and (c) the country whose tastes have changed is unstable in isolation. These conclusions, however, afford no clue to the probable change in the balance of trade. But from Eqs. (13) it is clear that if both countries would be stable in isolation, the shift of consumption must move the trade balance against the country with altered tastes; imports of Y, in other words, must be higher than in the previous equilibrium despite the decline of her income. It is also clear from Eqs. (13) that if either country would have been *unstable* in isolation, then the shift of consumption will move the balance in *favor* of the country with altered tastes. We may conclude that a decline in the propensity to consume domestic goods accompanied by a rise in the propensity to consume foreign goods will reduce foreign balances of the country with changed tastes only if both countries would be stable when isolated.

How is the situation altered if the rise in demand for foreign goods is accompanied by no decline in demand for domestic goods? The last equation of (13) shows that such a change (μ) causes the balance of trade to move in the same direction (though not necessarily by the same amount) as a similar increase of domestic investment (α). Hence this case need not be discussed further.

All results obtained above are summarized in Tables 1 and 2 where the directions of change of each of the variables of the system with respect to the parameters α, β, γ, and μ are indicated. Table 1a shows that, without a knowledge of stability conditions, it is difficult to predict the international repercussions of a particular domestic change. Hence in discussing such questions as the foreign-trade aspects of business cycles, effects of capital transfers, and the like, one should always

Table 1. Equilibrium movements of the system for the "general" and "normal" cases

Parameter	a. General stability conditions (7) satisfied							b. "Normal" case: both countries stable in isolation						
	u	v	y	u'	v'	y'	b	u	v	y	u'	v'	y'	b
α	+	?	+	+	?	+	?	+	+	+	+	+	+	-
β	+	?	+	+	?	+	?	+	?	+	+	+	+	-
γ	?	?	?	?	?	?	?	-	-	-	+	+	+	-
μ	+	?	+	+	?	+	?	+	?	+	+	+	+	-

Table 2. Equilibrium movements of the system with one country unstable in isolation

Parameter	a. Country with altered tastes (Y) unstable in isolation							b. Passive county (Y') unstable in isolation						
	u	v	y	u'	v'	y'	b	u	v	y	u'	v'	y'	b
α	+	?	+	+	+	+	-	+	+	+	+	?	+	+
β	+	?	+	+	+	+	-	+	+	+	+	?	+	+
γ	-	?	-	-	-	-	+	+	+	+	+	?	+	+
μ	+	?	+	+	+	+	-	+	+	+	+	?	+	+

specify which of the countries is assumed to be unstable in isolation and which stable. Many economists will probably prefer to assume that all countries are stable in isolation, in which case the results given in Table 1b are relevant.

With stability conditions specified, directions of change may be determined for all variables except investment in one of the two countries. This remaining ambiguity is attributable to the dual nature of such investment. That is, whenever the balance of trade of a country declines while domestic investment rises (or conversely), the direction of change of total investment cannot be determined without further information. Thus it will be found, upon examination of Tables 1 and 2, that the only uncertainty which remains when stability conditions are fully specified is the total investment change of the country whose balance of trade moves in a direction opposite to its income movement. But this is simply the case in which domestic and foreign investment move in opposite directions, for domestic investment is positively correlated with income. The final outcome under these circumstances depends, as noted above, upon such nonstability conditions as the relation between marginal propensity to invest and marginal propensity to import. In the special case in which the marginal propensity to invest domestically is zero, uncertainty regarding the direction of change of total investment is removed, since changes of foreign investment are then the only *economically determined* changes of total investment.[13] In other words, the induced change of investment for a particular country in a new position of equilibrium is then identical with the change of its trade balance. It follows that, with marginal propensities to invest equal to zero in both countries, changes in consuming habits can only increase investment in one country at the expense of investment in the other.

Apart from investment changes, other aspects of the tables are largely self-explanatory and further comment seems superfluous.

In closing, we may note that the use of certain equivalences affords a considerable simplification, provided one is interested in income changes alone. For an isolated community, a given increase in the propensity to consume is known to affect income in exactly the same manner as a corresponding amount of net investment.[14] Similar propositions may be developed for interdependent economies. The fact that $y \equiv u + v$ and $y' \equiv u' + v'$ enables us to write Eqs. (1) as follows:

$$(14) \qquad y = u_1(y) + v(y) + u_2'(y') + \alpha + \beta - \gamma,$$

and

$$y' = u_1'(y') + v'(y') + u_2(y) + \gamma + \mu.$$

From (14) it is easily shown that: (*a*) an increase in the propensity to consume domestic goods (β) is equivalent, in its income effect, to a corresponding amount of net domestic investment (α); (*b*) a shift in the propensity to consume from domestic to foreign goods (γ) is equivalent to net disinvestment of γ in the country whose tastes have changed, accompanied by net investment of the same amount in the second country; and (*c*) an increase in the average propensity of one of the countries to consume foreign goods (μ) is equivalent to a corresponding amount of net investment in the other country. Thus all of the changes which I have considered may be reduced, for income analysis, to combinations of net investment changes in the two countries.

13. This is the system envisaged by those who object to the inclusion of induced investment as a component of static equilibrium.

14. Cf. Paul A. Samuelson, "The Theory of Pump-Priming Reexamined," *American Economic Review*, 30 (September 1940), 492–506, esp. 505.

11 | Flexible Exchange Rates and the Theory of Employment

The monetary nationalism that grew so rapidly during the interwar years was largely a protest against the international gold standard, which was criticized on the ground that it served as an instrument for transmitting depressions from one country to another and thereby made it difficult, if not impossible, for any one country to pursue an independent fiscal and monetary program. At first the interwar criticisms were directed primarily at the difficulties of *price* stability under the gold standard, and the problem was viewed fundamentally as a conflict between domestic *monetary* policy and international equilibrium.[1] Later, however, the development of the theory of employment and its application to international problems made it apparent that the conflict between domestic stability and international equilibrium was really much deeper than the early discussion of monetary and price phenomena had indicated. Not only the quantity of money and the

Written jointly with Svend Laursen. Reprinted from *Review of Economics and Statistics*, 32 (November 1950), 281–299. Copyright President and Fellows of Harvard College, 1950.

1. The emphasis on money and prices in the early stages of the discussion is clearly apparent in the work of J. M. Keynes during the decade of the twenties, particularly in his *Monetary Reform*. An admirable survey of the evolution of Keynes's ideas on this subject may be found in Arthur I. Bloomfield, "Foreign Exchange Rate Theory and Policy," in *The New Economics*, ed. S. E. Harris (New York, Alfred A. Knopf, 1947), pp. 293–314. Further evidence of the importance attached to money and prices may be found in the famous purchasing-power-parity controversy which was precipitated largely by Cassel during the period of fluctuating exchange rates which followed World War I. See, for example, Gustav Cassel, *Money and Foreign Exchange after 1914* (New York, Macmillan, 1930), *passim*, esp. pp. 137–162.

level of prices but also the total demand for goods and services and the level of output and employment were subject to external influences, and the control of output and employment at home in the face of fluctuations arising abroad was usually beyond the powers of the traditional monetary devices. In other words, the theory of employment demonstrated that even if a country were willing and able, because of large international reserves, to pursue a policy of domestic stability, a mere stabilizing of the quantity of money would probably not be sufficient to offset the fluctuations in income arising from the changing demand for exports.

The gold standard was guilty of the charges made against it, not primarily because it permitted the vicissitudes of foreign trade to influence the quantity of money, but because there was a direct link under this standard between the demand for exports and the national income.[2] A decline in exports meant both a decline in the quantity of money and a fall of current income, and even if the first of these effects could be offset by appropriate neutralizing monetary policy, the second usually remained to be dealt with by other means. The basic conflict, then, was not merely between domestic *price* stability and international equilibrium, but also, and perhaps to a greater extent, between domestic *income* stability and international equilibrium. And the area of economic policy in which the conflict was important extended far beyond the traditional monetary sphere, embracing as it did all aspects of fiscal policy and taxation, as well as other measures to stabilize the total demand for a country's output.

The theory of employment, by revealing the true magnitude of the problem, thus heightened the demand for an international monetary system that would free individual countries from the shackles of the gold standard and enable them to pursue independent programs of domestic stabilization. Although several alternatives to the gold standard were proposed, most of them involved to one degree or another a system of flexible exchange rates. It was believed that under such a

---

2. The influence of the theory of employment on economists' ideas concerning the international transmission of business cycles is clearly seen in the voluminous discussion of the foreign trade multiplier, which followed publication of Keynes's *General Theory of Employment, Interest, and Money* in 1936. A more general treatment of the subject is given by William A. Salant, "Foreign Trade Policy in the Business Cycle," *Public Policy*, ed. C. J. Friedrich and E. S. Mason, 2 (1941), 208–231. See also League of Nations, *Economic Stability in the Postwar World* (Geneva, 1945), chap. 6.

system a "stable" country would be insulated to a considerable extent against economic fluctuations arising in the rest of the world.[3]

The purpose of the present study is to examine the claims made for fluctuating exchange rates, and particularly to examine these claims from the point of view of the theory of employment. Assuming that the price of each country's currency in the foreign-exchange market tends to settle at the level at which supply is equal to demand, we ask ourselves how cyclical movements of output in one part of the world would affect output elsewhere. In short, would stable countries be insulated from unstable ones under such a monetary arrangement, or would income and employment in every country still be dependent, as under the gold standard, upon economic conditions in the rest of the world?

The interrelations between exchange rates, employment, and prices in different countries cannot be studied without defining precisely what is meant by a "system of flexible exchange rates." Does the phrase refer to a foreign-exchange market which is open to all potential buyers and sellers, regardless of the purpose for which foreign exchange is being bought or sold, or does it refer to a more limited market? And does the "flexibility" of exchange rates imply that prices for foreign currencies rise and fall in response to day-to-day changes in supply and demand, as in competitive commodity markets, or are price adjustments made only occasionally in response to persistent and substantial discrepancies between supply and demand?

Both of these questions, as the reader may recognize, are prompted by problems which arose during the decade of the thirties. Exchange rates at that time underwent frequent and substantial fluctuations; and although the exchange rates were by no means free-market rates, the fluctuations that occurred nevertheless created serious doubts concerning the effectiveness of a flexible-exchange system in equalizing a country's international payments and receipts. The doubts arose, in the first place, because the upward and downward movement of exchange rates was considerably aggravated by speculative capital movements.[4] The second and more important element in the skepticism produced by the

---

3. See James E. Meade and Charles J. Hitch, *An Introduction to Economic Analysis and Policy*, American ed. (New York, Oxford University Press, 1938), pp. 344–355; R. F. Harrod, *International Economics*, ed. 2 (London, Nisbet, 1939), chap. 7; and Abba P. Lerner, *The Economics of Control* (New York, Macmillan, 1944), chaps. 28 and 29.

4. League of Nations, *International Currency Experience: Lessons of the Interwar Period* (Geneva, 1944), chap. 5.

interwar experience was the realization that the demand for exports and imports may not be responsive to changes in currency values. If the demand for imports in most countries were as inelastic as the interwar experience seemed to suggest, a system of fluctuating exchange rates would be an inefficient method of correcting a disequilibrium in the balance of payments; large movements of exchange rates would be needed to correct relatively modest deficits or surpluses. Indeed, the response of imports and exports might conceivably be so small that depreciation would augment rather than diminish the size of a country's deficit. In such an event, a system of free-market exchange rates would not be a self-adjusting mechanism; currency depreciation would create a situation leading to further depreciation, and the cumulative, unstable movement might well continue until the monetary system broke down completely.[5]

In view of these technical problems, we should attempt at the outset to determine what limitations it may be necessary to place upon the markets for foreign exchange to make these markets stable and workable. It seems highly probable, from the interwar experience, that a regime of flexible exchange rates would not be successful unless capital movements were subject to some type of control. It will accordingly be understood that, in speaking hereafter of a free-market exchange system or a flexible-exchange system, we mean a system in which foreign exchange may be purchased and sold freely *for all purposes except capital movements*. To simplify the problem, we shall assume that capital transactions are completely prohibited. It should be emphasized, however, that such an assumption is not absolutely necessary; our final conclusions would be altered only slightly if we had allowed for a steady rate of foreign lending or borrowing.[6]

5. The principal contributions during the interwar period to the discussion of exchange stability were as follows: C. F. Bickerdike, "The Instability of Foreign Exchange," *Economic Journal*, 30 (March 1920), 118–122; Joan Robinson, "The Foreign Exchanges," in *Essays in the Theory of Employment* (New York, Macmillan, 1937); and A. J. Brown, "Trade Balances and Exchange Stability," *Oxford Economic Papers*, 6 (April 1942), 57–76. A more recent contribution to this same subject is Arnold C. Harberger, "Currency Depreciation, Income, and the Balance of Trade," *Journal of Political Economy*, 58 (February 1950), 47–60.

6. The recent experience (1949) prior to devaluation of the pound sterling suggests that speculative capital movements under a regime of flexible exchange rates may be rather difficult to control. Even if the more common forms of speculative transfers can be avoided, the possibility remains that speculation in foreign exchange may occur through postponement or advancement of purchases of goods and services. To a considerable extent, the recent decline in British sales to the dollar area represents such a speculative postponement of purchases.

The second lesson from the interwar period of currency fluctuations is that short-run movements in exchange rates are likely to be unstable even apart from speculative capital movements. It is probable that the short-run demand for imports and exports is quite inelastic, and for this reason day-to-day or month-to-month fluctuations in currency values would not be an appropriate method of eliminating short-run discrepancies between international payments and receipts. Quite the contrary, such movements in exchange rates might easily aggravate the discrepancies they were intended to correct. In the long run, on the other hand, the presumption seems to be the other way. When the numerous possibilities of a long-run substitution between domestic and foreign goods, or between the goods of different countries, is considered, it seems rather unlikely that the long-run elasticities of demand will be so small as to render the foreign-exchange markets unstable. It is our view, then, that depreciation of a particular country's currency will ultimately improve that country's balance of payments, even though the short-run effects may well be adverse.[7] If correct, this view suggests that the appropriate foreign-exchange market is not a completely uncontrolled market, but a market in which foreign exchange rates are kept at fixed prices, with occasional changes made in these prices in response to persistent deficits or surpluses.[8]

In what follows, the relation between exchange rates and the level of economic activity in various countries will be investigated only in this rather long-run sense. Thus, when we ask how a depression or economic expansion in one country affects exchange rates and economic activity in other countries, the assumption will always be implicit, if not explicit, that the period of time under consideration is sufficiently long so that depreciation of a given country's currency will improve that country's balance of payments. In technical terms, this means that we shall take it for granted that the foreign exchange markets are stable.

An investigation of the interactions between exchange rates, prices, and employment is by no means a new field of endeavor. Both the

7. The long-run effects are particularly important in the theory of adjustment developed by Frank D. Graham. See *The Theory of International Values* (Princeton, N.J., Princeton University Press, 1948), *passim*.

8. The exchange market envisaged here is essentially the same as the one which, it is hoped, will eventually be established under the International Monetary Fund. The experience of the Fund up to the present time suggests that short-run rigidity of exchange rates may interfere somewhat with the necessary long-run flexibility. But this is a question which cannot be adequately treated in the present paper.

proposals made during the interwar period for a system of flexible exchange rates and the actual experience with fluctuating rates during that period stimulated a considerable amount of research in this field. Before we present our own work, it seems desirable to summarize, as far as possible, the principal conclusions of the earlier research. There seems to be general agreement, in the previous studies, that if cyclical fluctuations consist largely in price changes, with only minor changes in the level or composition of output, a system of flexible exchange rates will be a highly effective means of isolating one or more countries from the effects of cyclical fluctuations elsewhere. If the cyclical movements take the form of changes in output and employment, there is less agreement as to the extent to which one country's output and employment will be protected by such a system from changes in output and employment in other parts of the world.[9] The accepted opinion seems to be that under a system of flexible exchange rates the *total* monetary demand for a given country's output will be unaffected by a contraction abroad, but the *nature* of this demand may be considerably changed; and if the mobility of resources is low, a shift in demand from one segment of the economy to another may prove almost as disturbing as a general reduction of demand.[10]

The argument in favor of flexible exchange rates as a means of isolating price movements is extremely simple, for it is based entirely upon the familiar purchasing-power-parity theory of exchange rates. The view that flexible exchanges also isolate movements of output and employment, however, is based upon less obvious reasoning. Consider, for instance, a hypothetical case of trade between two countries, the United States and the United Kingdom. Suppose that the exchange rate between the two is $3 = £1$, and that at this rate the balance of payments between the two countries is in equilibrium. Since capital movements are assumed throughout to be negligible, all payments between the two countries consist in payments for goods and services.

9. Cf. the following statement by P. B. Whale: "So far as *price* movements are concerned, therefore, it is not impossible for a country with an independent currency to insulate itself from much of the effects of a world trade depression or to escape the especially acute deflation which might be its share. This is not to say, however, that such a country can escape the effects of the contraction in the volume of world trade." Quoted from p. 26, "The Theory of International Trade in the Absence of an International Standard," *Economica*, 3 (February 1936), 24–38.

10. Gottfried Haberler, in *Prosperity and Depression*, ed. 3 (Geneva, League of Nations, 1941), says on p. 446 that "under free exchanges without capital movements, there will be no tendency for prosperity or depression to communicate itself from country to country."

Suppose now that the balanced trade between the two countries is disturbed by an expansion of investment and income in the United Kingdom. In order to emphasize the role of output and employment in the process of adjustment, we shall assume that the expansion of the United Kingdom comprises exclusively a rise in output and that costs and selling prices remain unchanged. The final results would be altered only slightly, however, if we had allowed for a rise of prices and costs with rising output. The question to be answered is whether, under a regime of flexible exchange rates, the total demand for the output of the United States would be isolated from the economic expansion in the United Kingdom; and this question may conveniently be answered by considering first the demand for American exports.

Assuming that there are no internal inflationary forces in the United States, the expansion in the United Kingdom, by increasing the British demand for American goods, will cause the pound to depreciate in terms of dollars; that is, the dollar price of sterling will fall. The fall in the price of sterling will depress the British purchase of American goods and stimulate American purchase of British goods; and if the elasticities of demand are sufficiently large, a new, balanced state of trade will eventually be established. In this new equilibrium the volume of American exports will be subject to two influences working in opposite directions. American exports will initially be increased by the expansion in the United Kingdom, but this initial influence will be offset to some extent, or perhaps more than offset, by the reduced demand for American goods resulting from appreciation of the dollar. Thus in the new position of equilibrium the volume of American goods and services sold in the United Kingdom may be either larger or smaller than in the original equilibrium.

Since American exports may either rise or fall when output is expanded in the United Kingdom, it is apparent that output as a whole in the United States will not remain at its original level unless the change in exports is exactly offset by a change in the opposite direction in some other component of output. What are the reasons, in the traditional view, for believing that this will actually occur? If American exports are increased, for example, why should the output of domestic goods be reduced by a corresponding amount? In none of the prewar discussions of exchange rates have we been able to find an explicit statement of the reasons for believing that such offsetting movements will occur. For the most part, it seems to be accepted as self-evident that if a country's exports and imports change by the same amount, as they would under a system of flexible exchange rates, the demand for the country's total output necessarily remains at a constant level. If such an assertion is critically examined, it will be found to rest upon an implicit assumption concerning producers and consumers: it implicitly assumes that when the domestic prices of imports rise or fall, any consequent change in a country's total domestic-currency expenditure on imports is exactly offset by a change in the opposite direction in expenditure on home goods; if less is spent on imports, more is spent on home goods, and conversely.

The significance of this implicit assumption may be illustrated by considering the total demand for output in the United States. Suppose that in the new position of equilibrium, after the expansion of income in the United Kingdom has come to a halt and the pound sterling has been stabilized at a lower level, the value of American exports is $200,000 larger than in the original equilibrium. Under a flexible-exchange system, the value of imports must likewise be $200,000 larger, for otherwise the foreign exchange market will not be in a balanced position. In other words, as American import prices fall, the dollar value of imports must rise; this obviously implies that the American demand for imports is elastic. Suppose now that when producers and consumers in the United States increase their dollar expenditures on imports, they reduce their expenditures on domestic goods by the same amount. In the new equilibrium, American output of goods intended for the domestic market will then be $200,000 *less* than before, a decline which exactly offsets the rise in exports. Output as a whole in the United States thus remains at its former level; the only effect of the expansion in the United Kingdom on economic conditions in the United States is a shift of American resources from the industries producing for the home market to the export industries.

If American exports are *reduced* rather than increased by the expansion in the United Kingdom, the argument concerning total output and the composition of output in the United States must be applied in reverse. In this event, the dollar value of American imports must be *lower* than in the initial equilibrium in order to maintain balance in the foreign exchange market; and if the total dollar value of imports declines as import prices fall, the American demand for imports clearly must be inelastic. When dollar expenditure on imports falls in the United

States, additional income is available for other purposes, and according to our implicit expenditure condition the income thus freed is spent entirely on domestic goods. Thus when exports of the United States decline, the expenditure condition implies that the demand for domestic goods rises by the same amount. Again, therefore, the *total* demand for American goods is unaffected by the expansion in the United Kingdom.

From the foregoing it is evident that, as long as the expenditure condition is fulfilled, an expansion of output in the United Kingdom will have no influence, under a regime of flexible exchange rates, upon the total demand for American goods. This is true regardless of whether American exports rise or fall. If American exports rise, the expansion in that segment of the economy will be offset by an equal contraction in the industries producing for home use. And if American exports fall, the contraction in the export industries will be offset by an equivalent expansion of domestic goods industries. It must be emphasized again that this argument always assumes that the expenditure condition is fulfilled; any increase in American expenditure on imports is assumed to be exactly offset by an equal decrease in expenditure on domestic goods, and conversely. If this condition is not satisfied, it is easy to show that the total value of output in the United States as well as the composition of this output will be affected by the expansion in the United Kingdom.

In view of the importance of the expenditure condition, we should ask ourselves whether it is a condition likely to be fulfilled by the expenditure schedules of most countries. The answer to this question, we believe, is in the negative. The condition implies that at a given level of money income the total expenditure on home goods and imports together is a constant amount, regardless of whether import prices are high or low. It seems to us highly improbable that expenditures of most countries will behave in such a manner. Of course, special circumstances can be found under which the expenditure condition will be satisfied. If Say's Law of Markets is regarded as valid, for example, and every unit of money income is considered to be a direct or indirect demand for goods and services, the total potential expenditure out of a given income on all goods and services will always be exactly equal to the income itself; and in this event, a rise in expenditure on imports will necessarily be accompanied by an equal fall in expenditure on home goods and conversely.

But few economists today would accept such an interpretation of the expenditure condition, for few would regard Say's Law as an accurate statement of market forces. The choice available to a typical income-earner is not simply between expenditure on imports and expenditure on home goods; rather, it is a three-fold choice between imports, home goods, and saving. And a demand for saving is no longer considered to be inevitably an indirect demand for goods and services. From this it follows that a decision to spend, say, $200 more on imports does not necessarily imply a decision to spend $200 less on home goods; the additional expenditure on imports may come, in part or in total, out of income which would otherwise have been saved.

If a third variable, saving, must be taken into account, how will the three variables, expenditure on imports, expenditure on home goods and saving, normally be related to one another? It is impossible, from theoretical considerations alone to give a conclusive answer to this question; a wide variety of different relations is consistent with rational behavior on the part of both producers and consumers. Nevertheless, we believe there is a strong presumption, based in part upon statistical evidence, that expenditure and saving will be related to each other in one particular way.

Consider, for example, the expenditure of the United States in the preceding illustration. If American wages, prices, and costs are fixed at some given level, and if import prices are also given, we can conceive of an expenditure schedule relating the amount of money which United States residents want to spend on all goods and services to the American national income; the schedule includes expenditure on both foreign and domestic goods, and expenditure on investment goods as well as on consumers' goods. Suppose now that import prices fall as a result of currency appreciation. How will this price change affect the expenditure schedule? The *composition* of expenditure will, of course, be changed since the relatively cheaper imports will be substituted for home goods. But apart from the change in composition, we believe that a change will also occur in the total expenditure schedule itself. With given prices at home, a decline in import prices increases the real income corresponding to any given level of money income. The statistical evidence for the United States shows rather conclusively that the proportion of income saved tends to rise with a rise in real income and to fall with a fall in real income; and it seems likely that if the necessary statistics were available this relation would be verified for other countries also.[11] We therefore believe there is a strong presumption that, as import prices fall and the real income corresponding to a given money income increases, the amount spent on goods and services out of a given money income will fall. The argument is applicable in reverse, of course, to a rise of import prices. In short, our basic premise is that, other things being the same, the expenditure schedule of any given country rises when import prices rise and falls when import prices fall.[12]

It is unfortunate that we do not at present have sufficient statistical evidence to verify this premise empirically. We should therefore add, in adopting the premise, that there are a number of circumstances in which a country's expenditure schedule may not shift in the manner that we have assumed. Nothing has been said, for example, about the influence of import prices on the distribution of income, and about the influence of the distribution of income, in turn, on the expenditure schedule. Nor have we made allowance for possible shifts in the expenditure schedule which may be related to domestic investment. Unfortunately, both of these influences upon a country's expenditure schedule are extremely difficult to predict. Despite this uncertainty, however, we believe that there is a presumption that the expenditure schedule will behave as we have postulated. A rise in import prices, relative to domestic prices, is equivalent in its overall effects to a general decline in the productivity of the economy. And just as a decline in physical productivity will normally lead to an increase in employment, if not of real income, so also, we believe, will an increase of import prices.[13]

The significance of a country's expenditure schedule under a regime of flexible exchange rates will become apparent if we state our case

11. These remarks refer only to the saving and expenditure associated with major business cycles. With respect to extremely long-run or secular changes in income, such as the gradual rise in income in the United States during the second half of the nineteenth century, Kuznets has collected data which suggest that the proportion of income saved may be constant regardless of the level of income. See Simon Kuznets, *National Income, A Summary of Findings* (New York, National Bureau of Economic Research, 1946), p. 53. With respect to cyclical movements, on the other hand, there is no doubt that the proportion of income saved tends to rise and fall with rising and falling income. See J. S. Duesenberry, "Income-Consumption Relations and Their Implications," in *Income, Employment and Public Policy* (New York, W. W. Norton, 1948), pp. 54–81.

12. See Wolfgang F. Stolper, "The Volume of Foreign Trade and the Level of Income," *Quarterly Journal of Economics*, 56 (February 1947), 285–310.

13. Harberger reaches a similar conclusion, but bases his argument on the theory of consumers' choice. See his "Currency Depreciation" (reference 5), pp. 52–53.

in terms of national income. If we set aside governmental transactions, the net income of a given country consists in the following:[14]

Net income equals
>   consumers' expenditure on all goods and services, domestic and foreign,
> *plus*   net domestic investment in all goods and services,
> *plus*   exports of all goods and services,
> *less*   imports of all goods and services.

This formulation involves no special assumptions as to the nature of the international monetary system and is applicable alike to the gold standard and to a system of flexible exchange rates. Under a regime of flexible exchange rates, however, the definition of national income may be considerably simplified. If capital movements are prohibited, as we have assumed, the only components of supply and demand in the foreign exchange market will be exports and imports of goods and services. Now if the price of foreign exchange tends toward a point at which supply is equal to demand, the value of a country's exports invisible as well as visible, will be equal to the value of its imports, and the balance-of-payments items in the above definition of national income will accordingly cancel out. In a position of international equilibrium, national income may then be written as follows:

Net income equals
>   consumption of all goods and services,
> *plus*   net domestic investment in all goods and services.

Reduced to its simplest terms, the second statement of national income say that under a system of free-market exchange rates and prohibited capital movements, the national income of any country is equal to that country's own expenditure on goods and services, including investment expenditure as well as consumption expenditure, and including expenditure on foreign as well as on domestic goods and services.

Since a country's expenditure depends upon its income, and since income in turn is exactly equal to this same expenditure, it might seem that under a system of flexible exchange rates the circular flow of

14. See *Survey of Current Business* supplement, "National Income and Product Statistics of the United States, 1929–1946," prepared by National Income Division (July 1947), pp. 1–17.

income would be a closed or autonomous circuit, and that the principles governing the *level* if not the *composition* of income in an open economy would be the same as those governing the level of income in an isolated state. In short, it might seem that business cycles originating abroad would have no effect upon the size of output and employment at home.

The fallacy in such a view, as we have indicated above, is that it neglects the influence of the terms of trade on a country's expenditure schedule; it assumes, in other words, that the expenditure schedule is a function of income alone and is independent of the terms of trade. In contrast to this conception of the expenditure schedule, we have argued that, other things remaining the same, expenditure out of a given income tends to rise when import prices rise and to fall when import prices fall. Since a country's output under a system of flexible exchange rates is governed exclusively by its own expenditure on goods and services, and since such expenditure, in turn, is partly dependent upon import prices, it is clear that changes in economic conditions abroad will influence output and employment at home even though the value of exports is always equal to the value of imports.

These ideas may perhaps be clarified by contrasting the position of a country under the gold standard with that of a country under a regime of flexible exchange rates. From our first definition of income, it is apparent that under the gold standard a country's net income may be divided into two parts, its expenditure on goods and services and its balance of trade (or, more generally, its balance of payments on current account). Since the first of these parts is dependent to some extent upon the terms of trade, we may say that under the gold standard the foreign events which influence the rate of output in a particular country may be classified into two groups: the first group comprises all events which affect the *terms* of trade, while the second comprises events which affect the *balance* of trade. Under a flexible-exchange system, by contrast, the balance of trade remains constant, and the foreign events which influence a country's output are accordingly limited to the first group, namely those which affect the *terms* of trade.

With foreign influences reduced from two types to one, it might seem that under a regime of flexible exchange rates a country's output would be insulated to a considerable extent, if not completely, from the effects of foreign business cycles. On the whole, this argument is probably correct; the dependence of output in one country on economic conditions elsewhere is clearly more indirect and less powerful under flexible exchange rates than under the gold standard. Nevertheless, it must be remembered that while fluctuations in the *balance* of trade would be eliminated by a system of flexible exchange rates, fluctuations in the *terms* of trade would become much more important; for it is only through changes in the latter, brought about by currency depreciation or appreciation, that the movements in the *balance* of trade would be eliminated. In a regime of flexible exchange rates, the extent to which the circular flow of income of a particular country forms an autonomous circuit thus depends upon the sensitivity of the country's expenditure schedule to changes in the terms of trade. If total expenditure is highly sensitive to movements in the relative price of foreign and domestic goods, the level of national income will tend to rise and fall with changing economic conditions abroad, despite the fact that the balance of trade is maintained at a constant level. If expenditure depends only to an insignificant degree upon the terms of trade, however, then the level of output of the given country will be largely independent of economic conditions abroad.

We have seen that a country's expenditure schedule will normally be related in a certain way to the level of import prices; and we have argued that through this relationship total output will be influenced, even under a system of flexible exchange rates, by economic conditions in the rest of the world. Having established these interrelations, we may now go a step further and inquire more specifically into the exact type of dependence between output in different countries which may be expected under a regime of flexible exchange rates. If output and employment are expanded in one part of the world, for example, will the expansion be transmitted to the rest of the world, as under the gold standard, or will the dependence between output in different countries be of a different type?

In order to answer this question, we may return once more to our example of trade between the United States and the United Kingdom. Suppose, as before, that trade between the two countries is initially in balance at an exchange rate of $\$3 = \pounds1$, and suppose that this equilibrium is disturbed by an expansion of output and employment in the United Kingdom. When the expansion occurs, the British demand for imports will rise, and the resulting deficit in the British balance of payments will cause the price of the dollar to rise, or the pound sterling to depreciate. In this manner, the exchange rate will eventually reach a new equilibrium appropriate to the higher level of output and employment in the United Kingdom.

Assume that this new equilibrium is $2.40 = £1$. What can be said now about the effects of the expansion in the United Kingdom upon the level of output or employment in the United States? The volume of American exports, as we have seen earlier, is subject to two conflicting forces and may either rise or fall. But regardless of what happens to the volume of exports, the level of United States output as a whole depends exclusively, under a system of flexible exchange rates, upon the amount of American expenditure for goods and services. If we are interested in the overall expansion or contraction of the American economy, and not in the fate of particular industries, we must therefore concentrate our attention upon the American expenditure function. Depreciation of sterling, by reducing the dollar prices of British goods, increases the real value of a given money income in the United States. And we have argued above that such an increase in the purchasing power of money income will normally increase the proportion saved, and reduce the proportion spent on goods and services, out of a given money income.[15] In short, the expansion in the United Kingdom and the resulting depreciation of the pound sterling will lead to a *fall* in the American money expenditure function. Since the value of American output is equal, in equilibrium, to the American expenditure on goods and services, it follows that American output and employment must likewise fall. We have thus reached the somewhat paradoxical result that under a regime of flexible exchange rates an expansion of economic activity in one country leads to a slight contraction in the other.

Consider the contrast which this result suggests between the gold standard and a flexible-exchange standard. One of the principal objections to the gold standard, as we pointed out at the beginning of this paper, was that it served as the mechanism by which a depression originating in one part of the world was transmitted throughout the world economy. Under the gold standard, in other words, there was a high degree of positive correlation between the rate of output in one part of the world and output elsewhere. Flexible exchange rates were

15. As far as the United States is concerned, the effects of rising and falling import prices on real income are almost negligible, owing to the fact that a small proportion of income is spent on imports; for this reason, there is a danger that the example may be misleading. In other countries, however, the proportion of income spent on imports is much larger, and an increase or decrease in import prices relative to domestic prices therefore has a greater effect on real income.

proposed primarily to break this link which had bound the output of individual countries to the fluctuations of world demand. In the light of the conclusion reached above, it appears that flexible exchange rates would serve, in part at least, the purpose for which they were intended. To be sure, the effective demand and output of every country would be governed to some extent by economic conditions elsewhere. But the monetary system would not itself contribute to the world-wide depressions and inflations that characterized the gold standard. Quite the contrary, under an effective system of flexible exchange rates an expansion in one part of the world would lead to a slight contraction elsewhere, and vice versa.

This does not mean, of course, that under a regime of flexible exchange rates a world-wide depression or inflation could never occur. It is entirely conceivable that economic developments might be such that the demand for investment would rise or fall simultaneously in many parts of the world; if so, a general contraction or expansion would occur throughout the world economy under any monetary system. Moreover, even if the underlying conditions of technology and demand were quite diverse, a prolonged depression in one country might still lead, through its adverse effects on expectations elsewhere, to a general world depression. But these examples of possible world-wide depressions merely emphasize that changes in effective demand, operating through the international monetary system, are not the only means by which depression and inflation are transmitted from one country to another. The examples do not refute the view that, under a flexible exchange system, the monetary mechanism would provide a buffer against a general world depression or inflation.

The tendency under a regime of flexible exchange rates for output in different countries to move in opposite directions raises an interesting problem concerning the justification of depreciation by an individual country. Of course, if all exchange rates were free-market rates, we could not ask whether a particular depreciation was "justifiable" or not; each exchange rate would simply be the rate which equalized supply and demand in the foreign-exchange markets. In practice, however, exchange rates have seldom been completely free in this sense, and it is doubtful whether such a free system will ever prevail in the future. It seems probable that exchange rates will always be determined in part by governmental policy. Whenever exchange rates are determined by governmental policy, however, the question is likely to arise as to whether a given policy is justified by the condition of a particular country's balance of payments.

This question was particularly prominent during the Great Depression, when changes in currency values were employed for domestic rather than international purposes. Owing to the widespread unemployment which prevailed at that time, most countries were tempted to devalue their currencies as a means of assisting their export industries and their industries competing with imports; the temptation was so strong, in fact, that devaluation was sometimes undertaken regardless of the condition of a country's balance of payments. A wave of competitive devaluation thus occurred in which countries with balance-of-payments surpluses devalued along with the countries having deficits.[16] Devaluation by the countries having surpluses, particularly by the United States, was widely condemned as a "beggar-my-neighbor" policy on the ground that it was a predatory means of increasing employment in the devaluing countries at the expense of employment elsewhere.

In the course of the discussion two different circumstances were distinguished, and devaluation was held to be justifiable in only one of these. First, if a country devalued as a means of expanding employment, and if the devaluation was not required by the condition of the country's balance of payments, the act was regarded as unneighborly and antisocial. Second, if the country attempted to solve its employment problem by domestic measures such as public works or other forms of spending, and if a deficit in its balance of payments developed as a result of the expansion of income, devaluation was considered to be a justifiable means of eliminating the deficit. A devaluation of this second sort, according to the view that prevailed at the time, would not inflict hardships upon other countries but would merely permit the expanding country to enjoy the full benefits of its own expansion.[17]

Few economists would dispute the validity of such a distinction. Nevertheless, it is interesting to note that, according to the theory presented in this paper, even a "justifiable" devaluation may create a moderate amount of unemployment in other countries. Consider, for

16. See League of Nations, *International Currency Experience* (reference 4), pp. 122–131.

17. Cf. the following remark by Harrod in *International Economics* (reference 3), p. 161: "Exchange depreciation will not be injurious to the outer world if it is the consequence of an internal expansion and occurs under the influence of supply and demand. It will only be injurious if it is deliberately brought about by the authorities as a means of stimulating internal employment." On this same point, see also Salant, "Foreign Trade Policy" (reference 2), p. 217.

example, our previous illustration of trade between the United States and the United Kingdom. Starting from a position of international equilibrium, we found that, as output and employment expanded in the United Kingdom, depreciation of the pound sterling, relative to the dollar, was necessary to prevent a deficit in the British balance of payments. Such a depreciation is the prototype of what would have been regarded during the thirties as "justifiable." And yet, according to the argument presented above, a devaluation of the pound under such conditions would lead to unemployment in the United States. Is it, on that account, to be regarded as a predatory or beggar-my-neighbor policy?

The answer, we believe, is clearly in the negative. Output in the United States, in our imaginary example, declines because American expenditure on goods and services declines; and the decline in the latter is attributable in turn to the improvement in the American terms of trade. Now, as we have pointed out above, an improvement in a country's terms of trade is equivalent, economically, to an increase in the productivity of some of the country's factors of production; such resources, by producing a given quantity of goods for export, can acquire more imported goods for a given amount of effort than was formerly true. Basically, then, the decline in American output is attributable to the higher productivity of the country's resources. The situation is more or less similar to what would happen if a peculiar innovation should suddenly increase the output of each worker and each machine in a certain segment of the American economy *without increasing anyone's desire for goods and services.* The increase in productivity is a type which creates no additional demand for investment goods and, unless the spending habits of the country can be adjusted to the higher productivity, unemployment of some resources is bound to ensue. Unemployment of this sort is hardly to be "blamed" upon other countries, however, any more than a sharp increase in technical productivity would be condemned. While it is not an evil event, neither is it an unmixed blessing, for it requires an adjustment of spending and saving habits to the new conditions of production.

The fundamental problem of this paper has been the degree of economic insulation that can be achieved by a system of flexible exchange rates. We began by describing the optimistic attitude that prevailed toward such a system during the interwar years, and in concluding it seems appropriate to ask whether the theory as set out above supports or refutes the optimists.

If capital movements can be effectively controlled, there is hardly any doubt that flexible exchange rates will cushion some countries to a considerable extent against the economic shocks of business cycles in other parts of the world; on this score, then, the opinions of the optimists are justified. Nevertheless, the whole tenor of the preceding argument has been that the shock absorption performed by flexible exchange rates will by no means be perfect. Both the composition of a country's output and the level of its total output will be affected to some extent under such a system by economic fluctuations abroad. We have seen, however, that output will not rise and fall simultaneously in all parts of the world, as under the gold standard. Instead, the rate of economic activity will probably fall moderately in some parts of the world while other parts of the world are enjoying a period of expansion, and conversely.

The tendency under flexible exchanges for output and employment to rise in some parts of the world at the same time that a contraction is taking place elsewhere does not mean that *real* income necessarily moves in opposite directions in different parts of the world. Real income depends upon a country's terms of trade as well as upon its output and employment, and under a system of flexible exchange rates a country's output tends to fall when its terms of trade improve and to rise when its terms of trade deteriorate. The effect on real income of the change in terms of trade is thus opposite to the effect of the change in output, and the net result of the two changes together remains indeterminate.

When output rises in one region of the world as a result of a depression elsewhere, for example, the rise in output may well be accompanied by a fall in real income as a consequence of the unfavorable movement in the expanding region's terms of trade. Such an outcome is particularly likely in agricultural countries or countries which specialize in other primary products. The basic cyclical problems of these countries have never been fluctuations in employment, as in the industrial countries; their problems, rather, have been wide shifts in the terms of trade which resulted from fluctuating output in other parts of the world. And a system of flexible exchange rates would not in any way reduce the amplitude of the cyclical movements in the primary producers' terms of trade. Quite the contrary, the fluctuations in terms of trade would clearly be greater under flexible exchanges than under fixed exchanges. A system of fluctuating exchange rates cannot therefore be regarded as a means of insulating the countries producing primary products from business cycles in the industrial countries. The principal value of such a system will probably be found, instead, in its ability to insulate industrial countries against economic fluctuations in other industrial countries. But even in this respect, as we have seen, the degree of insulation is not perfect.

In applying these conclusions to practical problems, we must bear in mind a number of reservations or limitations. In the first place, we have considered only those changes in output associated with direct changes in the circular flow of income; this means that we have neglected such monetary influences as changes in interest rates and in the real value of cash balances. Closely related to this first limitation is the absence in the foregoing study of any discussion of price flexibility. Throughout our investigation we have assumed that selling prices and costs remain constant in terms of the currency of the selling country; the only price movements taken into account were the movements in buyers' prices of imports resulting from fluctuations in exchange rates. Third, in discussing the effects of a flexible-exchange system we have taken it for granted that such a system is workable in the sense that at some feasible pattern of exchange rates each country's demand for foreign exchange is equal to its supply. As we have indicated, serious doubts have arisen in recent years regarding the validity of this assumption. This is a technical question, which is discussed in the appendix below. Finally, we have not examined the problems of transferring resources from one industry to another within a given country; throughout the investigation we have considered only *total* demand and *total* output and have said little about shifts in the composition of demand and output.

It would be useful, if space permitted, to relax the assumption of fixed prices and selling costs and thereby to introduce a greater degree of price flexibility into the system. For this purpose, two fundamental types of price behavior ought to be considered. The first type, which might be called "cyclical price behavior," is characterized by a tendency for prices and costs to rise and fall with rising and falling output. In this type of price behavior, which can be found in many business cycles, prices and costs do not represent additional independent variables; rather, the price and cost variables are functionally dependent upon the level of output in each country. It follows that price flexibility of the first type does not alter the conclusions reached above in any fundamental respect. The second type of price behavior, for which empirical examples are more difficult to find, is represented by a situation in which prices and costs tend to fall whenever the demand for resources is less than the available supply at existing prices, and to rise when the demand for resources exceeds the available supply. If this second type of price flexibility were the prevalent type, equilibrium for the system as a whole would obviously be impossible at any level of output other than a full-employment level,[18] and the foregoing discussion of the theory of employment as it affects exchange rates would accordingly have to be replaced by the orthodox or classical theory of international trade. In brief, then, the theory developed above is valid either for fixed prices and costs or for price flexibility of the first type but not for price flexibility of the second type.

The results thus far have been presented in a nontechnical and non-mathematical manner. For this reason many of the difficult aspects of the subject have been dismissed with a few casual remarks, while other aspects have been omitted altogether. The investigation, for example, has been limited to purely static problems; we have compared one position of equilibrium with another, but we have said nothing about the dynamic process of adjustment when the economic system is not in equilibrium. Nor have we discussed the conditions of stability of the dynamic system. These technical problems will be presented in the appendix below.

Appendix

Consider a simplified case of trade between two countries, which we shall call country 1 and country 2. Let y_1 and y_2 be the net money incomes of the two countries, each income being measured in terms of the given country's own currency. We shall assume that money wages and the money returns to other factors of production remain constant and that all commodities are produced under conditions of constant costs. Under these conditions, changes in y_1 and y_2 will measure not only changes in money income but also changes in the physical output of goods and services and in the level of employment.

Let π represent the price in country 1 of the currency of country 2. A rise in π then indicates depreciation of country 1's currency, while a fall indicates appreciation. Since all goods and services are assumed to be produced and sold at constant costs in terms of the selling country's currency, the prices of imports in country 1 will vary in proportion to π, and π may

18. Equilibrium might also be impossible at full employment. But this question of the consistency or inconsistency of the classical theory cannot be discussed here.

accordingly be used as an index of import prices in that country; and by similar reasoning the index of import prices in country 2 will be $1/\pi$. With prices of domestic goods constant, the demand for imports in each country will be a function of two variables, money income and the given country's index of import prices. If $\hat{v}_1$ and $\hat{v}_2$ represent the domestic-currency expenditure of the two countries on imports, we may therefore write $\hat{v}_1 = \hat{v}_1(y_1, \pi)$ and $\hat{v}_2 = \hat{v}_2(y_2, 1/\pi)$ as the two import functions. The total money expenditure of each country on all goods and services will likewise depend upon the given country's national income and upon import prices. Letting $\hat{\omega}_1$ and $\hat{\omega}_2$ represent these total expenditures for the two countries, we have $\hat{\omega}_1 = \hat{\omega}_1(y_1, \pi)$ and $\hat{\omega}_2 = \hat{\omega}_2(y_2, 1/\pi)$. The symbol $\hat{\omega}_1$ as used here includes money expenditure for net investment as well as for consumption; and it includes expenditure on imports as well as on domestically produced goods and services. Since each country's national income is equal to its expenditure on goods and services *plus* its exports *minus* its imports, and since one country's imports are the other's exports, we may write the following equations:

$$(A1) \quad \begin{aligned} y_1 &= \hat{\omega}_1(y_1, \pi) + \pi\hat{v}_2(y_2, 1/\pi) - \hat{v}_1(y_1, \pi), \\ y_2 &= \hat{\omega}_2(y_2, 1/\pi) + (1/\pi)\hat{v}_1(y_1,\pi) - \hat{v}_2(y_2, 1/\pi), \end{aligned}$$

and $\quad b_2 = (1/\pi)\hat{v}_1(y_1, \pi) - \hat{v}_2(y_2, 1/\pi).$

With a given exchange rate, π, and with given expenditure functions and import functions in the two countries, Eqs. (A1) are sufficient to determine the equilibrium levels of income, $y_1{}^0$ and $y_2{}^0$, and the balance of payments on current account, b_2. The balance of payments as represented by (A1) is of course that of country 2, expressed in country 2's currency.

Suppose now that the exchange rate is a flexible rate, and that it accordingly takes on a value at which the international payments and receipts between the two countries are equalized. If capital movements are prohibited the equilibrium exchange rate will be that rate at which each country's exports are equal to its imports and we will have:

$$(A2) \quad \begin{aligned} y_1 &= \hat{\omega}_1(y_1, \pi) + \alpha_1, \\ y_2 &= \hat{\omega}_2(y_2, 1/\pi), \end{aligned}$$

and $\quad (1/\pi)\hat{v}_1(y_1, \pi) = \hat{v}_2(y_2, 1/\pi).$

Equations (A2) are the basic equations of our system. With given expenditure functions and price levels in both countries, these equations indicate the equilibrium levels of income as well as the equilibrium exchange rate. The problem discussed above was how the equilibrium values of the three variables are affected by a shift in the expenditure function of one of the countries. In order to analyze the problem mathematically, the quantity α_1 has been added to the first of Eqs. (A2). This quantity represents an increase in the demand for domestic goods in country 1. We want to know how a change in α_1 affects y_1, y_2, and π; that is, how an expansion of domestic demand in country 1 affects income at home and abroad, and how such an expansion affects the rate of exchange. To simplify our answers to these questions, we suppose that the units of currency in which money incomes are measured are chosen in such a way that in the initial equilibrium the rate of exchange is 1 for 1; in other words, that $\pi^0 = 1$. Differentiating (A2) with respect to α_1, we find:

$$\left(1 - \frac{\delta\hat{\omega}_1}{\delta y_1}\right)\frac{dy_1}{d\alpha_1} - \left(\frac{\delta\hat{\omega}_1}{\delta\pi}\right)\frac{d\pi}{d\alpha_1} = 1,$$

(A3)
$$\left(1 - \frac{\delta\hat{\omega}_2}{\delta y_2}\right)\frac{dy_2}{d\alpha_1} + \left(\frac{\delta\hat{\omega}_2}{\delta(1/\pi)}\right)\frac{d\pi}{d\alpha_1} = 0,$$

and
$$-\left(\frac{\delta\hat{v}_1}{\delta y_1}\right)\frac{dy_1}{d\alpha_1} + \left(\frac{\delta\hat{v}_2}{\delta y_2}\right)\frac{dy_2}{d\alpha_1} + \left(\hat{v}_1 - \frac{\delta\hat{v}_2}{\delta(1/\pi)} - \frac{\delta\hat{v}_1}{\delta\pi}\right)\frac{d\pi}{d\alpha_1} = 0.$$

Equations (A3) constitute three linear equations which may be solved for the three unknowns, $dy_1/d\alpha_1$, $dy_2/d\alpha_1$, and $d\pi/d\alpha_1$. Before solving the equations, however, we shall find it useful to consider the numerical limits that can be attached to the partial derivatives, which constitute what might be called "technical coefficients" of the system; and since these coefficients will appear frequently in the subsequent argument it is desirable to give them a simpler notation than the somewhat cumbersome partial derivatives of Eqs. (A3).

Consider first the changes in total expenditure with respect to changes in money income, such as $\delta\hat{\omega}_1/\delta y_1$, for example. In the terminology of the theory of employment, this partial derivative represents the marginal propensity to spend; it is the sum, if induced investment is taken into account, of the marginal propensity to consume and the marginal propensity to invest. It is always positive, of course, and unless the marginal propensity to invest is high it will normally be less than unity. Hereafter we shall substitute for this partial derivative the single letter w_1, with a similar notation for the second country. Thus we have $0 < w_1 \equiv \delta\hat{\omega}_1/\delta y_1 < 1$ and $0 < w_2 \equiv \delta\hat{\omega}_2/\delta y_2 < 1$.

The partial derivative $\delta\hat{v}_1/\delta y_1$ represents the marginal propensity of country 1 to import. With given prices, it indicates the increase in money expenditure on imports that occurs when money income is increased by a small amount. Like the marginal propensity to spend, the marginal propensity to import is normally positive, but less than unity. If m_1 and m_2 are used to designate the two marginal propensities to import, we have

$$0 < m_1 \equiv \delta\hat{v}_1/\delta y_1 < 1 \quad \text{and} \quad 0 < m_2 \equiv \delta\hat{v}_2/\delta y_2 < 1.$$

The changes in total expenditure with respect to changes in the price of foreign currency ($\delta\hat{\omega}_1/\delta\pi$ and $\delta\hat{\omega}_2/\delta[1/\pi]$) have no special name since they do not appear in the usual versions of the theory of employment. We shall call them simply the "price effects" of changes in the exchange rate. We have argued in the text that, with given money incomes and given domestic prices, an increase in import prices will probably increase total expenditure out of a given income. This means that $\delta\hat{\omega}_1/\delta\pi$ and $\delta\hat{\omega}_2/\delta(1/\pi)$ are assumed to be positive. Although there may be exceptions to this rule, positive values for the price effects of depreciation are the normal expectation. Hereafter s_1 and s_2 will be used to denote $\delta\hat{\omega}_1/\delta\pi$ and $\delta\hat{\omega}_2/\delta(1/\pi)$ respectively, with the understanding that both of these price effects are normally positive.

Consider finally the partial derivative of the balance of trade with respect to the exchange rate, in other words, expression $\hat{v}_1 - \delta\hat{v}_1/\delta\pi - \delta\hat{v}_2/\delta(1/\pi)$. This expression shows how a rise in the price of country 2's currency, with given money incomes and outputs in both countries, affects the balance of trade of country 1. The partial derivative $\delta\hat{v}_2/\delta(1/\pi)$ represents the change in money expenditure on imports that occurs in country 2 when the prices of imports in that country rise uniformly by a small amount. This expression will accordingly be negative or positive depending on whether country 2's demand for imports is elastic or inelastic. A similar argument applies, of course, to $\delta\hat{v}_1/\delta\pi$. In view of the role played by the ordinary elasticities of demand, it is useful to translate the above expression into such elasticities. Let η_1 and η_2 represent elasticities of demand for imports in countries 1 and 2, respectively. It is then easy to show that, in the neighborhood of equilibrium,[19]

$$(A4) \qquad \hat{v}_1 - \frac{\delta\hat{v}_1}{\delta\pi} - \frac{\delta\hat{v}_2}{\delta(1/\pi)} = \hat{v}_1(\eta_1 + \eta_2 - 1).$$

The symbols η_1 and η_2, being ordinary elasticities of demand, will normally be positive. It follows that (A4) will be positive whenever either country has an elastic demand for imports. If the demand for imports is *inelastic* in *both* countries, on the other hand, both η_1 and η_2 will be less than unity. In this event (A4) may be either positive or negative, depending upon whether

---

19. Suppose we are dealing with composite import commodities, and let x_1 and x_2 be the physical units of such imports in countries 1 and 2 respectively. The price of imports in country 1 being π, we then have $\hat{v} = \pi x_1$, whence $\delta\hat{v}_1/\delta\pi = x_1 + \pi\,\delta x_1/\delta\pi = x_1(1 - \eta_1)$. By an analogous argument $\delta\hat{v}_2/\delta(1/\pi) = x_2(1 - \eta_2)$. We have chosen our currency units in such a way that at the initial position of equilibrium the exchange rate π has a value of unity. From this it follows that $x_1 = \pi x_1 = \hat{v}_1$ and $x_2 = 1/\pi x_2 = \hat{v}_2$. Now when the foreign-exchange market is in equilibrium, we must have $\hat{v}_1 = \pi\hat{v}_2$ and since $\pi^\circ = 1$, this implies $\hat{v}_1 = \hat{v}_2$. From these relations we derive Eq. (4) above.

$\eta_1 + \eta_2$ is greater or less than unity. Since an inelastic demand for imports is by no means an impossibility, we cannot, without additional information, determine the sign of (A4). For the moment we shall assume that it may be either positive or negative.

Let us return now to Eqs. (A3). With the simplified notation, they may be written as follows:

$$(1 - w_1) \frac{dy_1}{d\alpha_1} \qquad\qquad - s_1 \frac{d\pi}{d\alpha_1} = 1,$$

(A5)
$$(1 - w_2) \frac{dy_2}{d\alpha_1} \qquad + s_2 \frac{d\pi}{d\alpha_1} = 0,$$

and
$$- m_1 \frac{dy_1}{d\alpha_1} + m_2 \frac{dy_2}{d\alpha_1} + \hat{v}_1(\eta_1 + \eta_2 - 1) \frac{d\pi}{d\alpha_1} = 0.$$

Solving (A5) for $dy_1/d\alpha_1$, $dy_2/d\alpha_1$, and $d\pi/d\alpha_1$, we find:

$$\frac{dy_1}{d\alpha_1} = \frac{1}{\Delta} \left\{ (1 - w_2)\hat{v}_1(\eta_1 + \eta_2 - 1) - m_2 s_2 \right\},$$

(A6)
$$\frac{dy_2}{d\alpha_1} = \frac{1}{\Delta} \left\{ - m_1 s_2 \right\},$$

and
$$\frac{d\pi}{d\alpha_1} = \frac{1}{\Delta} \left\{ m_1(1 - w_2) \right\},$$

where

$$\Delta \equiv \begin{vmatrix} 1 - w_1 & 0 & -s_1 \\ 0 & 1 - w_2 & s_2 \\ - m_1 & m_2 & \hat{v}_1(\eta_1 + \eta_2 - 1) \end{vmatrix}$$
$$\equiv (1 - w_1)(1 - w_2)\hat{v}_1(\eta_1 + \eta_2 - 1) - s_1 m_1(1 - w_2)$$
$$- s_2 m_2(1 - w_1).$$

It is apparent that we cannot evaluate the signs of (A6) from our knowledge of the technical coefficients alone. Both the numerators and the common denominator of the right-hand side of (A6) contain some expressions assumed to be positive, other expressions assumed to be negative, and one expression which may be positive, negative, or zero. Because of this uncertainty, we cannot give a direct answer to the question we set out to investigate.

The problem must therefore be approached indirectly by considering the conditions of stability; we must examine the behavior of a dynamic system before we can evaluate our static equations.[20] There is of course no assurance that the technical coefficients—the marginal propensities to spend, to import, and so forth, and the price elasticities—will in all cases have the amplitudes required to assure the stability of the system. As we intimated in the text, it is entirely possible, particularly in the short run, for the elasticities of demand for imports to be so small that a flexible-exchange system would be unstable and therefore unworkable. But there is no point in discussing the operation of a system that is fundamentally unworkable. We shall therefore make the optimistic assumption, as we did in the text, that elasticities of demand are sufficiently large and propensities to spend sufficiently small so that an economic system such as the one depicted in (A6) will be a stable system. The limitations which this assumption places upon our coefficients are discussed below. We leave it to the reader to judge whether these limitations are reasonable or unreasonable, probable or improbable.

The dynamic system that follows is based upon two familiar postulates concerning the behavior of prices and output when supply is not equal to demand. The first postulate is that the price of foreign exchange tends to rise whenever the demand for such exchange exceeds the supply, and to fall when supply exceeds demand, the speed of the price movement being proportional to the discrepancy between demand and supply. If country 1 and country 2 each had a well-developed market for the currency of the other, this postulate could easily be applied to both markets, with arbitrage activity introduced to make the prices in the two markets consistent. For present purposes, however, it will be convenient to assume that one currency tends to dominate the foreign-exchange markets, and international transactions are conducted primarily in this dominant currency. Suppose, in the present instance, that the dominant currency is that of country 2. The important foreign-exchange price will then be the price of country 2's currency in terms of country 1's currency, and changes in this price will be

---

20. The principle that static equations can frequently be evaluated from a knowledge of a corresponding dynamic system has been called by Samuelson the "correspondence principle." In a rather nontechnical way, this principle has a long history in the theory of international trade. Alfred Marshall, in his discussion of the familiar equations of reciprocal demand, was careful to distinguish between positions of stable and unstable equilibrium; and in describing the effects of tariffs or other disturbances in international trade, he always confined his arguments to the stable cases. See *The Pure Theory of Foreign Trade*, printed for private circulation in 1879; see also his *Money, Credit, and Commerce* (London, Macmillan, 1923), appendix J.

The correspondence principle has been employed more recently in the theory of prices and in the theory of employment. See J. R. Hicks, *Value and Capital* (Oxford, Clarendon Press, 1939), pt. 2; and A. C. Pigou, *Employment and Equilibrium* (London, Macmillan, 1941). The definitive formulation and rigorous proof of the correspondence principle was derived by Paul A. Samuelson, and can be found in his article "The Stability of Equilibrium: Comparative Statics and Dynamics," *Econometrica*, 9 (April 1941), 97–120.

governed by the balance of payments of country 2. We may therefore write, as our first dynamic postulate,

$$\frac{d\pi}{dt} = k_3 \left\{ (1/\pi)\hat{v}_1(y_1, \pi) - \hat{v}_2(y_2, 1(\pi)) \right\},$$

where k_3 is a positive constant, hereafter called the "speed of adjustment in the foreign-exchange market."

The second postulate is that the level of output in a given country tends to rise whenever the demand for goods and services as a whole exceeds the current rate of output, and to fall when demand falls short of current output. During the period of adjustment, when supply is not equal to demand, any discrepancy is assumed to be met by an appropriate movement of business inventories. Since we are now dealing with a dynamic system, we can no longer assume, as we did in the discussion of the static equations, that each country's balance of payments is always in equilibrium. It follows that the total demand for a country's output will not be equal, as it was in the static system, to that country's total expenditure for all goods and services. Total demand will be equal, instead, to domestic expenditure on all goods and services *plus* the domestic-currency value of exports *minus* the domestic-currency value of imports. In the notation of our earlier equations, we thus have two dynamic income equations, one for the income of country 1 and the other for the income of country 2. Together with the equation expressing the adjustment of foreign exchange rates, these equations form a complete dynamic system as follows:

(A7)
$$\frac{dy_1}{dt} = k_1 \left\{ \hat{\omega}_1(y_1, \pi) + \pi\hat{v}_2(y_2, 1/\pi) - \hat{v}_1(y_1, \pi) - y_1 \right\},$$

$$\frac{dy_2}{dt} = k_2 \left\{ \hat{\omega}_2(y_2, 1/\pi) + (1/\pi)\hat{v}_1(y_1, \pi) - \hat{v}_2(y_2, 1/\pi) - y_2 \right\},$$

and
$$\frac{d\pi}{dt} = k_3 \left\{ (1/\pi)\hat{v}_1(y_1, \pi) - \hat{v}_2(y_2, 1/\pi) \right\}.$$

Like k_3, the symbols k_1 and k_2 of (A7) are positive quantities which represent speeds of adjustment.

Without knowing the exact functional relations given by the demand functions of (A7)—that is, the total expenditure and import functions—it is impossible to solve (A7) so as to express income and exchange rates as explicit functions of time. In any event, we are interested not in the explicit solutions of (A7) but in the conditions of stability of such a system. And a necessary condition of stability is that the linear parts of (A7) form a stable system. Accordingly, we may expand the right-hand side of (A7) in a Taylor series about the equilibrium values $y_1{}^0$, $y_2{}^0$, and π^0, and omit all except the linear terms of the expansion, thus:

(A8)
$$\frac{dy_1}{dt} = k_1(w_1 - m_1 - 1)(y_1 - y_1^0) + k_1 m_2(y_2 - y_2^0)$$
$$+ k_1\left\{s_1 + \hat{v}_1(\eta_1 + \eta_2 - 1)\right\}\left\{\pi - \pi^0\right\},$$

$$\frac{dy_2}{dt} = k_2 m_1(y_1 - y_1^0) + k_2(w_2 - m_2 - 1)(y_2 - y_2^0)$$
$$- k_2\left\{s_2 + \hat{v}_1(\eta_1 + \eta_2 - 1)\right\}\left\{\pi - \pi^0\right\},$$

and
$$\frac{d\pi}{dt} = k_3 m_1(y_1 - y_1^0) - k_3 m_2(y_2 - y_2^0) - k_3 \hat{v}_1(\eta_1 + \eta_2 - 1)(\pi - \pi^0).$$

The solution of (A8) has the following form:

(A9)
$$y_1 = y_1^0 + A_{11}e^{\lambda_1 t} + A_{12}e^{\lambda_2 t} + A_{13}e^{\lambda_3 t},$$
$$y_2 = y_2^0 + A_{21}e^{\lambda_1 t} + A_{22}e^{\lambda_2 t} + A_{23}e^{\lambda_3 t},$$
$$\pi = \pi^0 + A_{31}e^{\lambda_1 t} + A_{32}e^{\lambda_2 t} + A_{33}e^{\lambda_3 t},$$

where the constants A_{ij} depend upon initial conditions at time $t = 0$, and where λ_1, λ_2, and λ_3 are roots of the following equation:

(A10)
$$\begin{vmatrix} k_1(w_1 - m_1 - 1) - \lambda & k_1 m_2 & k_1 s_1 + k_1\hat{v}_1(\eta_1 + \eta_2 - 1) \\ k_2 m_1 & k_2(w_2 - m_2 - 1) - \lambda & -k_2 s_2 - k_2\hat{v}_1(\eta_1 + \eta_2 - 1) = 0 \\ k_3 m_1 & -k_3 m_2 & k_3\hat{v}_1(\eta_1 + \eta_2 - 1) - \lambda \end{vmatrix}$$

It is apparent from (A9) that y_1, y_2, and π will not be stable, that is, they will not tend to approach the equilibrium values y_1^0, y_2^0, and π^0, unless the real parts of λ_1, λ_2, and λ_3, the roots of (A10), are all negative. In order to see what this means, we may expand the determinant (A10) and combine all like powers of λ. With a change of sign, (A10) may then be expressed in the following form:

(A11)
$$\lambda^3 + \alpha_1\lambda^2 + \alpha_2\lambda + \alpha_3 = 0,$$

where α_1 is the sum, with the sign changed, of all principal first-order minors of the determinant obtained from (A10) by putting $\lambda = 0$; α_2 is the sum, without change of sign, of similar second-order minors, and α_3 is simply $k_1 k_2 k_3 \Delta$. In order that the real parts of the roots of (A11) shall all be negative, it is known that the following conditions must be fulfilled: [21]

(A12)
$$\alpha_1 > 0; \quad \alpha_1\alpha_2 - \alpha_3 > 0; \quad \alpha_3 > 0.$$

21. The necessary and sufficient conditions for the real parts of the roots of an nth-degree equation to be negative were first given by E. J. Routh in *A Treatise on the Stability of a Given State of Motion* (London, Macmillan, 1877). The Routh conditions are discussed by Paul A. Samuelson in *Foundations of Economic Analysis* (Cambridge, Mass., Harvard University Press, 1947), appendix B. A convenient way of stating the conditions in terms of determinants may be found in R. A. Frazer, W. J. Duncan, and A. R. Collar, *Elementary Matrices and Some Applications to Dynamic and Differential Equations* (Cambridge, England, University Press, 1938), pp. 154–155.

Consider first the sign of α_3. Since $\alpha_3 \equiv k_1 k_2 k_3 \Delta$, we have

(A13) $\qquad \alpha_3 \equiv k_1 k_2 k_3 \{ (1 - w_1)(1 - w_2)\hat{v}_1(\eta_1 + \eta_2 - 1)$
$\qquad\qquad\qquad - s_1 m_1 (1 - w_2) - s_2 m_2 (1 - w_1) \} > 0.$

Thus, one of the conditions of stability of Eqs. (A8) is that Δ, the determinant of our static system, must be positive. We have argued above that w_1, w_2, m_1, and m_2 are all positive quantities each of which is normally less than unity, and that s_1 and s_2 are likewise positive. Under these circumstances it is easy to see from (A13) that Δ will not be positive, and the dynamic system will not be stable, unless the sum of the two import demand elasticities exceeds unity, and perhaps exceeds unity by a considerable amount.

This conclusion, as Harberger has emphasized in another connection, differs from most of the earlier discussions of exchange stability.[22] According to the traditional view, the dividing line between stability and instability, when commodities are produced and sold at constant cost, is the point at which $\eta_1 + \eta_2 = 1$. The earlier conclusions with respect to exchange stability differ from our own, and from those of Harberger, principally because the earlier discussions adopted a fixed set of demand schedules as a point of departure, whereas we have made allowance for the effects of changes in income on these demand schedules.[23] And, under the assumptions we have made with respect to the signs of our coefficients, the shifts in demand induced by changes in income exert a destabilizing influence.

To illustrate this argument, consider a system in which the sum of the two demand elasticities, $\eta_1 + \eta_2$, is exactly equal to unity. If the demand schedules for imports could be regarded as fixed, such a system would be in a state of neutral stability; that is, it would be on the borderline between a stable and an unstable system. If the balance of payments were initially in equilibrium, neither depreciation nor appreciation would affect this equilibrium. As soon as we allow for induced movements of income, however, it becomes apparent that a system that is neutral as of given demand schedules is unstable when all repercussions are taken into account.

Suppose, for example, that one of the two countries should depreciate its currency with respect to the other currency. Under the assumed demand conditions, the balance of payments would remain in equilibrium, but the domestic-currency prices of imports would rise in the depreciating country and fall in the second country. Now according to the discussion in the text

---

22. Harberger, "Currency Depreciation" (reference 5), pp. 50–55.
23. What we have called the "traditional view" of stability in international trade was first presented by Alfred Marshall. In his *Pure Theory of International Trade* (privately printed, 1879), he distinguished graphically between the stable and the unstable points of equilibrium; and later, in his *Money, Credit, and Commerce*, appendix J, he pointed out that in the stable cases the sum of the two price elasticities is greater than unity. For more recent contributions to the stability discussion, see note 20 above.

regarding the sign of s_1 and s_2, the rise of import prices in the depreciating country represents a decline in real income which, other things being the same, increases the proportion of income spent on goods and services. Income and employment accordingly tend to rise in the depreciating country, and the demand for imports is thereby increased. In the second country, where import prices have fallen, the proportion of income spent on goods and services declines somewhat, the level of output is reduced, and the demand for imports declines along with the decline in employment. Induced movements of income thus bring about a rise of imports in the depreciating country and a decline of that country's exports. From this it follows that if depreciation initially leaves the balance of payments unchanged, the final effect will be a deficit for the depreciating country. Income movements have converted a neutral situation into an unstable one. The dividing line between stable and unstable systems, in other words, occurs at a point of higher demand elasticity than the traditional argument would suggest.

The reader may object that in all the preceding discussion of stability and instability we have considered only one aspect of the problem and have neglected other, equally important, aspects. From an economic point of view, the world economy has been discussed as though its stability or instability depended entirely upon the foreign-exchange market, and nothing has been said about the possibility of an unstable situation arising from a cumulative movement of income in one or both countries. From a technical, mathematical point of view, the incompleteness of the conclusions reached thus far is reflected in the fact that we have examined only one of the conditions of stability given by (A12), namely, the condition that Δ shall be positive. What then can be said about the other two conditions? It can easily be shown (but proof is left to the reader) that, with the values of the coefficients assumed thus far, the third condition of stability, $\alpha_3 > 0$, is the critical one; if this condition is satisfied, the other two are necessarily satisfied also; and if the third condition is *not* satisfied, the system is of course unstable regardless of whether the first two conditions of stability are satisfied or not. In other words, if the marginal propensity to spend is less than unity in each country, and if the "price effects" s_1 and s_2 are both positive, the necessary and sufficient conditions of stability reduce to the single condition, $\alpha_3 > 0$. In economic terms, this means that, with the assumed values of the propensities to spend and the price effects, the dynamic system taken as a whole can be an unstable one only if there are inherent instabilities in the foreign-exchange market.

Consider now an alternative situation in which cumulative movements of income *may* be the source of instability. Suppose that the propensity to spend in one of the countries, say country 1, is greater than unity. What can be said, under this condition, about the stability of the entire system? Will a temporary rise of income in country 1 be the cause of a cumulative movement ending in a run-away inflation, or will income of that country be stabilized by economic events in the rest of the world? A question similar to this was discussed in the preceding paper dealing with the theory of employment under the gold standard,[24] and it was there shown that, with fixed exchange rates, the system *may* be stable even though the propensity to spend exceeds unity in one of the two countries. The fact that exchange rates under the gold standard are stationary means, as we emphasized in the text, that movements of income in one country are closely related to those of the other country, and a high propensity to spend in one country may therefore be offset, as far as it affects the stability of the entire system, by a low propensity to spend in the other country.

Under a system of flexible exchange rates, however, the conditions of stability are more restrictive. If a country's exports are always made equal in value to its imports by appropriate adjustments of exchange rates, there are no foreign-trade leakages to be taken into account, and an increase in a country's demand for imports is therefore almost equivalent, as far as its effects upon home income are concerned, to an increase in the demand for home goods. Thus, if country 1 and country 2 in the above example were trading under a free-market exchange system, the former could not rely upon the low propensity to spend in country 2 as a stabilizer. For each time country 1 increased its imports, the increase would be matched, as a result of exchange fluctuations, by an equivalent increase in exports. These propositions can be stated in technical language as follows: with minor and unrealistic exceptions, one or more of the stability conditions (A12) will fail to be satisfied whenever the marginal propensity to spend exceeds unity in one or both countries. The exceptions to this rule are so improbable and unrealistic that for all practical purposes they may be ignored.[25]

Assuming that the price effects s_1 and s_2 are both positive, the foregoing discussion of stability may be summarized in two propositions. First, stability of the system requires, except in a few highly unlikely cases, that the marginal

24. Lloyd A. Metzler, "Underemployment Equilibrium in International Trade," which appears as Chapter 10 of the present volume.

25. An exception might arise if the price effect of depreciation were very large in one country and very small in the other, and if, at the same time, the country with a small "price effect" had a marginal propensity to spend that was greater than unity while the other country had a small propensity to spend. Even under these circumstances, however, the system would not be stable unless the disparity in "price effects" between the two countries were quite large, and unless the speed of adjustment in the foreign-exchange market were low, relative to the speed of adjustment of income in each country. The unrealistic character of all these combined assumptions is reflected in the fact that if they were all realized simultaneously, an increase of investment in the country with the high propensity to spend would actually *reduce* incomes in both countries! See Eqs. (6) above.

propensity to spend be less than unity in each country. Second, the economic system taken as a whole cannot be stable unless the sum of the two elasticities of demand for imports, $\eta_1 + \eta_2$, is greater than unity, and perhaps considerably greater than unity. Hereafter, in discussing the static equations, it will be assumed that these two conditions of stability are met.

If one or both of the price effects should be negative, the preceding discussion of economic stability would require considerable modification. Perhaps most important of all, the system might be stable under such conditions, even when the sum of the two import demand elasticities was less than unity. Since we have argued in the text that the price effects are likely to be positive, however, there seems to be little point in discussing the conditions of stability under the opposite hypothesis that these coefficients are negative.

This completes our discussion of dynamic problems. Bearing in mind the conclusions reached concerning stability, we may now return to the problem of comparative statics which we originally set out to answer. The static problem, as the reader will recall, consisted of an attempt to determine the final effects of a rise in investment in one of the two countries on the three variables of the system.

Consider first the change of income in country 1. This change is given by the first equation of (A6). From the conditions of stability we know that Δ, the basic determinant of the system, must be positive. Moreover, if Δ is positive there is no difficulty in showing that, subject to the earlier restrictions placed upon our coefficients, the numerator of the expression for $dy_1/d\alpha_1$ must likewise be positive. It follows that $dy_1/d\alpha_1$ is a positive quantity. More than this, $dy_1/d\alpha_1$ is larger than the ordinary investment multiplier for a closed economy; in other words,

$$\text{(A14)} \qquad \frac{dy_1}{d\alpha_1} > \frac{1}{1 - w_1}.$$

The proof of (A14) follows from the fact that the numerator of the expression in (A6) for $dy_1/d\alpha_1$ is greater than $\Delta/(1 - w_1)$. Inequality (A14) has an important bearing upon the international aspects of business cycles; it shows that in countries with a highly fluctuating propensity to invest, the cyclical expansions and contractions of income are likely to be considerably aggravated by a system of free-market exchange rates. In view of the fact that such cyclical problems have been discussed in the text of this paper, there is no point in elaborating here. We may go on, instead, to a consideration of the other two variables of the system, namely, the exchange rate and the level of output in country 2. From Eqs. (A6) and from the stability conditions of our two-country system, it is apparent that the expansion of income in country 1 causes the price of foreign exchange in that country to rise, in other words, $d\pi/d\alpha_1 > 0$. Finally, the second of Eqs. (A6), together with the stability conditions, shows that output *falls* in country 2 as a result of the expansion in country 1, that is, $dy_2/d\alpha_1 < 0$. All of these results were discussed, in a nontechnical way, in the text above.

Our analysis in this appendix has been devoted, for the most part, to a rigorous proof of a number of propositions discussed in the main body of the paper. We have attempted to break new ground only in the dynamic aspects of the subject; the dynamic problems did not lend themselves readily to a nonmathematical treatment and consequently were not included in the paper itself. Study of the dynamic system, particularly of the stability conditions for such a system, has enabled us to define more accurately the circumstances under which our original conclusions hold true. But the stability conditions do not, we believe, cast doubt upon the validity or reasonableness of the original results.

Part II

Money, Interest, and Prices

12 | Wealth, Saving, and the Rate of Interest

The fundamental thesis of classical economics, that a free-market economy has an automatic tendency to approach a state of full employment, has been a subject of heated controversy in recent decades. Indeed after the publication of Keynes's *General Theory* there were many economists who rejected the classical thesis completely on the ground that it contained internal inconsistencies. Today, however, we are witnessing a renaissance of the classical doctrines. In part, this is attributable to world-wide economic developments since the end of the war, which have been characterized by a high level of demand and by full employment in almost all industrial countries. But the rebirth of classical theory is also attributable, in part, to attempts to reconstruct the classical doctrines along lines which make them immune to the Keynesian criticisms.

The principal architect of the reconstruction is Pigou;[1] but the basic idea of the remodeled classical theory can be found in the works of other economists as well, particularly those of Scitovszky[2] and Haberler.[3] The innovation which these economists introduced was a reconsideration, or perhaps I should say an elaboration, of the forces determining the

Reprinted from *Journal of Political Economy*, 59 (April 1951), 93–116. Copyright University of Chicago, 1951.

1. A. C. Pigou, *Employment and Equilibrium* (London, Macmillan, 1941), chap. 7; and "The Classical Stationary State," *Economic Journal*, 53 (December 1943), 343–351.
2. Tibor Scitovszky, "Capital Accumulation, Employment and Price Rigidity," *Review of Economic Studies*, 7 (February 1941), 69–88.
3. Gottfried Haberler, *Prosperity and Depression*, ed. 3 (Geneva, League of Nations, 1941), pp. 491–503.

quantity of real saving. In the classical theory the amounts of saving and investment out of a full-employment level of income were regarded as functions of the interest rate alone, and the latter was thus the primary governing force of the economic system as a whole. Equilibrium was attained, according to the classical theory, only when the interest rate was such that the quantity of real saving out of a full-employment income was equal to the quantity of real investment.[4] Scitovszky, Pigou, and Haberler retained this basic concept of equilibrium but argued that saving depends upon the real value of privately held wealth as well as upon the interest rate. Other things remaining the same, they said, real saving tends to be smaller and real expenditure for consumption tends to be larger, the larger the real value of private wealth. For convenience, I shall hereafter use the expression "saving-wealth relation" to designate such a functional connection between current saving and private wealth.

The saving-wealth relation was employed by Pigou and Haberler to defend the classical theory against the criticism of Keynesian economics. In particular, the relation was employed to show that a flexible-wage economy has an automatic tendency to approach a state of full employment, as postulated in the classical theory. On account of the special purpose which it originally served, the saving-wealth relation is now widely considered to be a modification, but not a fundamental change, in the classical theory. Indeed, Haberler even suggests that some sort of functional connection between saving and wealth is implicit in works on economics which preceded the explicit recognition of the saving-wealth relation.[5]

I do not share these views. In my opinion, the saving-wealth relation is more nonclassical in its implications than any of the contributions to the subject would lead one to believe. Although the Scitovszky-Pigou-

4. Consider, for example, the following remark of John Stuart Mill: "There must be, as in other cases of value, some rate [of interest] which . . . may be called the natural rate; some rate about which the market rate oscillates, and to which it always tends to return. This rate partly depends on the amount of accumulation going on in the hands of persons who cannot themselves attend to the employment of their savings, and partly on the comparative taste existing in the community for the active pursuits of industry, or for the leisure, ease, and independence of an annuitant" (*Principles of Political Economy*, reprinted from the 5th London ed. [New York, Appleton, 1893], bk. 3, chap. 23, sec. 1). Although Mill does not specify in this passage that the saving and investment which govern the interest rate are full-employment saving and full-employment investment, the tenor of his work strongly suggests that this is what he had in mind (see for example, his *Principles*, bk. 3, chap. 14).

5. Haberler, *Prosperity and Depression* (reference 3), p. 499, n. 2.

Haberler system resembles the classical system in its tendency toward a state of full employment, it is quite unlike the classical system in other respects, and these other respects have generally been overlooked. The most striking difference between the new system and the classical concerns the interest rate, and it is this subject which I wish to explore in the present paper.

The distinguishing feature of the classical theory of the interest rate is its emphasis upon so-called "real" conditions of demand and supply and its denial of the influence of monetary policy or banking policy. The classical economists believed that there exists a unique interest rate, or a unique pattern of long-term and short-term rates, at which the economic system is in equilibrium and that this unique interest rate cannot be influenced by changes in the quantity of money. The following quotation from Ricardo is representative of the classical opinion:

[Interest for money] . . . is not regulated by the rate at which the bank will lend, whether it be 5, 4, or 3 percent, but by the rate of profits which can be made by the employment of capital, and which is totally independent of the quantity or of the value of money. Whether a bank lent one million, ten million, or a hundred millions, they would not permanently alter the market rate of interest; they would alter only the value of money which they thus issued. In one case, ten or twenty times more money might be required to carry on the same business than what might be required in the other.[6]

In contrast to the classical doctrine, the theory of the interest rate implicit in the Scitovszky-Pigou-Haberler system is at least partly a monetary theory, as I shall demonstrate below. In this system there is no single interest rate and no single pattern of rates at which the economy is in equilibrium. Rather, there are an infinite number of different rates capable of performing the equilibrating function, and the particular rate that prevails at any given time depends to a considerable extent upon the policy of the banking authorities. Thus, in salvaging one feature of classical economics—the automatic tendency of the system to approach a state of full employment—Pigou and Haberler have destroyed another feature, namely, the real theory of the interest rate. In this respect Pigou, the archdefender of classical economics, has deserted

6. David Ricardo, *Principles of Political Economy and Taxation*, Everyman's Library ed. (London, Dent, 1911), p. 246.

Mill and Marshall and joined Schumpeter and Keynes![7] Although remnants of the classical, real theory of the interest rate remain, these are overshadowed, I believe, by the monetary feature which has been added. Moreover, the added feature which transforms the interest rate into a monetary rate is not liquidity preference, as in Keynesian economics, but the saving-wealth relation.

The subsequent analysis will be more understandable, I believe, if I digress from my principal theme long enough to indicate briefly the way in which the saving-wealth relation became prominent in economic theory. For this purpose consider an economic system in which the demand for investment is so low and the supply of saving so high that potential full-employment saving exceeds potential full-employment investment at all positive interest rates. In this event, there is no achievable interest rate which fulfils the classical condition of equilibrium. Whatever the interest rate may be, the demand for goods and services as a whole falls short of productive capacity—the Keynesian system in its simplest form. Moreover, the outcome of this situation, as envisaged by Keynes, is a cumulative reduction in output and employment, the reduction continuing until potential saving is reduced to the level of potential investment through a reduction in real income.

Suppose, however, that wages and other factor costs tend to fall when unemployment develops. To what extent will the reduction in costs stimulate output and move the system back toward full employment? Keynes argued that a general wage reduction affects output primarily through its influence on the interest rate. Any decline in wages and other costs is likely to result, he asserted, in a corresponding decline in other prices. In real terms, then, the only significant effect of the reduction in wages and other costs is an increase in the real value of money balances which tends, through liquidity preference, to reduce the interest rate. If full-employment saving exceeds full-employment investment at all possible interest rates, however, the reduction in the interest rate

---

7. Although Pigou is usually considered to be a defender of classical or neoclassical economic theory, his ideas concerning the interest rate were somewhat nonclassical even before the publication of his *Employment and Equilibrium*. He believed, in particular, that the banking system has a limited influence upon the equilibrium interest rate as well as upon the market rate. If the banks establish a market rate below the equilibrium rate, for example, prices and costs tend to rise, and the real expenditures of fixed-income groups are reduced. The resources thus freed are available for capital development, and the increased supply of capital reduces the equilibrium interest rate. Apart from this reservation, Pigou's earlier conception of the interest rate seems to be largely classical in its implications. See A. C. Pigou, *Industrial Fluctuations*, ed. 2 (London, Macmillan, 1929), *passim*, esp. p. 277.

cannot conceivably eliminate all the deflationary gap and restore output to the full-employment level. Keynes's theory thus leads to the conclusion that wage-and-cost reductions are not an effective remedy for deficient demand.[8]

Pigou attempted to refute this Keynesian view concerning wage-and-cost reductions, and in doing so he introduced the saving-wealth relation. He suggested that as wages and prices decline, the resulting increase in the real value of money balances will stimulate demand in a way which is independent of the change in the interest rate. Money balances constitute a part of private wealth, and the increase in the former accordingly implies an increase in the latter. As the real value of private wealth increases, the amount of saving out of a full-employment level of real income tends to decline. In this manner the excess of potential saving over potential investment which accounted for the initial unemployment is eventually eliminated. In the absence of barriers to price-and-cost reductions, the system thus has an automatic tendency to approach a state of full employment, as envisaged in the classical theory. Saving is brought into line with investment not primarily through a reduction of the interest rate but rather through a general deflation and a corresponding increase in the real value of the money supply.

I do not wish to discuss the relevance of the saving-wealth relation to the arguments frequently heard for a policy of overall flexibility of wages and prices. Other economists have pointed out that the portion of cash balances whose real value is increased by a general deflation normally constitutes a relatively small part of total assets and that an enormous reduction of prices would therefore be required to increase the real value of a country's total wealth by any substantial amount. They have argued, further, that the general increases or decreases in prices and costs required for the successful operation of such a system might easily lead to expectations of additional price increases or decreases which would upset the stability of the whole system.[9] Such questions of economic policy, however, are not the immediate concern of this paper. I mention them here only to avoid a possible misunderstanding of what

8. J. M. Keynes, *General Theory of Employment, Interest, and Money* (New York, Harcourt, Brace, 1936), chap. 19. On p. 267 of this chapter, Keynes says: "There is, therefore, no ground for the belief that a flexible wage policy is capable of maintaining a state of continuous full employment; . . . the economic system cannot be made self-adjusting along these lines."

9. Michael Kalecki, "Professor Pigou on 'The Classical Stationary State': A Comment," *Economic Journal*, 54 (April 1944), 131–132; and Don Patinkin, "Price Flexibility and Full Employment," *American Economic Review*, 38 (September 1948), 543–564.

I shall say later. In what follows, I shall make the most favorable assumptions possible as to the effects of price movements upon the demand for goods and services; I shall ignore the adverse influence of fluctuating prices upon expectations and assume that there is a substantial tendency for saving to decline when the real value of private wealth rises. Given these favorable assumptions, I shall then ask how an economic system containing the saving-wealth relation is related to classical theory.

Two Concepts of Monetary Theory

Before describing the theory of interest implicit in the Scitovszky-Pigou-Haberler system, I wish to say something about the meaning of a "monetary" theory of interest rates. A theory is usually regarded as a monetary theory if the economic system envisaged is one in which the equilibrium interest rate, or the equilibrium pattern of rates, can be altered by a change in the quantity of money. Although this definition is satisfactory for most purposes, it is not sufficiently accurate to characterize an economic system containing the saving-wealth relation. It is inadequate, in particular, because it does not indicate the manner in which the quantity of money is altered. As I shall demonstrate below, the influence of a change in the quantity of money in the Scitovszky-Pigou-Haberler system depends not only upon the magnitude of the change but also upon the way in which it is brought about. Some changes in the quantity of money will alter the equilibrium interest rate, while others will not.

We may distinguish, I believe, between two fundamentally different types of increase or decrease in the quantity of money. The first type is a change which takes place through open-market transactions of the central bank. The significant feature of this type of change is that it consists in an exchange of one form of asset for another. When money holdings are increased through central-bank purchase of securities, for example, holdings of securities outside the central bank are reduced by a corresponding amount. The second type of change consists in a direct increase or decrease in the money supply without any offsetting changes in private holdings of other assets. The supply of money may be reduced, for example, by a currency reform in which one unit of new money is exchanged for two units of old. Or the supply of money may be reduced by means of a governmental budgetary surplus, provided that the excess monetary receipts are impounded. In both these examples the supply of money is altered without altering private holdings of other assets, and it is this characteristic which distinguishes the second type of monetary change from the first.

I intend to show in subsequent parts of this paper that the theory of interest implicit in the Scitovszky-Pigou-Haberler system is a monetary theory if the change in the quantity of money is of the first type and a real theory if the change is of the second type. This means that open-market transactions of the central bank will have a *permanent* influence on the interest rate at which the system is in equilibrium, even after the bank has stopped its purchases or sales of securities. If the change in the quantity of money does not affect the private holdings of other assets, however, it will have no lasting influence on the interest rate.

With respect to the rate of interest, the Scitovszky-Pigou-Haberler theory thus occupies an intermediate position between the classical theory and the Keynesian. The classical theory is a real theory of the interest rate from the point of view of both types of monetary change. According to the classical doctrine, neither a central-bank purchase or sale of securities nor an arbitrary increase or decrease in the quantity of money can have any effect upon the interest rate at which the economic system returns to equilibrium. As I have indicated above, the equilibrium interest rate of the classical theory is the rate at which full-employment potential saving is equal to full-employment potential investment, and this equilibrium rate is independent of both the quantity of money and the policy of the central bank. The classical theory, then, is a non-monetary or real theory of the interest rate, regardless of whether the monetary disturbance is of the first type or the second type.

At the other extreme is Keynes's theory, which is a purely monetary theory from the point of view of either type of monetary disturbance. According to Keynes, the rate of interest is governed largely by the decisions of asset-holders concerning the proportions in which they wish to hold money and securities; that is, in Keynes's terminology, the rate is determined by liquidity preference.[10] Other things remaining unchanged, the desired ratio between money and securities tends to rise with a fall in the interest rate, and the equilibrium interest rate is the one at which the desired ratio of money to securities corresponds to the actual ratio. From this it follows that any monetary or banking policy which increases the actual quantity of money relative to the actual quantity of securities will reduce the interest rate at which the system is

10. Keynes, *General Theory* (reference 8), chaps. 13, 15, and 18.

in equilibrium. Thus, both an arbitrary increase in the quantity of money (a disturbance of the second type) and an increase in the quantity of money through a limited and temporary purchase of securities by the central bank (a disturbance of the first type) will reduce the equilibrium interest rate in Keynes's system.

This brief and somewhat elliptical summary of the Keynesian and classical theories of the interest rate is intended to emphasize the polar positions which the two theories occupy relative to the theory implicit in the Scitovszky-Pigou-Haberler system. The equilibrium interest rate in the classical theory is independent of monetary disturbances, regardless of whether such disturbances are of the first type or the second type. The equilibrium interest rate in Keynes's theory, on the other hand, can be permanently altered by a monetary disturbance of either type. In short, the classical theory is a real theory from the point of view of either type of disturbance, while the Keynesian theory is a monetary theory from the point of view of either type. The polar positions of the two theories explain, I believe, why no distinction has been made in the past between the two types of monetary disturbance.

A Geometric Presentation

The economic system which will be investigated below is one in which the capital market is subject to three main influences: (a) the influence of current saving and investment, as in the classical or neoclassical theory; (b) the influence of decisions concerning the holding of cash or securities, as in Keynes's doctrine of liquidity prererence; and (c) the influence of wealth on current saving, as in the Scitovszky-Pigou-Haberler reconstruction of the classical theory. I assume that the equilibrium rate of interest, or the equilibrium pattern of rates, is determined by the interplay of these three influences.

At the outset I wish to make a number of simplifying assumptions. Although these assumptions are somewhat unrealistic, few of them are absolutely essential, and most of them could be substantially modified without altering any of my principal results. I assume, in the first place, that the economy with which we are dealing is a closed economy with a fixed amount of labor. Second, I assume that the wage rate tends to rise whenever the demand for labor is greater than the fixed supply and to fall whenever the demand is smaller than the fixed supply. Third, I assume that all agents of production except labor are produced means of production and that all production is carried on at constant returns to scale. Under these conditions the relative prices of all commodities and services are determinate and independent of the commodity composition of the national income. We can therefore speak unambiguously of a rate of total output, or of a level of national income, at which the economy's resources are fully employed. Fourth, I assume that owners of private wealth hold such wealth in only two forms, money (including demand deposits) and common stock, and that all common stock involves approximately the same degree of risk.[11] Fifth, I assume that the central bank is legally authorized to buy and sell the common stock held by the owners of private wealth and that this common stock constitutes the only nonmonetary asset of the banking system.

Given these assumptions, one can readily construct a simple geometric interpretation of the forces governing the interest rate. These forces will operate in two different markets: a market for goods and services as a whole and a market for securities. Consider first the market for goods and services. Stability of the general price level in the goods-and-services market obviously requires that the total demand arising from a full-employment level of real income shall be equal to the economy's productive capacity; and this is equivalent to the requirement that potential saving out of a full-employment level of income shall be equal to potential investment. If potential investment at full employment exceeds potential saving, the demand for goods and services as a whole exceeds full-employment output; prices and costs accordingly tend to

11. Common stock has been selected as the typical security in order to avoid the difficulties associated with bonds during periods of inflation or deflation. Throughout the paper I assume that, in the absence of movements in interest rates, common-stock prices rise or fall to the same extent that other prices rise or fall, so that a general inflation or deflation does not affect the real value of securities. This means that the real value of a given quantity of securities is a function of the rate of interest alone (see below).

Although the theory is simplified in this respect by regarding common stock as the typical security, two new problems are thereby introduced and these must not be overlooked. Perhaps most important, when all investment is financed by issuing common stock, the idea of a functional relation between the rate of interest and the real volume of investment becomes somewhat vague. Under these circumstances businessmen do not commit themselves, as they do when they issue bonds, to the payment of fixed capital charges. Saying that investment depends upon the rate of interest when all securities are common stocks is equivalent to saying that businessmen undertake more investment when stock prices are high than when they are low.

Apart from the problem of defining an investment function, the use of common stock in our argument presents the further problem of separating risk payments from interest payments per se. I have attempted to avoid this second problem by assuming that the degree of risk is about the same for one stock as for another. I realize, however, that such an assumption does not meet the basic difficulty and that, in a more extended treatment of the subject, allowance should be made for differences in risk.

rise. If potential full-employment investment falls short of potential full-employment saving, on the other hand, this implies that the demand for goods and services as a whole falls short of full-employment output. Hence prices and costs tend to fall.

In the classical theory, real saving and real investment were functions of a single variable—the interest rate—and the economy was assumed to be in equilibrium at only one rate. In the theory now being investigated, however, the amount of real saving at full employment is regarded as a function of two variables—the interest rate and the real value of wealth in the hands of the savers. As soon as the second variable is introduced, the concept of a single interest rate at which the goods-and-services market is in equilibrium loses its meaning. In place of the equilibrium rate of classical theory, we now have a schedule of rates, or a functional relation between the interest rate and the real value of private wealth.

In order to see how such a schedule can be derived, suppose that on a certain date the total of all privately held wealth—money and securities combined—has a certain real value. If the value of private wealth is fixed, saving may be regarded as a function of the rate of interest alone, and I shall assume that with this given saving schedule a rate of interest can be found at which full-employment saving is equal to full-employment investment. Consider now what would happen if the interest rate were arbitrarily increased above its equilibrium level. At the higher interest rate potential saving out of a full-employment income would exceed potential investment, which means that, other things remaining the same, the community's demand for goods and services would fall short of its capacity to produce. In other words, the increase in the rate of interest, taken by itself, would bring about a deflationary gap. But if the community's combined holdings of money and securities were increased in some manner at the same time that the rate of interest were raised, then the deflationary gap might be avoided. The increase in asset holdings would tend to reduce the amount of saving corresponding to any given rate of interest, thereby offsetting (or perhaps more than offsetting) the tendency toward excessive saving attributable to the rise in the rate of interest. The rise in the rate of interest would reduce investment, but the increase in the value of private wealth would reduce saving; and it is thus conceivable that full-employment potential saving might equal potential investment at the higher interest rate as well as at the lower rate.

Many other combinations of the interest rate and the real value of private wealth will fulfil the condition that full-employment saving equals full-employment investment, and we may accordingly conceive of a schedule or a functional relation indicating what the real value of private wealth would have to be, for many different interest rates, in order to make the community's demand for goods and services as a whole equal to its capacity to produce. The real value of private wealth which fulfils this condition will be an increasing function of the rate of interest. Such a function is plotted as the line *WW* in Fig. 1.

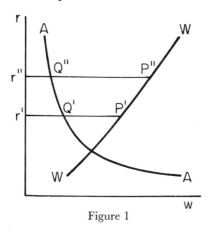

Figure 1

For convenience, *WW* will be called the "wealth-requirements schedule." At any point on this line potential saving out of full-employment income is equal to potential investment. But as we move upward and to the right along the line, both saving and investment decline. Investment declines because of the rise in the interest rate, while saving declines because of the increase in the real value of private wealth. Any point below *WW* in Fig. 1 represents a point of inflationary potential. At such a point the rate of interest is too low, given the value of private wealth, to bring about an equality between full-employment saving and investment. The demand for goods and services thus exceeds capacity, and prices tend to rise. In the same way one can show that any point *above WW* represents a point of *de*flationary potential. It follows that the demand for goods and services is equal to the economy's productive capacity only for combinations of the interest rate and the value of private wealth lying on *WW*.

The wealth-requirements schedule has been developed above in terms of the real value of private wealth as a whole, and no distinction has been made between private holdings of money and private holdings of securities. Such a distinction has thus far been unnecessary because saving was assumed to be a function of *total* asset holdings and not of the *composition* of these assets. When we later discuss the securities market, however, we shall find that the division of total assets between money and securities is the decisive factor in this market. Our later task will accordingly be simplified if the wealth-requirements schedule can be broken down into its two component parts, namely, money and common stock.

If the community holds a given amount of common stock, the real value of these stock holdings will obviously depend upon the interest rate. Indeed, the interest rate itself is nothing more than the yield of the stock, and this yield, in turn, is the ratio of the income earned by the stock to its market price. In the short run the income earned by the common stock is a given amount, determined by the fixed supplies of the various agents of production; and this means that the yield, or the rate of interest, varies inversely with the real value of the stock. To put the matter the other way round, we may say that the real value of the given common stock is inversely related to the prevailing rate of interest. The higher the rate of interest, the lower the real value of common-stock holdings and conversely. In Fig. 1 the value of the community's security holdings is expressed as such a function of the interest rate by the line AA.

I now wish to show how the wealth-requirements schedule WW can be expressed in terms of money and interest rates rather than in terms of total wealth and interest rates. For this purpose, suppose that the interest rate is temporarily set at r'' in Fig. 1. The wealth-requirements schedule tells us that, in order to prevent an excess or deficiency of demand from developing in the goods-and-services market at this interest rate, the community's holdings of money and securities combined will have to be $r''P''$. But the value of securities alone, at an interest rate of r'', is the distance $r''Q''$ in Fig. 1. If the community is to have a sufficient amount of total assets to maintain a balance between demand and supply in the goods-and-services market, its holdings of money will therefore have to equal the difference between $r''P''$ and $r''Q''$, or $Q''P''$.

This difference is plotted in Fig. 2 as the line $r''T''$. A similar construction for a rate of interest r' carries over the distance $Q'P'$ of Fig. 1 to $r'T'$ of Fig. 2. The line MM of Fig. 2 is the locus of all such points as T'

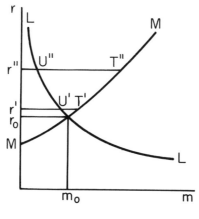

Figure 2

and T''. Given the community's private holdings of securities, MM indicates the amount of money which will have to be held, at any particular interest rate, in order to keep the amount of saving out of full-employment income equal to the amount of investment. For brevity, MM will be called the "money-requirements schedule." The money-requirements schedule is thus the horizontal difference between the wealth-requirements schedule, WW, and the schedule of the real value of securities, AA.

The Market for Goods and Services and the Market for Securities

The line MM of Fig. 2, like WW of Fig. 1, indicates the conditions needed to maintain a balance between supply and demand in the market for currently produced goods and services. In addition to this goods-and-services market, the market for securities must also be taken into account. The entire economic system cannot be in equilibrium unless the latter market, as well as the former has reached a balanced position. The market for *new* securities has already been allowed for, by implication, in the preceding discussion of saving and investment; in the absence of hoarding, equality between saving and investment implies equality between the supply of and the demand for new securities. But this new-securities market is usually a relatively small part of the total securities market; in many countries, indeed, the value of new securities offered on the market in a given year is an exceedingly small fraction of the value of previously issued, or old, securities. This means that decisions of asset-holders to augment or reduce their stocks of old securities will frequently exert a much greater influence on the rate of interest than will discrepancies between current saving and current investment. The old-securities market must therefore be taken into account, along with the market for goods and services as a whole, in order to complete the description of interest rates given by Figs. 1 and 2.

The existing stock of securities will influence security prices and the rate of interest only if asset-holders, on balance, decide to increase or decrease their holdings of securities, that is, only if the typical asset-holder wishes to substitute additional money for part of his security holdings or additional securities for part of his money holdings. Decisions of this sort depend largely upon the *composition* rather than the size of asset portfolios. Thus, in deciding whether to buy or sell securities, the typical asset-holder compares the existing ratio between his money holdings and his security holdings with the ratio which he regards as satisfactory under the given economic conditions. The degree of his actual liquidity, compared with a sort of optimum liquidity, governs his actions in the securities market.

I shall follow Keynes in assuming that, other things remaining the same, the typical asset-holder wishes to increase his liquidity as the rate of interest falls. Unless the banking authorities intervene, however, private asset-holders cannot, on balance, increase or decrease their holdings of old securities; as of a given moment of time, both the number of shares of stock and the quantity of money in private hands are fixed quantities. This means that, if the prevailing money-securities ratio differs from the desired ratio, security prices and the rate of interest must continue to change until the desired ratio is brought into line with the prevailing ratio; in short, the demand must be adjusted to the existing supply through appropriate movements in the rate of interest.

The influence of liquidity preference may be examined from another direction, and for present purposes this alternative point of view is more convenient. Instead of starting with a fixed amount of securities and a fixed quantity of money and asking how the rate of interest will be adjusted so that demand will equal supply, we may start with a fixed amount of securities and a fixed interest rate and ask what the total money holdings would have to be in order to satisfy the typical asset-holder with his money-securities ratio. By assuming a number of different interest rates and making similar calculations for each, we may thereby build up a liquidity-preference schedule, or a demand-for-money schedule.

Suppose, for example, that, at an interest rate of r'' (Fig. 1), the typical asset-holder wishes to hold money in an amount equal to two-thirds the value of his security holdings. At this interest rate the security holdings of the community as a whole have a real value of $r''Q''$, as shown in Fig. 1. It follows that asset-holders as a group will attempt to alter their security holdings and hence alter the rate of interest, unless the real value of money holdings amounts to two-thirds of $r''Q''$. Let the point U'' in Fig. 2 be chosen so as to make $r''U''$ equal to two-thirds of $r''Q''$. Suppose now that when the interest rate falls to r', the typical asset-holder wishes to hold money equal to the full value of his securities. The value of total securities at an interest rate of r' is $r'Q''$ (Fig. 1), and the condition of equilibrium in the old-securities market requires that money holdings shall equal this same amount. We may therefore select a point, U', in Fig. 2 such that $r'U'$ is equal to $r'Q'$. The liquidity-preference schedule LL in Fig. 2 is the locus of all such points as U'' and U'; it shows what the community's holdings of money would have to be, at any given interest rate, in order to create a proper balance between cash and securities.

From the construction of the diagram it is apparent that there are two reasons why the demand for money, LL (Fig. 2), tends to rise as the rate of interest falls. First, the typical asset-holder usually wants to hold a larger ratio of cash to securities at low interest rates than at high rates. And, second, the real value of securities, the denominator of the cash-securities ratio, is increased by a fall in the interest rate. In most discussions of liquidity preference only the first of these reasons is taken into account, but the second may be equally important.[12]

I have now discussed two different functional relations between the rate of interest and the real quantity of money; the first of these I called a money-requirements schedule, while the second is the usual liquidity-preference schedule. The money-requirements schedule represents all combinations of money balances and the rate of interest for which the community's demand for goods and services as a whole is exactly equal

12. The best account I have found of the second reason for the negative slope of the liquidity-preference schedule is that of E. Solomon in "Money, Liquidity, and the Long-Term Rate of Interest: An Empirical Study, 1909–38" (unpublished dissertation, University of Chicago, 1950).

to its capacity to produce. At any point not on this schedule there is either an excess or a deficiency of demand and consequently a tendency for prices and costs to rise or fall. The money-requirements schedule, MM, thus indicates the possible combinations of the interest rate and the quantity of real cash balances which will maintain over-all price equilibrium in the goods-and-services market. The liquidity-preference schedule, on the other hand, describes the conditions of price equilibrium in the *securities* market. If the actual quantity of real cash balances lies on LL, there will be no tendency for asset-holders as a whole to attempt to shift from securities to cash or from cash to securities, and accordingly no tendency for the price of securities or the rate of interest to change. At any point *not* on LL, however, the price of securities will either rise or fall, depending upon whether the demand for cash at the prevailing interest rate is smaller or greater than the actual amount.

From Fig. 2 it is now apparent that only one combination of the interest rate and the real value of money balances will satisfy the conditions of equilibrium in both the goods-and-services market and the securities market. I have denoted this combination by the two letters r_0 and m_0. If all prices, including wages and the costs of other agents of production, tend to rise when demand exceeds supply and to fall when supply exceeds demand, the combination r_0 and m_0 is the one toward which the economic system will gravitate. The nature of this market mechanism will be clarified, I believe, if we consider what happens to the system when the interest rate and the real value of money balances differ from the equilibrium combination r_0 and m_0.

This is done in Fig. 3, where I have reproduced the essential features of Fig. 2. The points B, C, D, and E in Fig. 3 represent four points which do not lie on either the liquidity-preference schedule or the money-requirements schedule. Suppose first that the actual situation with regard to the rate of interest and the real value of cash balances at a given moment of time can be represented by the point B. What happens, in this event, to the variables of our system? The liquidity-preference schedule shows that, at the rate of interest represented by B, the community's demand for real money balances falls short of actual money holdings. Asset-holders accordingly attempt to substitute securities for their excess cash holdings, thereby forcing up security prices and reducing the rate of interest. Moreover, in situation B the goods-and-services market as well as the securities market is out of balance. The diagram shows that, at the prevailing interest rate, money holdings are too large

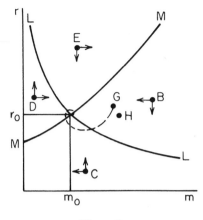

Figure 3

to bring about an equality between full-employment saving and full-employment investment. Saving is below the equilibrium level because of the excessive cash holdings, and the demand for goods and services thus exceeds the economy's capacity to produce. As a result, prices tend to rise and the real value of money balances is reduced. The movements in the rate of interest and in the real value of money balances are indicated by the short arrows emanating from point B.

By similar reasoning one can demonstrate that at point C, security prices tend to fall and the interest rate is correspondingly increased, while the prices of goods and services rise and the real value of cash balances is reduced. Likewise, at D, security prices fall, the rate of interest is increased, commodity prices and wages fall, and the real value of cash balances tends to rise. Finally, if the actual position of the variables is at E, security prices rise, the interest rate is reduced, commodity prices fall, and the real value of cash balances is thus increased. Movements of the variables in the neighborhood of the points C, D, and E have again been indicated by arrows.

Figure 3 demonstrates that when the economic system is out of balance, at least one force is always operating to bring the variables of the system closer to the equilibrium point, r_0, m_0. The other force, indicated by the second of the two arrows at each of the points B, C, D, and E, operates in such a way as to impart a circular or cyclical movement to the variables. This suggests that, if the rate of interest and the quantity of real cash balances were initially at some nonequilibrium point such as G, the approach to equilibrium might be a spiral or damped cycle like the one depicted in Fig. 3. Although such a damped cycle is possible, it is not inevitable, as I shall demonstrate in the appendix to this paper. In any event, I believe it is highly unlikely that the cyclical movement implied by Fig. 3 bears any close resemblance to the typical observed business cycle. Most observed cycles are cycles of output and employment, whereas the cycle depicted in Fig. 3 is largely a cycle of prices and interest rates.[13] I have presented the dynamic problem concerning the movements of prices and interest rates merely to show the tendency of the system to approach an equilibrium position and not as a contribution to the theory of business cycles.

Open-Market Operations

I have now shown that the market for goods and services and the market for securities can be in equilibrium simultaneously only at the point r_0, m_0 and that the economic system has an automatic tendency to approach this equilibrium. Superficially, this suggests a close analogy between the rate of interest r_0 and the classical concept of the equilibrium rate. Like the equilibrium rate of classical theory, the rate r_0 is the only one compatible, under the assumed conditions, with equilibrium of the economic system as a whole; that is, r_0 is the only rate which satisfies both the liquidity-preference requirement and the requirement that full-employment saving shall be equal to full-employment investment. Why then does r_0 not have as much claim to be regarded as a real rate as does the classical concept of the real rate of interest?

Whether the rate r_0 is a real rate or a monetary rate depends, as I have indicated earlier, upon the nature of the monetary disturbance. If the disturbance is of the first type—that is, if it is a change in the quantity of money associated with the purchase or sale of securities by the central bank—it will alter some of the functional relations of Figs. 1 and 2 and will accordingly change the equilibrium interest rate. The rate r_0 must therefore be regarded as a monetary rate from the point of view of monetary disturbances of this sort. On the other hand, if the monetary

13. Superficially, the cycle of interest rates and prices described above seems to be somewhat like the monetary part of Hicks's business cycle theory. In reality, however, the two cyclical processes are quite different. The process envisaged by Hicks involves movements of output and employment rather than movements of prices and costs; and savings in Hicks's theory depend upon the rate of interest and real income, whereas savings in the present paper depend upon the rate of interest and the real value of private wealth. See J. R. Hicks, *A Contribution to the Theory of Business Cycles* (London, Oxford University Press, 1949), chaps. 11 and 12.

disturbance is of the second type, which consists in an increase or decrease in the quantity of money without any offsetting changes in other assets, then it will not alter the functional relations of Figs. 1, 2, and 3 and will not permanently change the interest rate. The rate r_0 is thus a real rate from the point of view of monetary disturbances of the second type. Because it is simple to describe, I shall first consider a monetary disturbance of the second type.

Suppose that the economic system is initially in equilibrium at a rate of interest r_0 and a quantity of real cash balances m_0. And suppose that, while other things initially remain unchanged, the quantity of money is arbitrarily doubled by giving to each holder of money an additional quantity equal to the amount he already holds. Temporarily, the variables of the system will then be at point H of Fig. 3; except for the increase in the quantity of money, nothing in the system will have changed. As I have shown above, however, there will be an automatic tendency for the variables of the system to return eventually to the former equilibrium position, r_0 and m_0. At point H both the securities market and the goods-and-services market will be out of balance, and changes will therefore occur in the interest rate and in the level of prices. The changes in prices, in turn, will affect the real value of cash balances.

Consider first the securities market. After the initial monetary disturbance, the quantity of money held by the typical asset-holder is larger than he would like to hold at the prevailing interest rate r_0. Asset-holders as a group therefore attempt to convert some of their excess cash into securities. As a result, security prices rise, which means that the interest rate falls. The fall in the interest rate increases investment, while the initial increase in the real value of cash balances reduces saving. The demand for goods and services as a whole thus exceeds productive capacity, so that commodity prices and costs begin to rise. The rise in prices tends to reduce the real value of cash balances and thereby initiates a movement of the variables back toward the original equilibrium position. The details of this dynamic process need not concern us here. Suffice it to say that the system as a whole will not be restored to equilibrium until the real value of cash balances is reduced to m_0 and the rate of interest is restored to its former level, r_0.

If the central bank does not acquire or dispose of any assets during the period of adjustment, the real value of money balances can be reduced only by an increase in the price level. Since the real value of cash balances is ultimately restored to its former level m_0, we know that the increase in prices, in the final position of equilibrium, must be as large as the original increase in the quantity of money. In other words, doubling the nominal quantity of money must result eventually in doubling all money prices and costs, including the money prices of securities as well as the money prices of goods and services. The real variables of the system all return to their former equilibrium levels. The rate of interest, the real value of saving and investment, and the real value of securities, as well as the real value of cash balances, are all the same in the new equilibrium as before the monetary disturbance occurred. The only permanent effect of increasing the quantity of money is a proportionate increase in the general level of prices and costs.[14]

With respect to monetary disturbances of the second type, such as the one I have just described, the economic system embodying both a saving-wealth relation and a liquidity-preference schedule is evidently quite similar to the classical system. In both the classical system and the system depicted in Fig. 3, the values of all real variables are independent of the quantity of money. But this is true of the system in Fig. 3 only if the monetary disturbances are of the second type, whereas it is true of the classical system for both types of monetary disturbance. If the disturbance is of the first type, which consists of open-market transactions by the central bank, then the equilibrium interest rate will be altered, as I have suggested above. With respect to monetary disturbances of the first type, the equilibrium interest rate of Fig. 3 is therefore a monetary rate, and in this regard it resembles the Keynesian interest rate more closely than it does the classical. In other words, by purchasing or selling securities, the banking authorities can alter not only the temporary interest rate which prevails while the open-market transactions are taking place but also the rate at which the system will return to equilibrium after the bank's transactions in securities have ceased.

The power of the banking authorities to alter the equilibrium interest rate is attributable not to their influence upon the nominal quantity of money but to their influence upon the quantity and value of privately held securities. A central-bank purchase of securities, for example, reduces the quantity of privately held securities. This means that the *AA*

14. Using a model more complex than the one I have been considering, Don Patinkin previously demonstrated that if both the saving-wealth relation and liquidity preference are active forces, monetary disturbances of the second type will not affect the equilibrium interest rate. See "The Indeterminacy of Absolute Prices in Classical Economic Theory," *Econometrica*, 17 (January 1949), 23–27. Patinkin did not examine the effects of monetary disturbances of the first type and accordingly concluded that the model he had constructed was closer to the classical model than to the Keynesian.

schedule of Fig. 1 is shifted to the left. And since the liquidity-preference schedule *LL* and the money-requirements schedule *MM* were both derived, in part, from the *AA* schedule, a shift in the latter causes the former schedules to shift as well. The system as a whole therefore comes into balance, after the securities purchases have been made, at a different rate of interest.

The effect of open-market transactions upon the equilibrium of the system can be described in terms of a ratio indicating the proportion of the total supply of securities held in private hands. Let this ratio be represented by the letter λ. Consider first the situation in which λ has a value of 1.0. This means that the total available supply of securities is held by private asset-holders, so that the central bank's assets consist exclusively of currency. Given the holdings of securities by private asset-holders, the rate of interest at which the system is in equilibrium can be determined, as in our earlier illustration, by the intersection of a liquidity-preference schedule, *LL*, and a money-requirements schedule, *MM*. Assuming that the value of private asset holdings when $\lambda = 1.0$ is given in Fig. 4 by the solid line *AA* and that the wealth-requirements schedule

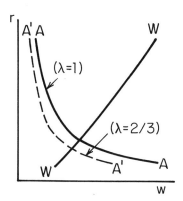

Figure 4

is *WW*, the liquidity-preference schedule and the money-requirements schedule can be derived as in my earlier illustration. These derived schedules, for $\lambda = 1.0$, are represented in Fig. 5 by the solid lines *LL* and *MM*, respectively. Under the assumed conditions with respect to security holdings, the equilibrium rate of interest is r_0, and the equilibrium value of real cash balances is m_0, as shown in Fig. 5.

Suppose that this equilibrium is disturbed by a substantial purchase of securities on the part of the central bank. The dynamic process by

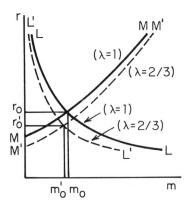

Figure 5

which the economy adapts itself to such open-market transactions will probably be highly complicated. The securities will be purchased at many different prices from the various asset-holders, and this means that we cannot predict exactly how the open-market transactions will affect the cash balances of all asset-holders together. In any event, the real value of cash balances will be influenced by price movements as well as by the central bank's dealings in securities, and it is the combined effect of both influences which ultimately governs the equilibrium value of the real money supply. In view of our interest in the equilibrium of the system, we may pass over the dynamic problems and investigate instead the influence of the central bank's security purchases upon the schedules in Figs. 4 and 5 which determine the ultimate resting places of our variables.

Suppose that the central bank continues to purchase securities until it has acquired one-third of the common stock available to the economy as a whole and that all transactions between asset-holders and the central bank cease at this point. When the securities market and the goods-and-services market are once again in equilibrium, how will the rate of interest compare with the rate that prevailed before the open-market transactions began? According to the classical theory, the rate of interest should return to its former level as soon as the bank's security purchases have ceased. According to the system depicted in Figs. 4 and 5, however the security purchases by the central bank will permanently *lower* the equilibrium rate of interest.

If the bank acquires one-third of all available securities, the security holdings of private asset-holders will of course be only two-thirds as large as they formerely were, so that λ will have a value of $\frac{2}{3}$. This means that at any given interest rate the real value of private security holdings will be two-thirds of its former value. The broken line $A'A'$ of Fig. 4 is drawn at two-thirds of the horizontal distance of the solid line AA from the vertical axis, and $A'A'$ thus represents the real value of private security holdings, expressed again as a function of the rate of interest, after the central bank has acquired its securities. The wealth-requirements schedule, WW, depends upon preferences and upon the savings and investment schedules and presumably will be unaffected by the open-market transactions.

Since the money-requirements schedule MM depends upon the value of private security holdings as well as upon WW, however, the MM schedule will be shifted. At any given rate of interest, the total assets—money and securities combined—needed to maintain equality between full-employment saving and full-employment investment will be the same as before. But the value of private security holdings has been reduced by the central bank's purchases, and this means that total assets cannot be maintained at the level needed for full employment unless private money holdings are increased by a corresponding amount. In short, the money-requirements schedule MM is moved to the right by the same amount that the securties schedule AA is moved to the left.[15] The new money-requirements schedule corresponding to $\lambda = \frac{2}{3}$ is shown in Fig. 5 as the broken line $M'M'$.

15. In describing the consequences of open-market transactions, I assume that the securities schedule AA is the only schedule of Fig. 4 which is *directly* influenced by the central bank's purchase or sale of securities; the other schedules (the wealth-requirements schedule, the money-requirements schedule, and the liquidity-preference schedule) are assumed to be affected only insofar as they are related to, or derived from, the securities schedule AA. This implies that the income available to the typical asset-holder is not altered by the central bank's dealings in securities. If disposable income tended to fall or to rise with an increase or decrease in the central bank's holdings of securities, the saving and investment schedules would also be affected, and the wealth-requirements schedule, which is derived from the saving and investment schedules, would tend to shift.

Taken by themselves, however, open-market transactions may well have a slight influence on disposable income. If the central bank buys securities, for example, the income on these securities is transferred from the former owners to the bank. In the absence of offsetting transactions, the security purchases thus reduce the disposable income of private asset-holders and increase the profits of the central bank by a corresponding amount. I do not wish to discuss the complications introduced by this connection between open-market transactions and disposable income. I therefore assume throughout that any additional profits which the central bank earns by reason of its acquisition of securites are ultimately passed on to private hands in the form of reduced taxes. Under these circumstances, the security purchases by the bank will redistribute income between former asset-owners and taxpayers but will not influence the total of disposable income.

The liquidity-preference schedule, as well as the money-requirements schedule, is affected by the central bank's purchase of securities. At any given interest rate, the proportions in which the typical asset-holder wishes to hold money and securities are presumably the same as in the old equilibrium. The value of private security holdings, however, is now only two-thirds of the former value at the same interest rate. The desired ratio between money holdings and security holdings will thus not be maintained unless the real value of money balances is reduced to two-thirds of its former value. In other words, the LL schedule in Fig. 5 is shifted to the left, the relative amount of the shift being the same as the leftward shift of the securities schedule AA. The new liquidity-preference schedule, for $\lambda = \frac{2}{3}$, is represented in Fig. 5 by the line $L'L'$.

The combined effect of the shift in the liquidity-preference schedule and of the shift in the money-requirements schedule is a reduction in the equilibrium rate of interest from r_0 to r'_0. Thus the banking authorities, by means of a limited purchase of securities, have *permanently* reduced the interest rate at which the economic system is in equilibrium. The dynamic process of adjustment by which the equilibrium interest rate moves from r_0 to r'_0 will probably be highly complex, as I have indicated earlier. Nevertheless, I believe that the influence of the central bank upon the equilibrium interest rate will stand out more clearly if we consider a greatly simplified dynamic sequence.

When the central bank begins to purchase securities, the first effect is a rise in security prices and a corresponding decline in the rate of interest. The actual security transactions themselves do not alter the total value of private asset holdings but merely change the form in which assets are held. The initial result of the bank's purchases, therefore, is a rise in the value of private asset holdings (capital gains) together with a reduction in the rate of interest and a shift on the part of asset-holders from securites to money. One may presume that at the new, lower rate of interest the asset-holders have exchanged securities for cash in such a way as to satisfy their demands for liquidity; for, if this were not true, the prices of securities would continue to rise, and the interest rate to fall, until the asset-holders were willing to part with the amount of securities that the central bank wanted to buy.

Although the point representing the new quantity of private money holdings and the new, temporary rate of interest will thus lie somewhere on the liquidity-preference schedule $L'L'$, it cannot at the same time lie on the money-requirements schedule $M'M'$, or the wealth-requirements schedule *WW*. The fall in the interest rate, taken by itself, would normally lead to an excess of full employment investment over full-employment saving and thus create an excess demand for goods and services. The inflationary pressure is further increased, however, by the capital gains, which increase the value of total private wealth holdings and thereby reduce current saving. As a result, prices and costs tend to rise, and the real value of the money supply is correspondingly reduced. The rise in prices and the reduction in the real value of private money holdings must continue until the real value of security-and-cash holdings combined is low enough to encourage a sufficient amount of saving to make full-employment saving once more equal to full-employment investment. The new equilibrium is finally achieved, as Figs. 4 and 5 demonstrate, at a permanently lower rate of interest.

Now since the new equilibrium must lie on the wealth-requirements schedule *WW*, as well as on the money requirements schedule *M'M'*, it is obvious that, when prices have finally stopped rising and the rate of interest has reached its new and lower equilibrium, the value of total private wealth must be smaller than in the old equilibrium. In short, the final result of the open-market security purchases by the central bank is a reduction in the real value of the total wealth in private hands. This reduction has occurred in two stages: the liquidity of the typical asset-holder has first been increased through the central bank purchase of securities; and the real value of the larger liquid balances has subsequently been reduced through inflation. Thus, under a regime of flexible prices, central-bank purchase of securities is an indirect means of reducing the real value of the total assets—cash and securities combined—in private hands. The reduction in the value of privately held wealth tends, in turn, to increase saving and thereby reduces the rate of interest at which full-employment saving is equal to full-employment investment. To summarize briefly, then, we may say that the central bank is able to alter the equilibrium rate of interest through its power to alter the real value of private wealth.

Conclusions

Assuming that saving depends upon the real value of private wealth as well as upon the interest rate, I have now demonstrated that the equilibrium interest rate is partly a real rate, as in the classical theory, and partly a monetary rate, as in Keynes's theory. Monetary disturbances of one type affect the equilibrium interest rate of the system, while disturbances of another type do not. In general, any monetary disturbance which alters the amount of securities held by the typical asset-holder tends also to affect the interest rate at which the economic system as a whole is in equilibrium. On the other hand, any monetary disturbance which does not affect private security holdings will leave the equilibrium interest rate unchanged.

The distinction which I have made between the two types of monetary disturbance suggests that the true cause of a change in the interest rate is not a change in the quantity of money per se, but a change in the amount of other assets held by the typical asset-holder. This conjecture is indeed correct. Open-market transactions of the central bank alter the equilibrium interest rate not because they affect the quantity of money but because they affect the quantity of privately held securities. Consider again, for example, the open-market transactions which I have described in Figs. 4 and 5. In those illustrations the central bank is assumed to purchase one-third of all privately held securities. As a consequence, the level of prices is increased, the real value of private wealth declines, the propensity to save increases, and real saving finally comes into balance with real investment at a permanently lower interest rate.

Suppose now that the amount of privately held securities were reduced without any offsetting change in the quantity of money. Such a reduction could be brought about by a capital levy of one-third on all securities, payable only in kind. In other words, the government could require that one-third of all privately held securities be turned over to it. In what respects would the effects of such a policy differ from the effects of the open-market transactions described in Figs. 4 and 5? Examination of the figures reveals that the interest rate, the volume of real investment, the real value of cash balances, and the other real variables of the system are affected in exactly the same way by a one-third levy in kind upon all securities as by a central-bank purchase of the same amount of securities. The nominal quantity of money is of course larger when the securities are acquired by purchase than when they are acquired by taxation. But the real value of bank balances is exactly the same, in the new position of equilibrium, in both cases. Thus the only difference between the effects of the two means of acquiring the securities is a difference in the level of prices and costs. The price level is higher when the securities are acquired by purchase than when they are acquired by taxation. In all other respects the two situations are identical as far as the final results are concerned.

The foregoing example reveals the close analogy between central-bank security purchases and a capital levy on securities. In the system investigated above, a purchase of securities by the central bank is a means of reducing the real value of privately held wealth and operates just as effectively in this direction as a corresponding capital levy payable in kind. Indeed, the central bank's power to alter the equilibrium interest rate arises exclusively from its influence on the real value of privately held securities.

Through its power to change the interest rate, the central bank can also affect the rate of growth of the economy as a whole. At each different equilibrium interest rate full-employment saving is of course equal to full-employment investment, but the amount of real saving and invest-ment varies with fluctuations in the equilibrium interest rate. When the equilibrium rate is increased, the economic system comes into balance at a lower real value of investment and saving; and when the equilib-rium rate is reduced, the real value of saving and investment tends to increase. By purchasing securities, the central bank can reduce the real value of private wealth, thereby increasing the propensity to save and causing the system to attain a new equilibrium at a permanently lower interest rate and a permanently higher rate of capital accumula-tion. In a similar manner, the bank, through sales of securities, can increase the real value of private wealth, lower the propensity to save, raise the equilibrium rate of interest, and reduce the rate of capital accumulation.

Whether the bank has a substantial influence or only a negligible influence upon the rate of growth of the system depends upon its authority to buy and sell securities and upon the magnitude of the saving-wealth relation. If the saving-wealth relation is large, so that the propensity to save increases or decreases appreciably as the real value of private wealth falls or rises, and if the bank is authorized to buy and sell securities in large quantities, then the rate of growth may be affected to a considerable extent by central-bank policy. In practice, however, there will usually be an institutional barrier to the amount of securities the bank can sell; it cannot sell more securities than it owns. And this means that when the bank has divested itself of all its securities, it has no further power to raise the equilibrium interest rate and lower the rate of growth. There may be a similar barrier to the amount of securities the bank can purchase, since only certain types of assets are eligible for the bank's portfolio. If the bank has acquired all the assets it is authorized to purchase, no further reduction of private wealth, and no further increase in private saving, can be accomplished by central-bank activity in the securities market.

In terms of the theory set out above, we may say that the central bank's power over the equilibrium interest rate and the equilibrium rate of growth will usually be determined by institutional arrangements which prevent it from purchasing more than a small fraction of private wealth or from selling more assets than it possesses. This might mean, for example, that the institutional arrangements were such that the value of λ would have to lie between 0.9 and 1.0. In most countries these institutional limits may well be so narrow that the actual power of the central bank to influence the equilibrium of the system is negligible. Nevertheless, if saving depends upon the real value of private wealth as described in the saving-wealth relation, the rate of interest must be regarded as partly a monetary rate. For if the institutional limits to central-bank action were removed or reduced, the possible variation in the equilibrium interest rate which could be brought about by the central bank would be correspondingly increased.

Appendix

The geometric methods employed in the text of this paper were not sufficiently powerful to deal with some of the more difficult problems encountered, particularly the dynamic problems. I am therefore adding an analytical appendix. The symbols used have the following meanings:

r represents the rate of interest, or the yield on common stock;

m represents the real value of private money holdings;

a represents the real value of all common stock, whether held by private owners or by the central bank;

λ represents the proportion of the total supply of common stock held by private owners;

w represents the real value of all privately held wealth, including both money and common stock;

S represents the real value of current saving; and

I represents the real value of current investment.

The amount of real saving out of a full-employment income is assumed to depend upon the real value of private wealth as well as upon the rate of interest, and we may accordingly write $S = S(r,w)$. Investment, under conditions of full employment, is assumed to depend only upon the rate of interest, and the investment function may therefore be written as follows: $I = I(r)$. If real national income under conditions of full employment is y_0, and if a proportion, c, of this consists of business profits, the real value of all common stock will be the capitalized value of these profits, thus: $a = cy_0/r$. The only remaining functional relation to be defined is the liquidity-preference function. Let $L(r)$ be such a function, indicating the proportion in which asset-holders as a group wish to hold money and common stock. With the aid of these definitions we may now write the following system of equations:

(A1) $$S(r, w) = I(r), \qquad L(r) = \frac{m}{\lambda a},$$

and $$w = \lambda a + m, \qquad a = \frac{cy_0}{r}.$$

The first of Eqs. (A1) expresses the condition that, in equilibrium, full-employment saving must equal full-employment investment. The second equation says that the rate of interest must be such that the desired proportion between money holdings and security holdings on the part of the owners of private wealth is equal to the actual proportion. The third equation is an identity, defining the real value of private wealth as the sum of private money holdings and private security holdings. Finally, the fourth of Eqs. (A1) says that the real value of all common stock is the capitalized value of business profits, where the capitalization is done at the prevailing rate of interest, r.

If the value of λ is given, Eqs. (A1) are sufficient to determine the equilibrium values of the four variables r, w, m, and a; that is, the equations determine the rate of interest, the total real value of privately held wealth, the real value of money balances, and the real value of all common stock. The price level does not enter explicitly into Eqs. (A1), since all variables are in real terms. Nevertheless, price movements are implicitly taken into account through movements of m, the real value of the money supply. In the absence of open-market transactions, indeed, m can change only by means of general inflation or deflation.

Security purchases or sales by the central bank are indicated in Eqs. (A1) by changes in the value of λ. An increase in λ, for example, indicates a larger proportion of total securities in private hands and hence signifies security sales by the central bank. Changes in λ will obviously alter the equilibrium values of all our variables. In order to see how a central-bank sale of securities affects these equilibrium values, we may differentiate (A1) with respect to λ, as follows:

$$\text{(A2)} \qquad (S_r - I_r)\frac{dr}{d\lambda} + S_w\frac{dw}{d\lambda} = 0,$$

$$-\frac{1}{\lambda a}\frac{dm}{d\lambda} + L_r\frac{dr}{d\lambda} + \frac{m}{\lambda a^2}\frac{da}{d\lambda} = -\frac{m}{\lambda^2 a},$$

$$\frac{dm}{d\lambda} - \frac{dw}{d\lambda} + \lambda\frac{da}{d\lambda} = -a,$$

$$\text{and} \qquad -\frac{a}{r}\frac{dr}{d\lambda} - \frac{da}{d\lambda} = 0.$$

Solving Eqs. (A2) for

$$\frac{dr}{d\lambda}, \quad \frac{dm}{d\lambda}, \quad \frac{dw}{d\lambda}, \quad \text{and} \quad \frac{da}{d\lambda},$$

we find:

$$\frac{dr}{d\lambda} = -\frac{S_w}{\Delta}\left(\frac{1}{\lambda} + \frac{m}{\lambda^2 a}\right),$$

$$\text{(A3)} \qquad \frac{dm}{d\lambda} = \frac{1}{\Delta}\left\{(S_r - I_r)\frac{m}{\lambda^2 a} - aS_w L_r\right\},$$

$$\frac{dw}{d\lambda} = \frac{1}{\Delta}(S_r - I_r)\left(\frac{1}{\lambda} + \frac{m}{\lambda^2 a}\right),$$

$$\text{and} \qquad \frac{da}{d\lambda} = \frac{1}{\Delta}\frac{aS_w}{r}\left(\frac{1}{\lambda} + \frac{m}{\lambda^2 a}\right).$$

The symbol Δ in Eqs. (A3) represents the basic determinant of the system, that is,

$$\text{(A4)} \qquad \Delta \equiv \begin{vmatrix} 0 & S_r - I_r & S_w & 0 \\ -\dfrac{1}{\lambda a} & L_r & 0 & \dfrac{m}{\lambda a^2} \\ 1 & 0 & -1 & \lambda \\ 0 & -\dfrac{a}{r} & 0 & -1 \end{vmatrix}$$

$$\equiv (S_r - I_r)\frac{1}{\lambda a} + S_w L_r - \frac{S_w}{r} - \frac{mS_w}{\lambda a r}.$$

The subscripts in Eqs. (A3) and (A4) indicate differentiation of the S, I, and L functions with respect to the variable appearing in the subscript. I assume the system is stable in the classic sense that an increase in the rate of interest creates an excess of potential saving over potential investment; this implies that $S_r - I_r$ is positive. The saving-wealth relation is represented in (A3) and (A4) by S_w, which is negative, indicating that an increase in the real value of private wealth reduces real saving. The slope L_r of the liquidity-preference schedule is assumed to be negative, which implies that an increase in the rate of interest reduces the desired ratio between money and securities.

With the given signs of S_r, I_r, and so on, one can see from (A4) that Δ is a positive determinant. Moreover, the direction of change of most of the variables of the system can be readily determined. Thus, Eqs. (A3) show that $dr/d\lambda$ is positive, $dw/d\lambda$ is positive, and $da/d\lambda$ is negative. This means that open-market sales of securities have increased the rate of interest, increased the real value of private wealth (cash and securities combined), and reduced the real value of the total supply of common stock.

The only change whose sign is indeterminate is $dm/d\lambda$, the change in the real value of private money holdings. The reason for this indeterminacy is not far to seek: the central-bank sales of securities have reduced private money balances, but the real value of the remaining private balances have subsequently been increased through a general deflation. The final position of real money balances thus depends upon the relative strength of these opposing forces. But whatever happens to the real value of privately held money, Eqs. (A3) show that privately held wealth as a whole has been increased by the central bank's sales of securities. The increase in the real value of private wealth has reduced the rate of saving, and it is this reduction of saving which accounts for the permanent rise in the equilibrium rate of interest.

Thus far I have investigated the stationary or equilibrium values of the system without saying anything about the dynamic process of adjustment. I shall conclude this appendix with a few remarks concerning the behavior of the variables through time, during intervals when the system is not in equilibrium.

Consider first the behavior of prices when total demand is different from productive capacity. The difference between demand and productive capacity is measured, of course, by the difference between potential full-employment saving and potential full-employment investment. If the former exceeds the latter, demand for goods and services falls short of productive capacity, and prices and costs accordingly tend to decline. Conversely, if full-employment investment exceeds full-employment saving, total demand exceeds capacity, and both prices and costs rise. In the absence of new borrowing or lending by the banking system, however, an increase in prices is equivalent to a fall in the real value of money balances, and the time movement of the general price level may therefore be described in terms of movements in the value of money. As a first dynamic postulate, then, I write:

(A5)
$$\frac{dm}{dt} = k_1[S\ (r,w) - I(r)\,].$$

Equation (A5) says that the price level tends to fall, and the real value of money balances tends to rise, whenever potential saving exceeds potential investment. Likewise, prices rise, and the real value of money balances falls, when potential saving falls short of potential investment. The speed of the price movement, in both cases, is assumed in (A5) to be proportional to the size of the inflationary or deflationary gap, and the constant, k_1, represents this speed of adjustment.

So much for the general price level in the commodity-and-service market. Consider next the movement of prices in the securities market. I assume, as I indicated in the text, that the securities market is dominated by transactions in old securities rather than by supply-and-demand conditions in the new-securities market. Specifically, I assume that security prices tend to rise whenever asset-holders on balance attempt to shift from money to securities and that security prices fall when asset-holders attempt a shift in the opposite direction. The attempted shift, in turn, depends upon whether the actual ratio of cash to securities is higher or lower than the desired ratio, as indicated by the liquidity-preference function. Since a rise in security prices is equivalent to a fall in the rate of interest, our second dynamic postulate may be written:

(A6)
$$\frac{dr}{dt} = k_2 \left[L(r) - \frac{m}{\lambda a} \right].$$

In words, Eq. (A6) says that the rate of interest rises, which means that security prices fall, when the desired ratio of money to securities exceeds the actual ratio. And, conversely, the rate of interest falls when the desired ratio is less than the actual ratio.

Equations (A5) and (A6) are the only equations of adjustment that we shall need. These two equations are the dynamic counterpart of the first two of Eqs. (A1). They do not form a complete system, however, since we have only two equations in four unknowns. Before we can solve our dynamic equations, we must have two more equations. The two missing equations are the third and fourth equations of our static system (A1). These are merely definitional equations and are assumed to be satisfied at any moment of time, without lag. The third equation defines private wealth at a given moment as the sum of private security holdings and private money holdings, while the fourth equation defines the rate of interest as the yield on securities. The complete dynamic system is as follows:

(A7)
$$\frac{dm}{dt} = k_1[S(r, w) - I(r)],$$

$$\frac{dr}{dt} = k_2\left[L(r) - \frac{m}{\lambda a}\right],$$

$$w = \lambda a + m,$$

and
$$a = \frac{cy_0}{r}.$$

Equations A7 cannot be explicitly solved, since we do not know the exact form of the functions S, I, and L. I shall therefore make a linear approximation of (A7), which will be valid only for small deviations from the equilibrium values of the variables. If r_0, w_0, m_0, and a_0 represent the equilibrium values, we may write, as such a linear approximation,

(A8)
$$\frac{dm}{dt} = k_1(S_r - I_r)(r - r_0) + k_1 S_w(w - w_0),$$

$$\frac{dr}{dt} = -k_2\frac{1}{\lambda a}(m - m_0) + k_2 L_r(r - r_0) \qquad\qquad + k_2\frac{m}{\lambda a^2}(a - a_0),$$

$$0 = (m - m_0) \qquad\qquad - (w - w_0) \qquad + \lambda(a - a_0),$$

$$0 = -\frac{a}{r}(r - r_0) \qquad\qquad - (a - a_0).$$

The solution of Eqs. (A8) takes the form

(A9)
$$m = m_0 + A_1 e^{\rho_1 t} + A_2 e^{\rho_2 t},$$

with similar results for r, a, and w, where A_1 and A_2 depend upon the initial values of the variables, and where ρ_1 and ρ_2 are the roots of the following equation:

(A10)
$$\begin{vmatrix} -\rho & k_1(S_r - I_r) & k_1 S_w & 0 \\ -\dfrac{k^2}{\lambda a} & k_2 L_r - \rho & 0 & \dfrac{k_2 m}{\lambda a^2} \\ 1 & 0 & -1 & \lambda \\ 0 & -\dfrac{a}{r} & 0 & -1 \end{vmatrix} = 0.$$

Equation (10) may be expanded in powers of ρ as follows:

(A11)
$$\rho^2 + \left(\frac{k_2 m}{\lambda ar} - k_2 L_r - k_1 S_w\right)\rho + k_1 k_2 \Delta = 0,$$

where Δ is the basic determinant of the static system, (A1).

The coefficients of the powers of ρ in Eq. (A11) are positive, which means that the real parts of the roots of Eq. (A11) are all negative. Thus the dynamic system is stable, for small deviations from equilibrium, regardless of the numerical values of L_r, S_w, and so forth. In other words, if the liquidity-preference function, the saving function, and the investment function do not alter their form or position as prices rise or fall, the dynamic system will eventually reach a stationary or static position.

This does not mean of course, that an economic system in which the saving-wealth relation is operative will always be a stable system in reality; for Eqs. (A7) and (A8) have made no allowance for expectations, and such expectations may exert a strongly destabilizing influence on the system. If prices of commodities are rising, for example, consumers and producers may anticipate further price increases; if so, saving will probably decline and investment will increase, thereby widening the inflationary gap and accelerating the price rise. Likewise, if security prices are rising, asset-holders may revise downward their estimate of what constitutes a normal ratio between money and securities; and if they do, the resulting attempt to shift from money to securities will cause a further rise in securities prices. These possibilities suggest that Eqs. (A7) and (A8) are stable only in a narrow sense.

Assuming that the system is stable, we may inquire in conclusion about the nature of the approach toward equilibrium. Is the solution of Eq. (A8) cyclical or noncyclical? The answer to this question depends upon the roots of Eq. (A10) or (A11). The dynamic system will not be cyclical unless these roots are complex numbers. This means that $b^2 - 4c$ is negative, where b is the coefficient of ρ in (A11) and c is the constant term. I leave it to the reader to prove the following propositions: (a) The roots of (A11) may be either real or complex, which means that the dynamic system may or may not have a cyclical solution. (b) If k_1 and k_2, the speeds of adjustment in the commodity market and the securities market respectively, are decidedly different in magnitude, the roots are likely to be real and the dynamic system is thus likely to be a noncyclical system. (c) If $S_r - I_r$ is large, so that a small rise in the rate of interest creates a substantial deflationary gap, the system will probably be cyclical.

13 | The Structure of Taxes, Open-Market Operations, and the Rate of Interest

Publication of the paper reproduced as Chapter 12 of this volume evoked a substantial amount of controversial literature.[1] This controversy no doubt reflects the fact that, in the field of monetary theory, every man is his own economist. Nevertheless, in view of the number of comments stimulated in one way or another by my examination of open-market operations, some sort of reply seems appropriate. Obviously, I cannot respond to every economist whose opinions differ from mine. I have therefore selected one, Robert A. Mundell,[2] whose contribution seemed to touch most closely upon the issues involved.

Open-Market Purchases and the Circular Flow of Income

The fundamental thesis of the preceding chapter is that open-market purchases of securities tend to lower the rate of interest because

---

Not previously published.

---

1. I shall mention only a few of the contributions to this literature: David M. Wright, "Professor Metzler and the Rate of Interest," *Journal of Political Economy*, 60 (June 1952), 247–249; Lloyd A. Metzler, "A Reply," *Journal of Political Economy*, 60 (June 1952), 249–252; Gottfried Haberler, "The Pigou Effect Once More," *Journal of Political Economy*, 60 (June 1952), 240–246; Don Patinkin, *Money, Interest, and Prices* (Evanston, Row, Peterson, 1956), pt. 2; Arnold Collery, "A Note on the Saving-Wealth Relation and the Rate of Interest," *Journal of Political Economy*, 68 (October 1960), 509–510; Robert A. Mundell, "The Public Debt, Corporate Income Taxes, and the Rate of Interest," *Journal of Political Economy*, 68 (December 1960), 622–626; George Horwich, "Real Assets and the Theory of Interest," *Journal of Political Economy*, 70 (April 1962), 157–169; and Harry G. Johnson, "Monetary Theory and Policy," *American Economic Review*, 52 (June 1962), 335–384.
2. Mundell, "The Public Debt" (reference 1).

they reduce the amount of privately held wealth and thereby stimulate saving. Thus the innovation of Chapter 12 is a demonstration that the power of the banking system to alter the rate of interest rests upon its ability to increase or decrease the value of privately held wealth and not upon its ability to increase or decrease the quantity of money. From this point of view, Chapter 12 represents a refutation of the classical notion of neutral money, even when the Keynesian inconsistencies do not exist and the market system operates in such a way as to ensure full employment.

Mundell objects to the arguments presented in Chapter 12 on two counts. First, he does not believe that an open-market purchase of securities is capable of reducing the value of privately held wealth; and second, he introduces an allocation element, to be described later, which he believes will cause the MM schedule of Fig. 5, Chapter 12, to shift leftward. His argument may be paraphrased as follows:

An open-market purchase of securities, by reducing the amount of stock held by private asset-holders, transfers the income earned by these securities from the former asset-holders to the central bank; and if the bank simply impounds such earnings, it is performing both a fiscal operation of surplus finance and a banking operation of open-market purchase. In order to isolate the influence of monetary policy, the bank must therefore divest itself of its fiscal operation, which is essentially a form of taxation.

It follows that, to analyze the problem of Chapter 12, the bank must be assumed to restore the circular flow of income by passing on to the agents of production the earnings which it acquires through open-market purchases. This can be done most easily by transferring additional earnings to the Treasury, provided that the Treasury, in turn, balances its budget and reduces taxes by an amount equivalent to its increased receipts from the central bank. But when taxes are reduced, as they must be to complete the analysis of monetary policy, the resulting capital gains may exactly offset the loss in the value of stocks, leaving the amount of privately held wealth the same as before the open-market operation. In this event, the central bank's purchase of securities will not alter the AA schedule of Fig. 4, Chapter 12; except for the effect of lower taxes on profits, the money-requirements schedule MM and the liquidity-preference schedule LL both remain unchanged. And when the profits effect (which Mundell calls an "allocation effect") is considered, the WW and MM schedules of Figs. 4 and 5 in the preceding chapter both move to the left, so that the equilibrium interest rate is raised, rather than lowered, by an open-market purchase of securities. The final outcome thus depends upon the types of taxes which are reduced.

Some taxes, like those on corporate profits, will be reflected immediately in the market prices of stocks; that is, they will be taxes on capitalizable sources of income. Others, like personal income taxes, will have no asset value attached to the source of income, since, in a free society, human beings cannot be bought or sold.

The ultimate consequence of an open-market purchase, combined with a transfer to the Treasury of excess bank profits and a corresponding reduction of taxes, thus depends upon the structure of the tax system. In short, it depends upon whether the reduced taxes apply to capitalizable or non-capitalizable sources of income.

As a matter of principle, I have no objection whatever to what has been said thus far. But as a matter of practical application, it seems to me that Mundell has distorted the picture to support his case. On several occasions he emphasizes the importance of the tax structure to his analysis. And yet he does not present an examination of these taxes. In this chapter I propose to show tht the actual structure of the federal tax system for the United States comes closer to supporting my conclusions than Mundell's. In particular, I shall demonstrate that a large proportion of federal tax receipts constitutes noncapitalizable taxes, such as personal income taxes; by contrast, the corporate profits tax, upon which Mundell places so much emphasis, is a relatively small part of total federal tax receipts.

Further, I shall demonstrate, from an examination of the conditions of production, that there is nothing capricious about this outcome. As contemporary economists are increasingly discovering, a large segment of net national product is produced by the personal efforts of human agents and only a small segment is attributable to capital, even in the most advanced economies. Quite apart from institutional tax arrangements, it therefore seems perfectly reasonable to suppose that a large segment of taxes should come from noncapitalizable human agents and only a small segment from capitalizable sources of income. Admittedly, the argument rests upon the particular structure of any given tax system. But to suppose that open-market purchases, accompanied by tax reductions, would leave private wealth unchanged, as Mundell at times seems to believe, one would have to suppose that 100 percent of all taxes were fully capitalizable. As I shall demonstrate from an examination of federal tax receipts, this is far from reality, at least in the United States.

Finally, I shall argue that, in his enthusiasm for corporate profits taxes, Mundell adopts a false criterion to determine whether or not the central bank's transfer of excess profits to the Treasury is offset by capital gains. Specifically, he compares the government's receipts from corporate profits taxes with its interest payments on the public debt. In doing so, he commits himself to the fallacious view that a given type of tax receipts can be identified with a specific type of expenditure. This proposition is true only for earmarked taxes or trust funds, such as social security contributions, and for specific charges made for the sale of government services. In general, particular types of taxes are for general expenditure, and this is about as far as one can go. An examination of tax receipts alone is therefore sufficient, and it is not necessary—indeed, it is often impossible—to compare a specific tax receipt with a specific expenditure.

In order to avoid a false impression, I should say at once that although I do not agree with Mundell's views, I have nevertheless been enlightened in reading his contribution to this controversial question and feel quite indebted to him for clarifying the issues which I left in an uncertain state. Moreover, my own examination of the United States federal tax structure revealed that corporate profits taxes are much larger, relative to total tax receipts, than I had supposed. Even so, I do not believe they are large enough to support Mundell's position, or to refute mine. But this is a question which must be left to the reader after an examination of the facts.

The Geometric Argument

Mundell summarizes his arguments ingeniously in a single diagram. I have discovered, however, that the single diagram omits part of the logic of Chapter 12 and is somewhat confusing, even for sophisticated economists. I propose therefore to return to the two diagrams employed in the preceding chapter.

Suppose first that all tax reductions apply to personal income taxes, and that income-earners do not capitalize their income streams. These are the implicit assumptions of my initial examination of open-market operations. In Figs. 1 and 2 below, I have reproduced Figs. 4 and 5 of Chapter 12. Enough has already been said about these figures to make further comment unnecessary.

Consider a situation in which the central bank purchases one-third of all existing securities. The schedule AA, which represents the capitalized value of corporate profits at various rates of interest, will then undergo a horizontal shift to the left, to the point where it is two-thirds of its

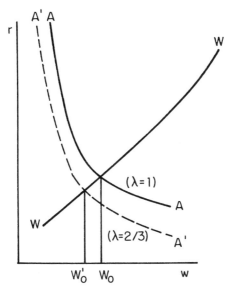

Figure 1

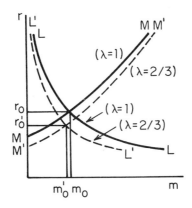

Figure 2

former value. The new schedule, after the open-market purchase has occurred, is shown by the broken line $A'A'$ of Fig. 1. In addition to the capital effect represented by $A'A'$, there is also an income effect to be considered. The asset-holders have transferred one-third of their securities to the central bank and, at a given rate of interest, their earnings have also been reduced in the same proportion. In short, the open-market purchase initially reduces both income and capital by one-third.

The central bank now earns more income while the asset-owners earn less. If the circular flow of income is restored by a transfer of additional earnings from the bank to the Treasury and an equivalent reduction of income taxes, the $A'A'$ schedule remains at its lower level; for the typical income-earner's *flow* of income cannot be transformed into a *stock* of assets. In other words, the personal income tax is a tax on a noncapitalizable source of income. Disposable income may rise or fall without affecting privately held assets in any manner.

Now since the securities component of wealth has fallen from AA to $A'A'$ in Fig. 2, the *total* wealth needed for a balance in the market for goods and services cannot be obtained unless the other component of wealth, real cash balances, *rises* to an equal degree. The altered money-requirements schedule is depicted in Fig. 2 as the broken line $M'M'$. For any rate of interest r, MM has moved to the right to the same extent that AA has moved to the left. Moreover, the liquidity-preference schedule LL must also move to the left. It is derived from an optimal ratio between cash and securities; since the denominator of this ratio has changed, the LL schedule must move in the same direction to the left. As a result of open-market security purchases combined with equal reductions of income taxes, the equilibrium rate of interest thus falls from r_0 to r_0' in Fig. 2.

Looking at Fig. 1, one sees that total wealth (cash balances and security holdings together) has decreased from W_0 to W_0'. Saving and investment both rise, and for two reasons. First, the rate of interest falls, and this stimulates investment; and second, the value of privately held wealth declines, and this causes saving to rise. In the end, then, an open-market purchase of securities together with a reduction of income taxes results in a fall in the interest rate, a rise in both saving and investment, and a fall in the real value of privately held wealth. The change in the real value of cash balances is indeterminate. Real balances may rise, fall, or remain unchanged, depending on the slopes of the LL and MM schedules in Fig. 2. This situation continues even after the open-market purchases have ceased.

The configuration represented by Figs. 1 and 2 supports my initial position. The real value of wealth is reduced by an open-market purchase of securities combined with a reduction of income taxes, because the ultimate effect of such transactions is a transfer of income from asset-owners to income-earners. Such a transfer reduces wealth for the economy as a whole, simply because the asset-holders are able to capitalize their income from securities whereas the income-earners are not.

Consider now the opposite situation to which Mundell attaches most importance. It is represented in Figs. 3 and 4. The reader will notice

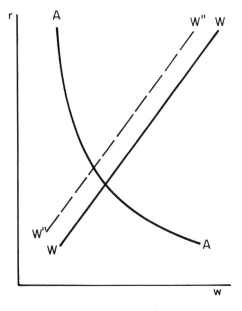

Figure 3

that an open-market purchase, under the premises of these figures, has no influence whatever upon the value of privately held securities; the schedule *AA* of Fig. 3 remains unaltered. The explanation of this fact lies in the peculiar nature of the tax system: when taxes are reduced to restore the circular flow of income, *the entire amount of the reduction is assumed to apply to corporate profits taxes*: no allowance is made for reductions in other forms of taxation. As a consequence, the income which the asset-owners lose when they sell their securities to the central bank is exactly offset by the income they gain from Treasury tax reductions. No redistribution of income is involved. Stockholders are left with the same amount of corporate income after taxes that they received before the open-market purchase began. Now since the *AA* schedule of Fig. 3 represents the capitalized value of corporate income after taxes, and

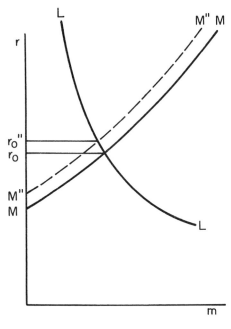

Figure 4

this type of income is unchanged, it follows that an open-market purchase, combined with an equivalent reduction in corporate profits
taxes, will have no influence upon AA, the security aspect of privately
held wealth. The liquidity-preference schedule LL in Fig. 4 is derived
from the AA schedule and will likewise be invariant under the combined
open-market purchase and corporate tax reduction.

This is not the whole story, however. As soon as we begin to examine
the influence of corporate profits taxes, an allowance must be made
for the systematic discrepancy between the private efficiency of investment and its social efficiency. The private investor receives only profits
after taxes, whereas the social efficiency of investment is some measure of
profits before taxes. Any reduction of corporate profits taxes narrows
this discrepancy and increases the incentives to invest at a given rate
of interest. The effects of this larger investment are shown as a shift to the
left of the wealth-requirements schedule WW in Fig. 3, and as an equal
shift of the money-requirements schedule MM in Fig. 4.

The reasons for these movements are not obvious intuitively, and I
therefore take the liberty of explaining them in detail. As the reader

will recall, the WW schedule represents all combinations of wealth and interest rate which are compatible with balance in the goods-and-services market under a full-employment rate of output. At any point on the schedule, potential real saving at full-employment income is equal to potential investment and there is neither inflation nor deflation in the market for currently produced commodities. Let us see what happens when corporate profits taxes are reduced as a consequence of open-market security purchases. Investments which were formerly not profitable at the higher tax rates now become profitable even though the social efficiency of investment remains unchanged. The initial effect of a reduction in corporate profits taxes is thus an increase in potential investment. At a given rate of interest, investment exceeds saving, and an inflationary gap arises in the market for commodities. In order to restore balance in this market, saving must rise as much as investment has risen. Again, at a given rate of interest, this can be accomplished only if privately held wealth falls enough to stimulate a higher rate of accumulation. Thus, as corporate profits taxes are reduced in conjunction with an open-market purchase of securities, the wealth-requirements schedule shifts to the left, from WW to $W''W''$ in Fig. 3. Since the money-requirements schedule MM in Fig. 4 is derived from the wealth-requirements schedule WW, it is obvious that MM must also shift to the left and to the same degree that WW shifts. The shift is shown in the broken line, $M''M''$, of Fig. 4.

Considering both the allocation effect on investment and the wealth effect on saving, we have seen that an open-market purchase of securities, accompanied by a reduction of corporate profits taxes, actually *increases* the rate of interest, rather than lowering it, as I concluded in Chapter 12. Again I must emphasize that this outcome is attributable to the fact that all tax reductions apply to fully capitalizable sources of income.

Consider now a third possibility. Suppose that the capital market is perfect in the sense that every source of income, including the services of human agents as well as the returns from securities, may be converted into a stock of capital at the prevailing rate of interest, r. The notion of a perfect capital market, usually attributed to Fisher,[3] is highly useful for some purposes, particularly when it is applied to the problem of determining how investment should be distributed between

3. Irving Fisher, *The Theory of Interest* (New York, Macmillan, 1930).

human and physical sources of income. My colleague, T. W. Schultz, for example, has made significant contributions in assessing the value of education along these lines.[4] But for the present purpose, the notion of a perfect capital market is so bizarre as to be virtually useless. Clearly there is no capital value arising from income earned by personal services, for in a free society human beings cannot be bought and sold as in a stock market. And, equally clearly, there is a significant portion of income attributable to these noncapitalizable sources. Despite the unreality of the concept of a perfect capital market, it is useful to consider (as an exercise) the effects of open-market operations, under the assumption that every agent of production has a capital value.

One may easily demonstrate that, in a perfect capital market, an open-market purchase of securities combined with an appropriate reduction of taxes[5] has no influence upon nonmonetary wealth. Every purchase of securities reduces the capital value of such securities to the full extent of the purchase. And every remission of taxes increases the capital value of the source of income by the same amount. For in a perfect capital market, every agent that earns an income has a capital value, so that the total wealth of an economy is simply the capitalized value of its national income.

The effects of open-market security purchases in a perfect capital market leave unchanged an asset schedule that is analogous to AA but more comprehensive, owing to the definition of privately held wealth as the capitalized value of the national income. All variables of

4. Professor Schultz has written extensively on the subject of investment in human beings by means of education. I shall not attempt a complete list of all his publications. Instead, I shall present only a few selected references: T. W. Schultz, "Investment in Man: An Economist's View," *Social Service Review*, 33 (June 1959), 110–117; "Capital Formation by Education," *Journal of Political Economy*, 68 (December 1960), 571–583; "Human Capital: A Growing Asset Inside the Soviet Union," *Saturday Review* (January 21, 1961); "Investment in Human Capital," *American Economic Review*, 51 (March 1961), 1–17; "U.S. Endeavors to Assist Low Income Countries to Improve the Economic Capabilities of Their People," *Journal of Farm Economics*, 43 (December 1961), pp. 1068–1077; "Investment in Human Capital in Poor Countries," J. E. Owens Memorial Foundation Lecture, in *Foreign Trade and Human Capital*, ed. Paul D. Jook (Dallas, Southern Methodist University Press, 1962); "Rise in the Capital Stock Represented by Education in the United States Between 1900 and 1957," in *The Economics of Higher Education*, ed. Selma J. Mushkin (Washington, D.C., U.S. Department of Health, Education, and Welfare, 1962); and *The Economic Value of Education* (New York, Columbia University Press, 1963).

5. If interest rates are to remain unchanged, the "appropriate reduction" of taxes must be a reduction of income taxes or some other form of noncapitalizable taxes. Otherwise, the tax reduction would have the same allocative effect on investment as that described above; that is, it would cause both the WW schedule and the MM schedule to shift leftward, thereby increasing the rate of interest.

the system, including the rate of interest, the real value of cash balances, the rate of saving and investment, and the total wealth of the society, are unaffected by the open-market purchase of securities combined with an equivalent reduction of income taxes.

This rather long discussion of the effects of open-market security purchases may be summarized as follows: when open-market purchases are combined with personal income tax reductions, the rate of interest falls; when the equilibrating tax reductions apply to corporate taxes, the rate of interest rises; and, finally, when the capital market is perfect according to Fisher's definition, the rate of interest remains unchanged. The final effect of open-market purchases thus depends entirely upon the nature of the tax reductions and upon the character of the capital market.

With respect to the capital market, I believe that for present purposes the concept of a perfect market may be dismissed altogether, without prejudice to its value for other purposes. We are thus left with the conclusion that the effects of open-market purchases and tax reductions depend upon the type of tax reductions. This raises the question of what criterion should be adopted in determining whether a given tax reduction falls upon capitalizable or noncapitalizable sources of income. And this is a point where Mundell and I differ.

It is true, indeed, that in Chapter 12 I assumed that all tax reductions were applicable to a noncapitalized tax, such as the income tax. But if we are to consider a more complicated tax system, including both noncapitalizable and capitalizable taxes, the only neutral way to reduce taxes is a flat proportional reduction of all types of taxes, whether capitalizable or not. Moreover, I would argue that such a proportional reduction is more than a convenient simplification; it is an absolute necessity if the effects of fiscal policy are to be separated from those of monetary policy. Suppose, for example, that corporate profits taxes account for 30 percent of the government's total receipts. If we assume, nevertheless, that 100 percent of all tax reductions are allocated to corporate taxes, we are then engaged in an operation consisting of two parts: a banking operation of open-market purchases and a fiscal operation of redistributing taxes between capitalizable and noncapitalizable sources of income.

In contrast to the argument I have presented here, that taxes must be reduced on a proportional basis in order to isolate the influence of monetary policy, Mundell considers a wide variety of tax reductions, some capitalizable and others not. I have argued that while all of Mundell's results are possible, the only one that is relevant to monetary policy is a proportional tax reduction. In order to see what this entails for the United States, we must begin with the federal tax structure, a classification of the various ways in which our government collects revenue.

The Structure of Federal Taxes

Federal receipts classified by type of tax are shown in Table 1 for the years 1946 to 1963 inclusive. Social insurance contributions are deducted from total receipts, simply because the social security system is regarded as a quasi-budgetary system in which the government acts as a trustee for the funds collected. In other words, the social insurance contributions are considered to be earmarked taxes; under this interpretation, it does not seem reasonable to include such taxes in any system of flat-rate deductions.

The relevant attributes of the personal income and corporate profits taxes have already been discussed. The third type of levy in Table 1, namely the excise tax, is difficult to classify, since there are differences of opinion among economists concerning its incidence. With respect to a uniform excise tax, however, there seems to be a rather broad consensus that the producer pays no part.[6] Thus, the ultimate effect of a uniform excise tax is either a uniform increase in the prices of final products, the returns to factors of production remaining unchanged, or a uniform reduction of the returns to factors of production, prices of final products remaining unchanged. Now it is to be noted that either of these alternatives is equivalent, as far as the agents of production are concerned, to a flat-rate increase of income taxes. On this basis, the excise tax should be classified as a tax on a noncapitalizable source of income.

Before reaching such a definite conclusion, however, there are several reservations that should be made. In the first place, the federal indirect business taxes are not all excise taxes in the ordinary sense;

6. Harry G. Brown, "The Incidence of a General Output or a General Sales Tax," *Journal of Political Economy*, 47 (April 1939), 254–262; Earl R. Rolph, "A Proposed Revision of Excise-Tax Theory," *Journal of Political Economy*, 60 (April 1952), 102–117; J. A. Stockfisch, "The Capitalization and Investment Aspects of Excise Taxes under Competition," *American Economic Review*, 44 (June 1954), 287–300; J. M. Buchanan, "The Capitalization and Investment Aspects of Excise Taxes Under Competition: Comment," *American Economic Review*, 46 (December 1956), 974–977; and J. A. Stockfisch, "Reply," *American Economic Review*, 46 (December 1956), 977–980.

Table 1. Federal government receipts, 1946 to 1963 (in millions of dollars)

Year	Total receipts, less social insurance	Personal income taxes		Corporate profits taxes		Excise (indirect business) taxes	
		Value	Percent	Value	Percent	Value	Percent
1946	33,707	17,162	50.9	8,649	25.7	7,896	23.4
1947	38,203	19,650	51.4	10,679	28.0	7,874	20.6
1948	38,900	18,997	48.8	11,813	30.4	8,090	20.8
1949	34,125	16,194	47.5	9,773	28.6	8,158	23.9
1950	44,309	18,179	41.0	17,098	38.6	9,032	20.4
1951	57,377	26,278	45.8	21,569	37.6	9,530	16.6
1952	60,329	31,165	51.7	18,639	30.9	10,525	17.4
1953	62,972	32,359	51.4	19,419	30.8	11,194	17.8
1954	55,665	29,155	52.4	16,455	29.6	10,055	18.1
1955	63,430	31,521	49.7	20,869	32.9	11,040	17.4
1956	68,226	35,244	51.7	21,381	31.3	11,601	17.0
1957	70,256	37,389	53.2	20,655	29.4	12,212	17.4
1958	66,173	36,640	55.4	27,657	26.7	11,876	17.9
1959	75,397	40,367	53.5	21,984	29.2	13,046	17.3
1960	78,963	44,043	55.8	20,967	26.6	13,953	17.7
1961	79,996	45,138	56.4	20,685	25.9	14,173	17.7
1962	85,032	49,029	57.7	20,769	34.4	15,234	17.9
1963	90,634	51,948	57.3	23,042	25.4	15,644	17.3

Sources: Data for 1946 to 1957, U.S. Income and Output (Washington, D.C., Office of Business Economics, U.S. Department of Commerce, 1958); data after 1957, Survey of Current Business (ibid., July 1964).

many are manufacturer's taxes which might conceivably have an allocative effect on investment. In the second place, the taxes are not uniform; they consist of taxes on such commodities or services as automobiles, liquor, tobacco, jewelry, transportation, cosmetics, and other luxuries. But perhaps the most important reservation of all is the fact that, when excise taxes reduce the returns of the factors of production, some of these returns will be the rents on capital goods. To the extent that this is true, the excise tax will reduce the market price of capital goods and it should therefore be regarded, at least partially, as a capitalizable tax. The degree of capitaliztion cannot be large, however, since the rents on capital goods constitute a small proportion of the net national product. I shall return to this question after an examination of Table 1.

There are two striking features of this table upon which I should like to comment. The first is the dominant position of the personal income tax as a source of federal receipts; the second is the stability of the proportion which a given type of tax contributed to the total in any particular year—with the exception of the years 1950 and 1951, when the United States was waging the Korean War without price controls and when, in addition, corporate profits taxes were temporarily increased.

For the period as a whole, the relative amounts which each of the three major taxes contributed to total receipts *less* social insurance payments were as follows:

Personal income taxes	52.6 percent
Corporate profits taxes	29.2 percent
Excise taxes	18.2 percent

These figures may slightly overstate the significance of the corporate profits tax, for they include the years 1950 and 1951 when this tax was abnormally high. In round numbers, the following figures may be taken as conservative estimates of the proportion of each tax to the total:

Personal income taxes	50 percent
Corporate profits taxes	30 percent
Excise taxes	20 percent

Thus, if all tax reductions are made on a proportional basis, at least 50 percent of the reductions will be allocated to personal income taxes which have no influence on private wealth; another 30 percent will be allocated to corporate profits taxes and will be reflected immediately in a rise of security prices. As I have pointed out above, the excise tax affects private wealth only to the extent that it reduces the rents on capital goods.

In order to estimate the capitalizable portion of this tax, we must obtain the shares of labor and of capital in the national income. On the whole, the interindustry application of the Cobb-Douglas production function yields a lower labor share than does the time-series analysis. In his presidential address to the American Economic Association, for example, Douglas presented a table showing that, in six versions of the interindustry study for various dates between 1889 and 1922, the value of the labor share varied between 0.53 and 0.75, the average being 0.65.[7] By contrast, the time-series analysis produced a magnitude between 0.69 and 0.90 for the period 1899 to 1922, the differences depending upon the definitions employed for labor, capital, and output. In round numbers, therefore, I assume that the labor share has a value of 0.75 and the capital share, 0.25.

With this information it is possible to determine the portion of the excise tax which is capitalizable and the portion which is not. A reduction of excise taxes is equivalent to an increment of income, so that 25 percent of the increment should normally accrue to capital goods and 75 percent to workers. If we assume that workers are income earners, and that the taxes they pay are income taxes, the federal tax structure, combined with the assumed income shares, enables us to divide tax reductions between noncapitalizable and capitalizable taxes. Bearing in mind that personal income taxes, corporate profits taxes, and excises account for 50 percent, 30 percent, and 20 percent of federal receipts *less* social insurance, the allocation of federal taxes between noncapitalizable and capitalizable taxes may be calculated as indicated below:

Noncapitalizable taxes
    Personal income taxes   50 percent
    Excise taxes allocated to personal incomes
        $(0.20)(0.75) = 0.15$ 15 percent
        Total noncapitalizable taxes   65 percent

7. Paul H. Douglas, "Are There Laws of Production?" *American Economic Review*, 38 (March 1948), 1–41.

Capitalizable taxes

Corporate profits taxes	30 percent
Excise taxes allocated to capital goods:	
$(0.20)(0.25) = 0.05$	5 percent
Total capitalizable taxes	35 percent

Total, all taxes *less* social insurance contributions   100 percent

It thus appears that 65 percent of all tax reductions have no influence upon privately held wealth. The tax reductions which increase capital values account for only 35 percent of the total. From the tax structure and the distribution of income, I conclude that an open-market purchase, combined with a proportional reduction of taxes, will substantially reduce the value of privately held wealth. The capital gains resulting from tax reductions will not by any means offset the capital losses arising from security purchases. The reduction is not so much as I assumed in Chapter 12, where all tax reductions were assumed to be noncapitalizable; nevertheless, it is a substantial amount which can hardly be neglected. Moreover, it lends strong support to my initial argument that an open-market purchase of securities reduces the value of privately held wealth and thus stimulates saving.

The income and capital effects of an open-market purchase will perhaps be clarified by a numerical example. The prevailing rate of interest is assumed to be 5 percent, and the central bank is assumed to purchase $20,000 worth of securities. Five percent of $20,000 is $1,000, and the latter is accordingly the amount of taxes which must be reduced to restore the circular flow of income. The combined effects of an open-market purchase and an equivalent proportional tax reduction on both income and privately held capital, are shown below.

	Income	Capital
Open-market purchase of $20,000	− $1,000	− $20,000
Tax reductions:		
Personal income tax (50 percent)	+ 500	000
Excise tax allocated to personal		
incomes (15 percent)	+ 150	000
Corporate profits tax (30 percent)	+ 300	+ 6,000
Excise tax allocated to capital		
goods (5 percent)	+ 50	+ 1,000
Balance	0	− $13,000

Even after tax reductions have been considered, the private wealth of asset-holders is still reduced by $13,000, or by 65 percent of the initial purchase. The capital loss may be explained as follows. First, when the central bank buys securities, it takes away a source of income which is 100 percent capitalizable; and second, when tax reductions are made on a proportional basis, only 35 percent of these reductions apply to capitalizable sources of income. As a consequence, the capital gains from tax reductions fall far short of the capital losses from security purchases.

This outcome will be true, to one degree or another, for any tax structure, provided only that there are some noncapitalizable taxes in the government's total receipts. But for the United States I have demonstrated that federal receipts are overwhelming noncapitalizable. For this reason, an open-market purchase and proportional tax reduction induces a considerable reduction in privately held wealth. It increases saving and investment and lowers the rate of interest, despite the presence of fully capitalizable taxes such as the corporate profits tax. The capitalizable taxes are simply too small to alter the results.

I suspect that this is true even when the allocation effect is taken into account, for the reduction of corporate profits taxes, which reduces the spread between the private efficiency and the social efficiency of capital, is subject to a 30 percent discount upon any rational basis of tax reductions. In short, if taxes are reduced proportionately, the holders of corporate securities will receive, as tax remissions, only 30 percent of the income lost from open-market purchases. While this will no doubt reduce the spread between the social and private efficiency of capital, the magnitude of the reduction is substantially smaller than Mundell implies.

An examination of the federal tax structure suggests that, even when capitalizable taxes are considered, these taxes are so small relative to the noncapitalizable taxes that the conclusions of my initial study will remain substantially unaltered: that is, an open-market purchase of securities reduces the value of privately held wealth and thereby stimulates saving; when the economy has adjusted to the new position, the rate of interest remains permanently lower than before the open-market purchase was initiated by the central bank; and finally, the power of the central bank to alter the rate of interest depends, as I have said in the preceding chapter, upon its ability to alter the value of privately held wealth, and not upon its ability to alter the quantity of money.

In emphasizing the complicated nature of federal tax receipts, Mundell has led me to a reappraisal of my initial position. For this I am grateful to him. After a careful study of these receipts, however, I am convinced, for the reasons presented above, that no substantial changes in my conclusions are required.

14 | The Rate of Interest and the Marginal Product of Capital

The doctrine of marginal productivity, in one form or another, is an essential feature of most modern theories of capital and interest. But in some of these theories the marginal product of capital enters only as a by-product of something else, while in others marginal product is the immediate determinant, or at least the direct measure, of the rate of interest. Whether the marginal product of capital is regarded as a direct measure of the rate of interest or is related only indirectly to this rate depends upon the concept of capital itself, and in this respect it is useful to divide capital theories into two broad groups.

First, there are those theories which conceive of capital as a coordinate factor of production having exactly the same status in the theoretical framework as land and labor. Perhaps the outstanding example of this type is the Cobb-Douglas theory of production, in which total output is considered to be a function of the total supply of labor and the total quantity of capital.[1] J. B. Clark's theory of distribution also belongs in this first group, although the purely descriptive parts of his

Reprinted from *Journal of Political Economy*, 58 (August 1950), 289–306, and 59 (February 1951), 67–68. Copyright University of Chicago, 1950 and 1951.

1. C. W. Cobb and Paul H. Douglas, "A Theory of Production," *American Economic Review Supplement*, 18 (March 1928), 139–165. For a summary of work subsequently done along these same lines, see Paul H. Douglas, "Are There Laws of Production?" *American Economic Review*, 38 (March 1948), 1–41. See also the excellent bibliography in *Readings in the Theory of Income Distribution*, ed. W. Fellner and B. F. Haley (Philadelphia, Blakiston, 1946), pp. 671–677.

major work, as distinct from the theory itself, frequently contain a somewhat different concept of capital.[2]

Second, there are those theories which conceive of capital as the value of a command over useful resources in general, without attempting to make a sharp distinction between capital goods and other agents of production. Each of the agents of production, in this view, has a capital value equal either to the discounted value of its expected return or to its cost of production, the two different measures, in equilibrium, giving the same result. The prototype of the second group is F. H. Knight's well-known theory of capital.[3] Ironically, the Austrian theory of capital,[4] which Professor Knight has consistently opposed, also belongs to this second group, and so does the closely related theory of discounted marginal productivity.[5]

In the first group of theories, which envisage capital, labor, and land as coordinate factors of production, the marginal product of capital is considered to be a direct measure or determinant of the rate of interest, just as the marginal products of labor and land are direct measures or determinants of wage rates and rents, respectively. In the second group, on the other hand, there is no such immediate link between marginal products and the returns to the agents of production. Since capital, according to the second view, does not represent any specific agent of production analogous to land or labor, it is impossible to regard the income per unit of capital as the marginal product of any specific agent. To be sure, the return to capital, being dependent upon the income earned by specific agents of production, is closely related to the marginal products of these agents; but the relation between marginal

2. J. B. Clark, *The Distribution of Wealth* (New York, Macmillan, 1899), chaps. 12–20. "As we have said, the addition to the product caused by the last unit of capital fixes the rate of interest. Every unit of capital can secure for its owner what the last unit produces, and it can secure no more. The principle of final productivity, in short, acts in two ways, affording a theory of wages and of interest" (p. 187).

3. Professor Knight has written so extensively on capital theory that it is difficult to select one or two articles as representative of his views. Perhaps the most representative are the following: F. H. Knight, "Interest," *Encyclopedia of the Social Sciences*, ed. E. R. A. Seligman and A. Johnson (New York, Macmillan, 1932), vol. 8, 131–143; "The Quantity of Capital and the Rate of Interest," *Journal of Political Economy*, 44 (August, October 1936), 433–463, 612–642. See also the bibliography in *Readings in Income Distribution* (reference 1), pp. 696–697.

4. E. von Böhm Bawerk, *The Positive Theory of Capital*, trans. William Smart (New York, Strechert, 1891), books 5–7. Perhaps the best exposition of the Austrian theory of capital is to be found in Knut Wicksell, *Lectures on Political Economy*, English ed. (New York, Macmillan, 1934), vol. 1, 144–180.

5. Wicksell, *Lectures* (reference 4), vol. 1, 181–182; and W. W. Leontief, "Interest on Capital and Distribution: A Problem in the Theory of Marginal Productivity," *Quarterly Journal of Economics*, 49 (November 1934), 147–161.

product and return is not necessarily one of complete equality. In this broader view of capital, in other words, the marginal product of "capital in general" is not necessarily the same thing as the marginal product of a particular type of machine or of a particular type of land. Wicksell long ago pointed out that, because of this discrepancy, the rate of interest may not be equal to the marginal social product of capital;[6] and his arguments were subsequently repeated by Åkerman,[7] Lange,[8] and Stigler.[9]

Despite this repetition, however, there is still a considerable amount of confusion concerning the exact relation between marginal productivity and interest. There is a tendency, in particular, to conclude that the final results reached by the second group of capital theories—by the theories which regard capital as a command over resources—are substantially the same as the final results reached by the first group of theories. No matter what the initial capital concept may be, in other words, interest is frequently held to be equal, in a state of equilibrium, to the marginal product of capital. This is true even in such a distinguished work as Abba P. Lerner's *The Economics of Control*.[10] After presenting what amounts essentially to a version of the Austrian theory of capital, Lerner argues that, in the long run when the stock of capital is in equilibrium and the economic system has accordingly reached a stationary state, the rate of interest is equal to the marginal product of capital. Using the Austrian theory of capital as a point of departure, Lerner thus teaches a final result identical with the result obtained from the Cobb-Douglas theory of production or from Clark's marginal productivity theory of interest and wages.

In citing this example from Lerner's major work, I do not mean to make an invidious comparison, for the same point of view can be found among many other economists. Indeed, it sometimes seems as though a marginal productivity schedule, relating the quantity of capital to its marginal product, has at one time or another been derived from almost every conceivable concept of capital. And, as a corollary, the interest

6. Knut Wicksell, *Über Wert, Kapital, und Rente* (Jena, G. Fischer, 1893), pp. 111–116. See also Wicksell's *Lectures* (reference 4), vol. 1, 180.

7. Gustav Åkerman, *Realkapital und Kapitalzins* (Stockholm, 1923), pp. 95–96.

8. Oskar Lange, "The Place of Interest in the Theory of Production," *Review of Economic Studies*, 3 (June 1936), 185.

9. G. J. Stigler, *Production and Distribution Theories* (New York, Macmillan, 1941), pp. 288–289.

10. Abba P. Lerner, *The Economics of Control* (New York, Macmillan, 1944): see chap. 25.

rate has then been ascribed to the marginal product of capital. Now for many practical purposes, including those which Lerner had in mind, there is probably no great harm in this procedure, since the rate of interest *is* closely related to the marginal product of capital. Nevertheless, the procedure is not entirely correct; and in view of the widespread misunderstanding on this point, it seems useful to present a more rigorous account of the relation between the rate of interest and the marginal product of capital.

It will be shown below that if capital is regarded as a command over useful resources, or as the investment value of a process of production, the rate of interest is never (except by accident) equal to the marginal social product of such capital. The reasons for this discrepancy will be discussed in some detail. Although the argument below repeats, in part, the earlier observations of Wicksell, I believe that such repetition is justified by the fact that Wicksell failed to make an impression upon later economists.

It is not always easy, at first glance, to see how a permanent discrepancy between the interest rate and the marginal product of capital can exist in a perfectly competitive market without calling into play some counteracting forces. Consider, for example, the economic decisions of an individual businessman. Suppose that this particular businessman produces a commodity that requires the use of a certain type of machine. If the capital market is competitive, the businessman will be faced with a given interest rate at which he can borrow or lend, and he will accordingly adjust his production plans so as to maximize the present value of his expected future income at this given interest rate. Among other things, this means employing such a number of machines that the marginal net product of each machine, expressed in terms of the price of the machine, is equal to the interest rate. In other words, the businessman will purchase and use additional machines up to the point where the marginal income derived from each machine, after making necessary expenditures for maintenance, is equal to the amount of interest that would have to be paid at the prevailing rate on the private capital invested in each machine.

Now this is surely the same as saying that, for an individual firm and for a particular type of capital good, the marginal product of capital is equal to the interest rate; and, if such a proposition is true for one firm and one agent of production, why is it not also true for all firms and all agents of production taken together? In other words, if the interest rate is equal to the marginal *private* product of capital, why is it not also equal to the marginal *social* product of capital?

The answer to this question is to be found, as might be expected, in a discrepancy between *private* and *social* products of capital. But the difference between the private and the social products is not of the type customarily considered in economic theory, for it has nothing to do either with the usual type of external economies and diseconomies or with imperfect competition. Even if all product and factor markets were perfectly competitive, and there were no external economies or diseconomies of production, it might still be true that the marginal private product of capital would differ from the marginal social product and that, as a consequence, the rate of interest would not be equal to the marginal social product of capital.

The divergence of the social from the private product of capital is attributable to the fact that it is impossible to find an invariant unit in which to measure the social quantity of capital. To put the matter another way, we may say that a change in the supply of capital—arising, for example, from new voluntary saving—alters the units in which all the previously existing capital is measured; and it is therefore incorrect to say that the supply of capital as a whole has increased by the amount of the voluntary saving. It is important to emphasize that this problem of measuring the quantity of capital is not an index-number problem. There are, to be sure, numerous index-number problems of the greatest complexity in the theory of capital. But the problem to which I now refer would exist even in the simplest economy in which all output consisted of a single type of consumers' goods and all firms were exactly alike.

The argument is perhaps most easily illustrated by an extremely simple version of the Austrian theory of capital. As will be shown later, however, the conclusions reached are valid for more general concepts of capital as well. Consider an economy in which all output consists of one commodity, timber, and suppose that the only costs of producing the timber are the labor costs of preparing the ground and planting the seedlings, and the interest charges on invested capital. The costs of felling the trees, in other words, are assumed to be negligible relative to initial expenditures for planting.[11] This is the point-input, point-output

---

11. I am well aware that these assumptions do not correspond at all to actual forestry practice. The simplified model of timber production is introduced simply because it brings out most clearly the relation between the rate of interest and the marginal product of capital. More realistic and more complicated models would in no way alter this fundamental relation.

version of the Austrian theory. The total output of timber obviously depends not only upon the number of workers employed in planting but also upon the period of time that the trees are allowed to grow.

Let the output *per worker* be represented in Fig. 1 by the line $w = \phi(t)$.

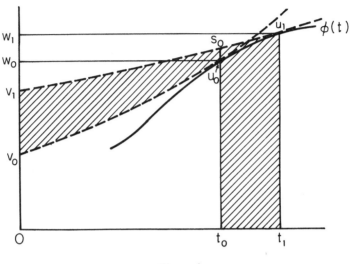

Figure 1

This line expresses the amount of timber that can be produced per year by each worker as a function of the length of time the trees are permitted to grow. If the age of the trees at the time of cutting is t_0, for example, output per worker will be w_0, while if the age is t_1, output will be w_1.

The length of time that the trees are permitted to grow will obviously depend upon the amount of capital that businessmen are willing and able to invest in their enterprises; that is, it will depend upon the economy's accumulated stock of wealth, expressed in units of income.[12] If a particular businessman wishes to produce an annual output per worker of w_0, for example, he will have to let his trees attain an age of t_0 before cutting. Suppose that t_0 is 35 years. In order to produce an annual output of w_0 per worker, the businessman will then have to have

12. Alternatively, we might say that the period of production is governed by the supply and demand for capital. The supply of capital, in turn, is determined by the preferences of income-earners for holding assets or consuming their wealth, which means that time preference or abstinence, or both, are ultimately determinants of the period of production.

35 woodlots with a uniform age distribution of trees varying between 1 and 35 years. In this way one of his woodlots will be ready for cutting and replanting each year.

Let v_0 in Fig. 1 be the wage rate per worker per year. The capital per worker that the businessman has invested in his one-year-old trees will then be the wage rate v_0 plus interest at the market rate for one year. Likewise, the capital per worker invested in the two-year-old trees will be v_0 plus interest *compounded* for two years, and so on for the older trees. If the dotted line $v_0 u_0$ represents the compound-interest line at the prevailing interest rate, it is clear that the amount of capital invested in trees of any particular age will be the distance of this line from the abscissa at the point representing the particular age of the trees. And if the woodlots have a uniform age distribution between unity and t_0, the total capital per worker required for an annual output of w_0 will be the sum of all such distances, which is the same as the area $o v_0 u_0 t_0$.

Suppose that the accumulated wealth per worker that the community as a whole is willing to hold is exactly equal to this area, and let ρ_0 be the interest rate at which the compound-interest line $v_0 u_0$ is computed. The output per worker w_0, the age of the trees at cutting t_0, the wage rate v_0, and the interest rate ρ_0 will then be in equilibrium in at least three different respects.

(1) For the given values of wages, interest, and the period of production, the amount of capital per worker is equal to the community's propensity to hold wealth, so that there is no tendency toward saving or dissaving, and accordingly no changes in methods of production.

(2) Since the accumulated value of wages, compounded for t_0 years, is equal to w_0, the businessmen are earning neither profits nor losses, and there is accordingly no incentive for a change in the number of firms. In other words, the amount of timber per worker felled at age t_0 is equal to the cost of planting these trees plus interest accumulated for t_0 years. In the discounted productivity doctrine, this second proposition is stated the other way round, by saying that the discounted value of the final product is equal to the wage rate. Whatever way it is stated, it means that the final product is equal to its cost of production, including the interest cost.

(3) Since the compound-interest line, or the discount line, $v_0 u_0$ is tangent to the production function at u_0, there is no other period of production which would be as profitable to the businessman as the period t_0. At the prevailing interest rate, in other words, the discounted value

of final output is maximized at t_0. In brief, the output w_0 is an equilibrium output in the sense that at this output the supply of capital per worker is equal to the demand, the revenue from the product is equal to the cost of production, and profits are being maximized.

Suppose now that this equilibrium is disturbed by an increase in capital arising from voluntary saving. According to the Austrian theory, the increase in capital leads to a sequence of events somewhat as follows. The interest rate falls as the prices of securities are bid up by the new savers, and the discounted value of the output w_0 rises above v_0. Or, to put the matter another way, the cost of production declines as a consequence of the lower interest rate, and businessmen earn excess profits. The excess profits attract new firms, whose competition for labor forces up the wage rate. Finally, at the new, lower interest rate the period of production t_0 is no longer the most profitable; it is now profitable to permit the trees to grow longer and consequently to employ more capital per worker.

In Fig. 1 I assume that the increase in capital eventually results in a new equilibrium at which the period of production is t_1, output per worker is w_1, wages are v_1, and the quantity of capital per worker is $ov_1u_1t_1$. The new interest rate, ρ_1, is not shown directly in the figure, but it governs the slope of the compound-interest line v_1u_1; in particular, the *relative* slope of the line at any point is equal to ρ_1.

We wish to see now how the interest rate ρ_1 is related to the marginal product of capital. The marginal product of capital, in absolute terms, is simply the difference between output w_1 and output w_0. The marginal product per unit of capital, on the other hand, is this amount $(w_1 - w_0)$ divided by the increase in the quantity of capital. The quantity of capital per worker has increased from $ov_0u_0t_0$ to $ov_1u_1t_1$, and this increase can be divided into two parts. The first part is the area, $v_0v_1s_0u_0$, which represents the excess of investment cost under the new wage and interest rates over investment cost under the old wage and interest rates of a process of production having a period t_0. (In other words, if businessmen in the new situation attempted to set up a production process with length t_0, their total investment per worker, including interest, would be $ov_1s_1t_0$, whereas the actual amount invested in such a process in the previous equilibrium was only $ov_0u_0t_0$. The difference between the two amounts is the shaded area, and this of course represents the *capital gains* per worker from all goods-in-process existing at the time the capital supply was increased.)

The other part of the capital increase, shown in Fig. 1 by the second shaded area, $t_0 s_0 u_1 t_1$, consists in the new voluntary savings. Although these voluntary savings were the initiating force which brought about a change in the period of production from t_0 to t_1, it is obvious from the figure that the total increase in capital is larger than the voluntary savings themselves. Moreover, the capital gains, which account for the excess of the total increase in capital over the new voluntary savings, are as much a part of real capital as are the voluntary savings. Under the new economic conditions, the investment cost, including interest, of a process of production having the new period t_1 is equal to $ov_1 u_1 t_1$; and it is this investment cost, rather than the actual amounts spent on earlier investments, which explains the value of both old and new investments in the new equilibrium.

It is apparent from Fig. 1 that the increase in product expressed as a percentage of the increase in total capital, or, more briefly, the marginal product of capital, is equal to the distance $w_1 - w_0$ divided by the sum of the two shaded areas of the figure. We wish to compare this ratio with the rate of interest. The rate of interest, as noted earlier, is equal to the *relative* slope of the compound-interest line, and in equilibrium this line is tangent to the production function $\phi(t)$. The relative slope of the production function is $(\Delta w / \Delta t) \cdot (1/w)$, where both Δw and Δt are assumed to be small; and it follows that in equilibrium $\rho_1 = (\Delta w / \Delta t) \cdot (1/w)$.

If the new voluntary savings are small, Δw may be taken to be equal to $w_1 - w_0$, while $\Delta t \cdot w$ will differ by only an infinitesimal amount from the shaded area $t_2 s_0 u_1 t_1$. Since the latter is the geometric representation of the new voluntary saving, we may say that the rate of interest is equal to the increase in product divided by the new voluntary saving. The marginal product of capital, on the other hand, is equal to the increase in product divided by the *total* increase in capital, and since the increase in capital includes capital gains as well as new saving, it is clear that the denominator of the ratio representing the marginal product of capital is larger than the denominator of the ratio representing the rate of interest. It follows that, for the type of investment process represented by Fig. 1, the rate of interest is always larger than the marginal product of capital.

The increase in capital in the preceding illustration has been divided into two parts, a voluntary increase consisting in new savings and an involuntary increase consisting in capital gains. These two parts might equally well be called respectively a primary and a secondary increase in capital; and as long as the distinction between the two remains valid, the rate of interest may be regarded as the marginal product of voluntary savings, or as the marginal product of the primary increase in capital, a quantity which is distinct from, and greater than, the marginal product of the increase in capital as a whole.

In the Austrian theory of capital, however, the total quantity of capital is considered to be a result of deliberate decisions of income-earners as to how much accumulated wealth they wish to hold. No place can be found in this theory for changes in the quantity of capital arising from such fortuitous events as capital gains and losses. Unless accompanied by a deliberate or voluntary increase in the desire to hold wealth, capital gains, in the Austrian view, would lead to consumption of part of accumulated wealth, while capital losses would stimulate further saving to make up such losses. Thus in comparing one position of equilibrium with another, as in Fig. 1, according to the Austrian theory we must consider the entire increase in capital to be voluntary savings. In this event, the rate of interest obviously cannot be described as the marginal product of voluntary savings, for such savings constitute the entire increase in capital. The new savings are used for two quite distinct purposes, and it is only one of these which affects the level of output and hence the rate of interest. In part, the new savings must be used to buy some of the assets of previous owners who are assumed to consume their capital gains. The remainder can then be used to lengthen the period of production or, more generally, to produce additional capital goods; it is this part which governs the rate of interest. Whether the entire increase in capital is deliberate, or whether part of it is accidental as in the earlier illustration, it remains true that the rate of interest is higher than the ratio of the increase in product to the increase in total capital. In short, the interest rate exceeds the marginal social product of capital.

Although the foregoing argument has been developed exclusively from the point of view of the Austrian theory of capital, it is equally applicable, as I have indicated earlier, to other capital concepts. Consider, for example, Professor Knight's theory of capital. Capital, according to this view, is an accumulated stock of purchasing power or command over resources, whose value, expressed in units of income, is equal both to the discounted value of the annual income earned by these resources and to the cost of producing the resources, with interest compounded at the market rate. For our purposes it is the second of these measures of capital that is the more important. If the value of a machine or other capital good is taken to be its potential cost of production under existing conditions, it follows (as in the Austrian theory) that no invariant unit can be found in which the capital value of agents of production can be measured. A 10-percent increase in capital, for example, will not normally be associated with an increase of exactly the same relative amount in machines or other capital goods, since the increase in machines will itself alter the units in which capital is measured. The proper measure of capital in Knight's theory is the value of the goods foregone, or the value of the potential income which would have to be sacrificed in bringing such capital into existence—and this potential income depends not only on the physical quantity of resources employed in producing capital goods but also upon the efficiency of these resources in the alternative employment of producing current income.

Now an increase in capital increases the productivity of the economic system as a whole and thereby alters the returns, expressed in current income, to the agents of production. An increase that took the form of additional machinery, for example, would increase the marginal productivity of labor and thereby lead to an increase in wages. The higher wage rate would mean that the employment of a given number of workers to produce machines rather than to produce for immediate consumption would involve a larger sacrifice of current income than was necessary before the increase in capital occurred. Insofar as labor cost is concerned, in other words, the accumulation of capital in the form of machines increases the cost of production of such machines and leads to capital gains. And (again as in the Austrian theory) the capital gains tend to keep the marginal social product of capital below the rate of interest.

Here, however, we are confronted with several complicating factors. The most important of these complications arises from the fact that machines are produced not only by the employment of labor but also by the employment of other agents of production, including machines themselves. Metalworking machines, for instance, are required to produce metalworking machines, trucks to produce trucks, and so on almost without limit. In the Austrian theory of capital this complication was ignored; the assumption was made, either explicitly or implicitly, that the investment cost of a particular process of production could be traced back to a combination of the so-called "original" factors of production, labor and land, plus accumulated compound interest. It was accordingly not difficult to show, as in Fig. 1 above, that an increase in wealth would bring about capital gains and that the return to capital as a whole would consequently exceed its marginal product. Higher wages and higher rents arising from an increase in capital are the direct cause, according to the Austrian theory, of an increase in the investment cost or replacement cost of every process of production and accordingly of capital gains for goods already in process. Moreover, the increased replacement costs and associated capital gains occur even though the rate of interest, which also enters into the cost of investment, tends to decline when the amount of capital is increased; the decline in interest cost does not completely offset the rise in wages and rents.

When we come to examine more complicated and more realistic situations in which machines as well as labor and land cooperate in the production of more machines, it is by no means certain that an increase in capital will bring about capital gains in the manner envisaged by the Austrian theory. For while wages and rents will probably rise as a result of the larger supply of capital, it is not clear that the price of machines will also rise. Indeed, since the increase in capital will normally raise the ratio of machines to other agents of production, there is a presumption that the marginal product of machines will decline, and the price of machines will therefore have to fall. In this event, the investment outlays required to produce a particular type of machine may well fall, rather than rise, when the amount of capital is augmented. In other words, if machines are used to produce machines, the decline in the price of such machines may more than offset the rise in wages and rents, with the result that the investment cost of a particular process is reduced. If this happens, an increase in capital will lead to capital losses rather than capital gains, and by the same sort of reasoning as above it follows that the rate of interest will fall short of the marginal social product of capital. As before, the rate of interest will equal the marginal return to new voluntary savings, but the increase in voluntary savings will now *exceed* the increase in capital as a whole.

It is apparent from the case just considered that the relation between marginal product and the rate of interest is exceedingly complex. A general increase in social capital may bring about either capital gains or capital losses, and the marginal product of social capital may accordingly exceed or fall short of the rate of interest. Whether the one or the other of these possibilities will occur depends upon a complicated set of economic and technical relations that almost defies description or generalization. The outcome depends, to a considerable extent, upon the ease or difficulty of substituting machines for labor in the various branches of production, and upon the ratios of high-capital agents of production to low-capital agents in different stages of production. For present purposes, however, it is sufficient to emphasize that an increase in capital alters the cost, in terms of foregone income, of producing various agents of production and that, as a consequence, the units in which capital is measured are also altered. The resulting capital gains or losses may conceivably more or less offset each other, so that the marginal social product of capital as a whole is not markedly different from the rate of interest. On the other hand, capital losses may predominate over capital gains, or conversely. In any event, it is clear that there is no assurance that the interest rate will necessarily equal the marginal social product of capital.

I have argued above that whether an increase in social capital leads to capital losses or to capital gains depends to a large extent upon the ease of substituting machines for labor. Since this process of substitution is not readily depicted in the Austrian theory of capital, the latter is capable of explaining only part of the relation between the rate of interest and the marginal social product of capital. Nevertheless, a slight modification of the Austrian theory can be found which shows, in a reasonably clear manner, how the rate of interest can sometimes be *below* the marginal product of capital. Suppose, as in our earlier discussion of the Austrian theory, that all capital consists in investment of labor in woodlots and that the only labor outlay in this process is that which occurs at the time the trees are planted.

In the present example, however, in place of the previous assumption that the national income consists exclusively of the output of lumber, I shall suppose that lumber is merely an intermediate product employed in the production of a final commodity X. Both labor and lumber are assumed to be employed in the production of the final product. In order to avoid complications arising from investment in the final stage of production, I assume that the time required to produce X is so short, relative to the growth period of the trees, that the capital investment in the final stage is negligible. As in our earlier example, social capital will then consist exclusively in the investment in growing trees.

Let the production function for lumber, expressing the output per worker as a function of the age of the trees when felled, be represented as before by the function $\phi(t)$. Since lumber in the present example is only an intermediate product, and since both the quantity of capital and the wage rate must ultimately be measured in terms of the final product, X, it is appropriate to express the production of lumber not in units of lumber but in the equivalent units of X. This means that the function $\phi(t)$ must be multiplied by the price of lumber in terms of X. Suppose that in the initial equilibrium a unit of lumber exchanges for p_0 units of X. The production function for lumber, expressed in units of the income commodity X, will then be represented by $p_0 \phi(t)$, as in Fig. 2. The initial position of equilibrium depicted by Fig. 2 is such that the optimum

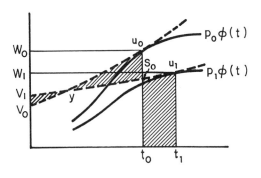

Figure 2

period of growth for the trees is t_0, the wage rate is v_0, the value of lumber output per worker in units of final income is w_0, the amount of capital per worker in the lumber industry is the area $ov_0 u_0 t_0$, and the rate of interest is the relative slope of the compound-interest line $v_0 y u_0$.

Suppose now that this equilibrium is disturbed by new savings. As in the earlier example, the new savings force down the rate of interest, entrepreneurs earn excess profits, and competition eventually eliminates these profits by forcing up wages. At the same time, the lower rate of interest makes it profitable for the entrepreneurs to extend the growth period of the trees; and lumber output per worker, in physical units, accordingly rises. Moreover, in the present example there is an additional equilibrating force at work: excess profits are eliminated not only by a rise in wages but also by a fall in the price of lumber in terms of the final product, X. Lumber is used exclusively in the production of this final product, and the price of lumber is governed by its marginal productivity in this employment. It is therefore clear that, as the supply of lumber increases, both its marginal product and its price, in terms of X, must decline. Let the new lower price be p_1. In Fig. 2 the decline in the price of lumber is shown by the downward shift of the "value product" curve, $p_1\phi(t)$. This downward shift is a uniform, relative shift throughout the length of the production function, the extent of the shift being equal to the relative decline in price.

When equilibrium is reestablished after the increase in the supply of capital, the period of production has been increased from t_0 to t_1, the wage rate has risen from v_0 to v_1, the price of lumber has declined from p_0 to p_1, the interest rate has fallen, and the amount of capital per worker has been increased to the area $ov_1u_1t_1$. Figure 2 has been so constructed that the *total value* of lumber output per worker is smaller in the new equilibrium than in the old, but this is by no means a necessary consequence of the increase in capital; whether the value of lumber output per worker rises or falls obviously depends largely upon the degree of the decline in the lumber price, and this in turn depends upon the difficulty or ease of substituting lumber for labor in the production of the final product X.

In any event, our primary concern is not with the movements of all the variables of the system but rather with the relation between the marginal social product of capital and the rate of interest; and this relation can be described, in part at least, in terms of capital gains and capital losses as in the earlier illustration. Since equilibrium in the market for the capital good, lumber, was reestablished partly by a fall in the lumber price and only partly by a rise in wages, it is evident from Fig. 2 that the rise in wages is not in itself sufficient to guarantee capital gains to the owners of the growing trees. Thus in Fig. 2 the cost, at the new wage and interest rates, of investing in the old process of production with length t_0 is $ov_1s_0t_0$, and, under the conditions assumed in the figure, this reproduction cost of the old investments is *smaller* than the former value of these investments; that is, the area of $ov_1s_0t_0$ is smaller than the area of $ov_0u_0t_0$. An increase in capital, under the conditions assumed in Fig. 2, thus leads to capital losses. To this extent the increase in capital as a whole tends to be smaller than the new voluntary savings, and by an argument opposite to the one presented earlier the marginal social product of capital tends to *exceed* the rate of interest.[13]

As in the earlier example, the rate of interest is equal to the value of the marginal product of the capital that is employed to extend the period of production; in the terminology of the Austrian theory, it is the marginal product of time. Unlike the earlier illustration, however, the amount of capital so used may be larger, because of capital losses, than the increase in capital as a whole. Moreover, the present example differs from the simple model given in Fig. 1 in still another respect: in the simple point-input, point-output model of Fig. 1, the capital employed in extending the period of production was identified with primary new saving, but in the more complex situation of Fig. 2 this identification is no longer possible. In Fig. 1 the entire labor force was assumed to be employed in capitalistic production—planting trees—and the proportionate increase in capital per worker was therefore the same as the proportionate increase in capital as a whole. In Fig. 2, on the other hand, only part of the labor force is employed in the production of lumber, the remainder being employed directly in the production of the income commodity X.

Figure 2 is drawn in terms of output and capital per worker in the lumber industry, and, since workers can shift back and forth from this industry to the X industry, capital per worker in the lumber industry can change not only because of an increase in the amount of capital available but also because of an increase or decrease in the number of workers in that industry. Thus, if the number of workers in the lumber

13. The economic system depicted in Fig. 2 resembles, in some respects, the model developed by Åkerman (*Realkapital und Kapitalzins*, reference 7, *passim*). Although Åkerman seemed to feel that his contribution to capital theory consisted in his analysis of *durable* capital goods, the feature of his approach which really distinguished it from the earlier work of Böhm Bawerk and Wicksell was the fact that his model envisaged competition and substitution between capital *goods* and labor in the final stages of production of consumers' goods. In contrast to Åkerman's system, the simplified period-of-production system of Böhm Bawerk and Wicksell allowed only for substitution between time (capital in general) and labor in the process of production as a whole.

The basic difference, then, between Wicksell and Åkerman is the same as the difference between Figs. 1 and 2 of this paper. Since he had considered only models similar to Fig. 1, Wicksell failed to understand how capital accumulation could lead to capital losses for the society as a whole, as in Fig. 2. In commenting on Åkerman's problem, Wicksell said, "I cannot enter now on the explanation of this very puzzling formula; presumably it belongs to the sphere of dynamic theory, where we cannot confine ourselves to the comparison of two different equilibria, but must also study the transition from one to the other" (*Lectures*, reference 4, vol. 1, 293). This explanation is wrong, of course, but I believe that it reveals the true difference between Wicksell's capital theory and Åkerman's.

industry declines, the amount of capital per worker employed in lengthening the period of production will exceed the amount of primary new savings. The excess, of course, represents capital that is freed when some of the woodlots are cut over and abandoned. Conversely, if the number of workers employed in the production of lumber *increases*, the capital available for extending the period of production will fall short of the new primary savings; in this event, part of the new savings will have to be used in planting new woodlots in order to employ the additional labor force.

Whether employment of labor in the lumber industry rises or falls when the amount of capital is increased depends upon a complex set of circumstances, particularly upon the character of the production function in the X industry. In the present problem, however, there is no need to analyze in detail the movements of the labor force between the lumber industry and the X industry. The point I wish to emphasize is that the rate of interest may *conceivably* fall short of the marginal social product of capital, and this point can be demonstrated by considering an intermediate situation in which the number of workers in the lumber industry is unaffected by the increased supply of capital. If the number of workers employed in producing lumber remains unchanged, the relative increase in the amount of capital available per worker will be the same as the relative increase in capital as a whole; Fig. 2, which is drawn in terms of output and capital per worker, can therefore be used to describe the movements in the total supply of capital and in the total value of lumber output.

As before, the marginal social product of capital and the rate of interest are equal, respectively, to the following ratios:

$$\text{Marginal social product of capital} = \frac{\text{Value of increase in lumber output}}{\text{Increase in capital}}$$

$$\text{and Rate of interest} = \frac{\text{Value of increase in lumber output}}{\text{Capital used in extending period of production}}.$$

The numerators of these expressions are the same, and the marginal social product of capital can therefore differ from the rate of interest only on account of differences in the denominators. Under the conditions assumed in Fig. 2, the first denominator is obviously smaller than the second; that is, the increase in capital as a whole is smaller than the amount of capital employed in extending the period of production. The increase in capital per worker in Fig. 2 is equal to the area $t_0 s_0 u_1 t_1$ *plus* $v_1 y v_0$ *minus* $u_0 y s_0$. The figure has been drawn in such a way that $u_0 y s_0$ exceeds $v_1 y v_0$, and it follows that the increase in capital per worker is *less* than $t_0 s_0 u_1 t_1$. But $t_0 s_0 u_1 t_1$ represents the amount of capital per worker employed in lengthening the period of production, and it is this quantity, rather than the increase in capital per worker, which is related to the rate of interest. Under the conditions assumed in Fig. 2, then, the rate of interest is less than the marginal social product of capital.

We have seen in the preceding discussion that the rate of interest may either exceed or fall short of the marginal social product of capital. This means that those capital theories which regard capital as a coordinate factor of production having the same status as the so-called "noncapital" factors, labor and land, are subject to a persistent bias in one direction or the other. Except by accident, the rate of interest cannot be described as the marginal product of capital in the sense that wages, in a noncapitalistic process of production, are the marginal product of labor. It is true, to be sure, that in a stationary state in which the demand for capital is equal to the supply, the rate of interest will equal the marginal *private* product of capital; for, if this were not the case, entrepreneurs would always have an incentive to expand or contract their employment of capital. But the nature of capital is such, as we have seen, that its marginal private product is never, except accidentally, equal to its marginal social product.

It is perhaps worth repeating that the discrepancy between the private and the social products is not attributable to monopoly. Nor is it attributable to complications arising from aggregating heterogeneous magnitudes into a social composite. Even in the simplest economy imaginable, in which production was limited to one final product and the process of production was exactly the same for all firms, it would still be true that the marginal private product of capital, and hence the rate of interest, would differ from the marginal social product.

The fundamental reason for the discrepancy is that the units in which social capital is measured—in other words the potential income foregone to produce the agents of production—have no invariant counterpart in the physical quantity of capital goods. In other words, a 10-percent increase in social capital need not mean a 10-percent increase in machines, even if all capital is devoted exclusively to the production of such machines; the relative increase in the number of machines may be either greater or less than 10 percent, depending upon whether the increase in capital leads to capital losses or to capital gains. The rate of interest is equal to the marginal product of the new machines, expressed as a percentage of the value of the new machines, whereas the marginal social product of capital is equal to the same marginal product of the new machines divided by the increase in value of all machines taken together. Since an increase in capital alters the value of machines already in existence, the total increase in capital is not necessarily the same as the value of the new machines.

Attempts have been made in two different ways to avoid the difficulty regarding the units of capital. First, Böhm Bawerk and those who followed his lead proposed the average period of production as a measure of the quantity of social capital, and the interest rate was then described as the marginal product of increasing this period of production. The ambiguities, both conceptual and statistical, involved in the concept of a period of production have been discussed so frequently that it is unnecessary for me to elaborate upon them here. It is sufficient to say that the period of production has not been widely adopted, even among the proponents of the Austrian theory of capital, as a practical or satisfactory measure of the quantity of capital.[14]

The second approach gives up all attempts to measure capital in value units and describes a country's capital endowment in terms of its physical units of machinery, equipment, and other capital goods. With this concept of capital, the return to a given type of capital good is a rental, the amount of which is equal to the marginal product of such equipment, just as the rent of land is equal to the marginal product of land. Although this procedure obviously avoids the difficulties of measuring capital, it is really no theory of capital at all, for it fails, on the one hand, to explain the rate of interest as a *ratio* of returns to value and, on the other hand, it provides no explanation of the tendency toward equality of interest rates among different types of investment.[15] Perhaps even more important, such an approach gives no clue as to how the

14. Wicksell, for example, developed a capital theory which was essentially the same as Böhm Bawerk's, and yet he measured the total quantity of capital either as the discounted value of its expected return or as the cost of production of the agents in which the capital was embodied. See his *Lectures* (reference 4).

15. In the terminology of Alfred Marshall, we might say that the physical concept of capital is capable of explaining the quasi-rents of various capital goods but not the rate of return on investment in such goods. See his *Principles of Economics*, ed. 8 (London, Macmillan, 1930), p. 421.

supply of capital goods as a whole is related to the willingness of income-earners to hold assets.

Value is thus the essence of the capital concept, and we are thrown back perforce upon some unit of value as the unit of measure of the quantity of capital. But, having accepted this proposition, it is important at the same time that we recognize that a one-to-one correspondence is not to be expected between changes in the quantity of capital, in the value sense, and corresponding changes in the quantity of the agents of production in which the capital is embodied. Discrepancies of this sort between the value measure and the physical measure of capital explain why the marginal productivity theory cannot be used, without modification, to describe the rate of interest.

Assuming then that the marginal social product of capital differs from the rate of interest, we may inquire, in concluding this paper, into the social consequences of this difference. One of the cardinal tenets of welfare economics is that an economic system cannot be in an optimal position unless the marginal return to each factor of production is equal to that factor's marginal social product; if the wages of a particular type of labor differ from marginal social product, for example, social welfare can usually be increased by a change in the amount of such labor performed.[16]

Although capital is not a factor of production in the ordinary sense, it is nevertheless useful to ask whether a similar proposition is true of the rate of interest; that is, if the rate of interest differs from the marginal social product of capital, does the "quantity" of services performed by capital tend, also, to differ from the social optimum? The answer to this question depends in part upon whether one is considering a stationary state or a growing economy. In a stationary state there is no doubt that a discrepancy between the rate of interest and the marginal social product of capital signifies a loss of economic welfare. It seems probable to me that this is also true in a growing economy. But in an expanding economic system there are a number of complications arising from uncertainty and from the unpredictable behavior of asset-holders, and these complications considerably reduce the force of our welfare proposition as applied to capital—if they do not destroy it entirely. It will

16. Lerner, *Economics of Control* (reference 10), pp. 102–105.

accordingly be convenient to begin with the simple if highly abstract case of the stationary state.

A stationary economy is characterized by the fact that the total wealth of the economy is equal to the amount which all its residents are willing to hold as a store of value. On balance, the residents consume all their current incomes, and no additional capital accumulation takes place. Now from the point of view of an individual income-earner, an act of personal saving is equivalent to a reduction in present consumption and an increase, in perpetuity, of future income; and the rate at which income in perpetuity can thus be substituted for present consumption is equal to the rate of interest. If the rate of interest is 5 percent, for example, new savings of $100 can be regarded as the substitution of an income of $5 per year in perpetuity for $100 of current consumption. In deciding whether to save or to dissave, an individual income-earner will presumably alter his asset holdings until the marginal satisfaction derived from $100 of current income is equal, for him, to the marginal satisfaction of $5 per year in perpetuity. More generally, if r is the rate of interest, we may say that r is also the marginal rate of substitution, for the typical income-earner, between future consumption and present consumption. I shall call this the private rate of substitution.

If the stationary economy is to be in an optimal position as far as the total quantity of capital is concerned, this private rate of substitution must be equal to the rate at which the economy as a whole can substitute future income in perpetuity for present income; that is, the private rate of substitution must equal the social rate. But the social rate of substitution is the marginal product of capital. Thus, if the rate of interest differs from the marginal product of capital, the private rate of substitution between future and present consumption will necessarily differ from the social rate of substitution, and the quantity of capital will accordingly differ from the optimum.

Suppose, for example, that the rate of interest is 5 percent, while the marginal product of capital is 7 percent. In this event an increase of social capital equal to $100 will enable the economy to produce additional income of $7 per year in future years. Asset holdings by individuals however, have presumably stopped at the point where $100 of additional assets yield a private return of only $5 per year. It follows that both society as a whole and the individual asset-holders can gain by any arrangement whereby the asset-holders are given a *marginal* return for additional savings equal to something between 5 and 7 percent. Such an arrangement obviously increases the welfare of the individual asset-holder, since the marginal rate at which he can substitute future income for present consumption exceeds his private rate of substitution. And the economy as a whole also benefits, since the marginal social product of the additional capital is larger than the return to the individual saver. To put the matter another way, any additional capital obtained by the means suggested yields a social return in excess of the amount needed to compensate the new savers. This surplus return constitutes a sort of social dividend which may be used to increase the welfare of the community as a whole.[17]

From the foregoing, it should be evident that, when the marginal product of capital exceeds the rate of interest, the quantity of capital in a stationary state falls short of the social optimum. By similar reasoning the converse of this proposition can easily be demonstrated; that is, it can be shown that when the marginal product of capital is *less* than the rate of interest, the quantity of capital, under stationary conditions, is *greater* than the optimal quantity. If the rate of interest is 6 percent, for example, while the marginal product of capital is 5 percent, an arrangement can be made whereby both the asset-holders and the rest of the society benefit from a reduction in the quantity of capital. The non-asset-holders benefit because the interest payments made to asset-holders on marginal assets exceed the social product of these assets. And the asset-holders gain because the private rate of substitution between current consumption and future consumption can be made more favorable to present consumption without eliminating completely the gain to the nonasset-holders.

Combining the results of the preceding paragraphs, we may formulate the general proposition that the quantity of capital in a stationary

17. It will no doubt be apparent to the reader that the concept of an optimal amount of capital that I have employed is not a highly sophisticated concept. A given change is regarded as an improvement of welfare if the Hicks-Kaldor condition is satisfied; that is, the new position is preferable to the old if those who suffered a loss in going from the old position to the new can be compensated by those who benefited and if a surplus remains after making such compensation. See Nicholas Kaldor, "Welfare Propositions of Economics and Interpersonal Comparisons of Utility," *Economic Journal*, 49 (September 1939), 549–552; and J. R. Hicks, "Foundations of Welfare Economics," *Economic Journal*, 49 (December 1939), 696–712. I doubt whether the broader types of welfare comparisons, such as those proposed by Scitovszky and Samuelson, would lead to definite conclusions in the present instance. See Tibor Scitovszky, "A Note on Welfare Propositions in Economics," *Review of Economic Studies*, 9 (November 1941), 77–88; and Paul A. Samuelson, *Foundations of Economic Analysis* (Cambridge, Mass., Harvard University Press, 1947), chap. 8.

state tends to exceed or fall short of the social optimum according as the rate of interest exceeds or falls short of the marginal product of capital. Stated in this way, the proposition bears a striking resemblance to the theory of external economies and diseconomies within an individual industry. It has been argued by Pigou and others, for example, that in an industry where the firms are subject to external diseconomies, the marginal social cost of the industry's output exceeds the marginal private cost, and output therefore exceeds the socially desirable level; and, conversely, when there are external economies output tends to be too small.[18]

The similarity between these well-known principles of welfare economics and the proposition I have presented concerning capital suggests that something akin to external economies and diseconomies may be present in the process of capital accumulation. And this is indeed true. To illustrate the point, suppose that the marginal product of capital is less than the rate of interest. In this case the marginal social product of capital is less than the marginal private product; this suggests, by analogy, that capital accumulation is subject to external diseconomies. What is the nature of these diseconomies?

If the marginal product of capital is less than the rate of interest, this can only mean, as I have argued above, that new savings bring about capital gains for assets already in existence. A capital gain arises because the cost in terms of foregone consumption of a given capital good has been increased, and this increase in cost represents a social cost analogous to an increase in the cost of producing a given commodity. Moreover, it is a cost which is not taken into account by the individual saver, and it may therefore be regarded as an external diseconomy of capital accumulation. Thus when the social product of capital is less than its private product, we may say that in a sense the production of capital is subject to external diseconomies. And, like ordinary diseconomies, the external diseconomies in the production of capital cause its quantity to exceed the socially desirable amount.

It is perhaps unnecessary to consider in detail the converse case in which the marginal product of capital exceeds the rate of interest. Suffice it to say that in this event an increase in capital leads to capital losses; and the capital losses represent a social economy in the sense that the

18. A. C. Pigou, *The Economics of Welfare*, ed. 4 (London, Macmillan, 1932), chaps. 9 and 11.

cost of capital goods, in terms of foregone current consumption, is reduced. Since the capital losses do not enter into the calculations of the individual saver, they constitute external economies in the production of capital. Like other external economies, they lead to a deficiency of "output," which in this instance means that the quantity of capital falls short of the optimal quantity.

Whether the amount of capital exceeds or falls short of an optimum is obviously a question which can be discussed rigorously only with reference to a stationary economy. In a growing economy the quantity of capital is continually increasing, and this means that the existing amount of assets is always less than the amount which savers wish, eventually, to hold. Of course, if the rate of growth of asset holdings were carefully planned by all savers, one might conceive of a sort of moving equilibrium representing the increasing amount of capital the savers wished to hold at different periods of time. In this event, the welfare propositions concerning the optimal *quantity* of capital could be translated into similar propositions concerning the optimal *rate of growth* of capital. If the marginal product of capital exceeds the rate of interest in such a growing economy, for example, it might be argued that the rate of growth is less than the socially desirable rate. Conversely, if the marginal product of capital is less than the rate of interest, the above reasoning would lead to the conclusion that capital is being accumulated too rapidly.

Although both these propositions concerning a growing economy appear to be logically sound, neither of them can be accepted without serious reservations. Perhaps most important of all, one cannot assume that the rate of accumulation of assets is always a result of careful planning on the part of savers. To some extent capital accumulation is a function of fortuitous circumstances such as capital gains and losses; and if savers simply hold whatever capital values happen to arise as the result of these gains and losses, there is no reason to suppose that the savers always equalize their private rate of substitution with the rate of interest. Such an equalization can be taken for granted only in a stationary state.

A second reservation must be made for the presence of uncertainty. If an uncertainty premium is added to the rate of interest, the combined uncertainty-and-interest charge may be so large that any possible discrepancy between the rate of interest and the marginal product of capital is relatively insignificant by comparison. When both uncertainty and the unpredictable response of savers to capital gains and losses are taken into account, it becomes apparent that a discrepancy between the rate of interest and the marginal product of capital in a growing economy does not imply anything very definite concerning the optimal rate of growth.

The Rate of Interest and the Marginal Product of Capital: A Correction

Mr. William Hamburger and M. Edmond Malinvaud have called my attention to an error in the preceding paper, which dealt with the reasons for a possible discrepancy between the rate of interest and the marginal product of social capital. Such a discrepancy arises, as I pointed out, because an increase or decrease in the supply of capital alters the units in which previously existing capital is measured. In other words, an increase in capital—attributable, let us say, to new voluntary saving—usually leads to capital gains or capital losses. The increase in social capital, which necessarily makes allowance for the capital gains or losses, thus differs from the primary saving; and this means that the rate of interest differs from the marginal social product of capital. The former is equal to the ratio of the increase in social product to the primary saving, whereas the latter is equal to the ratio of the increase in social product to the increase in social capital.

Suppose, for example, that primary or autonomous saving takes place to the extent of $1,000 and that the new saving is invested in machines having a net yield of $70 per year. The rate of interest is then 7 percent, and this rate, in turn, is equal to what I have called the "marginal private product of capital." The increase in machinery, however, will usually result in capital gains or losses for machines and other capital goods already in existence, and the change in social capital must take these gains or losses into account along with the primary saving. If capital gains occur to the extent of $400, for instance, and if these capital gains are not consumed, then the increase in social capital is $1,400, compared with the primary or autonomous saving of $1,000. The marginal social product of capital—or perhaps it should be called the "marginal product of social capital"—is the increase in social product, or $70, divided by the increase in social capital, or $1,500. In the present numerical example the marginal product of social capital is thus 5 percent, compared with a rate of interest of 7 percent.

The last section of my article was devoted to a discussion of the welfare implications of such a discrepancy between the rate of interest and the marginal product of social capital, and this section contained a fundamental error. I suggested that the discrepancy between the rate of interest and the marginal product of social capital is analogous to the familiar example from price theory in which the return to a factor of production differs from that factor's marginal social product. Thus if the rate of interest or the marginal private product of capital differs from the marginal social product, I argued that the quantity of capital tends to differ from the optimal quantity, just as the quantity of labor differs from the optimal quantity when wages differ from the marginal social product of labor.

My argument in this regard was based upon the erroneous belief that the marginal product of social capital, as I have defined it, measures the rate at which the economy as a whole can substitute future income in perpetuity for present consumption. Since the rate of interest measures the rate at which each individual saver can substitute future income for present consumption, a discrepancy between the rate of interest and the marginal social product of capital implies, according to my paper, that the social rate of substitution between present consumption and future income differs from the private rate of substitution. "Thus," I said, "if the rate of interest differs from the marginal product of capital, the private rate of substitution between future and present consumption will necessarily differ from the social rate of substitution, and the quantity of capital will accordingly differ from the optimum."[19]

As a result of conversations with Mr. Hamburger and M. Malinvaud, I now realize that all of this is a mistake. The basic error of my argument is the assertion that the marginal product of social capital measures the rate at which the economic system can substitute future for present consumption. This social rate of substitution between present and future is not measured, as I had supposed, by the marginal product of social capital but by the rate of interest itself. Consider, for example, the preceding numerical illustration. When new primary saving takes place to the extent of $1,000, the amount of current consumption foregone is exactly equal to this amount, even though the supply of capital, including the capital gains, is increased by $1,400. In other words, the capital gains or losses have nothing to do with the extent to which cur-

19. See above, p. 383.

rent consumption is reduced through new saving. The economy as a whole has given up $1,000 of potential current consumption in exchange for $70 of additional income per year in perpetuity. The social rate of substitution between present and future is thus equal to the rate of interest and not to the marginal product of social capital. This means that a discrepancy between the rate of interest and the marginal product of social capital does not imply a corresponding discrepancy between the social and the private rates of substitution. The total quantity of capital may therefore be an optimal quantity, at any given time, even though the rate of interest differs substantially from the marginal product of social capital.

The foregoing correction of my earlier views presupposes that capital is desirable only because of the income it yields. If capital is wanted for its own sake, apart from the income it yields, then I suspect that a discrepancy between the rate of interest and the marginal product of social capital may have some significance from the point of view of welfare economics. But this is a question which I did not discuss in my original paper, and it cannot be treated adequately in this brief note.

Part III

Business Cycles and Economic Fluctuations

15 | The Nature and Stability of Inventory Cycles

Business cycle explanations may conveniently be classified, for the purpose of comparison, according to their implicit stability assumptions. On this basis there are two principal groups, one in which the economy is assumed to be in unstable equilibrium and one in which market relations are assumed to be stable. Proponents of the first group envisage cyclical movements as the consequence of (a) an initial disturbance that sets in motion a cumulative process, and (b) certain limiting stabilizers which reverse the direction of the cumulative movement but which are not operative except in extreme positions, such as full employment and the like. Wicksell's analysis of prices and interest rates provides a good example of this type of theory. In the second group, on the other hand, movements of output and employment represent a process of adaptation to cyclical changes in the parameters of a system that would otherwise be stable. The idea of a determinate relation between changes in the level of noninduced investment and changes in total income, for example, belongs to this group.

Corresponding to either type of cycle theory are two sets of relations, a series of sequences defining time-paths for the variables of the system, and a set of simultaneous equations expressing equilibrium or stationary values of the variables.[1] From this point of view, the distinction between the unstable- and the stable-economy theories is largely one of emphasis.

Reprinted from *Review of Economic Statistics*, 23 (August 1941), 113–129. Copyright President and Fellows of Harvard College, 1941.

1. Cf. Paul A. Samuelson, "The Stability of Equilibrium: Comparative Statics and Dynamics," *Econometrica*, 9 (April 1941), 97–120.

No tendency exists, according to the former, for the economy to approach an equilibrium; consequently, the dynamic system receives most attention. And since an unstable economy obviously does not move steadily upward or downward, the analysis of "turning points" is highly important.[2] The stable-economy theories, on the other hand, emphasize the character of the static system; for this system is regarded as a norm toward which the economy is moving, and which would ultimately be attained except for disturbances in the parameters of the system. Dynamic sequences are relevant for this type of theory only insofar as they indicate the manner in which the economy moves from one equilibrium to another. Indeed, if the period of adjustment is relatively short, the dynamic system may be neglected entirely and time-movements attributed simply to changes in the parameters of the static system.

These relations of comparative statics to economic dynamics are presented in an interesting and important form in recent discussions of the determinants of total output. Use of the multiplier in analyzing income and investment obviously constitutes static analysis of a system that is assumed to be *stable* in equilibrium. That is, an equilibrium level of income is assumed to correspond to any given level of noninduced investment, and the system is assumed to move toward this equilibrium. Yet the implications of such a stability assumption have never been fully explored. From early formulations of the investment-income relation it is not apparent exactly *how* the system moves from one equilibrium to another and *why* it tends to approach equilibrium at all.[3] In Keynes's *General Theory*, for example, one searches in vain for a description of the time sequence of events by which an increase of net investment produces a rise of income. Thus, although static relations are worked out in some detail, the dynamic equivalent of the income equation is not fully specified.

Needless to say, an infinite number of dynamic sequences having the Keynes income-investment equation as an equilibrium limit could be formulated. In the group of possible models, however, two types of time

2. See Gottfried Haberler, *Prosperity and Depression*, ed. 3 (Geneva, League of Nations, 1941), *passim*, esp. chap. 11.

3. See R. F. Kahn, "The Relation of Home Investment to Unemployment," *Economic Journal*, 41 (June 1931), 173–198; Colin Clark, *National Income and Outlay* (London, Macmillan, 1936), chap. 12; and J. M. Keynes, *The General Theory of Employment, Interest, and Money* (New York, Harcourt, Brace, 1936), *passim*. The geometric series which Kahn uses in developing his employment multiplier suggests a dynamic sequence, but the exact character of the lag is never fully explained.

relation seem most important. The first of these is the lag in the expenditure of income behind its receipt. This receipts-expenditure period, associated as it is with the income velocity of circulation of money, has much to do with the rate at which a system moves from one equilibrium of income to another.[4] The second important lag is the period required for a change in revenue from sales to produce a change in total output. This period determines the time rate at which an alteration in money demand is converted into a change in income paid out.

Shortly after publication of the *General Theory*, both types of lag were utilized in the formulation of dynamic systems of which the Keynes scheme was a static limit. D. H. Robertson developed a sequence in which the first type was utilized,[5] while Erik Lundberg examined the consequences of a system containing the second.[6] Briefly, the Robertson sequence was built upon the following assumptions:[7] (*a*) The expenditure of income occurs one period after its receipt. (*b*) Businessmen respond to an increase in money demand with an immediate increase of output, so that income produced in a particular period can be measured by the sum of consumption plus net investment. Robertson assumed, in other words, a length of unity for the receipts-expenditure period and a zero lag in the response of output to a change in consumer demand.

Lundberg, on the other hand, built his models upon the following assumptions: (*a*) Consumers' demand responds immediately to a change of income (that is, the receipts-expenditure period was assumed to be zero). (*b*) The output of consumers' goods lags one period behind a change in revenue from sales. In other words, businessmen were assumed to base their production in period *t* upon sales in period *t* − 1. Thus a discrepancy between *total output* and *total sales* might arise. This discrepancy was assumed to be balanced by a change of inventories.

The foregoing summaries of the Robertson and Lundberg dynamic sequences should indicate clearly that the latter is in most respects the

4. I do not wish to imply that the lag of expenditure behind receipt of income is identical with the inverse of income velocity, but only that, other things being equal, a reduction of the receipt-expenditure lag increases income velocity. See Alvin H. Hansen, *Fiscal Policy and Business Cycles* (New York, W. W. Norton, 1941), pp. 268–270.

5. D. H. Robertson, "Some Notes on Mr. Keynes' General Theory of Employment," *Quarterly Journal of Economics*, 51 (November 1936), 168–191.

6. Erik Lundberg, *Studies in the Theory of Economic Expansion* (London, P. S. King, 1937), chap. 9.

7. In addition to the enumerated assumptions, both the Robertson and Lundberg sequences—as well as those developed in this paper—assume the existence of unemployed resources, so that output may be expanded without a rise of prices.

converse of the former. The Robertson model assumes a period of unity for the first type of lag (expenditure behind receipt of income) and a period of zero for the second (output behind revenue from sales), while Lundberg assumes a zero period for the first and a unit period for the second. For relatively simple sequences, both systems lead to substantially the same results—that is, a given increase of investment causes total income to approach steadily a new level determined by the multiplier and the amount of added investment. Both systems, in this case, are stable when the marginal propensity to consume is less than unity, and otherwise unstable. But when more complex sequences are considered, and particularly when allowance is made for the possibility of induced investment, the behavior of the two systems may differ even with the same values of the marginal propensity to consume and the accelerator. Hence it is important to know (*a*) which scheme more accurately describes the existing state of affairs, and (*b*) in what respects the two lead to different results.

No doubt some lag exists, in the real world, both in expenditure of income behind its receipt and in the output decisions of businessmen behind changes of monetary demand. Indeed, the mere fact of inventory fluctuations is adequate demonstration of the latter lag, while the periodic character of income payments lends support to the argument for the former. Logically, of course, there is no reason why a system including both types could not be devised. As a practical matter, the solutions of such hybrid systems are quite complex, and useful results from them are difficult to derive. Moreover, if the length of one of the lag periods is quite short compared with the other, either the Robertson or the Lundberg sequence will give a close approximation to the true situation, the selection depending upon which lag is the shorter. If, for example, businessmen make production plans on a yearly basis, while the average interval between receipt and expenditure of income is only one-half month, the assumptions of a zero length for the receipts-expenditure lag and a unit period for the sales-output lag will not be seriously unreal. Error will arise only on account of the half-month period at the end of the production year. In other words, except for this half-month interval, the assumption that income paid out within a given production period is spent (or saved) in the same production period is correct. In this case the Lundberg sequence is appropriate. Conversely, if businessmen revise their plans from day to day, so that the sales-output lag is short compared with the receipts-expenditure period, the Robertson sequence best fits the facts.

Which of the two lags is likely, in fact, to be the shorter? If we measure the receipts-expenditure period by one-half the average interval between income payments, this period is quite short. For wages are paid on a weekly or biweekly basis, salaries are paid monthly, and dividends and interest, which are paid out over longer intervals, represent a smaller proportion of the national income. From this point of view, the Lundberg sequence would seem more realistic. It must be remembered, however, that the length of the receipts-expenditure period is conditioned not only by the average interval between income payments, but also by the nature of consumer habits. In most cases, a rise of income will not lead to an immediate increase of consumption even with a very short payment interval, for some time is essential to adapt oneself to a higher standard of living. Likewise, a fall of income will usually take time to bring about a reduction of consumer demand.[8] Such consumer inertia makes an appraisal of the average lag between income receipt and expenditure extremely difficult. And even if this average could be determined empirically, the length of the second lag (sales-output) would still remain to be determined.

Because of uncertainty regarding the comparative lengths of the two periods, a contrast of the behavior of an economy subject to the Robertson lag with that of an economy where the Lundberg lag is assumed to be most important seems desirable. Since the Robertson model has been elaborated by Professors Hansen[9] and Samuelson,[10] through the introduction of induced investment, I shall confine myself to variants of the Lundberg sequence.

Consider, first, a dynamic model based upon the following assumptions:

(1) Entrepreneurs have adequate inventories so that any discrepancy between output and consumer demand may be met by inventory fluctuations rather than price changes.

(2) Output in a given period is based upon sales of the preceding period.

(3) Consumers' goods are produced entirely in anticipation of sales with no attempt to replenish inventory losses or to get rid of accumulated stocks.

8. Colin Clark finds a lag of about two years for changes in consumption of the British well-to-do behind changes in their incomes (*National Income and Outlay*, reference 3, p. 254).
9. Hansen, *Fiscal Policy and Business Cycles* (reference 4), chap. 12.
10. Paul A. Samuelson, "Interactions Between the Multiplier Analysis and the Principle of Acceleration," *Review of Economic Statistics*, 21 (May 1939), 75–78.

(4) Income is equal to the production of consumers' goods plus net investment.

(5) Consumption within the sales-output period depends upon income of the same period.

(6) All income produced is paid out, that is, there are no business savings.

These assumptions will be recognized as those of the Lundberg first sequence, except that I have excluded business savings. I make this change because it simplifies the numerical examples while retaining all of the essential features of the Lundberg models. In any case, if business savings represent permanent additions to (private) capital which never enter into the stream of income paid out, they may be considered in our models simply by changing the marginal propensity to consume. This amounts to assuming that corporations pay out income to themselves and that the community marginal propensity is computed by including such corporations as "persons" whose marginal propensity to consume is zero. For example, a community in which 75 percent of all income produced is paid out, and in which consumers spend all of the income they receive, will have a marginal propensity to consume of 75 percent, relative to income produced. Likewise, a community whose corporations pay out 80 percent of income produced, and whose citizens spend 90 percent of income received, will have a marginal propensity to consume of $(0.90)(0.80) = 0.72$, again relative to income produced. Thus, so long as business savings are *permanent*, their effect may be summarized in the marginal propensity to consume, and explicit recognition of them in our model sequence is unnecessary.[11]

If v_o represents the amount of noninduced net investment, while $y(t)$ and $u(t)$ represent total income produced and consumers' goods produced respectively (in period t), we know that[12]

$$y(t) = u(t) + v_o.$$

11. If undistributed profits are not permanently invested, but simply retained for a period longer than our "unit period," the dynamic sequence becomes quite complex. In this case, simply to change the marginal propensity to consume does not suffice, since business savings of a given period are likely to be balanced by subsequent disbursements in excess of earnings.

12. To compare net investment with consumption, we must specify a unit of measurement common to both. We may assume either that all magnitudes are in wage units or, alternatively, that they are in currency units which, because of unemployed resources and constant costs, do not change in value.

This relationship simply expresses the fact that income produced is equal to the output of consumers' goods plus net investment. But output of consumers' goods in a given period t is equal to sales of the preceding period, by assumption (2). Hence if β is the marginal propensity to consume, relative to income produced, $u(t) = \beta y(t-1)$ and

(1) $$y(t) = \beta y(t-1) + v_o.$$

Equation (1) shows how income of a given period is related to income of the preceding period and to the amount of net investment. It depicts a sequence identical with the Robertson model. Thus for simple dynamic systems, the behavior of a model is not changed by substituting a sales-output lag for a receipts-expenditure lag.

A numerical example of the way the system approaches equilibrium is given in Table 1. I assume there that the marginal propensity to

Table 1. Behavior of a system with passive inventory adjustments ($\beta = 0.6$)

(1) Production of consumers' goods for sale	(2) Net noninduced investment	(3) Income produced (1) + (2)	(4) Sales	(5) Inventories at close of period
600	400	1000	600	500
600	500	1100	660	440
660	500	1160	696	404
696	500	1196	718	382
718	500	1218	731	369
731	500	1231	739	361
739	500	1239	743	357
743	500	1243	746	354
746	500	1246	748	352
748	500	1248	749	351
..	..	..	..	..
..	..	..	..	..
..	..	..	..	..
750	500	1250	350	350

consume is 0.6, that net investment (v_o) is 400, and that the economy is initially in equilibrium with a total income of 1000, of which 600 represents consumers' goods. I assume also that inventories of consumers goods amount to 500. Equilibrium is disturbed, in the second period, by an increase of net investment to 500. Production of consumers' goods being 600, total income in period 2 is 1100. Hence consumption is 660, of which 600 represents current production and 60 a reduction of inventories. In the third period, entrepreneurs produce 660 units (last period's sales), and, assuming investment to be maintained at 500 per period, income of this period is 1160, so that sales amount to 696. Again, sales represent partly current production (660) and partly a reduction of inventories (36).

The sequence continues in this manner, with the increase of output and income of each period being smaller than that of the preceding period. Ultimately a new equilibrium of 1250 units of income is approached, and, as long as net investment remains at 500, this level of income will be maintained.

Changes of income and inventories are depicted in Fig. 1. For the moment, we need only note that (*a*) income approaches its new

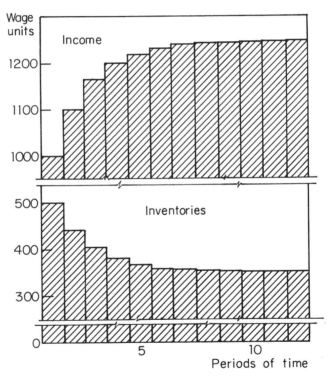

Figure 1. Behavior of a system with passive inventory adjustments: the basic Lundberg sequence

equilibrium steadily; (*b*) inventories decline by the exact amount of the increase in sales per period; and (*c*) the income equilibrium is not affected by the inventory reduction, since this represents only a temporary source of disinvestment. None of the conclusions based upon Table 1 is novel. All of them may be found in Lundberg's first sequence, and some of them in the Robertson analysis. I have, nevertheless, included the table and figure in order to facilitate comparison with more complex sequences to follow.

The passive nature of inventory changes in Table 1 makes the sequence rather unrealistic. Businessmen will ordinarily attempt to replenish inventories depleted by an unforeseen rise in demand, or to reduce inventory accumulations resulting from unpredicted depressions. We ought, therefore, to consider a dynamic model in which allowance is made for such adjustments. We may retain all of the assumptions of the first sequence except the third. Rather than assuming inventories to be completely passive, we shall now assume that an attempt is made to maintain them at a constant, "normal" level s_o. Otherwise, we shall assume as before that production for sale in a given period (as distinguished from production for stocks) is based upon sales of the preceding period. Thus we have the following value for income produced in period t:

$$y(t) = u(t) + s(t) + v_o,$$

where $u(t)$ represents production for sale, $s(t)$ production for inventory purposes, and v_o net noninduced investment.

We wish to know how production for sale, $u(t)$, and production for inventory, $s(t)$ are related to income and sales of preceding periods. As before, production for sale is assumed equal to sales of the preceding period so that $u(t) = \beta y(t-1)$.

The second item, $s(t)$, may be either positive or negative. If stocks exceed the normal level, s_o, which business wishes to maintain, businessmen will produce fewer consumers' goods than they expect to sell in the hope that by so doing they can reduce inventories. In this case $s(t)$ is negative. On the other hand, if stocks are lower than the normal level, an attempt will be made to replenish inventories so that $s(t)$ will be positive. Whether positive or negative, production for inventory in period t will equal the difference between the normal level and the actual level of stocks at the *close* of period $t-1$. But in period $t-1$, entrepreneurs *intended* to produce enough so that stocks at the close of that period would equal the normal level, s_o; in other words, they produced an amount sufficient to cover expected sales plus whatever was needed (positive or negative) to make stocks equal s_o. If actual sales exceeded those anticipated, entrepreneurs were forced to sell goods they had intended for inventories. Conversely, if actual sales fell short of expected sales, entrepreneurs were forced to hold goods they had intended for sale. In either case, the difference between the normal level and the actual level at the close of period $t - 1$ is simply the difference between actual and anticipated sales of that period.

It follows immediately that production for inventory in period t is equal to the difference between actual and anticipated sales of period $t - 1$. In common-sense terms, we say that production for stocks in a given period is equal to the unintended inventory loss of the preceding period. But anticipated sales of $t - 1$ were $\beta y(t - 2)$, while actual sales were $\beta y(t - 1)$. Hence

$$s(t) = \beta y(t - 1) - \beta y(t - 2).$$

Combining the expressions for $u(t)$ and $s(t)$, we find

(2) $$y(t) = 2\beta y(t - 1) - \beta y(t - 2) + v_o.$$

The behavior of this system may be illustrated by another numerical example. In Table 2, I assume as before that the marginal propensity to consume is 0.6, and that we start from a position of equilibrium in which net noninduced investment is equal to 400, income is 1000, total sales 600, production for sale 600, and production for inventory zero. These figures are in the first line of the table. In the second period, I assume that equilibrium is disturbed by an increase of noninduced investment to 500, an increase which is subsequently maintained. Total income thus rises to 1100, and sales to 660, causing an inventory reduction of 60, since anticipated sales (and hence output) in period 2 were only 600. Suppose now that entrepreneurs attempt to maintain their inventories at a level of 500. Then in period 3 they will produce 660 units for sale plus 60 units for inventory. Adding to this the 500 units of noninduced investment, we get a total income produced in period 3 of 1220, with sales of 732. Thus actual sales have once again exceeded anticipated sales, so that inventories remain below the normal level of 500.

This is characteristic of the early prosperity phase of a pure inventory

Table 2. Result of attempting to maintain inventories: the pure inventory cycle ($\beta = 0.6$)

(1) Production of consumers' goods for sale	(2) Production of consumers' goods for stocks	(3) Net noninduced investment	(4) Income produced (1) + (2) + (3)	(5) Sales	(6) Inventories at close of period
600	0	400	1000	600	500
600	0	500	1100	660	440
660	60	500	1220	732	428
732	72	500	1304	782	450
782	50	500	1332	799	483
799	17	500	1316	790	509
790	− 9	500	1281	769	521
769	− 21	500	1248	749	520
749	− 20	500	1229	737	512
737	− 12	500	1225	735	502
735	− 2	500	1233	740	495
740	5	500	1245	747	493
747	7	500	1254	752	495
752	5	500	1257	754	498
754	2	500	1256	754	500
754	0	500	1254	752	502
752	− 2	500	1250	750	502

cycle. For a time, added income generated by production for inventory plus the secondary effects of increased investment will cause sales to exceed those anticipated by more than production-for-inventory purposes. Hence inventories actually decline despite attempts to increase them. Sales, however, cannot continue to rise as rapidly as income because of the dampening influence of savings. As a result, the excess of actual sales over anticipated sales declines, and inventories begin slowly to accumulate. This causes income to rise at a still slower rate, since less is produced each period for inventory purposes. In turn, the decline of the *rate of growth* of income and sales accelerates the increase of stocks. Ultimately (period 6 of the table) actual sales fall short of those expected, and inventories rise above the normal level. Thereafter, attempts of entrepreneurs to reduce stocks lead to a cumulative decline of income because (*a*) less is produced than is expected to be sold, and (*b*) the initial decline reduces expectations and hence production for sale in subsequent periods. Moreover, once income begins to decline actual sales fall short of those anticipated so that attempts to reduce stocks are abortive.

Once again, however, the stabilizing influence of savings prevents a continuous movement in one direction. With a marginal propensity to consume less than unity, the decline of sales is less than the decline of total income, which means that the depression cannot continue to "feed upon itself." In other words, actual sales cannot continue to fall short of expected sales by as much as the inventory surplus. Eventually, therefore, attempts at inventory reduction will succeed, so that inventories are brought down slowly to the normal level. At this point income begins to rise by reason of the fact that entrepreneurs are no longer attempting to produce less than they sell. Thus the cycle repeats itself, but each time with a smaller amplitude.

This is the simplest form of inventory cycle. I have discussed it in some detail because it contains many features common to more complex sequences. The nature of the cycle is more clearly seen in Fig. 2. The following points may be noted:

(1) The cycles are damped, so that income eventually approaches a new equilibrium of 1250, determined by the multiplier and the increase of noninduced investment.

(2) Induced investment for purposes of inventory accumulation does not affect the income equilibrium.

(3) Inventories lag behind the movement of income. So long as inventories remain below the normal level, income rises; whenever they are above normal, income falls. Income reaches a maximum at the point where inventories have finally accumulated to the normal level, and a minimum at the point where they have *fallen* to this norm.

The cycle pictured in Fig. 2 is a pure inventory cycle in the sense that it is produced entirely by investment (or disinvestment) for inventory purposes. It may be shown that *any disturbance in a dynamic system such as that of Eq. (2) above will produce cyclical oscillations about a new level of income, provided the marginal propensity to consume is less than unity.* Thus the results of Table 2 do not depend upon any special values of our coefficients. If the marginal propensity to consume were greater than unity, the system would not oscillate when disturbed by an increase of noninduced investment, but would diverge steadily.

The dynamic models of Tables 1 and 2 introduce a somewhat

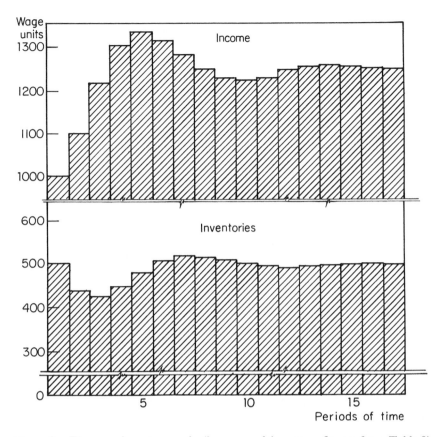

Figure 2. The pure inventory cycle (income and inventory figures from Table 2)

artificial assumption about business expectations. In both cases entre-preneurs are assumed to base their expectations of sales in a given period upon sales of the preceding period. It is natural to object that expectations of future sales may depend not only upon the past *level* of sales, but also upon the *direction of change* of such sales. Thus a level of sales of 500 in period $t - 1$ which was reached from a level of 400 in $t - 2$ might give rise to expectations in period t entirely different from what they would have been had the sales of 500 been approached from a level of 600 in $t - 2$. In the former case, sales would normally be expected to exceed 500 in period t, whereas in the latter they would probably be expected to fall short of 500.

To discuss the role of expectations, I shall make use of a coefficient of expectations, η, defined as the ratio between the expected change of sales between periods t and $t-1$ and the observed change of sales between periods $t-1$ and $t-2$. To see what this means, let us consider some examples. Suppose observed sales in periods $t-1$ and $t-2$ were 500 and 400 respectively. Then the expected change of sales between $t-1$ and t would be the product of the coefficient of expectations and the observed change of sales between $t-2$ and $t-1$ (100 units). If the coefficient were one-half, for example, sales would be expected to increase by 50 between $t-1$ and t; in other words, expected sales would be 550. Likewise, if the coefficient were zero, no change at all would be expected, so that anticipated sales in t would equal actual sales in $t-1$. Other results for this same example may be tabulated as follows:

Coefficient of expectations	Anticipated sales
-1	400
-0.5	450
0	500
0.5	550
1	600

Remembering that actual sales in $t-1$ and $t-2$ were 500 and 400 respectively, we may make the following observations: (*a*) if the coefficient of expectations is unity, a given rate of change is expected to continue undiminished; (*b*) if the coefficient of expectations is zero, a given level of sales is expected to continue; and (*c*) if the coefficient is -1, any change between $t-2$ and $t-1$ is expected to be only temporary, so that sales in period t are expected to return to the level of period $t-2$.

In the sequences to follow, the coefficient of expectations will be assumed to lie between the limits $-1 \leq \eta \leq 1$. Although the argument might easily be extended to other values, I believe that this range is sufficiently wide to include most actual cases.[13]

13. It is useful to compare this coefficient with J. R. Hicks's "elasticity of expectations" in his *Value and Capital* (London, Oxford University Press, 1939), p. 205. In my terminology, the Hicks elasticity concept is defined as the ratio of the expected relative change between $t-2$ and t to the *actual* relative change between $t-2$ and $t-1$. If a parameter has the values π_2 and π_1 in periods $t-2$ and $t-1$, and if these values lead to an expectation of π_0 in period t, the elasticity of expectations is $(\pi_0 - \pi_2)/\pi_2 \div (\pi_1 + \pi_2)/\pi_2$, whereas my coefficient of expectations is $(\pi_0 - \pi_1)/(\pi_1 - \pi_2)$. If e represents the elasticity of expectations while η, as above, represents the *coefficient* of expectations, it is easily shown that $\eta = e - 1$. Thus a range of variation for e between zero and unity (the range which Hicks considers) corresponds to a range for η between -1 and zero.

Again we may suppose, as in the first two sequences, that income is spent (or saved) in the period in which it is received. But rather than assuming production for sale to be determined by sales of the past period, we shall now suppose it is related by the coefficient of expectations to sales of the *two* preceding periods in the following manner:

$$u(t) = \beta y(t-1) + \eta[\beta y(t-1) - \beta y(t-2)]$$

or $\qquad u(t) = (1+\eta)\beta y(t-1) - \eta\beta y(t-2).$

If no attempt is made to adjust inventories, total income produced is equal to the output of consumers' goods for sale plus net noninduced investment. Hence

(3) $\qquad y(t) = (1+\eta)\beta y(t-1) - \eta\beta y(t-2) + v_o.$

Equation (3) is simply an extension of the Lundberg first sequence obtained by introducing a coefficient of expectations. In fact, the Lundberg sequence is the special case of Eq. (3) in which $\eta = 0$. It is therefore important to know how the behavior of this basic sequence changes with an alteration of the coefficient of expectations.

Three numerical examples illustrating Eq. (3) are presented in Table 3. In each example the marginal propensity to consume is 0.6. Hence any differences among the three cases presented may be attributed to the coefficient of expectations. The initial disturbance, as before, is a rise of 100 in the level of noninduced net investment.

An explanation of Table 3a will suffice, since all three parts of the table are constructed according to the same principles. We begin from a position of equilibrium, with sales per period of 600, non-induced investment of 400, and total income of 1000, and we suppose this equilibrium to be disturbed by an increase in net noninduced investment per period to 500. Income rises in the first period of added investment to 1100, and sales to 660, so that inventories decline to 440. Thus far the results are the same as in Table 1. The coefficient of expectations being positive, however, the rise of sales creates an expectation of a further rise. The coefficient assumed in Table 3a is 0.2. Thus expected sales in period 3 (and hence production of consumers' goods) are $660 + 0.2(660 - 600) = 672$. With production of consumers' goods of 672 and net noninduced investment of 500, total income produced in the third period is 1172, and sales are 703. These sales in turn create an expectation that revenue in the next period will be $703 + 0.2$ $(703 - 660) = 712$, and so on.

Table 3. Effect of expectations on the basic Lundberg sequence
Part a: $\beta = 0.6$; $\eta = 0.2$

(1) Production of consumers' goods for sale	(2) Net noninduced investment	(3) Income produced (1) + (2)	(4) Sales	(5) Inventories at close of period
600	400	1000	600	500
600	500	1100	660	440
672	500	1172	703	409
712	500	1212	727	394
732	500	1232	739	387
741	500	1241	745	383
746	500	1246	748	381
749	500	1249	749	381
749	500	1249	749	381
749	500	1249	749	381
..	..	..	..	..
..	..	..	..	..
..	..	..	..	..
750	500	1250	750	380

Part b: $\beta = 0.6$; $\eta = 0.5$

600	400	1000	600	500
600	500	1100	660	440
690	500	1190	714	416
741	500	1241	745	412
760	500	1260	756	416
762	500	1262	757	421
757	500	1257	754	424
752	500	1252	751	425
749	500	1249	749	425
748	500	1248	749	424
..	..	..	..	..
..	..	..	..	..
..	..	..	..	..
750	500	1250	750	425

The following features of the table may be noted. (*a*) Income approaches steadily a new equilibrium determined by the multiplier and the amount of net noninduced investment. (*b*) For the values of the coefficient of expectations and the marginal propensity to consume of Table 3a, dependence of output upon the rate of change of sales does not change the mode of approaching a new equilibrium, but

Part c: $\beta = 0.6$; $\eta = 1$

600	400	1000	600	500
600	500	1100	660	440
720	500	1220	732	428
804	500	1304	782	450
832	500	1332	799	483
816	500	1316	790	509
781	500	1281	769	521
748	500	1248	749	520
729	500	1229	737	512
725	500	1225	735	502
733	500	1233	740	495
745	500	1245	747	493
754	500	1254	752	495
757	500	1257	754	498
756	500	1256	754	500
754	500	1254	752	502
750	500	1250	750	502
..	..	..	..	..
..	..	..	..	..
..	..	..	..	..
750	500	1250	750	500

merely accelerates the speed with which the new level is approached. Thus with a positive coefficient of expectations, income moves more rapidly from the old equilibrium to the new than with a zero coefficient. (c) While sales advance by 150 in the new equilibrium, inventories decline only by 120 even though no attempt is made to maintain them.

The second and third parts of Table 3 differ from Table 3a only in the value of the coefficient of expectations. In 3b, η has a value of 0.5, while in 3c, the coefficient is unity. Comparison of 3b and 3c with 3a suggests the following points. (a) All three sequences are stable, for income approaches a new equilibrium in each case. (b) The income equilibrium is independent of the coefficient of expectations; it depends only upon the propensity to consume and the amount of noninduced investment. (c) For large values of the coefficient of expectations, income does not approach its new equilibrium steadily, but tends to oscillate about this new level in a series of damped cycles.

Explanation of these cycles may be found in the relation of η to the marginal propensity to consume. The initial rise of income leads to expectations of a further rise. And the combined influence of high expectations with the secondary effects of higher noninduced investment may create a level of income above the level justified by the amount of noninduced investment. When this happens, income must necessarily decline. For with a marginal propensity to consume less than unity, an expansion of production in anticipation of a rise in sales cannot *by itself* create an increase of sales as great as the increase in consumers' goods output. Hence expectations are disappointed, which leads to lower expectations in subsequent periods, with a slowing down in the rate of growth of incomes and further unrealized expectations. The process continues until income actually begins to decline.

Once the decline is started, a further decline is inevitable since businessmen restrict output in expectation of fewer sales. Again, however, savings act as a stabilizer and reverse the direction of change. With a marginal propensity to consume less than unity, the mere expectation of a decline cannot in itself lead to a reduction of sales as great as the reduction of output. Eventually, therefore, expectations become less pessimistic, owing to the fact that they have not been fully realized in the past. When this occurs, output—although still lower than sales of the previous period—may exceed *output* of the previous period so that income again begins to rise. And thus the cycle repeats itself, each time with a smaller amplitude, as indicated in Parts b and c of Table 3.

We have seen that a positive coefficient of expectations may lead to (*a*) a steady approach to equilibrium of the same type as in the Lundberg first sequence, only more rapid, or (*b*) cyclical oscillations about the new equilibrium. Whether the system behaves in the first manner

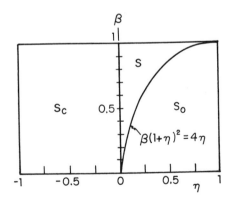

Figure 3. Influence of expectations upon a system with passive inventory adjustments

or the second depends upon the relation of the marginal propensity to consume to the coefficient of expectations. The nature of this relation is indicated in Fig. 3. A sequence of the type indicated by Eq. (3) will approach equilibrium steadily for any values of β and η in the region S, while it will oscillate about the new equilibrium if its β and η lie in the region S_o.[14] Thus a positive coefficient of expectations is more likely to lead to cyclical movements the smaller is the marginal propensity to consume. In other words, a smaller coefficient of expectations is required to "overstep the mark" if the system is damped by large savings than if most income is consumed.

With a negative coefficient of expectations, behavior of the system is quite different. The cycle is replaced by a cobweb movement. To show how this cobweb arises, suppose that an economy has a marginal propensity to consume of unity and a coefficient of expectations of -1. And suppose that, because of a change in noninduced investment, income and sales rise from 1000 to 1100 units. Since $\eta = -1$, we know that any change of sales is expected to be temporary, so that entrepreneurs anticipate sales of 1000 in the next period after the change. Consequently, they produce only 1000 units, and if the burst of noninduced investment is not maintained, actual income and sales are 1000. The drop in sales from 1100 to 1000, in turn, leads to sales expectations of 1100 for the next succeeding period; as a result, actual production and sales are 1100. In this manner an initial burst of investment produces an undamped cobweb with income and sales alternating between 1000 and 1100. The system is in *neutral* equilibrium. Had the marginal propensity to consume been less than unity, however, the cobwebs would have been damped, and equilibrium stable. More generally, any model whose β and η lie within the region S_c of Fig. 3 represents a stable system which approaches equilibrium through a combination of a damped cobweb and a steady change at an exponential rate.

Although expectations may temporarily be negative, the kind of alternate periods of optimism and pessimism depicted in a literal interpretation of a negative coefficient of expectations is probably seldom found in the actual world. Analysis of the case is included, nevertheless, to show that negative expectations do not change the condition of stability (that is, that $\beta < 1$).

14. The region S_0 is separated from S by the line $\beta(1 + \eta)^2 = 4\eta$. The inequality $\beta(1 + \eta)^2 < 4\eta$ is simply the condition that the roots of the "characteristic equation" $\rho^2 - (1 + \eta)\beta\rho + \eta\beta = 0$ shall be imaginary.

An interesting parallel is found between our third sequence and the Hansen-Samuelson extension of Robertson's dynamic model. Without attempting a detailed discussion of the Hansen-Samuelson case, we can enumerate its essential features as follows: (*a*) a lag of one period is assumed in the expenditure of income behind its receipt; (*b*) entrepreneurs are assumed to produce, in a given period, whatever amounts of consumers' goods are demanded in that period (the sales-output lag is zero); and (*c*) aside from noninduced investment, a part of the production of capital goods in a particular period is assumed to be a linear function of the rate of change of sales in the same period (the acceleration principle). With these assumptions, a dynamic model is constructed which is found to (*a*) converge steadily, (*b*) converge cyclically, (*c*) diverge cyclically, or (*d*) diverge steadily, according to the values of the marginal propensity to consume and the accelerator.

Comparison of Eq. (3) with the Samuelson equation reveals that the two are identical except that the coefficient of expectations (η) has replaced the accelerator (α in Samuelson's notation). Thus the coefficient of expectations apparently bears the same relation to the basic Lundberg sequence that the acceleration principle bears to the Robertson sequence. Indeed, the right half of my Fig. 3 is the same as Samuelson's figure (with η substituted for α) except that I have excluded values of η greater than unity.

So long as inventories are merely a passive factor of adjustment, our discussion of Eq. (3) demonstrates that a nonzero coefficient of expectations between -1 and $+1$, while changing the method of approach toward equilibrium, cannot alter either the level of equilibrium or the stability of the system. The situation is otherwise if entrepreneurs attempt to maintain their stocks of goods at a constant level. In this case, a positive coefficient places important restrictions upon the conditions of stability. The character of these restrictions may be determined by developing another model.

We may assume, as in the third sequence, that sales anticipations are related to sales of the two preceding periods through the coefficient of expectations η. Rather than supposing inventories to be entirely passive, however, we now assume that an attempt is made to maintain them at a constant level, s_o. Otherwise all assumptions of the basic Lundberg sequence are maintained.

We have seen above that income produced in the consumers' goods industries may be divided into two parts: an amount $u(t)$ produced in anticipation of sales, and an amount $s(t)$ produced for stocks. The first item, production for sale, is related to past sales through the coefficient of expectations, exactly as in our third sequence, so that

$$u(t) = (1 + \eta)\beta y(t - 1) - \eta\beta y(t - 2).$$

To complete the sequence, production for stocks, $s(t)$, must be related to income (or sales) of preceding periods. In developing our second sequence, we found that attempting to maintain inventories is equivalent to producing for stocks in each period an amount equal to unintended inventory reductions of the preceding period, and that unintended inventory reductions of a given period are simply the difference between actual and anticipated sales of that period. In other words, production for stocks in period t was found equal to the difference between actual and anticipated sales of period $t - 1$. So it is here. Only now, anticipated sales of period $t - 1$ are no longer equal to sales of $t - 2$, but are related to sales of the *two* preceding periods through the coefficient of expectations, as follows:

Expected sales in period $t - 1 = (1 + \eta)\beta y(t - 2) - \eta\beta y(t - 3)$.

Hence $s(t)$, the difference between actual and anticipated sales of period $t - 1$, is

$$s(t) = \beta y(t - 1) - (1 + \eta)\beta y(t - 2) + \eta\beta y(t - 3).$$

Remembering that income produced in period t is equal to total production of consumers' goods for all purposes plus net noninduced investment, we have

$$(4) \quad y(t) = (2 + \eta)\beta y(t - 1) - (1 + 2\eta)\beta y(t - 2) + \eta\beta y(t - 3) + v_o.$$

In Table 4 the behavior of Eq. (4) is illustrated by two numerical examples. The two examples differ only in the value of the coefficient of expectations; in Part a, η has a value of unity, while in Part b it is one-half. The marginal propensity to consume is 0.6 in both cases. Let us consider Part a. We begin, as always, from a position of equilibrium, with noninduced investment of 400, income of 1000, sales of 500, production for sale of 600, and production for inventory of zero. Equilibrium is disturbed in the second period by a rise of noninduced investment to 500. This increases sales to 660 and reduces inventories to 440. In the third period, production for sale is related to sales of the two

Table 4. Effect of expectations when entrepreneurs attempt to maintain inventories

Part a: Unstable case; $\beta = 0.6$; $\eta = 1$

(1) Production of consumers' goods for sale	(2) Production of consumers' goods for stocks	(3) Net noninduced investment	(4) Income produced (1) + (2) + (3)	(5) Sales	(6) Inventories at close of period
600	0	400	1000	600	500
600	0	500	1100	660	440
720	60	500	1280	768	452
876	48	500	1424	854	522
940	− 22	500	1418	851	589
848	− 89	500	1259	755	593
659	− 93	500	1066	640	519
525	− 19	500	1006	604	421
568	79	500	1147	688	380
772	120	500	1392	835	437
982	63	500	1545	927	555
1019	− 55	500	1464	878	641
829	−141	500	1188	713	616
548	−116	500	932	559	489
405	11	500	916	550	355
541	145	500	1186	712	329
874	171	500	1545	927	447

Part b: Stable case; $\beta = 0.6$; $\eta = 0.5$

600	0	400	1000	600	500
600	0	500	1100	660	440
690	60	500	1250	750	440
795	60	500	1355	813	482
845	18	500	1363	818	527
820	−27	500	1293	776	544
755	−44	500	1211	727	528
702	−28	500	1174	704	498
693	2	500	1195	717	476
724	24	500	1248	749	475
765	25	500	1290	774	491
786	9	500	1295	777	509
779	− 9	500	1270	762	517
754	−17	500	1237	742	512
732	−12	500	1220	732	500
727	0	500	1227	736	491
738	9	500	1247	748	490

preceding periods, just as in Table 3, by the coefficient of expectations. Since this coefficient is unity in Table 4a, sales of 600 and 660 in the first two periods create an expectation that sales of the third period will be 720. In addition to this amount produced for sale, 60 units are produced to make good the unintended inventory reduction of the previous period. Adding to these items the 500 units of noninduced investment, we obtain a total income produced of 1280 units for the third period. In this manner the entire sequence may be built up. Table 4b is constructed in exactly the same manner except that a coefficient of expectations of one-half is used in computing the column, "production of consumers' goods for sale."

Income and inventory figures from the two parts of the table are

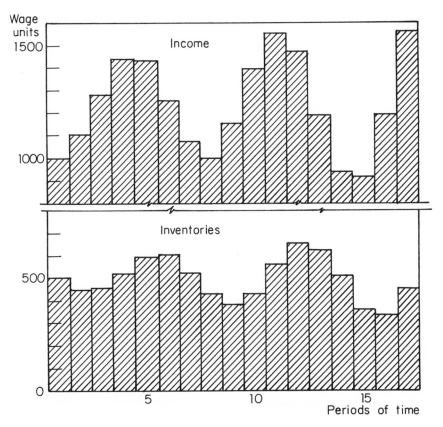

Figure 4. Income and inventory movements as described by data in Table 4a

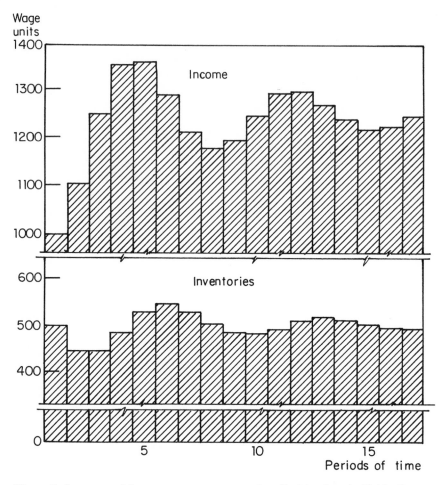

Figure 5. Income and inventory movements as described by data in Table 4b

plotted in Figs. 4 and 5. Both figures exhibit the characteristic inventory cycle, with changes in the level of stocks lagging one-fourth cycle behind changes of income. The figures differ, however, in an important respect. In Fig. 4 the amplitude of the cycles grows larger as the sequence develops, whereas in Fig. 5 the fluctuations are damped. In other words, the sequence in Table 4b represents a stable system, while 4a is essentially unstable. The destabilizer in 4a is obviously the coefficient of expectations, for the two parts of the table differ from each other only in the value of this coefficient. Thus, apparently, whenever entrepreneurs attempt to maintain inventories at a constant level, a high coefficient of expectations may create an unstable situation even with a marginal propensity to consume less than unity.

Exactly how large η must be to produce instability is indicated in Fig. 6. A system of the type in Eq. (4) is stable for any values of η and β contained in region S_o; disturbances of equilibrium in such cases produce damped inventory cycles.[15] A system with values of η and β in

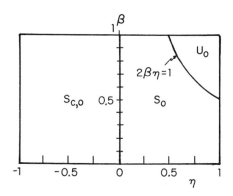

Figure 6. Stability diagram for sequence in Eq. (4)

region U_o, on the other hand, is unstable; disturbances of equilibrium here produce explosive cycles such as those of Fig. 4. Examination of our stability chart suggests the following points. (*a*) For values of the coefficient of expectations less than one-half, conditions of stability are no more restrictive than in our previous sequences; such models are stable for any marginal propensity to consume less than unity. (*b*) Severity of stability conditions increases very rapidly with an increase in the coefficient beyond one-half. In general, β, the marginal propensity to consume, must be less than $\frac{1}{2}\eta$. How severe this condition really is may be shown by a few numerical examples. If η is unity (that is, a given rate of change of sales is expected to continue), the system will not be stable unless the marginal propensity to consume is less than one-half. Likewise, with $\eta = \frac{3}{4}$, stability requires that β be less than two-thirds.

For negative expectations between 0 and -1, the system is stable,

15. The lines dividing the stable from the unstable regions are determined from the conditions that the roots of the characteristic equation $\rho^3 - (2 + \eta)\beta\rho^2 + (1 + 2\eta)\beta\rho - \eta\beta = 0$ shall lie within the unit circle of the complex plane.

in our sequence, for any marginal propensity to consume less than unity. This is the region $S_{c,o}$ of Fig. 6. Movement toward equilibrium in such cases is a combination of a damped cobweb and a cyclical movement, the former attributable to the negative coefficient of expectations and the latter representing a simple inventory cycle.

The inventory cycles analyzed above were a direct result of attempts by entrepreneurs to maintain stocks at a constant level, which in many cases probably represents a reasonable approximation to the actual situation, particularly if one considers only short-run adjustments. In other cases, however, the assumption that the desirable level of stocks is somehow related to the expected level of sales may be more accurate. In general, the amount of inventories which entrepreneurs regard as "normal" will vary directly with the expected volume of business. Thus the economy may be subject to the influence of an accelerator as well as a coefficient of expectations, for inventory production will then be related to the rate of change of sales. A complete examination of dynamic systems having a sales-output lag therefore requires analysis of the relations between the inventory accelerator and our coefficient of expectation.

We may begin with the inventory accelerator alone. Suppose that entrepreneurs attempt to maintain inventories at a constant proportion, α, of expected sales. Suppose further that sales in a given period (say t) are expected to equal sales of the preceding period (in other words, $\eta = 0$). Income produced, as before, is equal to production for sale, $u(t)$, plus production for stocks, $s(t)$, plus noninduced investment. Anticipated sales being equal to sales of the preceding period, we know that

$$u(t) = \beta y(t - 1).$$

Production for inventory purposes, on the other hand, is equal to the differences between the desired level of inventories, $\alpha\beta y(t - 1)$, and actual stocks on hand at the close of the previous period, $k(t - 1)$; that is,

$$s(t) = \alpha\beta y(t - 1) - k(t - 1).$$

But $k(t - 1)$ would have been equal to $\alpha\beta y(t - 2)$ except for unintended reductions or increases in stocks during the period $t - 1$. And, just as before, these unintended changes of inventories are the difference between actual sales, $\beta y(t-1)$, and expected sales, $\beta y(t-2)$. Hence

$$k(t-1) = \alpha\beta y(t-2) - \beta y(t-1) + \beta y(t-2),$$

so that

$$s(t) = (1+\alpha)\beta y(t-1) - (1+\alpha)\beta y(t-2).$$

Adding the amounts of production for sale, $u(t)$, and production for inventory, $s(t)$, to noninduced investment, v_o, we obtain the following expression for income of the period t:

(5) $$y(t) = (2+\alpha)\beta y(t-1) - (1+\alpha)\beta y(t-2) + v_o.$$

This equation, except for minor changes, is Lundberg's second sequence.

Two numerical examples of the model are given in Table 5. In Part a the assumption is made that $\beta = 0.5$ and $\alpha = 0.5$, while Part b is constructed upon the assumptions that $\beta = 0.6$ and $\alpha = 1$. The only feature of the tables requiring explanation is the second column, "production of consumers' goods for stocks." Amounts in this column are those needed to bring stocks up to the given proportion, α, of expected sales. In the third line of Part a, for example, expected sales are 550 and inventories of the previous period only 200. Since $\alpha = 0.5$, sales expectations of 550 should be accompanied by total inventories of 275. Consequently, production of stocks in the third period is 75.

Both parts of Table 5 reveal the usual inventory cycles. In Part a, however, the cycles are damped, while in Part b they are explosive. The inventory accelerator thus appears to act as a destabilizer in much the same manner as a positive coefficient of expectations. Stability of the economy cannot be discussed without knowing what combinations of α and β will produce damped cycles, as in Part a, and what combinations will lead to explosive cycles, as in Part b. Solution of this problem is depicted in Fig. 7. Any economy whose marginal propensity to consume and inventory accelerator lie in the region S_o is a stable economy that approaches equilibrium through a series of damped cycles. Both U_o and U, on the other hand, are regions of instability. No economy whose α and β lie in these regions has any tendency at all to approach equilibrium. Systems with α and β in U_o oscillate in explosive

Table 5. The inventory accelerator

Part a : Stable case ; $\alpha = 0.5$; $\beta = 0.5$

(1) Production of consumers' goods for sale	(2) Production of consumers' goods for stocks	(3) Net noninduced investment	(4) Income produced (1) + (2) + (3)	(5) Sales	(6) Inventories at close of period
500	0	500	1000	500	250
500	0	600	1100	550	200
550	75	600	1225	612	213
612	93	600	1305	652	266
652	60	600	1312	656	322
656	6	600	1262	631	353
631	− 38	600	1193	596	350
596	− 52	600	1144	572	322
572	− 36	600	1136	568	290
568	− 6	600	1162	581	271
581	19	600	1200	600	271
600	29	600	1229	614	286
614	21	600	1235	617	304
617	4	600	1221	610	315
610	− 10	600	1200	600	315
600	− 15	600	1185	592	308
592	− 12	600	1180	590	298

Part b : Unstable case ; $\alpha = 1$; $\beta = 0.6$

600	0	400	1000	600	600
600	0	500	1100	660	540
660	120	500	1280	768	552
768	216	500	1484	890	646
890	244	500	1634	980	800
980	180	500	1660	996	964
996	32	500	1528	917	1075
917	− 158	500	1259	755	1079
755	− 324	500	931	559	951
559	− 392	500	667	400	718
400	− 318	500	582	349	451
349	− 102	500	747	448	250
448	198	500	1146	688	208
688	480	500	1668	1001	375
1001	626	500	2127	1276	726
1276	550	500	2326	1396	1156
1396	240	500	2136	1282	1510

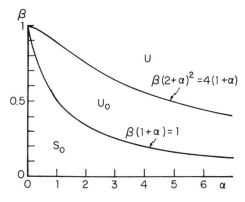

Figure 7. Stability diagram for sequence in Eq. (5)

cycles when disturbed, as in Part b of Table 5, while those with α and β in U diverge steadily.[16]

Introduction of the accelerator imposes severe limitations upon stability of the system, particularly if entrepreneurs attempt to maintain inventories at a large multiple of sales. If, for example, α is unity (that is, entrepreneurs attempt to maintain stocks equal to sales), the economy will not be stable unless the marginal propensity to consume is less than one-half. Likewise, if α is 2, stability requires a marginal propensity to consume less than one-third.[17]

16. Separation of the stable region from the unstable regions is determined from the condition that the roots of $\rho^2 - (2 + \alpha)\beta\rho + (1 + \alpha)\beta = 0$ shall lie within the unit circle of the complex plane. Separation of U_0 from U, on the other hand, is determined from the condition that the roots of the above equation shall be real.

17. Lundberg's failure to solve his difference equations has led him to draw an incorrect conclusion from one of his models. In his second sequence, which is the same as sequence (5) above, he assumes that 80 percent of all income produced is paid out, and that 90 percent of all income paid out is consumed. This amounts to assuming that our β, the marginal propensity to consume relative to income produced, is $(0.8)(0.9) = 0.72$. He also assumes that entrepreneurs attempt to maintain stocks at 50 percent of sales (that is, $\alpha = 0.5$).

From Fig. 7 it is evident that the point $\beta = 0.72$, $\alpha = 0.5$ lies in the region U_0. In other words, for these values of the marginal propensity to consume and the inventory accelerator, the economy is unstable; any disturbance produces a series of explosive cycles. And yet Lundberg concludes from his numerical example that the system approaches *asymptotically* a new equilibrium determined by the multiplier and the amount of noninduced investment. As a matter of fact, a sequence such as this never behaves in this manner, although it may approach a new equilibrium through a series of damped inventory cycles.

The Lundberg error provides a good illustration of the treacherous nature of numerical examples. It is unsafe to draw general conclusions from them, for one never knows to what extent the conclusions depend upon special characteristics of the examples chosen.

In Fig. 8, stability conditions for our fifth sequence are compared with those of its analogue, the Hansen-Samuelson model. The region S represents values of α and β which yield stable results for either model. Similarly, values of α and β in the region U produce instability in both sequences. Any pairs of the two parameters found in S', however, will yield stable results if applied to the Hansen-Samuelson model, but will represent an unstable system in the present case. If α is equal to unity, for example, the Hansen-Samuelson model will be stable for any β less than unity, whereas stability of sequence (5), as noted above, requires a β less than one-half. Thus an inventory accelerator places much more severe restrictions upon stability conditions of the basic

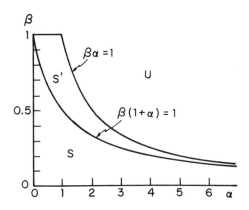

Figure 8. Stability of the Hansen-Samuelson model compared with that of sequence in Eq. (5)

Lundberg sequence than does the ordinary accelerator upon the Robertson sequence.

The explanation of this difference is simple. The acceleration principle is usually developed from the assumption that either technological or economic factors require a constant ratio between output of consumers' goods and certain types of capital goods. And then it is shown that, *ignoring changes in replacement demand*, the demand for capital goods is a linear function of the rate of change in demand for consumers' goods. This is the α of the Hansen-Samuelson model. If the capital goods in question are extremely durable, ignoring changes of replacement demand will not vitiate the results of a short-run analysis. In the present case, however, the capital goods subject to the acceleration principle are inventories, perhaps the least durable of all. Hence replacement demand should not be neglected.

The manner of considering such replacement is clearly seen in Eq. (5). In formulating this equation, production in period t of goods for stock was put equal to $(1 + \alpha)\beta y(t - 1) - (1 + \alpha)\beta y(t - 2)$. This expression may be divided into two parts. The first, $\alpha[\beta y(t - 1) - \beta y(t - 2)]$, is the simplified accelerator, which ignores replacement demand. The second, $\beta y(t - 1) - \beta y(t - 2)$, is the amount produced to replace unintended inventory reductions of the preceding period. Such unintended changes of stock occur, of course, because actual sales differ from those expected. Without this second item (production for replacement) the Lundberg second sequence would require exactly the same conditions for stability as the Hansen-Samuelson model. When unintended inventory changes are adjusted, however, the inventory accelerator becomes a destabilizer with the same force that is possessed by an ordinary accelerator, one unit larger. An inventory accelerator of unity, for example, imparts as much instability to a system as an ordinary accelerator of two.

The sequence summarized in Eq. (5) was developed from the assumption of a positive inventory accelerator and a zero coefficient of expectations. Development of the sequence of Eq. (4), on the other hand, required a positive coefficient of expectations and a zero inventory accelerator. A dynamic system more general than either (4) or (5) may be obtained by assuming both the coefficient of expectations and the inventory accelerator to be positive.

Let η and α, as above, represent these two parameters. Production of consumers' goods in a given period may now be divided into three parts: (a) production for anticipated sales; (b) production to replace unintended inventory losses; and (c) production to bring output up to the given proportion, α, of expected sales. Call these three items $u(t)$, $s_r(t)$, and $s(t)$, respectively. We have seen above that $u(t)$, production for sale, is related to sales of the two preceding periods in the following manner:

$$u(t) = (1 + \eta)\beta y(t - 1) - \eta\beta y(t - 2).$$

Likewise, unintended inventory reductions (or accumulations) in period $t - 1$ are equal to the difference between actual and anticipated sales in that period, so that

$$s_r(t) = \beta y(t - 1) - (1 + \eta)\beta y(t - 2) + \eta\beta y(t - 3).$$

Finally, $s_\alpha(t)$, production on account of the "pure accelerator," is equal to the difference between anticipated sales in period t and in period $t - 1$ multiplied by the accelerator; in other words,

$$s_\alpha(t) = \alpha[(1 + \eta)\beta y(t - 1) - (1 + 2\eta)\beta y(t - 2) + \eta \beta y(t - 3)].$$

Since total income produced equals production of consumers' goods for all purposes plus noninduced net investment, we have, upon adding the expressions for $u(t)$, $s_r(t)$, and $s_\alpha(t)$,

(6) $y(t) = [(1 + \eta)(1 + \alpha) + 1]\beta y(t - 1)$
$$- (1 + 2\eta)(1 + \alpha)\beta y(t - 2) + (1 + \alpha)\eta \beta y(t - 3) + v_o.$$

The difference equation (6) is the most general dynamic system to be considered. Many of our other sequences are simply special cases of this model. By putting $\eta = 0$ we obtain Eq. (5), while (4) is the special case in which $\alpha = 0$. Likewise, Eq. (3) may be obtained by setting both η and α equal to zero in (6).

Behavior of an economy subject to both an inventory accelerator and a coefficient of expectations might be illustrated, as in previous cases, by numerical examples. Both the method of constructing such examples and the character of inventory movements, however, should by now be thoroughly familiar. And inventory cycles corresponding to this more general model are not different in principle from those of the special cases. Consequently, I leave it to the reader to construct any examples which seem appropriate to verify the conclusions set out below.

Although income and inventory movements are much the same for the general case (6) as for (4) and (5), the range of values of the parameters α, β, and η within which an economy is stable requires further consideration. For stability of this general system, the marginal propensity to consume, the inventory accelerator, and the coefficient of expectations must satisfy the following inequalities:[18]

(7) $\qquad (1 + \alpha)(2 + \alpha)\eta \beta^2 - (1 + \alpha)(1 + 2\eta)\beta + 1 > 0$

and $\qquad\qquad\qquad\qquad 3 - \beta(2\alpha + 3) \qquad\qquad > 0.$

In order to grasp clearly just what this means, we may consider some special cases. Let us suppose, as before, that η may have any values

---

18. Again, stability of the system is determined from the condition that the roots of $f(p) = 0$ shall lie within the unit circle, where $f(p) = 0$ is the characteristic equation of Eq. (6).

between zero and unity; and let us consider only these limiting values. If $\eta = 0$, the system will be stable as in (5), provided only that $\beta < 1/1 + \alpha$. If $\eta = 1$, on the other hand, stability requires that $(1 + \alpha)(2 + \alpha)\beta^2 - 3(1 + \alpha)\beta + 1 > 0$ where, because of the second of the inequalities (7), the relevant root of the quadratic in β is the lowest positive root.

The nature of these restrictions is best understood by referring to Fig. 9. All values of the marginal propensity to consume and the inven-

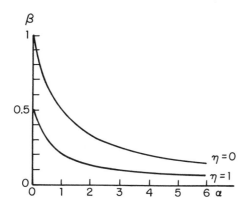

Figure 9. Influence of expectations upon the stability of a system containing an inventory accelerator such as the sequence in Eq. (6)

tory accelerator below the line marked $\eta = 0$ yield stable results when the coefficient of expectation is zero. This is simply case (5). If the coefficient of expectations is unity, however, the economy will not be stable unless β and α lie below the line $\eta = 1$. The figure shows clearly that the coefficient of expectations places very severe restrictions upon our stability conditions—so severe, indeed, that an economy with a coefficient of unity must almost certainly be unstable. Suppose, for example, that businessmen attempt to keep inventories equal to one-half of sales (or $\alpha = 0.5$). If $\eta = 1$, Fig. 9 shows that the economy will not be stable unless the marginal propensity to consume is less than (approximately) three-tenths. Even with $\alpha = 0$ (no inventory accelerator), stability of a system with a coefficient of expectations of unity requires a marginal propensity to consume less than one-half. It is doubtful whether propensities as low as these could be found, even in the most wealthy countries. We may conclude either (a) that the coefficient of expectations cannot conceivably be as large as unity, or (b) that the economy is essentially unstable except for the operation of certain limiting stabilizers.

If we accept conclusion (*a*), we place ourselves with the group who envisage cyclical fluctuations as a result of variations in the parameters of an otherwise stable economy. In this case discussions of an income equilibrium corresponding to a given level of noninduced investment are relevant. The multiplier, in other words, becomes an important if not a dominant factor in the determination of income. Acceptance of conclusion (*b*), on the other hand, makes necessary an explanation of why the economy exhibits any stability at all. The level of income and employment must be explained, not by the multiplier and the amount of noninduced net investment, but by the operation of limiting stabilizers. A comprehensive discussion of such stabilizers is beyond the scope of this paper. An enumeration of them, however, would certainly include flexible interest rates, full employment, credit restrictions (other than interest rate changes), and cyclical changes in the coefficient of expectations, to mention only a few. How important these stabilizers are, and at what points they begin to operate, are questions for empirical investigation. Probably no very useful generalizations may be made about them.

The dynamic sequences (1) through (6) were intended to show what types of behavior are possible for a system containing a sales-output lag. The following conclusions seem to be the most important:

(1) An economy in which businessmen attempt to recoup inventory losses will always undergo cyclical fluctuations when equilibrium is disturbed, provided the economy is stable. This is the pure inventory cycle.

(2) The assumption of stability imposes severe limitations upon the possible size of the marginal propensity to consume, particularly if the coefficient of expectations is positive.

(3) The inventory accelerator is a more powerful destabilizer than the ordinary acceleration principle. The difference in stability conditions is due to the fact that the former allows for replacement demand whereas the usual analytical formulation of the latter does not. Thus, for inventories, replacement demand acts as a destabilizer. Whether it does so for all types of capital goods is a moot question, but I believe cases may occur in which it does not.

(4) Investment for inventory purposes cannot alter the equilibrium

of income, which depends only upon the propensity to consume and the amount of noninduced investment.

(5) The apparent instability of a system containing both an accelerator and a coefficient of expectations makes further investigation of possible stabilizers highly desirable.

16 | Partial Adjustment and the Stability of Inventory Cycles

My first studies of inventory cycles seemed to place severe restrictions upon the parameters of the system if the cycles were to be stable.[1] In a system involving both a marginal propensity to consume, β, and a marginal inventory accelerator, α, for example, the cycles were found not stable unless the following relation exists between the parameters:

$$(1) \qquad\qquad (1 + \alpha)\beta < 1.$$

The inequality in (1) was based upon a second-order difference equation in a single variable, y, in which the stock of inventories disappeared entirely.

Before carrying the analysis further, let us present the notation to be used here:

$y(t)$ net income in period t

$I(t)$ the stock of inventories at the close of period t

α the marginal inventory accelerator, or the relation of desired inventories to anticipated sales

β the marginal propensity to consume

V_o net autonomous investment.

Following Lundberg's assumptions concerning the leads and lags in the circular flow of income, I demonstrated earlier that the inventory sequence could be represented by the following equation:

$$(2) \qquad y(t) = (2 + \alpha)\beta y(t - 1) - (1 + \alpha)\beta y(t - 2) + V_o.$$

Prepared for the International Statistical Institute, Dublin, September 1962. Not previously published.

---

1. See Chapter 15 above.

The condition of stability, represented by (1) above, was derived from the difference equation (2). My first theory of inventory cycles should be regarded as a complete-adjustment system, since producers were supposed to adjust output to the optimal level within a single planning period.

Professor Michael Lovell[2] has introduced a concept of partial adjustment which suggests that producers may not make a complete adjustment within a single planning period. Rather, they may adjust only partially, leaving either inventories or output for sales in a nonoptimal position. The purpose of this paper is to show how partial adjustment stabilizes an otherwise explosive cycle. Two types of partial adjustment are considered. In the first, producers are assumed to make a complete adjustment to expected sales, while adjusting inventories only partially to the optimal level. In the second, producers are assumed to make a partial adaptation of output for both inventories and sales. The former type of behavior is called "partial inventory adjustment" while the latter is given the designation "partial adjustment of induced output."

Partial inventory adjustment is shown to exert a much stronger stabilizing effect than partial adjustment of induced output. Partial adjustment, whether applied to inventories or to induced output, requires a new parameter, π, which I call the "coefficient of partial adjustment." It normally lies between zero and unity, and indicates the degree to which producers adapt output either for sales or for inventories to the optimal position.

Partial Inventory Adjustment

Because it is mathematically simple, I begin with a description of partial inventory adjustment. As soon as any type of partial adjustment is introduced, it becomes convenient to consider a dynamic situation which differs from the one which I originally analyzed. Specifically, in place of a second-order equation in one variable (national income), which formed the basis of my original study, a system of two first-order equations in two variables (net income and end-of-period inventories) proves to be more manageable. The first equation defines net income, which consists of output for sales, output for inventories, and net autonomous investment. If producers base their anticipated sales upon the

2. "Manufacturers' Inventories, Sales Expectations, and the Acceleration Principle," *Econometrica*, 29 (July 1961), 293–314.

realized sales of the previous period, production for sales in t will be equal to $\beta y(t-1)$. Similarly, if the optimal level of inventories bears a constant marginal ratio α to expected sales, the optimal stock of inventories in t will be $\alpha\beta y(t-1)$. And if the actual stock of inventories at the close of period $(t-1)$ is $I(t-1)$, the output needed to bring actual inventories to the level of the optimal quantity will be $\alpha\beta y(t-1) - I(t-1)$. Thus national income in period t, in terms of its three components becomes

$$(3) \qquad y(t) = \beta y(t-1) + [\alpha\beta y(t-1) - I(t-1)] + V_o.$$

Equation (3) is simply a definition of net income. In addition, we must have a similar definition for inventories. Inventories at the end of period t will be equal to inventories at the end of period $t-1$, plus output—positive or negative—for inventories in t, plus any unexpected changes in inventories which may arise because anticipated sales, $\beta y(t-1)$, differ from actual sales, $\beta y(t)$. The equation for the stock of inventories at the end of period t may accordingly be expressed as follows:

$$(4) \quad I(t) = I(t-1) + [\alpha\beta y(t-1) - I(t-1)] + [\beta y(t-1) - \beta y(t)].$$

Combining Eqs. (3) and (4), we obtain a system of two first-order equations in the two variables, y and I. This system is equivalent to Eq. (2) above, which is the equation of my first theory of inventory cycles. Indeed, Eq. (2) could easily be derived from Eqs. (3) and (4) by appropriate cancellations and substitutions. Nevertheless, the latter are useful, even though appearing more complicated than the former, simply because they enable us to describe partial inventory adjustment in a more direct fashion. In Eqs. (3) and (4), for example, the bracketed expression $[\alpha\beta y(t-1) - I(t-1)]$ represents output for inventories during period t. It also represents a complete adjustment of inventories, since the producers expect to alter the value of their inventories from the actual level to the optimal level within the span of a single planning period.

Suppose now that we introduce Lovell's concept of a partial adjustment, and let it apply to inventories alone. Suppose, further, that the coefficient of partial adjustment is π, where $0 < \pi < 1$. Output for inventories in both equations then becomes $\pi[\alpha\beta y(t-1) - I(t-1)]$ and Eqs. (3) and (4) become:

$$(5) \qquad y(t) = \beta y(t-1) + \pi[\alpha\beta y(t-1) - I(t-1)] + V_0$$

$$\text{and} \quad I(t) = I(t-1) + \pi[\alpha\beta y(t-1) - I(t-1)] + [\beta y(t-1) - \beta y(t)].$$

The reasons for the two-equation form should now be evident. First, it emphasizes the relation between the *flow* of income and the *stock* of inventories which forms the basis of the cyclical process; and, second, as I have mentioned above, the two-equation system greatly simplifies the analysis of partial inventory adjustment.

Combining the coefficients of y and I, Eqs. (5) may be expressed as follows:

(6) $$y(t) = (1 + \pi\alpha)\beta y(t - 1) - \pi I(t - 1) + V_o$$

and $$I(t) = (1 + \pi\alpha)\beta y(t - 1) + (1 - \pi)I(t - 1) - \beta y(t).$$

In order to put Eqs. (6) into normal form, we add $\beta y(t)$ to both sides of the second equation, multiply both sides of the first equation by β, and subtract the first equation, thus modified, from the second. The result is:

(7) $$y(t) = (1 + \pi\alpha)\beta y(t - 1) - \pi I(t - 1) + V_o$$

and $$I(t) = (1 + \pi\alpha)\beta(1 - \beta)y(t - 1) + [1 - \pi(1 - \beta)]I(t - 1) - \beta V_o.$$

The solution of the homogeneous part of Eqs. (7) is

(8) $$y(t) = A_1 \lambda_1{}^t + A_2 \lambda_2{}^t + K_2,$$

where λ_1 and λ_2 are latent roots of the following characteristic equation:

(9) $$\begin{vmatrix} (1 + \pi\alpha)\beta - \lambda & -\pi \\ (1 + \pi\alpha)\beta(1 - \beta) & [1 - \pi(1 - \beta)] - \lambda \end{vmatrix} = 0.$$

In expanded form, Eq. (9) may be written as:

(10) $$\lambda^2 - [(1 + \pi\alpha)\beta + 1 - \pi(1 - \beta)]\lambda + (1 + \pi\alpha)\beta = 0.$$

The roots of Eq. (10) will normally be cyclical for a wide variation of π. Thus at the upper limit, where $\pi = 1$, Eq. (10) is

(11) $$\lambda^2 - (2 + \alpha)\beta\lambda + (1 + \alpha)\beta = 0.$$

Equation (11) is the characteristic equation of my complete-adjustment theory of inventory cycles. The roots of Eq. (11) are known to be complex whenever the system is stable, that is, whenever $(1 + \alpha)\beta < 1$.

At the lower limit, where $\pi = 0$, it will not be true that the roots of Eq. (10) are complex. Indeed, when $\pi = 0$, Eq. (10) is transformed into the following:

(12) $$\lambda^2 - (1 + \beta)\lambda + \beta = 0.$$

By substitution, the reader may easily verify that Eq. (12) has two positive real roots, $\lambda_1 = \beta$, $\lambda_2 = 1$. Thus an extremely low value of π has eliminated the cycle altogether. Such a result is to be expected. A low value of π is equivalent to a passive attitude toward inventories, and I have shown that an active attempt to maintain inventories at some level with respect to anticipated sales is the essence of the cyclical process.

The table below shows in the two right-hand columns the critical minimum values of π, for the given values of α and β, below which partial inventory adjustment converts a cyclical system into a noncyclical one.

Marginal propensity to consume, β	Marginal inventory accelerator, α	
	$\alpha = 1.0$	$\alpha = 0.5$
0.9	0.0182	0.0214
0.8	0.0390	0.0455
0.7	0.0629	0.0732
0.6	0.0911	0.1053
0.5	0.1250	0.1430
0.4	0.1672	0.1905
0.3	0.2223	0.2507
0.2	0.3002	0.3340
0.1	0.4297	0.4676

We can see that unless the marginal propensity to consume is exceedingly small, the coefficient of partial inventory adjustment required to convert a cyclical process into a noncyclical one is so small that for practical purposes it may be neglected.

Considering the small values of π depicted above, it seems reasonable to suppose that for any reasonable value the system will probably be cyclical, despite the fact that producers display a degree of inertia in adjusting their inventories to the optimal level. This means that for most, but not all, cases, the roots of Eq. (10) will be complex conjugate roots of the form

$$(13) \qquad \lambda_1 = x + iy, \; \lambda_2 = x - iy.$$

The solution of Eq. (10) accordingly will be something like

$$(14) \qquad y(t) = A(r)^t \cos(\theta t + \phi),$$

where $r^2 = x^2 + y^2$ and $\theta = \arctan y/x$. Stability of Eq. (10) thus depends upon the value of r; more conveniently, it depends upon r^2, for $r^2 \gtreqless 1$ according as $r \gtreqless 1$.

Now from the theory of symmetric functions we know that the constant term in Eq. (10) is equal to the sum of the products of the roots of Eq. (10) taken two at a time. But Eq. (10) normally has only two roots, $x + yi$ and $x - iy$. It follows that

$$(15) \quad \lambda_1 \lambda_2 = (x + iy)(x - iy) = x^2 - (iy)^2 = x^2 + y^2 = r^2 = (1 + \pi\alpha)\beta.$$

The condition of stability for Eq. (10) therefore is given by the following inequality:

$$(16) \quad r^2 = (1 + \pi\alpha)\beta < 1.$$

For a complete-adjustment system the condition of stability is known to be

$$(17) \quad (1 + \alpha)\beta < 1.$$

Bearing in mind that π is less than unity, one sees immediately that partial inventory adjustment is capable of converting a potentially unstable system into a stable one. Indeed, regardless of whether the roots are real or complex, and whether the motions are oscillatory or exponential, it can be shown by analysis of the stability criteria for difference equations that lowering π can only increase the range of stability of the system: so long as $\beta < 1$ and π is positive, the boundary of stability becomes Eq. (16), in all cases.

The Routh-Schurr-Samuelson conditions for stability of difference equations[3] are

$$\pi(1 - \beta) \geq 0, \; 1 - \beta(1 + \pi\alpha) \geq 0, \text{ and } 2[1 + \beta(1 + \pi\alpha)] - \pi(1 - \beta) \geq 0.$$

Obviously, the first and last of these are assured for $\pi \geq 0$ and $\beta \leq 1$. Hence the middle condition alone is operative in all relevant cases.

Partial Adjustment of Induced Output

I turn now to a discussion of partial adjustment applied to output for both inventories and sales, or to partial adjustment of induced output. In considering partial inventory adjustment, we needed only two equations in two variables, net income and end-of-period inventories. When we begin to speak of induced output, we shall need two more variables, optimal induced output and actual induced output. Suppose that π again represents the coefficient of partial adjustment, with the reservation

3. Paul A. Samuelson, *Foundations of Economic Analysis* (Cambridge, Mass., Harvard University Press, 1947), p. 436.

that the coefficient now applies to output for both inventories and sales rather than to output for inventories alone. Let p_o represent optimal induced output.

We now have four variables, as follows:

p_o optimal induced output
p_a actual induced output
y net income
I end-of-period inventories.

Consider initially the relation between p_o and p_a. Actual induced output $p_a(t)$ in period t will be equal to actual induced output in period $t - 1$, plus a partial adjustment—positive or negative—of the difference between optimal induced output and actual induced output. Thus, considering p_o as a datum, we have:

(18)
$$p_a(t) = p_a(t-1) + \pi[p_o(t) - p_a(t-1)]$$
$$= (1 - \pi)p_a(t-1) + \pi p_o(t).$$

Optimal induced output can be related to past sales and inventories in much the same manner as in our earlier discussion of partial inventory adjustment. Thus the optimal level of output for both sales and inventories, again under Lundberg's premises concerning the circular flow of income, can be represented by the following equation:

(19)
$$p_o(t) = \beta y(t-1) + [\alpha\beta y(t-1) - I(t-1)].$$

The third variable, net income, is simply the sum of actual induced output and autonomous net investment:

(20)
$$y(t) = p_a(t) + V_o.$$

Finally, the fourth variable, end-of-period inventories, is as before the amount of inventories at the end of period $t - 1$, *plus* actual induced output for both inventories and expected sales in period t, *less* sales in t. The equation for inventories, there, is as follows:

(21)
$$I(t) = I(t-1) + p_a(t) - \beta y(t).$$

With Eqs. (18), (19), (20), and (21), we have four equations in four variables. Superficially, they appear to comprise a fourth-order system. In reality, however, it is not as imposing as it seems; the principal matrix is doubly degenerate, which means that its determinant vanishes until two variables are eliminated. In practice, the most convenient variables to eliminate are p_o and p_a. I shall not describe the process of elimination in detail. Suffice it to say that when the two variables have been eliminated by substitution, and when the remaining two equations are reduced to standard form by the method used above, the system appears as follows:

(22) $\quad y(t) = [1 - \pi + \pi(1 + \alpha)\beta]y(t - 1) - \pi I(t - 1) + \pi V_o$

and $\quad I(t) = [1 - \pi + \pi(1 + \alpha)\beta][1 - \beta]y(t - 1) + [1 - \pi(1 - \beta)]$
$$I(t - 1) - [1 - \pi(1 - \beta)]V_o.$$

The characteristic equation of the homogeneous part of Eq. (22) is

(23) $\quad \begin{vmatrix} [(1 - \pi) + \pi(1 + \alpha)\beta] - \lambda & -\pi \\ [(1 - \pi) + \pi(1 + \alpha)\beta][1 - \beta] & [1 - \pi(1 - \beta)] - \lambda \end{vmatrix} = 0.$

When expanded, the equation above becomes a second-degree equation in λ:

(24) $\quad \lambda^2 - [(1 - \pi) + \pi(1 + \alpha)\beta + 1 - \pi(1 - \beta)]\lambda$
$$+ [(1 - \pi) + \pi(1 + \alpha)\beta] = 0.$$

Equation (24) exhibits greater cyclical tendencies than the inventory system previously discussed. With respect to partial inventory adjustment, we saw that a low enough value of π would convert a cyclical process into a noncyclical one. For partial induced output systems, as represented by Eq. (24), this is no longer true. Indeed, as π falls, the roots of Eq. (24) remain complex up to the point where $\pi = 0$. No area exists, as in partial inventory adjustment, in which the characteristic equation has real roots. The economic sequence continues to oscillate, although at an extremely low amplitude, up to the point where $\pi = 0$. This can be seen by reorganizing the terms of Eq. (24) as follows:

(25) $\quad \lambda^2 - \{2 + \pi[(2 + \alpha)\beta - 2]\}\lambda + \{1 + \pi[(1 + \alpha)\beta - 1]\} = 0.$

No matter what the values of α and β may be, Eq. (25) may be written in the following form:

(26) $\quad \lambda^2 - (2 + \pi k_1)\lambda + (1 + \pi k_2) = 0.$

Consider the discriminant, $b^2 - 4ac$, of Eq. (26). When this expression is written out, it appears in the following form:

(27) $\quad b^2 - 4ac = 4 + 4k_1\pi + k_1{}^2\pi^2 - 4 - 4k_2\pi.$

Equation (27) is a second-degree equation in π. Moreover, no matter what its coefficients k_1 and k_2 may be, the constant term always cancels, so that the discriminant may be written in a generalized form, such as:

(28) $$b^2 - 4ac = a_0\pi^2 + a_1\pi.$$

If $b^2 - 4ac$ is set equal to zero, we have

(29) $$a_0\pi^2 + a_1\pi = 0.$$

One of the roots of Eq. (29) is $\pi = 0$, and this is true for any values of α and β. Let us look now at the upper limit where $\pi = 1$. It can be shown that at this upper limit both the inventory sequence and the induced-output sequence reduce to the same characteristic equation, namely,

(30) $$\lambda^2 - (2 + \alpha)\beta\lambda + (1 + \alpha)\beta = 0.$$

Equation (30) is the characteristic equation for my first complete-adjustment theory of inventory cycles. I have shown that, in the complete-adjustment system, the sequence of events will be oscillatory as long as the economic parameters, α and β, conform to the condition of stability. It would be tempting to say that oscillations must occur whenever $\pi = 1$. But of course no such statement can be made because of the possibility of instability at $\pi = 1$, under the premise of complete adjustment. I am therefore thrown back on the rather lame assertion that experiments with numerical examples confirm the view that the cycle remains oscillatory for wide ranges of π, particularly if β does not exceed some critical fraction and α is any positive fraction.

So much for the roots of the characteristic equation in the induced-output system. I turn now to an examination of the condition of stability for such a system. Again, from the theory of symmetric functions, we know that the constant term of Eq. (24), the characteristic equation for an induced-output system, must equal the sum of the products of the roots of that equation, taken two at a time. And again, Eq. (24) has only two roots, normally complex conjugates, of the form,

(31) $$\lambda_1 = x + iy, \qquad \lambda_2 = x - iy.$$

Hence it follows that

(32) $$\lambda_1\lambda_2 = x^2 + y^2 = r^2 = (1 - \pi) + \pi(1 + \alpha)\beta.$$

Thus the condition of stability is

(33) $$(1 - \pi) + \pi(1 + \alpha)\beta < 1.$$

Subtracting $1 - \pi$ from both sides of the above inequality, we find

(34) $$\pi(1 + \alpha)\beta < \pi.$$

Division of both sides of (34) by π produces a more simple inequality, thus:

(35) $$(1 + \alpha)\beta < 1.$$

From the above inequality we have reached the somewhat puzzling conclusion that the coefficient of partial adjustment has no effect whatever upon the stability of the system, at least as far as r^2 is concerned! A system which is potentially unstable under the premise of complete adjustment remains unstable even after partial adjustment of induced output is introduced. And this remains true for all values of the coefficient of partial adjustment except $\pi = 0$. Generally speaking, the partial induced-output system is stable, neutral, or unstable according as its counterpart complete-adjustment system is stable, neutral, or unstable.

To show that the magnitude of positive π cannot affect the qualitative property of stability, we write the Routh-Schurr-Samuelson stability inequalities for this general system as

$$\pi(1 - \beta) \geq 0, \ \pi[1 - \beta(1 + \alpha)] \geq 0, \text{ and } 4 - 3\pi(1 - \beta) + 2\pi\alpha\beta \geq 0.$$

The magnitude of π clearly has no effect on the first two of these. For $\beta \leq 1$ and $\pi \leq 1$, it is easy to verify that the last is assuredly satisfied. Hence the bracket in the middle expression is the only interesting stability boundary in the relevant cases.

By contrast, we have seen that partial inventory adjustment is capable of transforming an unstable sequence into a stable one, provided that the coefficient of partial adjustment is sufficiently small. Thus partial adjustment proves to be a more powerful stabilizing influence when applied to inventories than when applied to both inventories and sales. I should not like to conclude these remarks, however, without saying something about the concept of stability here used. We have seen that in an oscillating sequence the inventory cycle can be represented by an equation such as

(36) $$y(t) = A(r)^t \cos(\theta t + \phi).$$

In Eq. (36) the modulus, r, governs the rate at which the cyclical fluctuations expand or contract; in other words, r is a relative measure of the rate at which the cycles explode or converge. The constant, A, on the other hand, is a measure of the amplitude at which the cycles begin their fluctuations.

In the preceding discussion, stability was measured entirely in terms of r, or its transformation r^2. I have discovered that for certain standard initial conditions, whether a system is potentially stable, neutral, or unstable under conditions of complete adjustment, a reduction of π always diminishes the value of A. This means that whether the cycles converge, remain unchanged, or explode, the amplitude of such fluctuations is nevertheless reduced by a decline in π. In this sense, partial adjustment may be regarded as a stabilizing influence even though it does not affect the value of r.

Consequences for Policy

What are the consequences, with respect to economic policy, of the analysis of partial adjustment presented above? Economists are agreed, I believe, that the inventory cycle is essentially a structural phenomenon in the sense that it represents the inevitable consequence of economic disturbance. They are also agreed that something should be done about these structural cycles. But no one seems to know exactly what should be done and how. I should like to suggest that, from the point of view of stabilizing economic activity, a policy of partial adjustment greatly simplifies the problems of our economic regulators. Partial adjustment is essentially a frictional or an inertial influence, and it slows down the rate of movement of the economy in any direction. This gives the regulators more time to assess the situation. Moreover, it reduces the significance of any lag which may arise between the time a given policy is introduced and the time it is felt by the economy as a whole.

In the years since the end of World War II there has been an increasing tendency to regard the free-market economy as essentially an unstable system. In the Employment Act of 1946, for example, the assumption was implicit that in order to keep the American economy on an even keel, the central authorities would have to look ahead and forecast the shape of things to come. The chastening experience which most economists underwent in trying and failing to make appraisals for the future has convinced most of them that such forecasts are impractical for the purpose of regulating economic activity. At the same time, some sort of regulation is considered to be essential. In short, most economists do not believe that the free-market system contains an automatic mechanisn which will ensure full employment and optimal use of resources.

The answer to the dilemma of steady employment without forecasting seems to me to lie in Professor Abba P. Lerner's "economic steering wheel."[4] The driver of an automobile can keep his car on a straight course without knowing, at any given time, exactly where it is going. He simply waits until he sees that it has gone too far to the right, and then nudges it gently to the left. Conversely, when he sees that it has gone too far to the left, he gives a gentle nudge to the right. By alternately moving his car from the right to the left, he manages to steer a reasonably straight course.

Obviously I do not mean to imply that all dynamic systems—or all automobiles—behave in this way. I can recall vividly, as a youth, driving an old Model T Ford along the dirt roads of Kansas. This particular car had a disturbing habit of developing what we called the "shimmies." A push to the left would lead it to overshoot the mark, thereby requiring an even greater push to the right. When our Model T developed the shimmies, its driver had two alternatives: either stop the car or end up in the ditch. Had I known then what I know now about the movements of a system, I would have said that our Model T was dynamically unstable. And what I say now is that partial adjustment can readily transform an unstable economy into a stable one, thereby greatly reducing the incidence of ulcers among bankers and government officials.

4. Abba P. Lerner, *Economics of Employment* (New York, McGraw-Hill, 1951), chap. 1.

17 | Factors Governing the Length of Inventory Cycles

Empirical studies of fluctuations in American economic activity have revealed at least two types of business cycles. First, there are the major movements of income and employment which are generally associated with variations in the demand for such important types of investment as producers' plant and equipment. The length of these major movements is so difficult to determine that it is not even certain that they should be designated as "cycles." Most of them, however, appear to cover a period of seven to nine years. In addition to the major cycle, a shorter and less severe cycle, having a duration of three to three and one-half years, is also apparent in economic statistics for the United States.[1] While this short cycle has never been clearly understood, there has been a tendency in recent years to attribute it to fluctuations in the demand for business inventories.[2]

A theory of these short cycles, or inventory cycles, was presented in one of my earlier papers, where it was shown that cyclical movements of income result from the mere fact that producers are unable to adjust

Reprinted from *Review of Economic Statistics*, 29 (February 1947), 1–15. Copyright President and Fellows of Harvard College. 1947.

1. See, for example, Joseph A. Schumpeter, *Business Cycles*, ed. 1 (New York, McGraw-Hill, 1939), vol. 2, chap. 8. Professor Schumpeter calls the short cycle a Kitchin cycle, and the longer one a Juglar. In addition to Kitchins and Juglars, a much longer cycle associated with the name of Kondratieff is also discussed.
2. Alvin H. Hansen, *Fiscal Policy and Business Cycles* (New York, W. W. Norton, 1941), pp. 17 and 54–55.

output immediately to changes in demand.[3] When equilibrium is disturbed by an increase in demand, for example, output is not immediately increased, and business inventories decline. Later, the attempt to replace depleted stocks causes income and employment to rise above the level which can be permanently maintained. A subsequent recession is therefore inevitable. In the early stages of the decline, businessmen again are unable to make an immediate adaptation, and inventories rise above their normal level. In attempting to dispose of their abnormal stocks, producers force output and employment below equilibrium. When this occurs, inventories are gradually reduced, and the stage is set for a revival.

From this brief description, it is apparent that any disturbance in the underlying conditions of equilibrium creates a series of oscillations about a new equilibrium. Such cycles are the result of structural conditions of production and sales, and occur even without speculative movements of inventories or movements induced by changes in credit policy. Whether the observed short cycles of American economic activity are inventory cycles of the type described in my earlier paper (and summarized above) can be determined only by a careful empirical study. A comparison must be made of the actual movements of income, inventories, and prices with the movements to be expected from the theory of inventory cycles. As a prerequisite to such a study, the present paper discusses certain features of a typical inventory cycle which were not analyzed in the earlier paper. In particular, an account is given of the factors which determine the length of the cycle.

In general, the time interval from peak to peak or from trough to trough of an inventory cycle depends upon four principal factors: (a) the average length of what I have called the "production planning period," or the period of time which elapses between a change in demand and a change in the rate of output of the average producer; (b) the country's marginal propensity to consume; (c) the relation which producers and dealers attempt to maintain between sales (or expected sales) and inventories; and (d) the nature of producers' and dealers' expectations—or, in other words, the extent to which a rise or fall of sales creates expectations of a further rise or fall.

In the analysis which follows it will be convenient to measure the

3. Lloyd A. Metzler, "The Nature and Stability of Inventory Cycles," which appears as Chapter 15 of the present volume.

time interval in terms of average production planning periods. In other words, instead of speaking of a cycle as a 40-month cycle or a 30-month cycle, we shall say that the cycle includes a certain number of production planning periods. This procedure is equivalent to accepting the production planning period as a datum and not inquiring into the conditions which determine its length. Later, when the inventory cycle has been fully described in terms of the other factors, it will be possible to see what is implied with respect to the length of the average planning period.

For the technical aspects of the discussion, the same notation will be used as in my earlier paper. The marginal propensity to consume will be designated by the letter β. The relation between expected sales and the desired level of inventories will be called "the inventory accelerator" and will be designated by α. The term "accelerator" is used in this connection because the increase or decrease in the desired level of inventories which results from a given increase or decrease of sales is closely related to the acceleration principle. Finally, producers' expectations will be taken into account through a "coefficient of expectations," η, defined as the ratio of the expected change in the volume of sales to the actual change in sales during the past two planning periods. Thus if the coefficient of expectations were one-half, and if sales in the last production period and in the last period but one were $500 and $400 respectively, expected sales in the next following period would be $550; that is, the expected change in sales would be one-half the observed change over the past two periods.

In the following pages, the influence of the marginal propensity to consume, the inventory accelerator, and the coefficient of expectations upon the length of a typical inventory cycle will be considered in the order named.

The Marginal Propensity to Consume

In order to simplify the argument, I have based the discussion which follows upon an abstract set of assumptions. Although none of these assumptions corresponds exactly to the situation in the real world, it is nevertheless my opinion that all of them together represent a rough approximation to the actual behavior of the economy. In other words, the combined assumptions are, in my judgment, more realistic than a cursory examination might at first suggest.[4] The assumptions are as follows:

(1) The time interval under consideration is divided into production planning periods, and the assumption is made that the rate of production for all commodities is fixed at the beginning of each period and remains unchanged throughout the period.

(2) Within any given planning period, discrepancies between output and sales are offset by movements of inventories.

(3) Sales during each planning period depend upon income produced within the same period. In other words, the lag of sales behind income produced is so short that within any given planning period sales may be regarded as an instantaneous function of output.

(4) Production plans at the beginning of each period are made on the basis of past sales experience and the current state of inventories; such plans include a rate of output sufficient to cover expected sales plus a positive or negative amount for inventory adjustment.

These four assumptions are sufficient to explain the relation of inventories to the short cycle of income. They are the basis of all the numerical examples presented below. In addition to these general assumptions, two special assumptions are made in the present section in order to isolate the influence of the propensity to consume. First, output in any given period is assumed to equal the level of sales in the preceding period; in other words, the coefficient of expectations is assumed to be zero. Second, the assumption is made that businessmen attempt to maintain inventories at a constant level which is independent of the volume of sales; in technical language, this means that the inventory accelerator is zero.

Two numerical examples, involving different propensities to consume, are given in Table 1. In the first example, consumption in each period is equal to three-fourths of income produced in the same period, while in the second example consumption is equal to one-half of income produced.[5] In other words, β, the marginal propensity to consume, is first 0.75 and then 0.50. Since numerical illustrations of this type have

4. Empirical evidence with respect to some of these assumptions is presented in "Three Lags in the Circular Flow of Income," which appears as Chapter 18 of the present volume.

5. The consumption function has such a form, in other words, that the marginal propensity to consume is equal to the average propensity. This is not a necessary condition, but is merely a simplifying assumption.

Table 1. The propensity to consume and the inventory cycle

Part a: $\beta = 0.75$; $\alpha = 0$; $\eta = 0$

(1) Production of consumers' goods for sale	(2) Production of consumers' goods for stocks	(3) Net noninduced investment	(4) Income produced (1) + (2) + (3)	(5) Sales	(6) Inventories at close of period
750	0	250	1000	750	400
750	0	350	1100	825	325
825	75	350	1250	938	287
938	113	350	1401	1051	287
1051	113	350	1514	1136	315
1136	85	350	1571	1178	358
1178	42	350	1570	1178	400
1178	0	350	1528	1146	432
1146	−32	350	1464	1098	448
1098	−48	350	1400	1050	448
1050	−48	350	1352	1014	436
1014	−36	350	1328	996	418
996	−18	350	1328	996	400
996	0	350	1346	1010	386
1010	14	350	1374	1030	380
1030	20	350	1400	1050	380
1050	20	350	1420	1065	385
1065	15	350	1430	1072	393
1072	7	350	1429	1072	400
1072	0	350	1422	1067	405

Part b: $\beta = 0.50$; $\alpha = 0$; $\eta = 0$

500	0	500	1000	500	200
500	0	600	1100	550	150
550	50	600	1200	600	150
600	50	600	1250	625	175
625	25	600	1250	625	200
625	0	600	1225	612	213
612	−13	600	1199	599	213
599	−13	600	1186	593	206
593	−6	600	1187	593	200
593	0	600	1193	596	197
596	3	600	1199	599	197
599	3	600	1202	601	198
601	2	600	1203	601	200
601	0	600	1201	600	201
600	−1	600	1199	599	201
599	−1	600	1198	599	200
599	0	600	1199	599	200

been discussed in my earlier paper, it will be sufficient for present purposes to give a brief explanation of the first example.

The system is initially in equilibrium, with production of consumers' goods equal to sales, with no production for stocks, and with net noninduced investment equal to savings. Thus, when noninduced investment is 250, net income is in equilibrium at a level of 1,000. In the second production planning period, it is assumed that equilibrium is disturbed by an increase of noninduced investment to 350. Since production of consumers' goods remains at the level of sales in the preceding period, the rise of income is limited to the increase of investment; income produced rises to 1,100 and sales of consumers' goods rise to 825. Thus sales exceed production of consumers' goods, and inventories decline from their normal level of 400 to 325. In the third planning period, production of consumers' goods amounts to 900, of which 825 is produced to cover expected sales, and 75 is produced to restore inventories to normal. With noninduced investment of 350, total output is 1,250, and sales are 938, instead of the anticipated 825. Inventories thus decline further despite the attempts of producers to increase them.

In the fourth period, income produced has reached its new equilibrium corresponding to the higher level of noninduced investment. Nevertheless, the fact that inventories remain below normal means that a further rise of income is inevitable, since output will be increased in an effort to restore the depleted stocks. When income has risen above equilibrium, stocks begin to accumulate rapidly, as the example shows. As soon as inventories are restored to a normal level, businessmen cease producing for stock and total output declines. This leads to a further inventory accumulation, since producers tend to overestimate their sales. In attempting to reduce their excess stocks, businessmen produce less than they expect to sell, and the downward movement of income is accelerated.

Additional details of the numerical examples are left to the reader. It is sufficient at this point to call attention to a number of facts regarding the relation between the movement of income and the movement of inventories: (*a*) when income has reached its equilibrium level in the prosperity phase of the cycle, inventories remain below normal; (*b*) the peak of the cycle of income is reached at the point where inventories are restored to a normal level; (*c*) after income has begun to decline, inventories continue to rise despite attempts of businessmen

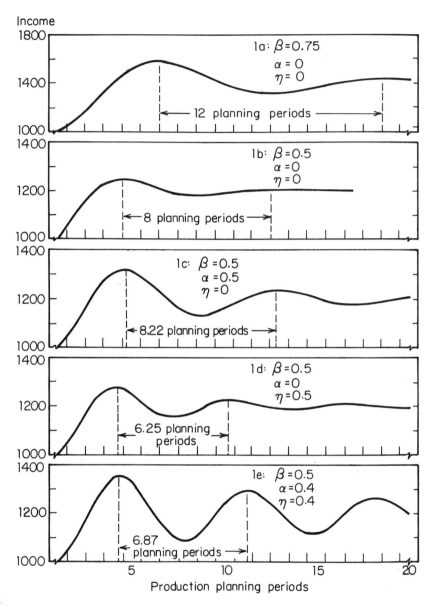

Figure 1. Cycles of income appropriate to various values of the marginal propensity to consume, β; inventory accelerator, α; and coefficient of expectations, η

to reduce them; the high point of inventory accumulation is reached when income has been reduced to its equilibrium level; (d) commodity stocks are reduced only after income has fallen below equilibrium; (e) the low point of income is reached just when stocks are reduced to a normal level; at this point, producers cease attempting to reduce stocks and output slowly rises. Thus a characteristic feature of inventory cycles is that changes in the level of inventories tend to lag one-quarter of a cycle behind changes in income produced.[6] Regardless of the intentions of producers, inventories continue to rise as long as income remains above equilibrium. Likewise, when income is below its equilibrium level, inventories always decline, even though a part of the decline is unintentional.

The second numerical example in Table 1 has the same characteristics as the first, except that the cycle is obviously shorter in duration and more highly damped. Income figures from the two examples are plotted in Figs. 1a and b. With a marginal propensity to consume of 0.75, the length of a typical cycle is twelve planning periods, whereas the length of the cycle in the second example is eight planning periods. This suggests that inventory cycles tend to be longer, the higher the marginal propensity to consume. The exact relation between the propensity to consume and the length of a typical cycle, for any value of the propensity to consume, is shown in line I of Fig. 2. We see that the length of the cycle increases quite rapidly as the marginal propensity to consume approaches unity.

It is not difficult to see why this should be the case. From the description of the cycle given above, it is apparent that, in the prosperity phase, income continues to rise as long as inventories are below their normal level. Now if the marginal propensity to consume is large, inventories are restored very slowly, for a given increase in output is accompanied by an almost equal increase in consumption. To some extent, in other words, the attempt to increase stocks is self-defeating, and the degree to which this is true is greater, the higher the marginal propensity to consume. Thus a high propensity to consume prolongs the prosperity phase of an inventory cycle by making it difficult for producers to increase their stocks.

6. It is important to bear in mind that these remarks refer to changes in the *level* of inventories, and not to changes in net inventory investment.

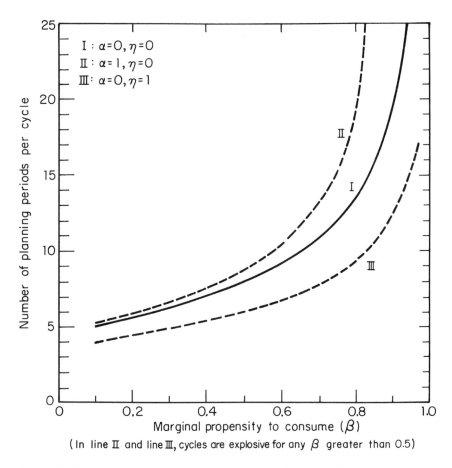

Figure 2. The marginal propensity to consume and the length of the cycle

An analogous argument is applicable to the downward phase of the cycle. Income declines as long as stocks remain above normal and, with a high marginal propensity to consume, the rate of reduction of such stocks is slow. A given reduction of output is accompanied by a substantial reduction in sales; inventories therefore remain high despite the attempts of producers to reduce them. A high marginal propensity to consume thus increases both the length and the severity of the depression phase of the cycle.

It may be useful to state these conclusions in another way. If the marginal propensity to consume is high, both the prosperity and recession phases of the inventory cycle are prolonged, and the upward and downward movements of income and employment tend to resemble the unstable cumulative movements envisaged by Wicksell. Indeed, in the extreme case where the propensity to consume is unity, the present theory cannot account for the turning points at all. In the absence of other factors, an attempt to increase inventories would lead, in this case, to a continuous upward movement, since a given increase in output would induce an equivalent increase in demand. Likewise, in the depression phase, an attempt to reduce inventories would lead to a continuous downward movement, since each reduction of output would be accompanied by a corresponding reduction of demand. In order to explain the turning points in this extreme case, it is necessary to introduce certain limiting factors which become operative only at high or low levels of output. This is essentially what Hawtrey does in his theory of the trade cycle;[7] cumulative upward or downward movements in the Hawtrey theory are reversed by changes in credit policy which alter the typical businessman's idea of what constitutes a "normal" level of inventories.

The Hawtrey theory is necessary only for extreme cases, however, for as long as the marginal propensity to consume is less than unity the turning points in the inventory cycle can be explained without recourse to limiting factors. Under such conditions, as we have seen, each prosperity phase establishes the conditions for a subsequent crisis and depression, and each depression leads to recovery. While credit contraction may accelerate the transition from prosperity to depression, it is not a necessary element in the explanation of the crisis. Nor is it necessary to account for the transition from depression to prosperity by assuming a general credit expansion. Cyclical movements are inherent in the structure of production and sales.

The Inventory Accelerator

The foregoing discussion assumes that producers attempt to maintain stocks at a constant level. In most cases it is probably more reasonable to assume that the "normal" level of inventories is related to sales in such a way that producers and dealers attempt to maintain higher stocks, the higher the level of their expected sales. This variability of

---

7. R. G. Hawtrey, *Trade and Credit* (New York, Longmans, Green, 1928), chap. 5.

normal stocks may be taken into account by means of the inventory accelerator.

The effects of such an accelerator upon a typical inventory cycle are shown in Table 2. The table differs from the second part of Table 1 only with respect to the normal level of inventories. The assumption has been made, in constructing Table 2, that producers and dealers attempt to maintain stocks equal to one-half the volume of expected sales in any given planning period; in other words, the inventory accelerator is 0.5 in Table 2, whereas in Table 1 it was zero.[8] This

Table 2. The inventory accelerator
$\beta = 0.5$; $\alpha = 0.5$; $\eta = 0$

(1) Production of consumers' goods for sale	(2) Production of consumers' goods for stocks	(3) Net noninduced investment	(4) Income produced (1) + (2) + (3)	(5) Sales	(6) Inventories at close of period
500	0	500	1000	500	250
500	0	600	1100	550	200
550	75	600	1225	612	213
612	93	600	1305	652	266
652	60	600	1312	656	322
656	6	600	1262	631	353
631	−38	600	1193	596	350
596	−52	600	1144	572	322
572	−36	600	1136	568	290
568	−6	600	1162	581	271
581	19	600	1200	600	271
600	29	600	1229	614	286
614	21	600	1235	617	304
617	4	600	1221	610	315
610	−10	600	1200	600	315
600	−15	600	1185	592	308
592	−12	600	1180	590	298
590	−3	600	1187	593	292
593	4	600	1197	599	290
599	9	600	1208	604	294

8. In accounting terminology, this means that the normal stock turnover per planning period is two. Actually, the rate of turnover probably varies with the level of output; empirical studies indicate that the normal turnover declines as output increases. This fact could easily be taken into account, in our numerical examples, by assuming a basic quantity of inventories which is independent of sales, and by assuming that intended deviations from this basic quantity depend upon expected sales.

means that in periods of rising income producers attempt not only to restore their inventory losses, but also to accumulate additional inventories appropriate to their higher sales. In the third planning period of Table 2, for example, production for stocks is 75, of which 50 are produced to restore the losses of the preceding period, while 25 are produced to bring inventories up to a level appropriate to the higher level of expected sales (550).

Figures for net income in Table 2 are plotted in Fig. 1c. When this series is compared with that shown in Fig. 1b, it is apparent that the inventory accelerator tends to increase the length of the cycle. In the present example, the fact that producers attempt to maintain inventories at one-half of expected sales leads to a cycle with a length of 8.22 planning periods, whereas in 1b, which was based upon the assumption of a constant normal level of stocks, the length of the cycle is eight periods. It is also worth noting that the inventory accelerator increases the severity as well as the length of the cycle.

The effect of the inventory accelerator upon the length of the cycle is shown in a different way by line II of Fig. 2. This line depicts the relation between the propensity to consume and the length of a typical cycle when the inventory accelerator is unity. In other words, it is based upon the assumption that producers attempt to maintain a volume of stocks just equal to their expected sales in each planning period. The inventory accelerator evidently increases the length of the cycle corresponding to any given value of the propensity to consume.

The influence of a high accelerator upon the length and severity of the cycle may be explained, as before, in terms of the relation between the change of income, the actual level of stocks, and the normal level. It is again true that income continues to rise as long as inventories remain below normal. For producers continue to increase output in an attempt to add to their depleted stocks. Now if the inventory accelerator is large, the volume of inventories which producers and dealers regard as normal is not a constant, but increases substantially as income and sales rise. In the prosperity phase of the cycle, producers and dealers attempt to increase their inventories even after such inventories have reached a level which, at a lower volume of sales, would have been considered satisfactory. Their goal is not a constant volume of stocks but a volume appropriate to their increasing sales. Under these circumstances, the time interval required to achieve a normal volume of inventories is naturally greater than it would have been with a zero accelerator. In their efforts to achieve a normal relation between inventories and sales, producers are pursuing a rising goal, and the downward phase of the cycle does not begin until this goal is reached.

Once the depression has set in, sales expectations of producers and dealers are disappointed, and inventories rise above normal. Moreover, as sales decline businessmen revise downward their estimates of a desirable volume of stocks; of course, the larger the inventory accelerator, the greater the extent of this downward revision. Thus a high inventory accelerator increases the volume of excess stocks to be worked off in the depression, just as it increases the deficiency of stocks to be made up in the prosperous phase of the cycle. These greater fluctuations in the demand for inventories inevitably increase both the duration and intensity of the cycle.

Business Expectations

Nothing has been said thus far about the role of expectations in business planning and the relation of such expectations to the inventory cycle. In the examples presented above, the assumption was always made that producers and dealers expect sales in any given period to be equal to sales in the preceding period. In other words, the coefficient of expectations was assumed to be zero. For many practical problems this is probably a reasonable assumption. Despite the emphasis which economists frequently place upon *rates of change* and their relation to business expectations, it is probable that inertia plays an important part in the formation of many production plans. The use of past sales as a guide to future production is both simple and effortless. Such a guide therefore has a strong appeal to the less venturesome and more conservative producers and dealers. For this reason, it is my belief that expectations of a short-run change have a smaller influence upon business plans than is sometimes imputed to them. Business plans show a surprising amount of conservatism even in periods of fairly rapid change.

Nevertheless, it would be a serious mistake to neglect expectations entirely and to assume, as above, that all production plans are based upon sales of the immediate past. Apart from the volume of sales, producers and dealers are also guided in making plans for the future by innumerable indicators or indexes of business trends. And one of the most important of these indexes is the rate of change of prices and sales.

It is well known that a period of expansion and rising prices tends to create expectations of further expansion, while contraction frequently engenders expectations of further contraction. The optimism or pessimism with which a producer or dealer views the immediate future is to some extent a direct function of the rate of change in his sales. Without attempting a complete analysis of the complex factors which govern business expectations, we may make a closer approach to reality by introducing a coefficient of expectations.

The coefficient of expectations has been defined as the ratio of the expected change in the volume of sales to the actual change in preceding periods. In order to isolate the effect of this coefficient upon the inventory cycle, it will be assumed in the example below that the inventory accelerator is zero; in other words, the assumption will be made that producers and dealers attempt to maintain their stocks at a constant level, a level which is independent of the volume of sales. Apart from the coefficient of expectations, Table 3 is based upon the same assumptions as the second part of Table 1. The marginal propensity to consume is 0.5, and the level of noninduced investment in the initial equilibrium is 500.

The coefficient of expectations in Table 3 is 0.5. This means that the expected change in sales between any two periods is half of the observed change between the last two planning periods. Thus when actual sales are 500 and 550 in the first and second periods respectively, production for sale in the third period is 575. Figures of income from Table 3 are plotted in Fig. 1d. A comparison of 1d with 1b shows that when business expectations are based upon the rate of change of sales, the inventory cycle tends to be shorter and sharper than would otherwise be the case. The time interval from peak to peak or from trough to trough is reduced, but the amplitude of the waves is increased. The length of the cycle in Table 3 is 6.25 planning periods, whereas the cycle depicted by 1b has a length of eight planning periods.

The effect of expectations upon the length of the cycle is shown, in a more general way, in Fig. 2. Line III shows the relation between the marginal propensity to consume and the length of the cycle when the coefficient of expectations is unity. The reduction in the length of the cycle attributable to the coefficient of expectations is simply the difference between line I and line III.

The manner in which expectations reduce the length of an inventory cycle is so obvious that it hardly requires an explanation. A positive

Table 3. The effect of expectations
$\beta = 0.5; \alpha = 0; \eta = 0.5$

(1) Production of consumers' goods for sale	(2) Production of consumers' goods for stocks	(3) Net noninduced investment	(4) Income produced (1) + (2) + (3)	(5) Sales	(6) Inventories at close of period
500	0	500	1000	500	250
500	0	600	1100	550	200
575	50	600	1225	612	213
643	37	600	1280	640	253
654	− 3	600	1251	625	279
618	− 29	600	1189	594	274
578	− 24	600	1154	577	251
569	− 1	600	1168	584	235
587	15	600	1202	601	236
609	14	600	1223	611	248
616	2	600	1218	609	257
608	− 7	600	1201	600	258
596	− 8	600	1188	594	252
591	− 2	600	1189	594	247
594	3	600	1197	598	246
600	4	600	1204	602	248
604	2	600	1206	603	251
603	− 1	600	1202	601	252
600	− 2	600	1198	599	251
598	− 1	600	1197	598	250

coefficient of expectations accelerates both the upward and the downward movement of income. In the prosperity phase of the cycle, a high coefficient of expectations means that income is forced above its equilibrium level more rapidly than would otherwise be the case. Inventories therefore accumulate more rapidly and the high point of the cycle, at which stocks have reached a normal level, is reached more quickly. The downward movement is accelerated in the same way. As sales decline, producers reduce output in anticipation of a further decline and income is quickly reduced to the point at which stocks can be reduced. In this way, the stage is set for an early revival.

The effect of business expectations on the inventory cycle is shown in Table 3 in a highly mechanical manner; the expected change of sales is always assumed to be one-half the observed change in the two preceding periods, regardless of the stage of the business cycle. It would be foolish to assert that such a mechanistic interpretation is realistic. The motives and moods of business planners are extremely complex, and no simple formulation can possibly be an accurate representation of the true situation. Expectations are subject to incessant change at all stages of the business cycle. Among other reasons, the mere fact that a given expectation is not realized is sufficient to account for a change in methods of forecasting.

Despite the complexity of the problem, however, it seems likely that the coefficient of expectations employed above gives at least a general indication of the influence of expectations on inventory cycles. For no matter how complex and varied the actual methods of forecasting may be, the broad effects of anticipations are probably similar to those indicated in Table 3. Producers as a group are clearly more optimistic about sales prospects in periods of rising sales than in periods of depression. When the economy as a whole is considered, an expansion or contraction of sales usually creates an expectation of a further expansion or contraction, even though the quantitative effects of expectations are not susceptible to the simple interpretation given above. Thus there is a strong presumption that business expectations will reduce the duration of a cycle and increase its intensity in the manner indicated.

Conclusions

Apart from the length of the production planning period, which is assumed to be given in the preceding discussion, the most important single factor governing the length of inventory cycles appears to be the marginal propensity to consume. In general, the cycle tends to be longer, the larger the propensity to consume. If the marginal propensity to consume is high, both the expansion phase and the contraction phase of the cycle are prolonged, since producers and dealers find it difficult to alter the volume of their inventories. During times of expansion in a high-consumption economy, for example, an increase of output induces a large increase of demand which, to a considerable extent, offsets the attempts of producers to restore their depleted inventories. Likewise, when income is contracting, a reduction of output leads to a substantial reduction of demand which partially frustrates producers' plans for disposing of excess stocks. Since the turning point of a cycle is not reached until inventories are normal, it is evident that a high propensity to consume increases the time interval from trough to peak and from peak to trough in a typical cycle.

The inventory accelerator and the coefficient of expectations affect the cycle in opposite ways; the former tends to lengthen the duration of the cycle, while the latter shortens it. Since little is known about the empirical values of these coefficients, it would be gratuitous to assert that the two opposite effects exactly offset each other. An offsetting tendency is apparent, however, and unless the two coefficients are quite large it may not be unreasonable to suppose that the true length of the cycle will be close to line I of Fig. 2, which assumes that both the inventory accelerator and the coefficient of expectations are zero.

The error, if any, from neglecting these coefficients is more likely to

Table 4. The combined influence of expectations and the inventory accelerator

$\beta = 0.5$; $\alpha = 0.4$; $\eta = 0.4$

(1) Production of consumers' goods for sale	(2) Production of consumers' goods for stocks	(3) Net noninduced investment	(4) Income produced (1) + (2) + (3)	(5) Sales	(6) Inventories at close of period
500	0	500	1000	500	200
500	0	600	1100	550	150
570	78	600	1248	624	174
654	88	600	1342	671	245
690	31	600	1321	660	306
656	−44	600	1212	606	312
584	−78	600	1106	553	265
531	−53	600	1078	539	204
533	9	600	1142	571	175
584	59	600	1243	621	197
641	59	600	1300	650	247
662	18	600	1280	640	287
636	−33	600	1203	601	289
585	−55	600	1130	565	254
551	−34	600	1117	559	212
557	11	600	1168	584	196
594	42	600	1236	618	214
632	39	600	1271	635	250
642	7	600	1249	628	271
625	−21	600	1204	602	273

be an overstatement of the length of the cycle than an understatement. This conclusion is corroborated in Table 4, where a hypothetical inventory cycle is developed on the assumption that both the accelerator and the coefficient of expectations have a value of 0.4. The length of this cycle, shown graphically in Fig. 1e, is 6.87 planning periods. If the coefficient of expectations and the accelerator had both been zero, the length of the cycle would have been eight planning periods.

In the construction of the numerical examples of Tables 1 to 4, it was necessary to assume that the production planning period has the same length and terminates on the same date for all businessmen. Such an assumption is obviously unrealistic. The production "season" for a commodity such as automobiles is clearly different from the season for summer clothes. Moreover, in some industries production plans are easily altered, while in others they are more or less rigidly fixed by technological considerations. In place of a single planning period, we are confronted with a whole series of planning periods, each with a different length and terminal date. While this complication destroys the simplicity of the theory of inventory cycles, it does not change its essential features. In place of concrete periods of production, the theory may be developed in terms of rates of change, the rates being dependent upon a sort of average planning period for the economy as a whole. The only indispensable assumption in the theory of inventory cycles is the assumption that businessmen do not immediately adapt their production plans to a change in sales. The inventory cycle is an inevitable consequence of this lag in output behind a change in sales.

Producers' plans and producers' expectations of future sales have been described throughout the present paper in terms of the physical volume of goods and services. The expected volume of sales in any planning period has been assumed to depend entirely upon the volume of sales in the preceding period and upon the rate at which the volume of sales is changing. Actual expectations are no doubt much more complicated than this simple procedure implies. Individual producers and individual industries are confronted not merely with a given physical volume of demand, but with a series of different volumes at different prices. In making plans for the future, we must take this price factor into account along with the physical volume of past sales.

The manner in which prices enter into producers' expectations depends upon competitive conditions in each individual industry or market. In a monopolistic market, the producer considers an expected demand schedule for his own product and chooses the volume and price which is most satisfactory in view of this expected schedule. Since marginal costs in such industries are frequently constant over a wide range of outputs, a shift in the schedule of expected demand is not likely to alter the most advantageous price unless the shift is accompanied by a substantial change in demand elasticity. In estimating the future volume of sales, a typical producer will therefore devote his attention primarily to the expected volume which corresponds to one particular price. Apart from cost changes, he will not have occasion to consider frequent changes in price policy. Thus the theory of inventory cycles is applicable principally to monopolistic or imperfectly competitive markets where prices are set by individual producers or groups of producers.

In perfectly competitive markets, such as the markets for many agricultural products, it is the expected *price* rather than the expected volume of sales which governs the individual producer's level of output. Since each producer can sell as much as he pleases at the prevailing price, his plans are naturally made with respect to price and not with respect to the amount he believes he can sell. For this reason, the theory of inventory cycles, in the form presented above, is obviously inapplicable to perfectly competitive markets. Even in a perfectly competitive economy, however, cyclical movements are associated with investment in stocks. In this case the inventories, in large part, are held by dealers and other middlemen rather than by producers, and inventory movements affect output primarily through their influence upon present and expected prices. Specifically, if the change in price at any given time is a function of both the level of stocks and the discrepancy between current output and current sales, it can be shown that a cyclical movement of prices and output very similar to the inventory cycle described in the present paper will develop whenever equilibrium is disturbed.[9] Cycles seem to be inherent in the process of inventory adjustment, regardless of whether the typical market structure is competitive or monopolistic.

In our description of inventory cycles in terms of production planning periods, no attempt has been made to determine the conditions which govern the length of a typical planning period. An accurate appraisal of this average lag between sales and output would require an extensive

9. Paul A. Samuelson, "The Stability of Equilibrium: Comparative Statics and Dynamics," *Econometrica*, 9 (April 1941), 97–120, exp. 113.

empirical investigation of individual industries as well as an interpretation of inventory figures for the economy as a whole. While such an investigation is beyond the scope of the present paper, it is possible to use the preceding results, together with a few basic facts concerning the American economy, to derive a rough estimate of the average length of the production planning period in the United States.

Statistics of income and price data for the interwar period in the United States reveal a short cycle with a length of 36 to 42 months. If this cycle is in fact an inventory cycle, it should be possible to get a general idea of the length of an average planning period by comparing the observed length of the short cycle with the number of planning periods to be expected in a typical cycle. In the period between the two world wars, the marginal propensity to consume, relative to income produced, was approximately 0.5.[10] If the length of the inventory cycle is determined largely by the propensity to consume, as suggested above, Fig. 2 shows that a typical cycle in the United States may be expected to have a length of eight planning periods. This means that eight planning periods, the length expected of the cycle, are equal to 36 to 42 months, the length of the observed cycle in the United States. It follows that the average planning period has a duration of approximately five months.

This figure is presented only as a general indication of the order of magnitude of the lag in production behind sales. It is subject to at least two important qualifications. In the first place, it makes no allowance for the influence of expectations and of the inventory accelerator upon the number of planning periods in a typical cycle; it assumes, in effect, that one of these factors offsets the other. If it were possible to make an empirical study of expectations and of the inventory accelerator, the results would probably indicate a smaller number of planning periods, relative to a given propensity to consume, than the figure given above. On the other hand, the second qualification to the preceding calculation involves an error in the opposite direction. In deriving a rough estimate of five months for the average planning period, the length of the cycle was related to the propensity to spend on consumers' goods. Since fluctuations occur in inventories of producers' goods as well as in inventories of consumers' goods, the

---

10. Paul A. Samuelson, "A Statistical Analysis of the Consumption Function," in Hansen, *Fiscal Policy and Business Cycles* (reference 2), appendix to chap. 11.

relevant propensity is not the propensity to consume, but the marginal propensity to spend on *all* goods, including investment goods as well as consumption goods. Unfortunately, it is almost impossible to derive an accurate estimate of this total propensity to spend.[11] If such a propensity were obtained, however, it would obviously be larger than the propensity to consume. Since the number of planning periods per cycle is larger, the larger the propensity to spend, it follows that failure to include investment goods in the propensity to spend involves an underestimation of the number of planning periods per cycle, and a corresponding overestimation of the average length of the planning period.

In view of these qualifications, it is apparent that an estimate of five months for the average planning period may involve a substantial margin of error. Nevertheless, as an indication of the order of magnitude of the average lag in output, it seems to be a reasonable estimate. A more accurate appraisal of business behavior from this point of view must await further empirical studies.

Appendix

The conclusions presented in the text were obtained from the solutions of a group of difference equations. Since these equations were given in my earlier paper, only a brief account of the method of derivation will be presented here.

Let $y(t)$ represent income produced in the tth planning period, and let β represent the marginal (and average) propensity to consume, relative to income produced. If sales expectations in any given period are based upon sales of the preceding period, production for sale in the tth period will be $\beta y(t-1)$, which is the actual level of sales of the $(t-1)$th period. Production for inventories may be positive or negative, depending upon the size of stocks relative to the normal level. In any case, however, inventories at the close of the $(t-1)$th period would have reached a normal level, except for the fact that actual sales during that period differed from expected sales. Hence production for stocks in the tth period is equal to the difference between actual sales and expected sales in the $(t-1)$th period; that is,

11. Cf. L. R. Klein, "Pitfalls in the Statistical Determination of the Investment Schedule," *Econometrica*, 11 (July–October 1943), 246–258.

$s(t) = \beta y(t - 1) - \beta y(t - 2)$. Combining this production for stocks with production for sales and adding the noninduced investment $v(t)$, we obtain national income of the tth period in terms of income of earlier periods, thus:

(A1) $$y(t) = 2\beta y(t - 1) - \beta y(t - 2) + v(t).$$

If $v(t)$ is subject to a single change in the first period and thereafter remains constant, as in the numerical examples, the solution of Eq. (A1) is

(A2) $$y(t) = y_o + A(\sqrt{\beta})^t \cos(\theta t + \theta_o),$$

where y_o is the new equilibrium, $\theta = \arccos \sqrt{\beta}$, and A and θ_o depend upon the initial position. Thus the system tends to oscillate about the new equilibrium, with a period of $2\pi/\theta$ and a damping factor of $\sqrt{\beta}$. Line I of Fig. 2 was derived from Eq. (A2).

If businessmen attempt to maintain a level of inventories which is a constant proportion, α, of their expected sales, production for stocks will include not only an amount sufficient to eliminate the unintended changes of the preceding period, but an additional (positive or negative) amount equal to α times the difference between expected sales in the tth and $(t - 1)$th periods. The difference equation then becomes

(A3) $$y(t) = (2 + \alpha)\beta y(t - 1) - (1 + \alpha)\beta y(t - 2) + v(t).$$

If the inventory accelerator α is sufficiently large, the income movements described by Eq. (A3) will not be cyclical. But in this case the system will be unstable, and a slight increase of income will set off a cumulative upward movement similar to the "vicious circles" envisaged by Hawtrey.[12] For the stable case, the solution of Eq. (A3) is

(A4) $$y(t) = y_o + A(\sqrt{(1 + \alpha)\beta})^t \cos(\theta t + \theta_o),$$

where $\theta = \arccos (2 + \alpha/2\sqrt{1 + \alpha})\sqrt{\beta}$. Comparing Eq. (A4) with Eq. (A2), it is evident that α increases both the period and the amplitude of a typical inventory cycle. Line II of Fig. 2 was obtained from Eq. (A4) by putting $\alpha = 1$.

In order to isolate the influence of expectations, we may assume now that the inventory accelerator is zero. If the coefficient of expectations is η, production in anticipation of sales in the tth period will be $\beta y(t - 1) + \eta[\beta y(t - 1) - \beta y(t - 2)]$. Likewise, production for stocks will be the difference between actual and expected sales in the preceding period, or $\beta y(t - 1)$

12. Hawtrey, *Trade and Credit* (reference 7), chap. 5.

$- (1 + \eta)\beta y(t - 2) + \eta\beta y(t - 3)$. Total income in the tth period is therefore given by

(A5) $\quad y(t) = (2 + \eta)\beta y(t - 1) - (1 + 2\eta)\beta y(t - 2) + \eta\beta y(t - 3) + v(t).$

Since the difference equation (A5) is more complicated than the two preceding equations, a complete solution has not been attempted. Even without a complete solution, however, a number of important characteristics of Eq. (A5) may be derived. Its auxiliary equation is

(A6) $\quad\quad\quad \lambda^3 - (2 + \eta)\beta\lambda^2 + (1 + 2\eta)\beta\lambda - \eta\beta = 0.$

While the roots of this equation may be either real or complex, in practice the equation is almost certain to have two complex roots and one real root. If both the coefficient of expectations and the propensity to consume are less than unity, for example, two of the roots are always complex. Moreover, even if the coefficient of expectations is as large as two, Eq. (A6) has two complex roots as long as the marginal propensity to consume is less than fifteen-sixteenths. Since such large coefficients are extremely unlikely, we may assume, for practical purposes, that Eq. (A6) has one real root and two complex roots.[13]

Let the complex roots be designated by r (cos $\theta \pm i$ sin θ), and let a represent the real root. With a single displacement of $v(t)$, the solution of Eq. (A5) then takes the form

(A7) $\quad\quad\quad\quad y(t) = y_o + \arccos(\theta t + \theta_o) + Ba^t,$

and the length of a typical cycle, in planning periods, is $2\pi/\theta$. In order to discuss the influence of expectations upon the length of the cycle, the theory of symmetric functions may be used to establish certain relations between the roots of Eq. (A6) and the coefficients of powers of λ, as follows:[14]

(A8)
$$a + 2r \cos \theta = (2 + \eta)\beta,$$
$$r^2 + 2ar \cos \theta = (1 + 2\eta)\beta,$$

and $\quad\quad\quad\quad\quad\quad\quad\quad\quad\quad ar^2 = \eta\beta.$

---

13. These conclusions with respect to the roots of Eq. (A6) were obtained from a consideration of the reduced equation corresponding to (A6). The reduced equation, $x^3 + px + q = 0$, has two complex roots provided $p^3/27 + q^2/4$ is positive. A sufficient but not a necessary condition for this to be true is that p shall be positive. When Eq. (A6) is written in the reduced form, it will be found that $p = \beta/3 \{3(1 + 2\eta) - (2 + \eta)^2\beta\}$. This expression is obviously positive as long as $\beta < 3(1 + 2\eta)/(2 + \eta)^2$. When $\eta = 1$, this reduces to $\beta < 1$, and when $\eta = 2$, it becomes $\beta < 15/16$.

14. See H. W. Turnbull, *Theory of Equations*, ed. 2 (New York, Interscience Publishers, 1944), p. 66. Also L. E. Dickson, *New First Course in the Theory of Equations* (New York, John Wiley and Sons, 1939), pp. 16–17.

Differentiating (A8) with respect to η, solving for $\partial\theta/\partial\eta$, and making certain obvious substitutions, we find

(A9)
$$\frac{\partial\theta}{\partial\eta} = \frac{\beta(1-\eta)\,(r-\cos\theta)}{r^2\sin\theta\{3\eta - a(2+\eta)\}}.$$

From Eq. (A6) it is easily shown that a lies between zero and η.[15] If $a < \eta$, it follows that $3\eta - a(2+\eta)$ is always positive. Moreover, from the third of equations (A8), $r^2 > \beta$. Writing k for $\cos\theta/r$ and substituting rk for $\cos\theta$ in the second of equations (A8), we find $r^2 + 2\eta\beta k = (1 + 2\eta)\beta$, or $r^2 = \beta + (1-k)2\eta\beta$. Since r^2 is known to exceed β, it follows that k must be less than unity; in other words, $\cos\theta$ must be less than r.

With these limitations upon r, $\cos\theta$, and a in mind, it is now possible to evaluate Eq. (A9). The expression $\partial\theta/\partial\eta$ is positive or negative according as the coefficient of expectations is less than or greater than unity. In economic terms, this means that the length of the inventory cycle is reduced as η is increased, *up to the point where $\eta = 1$*; thereafter a further increase in the coefficient of expectations *increases* the length of the cycle. Thus the statement in the text that the length of the cycle is reduced as η increases is valid only for coefficients of expectations less than unity. The relation of η to the length of the cycle, when η exceeds unity, was omitted from the original discussion because it was considered highly improbable that the coefficient of expectations, on the average, could be greater than unity. The influence of the coefficient of expectations upon the length of the cycle, for two different marginal propensities to consume, is shown in Fig. 3. Unless the marginal propensity to consume is low, inventory cycles tend to become unstable when η becomes large. For this reason, the region of the chart to the right of the minimum point, $\eta = 1$, probably has little practical significance.

A difference equation even more complicated than (A5) is obtained by considering a system containing both an inventory accelerator and a coefficient of expectations. If the method outlined above is used, the following equation may be derived for the movement of income in this more general case:

(A10) $\quad y(t) = [(1+\eta)(1+\alpha)+1]\beta y(t-1)$
$$- (1+2\eta)(1+\alpha)\beta y(t-2) + (1+\alpha)\eta\beta y(t-3) + v(t).$$

All of the difference equations discussed above are special cases of Eq. (A10). Equation (A1), for example, may be obtained from (A10) by giving both

---

15. If $f(\lambda) = 0$ represents Eq. (A6), then $f(0) = -\eta\beta$, which is necessarily negative, and $f(\eta) = \eta^3(1-\beta)$, which is positive. Hence the root a, for which $f(a) = 0$, must lie between 0 and η.

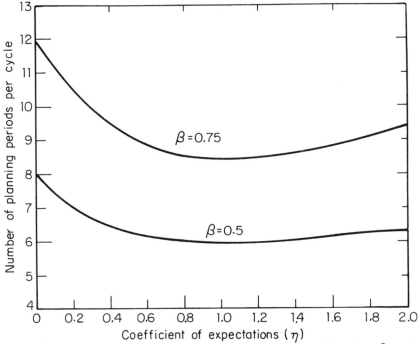

(When $\beta=0.75$, cycles are explosive for any η greater than 2/3; when $\beta=0.5$, cycles are explosive for any η greater than unity.)

Figure 3. The coefficient of expectations and the length of the cycle

α and η a value of zero. Equation (A3) is the special case of (A10) in which $\eta = 0$, while (A5) is the case in which $\alpha = 0$. The cycle shown in Fig. 1e was obtained from Eq. (A10) by giving numerical values to the coefficients and solving the resulting equation. Because of its complexity, a general solution of Eq. (A10) is omitted.

18 | Three Lags in the Circular Flow of Income

The theory of employment was first presented as a static theory of equilibrium, and this no doubt accounts for much of the confusion and controversy which occurred in its formative years. The disputes over the definitions of saving and investment, and whether the two are necessarily equal, could largely have been avoided had a more careful distinction been made at the outset between the equilibrium of income and movements about this equilibrium. In retrospect, it is perhaps surprising that the static theory should have been the source of so many differences of opinion since in another field, the field of price theory, economists were thoroughly accustomed to dealing with static relations and to distinguishing between the equilibrium itself and movements about this equilibrium. No economist, for example, would have said that the equality of purchases and sales of a particular commodity indicates that the price of that commodity is in equilibrium. And yet the equality of saving and investment over a given past period, which has no more significance in income theory than the equivalence of purchases and sales in price theory, created serious doubts as to whether the saving-investment relation could be used as a condition of equilibrium.[1]

In the end, the controversy was resolved by distinguishing between

Reprinted from *Income, Employment and Public Policy: Essays in Honor of Alvin H. Hansen* (New York, W. W. Norton, 1948), pp. 11–32. Copyright W. W. Norton, 1948.

1. See Gottfried Haberler, "Mr. Keynes' Theory of the 'Multiplier': A Methodological Criticism," *Zeitschrift für Nationalökonomie*, 7 (1936), 299–305. Reprinted in American Economic Association, *Readings in Business Cycle Theory* (Philadelphia, Blakiston, 1944), chap. 9.

actual saving and investment and the amounts which savers would like to save, and investors would like to invest, if income were maintained at the existing level over a considerable period of time. In other words, a distinction was made between actual investment and intended investment, and between actual saving and intended saving.[2] It was then found that the condition of equilibrium of income is the equality of intended saving and intended investment. If intended investment over a given period exceeds intended saving, income in subsequent periods rises; conversely, if intended saving exceeds intended investment, income falls. These conclusions may easily be demonstrated by showing how producers or income-earners react to a discrepancy between actual and intended investment, or between actual and intended savings. If intended investment exceeds intended savings, for example, the discrepancy may result from the fact that producers as a group have experienced an unforeseen reduction of inventories, and actual investment therefore has fallen short of intended investment. If so, the level of output and income in later periods will be increased, both to replace depleted stocks and to meet the higher level of demand which brought about the initial reduction of stocks.

The difference between intended saving and intended investment may, however, result from the fact that income-earners, for one reason or another, are temporarily saving a larger part of their incomes than they would if income were maintained at the present level. In this case the subsequent rise of income will be brought about by an increase of consumption, with a corresponding increase in output. Thus whatever the cause of the discrepancy, an excess of intended investment over intended saving leads to a rise of income. And conversely, it may be shown that an excess of intended saving over intended investment leads to a fall of income.

In later refinements of the theory of employment, these relations between intended and actual saving and investment were worked out by means of dynamic sequences in which lags were assumed in the circular flow of income. Although most of these sequences led to a discrepancy between intended saving and actual saving, a few of them

2. Although the Swedish economists did not use the terminology suggested above, the distinction between planned and unplanned (or intended and unintended) components of saving and investment is their principal contribution to the theory of employment. See Bertil Ohlin, "Some Notes on the Stockholm Theory of Saving and Investment: Part I and Part II," *Economic Journal*, 47 (March and June 1937), 53–69 and 221–240.

dealt, on the other side of the equation, with the relation between intended investment and actual investment. In general, the dynamic models were so highly simplified that they could not be regarded as complete theories of economic fluctuations. There can be little doubt, however, that the lags in the circular flow of income which were incorporated in these simple models will be basic features of more complicated and realistic business cycle theories of the future. An understanding of these lags, and of their relation to dynamic theories of income, is therefore a useful preliminary to the study of business cycles. To provide such an understanding is the purpose of the present paper. In the two sections which follow, a brief account is given of the principal lags in the circular flow, and of the way in which these lags have been used in dynamic theory. Finally, in the last section, statistical evidence is presented concerning the relative lengths of the principal lags.

Position of the Lags in the Circular Flow

The flow of income from business units to households, in the form of income payments to the factors of production, and back again to business units, in the form of purchases of goods and services, is a highly complicated process. If we examine it in detail, we shall find that it comprises not one or two income circuits, as sometimes assumed, but a very large number. Each circuit has distinctive characteristics of its own, particularly with respect to the length of time required to complete the flow.

In the purchase of certain services by households, for example, the income spent returns almost immediately to other households in the form of income earned in rendering such services. When income is used to buy highly fabricated goods such as automobiles, on the other hand, a considerable period of time may elapse before the sales of the automobile dealers become an equivalent amount of income for factors of production. To complete the circular flow in this latter case, the proceeds of the dealers' sales must pass through the hands of a large number of different business units. The dealers who find their sales increasing must increase their orders from automobile manufacturers, and the manufacturers in turn must increase their rate of output. In adding to their output, the manufacturers will of course increase their orders from other business units, such as steel mills. Thus the increase in retail sales is gradually translated into an increase in income payments to households through many different stages of the production process.[3]

In order to trace this flow of income in detail, we should need a new *Tableau Economique*, such as the one developed by Professor Leontief, showing how each industry's purchases from every other industry, and from households or factors of production, are related to that particular industry's level of output.[4] Dynamic studies of income and employment in the future will doubtless take the form of an elaboration and refinement of the Leontief tables. Only in this way can we expect to get a completely accurate picture of the flow of income and other money payments between factors of production and business units. At the present time, however, neither our statistical materials nor our economic theory are adequate for using the Leontief tables in business cycle studies. Leontief's technique, like that of Keynes in *The General Theory*, is essentially a static technique. While considerable progress has been made in incorporating Keynes's theory of employment into business cycle theory, the same cannot be said, as yet, of Leontief's system. It seems likely that for some time we shall have to·be content with business cycle theories which are considerably more crude and unrefined than those which will eventually be possible by elaborating Leontief's technique.

This means, in particular, that for dynamic studies of fluctuations in income and employment it may be necessary to treat all business units as a group, and not to concern ourselves too much with interfirm or interindustry purchases and sales. Although this is admittedly a drastic simplification, I believe it is justified by the fact that it enables us to concentrate our attention upon certain causes of economic fluctuations which would tend to be obscured in a more elaborate economic model. If the economy is envisaged in this simplified manner as a combination of households or factors of production, on the one hand, with business firms or productive units, on the other, the circular flow may be regarded, at least to a first approximation, as a simple flow of income pay-

3. Cf. Fritz Machlup, *International Trade and the National Income Multiplier* (Philadelphia, Blakiston, 1943), p. 1.

4. W. W. Leontief, *The Structure of American Economy, 1919–1929* (Cambridge, Mass., Harvard University Press, 1941), *passim*. esp. chap. 12. In this early version of his theory, Leontief assumed that the demand for investment goods, as well as the demand for goods-in-process, depends upon the rate of current output in each industry. In later versions, the household equation was deleted, and both household expenditures and investment expenditures were regarded as autonomous. See, for example, W. W. Leontief, "Output, Employment, Consumption and Investment," *Quarterly Journal of Economics*, 58 (February 1944), 290–314.

ments—wages, salaries, rents, dividends, and the like—from business units to households and as a reverse flow of consumption expenditures and security purchases from households to business units.

When a change occurs in the flow of income or in consumption expenditures, there are at least three points at which the transmission of this change to the rest of the economy may be temporarily stopped. Suppose, for example, that the initial change takes the form of additional income payments to the factors of production. When households receive such additional income, they will eventually increase their consumption expenditures. They may not do so immediately, however, and if not, the increase in the circular flow will be temporarily brought to a halt. This lag in consumers' expenditures behind income payments will be called a "household expenditure lag," or a "consumption lag." The principal explanation of the expenditure lag is to be found in the inertia of the average consumer. Consumers' expenditures are governed, to some extent at least, by habits or by customary standards of living, and these habits and customs are frequently difficult to alter. When income available for expenditure increases or decreases, a period of time may therefore elapse before a corresponding increase or decrease occurs in outlays for consumers' goods. In the meantime, the ratio of savings to income will have been temporarily changed.

The second important lag in the circular flow is the lag of output behind a change in the volume of sales. When the increase in income payments in the example above has been reflected in a greater demand for consumers' goods, there may still be no immediate increase in the level of production. A wholesale or retail dealer who finds his sales increasing does not immediately increase his orders by a corresponding amount. He usually waits for a while in order to be sure that the increase in demand is permanent. In the meantime, the discrepancy between sales and receipt of goods from manufacturers is offset by a decline in retail or wholesale inventories. Inertia on the part of retailers and wholesalers thus accounts for part of the lag in output behind a change in sales, but it is by no means the most important factor. Much more important is the fact that the production process itself requires time. Most manufactured goods are produced according to production schedules, and these schedules are not altered except in response to a large and sustained movement in the volume of orders from dealers. Thus, even after an increase in retail sales has been reflected in orders to manufacturers, a considerable period of time may still elapse before output is correspondingly increased. This lag in production behind sales will be called simply an "output lag."

When output is finally increased, income payments to the factors of production will normally increase as well. Wages, salaries, and other payments for services of the factors will increase as employment rises. In the case of at least one type of payment, however, there may be a considerable interval between the earning of income in the process of production and its distribution. Specifically, when business units earn higher profits as a result of expanded demand and production, they may not immediately adjust their dividend payments. This is the third important lag in the circular flow of income, and it will be referred to hereafter as an "earnings lag."

Starting with an assumed increase in income payments to the factors of production, we have considered three points in the circular flow at which the transmission of the increased money payments may be temporarily stopped or retarded. First, consumption expenditures may not respond immediately to the increase in income payments. Second, after consumption has increased, output may not be increased to meet the increase in sales; for a time, in other words, the increased level of consumption may be met from existing business inventories. Third, when output is increased, there may be a lag in the distribution of part of the income earned in production. This happens when dividend payments lag behind corporate profits. The different ways in which these lags have been incorporated into theories of income and business cycles are discussed below.

The Use of Lags in Dynamic Economics

In the development of dynamic sequences which show how income moves from one level of equilibrium to another, or how equilibrium in the circular flow is restored after a temporary disturbance, both the expenditure lag and the output lag have been widely employed. The expenditure lag is usually associated with the work of Professor D. H. Robertson, who introduced the concept of a consumption "day." Robertson defined his "day" in such a way that consumption expenditures of any given day depend upon the amount of income received in the preceding day.[5] In other words, he assumed a lag of one day in the expenditure of income behind its receipt.

---

5. D. H. Robertson, *Banking Policy and the Price Level* (London, Staples Press, 1926), p. 59.

After publication of *The General Theory*, the Robertson sequence was frequently used to depict the multiplier as the limit of a sequence of expenditures in successive income periods.[6] In these illustrative examples, the time interval was divided into consumption periods and it was assumed that all consumers plan their expenditures for a given period on the basis of the income which they received in the preceding period. In other words, a lag of one unit period was assumed in consumers' expenditures—compared with income receipts. The amount of net investment during a given expenditure period was assumed to depend upon independent influences, such as the rate of technological change and the nature of competition. National income for a given period was then computed by adding consumption expenditures of that period to investment of the same period. Thus it was implied that output of consumers' goods during a particular expenditure period is equal to sales of consumers' goods in the same period. No allowance was made, in other words, for a lag in output behind sales; if any such lag existed at all, it was either explicitly or implicitly assumed to be quite short relative to the length of the consumers' expenditure lag. The final assumption of the Robertson sequence was that income payments of a given expenditure period depend upon national income of the same period. This assumption is equivalent to stating that the lag in distribution of business profits is negligible, compared with the expenditure period.

Since the output lag is negligible in the Robertson sequence, there are no unintended increases or decreases of inventories to be taken into account. Intended investment within a particular expenditure period is equal to actual investment, and any discrepancy between intended saving and intended investment must be attributable to unintended components of saving.

The second important lag in the circular flow of income—the lag in output behind a change in sales—was first used as the basis of a dynamic sequence by Erik Lundberg. Instead of dividing the time interval into expenditure periods, as Robertson had done, Lundberg conceived a series of production planning periods.[7] He assumed that the level of

6. A few examples may be cited: (*a*) D. H. Robertson, "Some Notes on Mr. Keynes' Theory of Employment," *Quarterly Journal of Economics*, 51 (November 1936), 168–191; (*b*) Fritz Machlup, "Period Analysis and Multiplier Theory," *Quarterly Journal of Economics*, 54 (November 1939), 1–27; and (*c*) Alvin H. Hansen, *Fiscal Policy and Business Cycles* (New York, W. W. Norton, 1941), p. 273.

7. Erik Lundberg, *Studies in the Theory of Economic Expansion* (London, P. S. King, 1937), chap. 9.

output for any given planning period is determined at the beginning of the period and remains unchanged until the beginning of the next period. If sales differ from the planned level of output, the difference is assumed to be met by an appropriate adjustment of inventories. The planned level of output at the beginning of each planning period is assumed, in Lundberg's system, to be governed by the past level of sales and by requirements for inventory purposes. If business inventories are below the level which producers regard as normal, for example, planned output will include not only an amount sufficient to cover expected sales, but also an additional amount calculated to bring stocks up to a normal level. If inventories are abnormally high, on the other hand, it is assumed that producers as a group will plan to produce less than they expect to sell. Consumers' expenditures during a given planning period are assumed to depend solely upon the level of income produced, and hence upon the amount of income payments, within the same planning period. Lundberg thus assumes that both the expenditure lag and the lag in the distribution of profits are short, relative to the length of the lag in output behind a change in sales.

With the Lundberg system, it may be shown that when the equilibrium of an economy is disturbed, income always approaches its new equilibrium in a series of oscillations. This sequence has been used, in fact, as the basis for a theory of inventory cycles.[8] It is not my purpose here to discuss inventory cycles, but simply to indicate the relation of the Lundberg sequence to the saving-investment controversy.

Since consumers' expenditures within a given production planning period are assumed to depend entirely upon income produced, and income payments, of the same period, it follows that if we are looking at the components of income for any past planning period, actual saving and intended saving must be the same. That is, the amount of earnings which households and business units save during a given planning period are the same, in the Lundberg sequence, as the amounts which they would save if the given level of output and income were maintained over a longer period. From this it follows that any difference between intended saving and intended investment in a given planning period must be attributable to unintended components of investment. These unintended changes of investment take the form of movements of business

---

8. Lloyd A. Metzler, "The Nature and Stability of Inventory Cycles," which appears as Chapter 15 of the present volume.

stocks, which occur when there are discrepancies between planned production and the level of consumers' expenditures.

From the foregoing description of the Robertson and Lundberg models, it is evident that the latter is the complete converse of the former. Lundberg assumes that the time interval between receipt of income and its expenditure is short, relative to the interval between a change in sales and a change in output. Robertson, on the other hand, assumes that consumers' expenditure lags behind income, and that within a given expenditure period, output responds immediately to a change in sales. Both dynamic systems assume that the lag in the distribution of business profits is negligible. The difference between the two systems thus hinges entirely upon the length of the output lag relative to the expenditure lag.

It is obvious that neither the Robertson sequence nor the Lundberg sequence is sufficiently complex to provide anything like a complete explanation of fluctuations of income, even if the major factors in investment decisions are known. When income is rising or falling, unintended elements will normally be found in both saving and investment. Nevertheless, if one of the two major lags in the circular flow is large, relative to the other, the discrepancy between intended investment and intended saving in periods of fluctuating income may be attributable predominantly to one side or the other of the saving-investment equation. Statistical evidence concerning the size of these two lags, as well as evidence concerning the lag in the distribution of business profits, is presented in the section which follows.

Relative Lengths of the Three Lags

Although the lag in expenditures behind income payments has been widely employed in dynamic economics, few attempts have been made to determine its length empirically. This is largely attributable to the fact that most empirical expenditure studies have been divorced from dynamic economic theory. Empirical consumption functions have been investigated by one group of economists while the dynamic theory of income was being studied by another, and few attempts have been made at integration. Had economists tested their theories more carefully against statistics of income and expenditure, it seems doubtful that the expenditure lag would have survived for so long as a central feature of dynamic economics. Data for the United States, at any rate, indicate that the lag in consumption expenditure is probably insignificant, relative to the lag in output behind sales.

Most of the studies of the consumption function during the interwar period were based upon statistics of annual income and expenditures. These showed that consumers' expenditures seem to depend, without a significant lag, upon income of the current year.[9] This, of course, does not constitute a decisive proof that the lag in expenditure is insignificant, for the empirical consumption functions were based upon annual data, and monthly or quarterly figures of income and expenditures might conceivably show a different result. Even with quarterly data, however, surprisingly little evidence of a consumption lag may be found.

In Fig. 1 consumption by quarters is compared with income payments for the period 1929 to 1938. All figures are in terms of 1929 prices,

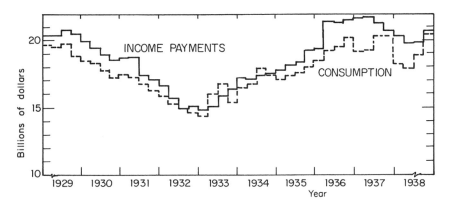

Figure 1. Consumption and income payments, 1929 to 1938

SOURCES:

(1) Consumption data are from Harold Barger, *Outlay and Income in the United States, 1921–1938*, New York, 1940, table 9, p. 93. Barger's figures, in current prices, were deflated by the Bureau of Labor Statistics index of retail prices. Since the B.L.S. index has been compiled only semiannually for some years, it was necessary to interpolate quarterly figures for these years. (See U.S. Dept. of Labor, *Changes in Cost of Living in Large Cities in the United States, 1913–41*, Bulletin No. 699, Washington, D.C., 1941.)

(2) Income payments data are U.S. Department of Commerce series for income payments, deflated by B.L.S. index of retail prices. The recent revisions which the Department of Commerce made in its statistics of national income were published too late to be included in this study, and income payments accordingly are unrevised estimates. (For revised data, see National Income Supplement to *Survey of Current Business*, July 1947.)

9. L. R. Klein, *A Macro-Economic System, U.S.A., 1921–1941* (mimeographed paper of the Cowles Commission for Research in Economics), pp. A2-A3; A. Smithies, "Forecasting Postwar Demand: I," *Econometrica*, 13 (January 1945), 4; and J. L. Mosak, "Forecasting Postwar Demand: III," *Econometrica*, 13 (January 1945), 33.

and both series are corrected for seasonal variation. The figure shows that, within a given quarter, consumption seems to be dependent largely upon income of the same quarter. In other words, the lag in consumption behind income payments is considerably less than three months. In 1929, for example, the decline in consumption occurred at the same time that income payments declined. Likewise, in 1933 the turning point at the bottom of the depression occurred in the same quarter for both consumption and income payments. Except for the beginning of the 1937–38 depression, the turning point of consumption coincided with the turning point of income payments throughout the entire period 1929 to 1938. No persistent lag in consumption is evident in the quarterly data.

The apparent absence of a consumption lag is shown in a different way in Fig. 2. The left-hand side of the figure is a scatter diagram of

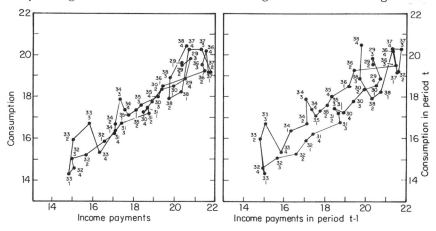

Figure 2. The relation between consumption and income payments (in billions of 1929 dollars)

SOURCES: Same as for Fig. 1.

Observations depicted are for quarters, with the quarter indicated by the small figure below the last two digits of the year.

quarterly consumption plotted against quarterly income payments, without lag. It represents the quarterly consumption function on the assumption that the lag in consumption is small, relative to a three-month period. In the right-hand side of the figure, consumption during each quarter is plotted against income payments of the preceding quarter. This would be the quarterly consumption function if one assumed that expenditures for consumption lagged one quarter behind income payments. It is apparent from the figure, however, that such an assumption is inadmissible; a much better relation is obtained from the unlagged data than from the lagged. From these figures it seems reasonable to conclude that if a lag in consumption exists, it is either short, relative to the quarterly interval, or it applies only to a small part of total consumption.

Empirically, the size of the second type of lag—the lag in output behind a change in sales—is somewhat more difficult to determine. If such a lag exists, it should be observable in the movement of business stocks. Thus, at the top of the prosperity phase of a cycle, when sales begin to decline, one should expect that output for a time would exceed sales and inventories would increase. A rise of business stocks after the close of a period of rising income is therefore prima facie evidence of a lag in output.[10] It is not conclusive evidence, however, for the increase in stocks may not be the result of business inertia but simply an *intended* increase for speculative or other reasons. No method exists for separating these intended changes in inventories from the changes which result from a temporary discrepancy between sales and output. Nevertheless it is possible to find a number of examples, in the period 1921 to 1938, when it seems highly improbable that a particular movement of inventories was an intended movement. In these cases, the best explanation of the inventory fluctuation is the presence of a lag in output behind sales.

Quarterly figures of net national product and of the total of manufacturers' and retailers' inventories are plotted in Fig. 3. Manufacturers' and retailers' inventories are here used to represent all business stocks, since comparable quarterly data for wholesale inventories are not available. The most striking example of a lag in output for the years shown in the chart is the period immediately following the downturn of 1929. Although national income began to fall in the fourth quarter of 1929, inventories continued to rise until the fourth quarter of 1930. While a small part of the rise in inventories may have been an intended increase for speculative purposes, it seems highly probable that most of the increase was a result of the failure of businessmen to adjust output to the sharp decline in sales. The year 1930 was a year of rapidly falling prices, and in this pessimistic atmosphere few businessmen could have been expected to increase their stocks in the hope of speculative gains. On the contrary, most of them would probably have been delighted to reduce

10. Similarly, a decline in business stocks at the bottom of the depression, after income has begun to rise, is evidence that producers have not adjusted their plans to the rise of sales.

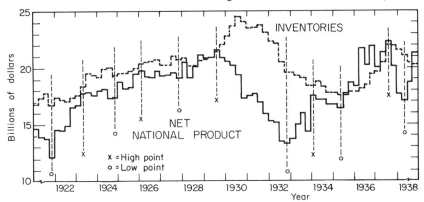

Figure 3. Manufacturers' and retailers' inventories compared with net national product (in 1929 dollars)

SOURCES:

(1) Net national product figures were derived from Harold Barger, *Outlay and Income in the United States*, table 11, pp. 114–119. Figures for net outlay (or product) in current prices were deflated by Kuznets' implicit price index interpolated from an annual to a quarterly basis.

(2) Inventory data were also derived from Barger, appendix C. Retail inventories were obtained from his table 34, p. 325. Manufacturers' inventories for the period 1929 to 1938 were obtained directly from his table 33. For the period 1921 to 1928, the Barger figures for inventories of six manufacturing groups (his table 31) were adjusted upward to agree with the Kuznets' year-end statistics by straight-line interpolations. (See Simon Kuznets, *Commodity Flow and Capital Formation*, tables 7 and 8.) The figures were then adjusted for seasonal variation by the link-relative method.

their stocks below the 1929 level. Thus the statistics for 1929 and 1930 provide strong evidence of a substantial lag in output behind sales.

Less striking but nonetheless important indications of the output lag may be found in the decade of the twenties. The rise of income which began in 1921 was brought to a temporary halt in the middle of 1923. But despite the ensuing mild depression of late 1923 and 1924, business stocks continued to increase throughout most of the year 1924. Again it seems doubtful that this was an intended increase, for the period was one of generally falling prices when business expectations must have been pessimistic. Between the second quarter of 1923 and the second quarter of 1924 the index of wholesale prices declined from 102 to 96.[11]

Other examples of the output lag may be found in Fig. 3, but the ones mentioned are sufficient to illustrate the significance of this lag.[12] It

11. U. S. Dept. of Labor, index of wholesale prices.

12. The output lag is more pronounced in the period 1921 to 1930 than in the later years of the interwar period. The absence of the lag in the decade of the thirties is probably attributable to speculation in business stocks. This matter, however, will be discussed more fully in a later paper.

is apparent from a comparison of Fig. 3 with Fig. 1 that the output lag is more pronounced than the expenditure lag. The lag in consumers' expenditures behind income payments cannot be discerned in the quarterly data whereas the lag in output behind sales is strongly indicated, if not decisively demonstrated, by quarterly statistics of net national product and inventories. Although wholesale inventory statistics, if available, might alter the results somewhat, it is doubtful that they would completely change the picture presented in Fig. 3, for the changes in wholesale inventories are small, relative to the changes in all business inventories.[13] The combination of retail and manufacturers' inventories shown in Fig. 3 comprises the predominant part of business stocks.

Empirical evidence concerning the third lag in the circular flow—the lag in the distribution of profits—is difficult to obtain, since several of the statistical series necessary for this purpose have not been published. Data for dividend payments, for example, are available only on an annual basis. Even more serious is the lack of information regarding the disposition of the profits of unincorporated business units; in the Department of Commerce statistics of noncorporate profits, no distinction is made between the total amount of such profits and the amounts withdrawn as personal income by entrepreneurs. With these gaps in our information, it is obviously impossible to determine by direct means whether the distribution of business profits lags behind their earning. It will be necessary instead to present partial information, and to infer from other information whether the lag is likely to be an important factor in the circular flow of income.

Consider first the relation between profits and the distribution of profits for the incorporated part of the economy. Corporate profits and dividend payments, on an annual basis, are presented in Fig. 4 for the years 1929 to 1938. Although the time interval for these data (one year) is too long to reveal accurately the relation in which we are interested, the figure nevertheless contains some evidence of a lag in dividend payments behind corporate profits. At the bottom of the depression, for example, the low point of corporate profits occurred in 1932, whereas the low point of dividend payments occurred in 1933. Except for the bottom of the depression, however, the turning point of dividend pay-

13. Annual figures for changes in wholesale, retail, and manufacturers' inventories may be derived from Harold Barger's *Outlay and Income in the United States, 1921–38* (New York, National Bureau of Economic Research, 1940), table 34 of appendix C. These figures show that in the years when the movements of total inventories were substantial, the change of wholesale inventories constituted 10 to 25 percent of the change in all business inventories.

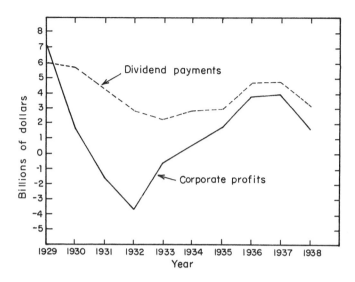

Figure 4. Corporate profits and dividends

SOURCE: U.S. Department of Commerce national income statistics, reprinted in the *Federal Reserve Bulletin*. As in Fig. 1, the statistics used in this figure are unrevised data.

ments appears to coincide with the turning point of profits, at least so far as these turning points are revealed by the annual data. This, of course, does not preclude the possibility that a lag may be present that is obscured in the annual data.

Much more significant than the suggestion of a lag is the picture which the figure presents of the stabilizing influence of dividend payments. Quite apart from the lag, the cyclical fluctuations of dividend payments are decidely smaller than the fluctuations of corporate profits. This means that in periods of rising or falling income a part of the increase or decrease in the value of total output is not passed on in the form of income to households, but is permanently absorbed by business units. Between 1929 and 1932, for example, corporate profits declined from $7.2 billion to $ −3.6 billion, a total decline of $10.8 billion. The decline of dividend payments, by contrast, was $3.7 billion, or slightly more than one-third of the decline in profits. In the subsequent economic expansion of 1932 to 1937, the increase in corporate profits was approximately $7.6 billion, compared with an increase of $2.6 billion in dividend payments.

In view of the small amplitude of fluctuations in dividend payments, relative to fluctuations of corporate profits, the exact length of the lag in dividend payments is perhaps not a matter of great importance. Since a large part of the fluctuations in corporate profits are never reflected in income payments to households, slight changes in the timing of the relatively smaller fluctuations in dividend payments will probably not have an appreciable effect upon the circular flow of income. In other words, the propensity of corporations to save is a more important regulator of the circular flow of income than the lag in dividend payments. This means that the error from ignoring the lag in dividend payments will probably be small, and that for certain problems of business cycles, dividends—along with other income payments—may conveniently be regarded as depending upon the current level of output. Whether this is also true of the distribution of noncorporate profits can be determined only when additional data are available.

Conclusions

The principal conclusion to be drawn from the preceding discussion is that the lag in consumers' expenditures is short, relative to the lag in output. Although some evidence of a lag in dividend payments is apparent in addition to the output lag, the influence of this earnings lag on the circular flow is reduced by the high propensity of business units to save. These results mean that if one examines the saving and investment components of national income during periods of fluctuating income and employment, the discrepancy between intended saving and intended investment will usually be found to be caused largely by unintended changes in investment, rather than by unintended changes in saving. In other words, it seems probable that unforeseen or unexpected changes in business inventories are the principal factor which equalizes actual saving and actual investment in periods when the discrepancies between intended saving and intended investment are large.

If this conclusion is correct, a reconsideration of dynamic economic systems in which unintended saving plays a dominant part would seem to be in order. Such systems do not appear to be in accord with the facts of American economic life. While no simple dynamic system, such as the Robertson or Lundberg sequence, can ever be an accurate representation of the complex events which comprise business cycles, the statistics presented above suggest that the Lundberg sequence is probably more realistic, as a first approximation, than the sequence which depends upon a lag in consumption. In other words, the consumption "day," which played such a prominent part in early explanations of the multiplier, is not, from an empirical point of view, a particularly useful concept.

The fact that the household-expenditure lag is short, relative to the lag in output, is important from the point of view of business cycle theory, for it provides an empirical foundation for the theory of inventory cycles. With a circular flow mechanism such as that postulated by Lundberg, it is easily shown that disturbances in the level of income create a series of cycles of diminishing amplitude. These cycles are inherent in the structure of production and sales, and for this reason might be regarded in the traditional way as endogenous cycles. Although they depend upon an initial impulse or disturbance to get them started, they are self-propagating once they are started. In the years since the presentation of the theory of employment, there has been a tendency to neglect such self-propagating or internal cycles, and to assume, for the most part, that observed movements of income represent a sort of moving equilibrium defined by the propensity to consume and the amount of autonomous investment. With this conception, the important determinant of economic fluctuations is the movement of autonomous investment; fluctuations of income are simply an expanded reflection of the change in the basic investment series, or the marginal efficiency of capital.

Although it is no doubt true that changes of long-run investment account for the major fluctuations of economic activity, considerable evidence is accumulating to suggest that the shorter and less violent fluctuations may be internal or endogenous cycles. If so, the output lag discussed above assumes an increasing importance, for it is the basis of at least one theory of short-run fluctuations.

19 | Business Cycles and the Theory of Employment

The theory of employment and income, which explains the level of total output in terms of investment and consumption, is generally regarded as a static theory. It is widely believed that the propensity to consume and the level of investment provide a broad explanation of the *level* of total economic activity achieved by an economy in equilibrium, but do not account for *fluctuations* in such activity.[1] In the study of cumulative processes of expansion and contraction—prosperity and depression—most economists feel that the popular discussion of savings and investment must be supplemented by other methods of investigation. When prices and production are rising or falling, for example, the effects of changing expectations upon the output decisions of businessmen must be taken into account. This means, among other things, that the rates of change of prices and sales are important factors in the volume of total production.

The Propensity to Consume in Business Cycle Theory

The "multiplier" explanation of output and employment has frequently been criticized on the ground that it neglects the dynamic

---

Reprinted from *American Economic Review*, 36 (June 1946), 278–291. Copyright American Economic Association, 1946.

---

1. See, e.g., Gottfried Haberler, *Prosperity and Depression*, ed. 3 (Geneva, League of Nations, 1941), p. 168.

aspects of economic activity.[2] To some extent the criticism is probably justified, for much of the present analysis of income and employment consists simply of static supply-and-demand relations. Nevertheless, in concentrating on the static character of the multiplier, it is easy to lose sight of the fact that the basis of this multiplier—the marginal propensity to consume—not only provides a static explanation of the equilibrium level of employment but also supplies the framework for important extensions of the theory of business fluctuations. In other words, the development of the static theory of employment has been accompanied by corresponding changes in the theory of business cycles.

The changes in business cycle theory are of two sorts. First, the modern theory of employment establishes a definition of a norm about which the economic system fluctuates: at any given time, the equilibrium level of income is the level at which intended savings are equal to intended noninduced investment. Business cycles consist simply of fluctuations about this norm or equilibrium. It is true, of course, that this definition of equilibrium presents a number of serious statistical problems. Difficulties arise, for example, in distinguishing between induced and non-induced investment. Despite the statistical problems, however, the establishment of a conceptual normal level of activity constitutes an important advance in the theory of economic fluctuations. In the absence of this norm, it was previously necessary either to rely upon purely empirical concepts of equilibrium or to assume that the system tends automatically toward full employment and that any deviation from full employment is therefore an evidence of disequilibrium.

Both of these alternatives are clearly inadequate. The first is inadequate because the usual empirical distinction between secular trend and cyclical fluctuations about the trend cannot be justified without an explanation of the trend itself; a mere fitting of a curve by "least squares" or other methods does not suffice to establish the nature of the

2. Much of the criticism resulted from the fact that no distinction was made, in the theory expounded by Lord Keynes, between intended and unintended components of savings and investment. As a result of this lack of precision, the theory that the level of income is determined by the condition that savings shall be equal to investment seemed either false or tautological when applied to dynamic problems. See Haberler, reference 1, chap. 8; Fritz Machlup, "Period Analysis and Multiplier Theory," *Quarterly Journal of Economics*, 54 (November 1939), 1–27; and Friedrich A. Lutz, "The Outcome of the Saving-Investment Discussion," *Quarterly Journal of Economics*, 52 (August 1938), 588–614.

trend movements.[3] The second alternative—a norm of full employment —is inadequate because it is now clear that income may be in equilibrium at a level of output considerably below full employment. The theory of income and employment, by providing a concept of an equilibrium level of employment, thus fills a serious gap in the study of business cycles.

The second important contribution of the theory of employment to business cycle analysis is in the explanation of turning points of the cycle. Prior to development of the concepts of propensity to consume and propensity to save, an explanation of these turning points was perhaps the most difficult task of business cycle analysis. Traditional theory usually assumed that the economic system is inherently unstable in the sense that a slight upward or downward movement of income and employment tends to initiate a cumulative and self-reinforcing process of expansion or contraction. In other words, it was commonly believed that an initial increase of income, employment, and prices would stimulate a further increase, and that income would continue to rise at an accelerated rate until the limits of possible expansion were reached, or until some outside force put a stop to the cumulative process.[4] The converse of this argument is, of course, that a slight downward movement is also self-aggravating, and that a depression, once started, tends to continue until some factor or factors which operate only at low levels of employment reverse the movement.

Traditional business cycle theory thus conceived of the economic world as a world subject to cumulative upward and downward movements as a result of relatively small disturbances. From this conception, it followed that an explanation of the cycle was to be found in the factors which reverse the direction of the cumulative movement. Once a process of expansion or contraction was started, it was widely believed that an explanation of further movements in the same direction was relatively

3. Edwin Frickey, "The Problem of Secular Trend," *Review of Economics and Statistics*, 16 (October 1934), 199–206.

4. The classic example of such an unstable economy is given by Wicksell, in his description of the cumulative change in prices which results from a discrepancy between the real rate of interest and the bank rate. See Knut Wicksell, *Interest and Prices*, transl. R. F. Kahn (London, Macmillan for the Royal Economic Society, 1936), chap. 9. While the cumulative process envisaged by Wicksell is a movement of prices and not of output or employment, unstable systems involving output may also be found in the writings of nineteenth-century economists. See, for example, the discussion by Pigou of a quotation from Walter Bagehot's *Lombard Street* (London, J. Murray, 1927), in which Bagehot argues that·a decline in output in one industry spreads through other industries in a self-reinforcing sequence of reduced demands. (A. C. Pigou, *Employment and Equilibrium* (London, Macmillan, 1941), p. 236).

simple. In an expansion process, for example, the rise of income was believed to be reinforced by optimistic expectations as well as by the effect of higher demand upon the output of investment goods (the acceleration principle). And since Say's Law (supply creates its own demand) was generally accepted, it was difficult to see how producers' expectations, in the aggregate, could be disappointed. While particular industries might suffer from overproduction, this would be offset by increased demand in other industries. The cumulative movement of income and prices was thus regarded as an obvious process; the real difficulty lay in an explanation of the turning points.[5]

To explain how a process of expansion is stopped and a depression initiated, economists usually introduced certain limiting factors which become operative only at high levels of economic activity. It was frequently asserted, for example, that a period of prosperity and rising income is brought to a close by the inability of the banking system to make additional loans. Faced with a declining reserve ratio as a result of previous loans and as a result of cash drains to support a higher volume of transactions, the banks become reluctant to make further loans. Interest rates rise and a period of credit contraction ensues. By reducing the level of total demand for goods, this credit contraction brings all of the forces of cumulative contraction into play, and the level of output declines. Thus, according to this view, the immediate cause of the crisis was the inflexibility of the banking system. Alternatively, the cause of the downturn was frequently found in a shortage of certain factors of production which made a continuation of the expansion process impossible. If the rise of output in certain segments of the economy were brought to a halt through the appearance of bottlenecks, it was widely believed that this would lead to a decline in total output through the operation of the acceleration principle.

At the other turning point, when depression ends and a revival begins, economists were much less certain about the immediate cause of revival. In some cases, the upturn was attributed to a resumption of investment activity induced by an accumulated shortage of equipment. In other cases, more liberal lending policies by the banking system were believed to be the immediate cause of recovery. And in still other cases, the revival was attributed simply to a return of business confidence and to more optimistic expectations in general. But whatever the immediate

5. Cf. Jan Tinbergen, "Econometric Business Cycle Research," *Review of Economic Studies,* 7 (February 1940), 73–90.

cause of revival, the important fact is that in traditional business cycle theory it was thought to be necessary to introduce limiting factors which brought the period of cumulative contraction to a close.

Like all brief generalizations, this explanation of traditional business cycle theory is no doubt an oversimplification. The problem is so complex, and the explanations which have been given for the cycle are so numerous, that no short summary could possibly be complete.[6] For this reason, the foregoing discussion is not to be interpreted as a summary of traditional theory. It is intended, rather, to point out one feature which most theories had in common: *the failure to develop explicitly the relation between consumption and income frequently gave an exaggerated appearance of instability to the economic system.* This led to a preoccupation with the causes of the turning points of the cycle, and to the introduction of limiting economic forces which were assumed to be operative only in periods of high prosperity or extreme depression.[7] Thus the acceptance of Say's Law, either explicitly or by implication, frequently disguised the structural nature of cycles, and created the impression that the turning points resulted largely from special factors.

From this point of view, explicit recognition of the relation between income and consumption was an important development. When the concept of a propensity to consume was introduced, the economic system was recognized as an essentially stable system which is subject to more or less regular oscillations about a moving equilibrium. The turning points of these cyclical oscillations were then frequently found to be no more difficult to explain than the cumulative processes of expansion and contraction. In other words, the entire cyclical process was recognized as a process of adjustment to irregular disturbances of the system. The turning points of the cycles, like the periods of expansion and con-

6. One of the best summaries of the state of business cycle theory prior to the development of the theory of employment may be found in Alvin H. Hansen, *Business Cycle Theory* (Boston, Ginn, 1927), chap. 8. Professor Hansen pointed out that despite the diversity of opinion concerning business cycles, there was a fair amount of agreement with respect to three points: (*a*) the factors instigating an expansion or contraction; (*b*) the nature of the cumulative process; and (*c*) the self-limitation of expansion or contraction. The most controversial and least convincing arguments in this summary were those advanced in explanation of the turning points, which were essentially the same as those mentioned in the text above.

7. An important exception to this statement must be made for the theory of Joseph A. Schumpeter in his *Business Cycles*, ed. 1 (New York, McGraw-Hill, 1939), vol. 1. Professor Schumpeter repeatedly emphasizes the significance of the norm about which the economy fluctuates and holds that, when this norm is clearly defined, the turning points require no special explanation. His conception of a normal level of activity differs from the one accepted in this paper, however, in that it assumes full employment, apart from monopolistic restrictions.

traction, were seen to be inherent in the structure of the system and were no longer regarded as dependent upon limiting factors such as an inflexible banking system or the appearance of bottlenecks.[8]

This does not imply, of course, that cyclical movements of income and employment are the result of a single cause, or that a single cyclical movement can be isolated as "the" business cycle. On the contrary, most recent studies of business cycles have emphasized the complexity of the actual economic system and have shown that oscillations of income about equilibrium may consist in a number of cycles of different lengths superimposed upon one another. Individual cycles have been attributed, for example, to the demand for producers' equipment, to the demand for housing, and to the demand for inventories.

All of these cycles were known in a general way before the theory of income and employment had been developed. Nevertheless, a clear understanding of the nature of the cyclical processes was not obtained until the theory of employment provided a concept of equilibrium. Prior to that time, it was usually found that the derived demand for such things as producers' equipment and inventories provided theories of unstable or cumulative processes, but not of cyclical movements. Turning points in these processes could be explained only by introducing new factors. Development of the theory of employment changed all this by showing, first, that the economic system is probably a stable system, and, second, that cyclical movements of income, employment, and prices are inherent in the nature of the system, and do not depend upon special circumstances.

The importance of the theory of employment in business cycle analysis is well illustrated by changes in the theory of inventory cycles. I turn now to a consideration of these developments.

The Theory of Inventory Cycles

In the period which preceded the development of the theory of employment, the most extensive discussion of inventory cycles was that

8. See, for example, the discussion of the acceleration principle by Ragnar Frisch, "The Interrelation between Capital Production and Consumer-Taking," *Journal of Political Economy*, 39 (October 1931), 646–654; and J. M. Clark, "Capital Production and Consumer-Taking—A Reply," *Journal of Political Economy*, 39 (December 1931), 814–816. The advance in business cycle theory brought about by the theory of employment is clearly seen by comparing these earlier writings with later work on the same subject, such as that of Paul A. Samuelson, "A Synthesis of the Principle of Acceleration and the Multiplier," *Journal of Political Economy*, 47 (December 1939), 786–797. See also R. F. Harrod, *The Trade Cycle* (Oxford, Clarendon Press, 1939).

of R. G. Hawtrey. It is well known that Hawtrey regards the attempts of businessmen to increase or decrease their inventories as the principal cause of economic expansion and contraction. In this respect, his analysis of business cycles differs from that of most other economists, who usually consider inventory fluctuation as one among many such causes. Nevertheless, from one point of view, the Hawtrey analysis is typical of the business cycle studies which preceded the theory of employment: his is essentially a theory of cumulative processes of expansion and contraction, and the turning points in these cumulative processes depend upon certain limiting factors which become operative only in periods of high prosperity or deep depression.

The essential feature of the Hawtrey theory is a slightly qualified acceptance of Say's Law. In one explanation of his theory, he says:

> The money of which demand consists is provided directly or indirectly from people's incomes. The total of the incomes which people in any community have to spend I call the *consumers' income*; the total which they do spend I call the *consumers' outlay*. Consumers' income and consumers' outlay tend to be equal. The means of payment (comprising money and bank credit), which people have on hand, I call the *unspent margin*. Consumers' income and consumers' outlay can only differ in amount when the unspent margin changes.
>
> The term consumer as here used must not be interpreted too narrowly. People spend their incomes not only on consumable products, but on investment. "Consumer" must be regarded as including "investor" and the consumers' outlay as including investment. For money invested is *spent*. It is spent on capital goods.[9]

With this conception of total demand, it is easy to see how a small disturbance may start a cumulative process of expansion or contraction. Suppose, for example, that businessmen decide to increase their inventories. In order to do so, they must produce more than they expect to sell. But in expanding output, businessmen also expand income by the same amount. Hawtrey argues that this increase of income is either spent on consumption or saved, and that most, if not all, of the added savings constitute a demand for capital goods. Considering both the demand for investment goods and the demand for consumers' goods, total demand therefore increases *pari passu* with the increase of income. As a result, producers find that their attempt to increase inventories has

9. R. G. Hawtrey, *Trade and Credit* (New York, Longmans, Green, 1928), pp. 83–84.

been frustrated by a corresponding increase in demand. Their subsequent production plans include not only a level of output sufficient to satisfy the higher demand, but also an additional output for inventories. Again, however, demand is increased by the higher level of output, and inventories remain low despite attempts of businessmen to increase them. Thus a cumulative process of expansion is set in motion, and continues as long as businessmen attempt to increase their inventories.

A similar argument is applicable to the process of contraction. When businessmen attempt to reduce inventories by producing less than they expect to sell, they find that their total sales are correspondingly reduced and inventories remain unchanged. "The dealers want to diminish their stocks of goods, but, when they restrict the orders they give to producers, the consumers' outlay falls off, and their sales are so reduced that their stocks are little diminished."[10]

Acceptance of Say's Law thus leads to a conception of the economy as an unstable system in which a slight contraction leads to further contraction, and a slight expansion sets off a cumulative upward movement. Hawtrey's theory is less extreme than this, for he allows total demand to differ from total output to the extent that there is a change in the unspent margin. When production and income are increasing, this means that the increase in demand is slightly less than the increase in the value of output, since a small part of the new income will be added to idle balances. In discussing the effects of expansion, Hawtrey says:

A little of the [added] money would remain behind in balances, for a man whose earnings are increased would hold on the average somewhat larger amounts of cash in hand than before; but probably much the greater part of the additional income is immediately in one way or another spent. . . .

The net effect in increasing stocks will [therefore] be limited to so much of this income as is kept in hand by the recipients in balances.[11]

An increase in unspent balances constitutes a leakage from the stream of income, and if carried to its logical end, analysis of this leakage might, with modifications, lead to a theory of inventory cycles which does not differ substantially from the present theory. Despite this fact, it is obvious from his writings that Hawtrey envisaged an unstable system. At one point, in fact, he speaks of the credit system as "inherently unstable." And throughout his writings he discusses "vicious

10. *Ibid.*, p. 93.
11. *Ibid.*, pp. 91–92.

circles" of expansion and contraction. In Hawtrey's opinion, these periods of expansion and contraction are brought to a close by changes in the credit policy of the banking system. During a period of rising income and prices, the banks find their cash reserves diminished both by an increase in deposits and by a drain of cash into circulation. Hawtrey argues that sooner or later the reduction of their reserves forces the banks to restrict credit. This means, among other things, that interest rates tend to rise, and with higher interest rates the carrying costs of inventories are considerably increased. Traders attempt to economize by reducing their inventories and, as a result, the cumulative process of contraction described above is set in motion. During the period of contraction, debts are gradually liquidated, bank deposits are reduced, and cash flows back into the banks as a consequence of the decline in income and prices. Eventually the increased liquidity of the banking system leads to lower interest rates and to more liberal lending policies in general. Finding their carrying costs reduced, traders decide to hold more inventories, and a period of economic expansion ensues.

The foregoing description of Hawtrey's theory of inventory cycles is intended primarily to emphasize the assumption of instability which is inherent in this theory. Hawtrey envisages an economic world in which a slight expansion or contraction leads to further expansion or contraction in a cumulative process which is reversed only by the action of the banking system. In discussing the end of a period of prosperity, he says: "If the restriction of credit did not occur, the active phase of the trade cycle could be indefinitely prolonged, at the cost, no doubt, of an indefinite rise of prices and an abandonment of the gold standard."[12]

This point of view, as noted earlier, is a logical consequence of Say's Law of Markets. If the proposition is accepted that supply creates its own demand, which means that savings constitute a demand for capital goods, then it is obvious that production cannot outrun demand, for any increase in output will be accompanied by a corresponding increase in demand. It follows that any attempt by businessmen to increase their inventories must lead to a cumulative process of expansion, while every attempt to reduce inventories must result in cumulative contraction. Thus Hawtrey's theory of inventory cycles is intimately connected with the classical proposition that general overproduction is impossible.

It is hardly necessary to point out that Say's Law of Markets is no

12. *Ibid.*, p. 98.

longer a widely accepted economic doctrine. One of the principal achievements of the theory of income and employment was to emphasize that savings do not constitute a demand for capital goods; in large part, they constitute a demand for legal evidences of wealth, such as stocks, bonds, and savings accounts. A substantial portion of the demand for investment goods comes from businessmen and is not directly related to the level of income. It is therefore entirely possible, indeed at most times probable, that an increase in total output will increase the total supply of goods more than it increases total demand; some of the increased income will be used in the purchase of previously existing assets and will not represent a demand for currently produced goods. Hence general overproduction is a possibility which must be taken into account.

If Say's Law of Markets is rejected, what happens to the theory of inventory cycles presented above? A partial answer to this question may be found in an earlier paper, in which I developed a simple theory of inventory cycles based upon the theory of employment.[13] The assumptions in that paper with respect to the behavior of businessmen were very similar to those of Hawtrey. It was assumed, for example, that businessmen make production plans in anticipation of future sales, and that anticipated sales depend partly upon the present level of sales and partly upon the rate of change of such sales. It was assumed further that the amount of inventories which businessmen desire to hold is related to the level of their sales. The theory of inventory cycles which I developed differs from Hawtrey's theory primarily in its rejection of Say's Law. In place of the proposition that supply creates its own demand, I substituted the proposition that only a part of total demand is directly related to the level of income. In other words, it was assumed that income-receivers use part, but not all, of their increments of income in the purchase of commodities, and that income which is used to purchase legal evidences of wealth does not represent a demand for current output.

To simplify the discussion, I divided the interval of time under consideration into "production planning periods;" I assumed that the rate of output in each planning period is determined at the beginning of the period and remains unchanged until the beginning of the next period. The economy was divided into consumers'-goods industries and

---

13. Lloyd A. Metzler, "The Nature and Stability of Inventory Cycles," which appears as Chapter 15 of the present volume.

investment-goods industries, and it was postulated that within any given planning period the demand for consumers' goods depends upon the level of total output during that period. Finally, the assumption was made that the demand for all investment goods is autonomous, in the sense that it is taken as a given factor in the situation, independent of the level of income. This last assumption is obviously not necessary, since the induced demand for investment goods may be included with the demand for consumers' goods in a general "propensity to spend." Nevertheless, it will simplify the subsequent analysis without altering the final results if we retain the assumption that all investment (except inventory investment) is noninduced or autonomous.

With these assumptions, it is possible to follow through the sequence of events in a typical inventory cycle. Suppose that the economy is initially in equilibrium, in the sense that the total output of goods and services is equal to the total demand for such goods and services. Consider what happens when this equilibrium is disturbed by an increase in the demand for and supply of noninduced investment. Although equilibrium is reestablished in the investment industries (since demand and supply increase in the same proportion), producers of consumers' goods find their stocks depleted by the increase of income and demand. This is characteristic of the early prosperity phase of an inventory cycle; producers are unable to adjust their output immediately to the increase in demand, and stocks therefore decline. In subsequent periods, production plans are revised upward, for two reasons: to meet the anticipated higher level of demand, and to replenish depleted inventories. As output is increased, total demand also rises, and businessmen find that their stocks remain abnormally low despite their efforts to increase them.

Up to this point, the description of inventory cycles closely resembles Hawtrey's theory; the rise of income and employment induced by the attempts of businessmen to expand their inventories has much in common with the cumulative expansion envisaged by Hawtrey. Nevertheless, there is an important difference between the two theories: Hawtrey assumes that in the absence of outside influences the cumulative expansion could continue indefinitely, whereas in the present theory the expansion itself sets up conditions which make a later decline inevitable. It is true that as income rises, total demand also rises; but the increase in the latter is smaller than the increase of total output. Inventories therefore begin to accumulate slowly, although actual additions to stocks are smaller than producers intend them to be. Even when income has risen to a level appropriate to the new level of noninduced investment, however, inventories remain abnormally low. This means that total income must rise still further, since businessmen attempt not only to produce enough to satisfy the higher demand at the new equilibrium, but also to produce an additional amount for replenishing their depleted inventories. In other words, in the process of expansion from the old equilibrium to the new, output and employment inevitably "overshoot the mark."

Once the level of income has risen above its new equilibrium, a subsequent decline is inevitable. The inflated level of income is sustained and increased only by investment in inventories, and such investment cannot be continued indefinitely. As income rises, inventories also rise, and this process continues until a normal relation between inventories and expected sales is established. Thereafter, businessmen plan no further increases in stocks; they attempt, instead, to produce only what they expect to sell. Since production plans in earlier periods included production for stocks as well as for sale, the decision to produce only for sale means an absolute decline in total output. As a result, income in the hands of consumers declines, sales are reduced, and a period of general contraction develops. The contraction is accelerated by the fact that sales fall below expectations, since this causes inventories to become abnormally large and businessmen therefore reduce output still further in an attempt to restore their stocks to a normal level.

In the early stages of depression, inventories continue to rise despite attempts to reduce them. In other words, the contraction of output is more than offset by an induced contraction of sales. For a time, the attempt to reduce inventories is self-defeating, serving merely to accelerate the downward movement of output and income. When output and employment have declined to the normal or equilibrium level at which savings are equal to autonomous investment, commodity stocks are still abnormally high. A further decline is inevitable, since businessmen will continue to reduce output in an attempt to dispose of their excess stocks. Thus income falls below equilibrium in the downward phase of an inventory cycle, just as it rose above equilibrium in the prosperity phase.

The downward movement cannot continue indefinitely, however, for eventually businessmen will succeed in reducing their stocks. To explain why this is true, let us refer again to the static theory of employment. The fact that income-receivers spend only part of their incomes means that, as output declines, the induced reduction of sales is smaller in absolute amount than the decline of output. Inventories are slowly reduced, and in subsequent periods the gap between production plans and expected sales is correspondingly narrowed. In other words, when businessmen find their stocks declining, they are relieved of the necessity of planning large stock reductions in the future and can make their production plans more nearly in accord with what they expect to sell. Income continues to fall, since further reduction of stocks is still considered desirable, but the *rate* of decline is arrested.

The downward movement continues, at a reduced rate, until inventories have fallen to their normal level, in relation to sales. At this point businessmen plan no further reductions in stocks. Since production is now equal to expected sales, whereas in earlier periods it was less than sales, it follows that income must begin to rise. Thus the mere fact that inventories have fallen to a normal level is sufficient to account for a turning point in the cycle from depression to recovery.

The cycle is now complete. I have explained how the prosperity phase of an inventory cycle inevitably leads to a crisis and to depression, and how the depression must be followed by a period of prosperity. The self-perpetuating character of such cycles is thus established. When the equilibrium of income is disturbed, output and employment tend to fluctuate about a new equilibrium in a series of damped cycles. In describing these cycles, we have said nothing about the influence of the banking system or of other limiting factors. The turning points of the cycle do not depend upon such things as changes in credit policy or bottlenecks in the supply of resources. In the prosperity phase of the cycle, for example, it is not necessary to assume a policy of credit restriction in order to show how prosperity leads to a crisis and to depression. The crisis is inherent in the nature of the expansion process, since this process invariably raises output above the stationary or equilibrium level. An analogous argument holds for the depression phase of the cycle. As income falls below equilibrium, inventories are gradually reduced, and this is sufficient to account for a revival, quite apart from changes in bank policy or in the supply of resources.

Thus the cycles described above are distinguished from Hawtrey's inventory cycles primarily by the nature of their turning points. Inventory cycles in the present theory are inherent in the structure of production and sales, whereas Hawtrey envisages the turning points as a result of credit policies and cost changes which become operative only in the extremes of prosperity and depression. The present theory can easily account for mild but persistent fluctuations of income about a moving equilibrium, even with no changes in credit policy, wage policy, or conditions of employment. By contrast, the Hawtrey theory speaks of "vicious circles" of expansion and contraction, which can be reversed only by the influence of limiting factors. In Hawtrey's theory, the length of a period of expansion is governed largely by the flexibility of the banking system and by the extent of unemployment when the expansion begins; the expansion is not brought to a close until the banks are forced to restrict credit. In the present theory, on the other hand, it is necessary to explain the length of the average cycle in terms of factors which are a part of the process of production and sales. While changes in banking policy may play some part in the turning points of the cycle, much greater emphasis, is placed in the present theory, upon the relation of output to sales and upon the relation of sales to production plans.

Conclusions

The changes in the theory of inventory cycles described above are typical examples of changes in business cycle theory in general. They illustrate the far-reaching influence which the theory of employment has exerted upon dynamic economics. As a result of these developments, the Wicksellian concept of an unstable cumulative process which was formerly the basis of many business cycle theories has in large part been replaced by the concept of oscillation about a normal or equilibrium level of income and employment. The normal level itself has been more clearly defined than was possible at an earlier date, and the relation of the actual level of income to this norm has assumed increasing importance.

While the cycles described by theories such as the theory of inventory cycles are conceptually perpetual, in practice they are probably damped. In the absence of disturbances to the underlying conditions of equilibrium, such cycles would tend to disappear. Moreover, the amplitude of any given cycle is directly related to the size of the initial disturbance. Small disturbances produce only small cycles, which means that large cyclical movements can be explained only by explaining the large initial disturbances. From this point of view, the cycle theories described in the present paper are incomplete. They explain how the economic system adapts itself to changes in the conditions of equilibrium, and give strong reasons for believing that the process of adaptation will be cyclical, but they do not explain the disturbing factors which initiate the cycles. In the words of Professor Schumpeter, they are "waves of adaptation."[14]

A wave of adaptation may be started by a change in any of the economic relations which determine the equilibrium level of income and employment. Changes in consumer tastes, for example, or in methods of production, may upset an existing equilibrium and lead to cyclical movements about a new equilibrium. It seems likely, however, that a very large proportion of actual business cycles has been initiated by disturbances in the willingness of businessmen to invest. The ultimate cause of cyclical fluctuations must therefore be sought in the investment motives of the business world or, in other words, in the causes of a fluctuating propensity to invest. But this complex problem is beyond the scope of the present discussion. In describing cycles of adaptation, and in comparing present theories of such cycles with earlier theories, we have simply accepted changes in the propensity to invest as disturbing factors to which the economic system eventually adapts itself. A complete explanation of all movements of income, prices, and employment would of course have to include an explanation of these disturbing factors, as well as a discussion of the adaptation process described above.

14. Schumpeter, *Business Cycles* (reference 7), pp. 179–180.

Part IV

Mathematical Economics and Statistics

20 | Stability of Multiple Markets: The Hicks Conditions

One of the most important achievements of modern economics is the integration of dynamic theory with the method of comparative statics. Until recently, dynamics and statics were two separate and distinct fields of inquiry with virtually no connection.

The separation of the two types of analysis is exemplified by the differences between traditional price theory and traditional business cycle theory. The former dealt with equilibrium prices and quantities and described how these equilibria were altered by changes in tastes, costs, and methods of production. The behavior of prices when supply is not equal to demand was seldom discussed. In contrast, traditional business cycle theory described cumulative processes of expansion and contraction, placing much emphasis upon the time sequence by which a rise in prices or incomes leads to a further rise, or a fall to a further fall. While oscillations of the system about some normal level were analyzed, the nature of this norm was not clearly established. Nor was the cumulative process itself related to the equilibrium of the system. Dynamic economics, as exemplified by business cycle theory, thus had little in common with comparative statics, the method of the classical economists.

One of the first steps toward an integration of statics and dynamics was taken by Professor J. R. Hicks in his *Value and Capital*.[1] Hicks

---

Reprinted from *Econometrica*, 13 (October 1945), 277–292. Copyright Econometric Society, 1945.

---

1. J. R. Hicks, *Value and Capital* (London, Oxford University Press, 1939).

insisted that comparative statics has no meaning unless the economic system is dynamically stable. In Chapter 5 he said: "The laws of change of the price-system, like the laws of change of individual demand, have to be derived from stability conditions. We first examine what changes are necessary in order that a given equilibrium system should be stable; then we make an assumption of regularity, that positions in the neighborhood of the equilibrium position will be stable also; and thence we deduce rules about the way in which the price system will react to changes in tastes and resources."

The important innovation in Hicks's analysis is thus the derivation of properties of the equilibrium system from the conditions of stability of a corresponding dynamic system. He argues that, since only stable systems tend to approach equilibrium when disturbed, static analysis really implies stability; and the conditions of stability provide important information about the static system.

While the usefulness of dynamic economics in describing displacements of a static system was clearly demonstrated by Professor Hicks, his method remained incomplete, as Professor Samuelson pointed out, because in the most general case it lacked an explicit dynamic system.[2] Starting with the case of a single commodity, Hicks made the assumption that price tends to fall whenever supply exceeds demand and to rise whenever demand exceeds supply. From this assumption it follows that a market involving only one commodity is stable provided a rise in price above equilibrium creates an excess supply, while a fall in price below equilibrium creates an excess demand. For under such conditions a displacement of price from equilibrium tends to be self-corrective; it sets in motion forces which restore equilibrium.

Hicks attributes these conclusions with respect to a single-commodity market to Walras and Marshall; he regards his own discussion in *Value and Capital* as simply a restatement of their conclusions. He then attempts to generalize the Walras-Marshall results to a market system involving a large number of commodities. Unfortunately, the generalization is attempted without the aid of an explicit dynamic system; instead of discussing the stability of a true dynamic system involving a large number of commodities, Hicks simply extends the Walras-Marshall conclusions to the case involving several commodities. In

2. See Paul A. Samuelson, "The Stability of Equilibrium: Comparative Statics and Dynamics," *Econometrica,* 9 (April 1941), 97–120, esp. 111–112.

other words, he assumes—but does not prove—that an individual market within the system is stable, as in the single-commodity case, provided a reduction in price below equilibrium creates an excess demand for that particular commodity, while an increase in price creates an excess supply.

Hicks realizes, of course, that in systems comprising several commodities the excess demand for and supply of a particular commodity cannot be discussed without reference to the prices of the other commodities. He therefore presents two definitions of stability, distinguishing one from the other according to the behavior of the other prices in the system. First, a market is defined as *imperfectly stable* if a fall in the price of a particular commodity creates an excess demand for that commodity, *after all other prices have adjusted themselves so that supply is again equal to demand in all markets except the one in question.* It is then tacitly assumed that the whole system of markets is dynamically stable if each market taken by itself is imperfectly stable according to this definition.[3] Second, a market is defined as *perfectly stable* if a fall in price below equilibrium creates an excess demand *after any given subset of prices in other markets is adjusted so that supply again equals demand, with all remaining prices held constant.* And again it is assumed that if each single market is stable in this sense, the entire system will be dynamically stable.

Superficially, this seems plausible. In reality, however, the one-thing-at-a-time method cannot always be applied to a multiple-market system in the manner proposed by Hicks. It cannot be assumed, as in the Hicks analysis, that when the price of one commodity is out of equilibrium the prices of all other commodities are either unchanged or are instantaneously adjusted to their new equilibria. For this reason the Hicks stability conditions cannot be accepted unless it is shown that they are related to the stability of a true dynamic system.

The errors of the Hicks method were first demonstrated by Samuelson in his pioneer article on the significance of dynamics to static analysis.[4] It was there shown that imperfect stability, in the Hicks sense, is neither a necessary nor a sufficient condition for true dynamic stability. An example was given of a dynamic system which was unstable despite

3. Hicks, *Value and Capital* (reference 1), p. 67.
4. Samuelson, "The Stability of Equilibrium" (reference 2), pp. 111–112. This article presents the first complete synthesis of dynamics and comparative statics.

the fact that it was imperfectly stable in the Hicks sense. Another example was given of a system which was dynamically stable even though it was neither perfectly nor imperfectly stable according to Professor Hicks's definitions. In a later note Professor Samuelson demonstrated that even perfect stability is insufficient to ensure true dynamic stability under all circumstances.[5]

From the Samuelson examples one might infer that Hicksian stability is only remotely connected with true dynamic stability. For some problems, this is correct. But for others, the Hicks conditions are highly useful despite their lack of generality. Their usefulness in economics results from two circumstances. In the first place, they provide a set of stability conditions which are independent of the speed of response of individual prices to discrepancies between supply and demand. In the following section it will be shown that the Hicks conditions of perfect stability are necessary if stability is to be independent of such price responsiveness. Second, and more important, in a certain class of market systems Hicksian perfect stability is both necessary and sufficient for true dynamic stability. In particular, if all commodities are gross substitutes, the conditions of true dynamic stability are identical with the Hicks conditions of perfect stability.[6] This proposition is demonstrated further on in this paper.

Stability and Relative Price Flexibility

Consider a market for n commodities and suppose that the demand and supply for the ith of these are $D_i(p_1, p_2, \ldots, p_n)$ and $S_i(p_1, p_2, \ldots, p_n)$ respectively, where $p_1, p_2, \ldots, p_n$ are the prices of the n commodities. For any given set of prices, the excess demand for the ith commodity is

$$x_i = D_i(p_1, p_2, \ldots, p_n) - S_i(p_1, p_2, \ldots, p_n).$$

In the neighborhood of equilibrium, the change in this excess demand with respect to a change in p_i, *after all other prices have adjusted themselves so that supply is equal to demand in the other markets*, is

---

5. Paul A. Samuelson, "The Relation Between Hicksian Stability and True Dynamic Stability," *Econometrica*, 12 (July–October 1944), 256–257.

6. The jth commodity in a group is defined as a gross substitute for the ith commodity if an increase in the price of the former creates excess demand for the latter.

(1)
$$\frac{dx_i}{dp_i} = \frac{\Delta}{\Delta_{ii}},$$

where $\Delta \equiv$
$$\begin{vmatrix} a_{11} & a_{12} & \cdots & a_{1n} \\ a_{21} & a_{22} & \cdots & a_{2n} \\ \cdot & \cdot & \cdot & \cdot \\ \cdot & \cdot & \cdot & \cdot \\ \cdot & \cdot & \cdot & \cdot \\ a_{n1} & a_{n2} & \cdots & a_{nn} \end{vmatrix}$$
and where $a_{ij} \equiv \dfrac{\partial(D_i - S_i)}{\partial p_j} \equiv \dfrac{\partial x_i}{\partial p_j}.$

Since a rise in price must reduce excess demand when the system is imperfectly stable, imperfect stability in the Hicks sense implies that the minors, Δ_{ii}, of Δ all have signs opposite to the sign of Δ. Likewise, perfect stability means that for any mth-order principal minor, $^m\Delta$, of Δ $(m < n)$ the cofactors $^m\Delta_{ii}$ have signs opposite the sign of $^m\Delta$. Thus, if the system is perfectly stable in the Hicks sense, the principal minors of Δ will alternate in sign as follows:[7]

$$a_{ii} < 0, \quad \begin{vmatrix} a_{ii} & a_{ij} \\ a_{ji} & a_{jj} \end{vmatrix} > 0, \quad \begin{vmatrix} a_{ii} & a_{ij} & a_{ik} \\ a_{ji} & a_{jj} & a_{jk} \\ a_{ki} & a_{kj} & a_{kk} \end{vmatrix} < 0, \text{ and so on,}$$

so that the sign of Δ must be the same as the sign of $(-1)^n$.

The difficulty with these stability conditions, as Samuelson has shown, is that they are not derived from any explicit dynamic system. When a true dynamic system is introduced, it becomes apparent that stability depends not only upon the slopes a_{ij} of the excess-demand functions, but also upon relative speeds of adjustment in the individual markets.[8] Suppose, for example, that the rate of change of price in each market is directly proportional to the difference between demand and supply in that market. Then for the ith commodity we have

(2)
$$\frac{dp_i}{dt} = \kappa_i[D_i(p_1, p_2, \ldots, p_n) - S_i(p_i, p_2, \ldots, p_n)].$$

The factor κ_i in Eq. (2) is the "speed of adjustment" in the ith market. It measures the speed with which the price responds to a given

---

7. Hicks, *Value and Capital* (reference 1), p. 315.
8. This was first pointed out by Professor Oscar Lange, in *Price Flexibility and Employment* (Bloomington, Ind., Principia Press, 1944), pp. 94–99.

discrepancy between demand and supply. For small deviations from equilibrium, (2) may be written[9]

(3) $\quad \dfrac{dp_i}{dt} = \kappa_i a_{i1}(p_1 - p_1{}^0) + \kappa_i a_{i2}(p_2 - p_2{}^0)$
$$+ \cdots + \kappa_i a_{in}(p_n - p_n{}^0) \ (i = 1, 2, \ldots, n),$$

where the superscripts indicate equilibrium prices. The stability of this system obviously depends both upon the speeds of adjustment κ_i, and upon the slopes a_{ij} of the excess-demand functions.

The Hicks conditions are stated entirely in terms of the slopes a_{ij}. This means that the Hicks conditions can be true stability conditions only in systems in which stability is independent of the relative speeds of adjustment in the separate markets. In general, this will not be the case. Consider, for example, the following dynamic system:

(4) $\qquad\qquad\qquad \dfrac{dp_1}{dt} = -\kappa_1(p_1 - p_1{}^0) - \kappa_1(p_2 - p_2{}^0)$

and $\qquad\qquad\qquad \dfrac{dp_2}{dt} = 2\kappa_2(p_1 - p_1{}^0) + \kappa_2(p_2 - p_2{}^0).$

This system possesses neither perfect nor imperfect stability in the Hicks sense. Actually, it may be shown that the system is stable or unstable in the true dynamic sense according as κ_1, the speed of adjustment in the first market, is greater or less than κ_2, the speed of adjustment in the second market.[10]

Since Hicks does not mention these speeds of adjustment explicitly, his analysis may be interpreted as an attempt to develop stability conditions which are independent of relative speeds of adjustment in individual markets. Indeed, the method of exposition which he uses

9. The use of linear approximations in dynamic analysis is frequently criticized, particularly by those who have little appreciation of the difficulties presented by more complex systems. I believe the case for linear systems is much stronger than is commonly supposed. Most of the statistical investigations of such important functions as the propensity to consume and the propensity to import fail to show any significant departure from linearity. In business cycle studies, the use of linear systems therefore has empirical support. In any case, Samuelson has shown that stability of linear approximations is a necessary condition, if not a sufficient one, for stability of more complicated dynamic systems. See Paul A. Samuelson, "The Stability of Equilibrium: Linear and Nonlinear Systems," *Econometrica*, 10 (January 1942), 1–25.

10. The characteristic equation of Eqs. (4) is $\lambda^2 + (\kappa_1 - \kappa_2)\lambda + \kappa_1\kappa_2 = 0$. The real parts of the solutions of this equation are positive or negative according as κ_2 is greater or less than κ_1.

clearly implies such independence. In discussing the effects of a change in the price of the ith commodity upon the excess demand for that commodity, he assumes that prices of all other commodities are adjusted to their new equilibria while no further change occurs—initially at least—in the price of the ith commodity. In other words he assumes that the speed of adjustment in the ith market is very small relative to the speeds of adjustment in the other markets of the system. But when he considers the stability of any other market in the system, such as the jth market for example, he likewise assumes that the speed of adjustment in this market is small relative to the other markets. These assumptions are obviously inconsistent; the speed of adjustment in the ith market cannot be small relative to the speed in the jth market at the same time that the speed of adjustment in j is small relative to the speed in i. In reality, Hicks is considering a different dynamic system corresponding to the excess demand of each separate market. For this reason the stability conditions he derives cannot be applicable to the entire system of markets unless true dynamic stability is independent of relative speeds of adjustment in the separate markets.

More than this can be said, however. While the Hicks conditions may not be identical with true dynamic stability conditions, it is easily demonstrated that *perfect stability, in the Hicks sense, is necessary for true stability if the market system is to be stable for all possible sets of speeds of adjustment.* To prove this proposition, consider the characteristic equation corresponding to the n-commodity system of Eq. (3). This market system is stable, for any initial prices, provided the roots of the following equation have no positive or zero real parts:

$$(5) \quad \begin{vmatrix} \kappa_1 a_{11} - \lambda & \kappa_1 a_{12} & \cdots & \kappa_1 a_{1n} \\ \kappa_2 a_{21} & \kappa_2 a_{22} - \lambda & \cdots & \kappa_2 a_{2n} \\ \cdot \cdot \cdot & \cdot \cdot \cdot & \cdot \cdot \cdot & \cdot \cdot \cdot \\ \kappa_n a_{n1} & \kappa_n a_{n2} & \cdots & \kappa_n a_{nn} - \lambda \end{vmatrix} \equiv \left| \kappa_i a_{ij} - \delta_{ij}\lambda \right| = 0.$$

This obviously requires that $A \equiv |\kappa_i a_{ij}|$ shall have the same sign as $(-1)^n$. For when λ becomes sufficiently large, the sign of $|\kappa_i a_{ij} - \delta_{ij}\lambda|$ is the same as the sign of $(-1)^n$, as may be seen by expanding Eq. (5). Hence if A, the determinant obtained by putting $\lambda = 0$ in (5), has a sign opposite to $(-1)^n$, $|\kappa_i a_{ij} - \delta_{ij}\lambda|$ must be equal to zero for some positive real value of λ. In other words, Eq. (5) must have a positive real root, and the system (3) must be unstable. Likewise, if $A = 0$, then

$\lambda = 0$ is one root of Eq. (5), and the system is on the borderline between stability and instability. Thus the system (3) cannot be stable unless its determinant A has the same sign as $(-1)^n$. But A is the same as the determinant of the Hicks static equations, except for multiplication by the positive speeds of adjustment $\kappa_1 \kappa_2 \ldots \kappa_n$. Hence, sign $A = \text{sign } (-1)^n$ is the last of the Hicks conditions of perfect stability.

Consider now what happens to the stability of Eq. (3) when the speeds of adjustment are changed. If the market system is to be stable for any set of speeds of adjustment, it must be stable when some of the κ_i are quite small relative to others in the set. In other words, the system must be stable even when any subgroup of prices is completely inflexible. Suppose, for example, that the speeds of adjustment $\kappa_{m+1}, \kappa_{m+2}, \ldots, \kappa_n$ are all put equal to zero. The system (3) then becomes an mth-order system in the variables $p_1, p_2, \ldots, p_m$, and the determinant corresponding to the subset is

$$\begin{vmatrix} \kappa_1 a_{11} & \kappa_1 a_{12} & \cdots & \kappa_1 a_{1m} \\ \kappa_2 a_{21} & \kappa_2 a_{22} & \cdots & \kappa_2 a_{2m} \\ \cdot & \cdot & \cdots & \cdot \\ \kappa_m a_{m1} & \kappa_m a_{m2} & \cdots & \kappa_m a_{mm} \end{vmatrix}.$$

From the preceding analysis, it is clear that stability requires that this determinant shall have the sign of $(-1)^m$. But apart from a positive factor $\kappa_1 \kappa_2 \ldots \kappa_m$, the determinant is simply an mth-order principal minor of the determinant of the Hicks static equations. Since the argument holds for any value of m from 1 to n, it follows immediately that stability of a multiple-market system cannot be independent of relative speeds of adjustment in the separate markets unless the Hicks conditions of perfect stability are satisfied.[11]

What is the economic significance of this result? Why should anyone be interested in stability conditions which do not depend upon speeds of adjustment in individual markets? In describing a given market system, an economist is always confronted with a given set of relative speeds. Why not determine the stability conditions for this system simply in terms of these given speeds of adjustment? In other words, why

11. Cf. Lange, *Price Flexibility and Employment* (reference 8), p. 96. The proof just given of the necessity of the Hicks conditions is closely related to the Lange concept of *partial* stability of any given order. It is equivalent to the statement that stability cannot be independent of relative speeds of adjustment unless the system possesses partial stability of all orders.

should the economist be concerned about the effects of changes in relative speeds of adjustment?

Two answers may be given to these questions. First, the extent to which the stability of a group of markets depends upon speeds of adjustment is a question of considerable interest. It is important to know, for example, whether the inflexibility of certain prices is a stabilizing factor or whether the markets would be stable even if all prices were responsive to discrepancies between supply and demand. If the Hicks conditions of perfect stability are not satisfied, stability of the system clearly depends upon a relative inflexibility of certain prices. Second, and more important, the conditions which govern price responsiveness are much more obscure than are the static supply and demand conditions in individual markets. To a large extent, speeds of adjustment are determined by institutional factors such as the willingness or ability of buyers and sellers to hold or to reduce inventories. Static conditions of supply and demand, on the other hand, depend largely upon maximum-profits conditions of producers and consumers. For this reason economists are usually more confident of their knowledge of supply and demand conditions than of their knowledge of such dynamic factors as speeds of adjustment. If possible, it is therefore desirable to describe market systems in terms which are independent of speeds of adjustment.

Nevertheless, an uncritical acceptance of the Hicks conditions may lead to serious errors, particularly if there is a high degree of complementarity between certain goods. While the Hicks conditions of perfect stability are *necessary* if stability is to be independent of relative speeds of adjustment, they are not always *sufficient*. In other words, a market may be unstable for certain speeds of adjustment even though it possesses perfect stability according to the Hicks criteria.

Consider, for example, the following system:

$$\frac{dp_1}{dt} = -\kappa_1(p_1 - p_1^0) - 0.8\kappa_1(p_2 - p_2^0),$$

(6) $$\frac{dp_2}{dt} = \qquad\qquad -\kappa_2(p_2 - p_2^0) - 0.8\kappa_2(p_3 - p_3^0),$$

and $$\frac{dp_3}{dt} = -10\kappa_3(p_1 - p_1^0) - \kappa_3(p_2 - p_2^0) - \kappa_3(p_3 - p_3^0).$$

This system possesses perfect Hicksian stability, yet it may be either stable or unstable dynamically, the outcome depending upon relative speeds of adjustment in the individual markets. If the three speeds of adjustment in the first, second, and third markets respectively are proportional to the three numbers 2, 2, 1, the system is stable. On the other hand, if the speeds of adjustment are proportional to 2, 2, 3, it may easily be shown that the system is unstable dynamically despite the fact that it satisfies the Hicks conditions for perfect stability.[12]

The preceding analysis has demonstrated two propositions. First, the Hicks conditions for perfect stability are necessary if a market system is to be stable for any set of relative speeds of adjustment. Second, the Hicks conditions are not always sufficient; some market systems may be stable with one set of relative speeds, and unstable with another, even though the static system is perfectly stable (in the Hicks sense) in both cases. If this were all that could be said, the usefulness of the Hicks conditions would be seriously limited, for true dynamic stability conditions would not be directly related to the Hicks conditions. In the following section, however, it will be shown that for at least one class of market systems, the Hicks conditions of perfect stability are identical with the true dynamic conditions. This fact gives the Hicks conditions an important application, particularly in the field of income analysis.

Substitution and Stability Conditions

In the present section, the following proposition will be proved: *If all commodities in a market system are gross substitutes, the conditions for true dynamic stability are identical with the Hicks conditions for perfect stability.*

12. With the first set of speeds of adjustment (2, 2, 1), the characteristic equation of Eq. (6) is

$$\lambda^3 + 5\lambda^2 + 6.4\lambda + 26.4 = 0.$$

By Descartes's rule of signs this equation has no positive or zero real roots. Moreover, by application of the Routh stability conditions, it may be shown that the above equation has no complex roots with nonnegative real parts. The system is therefore stable. See E. J. Routh, *The Advanced Part of a Treatise on the Dynamics of a System of Rigid Bodies*, ed. 5 (London, Macmillan, 1905), pp. 297–301. With the second set of speeds of adjustment (2, 2, 3), the characteristic equation of Eq. (6) is

$$\lambda^3 + 7\lambda^2 + 11.2\lambda + 79.2 = 0.$$

While the equation has no nonnegative real roots, it fails to satisfy the Routh conditions and must therefore have complex roots with positive real parts.

A discussion of the Routh conditions may be found in R. A. Frazer, W. J. Duncan, and A. R. Collar, *Elementary Matrices* (Cambridge, England, University Press, 1938), p. 154. Readers unfamiliar with Routh's work on dynamics may easily verify the conclusions just presented by solving the two numerical equations.

The fact that all commodities are gross substitutes means that a rise in price of the ith commodity, all other prices remaining unchanged, reduces the excess demand for that commodity and increases the excess demand for all other commodities. Thus $a_{ii} < 0$ and $a_{ij} > 0$ for any i and any j. Consider again the dynamic system (3), repeated below for convenience:

$$(7) \qquad \frac{dp_i}{dt} = \kappa_i \sum_{j=1}^{n} a_{ij}(p_j - p_j^{\,0}) \qquad\qquad (i = 1, 2, \ldots, n).$$

The speeds of adjustment κ_i in this system are determined partly by the units in which time is measured. But stability of the system is obviously independent of the time unit. Without loss of generality, we may therefore choose our time unit in such a way that $\kappa_i a_{ii}$ is less than unity in absolute value for all i. It is then possible to prove our theorem by consideration of the following related system of difference equations:

$$(8) \quad \begin{aligned} y_1(t) &= (\kappa_1 a_{11} + 1)y_1(t-1) + \kappa_1 a_{12} y_2(t-1) + \cdots + \kappa_1 a_{1n} y_n(t-1), \\ y_2(t) &= \kappa_2 a_{21} y_1(t-1) + (\kappa_2 a_{22} + 1)y_2(t-1) + \cdots + \kappa_2 a_{2n} y_n(t-1), \\ &\;\cdot \quad \cdot \quad \cdot \quad \cdot \quad \cdot \quad \cdot \quad \cdot \quad \cdot \quad \cdot \quad \cdot \quad \cdot \quad \cdot \quad \cdot \quad \cdot \quad \cdot \\ y_n(t) &= \kappa_n a_{n1} y_1(t-1) + \kappa_n a_{n2} y_2(t-1) + \cdots + (k_n a_{nn} + 1)y_n(t-1). \end{aligned}$$

The proof will be accomplished in two stages. First, it will be shown that the differential equations (7) are stable or unstable according as the difference equations (8) are stable or unstable. Second, it will be shown that the Hicks conditions of perfect stability are necessary and sufficient for stability of the difference equations (8).

The characteristic equation of the difference equations (8) is

$$(9) \quad \begin{vmatrix} \kappa_1 a_{11} + 1 - \rho & \kappa_1 a_{12} & \cdots & \kappa_1 a_{1n} \\ \kappa_2 a_{21} & \kappa_2 a_{22} + 1 - \rho & \cdots & \kappa_2 a_{2n} \\ \cdot \quad \cdot \quad \cdot & \cdot \quad \cdot \quad \cdot & \cdots & \cdot \quad \cdot \quad \cdot \\ \kappa_n a_{n1} & \kappa_n a_{n2} & \cdots & \kappa_n a_{nn} + 1 - \rho \end{vmatrix} = 0.$$

If we substitute $\lambda = \rho - 1$ in (9), we obtain Eq. (5), which is the characteristic equation of the differential system (7). Thus the roots of (9) are greater by unity than the roots of (5), the characteristic equation of (7).

Now stability of the difference system (8) requires that the moduli of all roots of (9) be less than unity (that is, that all roots lie within the unit circle of the complex plane), whereas stability of (7) requires that the real parts of the roots of (5) be negative. If all the roots of (9) lie within the unit circle of the complex plane, it is obvious that the real parts of the roots of (5) will all be negative. Hence stability of the difference equations (8) is sufficient to ensure stability of the differential equations (7).

Is it also necessary? Conceivably, one of the roots of (9) could lie outside the unit circle (if its value were $2\sqrt{(-1+i)}$, for example) and yet all the roots of (5) could have negative real parts. In this case the differential equations would be stable even though the corresponding difference equations were unstable. But this is impossible in the present case, for it may be shown that *under the restrictions placed upon a_{ij} and a_{ii}, the root of Eq. (9) with the largest modulus is a positive real root.* From this proposition it follows that if one of the complex roots of (9) has a modulus which is equal to or greater than unity, there must also be a positive real root equal to or greater than unity. And in this case (5) will have a root with a zero or positive real part, and the differential equations (7) will be unstable.

To prove that the root of (9) with the largest modulus is a positive real root, consider the behavior of the difference equations (8). Suppose that initially $y_1, y_2, \ldots, y_n$ are all positive and that no further disturbances occur from outside the system. Then, since all the coefficients on the right of (8) are positive, $y_k(t)$ remains positive throughout. That is, (8) shows that $y_k(t) \geq 0$ whenever $y_1(t-1), y_2(t-1), \ldots, y_n(t-1)$ are all greater than or equal to zero. Now the general solution of these difference equations, for y_k, is

$$(10) \qquad y_k(t) = \sum r_i{}'[g_i(t)\cos(\theta_i t) + h_i(t)\sin(\theta_i t)],$$

where r_i is the modulus of the ith distinct root of (9), and $g_i(t)$ and $h_i(t)$ are polynomials of degree one less than the multiplicity of the ith root, with coefficients dependent upon initial conditions. The solution, (10), includes real as well as complex roots. For positive real roots, $\theta_i = 0$, while for negative real roots, $\theta_i = \pi$.

Suppose that r_1 is the largest modulus, and rewrite (10) as follows:

$$(11) \qquad y_k(t) = r_1{}'\left[g_1(t)\cos(\theta_1 t) + h_1(t)\sin(\theta_1 t) \right.$$
$$\left. + \sum_{i \neq 1} \left(\frac{r_i}{r_1}\right)^t \{g_i(t)\cos(\theta_i t) + h_i(t)\sin(\theta_i t)\} \right].$$

Since r_i/r_1 is less than unity for all i included in the summation,

$$\sum_{i \neq 1} \left(\frac{r_i}{r_1}\right)^t \{g_i(t)\cos(\theta_i t) + h_i(t)\sin(\theta_i t)\}$$

can be made as small as we please by taking t sufficiently large. Beyond a certain time interval, the sign of $y_k(t)$ will therefore be the same as the sign of $g_1(t)\cos(\theta_1 t) + h_1(t)\sin(\theta_1 t)$ for at least some values of t. This latter expression in turn is dominated, for sufficiently large t, by the parts of $g_1(t)$ and $h_1(t)$ with the highest power of t. If the dominant root (or dominant pair of conjugate complex roots) is repeated v times, this leading expression will take the form $t^{v-1}[A\cos(\theta_1 t) + B\sin(\theta_1 t)] \equiv t^{v-1}C\cos(\theta_1 t + \phi_1)$. Thus if t becomes sufficiently large, $y_k(t)$ will have the same sign as $C\cos(\theta_1 t + \phi_1)$ for at least some values of t. But unless θ_1 is zero, $\cos(\theta_1 t + \phi_1)$ assumes both positive and negative values for different integral values of t, and $y_k(t)$ therefore becomes negative for certain intervals of t regardless of whether C is positive or negative. Since this is clearly impossible when all the y_k's are initially positive, it follows that θ_1, the amplitude of the root with the largest modulus, must be zero, and this root must therefore be a positive real root.[13]

This completes the first part of our proof. Before presenting the second part, let us summarize briefly the preceding results. First, if the difference equations (8) are stable, all the roots of (9) must lie within the unit circle of the complex plane. In this case, no roots of (5), the characteristic equation of our differential system, can have positive or zero real parts, since the roots of the latter are less than those of (9) by exactly unity. It follows that stability of the difference equations (8) is sufficient to ensure stability of the corresponding differential equations (7). Second, if the difference equations (8) are unstable, (9) must have at least one positive real root greater than unity, since the root of (9)

13. This proof assumes that the coefficient C is not zero. While this may not be true for certain initial conditions, it is easily shown that C cannot be identically zero for all possible positive values of $y_1(0), y_2(0), \ldots, y_n(0)$. The coefficients such as C are linear functions of the initial values, which means that C can be zero only when the initial conditions satisfy an equation of the form $\alpha_1 y_1(0) + \alpha_2 y_2(0) + \ldots + \alpha_n y_n(0) = 0$. This equation defines a plane in n-dimensional space; any combination of $y_1(0), y_2(0), \ldots y_n(0)$ which lies on this plane yields a zero value for C, while all other combinations yield nonzero values. Now it is obvious intuitively that no plane in n-dimensional space can include all combinations of the n variables which lie in the positive hyperquadrant. In other words, sets of positive values of $y_1(0), y_2(0), \ldots, y_n(0)$ may always be found outside the plane. Since the proof given in the text is valid for any combination of positive initial conditions, the values of $y_1(0), y_2(0), \ldots, y_n(0)$ may always be selected so as to make C nonzero. I am indebted to Professor Samuelson for pointing this out.

with the largest modulus is a positive real root. But if (9) has a positive real root greater than unity, (5) will have a real root greater than zero and the differential equations (7) will therefore be unstable. Thus if the difference equations are unstable, the corresponding differential equations will likewise be unstable.

It has now been demonstrated that the differential system (7) is stable or unstable whenever the corresponding difference equations (8) are stable or unstable. To complete the proof that the Hicks conditions of perfect stability are necessary and sufficient for stability of both the differential and the difference equations, it remains only to prove that they are necessary and sufficient for stability of the difference equations (8).

Consider again the characteristic equation (9). In its expanded form, this equation may be written

$$(12) \quad (\rho - 1)^n - \sum \kappa_i a_{ii}(\rho - 1)^{n-1} + \sum \kappa_i \kappa_j \begin{vmatrix} a_{ii} & a_{ij} \\ a_{ji} & a_{jj} \end{vmatrix} (\rho - 1)^{n-2}$$
$$+ \cdots + (-1)^n \kappa_1 \kappa_2 \ldots \kappa_n \Delta = 0,$$

where $\Delta \equiv |a_{ij}|$ as before.

We have seen that the difference equations (8) are stable provided this equation has no positive real roots equal to or greater than unity. Or, what amounts to the same thing, the system will be stable if the equation

$$(13) \quad \lambda^n - \sum \kappa_i a_{ii} \lambda^{n-1} + \sum \kappa_i \kappa_j \begin{vmatrix} a_{ii} & a_{ij} \\ a_{ji} & a_{jj} \end{vmatrix} \lambda^{n-2} + \cdots$$
$$+ (-1)^n \kappa_1 \kappa_2 \ldots \kappa_n \Delta = 0$$

has no positive or zero real roots. Since the κ_i are all positive, we know by Descartes's rule of signs that Eq. (13) can have no positive or zero real roots if the determinants,

$$a_{ii}, \quad \begin{vmatrix} a_{ii} & a_{ij} \\ a_{ji} & a_{jj} \end{vmatrix}, \quad \begin{vmatrix} a_{ii} & a_{ij} & a_{ik} \\ a_{ji} & a_{jj} & a_{jk} \\ a_{ki} & a_{kj} & a_{kk} \end{vmatrix}, \text{ and so on,}$$

are alternately negative and positive. But these are the Hicks conditions of perfect stability. We have thus proved that perfect stability in the Hicks sense is sufficient for stability of both the difference equations (9) and the differential equations (7).

To prove that the Hicks conditions are also necessary, consider a system of m difference equations comprising a subset of the system (8):

$$\hat{y}_1(t) = (\kappa_1 a_{11} + 1)\hat{y}_1(t - 1) + \kappa_1 a_{12}\hat{y}_2(t - 1) + \cdots + \kappa_1 a_{1m}\hat{y}_m(t - 1),$$
$$\hat{y}_2(t) = \kappa_2 a_{21}\hat{y}_1(t - 1) + (\kappa_2 a_{22} + 1)\hat{y}_2(t - 1) + \cdots + \kappa_2 a_{2m}\hat{y}_m(t - 1),$$

(14) . . . .

$$\hat{y}_m(t) = \kappa_m a_{m1}\hat{y}_1(t - 1) + \kappa_m a_{m2}\hat{y}_2(t - 1) + \cdots + (\kappa_m a_{mm} + 1)\hat{y}_m(t - 1).$$

It can easily be shown that the complete system (8) is not stable unless subsystem (14) is also stable. To demonstrate this, we need only suppose again that all y_i of the complete system and all $\hat{y}_i$ of the subsystem are initially positive, and that each y_i of the complete system is initially greater than the corresponding $\hat{y}_i$ of the subsystem. Then at any time, t, $y_i(t) \geq \hat{y}_i(t)$; that is, for the initial conditions postulated, $y_i(t)$ of the complete system remains permanently greater than or equal to $\hat{y}_i(t)$ of the subset. The proof is a simple proof by induction. If $y_j(t - 1) \geq \hat{y}_j(t - 1)$ holds for all j from 1 to m, then $y_i(t)$ is a sum of n positive or zero terms, of which m terms are greater than or equal to the corresponding terms in the summation for $\hat{y}_i(t)$. Hence, $y_i(t) \geq \hat{y}_i(t)$ for all i from 1 to m.

If this is true, then clearly the complete system is not stable unless the subset is also stable. And a necessary condition for stability of the subset, as we have seen earlier, is that the mth-order determinant,

$$\begin{vmatrix} a_{11} & a_{12} \cdots a_{1m} \\ a_{21} & a_{22} \cdots a_{2m} \\ \cdot & \cdot \quad \cdot \quad \cdot \quad \cdot \\ a_{m1} & a_{m2} \cdots a_{mm} \end{vmatrix},$$

shall have the same sign as $(-1)^m$. This must be true for any subset and for any value of m from 1 to n. Since the complete system is not stable unless all such subsets are stable, it follows that all mth-order principal minors of Δ must have the sign of $(-1)^m$. Thus perfect stability in the Hicks sense is necessary for true dynamic stability of both the difference equations (8) and the differential equations (7).

Conclusions

The fundamental assumption in the foregoing analysis is that the price of a particular commodity tends to rise whenever demand exceeds supply and to fall whenever supply exceeds demand. This assumption is accepted by Hicks as the basis for his conclusion that a single-commodity market is not stable unless demand and supply conditions are such that a rise in price above equilibrium creates an excess supply, while a fall in price below equilibrium creates an excess demand. Although the Hicks conclusion is valid for a system involving only one commodity, it cannot be generalized, in the manner attempted by Hicks, to a market system involving *n* commodities.

In other words, it is inadmissible to assume, as Professor Hicks does in his discussion of *imperfect* stability, that a system of markets is necessarily stable if a fall in the price of a particular product leads to an excess demand for that product after all other prices have been adjusted so that supply is again equal to demand for each of the other commodities. Nor is it correct to assume, as in the Hicks discussion of *perfect* stability, that a market system is dynamically stable whenever a fall in the price of a given commodity leads to excess demand for that product after any given subset of prices of other commodities is adjusted so that supply again equals demand for these other commodities, with all remaining prices held constant. The Hicks discussion of perfect and imperfect stability tacitly assumes that whenever the price of a particular product deviates from equilibrium, the prices of all remaining products either remain unchanged or are adjusted instantaneously to their new levels of equilibrium. Thus the concepts of perfect and imperfect stability developed by Professor Hicks make no allowance for the fact that all prices may be out of equilibrium at the same time.

The error in Hicks's analysis of multiple-market systems is attributable to the fact that he generalizes the *conclusion* which was derived for a single-commodity market rather than the *method of analysis* for such a market. The correct generalization of the one-commodity case is a dynamic system which expresses the rate of change of the price of each commodity as a function of the discrepancy between demand for and supply of that commodity. The true conditions of stability are to be derived from this dynamic system, rather than from the properties of the corresponding static system. Samuelson has shown that these true stability conditions may differ from the Hicks conditions of perfect and imperfect stability.

Nevertheless, the foregoing analysis has demonstrated that, despite the error in the Hicks method, the Hicks conditions of perfect stability are applicable to certain economic problems. In the first place, a market system must be perfectly stable, in the Hicks sense, if the true dynamic system is to be stable for all possible speeds of price adjustment in individual markets. This means that in a market system which does not possess perfect Hicksian stability, true dynamic stability depends partly upon the fact that certain prices are relatively unresponsive to discrepancies between demand and supply; if these inflexible prices became more responsive, such a system might become unstable. A dynamic system can be stable for all possible speeds of adjustment only if it is perfectly stable in the Hicks sense.

Second, the analysis has shown that for at least one type of multiple market system the Hicks conditions of perfect stability are identical with the true dynamic conditions. In particular, if all commodities are gross substitutes, the Hicks conditions are both necessary and sufficient for stability of the dynamic system. In most price problems, this conclusion may not be significant, for almost all markets have some degree of complementarity. In other problems, however, the Hicks conditions are highly useful. The study of income movements between countries, for example, requires the analysis of differential and difference equations which conform to the conditions described above. In other words, in a large part of income analysis the Hicks conditions of perfect stability are both necessary and sufficient for true dynamic stability. These problems will be discussed in a later paper.

Since the Hicks conditions of perfect stability are now known to be necessary and sufficient for true stability of at least one class of markets, it is natural to speculate about their usefulness for other classes of markets as well. The analysis presented above does not preclude the possibility that the Hicks conditions may be identical with the true dynamic conditions for certain classes of markets in which some goods are complementary. Indeed, Samuelson has previously demonstrated one such case; he has shown that if the static system is symmetrical, in the sense that $a_{ij} = a_{ji}$, and if the speed of adjustment is the same in all markets, the Hicks conditions of perfect stability are both necessary and sufficient, regardless of whether a_{ij} is positive or negative.[14] Further investigation may reveal other cases of a similar nature. In any event, an investigation which relates the true stability conditions to the minors of the static system will be highly useful, whether or not the final results are in accord with the Hicks conditions.

14. Samuelson, "The Stability of Equilibrium" (reference 2), p. 111.

21 | A Multiple-Region Theory of Income and Trade[1]

The theory of employment and income that was developed during the decade of the thirties was concerned primarily with the economic forces governing the level of output in a closed economic system. From the outset, however, it was apparent that the new ideas had important applications to interregional and international problems. In particular, the theory of employment added considerably to our understanding of the mechanism by which an expansion or contraction of income in one region or country is transmitted to other regions or countries.

Much of the early discussion of such problems was devoted to a highly simplified model in which the world was divided into two regions or countries; in this model an expansion or contraction of income was assumed to originate in one of the two regions or countries, and the repercussions upon income in the other region or country and upon the balance of payments between the two were then examined in some

Reprinted from *Econometrica*, 18 (October 1950), 329–354. Copyright Econometric Society, 1950.

1. This paper was written in 1945 but was not submitted for publication because there seemed to be no widespread interest in the subject. Later, however, it became apparent that the general principles of regional income movements are applicable to many fields other than international trade. Most of the propositions developed in this paper, as an example, are applicable to the theory of linear programming and to input-output studies within a single country. See, for instance, David Hawkins and Herbert A. Simon, "Note: Some Conditions of Macroeconomic Stability," *Econometrica*, 17 (July–October 1949), 245–248; R. M. Goodwin, "The Multiplier as Matrix," *Economic Journal*, 59 (December 1949), 537–555; and John S. Chipman, "The Multi-Sector Multiplier," *Econometrica*, 18 (October 1950), 355–374. In addition to these published papers, I have recently read an unpublished manuscript by H. A. John Green dealing with some aspects of the problem discussed in the present paper. In view of the renewed interest in the subject, it seems to me appropriate to present the results of my own investigation.

detail.[2] The purpose of the present paper is to generalize the earlier discussion by considering a model of an economic system composed of n regions or countries, where n may be either large or small. Although I shall speak hereafter of "n countries," I assume it is clear that the conclusions apply without modification to the regions within a single country or, indeed, to any regional classification of the world economy, such as the economy composed of Eastern Europe, Western Europe, Latin America, and the like.

The procedure followed in this paper is essentially the same as that employed in the earlier discussions of the two-country model. The level of output in each of the n countries is assumed, initially, to be in a state of balance in the sense that the country's rate of output of goods and services is equal to the demand for such goods and services. A disturbance of the economic forces governing income is then assumed to take place in one of the countries, and the effects of this disturbance are traced throughout the n-country system. Both movements of real income or employment and movements of the international balance of trade are taken into account. In order to isolate the effects of employment and real income, the assumption is made that all prices, costs, and exchange rates remain unaltered. In other words, commodities and services are assumed to be produced and sold at constant supply prices. Exchange rates are assumed to be kept at fixed levels, either by central bank activity or by the normal operations of the gold standard. A free market for foreign exchange is postulated for each of the n countries, and imports are thus supposed to be limited by a country's income or purchasing power, and not by the size of its foreign-exchange reserves.

In the present world of unbalanced trade, dollar shortages, exchange controls, and "hard" or "soft" currencies, this last assumption will doubtless strike the reader as highly unrealistic. I should therefore add that the model of international trade discussed below is not intended as a description of the abnormal conditions prevailing today. Whether the model will or will not be a reasonable description of world trade and

---

2. See, for example, my own papers, "The Transfer Problem Reconsidered," and "Underemployment Equilibrium in International Trade," included in the present volume as Chapters 2 and 10. See also Fritz Machlup, *International Trade and the National Income Multiplier* (Philadelphia, Blakiston, 1943). Machlup presents an economic model involving three countries and has also described models involving a larger number. In his more complex models, however, a considerable amount of symmetry is assumed with respect to propensities to spend and to import, and for this reason his results cannot be regarded as completely general.

employment in the future is a question that can hardly be answered at the present time; the answer obviously depends upon numerous and unpredictable political influences as well as upon more narrow economic considerations such as the fate of exchange controls, import quotas, and other governmental measures for controlling world trade.

Whatever the future development of international trade may be, there are two reasons, it seems to me, why economic models such as the one given in this paper are useful. In the first place, there are almost certain to be large areas of the world, even in an economic system having extensive trade controls, in which payments between one region and another are made more or less freely. It is unlikely, for example, that any limitations other than that of purchasing power will ever be placed upon transactions between Kansas and Nebraska or upon payments between the North Central States and the New England States in the United States. Likewise, payments between members of the sterling area of the British Commonwealth now occur quite freely despite the limitations upon payments outside the area.[3] Thus whatever happens to inter*national* trade, the model discussed below remains useful as a description of inter*regional* trade. The second and less important reason for regarding the model as useful is the fact that it can be helpful in interpreting economic events of the past. There have been long periods of time—the period under the gold standard before the first world war is an example—when international payments were made without restriction throughout the world. There is no doubt that during these periods limited income was the principal constraint upon imports, and the assumption made above regarding foreign-exchange markets is accordingly appropriate for describing such periods.

The international theory of income to be presented below is, in at least two respects, a short-run theory. It is short-run, in the first place, in the same sense that Keynes's *General Theory* is short-run: it takes the rate of current investment in each country either as a given amount or as a given function of income in that country and makes no allowances either for the effects of continuous investment upon a country's capacity to produce or for the repercussions of a change in such capacity upon the demand for new investment. The theory, in brief, is a *static* theory

3. This second example is perhaps slightly misleading, inasmuch as all of the countries concerned have far-reaching import controls which to a considerable extent take the place of exchange controls. It does not seem overly optimistic, however, to conjecture that the import controls within the area, if not those pertaining to imports from countries outside the area, will be gradually relaxed.

of income and not a theory of growth; for this reason it is obviously inapplicable over an extended period of economic development.

The theory given below is short-run, in the second place, in its treatment of each country's balance of payments. The procedure followed in this regard is simply to investigate the effects of a given disturbance upon each country's balance of payments on current account, and not to inquire about how a given deficit or surplus in this balance is offset. Nothing is said, in other words, about the role of capital movements in establishing and maintaining equilibrium in the flow of international payments and receipts. Thus, quite apart from the problems of growth, the position of equilibrium described below must be regarded as temporary. For unless capital movements occur more or less automatically in response to discrepancies in a country's balance of payments on current account, a country with a deficit in its current account will sooner or later have to take measures such as cost deflation or currency depreciation to eliminate the deficit; and these measures in turn will affect the equilibrium of income. In other words, the equilibrium of income to be discussed in this paper can exist over a considerable period of time only if international monetary reserves are large or if capital movements are of the equilibrating type.

In demonstrating how an economic disturbance in one country affects income and employment throughout the world, we might select any one of a considerable number of economic events as the disturbing force. We might, for example, investigate the repercussions of an increase in domestic investment in one of the n countries or of an increase in the consumption of domestic goods; or we might consider the effects of technological changes or changes in taste which tend to shift the demand for goods and services in some particular country from domestic goods to imports; or we might, following more traditional lines, examine the economic consequences of reparations payments or some other form of income transfer between countries. The international repercussions of all such disturbances, however, have many common features, and it would be needlessly repetitious to consider each of them separately.

Indeed, it seems to me that the important elements of an interregional or international theory of employment can, for the most part, be demonstrated by considering only one type of disturbance, namely, a change in domestic investment in one of the n countries. The effects of other, more complex types of disturbances can then be determined by regarding these complex disturbances as combinations of movements of investment in one or more countries. Thus, for the purpose of income analysis, a reparations payment may be regarded as a combination of investment in the receiving country and disinvestment of the same amount in the paying country. In view of this possibility of transforming other disturbing forces into combinations of movements in investment, the international theory of employment presented below is developed entirely by considering the adjustment of the world economy to a change in investment in one country. The conclusions reached for this particular disturbance are readily applicable to other disturbances as well.

A System of Income Equations

Neglecting income transfers between countries, the current net income of a particular country is simply the market value of that country's net output of goods and services. The word "net" as used in this connection implies that two deductions are made from the total value of goods and services produced. First, the usual allowance is made for the depreciation of capital. Second, and more important for present purposes, the value of all imported goods and services employed in production is deducted from the market value of such production. This second deduction is necessary because a country's output incorporates not only the services of domestic factors of production, but also many materials and services purchased abroad; and the latter do not constitute income produced within the given country. The concept of income in an open economy is thus a sort of value-added-by-manufacture concept, except that the unit of account is a country or region rather than an industry.

Consider now a sum of values comprising the following items: (a) all expenditures by the residents of a particular country upon consumers' goods and services, including imported as well as domestic goods and services; (b) net investment in plant, equipment, inventories, and the like, including investment in equipment produced abroad as well as investment in things domestically produced; (c) exports of goods and services. In what respects does this sum differ from net income as defined in the preceding paragraph? The sum includes, in the first place, the value of imported materials and services employed in domestic production, and these obviously must be deducted in computing the net income produced within the given country. The sum also includes, in the second place, imported finished goods which may have been used either for consumption, for net investment, or for re-export; since these imported finished goods obviously do not constitute a part of the particular country's current production, their value must likewise be deducted from the total in computing national income. Thus we find that the total of domestic expenditures for consumption and investment plus receipts from exports exceeds national income by the value of imports, including both imports of finished goods and services and imports of intermediate goods and services. In terms of the final uses of goods and services, national income may accordingly be written as follows:

National income *equals* expenditures on consumers' goods and services
plus net investment *plus* exports of goods and services
less imports of goods and services.

Three of the items in this summation—consumption, net investment, and imports—are dependent upon the level of income and employment at home, while the remaining item, exports, depends upon income in all of the countries to which the given country is selling goods and services.[4] This immediately suggests that for the world economy it might be convenient to set up a tabular presentation of income similar to the input-output tables developed by Leontief in the study of interindustry relations.[5] Such a table would show how each country's income is *earned* —in sales at home and sales to other countries—and how income is *spent*—in purchases at home and purchases from other countries. Individual countries or regions, in other words, would replace the individual industries in the Leontief tables; and imports and exports would replace inputs and outputs.

Let $m_i(y_i)$ be the function which shows how *total* imports of the ith country from all other countries in the table are related to national income, y_i, of the importing country. This total import function will be composed of a number of subfunctions showing how imports from each of the other countries are related to income in the ith country. Thus, if

4. If the import content of a country's exports differs from the import content of the goods and services produced for home use, total imports will depend not only upon income but also on the composition of income—that is, upon the way output is divided between exports and goods or services produced for domestic use. Since the demand for the given country's exports is governed in part by income in other countries, and since imports in this instance depend partly upon exports, it follows that imports should really be expressed as a function of income in all countries. But this is a refinement which cannot be incorporated in the present model without complicating it unduly.

5. W. W. Leontief, *The Structure of American Economy, 1919–1929* (Cambridge, Mass., Harvard University Press, 1941), *passim*.

$m_{ji}(y_i)$ represents the imports of the ith country from the jth country, stated as a function of income in the ith country, we will have $m_i(y_i) \equiv m_{1i}(y_i) + m_{2i}(y_i) + \ldots$, where the summation is extended over all countries from which the ith country imports goods or services. Since one country's imports are another country's exports, the entire pattern of world trade may be described in terms of the import functions $m_{ij}(y_i)$. The tabular presentation of world income may then be completed by inserting functional relations for each country's expenditures on *all* goods and services.

In setting up such total expenditure functions, we do not need to distinguish between consumers' goods and net investment, since the one affects income in the same way as the other. Suppose that both consumers' goods expenditures and net investment are dependent to some extent upon income at home, and let $u_i(y_i)$ represent such an expenditure function; $u_i(y_i)$, in other words, shows how expenditure in the ith country on *both* consumers' goods and net investment is related to the ith country's income. Hereafter the function $u_i(y_i)$ will be called simply an "expenditure function"; it plays the same role in the present theory of employment that is usually attributed to the consumption

Table 1. Notation for components of income, expenditure, and trade in the multiple-region model

	Expenditures by country 1 (1)	Expenditures by country 2 (2)	Expenditures by country 3 (3)	National income (1) + (2) + (3)
Receipts from sales by country 1 (1)	$u_1(y_1) - m_1(y_1)$	$m_{12}(y_2)$	$m_{13}(y_3)$	y_1
Receipts from sales by country 2 (2)	$m_{21}(y_1)$	$u_2(y_2) - m_2(y_2)$	$m_{23}(y_3)$	y_2
Receipts from sales by country 3 (3)	$m_{31}(y_1)$	$m_{32}(y_2)$	$u_3(y_3) - m_3(y_3)$	y_3
Total expenditures of each country (1) + (2) + (3)	$u_1(y_1)$	$u_2(y_2)$	$u_3(y_3)$	

function. The quantity $u_i(y_i)$ represents *all* expenditures of the *i*th country on consumers' goods and net investment, irrespective of the source of goods and services purchased. It includes imported finished goods as well as the import content of domestic production. In order to show how expenditure by a given country affects that country's net income, total imports, $m_i(y_i)$, must therefore be subtracted from the expenditure function, $u_i(y_i)$.

The foregoing relations are summarized in Table 1, which presents a hypothetical case of a world economy consisting of three countries. The items in a given *row* of this table provide a classification of the components of a country's national income according to the *sources* from which it was earned, while the items in the corresponding *column* indicate the *uses* of national income. The sum of the items in row 1 thus represents national income of country 1, while the sum of the items in column 1 shows the total expenditures of country 1 on all goods and services. When we sum column 1, the positive items of imports, $m_{21}(y_1)$ and $m_{31}(y_1)$, will exactly cancel against total imports, which enter negatively in row 1, column 1, leaving only the total expenditure, $u_1(y_1)$.

Consider now a more general economic system consisting of *n* countries. Using the same notation as in the table, we can set up *n* equations which express the fact that, in equilibrium, each country's output is equal to the demand for this output. Thus we have

$$
\begin{aligned}
y_1 &= [u_1(y_1) - m_1(y_1)] + m_{12}(y_2) && + \cdots + m_{1n}(y_n), \\
y_2 &= m_{21}(y_1) && + [u_2(y_2) - m_2(y_2)] + \cdots + m_{2n}(y_n), \\
&\cdots\cdots\cdots\cdots\cdots\cdots\cdots\cdots\cdots\cdots\cdots\cdots\cdots\cdots\cdots\cdots \\
y_n &= m_{n1}(y_1) && + m_{n2}(y_2) && + \cdots \\
& && && + [u_n(y_n) - m_n(y_n)].
\end{aligned}
$$

(1)

Since there are *n* countries in all, these *n* equations are sufficient, with given prices and exchange rates, to determine the level of income in each country.

Stability of the System

Equations (1) are *static* equations; they indicate the levels of income which the system would achieve if consuming and investing habits remained unchanged over a sufficient period of time. They are accordingly useful in solving economic problems such as the ones mentioned earlier.

Suppose, for example, that the propensity to consume or to invest in domestic goods were to increase in country 1; the demand for goods and services would then rise throughout the world economy, and if the system were stable a new equilibrium, corresponding to the higher level of demand in country 1, would eventually be established in all countries. Equations (1) enable us to show how the new position of equilibrium in each of the n countries compares with the old. This problem is nothing more than a generalization of the familiar investment multiplier.

Before we discuss the static theory of income, however, there is a closely related dynamic problem that it will be useful to examine first. As we shall see, solution of the dynamic problem provides a considerable amount of information about the static theory. If income in one or more of the n countries is not in a state of equilibrium, so that the current level of output differs from the current demand, then the current levels of income, $y_1, y_2, \ldots, y_n$, will not satisfy Eqs. (1). In some instances, the level of output or income, y_i, may fall short of demand, while in other instances output will probably be in excess of current demand. Under these circumstances there will be a tendency for the level of output in each country to change, as producers try to bring their production plans in line with current requirements. The changes in output in turn will alter the level of income in each country, thereby bringing about shifts of demand and creating further discrepancies between supply and demand. The dynamic problem I wish to discuss is whether such a system has a natural tendency to approach a balanced state or whether discrepancies between demand and supply tend to produce still larger discrepancies. In short, is the system of income equations stable or unstable?

In order to answer this question, some assumptions must be made as to what happens in each country when output differs from current demand. Although no simple model can possibly do justice to such a complex problem, it seems to me reasonable to suppose that producers as a group will react to a discrepancy between output and demand by altering the rate of output. I shall therefore assume that output, and hence income, increases whenever demand exceeds current output and falls when demand is less than current output. Moreover, I shall assume that the speed with which output plans are altered is directly proportional to the size of the discrepancy between demand and supply; a big discrepancy, in other words, leads to a more rapid response than a small one. Although this second assumption is not absolutely essential, it is an assumption which will simplify our problem somewhat without altering the results in any important respect. Throughout the period when income is out of equilibrium, discrepancies between demand and supply are assumed to be met by appropriate adjustments of business inventories.

For any given country, say country 1, the rate of current net output or national income is y_1, while the net demand for this output is $u_1(y_1)$ $- m_1(y_1) + m_{12}(y_2) + \cdots + m_{1n}(y_n)$. The preceding assumptions concerning the behavior of producers may therefore be embodied, as a first approximation, in the following system of dynamic equations:

(2)

$$\frac{dy_1}{dt} = k_1[u_1(y_1) - m_1(y_1) + m_{12}(y_2) + \cdots + m_{1n}(y_n) - y_1],$$

$$\frac{dy_2}{dt} = k_2[u_2(y_2) - m_2(y_2) + m_{21}(y_1) + \cdots + m_{2n}(y_n) - y_2],$$

$$\cdots\cdots\cdots\cdots\cdots\cdots\cdots\cdots\cdots\cdots\cdots\cdots\cdots\cdots\cdots\cdots$$

$$\frac{dy_n}{dt} = k_n[u_n(y_n) - m_n(y_n) + m_{n1}(y_1) + \cdots + m_{n,n-1}(y_{n-1}) - y_n].$$

The constants k_i in these equations are positive numbers which represent the speeds of adjustment of output in the various countries.

Equations (2) cannot be solved without knowing the explicit form of the expenditure functions and import functions. Since we are primarily interested in the stability of the system and not in its explicit solution, however, we may consider only a linear approximation to (2). Stability of the linear approximation is obviously a necessary condition, although not always a sufficient condition, for stability of Eqs. (2). Expanding the right-hand side of (2) in a Taylor expansion about the equilibrium values $y_1^0, y_2^0, \ldots, y_n^0$, and dropping all except linear terms, we have

(3)

$$\frac{dy_1}{dt} = k_1(u_1' - m_1' - 1)(y_1 - y_1^0)$$
$$+ k_1 m_{12}'(y_2 - y_2^0) + \cdots + k_1 m_{1n}'(y_n - y_n^0),$$

$$\frac{dy_2}{dt} = k_2 m_{21}'(y_1 - y_1^0)$$
$$+ k_2(u_2' - m_2' - 1)(y_2 - y_2^0) + \cdots + k_2 m_{2n}'(y_n - y_n^0),$$

$$\cdots\cdots\cdots\cdots\cdots\cdots\cdots\cdots\cdots\cdots\cdots\cdots\cdots\cdots\cdots\cdots$$

$$\frac{dy_n}{dt} = k_n m_{n1}'(y_1 - y_1^0)$$
$$+ k_n m_{n2}'(y_2 - y_2^0) + \cdots + k_n(u_n' - m_n' - 1)(y_n - y_n^0),$$

where $u_i' \equiv (du_i/dy_i)_{y_i}{}^0$, $m_{ji}' \equiv (dm_{ji}/dy_i)_{y_i}{}^0$, and so forth. Equations (3), being linear with constant coefficients, can be solved for any given initial conditions so as to express each of the incomes y_i as a function of time, as follows:

$$(4) \qquad y_i(t) = y_i^0 + A_{i1}e^{\lambda_1 t} + A_{i2}{}^{\lambda_2 t} + \cdots + A_{in}e^{\lambda_n t},$$

where the A_{ij} are constants dependent upon the initial value of income at time $t = 0$, and where the λ_j are roots of the following equation:

$$(5) \quad \begin{vmatrix} k_1(1 + m_1' - u_1') + \lambda & -k_1 m_{12}' & & -k_1 m_{1n}' \\ -k_2 m_{21}' & k_2(1 + m_2' - u_2') + \lambda \ldots & & -k_2 m_{2n}' \\ \cdots\cdots\cdots\cdots\cdots\cdots\cdots\cdots\cdots\cdots\cdots\cdots\cdots\cdots\cdots \\ -k_n n_{n1}' & & -k_n m_{n2}' & \ldots k_n(1 + m_n' - u_n') + \lambda \end{vmatrix} = 0.$$

In order for $y_i(t)$ to approach its equilibrium value y_i^0 as t increases, it is apparent from Eq. (4) that the real parts of $\lambda_1, \lambda_2, \ldots, \lambda_n$ must all be negative. The necessary and sufficient conditions for this to be true may conveniently be expressed in terms of the following nth-order determinant:

$$(6) \quad M \equiv \begin{vmatrix} 1 + m_1' - u_1' & -m_{12}' & \cdots & -m_{1n}' \\ -m_{21}' & 1 + m_2' - u_2' \ldots & & -m_{2n}' \\ \cdots\cdots\cdots\cdots\cdots\cdots\cdots\cdots\cdots\cdots\cdots\cdots\cdots \\ -m_{n1}' & -m_{n2}' & \ldots 1 + m_n' - u_n' \end{vmatrix}.$$

The coefficient m_{ij}' of the determinant (6) represents, of course, the marginal propensity of the jth country to import from the ith country; that is, it shows how the demand in country j for imports from country i is affected by a small increase in the former country's income. Similarly, the coefficient m_j' represents the marginal propensity of the jth country to import from all other countries together, so that $m_j' \equiv m_{1j}' + m_{2j}' + \cdots + m_{nj}'$. Throughout this paper coefficients such as m_{ij}' are assumed to be positive or zero, which means that all the off-diagonal elements of M are negative or zero.[6] The coefficient u_j' represents the

---

6. If one country's imports from another consisted predominantly of inferior commodities, the former's propensity to import from the latter might conceivably be negative. In this event many of the theorems of the present paper would be invalid. The presence of negative propensities to import makes the conditions of stability considerably more complicated. Compare, for example, my conclusions concerning stability with those of John S. Chipman, "The Multi-Sector Multiplier" (reference 1).

marginal propensity of the jth country to spend, including the marginal propensity to invest (if any) as well as the marginal propensity to consume, and including expenditure on imported finished goods as well as upon domestic goods. Normally u_j' will be less than unity, but if the propensity to invest is large, this need not be true.

I have demonstrated in an earlier paper that for dynamic systems such as (3) in which all off-diagonal coefficients of the y_i are positive or zero, the necessary and sufficient conditions of stability are identical with the so-called Hicksian conditions of perfect stability.[7] This means that the determinant M and any set of its principal minors such as

$$1 + m_i' - u_i', \quad \begin{vmatrix} 1 + m_i' - u_i' & -m_{ij}' \\ -m_{ji}' & 1 + m_j' - u_j' \end{vmatrix},$$

$$\begin{vmatrix} 1 + m_i' - u_i' & -m_{ij}' & -m_{ik}' \\ -m_{ji}' & 1 + m_j' - u_j' & -m_{jk}' \\ -m_{ki}' & -m_{kj}' & 1 + m_k' - u_k' \end{vmatrix},$$

and so on, must be positive. Hereafter any determinant satisfying these conditions will be called a "Hicksian determinant."[8]

Since the speeds of adaptation k_j do not appear in the Hicks conditions, it follows that stability of (3) is independent of such speeds. A system which is stable for one set of speeds of adaptation will therefore be stable for all other possible sets. The fact that producers in one country change their production plans more rapidly than producers in another country has no effect upon the stability of the system.

Having established a general set of conditions which must be fulfilled in order that the income equations shall be stable, we can now go a step further and show that these Hicksian conditions depend, in a unique way, upon the propensities to spend in all countries. In particular, two propositions will be demonstrated. First, if the marginal propensity to spend, including expenditure on investment goods as well as on

7. Lloyd A. Metzler, "Stability of Multiple Markets: The Hicks Conditions," included as Chapter 20 of the present volume.

8. In my earlier paper the conditions of stability were expressed in terms of a determinant whose elements all had signs opposite to the signs of the corresponding elements of M. As a result, the formal appearance of the stability conditions was not the same as in the present paper. In the terminology of my earlier paper, stability of the system required that the principal minors, when arranged as above, should be alternately negative and positive and that the basic determinant itself should have the sign of $(-1)^n$. By changing the sign of each of the elements of M, the reader can easily verify that these earlier stability conditions are identical with the ones given in the present paper.

consumers' goods, is less than unity in every country, the system is necessarily Hicksian and therefore stable. Second, if the marginal propensity to spend is *greater* than unity in every country, the system cannot be Hicksian and must therefore be unstable.

To prove these propositions, it is convenient to use a theorem developed by Mosak.[9] Mosak's theorem, in slightly modified form, is as follows. If an nth-order determinant is Hicksian, and if the off-diagonal elements $-m_{ij}'$ are all negative, then the cofactor M_{ij} of the element $-m_{ij}'$ is positive for all i and j. The proof of this theorem is a simple proof by induction. Expanding M_{ij} about the row containing the elements $-m_{j1}', -m_{j2}', \ldots, -m_{jn}'$, we may write

$$(7) \qquad M_{ij} \equiv \sum_k -m_{jk}' M_{ij,jk},$$

where $M_{ij,jk}$ is the cofactor of the element $-m_{jk}'$ in the determinant M_{ij} and where the summation extends over all values of k from 1 to n except $k = j$. Since $M_{ij,jk} \equiv -M_{jj,ik}$, Eq. (7) may be written as follows:

$$(8) \qquad M_{ij} \equiv \sum_k m_{ik}' M_{jj,ik}.$$

Now M_{jj} is a Hicksian determinant of order $n - 1$. Suppose that Mosak's theorem is true for such an $(n - 1)$th-order determinant. Then $M_{jj,ik}$ is positive, and it follows, from Eq. (8), that M_{ij} must likewise be positive. Thus if the theorem is true for the cofactors of an $(n - 1)$th-order determinant obtained by deleting the jth row and jth column of M, it is also true for the cofactors of the nth-order determinant M. A similar argument applies, of course, to the cofactors of any lower-order Hicksian determinants obtained from M by deleting like rows and columns. To complete the proof, we must show that the theorem is true for a low-order principal minor of M, such as a second-order minor. A typical second-order minor of M is

$$\begin{vmatrix} 1 + m_i' - u_i' & -m_{ij}' \\ -m_{ji}' & 1 + m_j' - u_j' \end{vmatrix}.$$

The cofactors of the off-diagonal elements of this minor are m_{ij}' and m_{ji}' respectively, and these are both positive. Thus Mosak's theorem is proved; that is, we have shown that if the nth-order determinant is Hicksian, the cofactors of its off-diagonal elements are all positive.

9. Jacob L. Mosak, *General-Equilibrium Theory in International Trade*, Cowles Commission Monograph No. 7 (Bloomington, Ind., Principia Press, 1944), pp. 49–51.

With the aid of this theorem, the two propositions stated above concerning the relations between marginal propensities to spend and the determinant M may easily be proved. Consider first the case in which the marginal propensity to spend is *less* than unity in each country. According to our first proposition, the determinant M is necessarily Hicksian and the dynamic system (3) is therefore stable under these conditions. The proposition will be proved by induction.

Since $m_i' \equiv m_{1i}' + m_{2i}' + \cdots + m_{ni}'$, it is clear that the sum of the elements of the ith column of M is equal to $1 - u_i'$, where u_i' is the marginal propensity to spend of the ith country. Thus if all u_i' are less than unity, the sum of the elements of each column of M will be positive. Adding all other rows of M to the first row, we may write:

$$(9) \qquad M \equiv \begin{vmatrix} 1 - u_1' & 1 - u_2' & 1 - u_3' \dots 1 - u_n' \\ -m_{21}' & & \\ -m_{31}' & & M_{11} \\ \dots & & \\ -m_{n1}' & & \end{vmatrix},$$

where M_{11} denotes the cofactor of M obtained by deleting the first row and first column. Now it is evident that under our assumed conditions M_{11} is an $(n-1)$th-order determinant having the same essential characteristics as M itself; in other words, that the sum of the elements of each column of M_{11} is positive. The first column of M_{11}, for example, contains all of the elements of the corresponding column of M except the negative quantity $-m_{12}'$, and similarly for all other columns. It follows that if the sum of the elements of a given column of M is positive, the same will be true a fortiori of the sum of the elements in the corresponding column of M_{11}. Any theorems concerning M which are based upon this characteristic will therefore be equally applicable to M_{11}. And a similar argument applies to lower-order principal minors of M, such as $M_{11,22}$, $M_{11,22,33}$, and so on.

Suppose now that our theorem is true for the $(n-1)$th-order determinant, M_{11}; that is, suppose that M_{11} is Hicksian. It can then be shown that the nth-order determinant, M, is also Hicksian. Expanding (9) on the first row and first column in a Cauchy expansion, we find:[10]

$$(10) \qquad M \equiv (1 - u_1')M_{11} + \sum_k \sum_j m_{j1}'(1 - u_k')M_{11,jk}.$$

10. See A. C. Aitken, *Determinants and Matrices* (New York, Interscience Publishers, 1944), pp. 74–75.

If M_{11} is a Hicksian determinant it must be positive, and $M_{11,jj}$, $M_{11,kk}$, and so forth, must likewise be positive. Moreover, by Mosak's theorem, $M_{11,jk}$ is positive. Since the m_{j1}' are positive or zero, and since $1 - u_1'$ and $1 - u_k'$ are positive by hypothesis, it follows immediately from Eq. (10) that if M_{11} is a Hicksian determinant, M is positive and is therefore Hicksian.

It has now been demonstrated that if all u_k' are less than unity, and if M_{11} is Hicksian, then M is likewise Hicksian. By a similar argument it can be shown that, if $M_{11,22}$ is Hicksian and if the u_k' are less than unity, M_{11} is necessarily Hicksian. To complete the proof that M is always a Hicksian determinant when the marginal propensity to spend, u_k', is less than unity in every country, it is sufficient to show that the theorem is true for any low-order principal minor of M. Consider, for example, the following second-order minor:

$$\begin{vmatrix} 1 + m_i' - u_i' & -m_{ij}' \\ -m_{ji}' & 1 + m_j' - u_j' \end{vmatrix}.$$

Since $m_i' \geq m_{ji}'$ and $m' \geq m_{ij}'$, it is easy to show by expanding the above determinant that it is necessarily positive whenever u_i' and u_j' are both less than unity. Moreover, it may be seen by inspection that, under the prescribed conditions, the principal minors are positive. The second-order minor of M is therefore Hicksian, and our proof that M is a Hicksian determinant is complete.

If M is a Hicksian determinant, it follows from the results of my earlier paper that the dynamic system represented by Eqs. (3) is a stable system. This conclusion will perhaps not surprise anyone, since it is simply a generalization of the theory of income stability of a single, closed economic system. It is well known that the multiplier in such a one-country system cannot have a finite value unless the country's marginal propensity to spend is less than unity. I have now established an analogous condition—sufficient but not necessary—for the case of an n-country economy.

Consider now an extreme case in which the marginal propensity to spend is *greater* than unity in every country. I have suggested above that in this event the determinant M cannot be Hicksian and the dynamic system (3) must therefore be unstable. The proof of this proposition consists in showing that if all u_k' exceed unity, the assumption that M is Hicksian involves a contradiction. If M is Hicksian, the principal minor M_{11} is, of course, also Hicksian, which means that $M_{11,jk}$ and M_{11} are both positive. But if the marginal propensity to spend is greater than unity in all countries, $1 - u_k'$ is negative for all values of k. From Eq. (10) it follows that M must be negative. This contradicts the assumption that M is a Hicksian determinant and proves, in fact, that M cannot be Hicksian. It shows, in other words, that if the determinant is Hicksian so far as its principal minors are concerned, and if all marginal propensities to spend exceed unity, the determinant itself is negative and is therefore non-Hicksian. Again, from the results of my previous paper it is clear that under such conditions the dynamic system (3) must necessarily be unstable.

I have now examined the stability of income for two different situations. The first, which might be called the normal situation, is the case in which the marginal propensity to spend is less than unity in every country. The second, which goes to the opposite extreme, is the case in which every country has a marginal propensity to spend exceeding unity. In the first situation the system was found to be Hicksian, and therefore stable, while in the second it was found to be non-Hicksian and therefore unstable. Between these two extremes may be found a large number of intermediate situations in which the propensity to spend is less than unity in some countries and greater than unity in others. The basic determinant M of these intermediate systems may or may not be Hicksian, which means that the systems may or may not be dynamically stable. Broadly speaking, we may say that M will be Hicksian and the system will be stable if the countries with low propensities to spend dominate, while in the converse case M will be non-Hicksian and the system unstable.

In any event, the discussion that follows below concerning the international repercussions of added investment in one of the n countries is based upon the explicit assumption that the income equations form a dynamically stable system. In other words, the assumption is made that an increase of investment in one of the countries leads ultimately to a new equilibrium of income in all countries and does not set off a continuous process of expansion culminating in a runaway inflation. This means that, while the propensity to spend may exceed unity in some countries, it cannot do so in all countries; at least one of the countries must have a propensity to spend of less than unity, and the low-propensity countries must be sufficiently important so that the basic determinant M is a Hicksian determinant.

Investment and Income

Having examined the conditions of stability of our income equations, we are now in a position to investigate some problems of comparative statics. Suppose that national income is initially in equilibrium in all countries and that this equilibrium is disturbed by an increase of investment in one of the countries, say in country 1. If the increase of investment is sustained over a sufficient period of time, and if the income equations are dynamically stable, a new equilibrium corresponding to the higher rate of investment will eventually be established throughout the system. The income of every country will probably be affected to some extent by the expansion of investment in country 1; and, as national incomes are altered, each country's exports and imports, or its balance of payments on current account, will likewise be changed. The present section is concerned with the changes in income brought about by the higher level of investment in country 1.

Let α_1 represent autonomous or noninduced investment in country 1. The first equation of the static system (1), including the additional investment, then becomes:

$$(11) \qquad y_1 = u_1(y_1) - m_1(y_1) + m_{12}(y_2) + \cdots + m_{1n}(y_n) + \alpha_1.$$

Assuming no change in autonomous investment in the other countries, the remaining $n - 1$ equations of (1) are unaltered. Equation (11) and the last $n - 1$ equations of (1) thus form a closed system of n equations in which the income of each country may be regarded as a function of α_1. In order to see how the increase of investment in country 1 affects each country, we may differentiate Eq. (11) and the last $n - 1$ equations of (1) with respect to α_1, and solve the resulting linear equations for $dy_1/d\alpha_1$ and $dy_k/d\alpha_1$. It will then be found that

$$(12) \qquad \frac{dy_1}{d\alpha_1} = \frac{M_{11}}{M}, \qquad \frac{dy_k}{d\alpha_1} = \frac{M_{1k}}{M},$$

where, as before, M is the determinant of marginal propensities given by Eq. (6). We know from the conditions of stability and from Mosak's theorem that M_{11}, M_{1k}, and M must all be positive. Both $dy_1/d\alpha_1$ and $dy_k/d\alpha_1$ must therefore be positive, which shows that an increase in investment in one of the n countries increases the level of income in every country in the system. There is, of course, nothing startling or profound about this conclusion; indeed, it is a conclusion which could have been reached intuitively without any mathematics at all.[11] It is therefore important only insofar as it leads to less obvious relations.

The expression M_{11}/M, which shows how income in the first country is affected by an increase of investment in that country, is a generalized form of the investment multiplier. I wish to show how this generalized multiplier is related to two simpler multipliers that one encounters frequently in the theory of employment. The first of these simple multipliers is the ordinary investment multiplier of a closed economic system, that is, the multiplier which ignores foreign trade leakages; the second is the so-called foreign trade multiplier, which makes allowance for foreign trade leakages but does not take into account the effects of income movements in other countries upon the demand for a given country's exports.

If, as before, u_1' denotes the marginal propensity to spend of the first country, and m_1' denotes that country's marginal propensity to import, the ordinary investment multiplier, which assumes that all demand is for home goods, is simply $1/(1 - u_1')$. The foreign trade multiplier, on the other hand, is $1/(1 - u_1' + m_1')$. What is the relation of these two simple multipliers to the generalized multiplier given by Eqs. (12)? Using the stability conditions and Mosak's theorem, it may be shown that, in the normal case in which the marginal propensity to spend is less than unity in every country, the value of the generalized multiplier lies between the ordinary multiplier and the foreign trade multiplier.

To prove this proposition, notice first that by adding all other rows to the first row of M, expanding on the elements of this new row, and dividing both numerator and denominator by M_{11}, we may write:

$$(13) \quad \frac{dy_1}{d\alpha_1} \equiv \frac{M_{11}}{M}$$

$$\equiv \frac{1}{(1 - u_1') + [(1 - u_2')M_{12}/M_{11}] + \cdots + [(1 - u_n')M_{1n}/M_{11}]}.$$

11. Any economist who gives the matter any thought will probably feel that to develop the rather complicated theorems of the previous section concerning Hicksian determinants and conditions of stability simply in order to prove that an increase in investment in one country causes income to rise in all countries is like using a bulldozer to move an anthill. His intuitive feeling may be so strong, in fact, that he will prefer to reverse the procedure of the present paper and use what he "knows" about the economic system to prove the theorems concerning determinants! While the mathematician will doubtless object to this procedure as completely lacking in rigor, I must confess that I have considerable confidence in it, particularly since it was substantially such a trend of thought which first led me to suspect the truth of the mathematical propositions given in the preceding section.

Since M_{1k}/M_{11} is positive for any value of k, and since all of the u_k' are assumed to be less than unity, it is clear that the expression in (13) is less than the ordinary investment multiplier, which in this instance has a value of $1/(1 - u_1')$.

The second limit to $dy_1/d\alpha_1$ may be found by expanding M on its first *column* and again dividing both numerator and denominator of the resulting expression for $dy_1/d\alpha_1$ by M_{11}. It will then be found that

$$(14) \qquad \frac{dy_1}{d\alpha_1} = \frac{1}{1 - u_1' + m_1' - [m_{21}'M_{21}/M_{11}] - \cdots - [m_{n1}'M_{n1}/M_{11}]}.$$

Again, since M_{k1}/M_{11} is positive, the value of $dy_1/d\alpha_1$ given by Eq. (14) is clearly *greater* than the foreign trade multiplier, $1/(1 - u_1' + m_1')$. Thus I have shown that in the normal case in which all marginal propensities to spend are less than unity, the generalized investment multiplier has the following limits:

$$(15) \qquad \frac{1}{1 - u_1' + m_1'} < \frac{dy_1}{d\alpha_1} < \frac{1}{1 - u_1'}.$$

These limits derive their importance from the fact that they represent two forms of the multiplier which have played prominent roles in the historical development of the theory of employment.

If one or more of the other countries—that is, countries 2, 3, ..., n —has a marginal propensity to spend greater than unity, one of the limits given by (15) *may* not hold. In particular, while the generalized multiplier is always greater than the foreign trade multiplier, as Eq. (14) shows, it may in special cases also be greater than the ordinary investment multiplier. Consider, for example, the following system:

$$(16) \qquad y_1 = 0.4y_1 + 0.5y_2 + \alpha_1, \qquad y_2 = 0.2y_1 + 0.7y_2.$$

For this system, $dy_1/d\alpha_1 = 3.75$, while $1/(1 - u_1') = 2.5$. Thus when the marginal propensity to spend of one or more of the "other" countries exceeds unity, the true investment multiplier for a given country may be larger than the ordinary investment multiplier. In most cases, however, it seems probable that the true multiplier will lie between the two simple multipliers, as indicated in (15).

It may be useful at this point to give a brief intuitive explanation of the relations among the three multipliers. The foreign trade multiplier is the smallest of the three because it assumes that a country's exports are given and independent of its imports. In a period of rising domestic income, in other words, the foreign trade multiplier tacitly assumes that increased expenditures on imports represent net leakages from the country's circular flow of income; no allowance is made for the fact that as imports rise the level of income in other countries also rises, and the demand for the particular country's exports therefore rises, to some extent, along with its imports. The generalized multiplier takes account of this secondary rise in the country's exports, and it is therefore larger than the foreign trade multiplier. The ordinary investment multiplier, on the other hand, makes no allowance either for the leakages from the circular flow of income arising from increased imports or for the return of some of these leakages in the form of increased exports; it assumes, instead, that every increase in expenditure represents an equivalent increase in domestic income. Since the secondary rise in exports is normally smaller than the increase in imports with which it is associated, it follows that foreign trade usually exerts a retarding effect upon a rise in income originating in domestic investment. In short, the effect of foreign trade is to spread the stimulating effects of investment in one country over the entire economic system, thereby diluting to some extent the stimulus to income in the country originating the expansion. And because it ignores this diluting effect, the ordinary investment multiplier overstates the rise in income at home to be expected from a given increase in domestic investment.

Investment and the Pattern of Trade

So much for the effects of investment upon income and employment. I turn now to the related problem of the pattern of trade. As income expands throughout the system, each country's exports and imports will rise, and it is almost inevitable under such conditions that the balance of trade of most if not all of the countries will be affected. In the new position of equilibrium, some countries will have more favorable balances while others will have less favorable balances than in the old. What can be said, in a general way, about the new network of trade compared with the old?

With respect to bilateral balances between individual pairs of countries, there is very little that a general theory such as the one outlined in this paper can predict. The outcome depends entirely upon the particular values of the propensities to spend and to import, and may show wide variation from one economic system to another. With respect to each country's balance of trade as a whole, on the other hand, certain broad generalizations are possible. In particular, we can specify the conditions under which a general expansion originating in country 1 is likely to lead to an improvement or to a deterioration in a given country's balance of trade with the rest of the world. Since there is no difficulty in forecasting how a given expansion will *initially* affect the balance of international payments, the problem before us is essentially a problem of comparing the initial, or primary, effects with the secondary repercussions. We want to know, in particular, whether the secondary repercussions are likely to reinforce or to offset the primary effects.

Consider, for example, the balance of payments of some country other than country 1, say country k. As investment and income expand in country 1, the initial effect will probably be an increase in exports from country k to the expanding country, thereby giving the latter a temporary surplus in its balance of payments. A similar initial effect may be anticipated, of course, in all of the other countries dealing with country 1. But as the other countries' exports to country 1 rise, their incomes will also rise, and the increase in incomes in turn will increase the demand for imports in these countries. The secondary income movements thus tend to offset the initial changes in balances of payments of the other countries.[12] There is no obvious reason, however, why the offsetting movement in each country's balance of payments should always be exactly equal to the initial disturbance. In the new equilibrium some countries will probably have more favorable balances of payments while others will have less favorable ones. What are the circumstances that distinguish the "surplus" countries from the "deficit" countries?

The question may be answered by considering the interrelations between balances of payments and incomes. Although the balance of trade of a given country depends upon the incomes of all countries in the system, there is a convenient way of relating each country's balance of trade to the *income of that country alone*. Thus, from the definition of national income given in Eqs. (1) above, it follows that the excess of a country's exports over its imports is equal to the excess of its national income over its total expenditure on both consumers' goods and net in-

12. It was no doubt this offsetting tendency that Nurkse had in mind when he said that the theory of employment provides both an explanation of the adjusting process of the balance of payments and a theory of the transmission of business cycles from one country to another. See Ragnar Nurkse, "Domestic and International Equilibrium," in *The New Economics*, ed. S. E. Harris (New York, Alfred A. Knopf, 1947), p. 264.

vestment. This is no more than a technical way of stating the common-sense proposition that a country with an export surplus is producing more than it uses itself, while a country with an import surplus is using more than it produces. But it is a technique, as we shall see, which saves a good deal of tedious algebra.

Consider, for example, the balance of payments of country k. If b_k denotes this balance, then it is clear from Eqs. (1) that

$$(17) \qquad b_k = y_k - u_k(y_k),$$

whence

$$(18) \qquad \frac{db_k}{d\alpha_1} = (1 - u_k') \frac{dy_k}{d\alpha_1}.$$

Since $dy_k/d\alpha_1$ is positive, Eq. (18) shows that the direction of change of country k's balance of payments depends upon that country's marginal propensity to spend. If its propensity to spend is less than unity, as will normally be the case, the balance of payments of country k will be improved by the expansion in country 1 even after allowing for the secondary rise of imports. But if the country's propensity to spend is *greater* than unity, Eq. (18) shows that its balance of payments on current account will be worsened by the expansion in country 1. In this instance the secondary rise of country k's imports will be *more* than sufficient to offset the initial rise of its exports.

Now suppose that the marginal propensity to spend of each of the countries 2, 3, . . . , n is less than unity. Under such conditions, the expansion of income in country 1 improves the trade balances of all other countries in the system; from this it follows that the trade balance of the country initiating the expansion must be less favorable than before the expansion began. In short, an expansion of income originating in one country normally moves the balance of trade *against* that country and *in favor of* all other countries in the system; as long as marginal propensities to spend are all less than unity, this proposition holds true regardless of the relative sizes of the marginal propensities to import. For this reason we cannot say that if the other countries' propensities to import from country 1 are high, the induced expansion of their imports is likely to overbalance the initial rise of their exports, leaving them with less favorable trade balances than before the expansion began. The outcome depends not upon the relative magnitudes of import propensities, but upon the absolute size of each of the propensities to spend. If the marginal propensities to spend are less than unity, the result will be an improvement in the balances of payments of all countries except country 1, irrespective of the size of import propensities.

If marginal propensities to spend in some of the countries exceed unity, on the other hand, it is possible that some or all of the conclusions of the preceding paragraph will have to be reversed. Consider first an extreme case. Suppose that the propensities to spend exceed unity in *all* of the countries 2, 3, ..., n. Under these circumstances it is clear from Eq. (18) that the balance of trade of each of these countries would become less favorable as a result of expansion in country 1; the secondary rise of imports in each of the countries would overbalance the primary increase in exports. But if countries 2, 3, ..., n all have less favorable balances of payments, country 1 must necessarily have a *more* favorable balance. After allowing for all repercussions, in other words, expansion of income in country 1 increases that country's exports more than its imports are increased. Public works, encouragement of private investment, and other measures to expand the employment of resources in country 1 would not, under the circumstances, create a balance-of-payments problem for the expanding country. Each time country 1 increased its imports, it could count upon an even larger secondary increase in its exports.

It is conceivable that this conclusion would be valid even under less extreme circumstances. Suppose, for example, that some of the countries 2, 3, ..., n had propensities to spend greater than unity while others had spending propensities less than unity. From Eq. (18) it is clear that some of these countries would then suffer a worsening of their balances of payments when country 1 started an expansion, while others would find their balances of payments improved. And if the sum of all the adverse and favorable changes together were adverse, then country 1 would obviously have a more favorable balance of payments than in the initial equilibrium. On the other hand, if the sum of changes in the balances of payments of countries 2, 3, ..., n were favorable, then the movement of country 1's balance would necessarily be adverse. Thus when some of the spending propensities of countries 2, 3, ..., n exceed unity, while others are less than unity, it is impossible without additional information to predict the effect of expansion on the balance of payments of the country initiating the expansion. The outcome depends upon a balancing of forces, that is, upon a balancing of the influence of the stable countries against the influence of the unstable ones.

Thus far we have regarded the balance of payments of country 1 as a sort of residual; we have described its movement only after seeing what happened to the balances of payments of the other countries in the system. Although this procedure is satisfactory for some purposes, it does not allow us to say much about the *magnitude* of the movement in country 1's balance of payments. It is therefore useful to examine this balance directly. From Eqs. (11) and (1) the balance of payments of country 1 may be written as follows:

(19) $$b_1 = y_1 - u_1(y_1) - \alpha_1.$$

In words, this says that country 1's balance of payments on current account is the difference between its income and its total expenditure on goods and services, *including in the latter autonomous expenditures*, α_1, as well as $u_1(y_1)$. Differentiating b_1 with respect to α_1, we find:

(20) $$\frac{db_1}{d\alpha_1} = (1 - u_1') \frac{dy_1}{d\alpha_1} - 1.$$

In evaluating Eq. (20) we may begin with what I have called the normal case, namely, the case in which all marginal propensities to spend are less than unity. In this case we know that $dy_1/d\alpha_1$ is less than the ordinary investment multiplier; that is, it is less than $1(1 - u_1')$. From this fact we can derive the following limits for the movement of the balance of payments on current account of country 1:

(21) $$-1 < \frac{db_1}{d\alpha_1} < 0.$$

These limits show that in the normal case an increase of investment in country 1 moves the balance of payments on current account *against* the expanding country; and the amount of unfavorable movement is normally less than the increase of investment. A billion-dollar public works program consisting exclusively in expenditure on domestic goods and services, for example, could not under normal circumstances create a foreign trade deficit in the expanding country greater than the amount of public works.

If the marginal propensity to spend in the expanding country is *greater* than unity, however, the limits given by inequality (21) no longer apply. It is apparent from Eq. (20) that under such a condition $db_1/d\alpha_1$ is less, algebraically, than -1. The unfavorable movement of country 1's balance of payment on current account would thus be *greater* than the amount of autonomous investment. An economy characterized by such a high propensity to spend would, of course, be highly unstable, and its instability in turn would lead to frequent and severe balance-of-payments problems vis-à-vis the rest of the world.

If the instability is in the rest of the world rather than in country 1, there may be no balance-of-payments problem at all in the country initiating the expansion. In other words, if a larger number of the "other countries" have marginal propensities to spend greater than unity, while country 1 has a propensity to spend *less* than unity, Eq .(20) shows that the change in the balance of payments of country 1 may be favorable rather than unfavorable. This would be true whenever $dy_1/d\alpha_1$ is greater than $1/(1 - u_1')$. In such a situation the secondary rise in exports of the expanding country would exceed the rise in imports; the secondary effects, in other words, would more than offset the primary effects. But such an outcome could be expected only under the rather unusual circumstances of high propensities to spend in a considerable number of the other countries.

Two-Country and Multiple-Country Models Compared

The classical theory of international trade, including the theory of comparative advantage as well as the closely related theory of the international price mechanism, was developed almost entirely in terms of two countries. Most of the important problems in international economics during the nineteenth century were discussed as though the world economy were divided into two regions, one region being the home country— usually England—and the other region being the "rest of the world." During the interwar period of the present century, this classical procedure came under heavy attack, particularly by the late Professor Graham, who argued with considerable cogency and force that the classical procedure involved a persistent bias.[13] Graham insisted that the traditional, two-country theory greatly exaggerated the role of international demand and neglected the role of shifts in output in determining the terms of international exchange. He argued specifically that if one considers a complex world economy in which a large number of coun-

13. Frank D. Graham, "The Theory of International Values Re-examined," *Quarterly Journal of Economics*, 38 (November 1923), 54–86, and "The Theory of International Values," *Quarterly Journal of Economics*, 46 (August 1932), 581–616. The ideas contained in these two articles were considerably elaborated in book form: Frank D. Graham, *The Theory of International Values* (Princeton, N.J., Princeton University Press, 1948).

tries are trading in a considerable number of commodities, the process of adjustment to a disturbing event in international trade is fundamentally similar to the process of adjustment within a single country. In Graham's view, then, the fact that resources, particularly labor, are more or less immobile between countries does not require, as the classical economists had supposed, a theory of *international* prices, separate and distinct from the theory of prices within a single country.

In concluding the present paper, which has dealt with an international theory of income rather than a theory of prices, there is no need to discuss at length the controversy between Graham and the classical economists. My purpose in raising the issue is not to try to settle it, but to raise a similar issue with respect to the international theory of income. If it is true, as Graham argues, that the traditional two-country model of international *price* theory involves a persistent and significant bias, is it also true that an analogous two-country model of international *income* theory involves a similar bias? To put the question another way, is a theory of international income that is founded upon the simplifying assumption that the world economy consists of two regions likely to involve any fundamental errors? The two-country income model, as I indicated earlier, has been discussed by a number of economists, and it should be possible to answer the question raised above by comparing the results of the two-country analysis with those of the generalized theory presented here. Since I am most familiar with my own version of the two-country model, I shall employ it to make the comparison.[14]

On the whole, the comparison does not reveal any basic flaws in the two-country model.[15] There are no processes of income adjustment in the *n*-country model which are not also revealed by the simple two-country model, and in the main the conclusions reached by employing the latter are the same as those reached by employing the former. In my earlier paper, using a terminology slightly different from that used here, I considered altogether three different cases of the two-country model. The first, or "normal," case was one in which the marginal propensity to spend was less than unity in both countries. The analogue of this case for the *n*-country model is the situation in which the propensity to spend is less than unity in each of the *n* countries. Under these circumstances both models reveal that an autonomous

14. Metzler, "Underemployment Equilibrium in International Trade," Chapter 10 of the present volume.
15. Machlup, *International Trade* (reference 2), p. 197.

increase of investment in one country creates a deficit in that country's balance of payments on current account and that the amount of the deficit is less than the autonomous investment. This conclusion using the two-country model, in other words, is in no way vitiated by the complex interactions of trade among a large number of countries.

The second case, in the two-country model, was one in which the propensity to spend of the country initiating the expansion, say country 1, was less than unity, while the propensity to spend of the second country was greater than unity. The analogous situation, in the n-country model, is that in which the propensity to spend is less than unity in country 1 but greater than unity in all other countries. Again, both the two-country and the n-country models lead to the same conclusion: autonomous investment in country 1 actually *improves* the balance of trade of that country; the induced rise of country 1's exports exceeds the rise of its imports.

The third and final case, in the two-country model, was a situation in which the propensity to spend in country 1 was greater than unity, while the propensity to spend in country 2 was less than unity; the analogue of this situation, in the n-country model, is the situation in which country 1 has a propensity to spend greater than unity, while all other countries have propensities less than unity. In this case also, as in the two preceding ones, the results of the two-country model are consistent with those of the n-country model. Either model supports the conclusion that, under the assumed conditions with respect to the propensities to spend, an increase in autonomous investment in country 1 leads to an unfavorable movement in that country's balance of trade, the amount of the unfavorable movement being greater than the amount of autonomous investment.

Considering the large measure of agreement between the two-country and the n-country models, the reader may wonder what purpose is served by studying the generalized theory at all. If the simple theory and the general one both lead to the same results, why bother with the latter? To this question a number of answers may be given. The first and most obvious one is that hindsight is better than foresight. While we might have felt intuitively that the two-country model is satisfactory for most purposes, I doubt whether we could have been sure of this without a careful study of the more general system.

A second reason for studying the general theory is that there are certain situations in the n-country model for which no analogue exists in the two-country model. This is true, for example, if the marginal propensity to spend is less than unity in country 1 and in some but not all of the remaining countries. In situations such as this the effects of expansion can be described only by the general, n-country model.

A third reason for preferring the n-country model to the two-country model is that the former provides a good deal more information than the latter about the dynamic stability of our income equations. Although I have used the stability conditions developed above primarily in studying the characteristics of the static equations, these stability conditions are also interesting and useful in other connections as well. It is useful, for example, to know that if the propensity to spend is less than unity in all regions or subregions of the system, the stability of the income equations does not depend in any way upon how the world economy happens to be divided into national units. As a second example, it could easily be shown from the discussion above and from my earlier paper on the stability of multiple markets that any cyclical solutions of the dynamic system are likely to be overshadowed by noncyclical solutions. This means, I believe, that the answer to the riddle of the business cycle is not to be found in horizontal transactions between one region and another, such as those depicted in our n-country system.

Perhaps the most important reason of all for studying the n-country model is that such a model will probably prove to be the most satisfactory theoretical foundation for an empirical study of the international aspects of income and employment. Although our study of the n-country model has not taken us very far, it has, I fear, taken us about as far as we can expect to go without introducing actual numbers in place of our hypothetical propensities to import and to spend. Unfortunately, the limits that we can expect to place upon the movements of our variables from a study of the theory alone are far too broad to be of much practical assistance in the formulation of economic policy. To a country considering the feasibility of a public works program, for example, it is little comfort to know that the unfavorable movement in its balance of trade engendered by such a program will normally be less than the amount of the public works. The country needs to know, in addition, what the approximate magnitude of its trade deficit will be and what the repercussions will be on incomes and trade balances in other countries.

In order to answer questions such as these, it is obvious that the theory described above must be transformed into an empirical system; and for this purpose the n-country system is clearly the appropriate one.

Eventually, then, an import-export matrix, similar in many respects to Leontief's input-output matrix for a single country, must be developed for the world economy. Many of the facts needed for such a table are already at hand. Reasonably accurate figures are available, for example, regarding the network of world trade. If these trade figures are to be transformed into propensities to import and to spend, however, they must be supplemented by statistics of national income for each of the countries. Lack of such income statistics has been responsible, more than anything else, for our inability to provide the empirical counterpart of the international theory of income set out above. With the improvement in statistics throughout the world since the end of World War II, it is to be hoped that this gap in our knowledge will soon be filled.

22 | A Multiple-Country Theory of Income Transfers

Nine years ago I presented a paper dealing with the effects of income transfers between countries.[1] In some respects the paper was simply a reconsideration of the controversy between Keynes and Ohlin concerning the effects of German reparations after the First World War;[2] and, like the Keynes-Ohlin discussion, my own contribution to the subject was limited to a simplified model consisting of only two countries. I now propose to investigate the same problem under somewhat more general conditions. Assuming that the world economy consists of n countries, I shall attempt to show how a transfer of money income from one of these countries to another influences the level of output and the balance of payments of each of the n countries. Repercussions of each transfer upon nonparticipating countries will thus be taken into account, along with the direct and indirect effects upon the paying and receiving countries themselves. Before I discuss the n-country model, however, let me summarize briefly the principal conclusions of my earlier investigation of the two-country model.

Reprinted from *Journal of Political Economy*, 59 (February 1951), 14–29. Copyright University of Chicago, 1951.

1. Lloyd A. Metzler, "The Transfer Problem Reconsidered," included as Chapter 2 of the present volume.
2. J. M. Keynes, "The German Transfer Problem," *Economic Journal*, 39 (March 1929), 1–7; Bertil Ohlin, "The Reparation Problem: A Discussion. I. Transfer Difficulties, Real and Imagined," *Economic Journal*, 39 (June 1929), 172–178; J. M. Keynes, "The Reparation Problem: A Discussion. II. A Rejoinder," *Economic Journal*, 39 (June 1929), 179–182; Bertil Ohlin, "Mr. Keynes' Views on the Transfer Problem. II. A Rejoinder," *Economic Journal*, 39 (September 1929), 400–404; and J. M. Keynes, "Mr. Keynes' Views on the Transfer Problem. III. A Reply," *Economic Journal*, 39 (September 1929), 404–408.

A transfer of money income between countries is unique in at least one respect: unlike other disturbances in international trade, such a transfer brings about a shift in purchasing power which is not associated with movements of prices or with movements of output and employment. In other words, even if prices and the volume of output remain constant in both countries, money income nevertheless falls in the paying country, as a result of the transfer, and rises by the same amount in the receiving country. The shift of purchasing power in turn affects each country's balance of payments. In the paying country, where money income has fallen, the demand for imports tends to decline; and in the receiving country, where money income has risen, the demand for imports rises.

An income transfer thus has a tendency, even before price movements or movements of output occur, to increase the exports and reduce the imports of the paying country and thereby to initiate the "real" transfer of goods and services which is necessary to restore equilibrium in the balance of payments between the two countries. The question at issue in my earlier paper was whether the improvement brought about in the paying country's balance of payments is likely to be greater than, equal to, or less than the amount of the transfer itself. In other words, does the shift of purchasing power constitute a complete, or only a partial, explanation of the transfer process?

Paradoxically, the answer to this question depends less upon the primary shift in purchasing power than upon its secondary repercussions; it was with respect to these secondary repercussions that my investigation of the transfer mechanism differed from the investigations of Keynes, Ohlin, and others. In the Keynes-Ohlin controversy and in most other interwar contributions to the subject, the secondary repercussions were assumed to take the form of movements of prices and money costs and the principal emphasis was accordingly placed upon changes in the terms of trade. In my own investigation, on the other hand, prices and money costs were assumed to remain constant. Hence discrepancies between supply and demand affected output and employment rather than the terms of trade.[3] The move-

---

3. Whether the one or the other of these two contrasting assumptions is the more realistic is an exceedingly difficult question. The answer depends in part upon institutional factors, such as the flexibility or rigidity of wages; it also depends to some extent upon problems of economic theory, such as the consistency or inconsistency of the full-employment system. But these are issues I do not wish to discuss here.

ments of output and employment in turn influenced each country's balance of payments, the exact changes being dependent upon the extent of the movements in income and upon the marginal propensities to import. The basic problem of my earlier paper was whether such income-induced movements in the volume and value of international trade tended automatically to restore equilibrium or whether a discrepancy between supply and demand in the international markets remained, even after all secondary repercussions of the transfer upon output and employment had been taken into account.

In order to isolate the effects of changes in output and employment from the effects of price changes, an extremely rigid model was considered in which the money demand for imports in each country was assumed to depend only upon the level of money income. Factor prices and exchange rates were assumed to remain constant, and all goods and services were assumed to be produced at constant-supply prices, so that no changes in the pattern of relative prices resulted from the shifts in demand.

If induced movements in output are allowed for, the effects of the money transfer upon purchasing power in the two countries become quite complex. It is no longer true, as was so frequently supposed in the interwar discussion of the transfer mechanism, that with given prices, the purchasing power of the paying country necessarily falls by exactly the amount of the transfer, while that of the receiving country rises by the same amount. Indeed, it is not even clear that the paying country's purchasing power falls at all or that the purchasing power of the receiving country necessarily rises; for in an economic system where output and employment are subject to fluctuations, the movement of purchasing power depends upon these fluctuations as well as upon the income transfer itself.

In the paying country, purchasing power initially falls by exactly the amount of the transfer, just as it was assumed to do in the interwar discussion. But this primary movement is later accompanied by a series of secondary movements which tend, in part, to reinforce the primary change and, in part, to offset it. On the one hand, the initial reduction of money income tends to reduce the paying country's demand for domestic goods, and the reduced demand leads to reduced output, which tends to depress income or purchasing power still further. On the other hand, the initial increase of income in the receiving country tends to increase the exports of the paying country; and the

rise of exports increases output, employment, and income in that segment of the paying country's economy. The ultimate effect of the
transfer on the paying country's income or purchasing power as a whole
thus depends upon a balancing of forces; the country's income may
either rise or fall, depending upon whether the stimulating effect of the
rise in exports is more important or less important than the depressing
effect of the transfer itself. A similar argument applies, of course, in
the receiving country, where the stimulating effect of the new income
receipt must be weighed against the retarding effect of a decline in exports. The final outcome is therefore somewhat doubtful in both
countries, so far as income effects are concerned.

Whether a given country's income rises or falls and whether the
favorable movement in the paying country's balance of payments is
less, or greater, than the annual income transfer depend (as I showed
in my earlier paper) upon what may be called the "propensity to spend"
in each of the countries. A country's marginal propensity to spend measures the increase in demand for all goods and services—imported as
well as domestic—which results from a one-unit increase of income.
Normally such propensities will be less than unity, that is, a given
increase of income will usually call forth a smaller increase in demand
for goods and services. If this were not true, each country's income and
employment would be inherently unstable, and except for the stabilizing
influence of countries with lower propensities to spend, there would be
no equilibrium of income at all. In exceptional cases, however, and for
rather short periods of time it is conceivable that the marginal propensity to spend of one or more countries may exceed unity without creating
an unstable situation, provided that there are some countries in the
world economy whose propensities to spend are small.

Thus in the two-country model we may consider three possible
cases with respect to propensities to spend. In the first case, which I have
called the "normal" case, the marginal propensity to spend is assumed
to be less than unity in each country. In the second case the marginal
propensity to spend is assumed to exceed unity in the receiving country
but to be less than unity in the paying. Finally, in the third case the
marginal propensity to spend is assumed to be less than unity in the
receiving country and greater than unity in the paying country. The
fourth possible case of a marginal propensity to spend greater than unity
in both countries must be rejected as incompatible with stability of
income for the world economy.

All these possibilities were investigated in my previous analysis of income transfers. In the first, or normal, case it was found that after all secondary repercussions had been taken into account, income fell in the paying country and increased in the receiving country. In other words, when the marginal propensity to spend was less than unity in each country, the secondary change in exports was not sufficient in either country to offset completely the initial effect of the transfer itself. The direction of change of income was the same as the direction of the primary shift of purchasing power, but the magnitude of the income movement might be either greater, or less, than the magnitude of the primary shift, depending upon the numerical values of the propensities to spend and to import in the two countries. The balance of payments on current account, exclusive of the transfer, tended in the normal case to move in favor of the paying country, both through an increase of exports and through a decline of imports; but the favorable movement was not equal in magnitude to the size of the transfer, and the paying country was accordingly left with a "transfer problem."

In the second and third cases, which I regarded—and still regard—as somewhat unusual, the balance of payments on current account again was found to move in favor of the paying country; and in these cases the favorable movement was greater than the transfer itself. The movements of income in these exceptional cases were somewhat peculiar. When the paying country was the one with the high propensity to spend, the transfer caused income to decline in the receiving country as well as in the paying country. Under these circumstances, the depression in the paying country was found to be so great that the receiving country, on balance, was affected adversely by the transfer;[4] in other words, the decline in the receiving country's exports was so large that it more than offset the stimulating effect in the receiving country of the transfer itself.

When the receiving country was the one with the high propensity to spend, on the other hand, the final effect of the transfer was a general expansion of income in both countries. Receipt of the transfer then brought about a large secondary increase in the receiving country's

4. This possibility corresponds to an argument sometimes advanced during the period after the First World War against the payment of German reparations, wherein it was claimed that the reparations payments would cause a world-wide depression. According to this argument, the depression would originate in Germany, as a consequence of the collection of the reparations sums, and would spread from Germany to the Allied countries through reduction in the latter's exports to Germany.

demand for goods and services, including the demand for imports as well as the demand for domestic goods. As a result, the exports of the paying country increased so much that, on balance, that country's income rose despite the initial depressing effect of the transfer payment. In the exceptional case in which the receiving country had a propensity to spend exceeding unity, the secondary rise of exports from the paying country thus overbalanced the transfer and income tended to rise in that country as well as in the receiving country.

If one of the two countries had a propensity to spend greater than unity, the final movements of income throughout the world economy were accordingly found to be dominated by the initial effect of the transfer in this unstable economy. When the paying country was the unstable one, income fell in both countries; and when the receiving country was the unstable one, income rose in both. Regardless of whether incomes of the two countries increased or decreased, the balance of payments on current account, exclusive of the transfer, moved in favor of the paying country, and as long as one of the two propensities to spend exceeded unity, the favorable movement in the balance of payments was greater than the annual transfer. In other words, if the paying country's imports increased as well as its exports because of an all-round increase in world income, the increase in exports was found to exceed the increase in imports by more than the amount of the transfer. And if both exports and imports of the paying country declined because of an all-round reduction of world income, the reduction of imports exceeded the reduction of exports by more than the amount of the transfer.

The circumstances, then, in which the full "real" transfer of goods and services could be brought about by the primary movement in purchasing power and the secondary movement of output were the somewhat unusual circumstances in which the propensity to spend exceeded unity in one of the two countries. In the normal case, in which the propensities to spend were less than unity in both countries, my examination of the fluctuating-employment model showed that the favorable movement in the paying country's balance of payments would be less than the annual transfer. When secondary as well as primary movements of income were taken into account, in other words, the transfer of purchasing power was found to be inadequate, except under unusual conditions, to bring about the real transfer of goods and services required to restore equilibrium in the balance of

Table 1. Summary of effects of income transfer in the two-country model

	Normal case: propensity to spend less than unity in each country	First special case: propensity to spend greater than unity in receiving country	Second special case: propensity to spend greater than unity in paying country
Income of paying country—	Falls	Rises	Falls
Income of receiving country—	Rises	Rises	Falls
Paying country's balance of payments on current account, exclusive of the transfer—	Exports rise; imports fall; improvement in balance of payments is *less* than amount of transfer	Exports and imports both rise, but exports rise more than imports; improvement in balance of payments is *greater* than amount of transfer	Exports and imports both fall, but decline of imports is greater than decline of exports; improvement in balance of payments is *greater* than amount of transfer

payments.[5] These results for the two-country model are summarized in Table 1, which is adapted from one of the tables in my earlier paper.

It is apparent from Table 1 that if all propensities to spend are assumed to be less than unity—and I believe this will usually be true— the transfer of purchasing power and the resulting secondary changes in income and employment cannot be regarded as a complete explanation of the transfer process. The paying country, which initially has a deficit in its balance of payments, will usually be left with a deficit, albeit a somewhat smaller one, even after all secondary movements in its exports and imports have taken place. With this principal conclusion of my earlier paper in mind, I turn now to a consideration of the transfer process in an economic system comprising n countries.

Let $y_1, y_2, \ldots, y_n$ be the net national incomes of the n countries. As before, I assume that exchange rates, prices, and costs are all constant. With given exchange rates, the national income of all countries may be expressed in a common currency unit, and for present purposes the currency of country 1 will be used as the common unit of measurement. If all prices remain constant, the total demand for goods and services and the demand for imports in a given country may be regarded as functions of that country's income. Let $u_i(y_i)$ be the function which shows how the ith country's expenditure on all goods and services is related to that country's net income, y_i. The quantity $u_i(y_i)$ includes net investment expenditure as well as expenditure on consumer's goods; and it includes expenditure on imports of finished goods as well as expenditure on domestic goods.

Let $m_i(y_i)$ be the expenditure on all imports of the ith country, again expressed as a function of the ith country's income. Let $m_{ji}(y_i)$ be the part of the ith country's imports which is obtained from the jth country. Then for any country we will have

(1)
$$m_i(y_i) \equiv \sum_j m_{ji}(v_i),$$

where the summation is extended over all j except $j = i$. In words, Eq. (1) says that the ith country's propensity to import is simply the sum of its partial propensities to import from individual countries. Since each country's income, in equilibrium, is equal to its net expenditure on goods

---

5. Metzler, "The Transfer Problem Reconsidered" (reference 1).

and services *plus* its exports *less* its imports, we may write the equations for the *n*-country model shown in Eqs. (2).

$$
\begin{aligned}
y_1 &= u_1(y_1) - m_1(y_1) &&+ m_{12}(y_2) &&+\cdots &&+ m_{1n}(y_n) &&- \tau, \\
y_2 &= &&m_{21}(y_1) + u_2(y_2) - m_2(y_2) &&+\cdots &&+ m_{2n}(y_n) &&+ \tau, \\
&\;\cdots &&\;\cdots &&\;\cdots &&\;\cdots &&\;\cdots, \\
y_n &= &&m_{n1}(y_1) &&+ m_{n2}(y_2) &&+\cdots + u_n(y_n) - m_n(y_n).
\end{aligned}
$$

(2)

With constant exchange rates, costs, and prices, Eqs. (2) are sufficient to determine the equilibrium level of income in each of the *n* countries. In these equations an autonomous element τ has been subtracted from the income of country 1 and added to the income of country 2. The amount τ represents an income transfer from the first country to the second. The size of τ will, of course, have a direct influence upon the incomes and the trade balances of the two countries between which the transfer takes place; and τ will also indirectly influence the incomes and trade balances of all other countries, through its effects upon their exports. Other things remaining the same, the *n* incomes, $y_1, y_2, \ldots, y_n$, may thus be regarded as functions of the income transfer τ.

In order to see how the income of each country is affected by a change in the size of the income transfer, we may differentiate Eqs. (2) with respect to τ as shown in Eqs. (3).

$$
\begin{aligned}
(1 + m_1' - u_1')\frac{dy_1}{d\tau} &- m_{12}'\frac{dy_2}{d\tau} &- \cdots &- m_{1n}'\frac{dy_n}{d\tau} &= -1, \\
- m_{21}'\frac{dy_1}{d\tau} &+ (1 + m_2' - u_2')\frac{dy_2}{d\tau} - \cdots &&- m_{2n}'\frac{dy_n}{d\tau} &= 1, \\
&\;\cdots &&\;\cdots &&\;\cdots, \\
- m_{n1}'\frac{dy_1}{d\tau} &- m_{n2}'\frac{dy_2}{d\tau} &- \cdots + (1 + m_n' - u_n')\frac{dy_n}{d\tau} &= 0.
\end{aligned}
$$

(3)

The expression u_i' of Eqs. (3) represents the marginal propensity of the *i*th country to spend; in other words, $u_i' \equiv [du_i(y_i)]/dy_i$. Similarly, m_i' is the marginal propensity to import of the *i*th country, which is defined as $[dm_i(y_i)]/dy_i$, and m_{ji}' is the marginal propensity of the *i*th country to import from the *j*th country, or $[dm_{ji}(y_i)]/dy_i$. Solving Eqs. (3) for $dy_1/d\tau$, $dy_2/d\tau$, and $dy_i/d\tau$, where y_i is taken to represent the income of any country not participating in the transfer we find

$$\frac{dy_1}{d\tau} = \frac{M_{21} - M_{11}}{M},$$

$$\frac{dy_2}{d\tau} = \frac{M_{22} - M_{12}}{M},$$

(4)

and

$$\frac{dy_i}{d\tau} = \frac{M_{2i} - M_{1i}}{M},$$

where

(5) $$M \equiv \begin{vmatrix} 1 + m_1' - u_1' & -m_{12}' & \cdots & -m_{1n}' \\ -m_{21}' & 1 + m_2' - u_2' & \cdots & -m_{2n}' \\ \cdots & \cdots & \cdots & \cdots \\ -m_{n1}' & -m_{n2}' & \cdots & 1 + m_n' - u_n' \end{vmatrix}$$

and where M_{rs} is the cofactor of the element in the rth row and sth column of M.

When we attempt to evaluate Eqs. (4) in order to see how the transfer has affected the levels of income in the paying country, the receiving country, and a nonparticipating country (country i), we find that neither the sign of M nor that of any of the cofactors of M is unambiguous If we place certain limitations on the values of the propensities to spend, however, the sign of M and its cofactors may readily be determined. Suppose, in particular, that we consider what I have called the "normal" case, that is, the case in which the marginal propensity to spend is less than unity in each country. Mathematically, this means that u_1', u_2', ..., u_n' are all less than unity, and from Eq. (5) it is clear that this implies that all the elements in the principal diagonal of M are positive quantities. If the partial propensities to import, m_{ji}', are positive or zero (as they will usually be) then the off-diagonal elements of M are either negative or zero. Consider, finally, the sum of the elements in a given column of M, say the kth column. This sum is equal to

$$1 + m_k' - u_k' - \sum_j m_{jk}'.$$

From Identity (1) it is apparent that $\sum m_{jk}' = m_k'$, and the sum of all elements in the kth column of M is accordingly equal to $1 - u_k'$. If u_k' is less than unity, as it is here assumed to be, this sum is clearly positive.

In the normal case, then, in which the propensity to spend in each country is less than unity, the determinant M has the following characteristics: (a) its off-diagonal elements are negative or zero; (b) its diagonal elements are positive; (c) the sum of the elements of each column is positive. Now I have shown elsewhere that a determinant with these characteristics is necessarily positive and that its cofactors are also positive.[6] Even this amount of information, however, is insufficient to evaluate Eqs. (4), for the numerators of these equations all contain one term which is positive and one which is negative. The numerators of Eqs. (4) must therefore be examined in more detail. By writing out the full expressions for M_{11} and M_{21}, the reader may easily verify that

$$
(6)\quad M_{11} - M_{21} =
\begin{vmatrix}
1 + m_2' - m_{12}' - u_2' & -m_{13}' - m_{23}' & \cdots & -m_{1n}' - m_{2n}' \\
-m_{32}' & 1 + m_3' - u_3' & \cdots & -m_{3n}' \\
\cdots & \cdots & \cdots & \cdots \\
-m_{n2}' & -m_{n3}' & \cdots & 1 + m_n' - u_n'
\end{vmatrix}.
$$

It is apparent by inspection that, if the marginal propensities to spend, u_k', are all less than unity, the determinant in Eq. (6) is an $(n-1)$th-order determinant having the same essential characteristics as M. Its off-diagonal elements are negative or zero, its diagonal elements are positive, and the sum of the elements of each column is positive. From the results of my earlier paper it follows that $M_{11} - M_{21}$ is a positive quantity. Since M is likewise positive, it is clear from Eqs. (4) that $dy_1/d\tau$ is negative. By a similar argument it may be shown that, in the normal case, $M_{22} - M_{12}$ is positive and $dy_2/d\tau$ is therefore positive. The sign of the third numerator of Eqs. (4) remains indeterminate, which means that $dy_i/d\tau$ may be either positive or negative.

It may be useful at this point to summarize the conclusions reached thus far. Assuming that the propensity to spend is less than unity in every country, I have demonstrated that a transfer of income between one country and another in an economic system involving n countries reduces the income of the paying country while increasing that of the receiving country. This means that, in the final position of equilibrium, after allowance has been made for all secondary repercussions of the transfer, the secondary movements of exports in each country are necessarily less important than the primary movement of income associated with the transfer itself. In the paying country, for example, exports

6. Lloyd A. Metzler, "A Multiple-Region Theory of Income and Trade," included as Chapter 21 of the present volume.

may rise as a result of higher income in other countries; but the secondary rise of exports cannot be large enough under the conditions assumed, to offset the depressing effects of the transfer. Likewise, in the receiving country exports may decline; but if they do, the decline in exports will be less important than the stimulating effect which the receiving country enjoys from receipt of the transfer. In short, the ultimate movement of income in both the paying and the receiving country is dominated by the primary effect. In countries which are not directly involved in the transfer, income may either rise or fall. Superficially, it would seem that countries whose exports are sold largely in the paying country would undergo a decline of income, while countries largely dependent upon the markets of the receiving country would find their incomes increasing. Although this is undoubtedly true as a first approximation, it is a proposition which, in a complex system of trade among many countries, can be neither precisely stated nor rigorously proved. The transfer, indeed, may affect nonparticipating countries in quite unexpected ways.

As far as income movements alone are concerned, it is obvious from the foregoing that, in the normal case in which the propensities to spend of all countries are less than unity, the n-country model leads to the same conclusions as the simple two-country model. Our primary interest, however, is not in the movements of income but in the movements of each country's balance of payments. For present purposes the income movements are important only because they affect the network of international payments and receipts. The basic issues, as in the interwar discussion of the transfer mechanism, are whether the income movements in all countries will bring about an export surplus in the paying country and an import surplus in the receiving country and whether the export surplus of the former and the import surplus of the latter will be equal to, greater than, or less than the amount of the annual transfer. With respect to these balance-of-payments problems, there is no difficulty in showing that, in the normal case, the n-country model again confirms the results of the two-country model.

In a transfer involving only two countries, the exports of the paying country will normally rise, while its imports will fall, as I have indicated above; and if each country's propensity to spend is less than unity, the export surplus achieved in this manner will be less than the amount of the annual transfer, regardless of how large the propensities to import may be. In attempting to reach similar results for the n-country model, a number of complications are encountered. We cannot be certain, for example, that the exports of the paying country will rise, as they normally do in the two-country model; for the paying country's exports depend upon the incomes of many countries which do not participate directly in the transfer, and in some of these countries income may fall as a result of the transfer. Unless the paying country is trading predominantly with the receiving country, therefore, it is impossible to say that its exports will necessarily rise. But regardless of whether its exports rise or fall, its imports will fall, and it may readily be shown that in this manner the paying country will achieve an export surplus. Moreover, the export surplus, as in the two-country model, will be less than the amount of the annual transfer, so that a "transfer problem" remains even after all primary and secondary changes in income in all the n countries have been taken into account.

In the receiving country also, exports may either rise or fall, depending upon whether that country's foreign markets are predominantly in countries whose incomes have risen or in countries whose incomes have fallen. But in the normal case the receiving country's imports will rise regardless of what happens to its exports, and it can be shown that the final result of the changes in both exports and imports is an import surplus. And just as the export surplus of the paying country is normally smaller than the annual transfer, so also will the import surplus of the receiving country be smaller than the transfer. From this it follows that a transfer problem remains to be solved in the receiving country as well as in the paying country. In an n-country model, however, the export surplus of the paying country will not necessarily be equal, in absolute magnitude, to the import surplus of the receiving country, and the severity of the transfer problem accordingly may differ between the two countries.

In order to demonstrate these propositions mathematically, let b_1, b_2, and b_i represent the balances of payments on current account, exclusive of the transfer, of the paying country, the receiving country, and any third country, respectively. We may then write

$$b_1 = \sum_j m_{1j}(y_j) - m_1(y_1),$$

(7)
$$b_2 = \sum_j m_{2j}(y_j) - m_2(y_2),$$

and
$$b_i = \sum_j m_{ij}(y_j) - m_i(y_i).$$

From Eqs. (2), however, it is apparent that Eqs. (7) may be written in the following more convenient form:

$$b_1 = y_1 - u_1(y_1) + \tau,$$

(8)
$$b_2 = y_2 - u_2(y_2) - \tau,$$

and
$$b_i = y_i - u_i(y_i).$$

Equations (8) express the familiar proposition that each country's balance of payments on current account is equal to the difference between the value of its total output and its own expenditure on all goods and services. In order to see how the transfer influences the three balances of payments, we may differentiate Eqs. (8) with respect to τ as follows:

$$\frac{db_1}{d\tau} = (1 - u_1')\frac{dy_1}{d\tau} + 1,$$

(9)
$$\frac{db_2}{d\tau} = (1 - u_2')\frac{dy_2}{d\tau} - 1,$$

and
$$\frac{db_i}{d\tau} = (1 - u_i')\frac{dy_i}{d\tau}.$$

Substituting in Eqs. (9) the values of $dy_1/d\tau$, $dy_2/d\tau$, and $dy_i/d\tau$ given by Eqs. (4), we have

$$\frac{db_1}{d\tau} = (1 - u_1')\left(\frac{M_{21} - M_{11}}{M}\right) + 1,$$

(10)
$$\frac{db_2}{d\tau} = (1 - u_2')\left(\frac{M_{22} - M_{12}}{M}\right) - 1,$$

and
$$\frac{db_i}{d\tau} = (1 - u_i')\left(\frac{M_{2i} - M_{1i}}{M}\right).$$

Consider first the change in the paying country's balance of payments, $db_1/d\tau$. The value of $db_1/d\tau$ is given in Eqs. (10) by two terms; and if the propensity to spend is less than unity in every country, the first of these terms is negative while the second is positive. I have shown elsewhere,[7] however, that under these so-called "normal" conditions $M_{11}/M < 1/(1 - u_1')$, and it follows that

$$\frac{M_{11} - M_{21}}{M} < \frac{1}{1 - u_1'}.$$

7. *Ibid.*

From this inequality it is apparent that the negative term of $db_1/d\tau$ is necessarily smaller than unity in absolute value. Since the second term of $db_1/d\tau$ is equal to unity, $db_1/d\tau$ is positive and lies between the following limits:

$$(11) \qquad 0 < \frac{db_1}{d\tau} < 1.$$

In words, Inequality (11) says that in the normal case the paying country's balance of payments, exclusive of the transfer, moves in a favorable direction but that the export surplus thus achieved is less than the amount of the annual income transfer. The first of Eqs. (10) thus establishes rigorously that the movements of income induced by a shift of purchasing power will normally give the paying country an export surplus somewhat smaller than the transfer itself. This is true regardless of the number of countries involved in the economic system; it applies equally to the n-country and to the two-country models. In short, the income movements, secondary as well as primary, are normally insufficient to bring about the full "real" transfer of goods and services required to restore equilibrium in the paying country's balance of payments.

An analogous proposition applies to $db_2/d\tau$, the movement in the balance of payments, exclusive of the transfer, of the receiving country. In the receiving country, as in the paying, the balance of payments moves in the direction required to restore equilibrium; again the size of the movement is less than the transfer itself, that is, in the new equilibrium the receiving country has an *import* surplus which is less than the amount of the transfer. The expression in Eqs. (10) for $db_2/d\tau$ consists of two terms, one of which is -1, while the other is positive. But the positive term may be shown to be less than unity. This conclusion follows from two inequalities. If all propensities to spend are less than unity, M_{22}/M is less than $1/(1 - u_2')$, whence

$$\frac{M_{22} - M_{12}}{M} < \frac{1}{1 - u_2'}.$$

From these inequalities and from Eqs. (10) it is apparent that

$$(12) \qquad -1 < \frac{db_2}{d\tau} < 0,$$

which shows that the import surplus in the receiving country's balance of payments is less than the annual transfer. Again, therefore, the results in the n-country system agree with the earlier results which I obtained for a simple two-country model.

In any country not directly involved in the transfer, the balance of payments may move in either direction. From Eqs. (9), however, it is clear that if the propensities to spend are less than unity, the balance of payments of each of the nonparticipating countries moves in the same direction as its income. If a country's income declines as a result of the transfer, for example, its balance of payments must be more unfavorable than in the original equilibrium. Or perhaps it would be more accurate in this case to say that the country's income has declined *because* its balance of payments has deteriorated.

The conclusions reached thus far are valid only for the case in which the marginal propensities to spend are less than unity in all countries. Although this normal case appears to be the most probable one, it is possible in the short run that the propensity to spend in some of the n countries may exceed unity. In a poor country, for example, the propensity to consume will be close to unity, and if any induced investment takes place at all the country's total propensity to spend may well exceed unity. We ought therefore to examine the transfer mechanism under the alternative hypothesis that some of the propensities to spend are greater than unity.

If all the propensities to spend exceeded unity, it is obvious intuitively that the n-country economy would be an unstable one, and in this event neither the concept of an equilibrium level of income nor the concept of equilibrium in the balance of international payments would have any meaning. Because it is beyond the powers of our present technique, this extreme case will be excluded from our investigation. If some of the propensities to spend are greater than unity while others are less than unity, however, it is possible that the n-country system, taken as a whole, may be stable despite the inherent instability of the high-propensity countries. The latter countries, in other words, may be stabilized by low propensities to spend in other countries. I turn now to an examination of such mixed, but stable, systems.

In the mixed cases in which some of the propensities to spend are greater than unity, the results of an income transfer are difficult to predict. Mathematically we cannot prove, as we can in the normal case, that the determinant M and its cofactors M_{rs} are all positive. If we assume that the n-country system is dynamically stable, however, the conditions which must be fulfilled to ensure stability will place certain useful limitations on the basic determinant and its cofactors. In particular, I have shown elsewhere that stability of the system requires that the determinant M and any set of its principal minors, such as M_{11}, $M_{11,22}$, $M_{11,22,33}$, and so on, shall all be positive.[8] From a theorem derived by Mosak[9] it follows that under these conditions the cofactors of the off-diagonal elements, such as M_{rs}, are also positive. In short, if the system is stable, M and its cofactors will have the same signs that they have in the normal case; and this is true regardless of which countries are the high-propensity countries.

To know the signs of M and its cofactors is not in itself sufficient to determine how an income transfer affects the national incomes and the balances of payments of the n countries. We must also know the signs of the differences of some of the cofactors, such as $M_{21} - M_{11}$, $M_{22} - M_{12}$, $M_{2i} - M_{1i}$, and the like. The necessary conditions of stability do not place any limitations upon the signs of such expressions, and for this reason a wide variety of results is possible. In view of the large number of possibilities, it is obviously difficult to summarize the effects of an income transfer in the exceptional cases in which some of the propensities to spend are greater than unity. However, there is a method of approaching the problem which enables one to see the similarities between the n-country and the two-country models even in these exceptional cases. In summarizing the results obtained from the two-country model, I pointed out that under some circumstances an income transfer would result in an expansion of income in both countries, while under other circumstances the effect of the transfer would be a contraction in both countries. We may now ask whether there are similar possibilities in the more complex model involving trade among n countries. What are the circumstances, in other words, under which an income transfer would result in an expansion of income in all n countries? And what are the circumstances under which incomes in all countries would contract?

In order to answer these questions, consider again the determinant in Eq. (6) formed of the difference $M_{11} - M_{21}$ of two $(n-1)$th-order determinants. Inspection will show that in a sense this determinant may

8. *Ibid.*
9. Jacob L. Mosak, *General-Equilibrium Theory in International Trade*, Cowles Commission Monograph No. 7 (Bloomington, Ind., Principia Press, 1944), pp. 49–51.

be regarded as the basic determinant, analogous to M, of a trading system involving $n - 1$ countries. In particular, it is the determinant that would result if country 1 could be withdrawn from the n-country system and if all the import demands of the other $n - 1$ countries for the goods and services of country 1 could be transferred to country 2. More briefly, we may say that it is the basic determinant of a system in which country 1 has been withdrawn in favor of country 2. (Although no country will *actually* be withdrawn from the system in such a manner, it will be helpful to think of the problem as though this could be done.)

Now in order for the system involving countries 2, 3, . . . , n to form a stable system, it is necessary, though not sufficient, that the determinant (6) be positive. If this is actually true, we may say, in a somewhat elliptical manner, that the system would be stable when country 1 was withdrawn in favor of country 2. But if some of the propensities to spend exceed unity, it is possible that $M_{11} - M_{21}$ may be negative even when M itself is positive and even when the n-country system as a whole is stable. If so, the system obtained by withdrawing country 1 in favor of country 2 would be an unstable system despite the stability of the n-country model.

The exact conditions under which such hypothetical instability may arise are difficult to formulate. It seems likely, though I have not found a rigorous proof, that the instability of an $(n - 1)$-country system in which country 1 has been withdrawn in favor of country 2 implies that the propensity to spend of country 2 exceeds that of country 1. Thus, if country 1 were a low-propensity country while country 2 were a high-propensity country, the presence of the former country would tend to stabilize the entire system; and if country 1 were withdrawn from the system in favor of country 2, the resulting increase in demand for the output of an inherently unstable country might lead to instability of the system as a whole. But this conclusion is based upon intuition and not upon mathematical proof, and it may not even be correct under all circumstances.

It will now be demonstrated that *if the system is unstable when the paying country is withdrawn in favor of the receiving country, a money transfer will increase the level of income of each of the n countries.* In order to prove this proposition, consider again Eqs. (4), which depict the movements of income in the paying country, the receiving country, and any third country. By hypothesis, $M_{11} - M_{21}$ is negative; this condition, indeed, is our definition of the hypothetical instability of the $(n - 1)$-country system. Hence from Eqs. (4) it follows immediately that $db_1/d\tau$ is positive, that is, the transfer increases the income of the paying country. This means that the secondary rise in the paying country's exports is more important to that country than the depressing effect of the transfer itself; or, in other words, the secondary movement overbalances the primary disturbance.

In order to show what happens to the incomes of the other countries, we must employ the following identity, which is true for any determinant:[10]

$$(13) \qquad MM_{11,2i} \equiv M_{11} M_{2i} - M_{21} M_{1i}.$$

From the conditions of stability of the n-country system and from Mosak's theorem, we know that both M and $M_{11,2i}$ are positive, from which it follows that

$$(14) \qquad M_{11} M_{2i} - M_{21} M_{1i} > 0, \qquad i \neq 1.$$

All the cofactors of M are necessarily positive, and if M_{21} exceeds M_{11}, as it does when $M_{11} - M_{21}$ is negative, we must have

$$(15) \qquad M_{11} M_{2i} - M_{11} M_{1i} > 0,$$

or

$$(16) \qquad M_{2i} - M_{1i} > 0, \qquad i \neq 1.$$

If we put $i = 2$ in (16), we have

$$(17) \qquad M_{22} - M_{12} \equiv M \frac{dy_2}{d\tau} > 0,$$

which shows that the transfer increases the income of the receiving country. And the same is obviously true of the income of any other country, such as country i.

I have now shown that if the hypothetical system obtained by withdrawing the paying country in favor of the receiving country is unstable, an income transfer in the actual n-country system necessarily increases the incomes of all countries. The economic rationale of this result is simple. The fact that the system would be unstable if the paying country were withdrawn means that that country has a stabilizing effect upon the world economy; in other words, its propensity to spend is low, compared with propensities to spend in other countries. For this reason the

10. See Maxime Bocher, *Introduction to Higher Algebra* (New York, Macmillan, 1907), p. 33.

Table 2. Summary of possible income movements in the n-country system

	Normal case: all marginal propensities to spend less than unity	First special case: system unstable when paying country is withdrawn in favor of receiving country	Second special case: system unstable when receiving country is withdrawn in favor of paying country
Income of paying country—	Falls	Rises	Falls
Income of receiving country—	Rises	Rises	Falls
Income of other countries—	?	Rises	Falls

depressing effects of the transfer in the paying country are small, while the stimulating effects in the receiving country and in the rest of the world are large. The stimulating effects thus offset the depressing effects, and income rises throughout the entire system.

Consider next the converse of the above situation; in other words, suppose that the income transfer causes a general contraction of all incomes of the system. Under what circumstances can this result be expected? It can easily be shown that a general contraction will occur, as a consequence of the transfer, if the propensities to spend of the various countries are such that the system is unstable when the *receiving* country is withdrawn in favor of the *paying* country. Such a situation might arise if the receiving country had a relatively low propensity to spend, while the paying country had a high propensity. Receipt of the transfer would then give only a small stimulus to income in the receiving country, whereas the depressing effects in the paying country might be substantial. Under such conditions, income would decline in all countries.

This converse proposition may be proved from the original proposition simply by changing the sign of the income transfer. If a positive transfer from country 1 to country 2 causes all incomes to *rise*, a negative transfer will necessarily cause all incomes to fall. But a negative transfer from country 1 to country 2 is really a positive transfer in the opposite direction. By changing the sign of the transfer, we have thus reversed the roles of payer and receiver and proved that, *if the system is unstable when the receiving country is withdrawn in favor of the paying country, the income transfer causes incomes in all countries to decline.*

With respect to movements of income, three different possibilities have now been discussed: (*a*) an income transfer may reduce the income of the paying country and increase that of the receiving country, while incomes of other countries either rise or fall; (*b*) the transfer may increase the income of every country in the system; and (*c*) the transfer may result in a net decline in all incomes. The circumstances under which each of these three results will occur are summarized in Table 2. Although I do not believe that the special cases in which incomes of all countries rise or fall simultaneously are very probable, I have nevertheless presented them, along with what seems to be the most likely result, in order to indicate the rather unusual conditions in which secondary income movements may overbalance the primary movements.

With respect to movements of each country's balance of payments, it is impossible to present any such summary as that given in Table 2. In the normal case in which all propensities to spend are less than unity, one can predict the direction of and the limits of the balance-of-payments movement in the receiving country and the paying country. But in the two special cases, even this amount of prediction is beyond the capacity of our model. The balance-of-payments movement of a given country is described in terms of its propensity to spend as well as its income movement; and in the special cases the propensity to spend of a given country may be either greater or less than unity.

If the incomes of all countries rise (first special case) and if the propensity to spend of the paying country is less than unity, then it is clear from Eqs. (4) that the balance of payments of the paying country, exclusive of the transfer, will move in a favorable direction and that the amount of such favorable movement will be larger than the transfer itself. But there is no assurance, in this event, that the receiving country will necessarily have an *un*favorable balance of payments *greater* than the transfer. A substantial part of the adjustment may be forced upon the nonparticipating countries. Similarly, if the transfer leads to a general *decline* of all incomes (second special case) and if the *receiving* country has a propensity to spend which is less than unity, it is again clear from Eqs. (4) that the change in the receiving country's balance of payments will be larger than would be required to restore equilibrium in its international transactions.

Although such possibilities as these reveal the analogy between the *n*-country model and the two-country model, they are not by any means the only conceivable results. It is thus apparent that when the propensity to spend exceeds unity in one or more countries, the theory presented above cannot, by itself, provide much useful information about the effects of a transfer upon the network of multilateral payments.

The foregoing account of the transfer mechanism in an economic system consisting of *n* countries has been presented as a generalization of my earlier paper, which considered only two countries. I have examined the *n*-country model in some detail in order to see whether the repercussions of the transfer upon nonparticipating countries would alter the conclusions reached in my earlier and simpler model. Although the number of *possible* results is naturally increased by the increase in the number of countries, the practical conclusions to be drawn from the *n*-country model are substantially the same, I believe, as those to be drawn from the two-country model. Both the simple model and the more complex one have shown that, except under unusual circumstances the income movements brought about by an income transfer will be insufficient to effect a corresponding "real" transfer of goods and services. In short, the movements of income will normally bring about only a partial adjustment of the balance of payments of the paying country and the receiving country; and this is true regardless of the number of countries in the economic system.

If the transfer of purchasing power is only a partial explanation of the process of adjustment, the question naturally arises as to how the remaining discrepancy between the international payments and the international receipts of the two participating countries can be eliminated. Suppose, for example, that after all income movements have been allowed for, the shifts in purchasing power account for an improvement in the paying country's balance of payments equal to 70 percent of the annual transfer. Can we say, in this event, that 70 percent of the adjustment of the paying country's balance of payments will take place through shifts in the demand schedules, while the remaining 30 percent is brought about by movements in prices at home and abroad? At first glance this seems to be a reasonable conclusion, but actually it is misleading. For the price changes will themselves bring about further movements of income and employment, which tend to offset the initial income movements. In other words, the price effects and the income effects are not additive, since they react upon one another in a rather complicated manner. This means that the description of the transfer mechanism presented above is valid only if the terms of trade between countries remain relatively constant. A theory of complete adjustment is rather different from the theory of partial adjustment presented in this paper. Interesting as it is, such a theory is beyond the scope of my present investigation.[11]

11. See A. J. Brown, "Trade Balances and Exchange Stability," *Oxford Economic Papers*, 6 (April 1942), 66–67.

23 | Taxes and Subsidies in Leontief's Input-Output Model

If a tax is imposed on the output of one industry and the proceeds are used to subsidize the output of another industry, the final effects of the combined tax and subsidy upon prices in the economic system as a whole are usually exceedingly difficult to predict. The outcome depends, in part, upon the importance of the taxed and subsidized commodities in the production of other commodities and upon the importance of the latter commodities in the production of the taxed and subsidized goods. It also depends, in part, upon the ability of producers and consumers to alter the proportions in which they purchase various commodities in response to the changing configuration of prices. In the present note I shall ignore these substitution effects by assuming, on the one hand, that the inputs of various commodities required to produce a unit of a given commodity are fixed amounts which cannot be altered by the producers, and, on the other hand, that the demand for the final output of the economic system as a whole is fixed and independent of the price movements. That is, I shall assume that the so-called coefficients of production as well as the commodity composition of national income are constants, as in Leontief's input-output models.[1]

Reprinted from *Quarterly Journal of Economics*, 65 (August 1951), 433–438. Copyright President and Fellows of Harvard College, 1951.

---

1. The economic system described in this paper is homogeneous of the *zero*th degree with respect to prices but, unlike Leontief's earlier models, it is not homogeneous with respect to output. In this regard, the system presented here resembles Leontief's later studies. See, for example, his "Output, Employment, Consumption and Investment," *Quarterly Journal of Economics*, 58 (February 1944), 290–314; and "Wages, Profit and Prices," *Quarterly Journal of Economics*, 61 (November 1946), 26–39.

Even under these highly simplified conditions, it is not obvious intuitively how prices in the system will be affected by a tax-and-subsidy scheme such as the one suggested in the preceding paragraph. Under competitive conditions, the price of each product will of course be altered in such a way that the new price will be equal to average cost of production *plus* any tax or *less* any subsidy that may be involved. But the cost of production of a given commodity, exclusive of the tax or subsidy, will be influenced by the movements of many other prices in the system, and the combined effects of all these price movements are sometimes quite complex. Consider, for example, the effect of the tax and subsidy upon the price of the taxed commodity. In the new position of equilibrium, after all prices have been adjusted to the tax and subsidy, the price of the taxed commodity must of course exceed cost of production by the amount of the tax per unit, and this suggests superficially that the tax and subsidy will increase the price of the taxed good.

Suppose, however, that the taxed commodity is one which requires a substantial amount of the subsidized commodity in its output. If the price of the subsidized commodity falls as a result of the new fiscal arrangements, the cost of production of the taxed commodity will thereby be reduced, and the question arises as to whether this secondary effect upon the price of the taxed article may not be more important than the primary effect of the tax itself. Is it possible, in other words, that the price of the taxed commodity may fall as a result of a secondary fall in its cost of production exceeding the amount of the tax itself? This outcome would appear to be more probable, the more important is the subsidized commodity, and the more important are other commodities whose cost of production is reduced, in the production of the taxed commodity.

A similar problem arises concerning the price of the subsidized commodity. This price, like that of the taxed article, will be subject to both a primary and a secondary effect. And while the primary effect—the subsidy—will always tend to reduce the price of the subsidized article, it is conceivable that the secondary movement of other prices may increase the cost of production of the subsidized good. If so, we should like to know whether such a secondary rise in cost of production could exceed the amount of the subsidy, and whether, as a consequence, the combined effect of the tax and subsidy might be a rise in the price of the article subsidized.

This problem, as I have formulated it, bears a close resemblance to the so-called "transfer problem" in international trade. Since I have previously investigated the transfer problem in a generalized economic system involving n countries, the results of that investigation can be applied, without modification, to the case of a tax and subsidy within a single country.[2] This procedure leads to the conclusion, as I shall show below, that if each industry in the economy produces a surplus in the sense that not all of its current output is required in the current production of other commodities, then the secondary effects of the tax and subsidy cannot completely offset the primary effects. If the cost of production of the taxed commodity falls, the magnitude of such a fall cannot, under the conditions postulated, be as large as the tax itself. Likewise, if the cost of production of the subsidized good rises, the amount of the rise is necessarily smaller than the amount of the subsidy. It follows that, after all secondary repercussions have been considered, the tax and subsidy scheme increases the price of the taxed commodity and reduces the price of the subsidized commodity.

Consider an economic system consisting of n industries producing n different commodities. Let $x_1, x_2, \ldots, x_n$ be the annual output of these n industries, and let $x_1', x_2', \ldots, x_n'$ be the part of this output which enters into the net national product of the economy. The amounts x_1', $x_2', \ldots, x_n'$, in other words, represent the amounts of the output of the n industries which are not consumed in the process of production itself. The difference, $x_i - x_i'$, thus represents that part of the ith industry's output which is consumed in the production of other commodities.

Let a_{ij} represent the amount of the ith commodity required, per unit, in the production of the jth commodity; the constants a_{ij} are thus the coefficients of production. If the total output of the jth industry is x_j, the demand in that industry for the product of the ith industry will then be $a_{ij}x_j$, and this will be true for any i and any j. In equilibrium, the output of each product will be equal to the demand for that product, including the demand in other industries as well as the so-called "final" demand. Applied to each of the n industries, this condition of equilibrium yields n equations as follows:

2. Lloyd A. Metzler, "A Multiple-Country Theory of Income Transfers," included as Chapter 22 of the present volume.

$$
\begin{aligned}
x_1 &= & a_{12}x_2 + a_{13}x_3 + \cdots + a_{1,n-1}x_{n-1} + a_{1n}x_n + x_1', \\
x_2 &= a_{21}x_1 & + a_{23}x_3 + \cdots + a_{2,n-1}x_{n-1} + a_{2n}x_n + x_2', \\
&\cdots \quad \cdots \qquad \cdots \qquad \cdots \qquad \cdots \qquad \cdots \qquad \cdots \quad \cdots, \\
x_n &= a_{n1}x_1 + a_{n2}x_2 + a_{n3}x_3 + \cdots \quad + a_{n,n-1}x_{n-1} \quad + x_n'.
\end{aligned}
$$

(1)

Equations (1) are Leontief's basic input-output equations. Since we are concerned with price movements rather than movements of output, Eqs. (1) will be useful for present purposes only insofar as they contribute to an understanding of such price movements. The units in which output is measured are of course arbitrary, but if these units are altered, corresponding changes must be made in each of the coefficients a_{ij}. Suppose that the units of output are chosen in such a way that in the position of equilibrium the total output of each industry is equal to one unit; in other words, let the equilibrium output be the unit of output in each industry. Let α_{ij} represent the coefficients of production corresponding to these new units of measurement. Equations (1) will then read as follows:

$$
\begin{aligned}
1 &= & \alpha_{12} + \alpha_{13} + \cdots + \alpha_{1,n-1} + \alpha_{1n} + u_1', \\
1 &= \alpha_{21} & + \alpha_{23} + \cdots + \alpha_{2,n-1} + \alpha_{2n} + u_2', \\
&\cdots \quad \cdots \qquad \cdots \qquad \cdots \qquad \cdots \qquad \cdots \qquad \cdots \quad \cdots \\
1 &= \alpha_{n1} + \alpha_{n2} + \alpha_{n3} + \cdots + \alpha_{n,n-1} \quad + u_n'.
\end{aligned}
$$

(2)

The u_i' of Eqs. (2) represent the elements of final output measured in the new units.

Suppose that commodity 1 is the taxed commodity and commodity 2 is the product subsidized. Let τ be the amount of this tax and subsidy and let $p_1, p_2, \ldots, p_n$ be the prices of the n commodities. Since total output of each industry is equal to one unit, the p_i also represent the total values, in equilibrium, of the outputs of the n industries. Finally, let $\lambda_1, \lambda_2, \ldots, \lambda_n$ represent the wages-and-normal-profits cost per unit of output in the n industries. Like the coefficients of production, the λ_i are assumed to be constants.

The price per unit of a given commodity must be sufficient to cover wages and normal profits and also to pay for the products of other industries employed in the production of the given commodity. In the jth industry, for example, the amount of the ith product required per unit of output is α_{ij}, and the cost of this amount is $\alpha_{ij}p_i$. When the price in each industry is equal to cost of production, inclusive of taxes and subsidies, the following equations will then be satisfied:

$$p_1 = \alpha_{21}p_2 + \alpha_{31}p_3 + \cdots + \alpha_{n-1,1}p_{n-1} + \alpha_{n1}p_n + \lambda_1 + \tau,$$

(3)
$$p_2 = \alpha_{12}p_1 \qquad + \alpha_{32}p_3 + \cdots + \alpha_{n-1,2}p_{n-1} + \alpha_{n2}p_n + \lambda_2 - \tau,$$

$$\cdots$$

$$p_n = \alpha_{1n}p_1 + \alpha_{2n}p_2 + \alpha_{3n}p_3 + \cdots + \alpha_{n-1,n}p_{n-1} \qquad + \lambda_n.$$

In order to show how the tax and subsidy affects the price of each commodity, we may differentiate Eqs. (3) with respect to τ. For this purpose let the basic determinant of the coefficients in Eqs. (2) be represented by Δ, thus:

(4)
$$\Delta \equiv \begin{vmatrix} 1 & -\alpha_{12} & -\alpha_{13} & \cdots & -\alpha_{1n} \\ -\alpha_{21} & 1 & -\alpha_{23} & \cdots & -\alpha_{2n} \\ \cdots & \cdots & \cdots & \cdots & \cdots \\ -\alpha_{n1} & -\alpha_{n2} & -\alpha_{n3} & \cdots & 1 \end{vmatrix}.$$

The determinant of the price equations (3) will then be the transpose of Δ, that is, the determinant obtained by interchanging the rows and columns of Δ. Call this second determinant Δ'. Upon differentiation of Eqs. (3) with respect to τ, we find:

$$\frac{dp_1}{d\tau} = \frac{\Delta_{11}' - \Delta_{21}'}{\Delta'} = \frac{\Delta_{11} = \Delta_{12}}{\Delta},$$

(5)
$$\frac{dp_2}{d\tau} = \frac{\Delta_{12}' - \Delta_{22}'}{\Delta'} = \frac{\Delta_{21} - \Delta_{22}}{\Delta},$$

$$\cdots \cdots \cdots \cdots \cdots$$

$$\frac{dp_i}{d\tau} = \frac{\Delta_{1i}' - \Delta_{2i}'}{\Delta'} = \frac{\Delta_{i1} - \Delta_{i2}}{\Delta}.$$

The determinant Δ has the following properties: (a) all its off-diagonal elements are negative or zero and all the elements in the principal diagonal are positive; (b) from Eqs. (2) it is evident that the sum of the off-diagonal elements in each row of Δ is negative and less, in absolute value, than unity; from this it follows that the sum of all elements of each row of Δ is necessarily positive—in other words, the positive element in the principal diagonal is larger, in absolute value, than the sum of all other elements of the row. I have shown in an earlier paper that a determinant having these properties is always a positive determinant, and that all its cofactors are also positive.[3] I have also shown that for such a determinant the cofactor Δ_{ii} of the element in the principal diagonal of the ith row is always larger than the cofactor Δ_{ij} of any other element in the same row.[4] Applied to the present problem, these properties mean that $\Delta_{11} - \Delta_{12}$ is positive and that $\Delta_{21} - \Delta_{22}$ is negative.

Referring back to Eqs. (5), we now see that $dp_1/d\tau$ is positive and $dp_2/d\tau$ is negative. In other words, after all secondary repercussions have been taken into account and the price system has adjusted itself to a new equilibrium, the price of the taxed commodity is permanently higher than before the tax was imposed, while the price of the subsidized commodity is permanently lower. The secondary effects cannot completely offset the primary effects of the tax and subsidy either in the taxed industry or in the subsidized industry. As far as other industries are concerned, prices may either rise or fall, as the reader can verify by constructing numerical examples.

The results obtained in this note are of course based upon highly restrictive assumptions. Money wages and normal profits—the λ_i of our equations—are assumed to remain constant, which means that the tax and subsidy affects income-earners only through the prices which they pay for goods and services. The coefficients of production are also held constant, which means that no industry can alter its methods of production. Finally, the commodity composition of national income, u'_1, $u'_2, \ldots, u'_n$, is held constant, which implies that consumers do not attempt to substitute relatively cheaper goods for relatively more expensive goods. Of course, if all commodities are produced under constant-cost conditions, a change in output such as might arise from a change in final demand will have no effect upon prices. Such a change, however, if it affects the output of the taxed and subsidized commodities, will alter the *rate* of the tax or subsidy and thereby bring about further price movements. Suppose, for example, that the output of the taxed commodity remains unchanged, while the output of the subsidized commodity increases. In this event either the rate of the tax will have to be increased, in order to make total subsidy expenditures balance

3. Lloyd A. Metzler, "A Multiple-Region Theory of Income and Trade," included as Chapter 21 of the present volume.
4. Metzler, "Multiple-Country Income Transfers" (reference 2). There the properties of the basic determinant Δ are stated in terms of *column* sums rather than *row* sums. The cofactors whose magnitude is compared with Δ_{ii} are thus the cofactors of the ith *column* rather than those of the ith *row*.

against tax receipts, or the rate of the subsidy will have to be reduced. Whether such changes will alter my original conclusions concerning price movements in the taxed and subsidized industries is a question that I have not been able to answer.

24 | The Assumptions Implied in Least-Squares Demand Techniques

Since the development of Professor H. L. Moore's partial correlation technique for deriving elasticities of demand,[1] numerous related procedures have been used extensively in empirical demand studies. Among the more common of these are the correlation of residuals from trend, multiple correlation, and the correlation of trend ratios. All such methods have one thing in common: they attempt to impute fixity to the demand curve by removing from the market data the effects of time shifts. The purpose of this article is not to suggest a new technique but to examine the assumptions about the nature of the supply and demand shifts which are implied in the methods enumerated above.[2]

The following four types of supply or demand time shifts will be considered in the analysis: (*a*) the curves remain fixed; (*b*) the curves shift in a "regular" manner; (*c*) the curves shift in a "random" manner;[3] (*d*) the curves shift in a compound manner, the components of the shifts being of the nature outlined in (*b*) and (*c*). Since each of the two curves

1. *Economic Cycles: Their Law and Cause* (New York, Macmillan, 1914), pp. 62–88.
2. Although some indication of the implied assumptions has previously been given, no attempt has been made, so far as I am aware, to systematize the results. See, for example, Mordecai Ezekiel, "Statistical Analyses and the 'Laws' of Price," *Quarterly Journal of Economics*, 42 (February 1928), 199–227; and Elizabeth W. Gilboy, "The Leontief and Schultz Methods of Deriving 'Demand' Curves," *Quarterly Journal of Economics*, 45 (February 1931), 218–261.
3. The distinction between "regular" and "random" shifts depends largely on the smoothness of a curve—as measured by successive differences—which might be fitted to the series of parameters describing the shifts. For a more precise definition, see note 7.

may shift in any of the four ways outlined above, sixteen different combinations of supply and demand shifts are possible. The results of the demand analysis for each of these combinations will be evaluated.[4]

The analysis below shows that, for those cases in which the correlation of price and quantity trend residuals has a meaning, the trend ratio, trend residual, and multiple correlation techniques yield substantially the same results. Hence the discussion may be confined, for the moment, to the method of correlating residuals from trend lines of prices and quantities.[5]

Refined statistical techniques obviously have no relevance for cases in which demand elasticities may be obtained directly from price-quantity scatters. Situations in which the demand curve has remained fixed may therefore be eliminated from consideration at the outset. Demand stability represents a sort of ideal, to which the statistical demand techniques attempt an approximation. The same reasoning applies to supply stability if the purpose of a statistical study is to determine supply elasticity.

If both supply and demand have shifted during the time interval included in the study, temporal changes in prices and quantities may then be represented as functions of such shifts. It is generally recognized that the purpose of fitting trend lines to the price and quantity time series is to remove the effects of demand shifts from the observed prices and quantities, while leaving in the data as much of the influence of supply shifts as possible. The success of the method clearly depends upon the nature of the supply and demand shifts.

If the supply and demand shifts contain no random or cyclical elements, so that such shifts may be represented by a reasonably smooth curve, the price and quantity time series will show "smooth" variation

4. The late Professor Henry Schultz analyzed such shift assumptions graphically by using a model which contained four possible combinations of supply and demand shift. See his *The Theory and Measurement of Demand* (Chicago, University of Chicago Press, 1937), pp. 73–81. His results differ from mine, however, because he assumed a cobweb relation, whereas I have assumed that the observed prices and quantities are equilibrium values in the neoclassical sense. Furthermore, his classification of shifts is oversimplified, as the results differ materially for different types of shifts. Cf. Table 2 further on in this paper.

5. The remainder of the present section is a nontechnical explanation of results obtained more rigorously in subsequent parts of the paper. To some extent the conclusions are identical with those obtained by Professor Ragnar Frisch in his discussion of the Leontief method. See his "Pitfalls in the Statistical Construction of Demand and Supply Curves," *Veröffentlichungen der Frankfurter Gesellschaft für Konjunkturforschung* (Neue Folge, 1933), no. 5. Because of space limitations I have not attempted to distinguish between those conclusions which are novel and those which represent an application of the Frisch results to the present problem.

and parabolas fitted to these series will pass through all the observed points. Residuals will consequently be zero and correlation of such residuals becomes indeterminate.

On the other hand, if both the supply and demand shifts contain random elements, the trend lines fitted to prices and quantities will not remove completely the effects of either the supply or the demand shifts, since such trend lines can remove only changes which occur in a more or less "regular" manner. Changes in the residuals may therefore be attributed to both supply and demand shifts, and the statistical technique has not succeeded in attaining the ideal of demand stability. The elementary regressions of the scatter of price residuals and quantity residuals will approximate the true demand slope only if the random elements contained in the demand shifts are small relative to the magnitudes of the random supply shifts.[6] Conversely, if the random supply shifts are small relative to the random demand shifts, the elementary regression coefficients will approximate the slope of the supply curves. In this case, the residuals are influenced more by demand changes than by supply changes; hence the scatter of price residuals and quantity residuals approaches the ideal of supply stability.

Correlation between price residuals and quantity residuals will be high (and negative) if random supply fluctuations are large relative to random demand fluctuations. Intuitively, this is evident from the fact that the shift conditions postulated lead to the imputation of a high degree of stability to the demand curves after removal of trend. In the converse case of high relative random demand shifts, the trend elimination imputes a high degree of stability to the supply curves, causing the residual values to cluster closely about a positively sloped line, and leading consequently to a high positive correlation between price residuals and quantity residuals. The correlation of the residual scatter will be low in intermediate cases in which random supply and demand fluctuations have about the same magnitude.

The preceding discussion is based on the assumption that demand and supply fluctuations which are random (or cyclical) with respect to time are not correlated among themselves. If correlation exists between the erratic demand and supply shifts—as is likely to be the case if these shifts have a cyclical basis—then the observed correlation between price residuals and quantity residuals will always be high regardless of the

6. Frisch, "Pitfalls in Statistical Construction" (reference 5), p. 14, calls this a "Cournot effect on the demand side."

relative sizes of supply and demand shifts. Moreover, there is no reason in this case to expect that the true slope will lie between the two elementary regressions of the residual scatter.

Finally, it should be noted that the use of least-squares procedures in fitting trend lines and the classification of shifts as random or regular place certain restrictions upon the nature of the trends. If the regular changes in demand and supply cannot be described by relatively simple parabolas, then the results will be distorted—either by "smoothing" into the trend a part of the random elements, if a high-degree parabola is fitted, or by leaving a part of the trend effect in the residuals, if a low-degree parabola is fitted.

Elimination of Trend

Assume that both the supply and demand curves are constant elasticity curves whose elasticity does not change with shifts through time. The two curves for the ith period may then be represented logarithmically by straight lines.

(1)
$$\text{Supply:} \qquad x = a_{1i}' + b_1 y$$
$$\text{Demand:} \qquad x = a_{2i}' + b_2 y.$$

The terms x and y of Eqs. (1) represent the logarithms of quantities and marginal costs (or prices) respectively. Elasticities of supply and demand are represented by b_1 and b_2, and these values are assumed to remain constant so that the equilibrium values of x and y may be represented as functions of a_{2i}' and a_{1i}'. Solving Eqs. (1) for the equilibrium values of x and y, we find

(2)
$$x_i = \gamma(b_1 a_{2i}' - b_2 a_{1i}') \quad \text{and} \quad y_i = \gamma(a_{2i}' - a_{1i}')$$
where $\gamma \equiv (b_1 - b_2)^{-1}$.

Shifts in a_1' and a_2' will be represented as the resultant of two components, one of which obeys a regular "law" in the sense that its movements may be described by an nth-degree parabola with time as a variable and the other of which is assumed to be "erratic" or "random." Thus

(3)
$$a_{1i}' = a_{1i} + \varepsilon_{1i} \quad \text{and} \quad a_{2i}' = a_{2i} + \varepsilon_{2i}.$$

In Eqs. (3) ε_1 and ε_2 are random fluctuations about the regular changes in demand and supply depicted by changes in a_1 and a_2. Since a_1 and a_2

change in ways which may be described by nth-degree parabolas, we may write

(4)
$$a_{1i} = \alpha_{10} + \alpha_{11}t_i + \alpha_{12}t_i^2 + \cdots + \alpha_{1n}t_i^n$$
and
$$a_{2i} = \alpha_{20} + \alpha_{21}t_i + \alpha_{22}t_i^2 + \cdots + \alpha_{2n}t_i^n.$$

Consider the determinant

$$\Delta \equiv \begin{vmatrix} 1 & m_1 & m_2 & \cdots m_n \\ m_1 & m_2 & m_3 & \cdots m_{n+1} \\ m_2 & m_3 & m_4 & \cdots m_{n+2} \\ \cdot & \cdot & \cdot & \cdots \cdot \\ m_n & m_{n+1} & m_{n+2} & \cdots m_{2n} \end{vmatrix}$$

where $m_r \equiv \overline{t^r}$ represents the average value of t_i^r.

Suppose that parabolas are fitted to the time series of quantity logarithms and price logarithms, thus:

(5)
$$T_{xi} = \beta_{x0} + \beta_{x1}t_i + \beta_{x2}t_i^2 + \cdots + \beta_{xn}t_r^n$$
and
$$T_{yi} = \beta_{y0} + \beta_{y1}t_i + \beta_{y2}t_i^2 + \cdots + \beta_{yn}t_i^n.$$

By setting up the "normal" least-squares, equations we may verify that

(6)
$$\beta_{xk} = \sum_{r=0}^{n} m_{xr}\Delta_{(r+1)\ (k+1)} \quad \text{and} \quad \beta_{yk} = \sum_{r=0}^{n} m_{yr}\Delta_{(r+1)\ (k+1)}$$

where Δ_{ij}' is the quotient obtained by dividing the algebraic cofactor of the element in the ith row and jth column of Δ, by the determinant itself, and $m_{xr} \equiv \overline{xt^r}$, $m_{yr} = \overline{yt^r}$, and so on, the bars in each case denoting averaging. Substituting Eqs. (3) in Eqs. (2), multiplying by t_i^r, and summing for all values of i, we have:[7]

(7)
$$m_{xr} = \gamma(b_1 m_{a_2r} - b_2 m_{a_1r}) \quad \text{and} \quad m_{yr} = \gamma(m_{a_2r} - m_{a_1r}).$$

Multiply Eqs. (4) by t_i^r, $(r = 0, 1, \ldots, n)$, sum for all values of i, and solve the resulting systems of simultaneous equations for α_{2k} and α_{1k}:

7. Equations (7) assume that the moments $m_{\varepsilon_2 r}$ and $m_{\varepsilon_1 r}$ both have values of zero, an assumption which would hold rigidly only if ε_2 and ε_1 were random with respect to t. Since one of the variables is time, however, the statistical relations between the ε's and t may not be described by normal bivariate surfaces. But if ε_2 and ε_1 are random in the sense that, within the limits of fluctuation, any one value is as likely to occur in a given period as any other, then the correlation between the ε's and t^r will be negligible up to the point where r is nearly as large as the number of observations.

(8) $\quad \alpha_{2k} = \sum_{r=0}^{n} m_{\alpha_2 r} \Delta'_{(r+1)(k+1)} \quad \text{and} \quad \alpha_{1k} = \sum_{r=0}^{n} m_{\alpha_1 r} \Delta'_{(r+1)(k+1)}.$

Finally, combining the results of Eqs. (6), (7), and (8), we may write

(9) $\quad \beta_{xk} = \gamma(b_1 \alpha_{2k} - b_2 \alpha_{1k}) \quad \text{and} \quad \beta_{yk} = \gamma(\alpha_{2k} - \alpha_{1k}).$

Substituting Eqs. (9) in Eqs. (5), it appears that

(10) $$T_{x_i} = \gamma \left(b_1 \sum_{k=0}^{n} \alpha_{2k} t_i^{\,k} - b_2 \sum_{k=0}^{n} \alpha_{1k} t_i^{\,k} \right)$$

and $$T_{y_i} = \gamma \left(\sum_{k=0}^{n} \alpha_{2k} t_i^{\,k} - \sum_{k=0}^{n} \alpha_{1k} t_i^{\,k} \right).$$

But $\quad \sum_{k=0}^{n} \alpha_{2k} t_i^{\,k} = a_{2i} \text{ and } \sum_{k=0}^{n} \alpha_{1k} t_i^{\,k} = a_{1i} \text{ from Eqs. (4).}$

Hence

(11) $\quad T_{x_i} = \gamma(b_1 a_{2i} - b_2 a_{1i}) \quad \text{and} \quad T_{y_i} = \gamma(a_{2i} - a_{1i}).$

Returning to Eqs. (2) and substituting (3) in (2), we have

(12) $\quad x_i = \gamma[b_1(a_{2i} + \varepsilon_{2i}) - b_2(a_{1i} + \varepsilon_{1i})]$

and $\quad y_i = \gamma[(a_{2i} + \varepsilon_{2i}) - (a_{1i} + \varepsilon_{1i})].$

Thus both the equilibrium values of prices and quantities and their trend values may be expressed as functions of a_{2i}, a_{1i}, ε_{2i}, and ε_{1i}. In the following analysis, the relations established above will be used to examine the results of three methods for deriving demand curves: correlation of residuals from trend, multiple correlation, and correlation of trend ratios.

The Method of Trend Residuals

Let

(13) $\quad X_i = x_i - T_{xi} \quad \text{and} \quad Y_i = y_i - T_{yi}.$

From Eqs. (11) and (12) it follows that

(14) $\quad X_i = \gamma(b_1 \varepsilon_{2i} - b_2 \varepsilon_{1i}) \quad \text{and} \quad Y_i = \gamma(\varepsilon_{2i} - \varepsilon_{1i}).$

Denote the coefficient of regression of X on Y by B_{XY}, and let B_{YX} be the *reciprocal* of the coefficient of regression of Y on X. Let b_{xy} represent the coefficient of regression of quantities on prices and b_{yx} the *reciprocal* of the coefficient of regression of prices on quantities (in logarithms). From Eqs. (12) and (14), we may express the regression coefficients B_{XY}, B_{YX}, b_{xy}, and b_{yx} as functions of the parameters of the demand and supply curves.

$$B_{XY} = \frac{b_1\sigma_{\varepsilon_2}^2 - (b_1 + b_2)r_{\varepsilon_1\varepsilon_2}\sigma_{\varepsilon_1}\sigma_{\varepsilon_2} + b_2\sigma_{\varepsilon_1}^2}{\sigma_{\varepsilon_2}^2 - 2r_{\varepsilon_1\varepsilon_2}\sigma_{\varepsilon_1}\sigma_{\varepsilon_2} + \sigma_{\varepsilon_1}^2},$$

$$B_{YX} = \frac{b_1^2\sigma_{\varepsilon_2}^2 - 2b_1b_2r_{\varepsilon_1\varepsilon_2}\sigma_{\varepsilon_1}\sigma_{\varepsilon_2} + b_2^2\sigma_{\varepsilon_1}^2}{b_1\sigma_{\varepsilon_2}^2 - (b_1 + b_2)r_{\varepsilon_1\varepsilon_2}\sigma_{\varepsilon_1}\sigma_{\varepsilon_2} + b_2\sigma_{\varepsilon_1}^2},$$

(15)

$$b_{xy} = \frac{b_1\sigma_{\alpha_2'}^2 - (b_1 + b_2)r_{\alpha_1'\alpha_2'}\sigma_{\alpha_1'}\sigma_{\alpha_2'} + b_2\sigma_{\alpha_1'}^2}{\sigma_{\alpha_2'}^2 - 2r_{\alpha_1'\alpha_2'}\sigma_{\alpha_1'}\sigma_{\alpha_2'} + \sigma_{\alpha_1'}^2},$$

and

$$b_{yx} = \frac{b_1^2\sigma_{\alpha_2'}^2 - 2b_1b_2r_{\alpha_1'\alpha_2'}\sigma_{\alpha_1'}\sigma_{\alpha_2'} + b_2^2\sigma_{\alpha_1'}^2}{b_1\sigma_{\alpha_2'}^2 - (b_1 + b_2)r_{\alpha_1'\alpha_2'}\sigma_{\alpha_1'}\sigma_{\alpha_2'} + b_2\sigma_{\alpha_1'}^2},$$

where $\sigma_{\alpha_2'} = \sigma_{(\alpha_2 + \varepsilon_1)}$, $\sigma_{\alpha_1'} = \sigma_{(\alpha_1 + \varepsilon_1)}$, and so forth.

Any one of the four types of supply and demand conditions considered in the introduction may be described in terms of σ_{α_1}, σ_{α_2}, σ_{ε_1}, σ_{ε_2}, $\sigma_{\alpha_1'}$, and $\sigma_{\alpha_2'}$ as indicated in Table 1. By substituting in Eqs. (15) the values of

Table 1. Description of demand and supply movements in terms of the standard deviations of their shifts

	Demand conditions	*Description*
Fixed		$\sigma_{\alpha_2} = 0$; $\sigma_{\varepsilon_2} = 0$; $\sigma_{\alpha_2'} = 0$
Random shifts		$\sigma_{\alpha_2} = 0$; $\sigma_{\varepsilon_2} > 0$; $\sigma_{\alpha_2'} = \sigma_{\varepsilon_2}$
Regular shifts		$\sigma_{\alpha_2} > 0$; $\sigma_{\varepsilon_2} = 0$; $\sigma_{\alpha_2'} = \sigma_{\alpha_2}$
Regular plus random shifts		$\sigma_{\alpha_2} > 0$; $\sigma_{\varepsilon_2} > 0$; $\sigma_{\alpha_2'} = \sigma_{\alpha_2 + \varepsilon_2}$
	Supply conditions	
Fixed		$\sigma_{\alpha_1} = 0$; $\sigma_{\varepsilon_1} = 0$; $\sigma_{\alpha_1'} = 0$
Random shifts		$\sigma_{\alpha_1} = 0$; $\sigma_{\varepsilon_1} > 0$; $\sigma_{\alpha_1'} = \sigma_{\varepsilon_1}$
Regular shifts		$\sigma_{\alpha_1} > 0$; $\sigma_{\varepsilon_1} = 0$; $\sigma_{\alpha_1'} = \sigma_{\alpha_1}$
Regular plus random shifts		$\sigma_{\alpha_1} > 0$; $\sigma_{\varepsilon_1} > 0$; $\sigma_{\alpha_1'} = \sigma_{\alpha_1 + \varepsilon_1}$

the standard deviations given in Table 1 for any hypothesis as to the nature of demand and supply shifts, we obtain a set of regression coefficients stated in terms of the parameters of the supply and demand functions for the particular hypothesis involved. Regression coefficients for the XY scatter and the xy scatter have been computed in this manner and the results are summarized in Table 2 for various assumptions about supply and demand shifts. The coefficients marked "meaningless" in the table are those for which the derived coefficient has no necessary relation to the supply or demand elasticity.

When we analyze Table 2, all situations in which the XY coefficients are equal to the xy coefficients may be discarded immediately, since the correlated residuals in such cases yield no information which may not be determined directly from the price-quantity scatter. The discarded cases are as follows: (a) supply fixed, random demand shifts; (b) supply fixed, random plus regular demand shifts; (c) demand fixed, random supply shifts; (d) demand fixed, random plus regular supply shifts; (e) random shifts in both supply and demand. The cases where there are no random shifts in either supply or demand may also be eliminated, as they yield indeterminate results.[8] The remaining cases are those in which one of the curves shifts in a regular manner while the shift in the other contains a random element.

Where one of the curves is subject to random shifts while the other is not, the method yields the elasticity of the curve which does not shift in a random manner.[9] Thus if supply is subject to random shifts while demand shifts in a regular manner, the method yields the elasticity of demand. Further, the results are not altered if there is a regular change in supply in addition to the random shifts. Likewise, a situation in which random shifts in demand are accompanied by regular shifts in supply will make possible the derivation of the supply elasticity regardless of whether or not the random demand shifts are accompanied by additional regular changes. The cases in which the method yields the demand elasticity, and where the same information may not be obtained directly from the price-quantity scatter are (a) random shifts in supply, regular shifts in demand; and (b) random plus regular shifts in supply, regular shifts in demand. In an analogous manner, the method may be used for deriving the supply elasticity in the following cases; (a) random shifts in demand, regular shifts in supply; (b) random plus regular shifts in demand, regular shifts in supply.

8. Indeterminateness results from the fact that the price and quantity trend lines fit the data perfectly so that all residuals are zero.

9. R. G. D. Allen has shown that Professor Pigou's "logarithmic" method yields similar results, where the shifts which I have characterized as "regular" are approximately linear. See Allen's "A Critical Examination of Professor Pigou's Method of Deriving Demand Elasticity," *Econometrica*, 2 (July 1934), 249–257.

Table 2. A comparison of the regression coefficients of residuals with regression coefficients of price-quantity scatter for various assumptions regarding supply and demand shifts

Condition	Demand fixed	Regular demand shifts	Random demand shifts	Regular plus random demand shifts
Supply fixed	$\left.\begin{array}{l}B_{XY}\\B_{YX}\\b_{xy}\\b_{yx}\end{array}\right\}$ Indeterminate	$\left.\begin{array}{l}B_{XY}\\B_{YX}\end{array}\right\}$ Indeterminate $\left.\begin{array}{l}b_{xy}\\b_{yx}\end{array}\right\}=b_1$	$\left.\begin{array}{l}B_{XY}\\B_{YX}\\b_{xy}\\b_{yx}\end{array}\right\}=b_1$	$\left.\begin{array}{l}B_{XY}\\B_{YX}\\b_{xy}\\b_{yx}\end{array}\right\}=b_1$
Regular supply shifts	$\left.\begin{array}{l}B_{XY}\\B_{YX}\end{array}\right\}$ Indeterminate $\left.\begin{array}{l}b_{xy}\\b_{yx}\end{array}\right\}=b_2$	$\left.\begin{array}{l}B_{XY}\\B_{YX}\end{array}\right\}$ Indeterminate $\left.\begin{array}{l}b_{xy}\\b_{yx}\end{array}\right\}$ Meaningless	$\left.\begin{array}{l}B_{XY}\\B_{YX}\end{array}\right\}=b_1$ $\left.\begin{array}{l}b_{xy}\\b_{yx}\end{array}\right\}$ Meaningless	$\left.\begin{array}{l}B_{XY}\\B_{YX}\end{array}\right\}=b_1$ $\left.\begin{array}{l}b_{xy}\\b_{yx}\end{array}\right\}$ Meaningless
Random supply shifts	$\left.\begin{array}{l}B_{XY}\\B_{YX}\\b_{xy}\\b_{yx}\end{array}\right\}=b_2$	$\left.\begin{array}{l}B_{XY}\\B_{YX}\end{array}\right\}=b_2$ $\left.\begin{array}{l}b_{xy}\\b_{yx}\end{array}\right\}$ Meaningless	$\begin{array}{l}B_{XY}=b_{xy}*\\B_{YX}=b_{yx}*\end{array}$	$\left.\begin{array}{l}B_{XY}\\B_{YX}\end{array}\right\}$ * $\left.\begin{array}{l}b_{xy}\\b_{yx}\end{array}\right\}$ Meaningless
Regular plus random supply shifts	$\left.\begin{array}{l}B_{XY}\\B_{YX}\end{array}\right\}=b_2$ $\left.\begin{array}{l}b_{xy}\\b_{yx}\end{array}\right\}$ Meaningless	$\left.\begin{array}{l}B_{XY}\\B_{YX}\end{array}\right\}=b_2$ $\left.\begin{array}{l}b_{xy}\\b_{yx}\end{array}\right\}$ Meaningless	$\left.\begin{array}{l}B_{XY}\\B_{YX}\end{array}\right\}$ * $\left.\begin{array}{l}b_{xy}\\b_{yx}\end{array}\right\}$ Meaningless	$\left.\begin{array}{l}B_{XY}\\B_{YX}\end{array}\right\}$ * $\left.\begin{array}{l}b_{xy}\\b_{yx}\end{array}\right\}$ Meaningless

* The degree to which these cases approach either the demand or the supply elasticity depends upon the size of the random demand shifts as compared with the random supply shifts. See Table 3.

Consider now the cases in which there are random shifts in both supply and demand. The results in such circumstances depend upon whether the shifts which are random with respect to time are also uncorrelated with one another. Consider first the case in which there is no correlation between ε_2 and ε_1. The first two equations of (15) then become

(16)
$$B_{XY} = \frac{b_1 \sigma_{\varepsilon_2}^2 + b_2 \sigma_{\varepsilon_1}^2}{\sigma_{\varepsilon_2}^2 + \sigma_{\varepsilon_1}^2}$$

and
$$B_{YX} = \frac{b_1^2 \sigma_{\varepsilon_2}^2 + b_2^2 \sigma_{\varepsilon_1}^2}{b_1 \sigma_{\varepsilon_2}^2 + b_2 \sigma_{\varepsilon_1}^2}.$$

Thus the degree to which the derived coefficients approach either the elasticity of supply or the elasticity of demand depends upon the size of the random shifts in demand as compared with the random shifts in supply. Call the ratio between the second moment of the random demand shifts and the second moment of the random supply shifts ρ. Equations (16) may then be rewritten

(17)
$$B_{XY} = \frac{b_1 \rho + b_2}{\rho + 1}$$

and
$$B_{YX} = \frac{b_1^2 \rho + b_2^2}{b_1 \rho + b_2}.$$

Two extreme cases may be noted immediately: (a) If the random demand fluctuations are very large compared with the random supply fluctuations, so that ρ approaches an infinite value, both the regression coefficients will approach the value of the elasticity of supply. (b) If the random demand fluctuations are negligible compared with the random supply fluctuations, so that ρ approaches zero, both the regression coefficients will approach the value of the elasticity of demand. Between these two limits, the derived coefficients may approach one or the other of the two elasticities, or may be entirely meaningless, depending upon the relative sizes of the random shifts. The amplitude of such shifts cannot be measured entirely by the standard deviations of the intercepts unless the shifts are defined exclusively in a horizontal direction. The proposition is illustrated graphically in Fig. 1 where the shift of curve I to I' is seen to be larger than the shift of H to H', although both sets of curves show the same amplitude of horizontal shift. In other words, ρ is

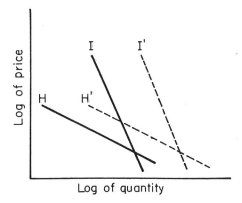

Figure 1. Influence of slope on amplitude shift

an inadequate measure of relative random shifts for our purpose; we must also assume something about the relative steepness of the curves.

Let $\pi = -b_2/b_1$. Rewrite Eq. (17) as follows:[10]

(18) $$B_{XY} = \frac{b_1(\rho - \pi)}{\rho + 1} \equiv \frac{b_2(\pi - \rho)}{\pi(\rho + 1)}$$

and $$B_{YX} = \frac{b_1(\rho + \pi^2)}{\rho - \pi} \equiv \frac{b_2(\rho + \pi^2)}{\pi(\pi - \rho)}.$$

When $\rho = \pi$ it is apparent the B_{XY} has a value of zero and B_{YX} an infinite value. This situation will be defined as one of equal amplitude in shifts; it is characterized by the fact that the correlation between the trend residuals is zero. Where $\rho > \pi$, both coefficients of regression are positive; this is the case of greater relative random fluctuations in demand. When $\rho < \pi$, the regression coefficients are both negative, and we have a situation in which the relative amplitudes of random supply fluctuations are larger.[11]

In Table 3 the degree to which the regression coefficients approximate the demand or supply elasticity has been recorded. The table may best be explained by considering the cases where the supply and demand elasticities are equal (that is, $\pi = 1$). For such cases, a good

10. Part of the transformations in Eqs. (18) are valid only for finite values of π other than zero; in other words, I am assuming that neither the supply nor the demand curve has an elasticity of zero or an infinite elasticity.

11. For a more complete discussion of the relation between the correlation of a price-quantity scatter diagram, the correlation of residuals, and the relative amplitudes of random shifts, see Frisch, "Pitfalls in Statistical Construction" (reference 5), pp. 14–20.

Table 3. Approximations to supply and demand elasticities: cases involving random fluctuations in both supply and demand

Ratio of demand elasticity to supply elasticity (π)

ρ \ π	∞		$\frac{1}{16}$		$\frac{1}{4}$		1		4		16	
	B_{XY}	B_{YX}	B_{XY}	B_{YX}	B_{XY}	B_{YX}	B_{XY}	B_{YX}	B_{XY}	B_{YX}	B_{XY}	B_{YX}
∞	b_1	b_1	b_1	b_1	b_1	b_1	b_1	b_1	b_1	b_1	b_1	b_1
16	b_1	b_1	$0.94b_1$	$1.01b_1$	$0.93b_1$	$1.02b_1$	$0.88b_1$	$1.13b_1$	$0.71b_1$	$2.67b_1$	0	∞
4	b_1	b_1	$0.79b_1$	$1.02b_1$	$0.75b_1$	$1.08b_1$	$0.60b_1$	$1.67b_1$	0	∞	$0.15b_2$	$1.35b_2$
1	b_1	b_1	$0.47b_1$	$1.07b_1$	$0.37b_1$	$1.42b_1$	0	∞	$0.37b_2$	$1.42b_2$	$0.47b_2$	$1.07b_2$
$\frac{1}{4}$	b_1	b_1	$0.15b_1$	$1.35b_1$	0	∞	$0.60b_2$	$1.67b_2$	$0.75b_2$	$1.08b_2$	$0.79b_2$	$1.02b_2$
$\frac{1}{16}$	b_1	b_1	0	∞	$0.71b_2$	$2.67b_2$	$0.88b_2$	$1.13b_2$	$0.93b_2$	$1.02b_2$	$0.94b_2$	$1.01b_2$
0	b_2	b_2	b_2	b_2	b_2	b_2	b_2	b_2	b_2	b_2	b_2	b_2

Ratio of variances of random demand and supply shifts (ρ)

approximation to the demand elasticity is obtained if the random fluctuations in supply are at least four times as large as the random fluctuations in demand (in other words, $\rho = 1/16$). Likewise, where the random demand fluctuations are at least four times the size of the random supply fluctuations, the regression coefficients approximate the elasticity of supply. One of the regression coefficients will always be larger than the true elasticity while the other will be smaller. Some kind of average of the regression coefficients may therefore give better results than either of the coefficients alone.[12]

Moreover, as the regression coefficients approach the value of the supply or demand elasticity, the coefficient of correlation between trend residuals of prices and trend residuals of quantities becomes large, having a positive value if the results approximate the elasticity of supply and a negative value if the results approximate the elasticity of demand. It might seem, therefore, that the coefficient of correlation could be used as an indication of the reliability of results. Such, indeed, would be the·case were it not for the possibility, first that other than random fluctuations be included in the residuals, and second that the random movements, while uncorrelated with time, be correlated among themselves. We shall next consider the second of these two possibilities, deferring the first to a later stage of the discussion.

Consider the limiting case in which there is perfect linear correlation between the random supply shifts and the random demand shifts. Let $\varepsilon_1 = \omega \varepsilon_2$ be the relation between the shifts. From Eqs. (15) it appears that[13]

$$(19) \qquad B_{XY} = B_{YX} = \frac{b_1 - \omega b_2}{1 - \omega}.$$

The coefficient of correlation between trend residuals of price and trend residuals of quantity has a value of ± 1 in this situation, but the high coefficient does not indicate that the regression coefficients approximate either the demand or supply elasticity. Equation (19) shows that the regression coefficients will approach the value of the demand elasticity when ω becomes large (that is, when the random fluctuations of supply

12. Professor Henry Schultz, *Theory and Measurement of Demand* (reference 4), p. 148, suggested a curve which minimizes the squares of the normals.

13. R. G. D. Allen derives similar results for the case of correlated price-quantity observation errors. Cf. his "The Assumptions of Linear Regression," *Economica*, 6 (May 1939), 197. Cf. also Frisch, "Pitfalls in Statistical Construction (reference 5), p. 18.

are much greater than the random demand fluctuations). Similarly, the derived coefficients approach the supply elasticity when ω is small.

In Fig. 2 B_{XY} has been plotted as a function of ω for the case in which $b_1 = 4$ and $b_2 = -2$. The figure shows that the regression coefficients

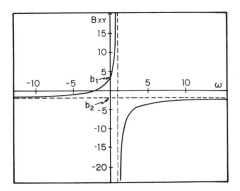

Figure 2. Approximation to supply or demand elasticity where the "random" shifts are linearly correlated. In this instance, $b_1 = 4$ and $b_2 = -2$.

may deviate very far from either the supply or the demand elasticity, even when the coefficient of partial correlation has a value of unity. Hence a high partial correlation between X and Y may indicate one of two possibilities: (a) The random fluctuations in one of the two curves are much smaller than the random fluctuations in the other, in which case the derived regression coefficients will be good approximations to the elasticity of the curve whose random fluctuations are the smaller; or (b) the random fluctuations, while uncorrelated with time, are correlated with one another, in which case no significance attaches to the derived regression coefficients. Thus we may conclude that the partial coefficient of correlation between trend residuals is not a reliable measure of the degree to which the regression coefficients approximate the supply or demand elasticity, except where it is reasonable to assume that no correlation exists between the parts of the supply and demand shifts which are random with respect to time.[14]

Throughout the preceding discussion the assumption has been made that the regular parts of supply and demand shifts could be described

14. It may be argued that cases of correlated supply and demand shifts have no theoretical significance for statistical demand studies, since the invariant relation in such cases is not between the price of a good and the amount demanded, but between shifts in supply and shifts in demand. I am indebted to Professor W. W. Leontief for this way of looking at the matter. Cf. Leontief, "Pitfalls in the Construction of Demand and Supply Curves: A Reply," *Quarterly Journal of Economics*, 48 (February 1934), 357–359.

by nth-degree polynomials, and that polynomials of this degree actually were fitted to the time series of price and quantity logarithms. We shall now see in what respects the conclusions will be altered if the "degree" of the fitted trend lines differs from the "degree" of the regular shift elements.

Consider first the case where the polynomials describing supply and demand shifts are of higher degree than the polynomials fitted to the price and quantity series. Write

(20)
$$a_{2i} = \alpha_{20} + \alpha_{21}t_i + \alpha_{22}t_i^2 + \cdots + \alpha_{2u}t_i^u$$

and
$$a_{1i} = \alpha_{10} + \alpha_{11}t_i + \alpha_{12}t_i^2 + \cdots + \alpha_{1v}t_i^v.$$
$$(n < u < v)$$

Suppose that nth-degree polynomials are fitted to the x and y series. Let U and V denote symmetrical $(u + 1)$th and $(v + 1)$th order determinants in the moments of t, of the same type as Δ. By the method previously demonstrated, it may be shown that

(21)
$$\alpha_{2k} = \sum_{r=0}^{u} m_{\alpha_2 r} U'_{(r+1)(k+1)}$$

and
$$\alpha_{1k} = \sum_{r=0}^{v} m_{\alpha_1 r} V'_{(r+1)(k+1)}.$$

Here, however, no simple linear relation exists between the β's and the α's, since the determinants which enter into the α's are now of a different order from those which enter into the β's. Hence it follows that T_x and T_y cannot be expressed as linear functions of a_1 and a_2.

The problem may be restated thus. Since a_1 is a vth-degree polynomial in t, no polynomial of degree less than v will remove completely from the price series and the quantity series the effects of regular shifts in supply. Similarly, no polynomial of degree less than u will remove completely the effects of regular shifts in demand. Accordingly, if the polynomials fitted to the price and quantity series are not sufficiently flexible, the residuals will contain not only the effects of random shifts in supply and demand, but a part of the "trend effect" as well. There is no reason, in such cases, for the derived coefficients of regression to approximate either the supply or demand elasticity.

We may now examine the effect of choosing a trend polynomial which contains more degrees of freedom than are necessary to remove the regular demand and supply shifts. Suppose, for example, that a_1 and a_2 may be described by λth-degree polynomials in t, while nth-degree polynomials are fitted to the price and quantity series ($\lambda < n$). It may be shown that no theoretical distortion would arise in this case, provided that ε_1 and ε_2 actually were random with respect to time. For the λth-degree polynomials describing a_1 and a_2 may always be extended to nth-degree polynomials simply by adding new terms whose coefficients are zero. The relations established in Eq. (9) between the β's and the α's will hold as before. Since α_{1k} and α_{2k} are both zero for all values of k greater than λ, it follows that the empirically determined coefficients β_{xk} and β_{yk} should also be zero for values of k greater than λ. In other words, the investigator should discover that he has fitted a polynomial whose degree is higher than necessary to describe the regular fluctuations.

Actually, however, the coefficients of $t^{\lambda+1}, \ldots, t^n$ will never be exactly equal to zero, since the "random" fluctuations ε_1 and ε_2 can never be entirely random (in the correlation sense) with respect to the powers of t. Thus both $m_{\varepsilon_2 r}$ and $m_{\varepsilon_1 r}$ will diverge from zero for large values of r. In other words, if the polynomials fitted to the data are high-degree polynomials, the trend lines not only will remove the effects of regular supply and demand shifts, but will also "smooth" into the trend lines a part of the random elements which should be left as residuals.

Two conflicting considerations therefore affect the selection of trend lines. If the curves fitted to the data are parabolas of low degree, a part of the "regular" supply and demand shifts which it is intended to remove will remain in the residuals. On the other hand, if high-degree parabolas are fitted, the curves will remove not only the trend effect but also a portion of the random element. A distortion of the results will occur in all cases except those in which the trend movements can be described by simple parabolas. In other words, the method is limited to those situations in which the trend effect may be eliminated by parabolas of low degree.[15]

The manner in which the preceding results are changed by the presence of errors of observation may now be examined.[16] Suppose that the ith-quantity observation differs from its equilibrium value by an

---

15. See Henry Schultz, *Statistical Laws of Demand and Supply* (Chicago, University of Chicago Press, 1928), pp. 47–54.

16. For a discussion of the influence of observation errors, see Allen, "Assumptions of Linear Regression" (reference 13), pp. 191–201. Allen, however, confines his analysis to the case of a linear relation obscured by observation errors and does not consider the possibility that other elements may be included in the residuals.

error of observation, θ_i, and that the ith price contains an error, τ_i. If the observational errors are random, it follows that $m_{\theta r}$ and $m_{\tau r}$ are equal to zero for small values of r, so that the shapes of the price and quantity trend lines are unaffected by the errors. Hence

(22)
$$X_i = \gamma(b_1\varepsilon_{2i} - b_2\varepsilon_{1i}) + \theta_i$$
and
$$Y_i = \gamma(\varepsilon_{2i} - \varepsilon_{1i}) + \tau_i.$$

Consider the special case in which demand shifts are regular while supply shifts are random, so that $\varepsilon_{2i} = 0$. Assuming no correlation between θ and τ, we may write

(23)
$$B_{XY} = \frac{b_2\gamma^2\sigma_{\varepsilon_1}^2}{\gamma^2\sigma_{\varepsilon_1}^2 + \sigma_\tau^2}$$

and
$$B_{YX} = \frac{b_2^2\gamma^2\sigma_{\varepsilon_1}^2 + \sigma_\theta^2}{b_2\gamma^2\sigma_{\varepsilon_1}^2}.$$

The extent of the error in the regression coefficients is thus seen to depend upon the size of the observation errors *as compared with the random supply fluctuations*. If the random supply fluctuations are large, errors of observation may not distort the results materially, while a small random supply fluctuation means that errors of observation will play an important role in the determination of B_{XY} and B_{YX}.[17] It seems then that random supply fluctuations not only are necessary to the derivation of the demand elasticity, but that the reliability of the derived coefficient varies directly with the square of such supply fluctuations whenever the problem is complicated by errors of observation.

In the extreme case where there are no random fluctuations in either supply or demand—the indeterminate case previously considered—the regression coefficients will be determinate but will represent the results of correlating the observational errors θ and τ. This is the case of "fictitious determinateness created by random errors."[18] Unlike the cases of meaningless coefficients determined from random shifts which are correlated with one another, the cases of "fictitious determinateness" may be detected quite readily by the Frisch "bunch map"

17. Once again, the Moore-Schultz correlation technique yields results similar to those obtained by the Pigou method. Cf. Allen, "A Critical Examination" (reference 9), p. 253.
18. Frisch, "Pitfalls in Statistical Construction" (reference 5), pp. 7–10.

technique, treating $t, t^2, \ldots, t^n$ as independent variables and correlating them with x and y.[19]

To summarize the results thus far, we have seen that the method of correlating trend residuals yields a derivation of the elasticity of demand for all situations in which the supply curve shifts in a random manner while the demand fluctuations are regular. A good approximation to the demand elasticity is obtained where there are also random demand fluctuations, provided that the random supply fluctuations are at least four times as large, on the average, as the random demand fluctuations. The validity of our conclusions is limited, however, to those products whose underlying "regular" supply and demand shifts are fairly simple; otherwise errors arise, either from smoothing a part of the random element into the trends when a sufficiently complicated trend line is chosen, or from leaving a part of the trend effect in the residuals when the trend line is too simple. Finally, the magnitude of the distortion arising from observational errors depends not only upon the size of such errors, but also upon the size of the random supply and demand fluctuations. In the following sections the method of trend residuals analyzed above will be compared with the multiple correlation and trend ratio methods.

The Method of Multiple Correlation

Demand studies sometimes allow for the effects of demand and supply shifts by fitting to the data a surface of the form,

$$(24) \qquad x = hy + \delta_0 + \delta_1 t + \delta_2 t + \cdots + \delta_n t^n.$$

Professor Ragnar Frisch and Dr. Frederick V. Waugh have shown that for those cases in which $n = 1$, this method is equivalent to correlating the trend residuals.[20] Their conclusions may be extended to the more general case, provided that the supply and demand shifts are of the types characterized in the introduction. By the least-squares technique, it is easily established that

19. Ragnar Frisch, *Statistical Confluence Analysis by Means of Complete Regression Systems*, Publication No. 5 (Oslo, University Economic Institute, 1934), 83–115.

20. Frisch and Waugh, "Partial Time Regressions as Compared with Individual Trends," *Econometrica*, I (October 1933), 387–401.

$$(25) \qquad h = \frac{\begin{vmatrix} m_{xy} & m_{yo} & \cdots & m_{yn} \\ m_{xo} & & & \\ \cdot & & & \\ \cdot & & \Delta & \\ \cdot & & & \\ m_{xn} & & & \end{vmatrix}}{\begin{vmatrix} m_{yy} & m_{yo} & \cdots & m_{yn} \\ m_{yo} & & & \\ \cdot & & & \\ \cdot & & \Delta & \\ \cdot & & & \\ m_{yn} & & & \end{vmatrix}}.$$

Expanding both numerator and denominator on the first row and simplifying the result, we have

$$(26) \qquad h = \frac{m_{xy} - \beta_{xo} m_{yo} - \beta_{x1} m_{y1} - \cdots - \beta_{xn} m_{yn}}{m_{yy} - \beta_{yo} m_{yo} - \beta_{y1} m_{y1} - \cdots - \beta_{yn} m_{yn}},$$

which may be written more conveniently

$$(27) \qquad h = \frac{m_{xy} - m_{yTx}}{m_{yy} - m_{yTy}}.$$

The value of h obtained above may be compared with the regression coefficient B_{XY} obtained earlier. From Eq. (13) it appears that

$$(28) \qquad B_{XY} = \frac{m_{xy} - m_{yTx} - m_{xTy} + m_{TxTy}}{m_{yy} - 2m_{yTy} + m_{TyTy}}.$$

But from Eqs. (11) and (12) we find

$$(29) \qquad m_{yTx} = m_{xTy} = m_{TxTy}$$

and

$$m_{yTy} = m_{TyTy}.$$

Whence

$$(30) \qquad B_{XY} = \frac{m_{xy} - m_{yTx}}{m_{yy} - m_{yTy}} = h.$$

We have thus shown that where the demand and supply fluctuations may be described as compositions of regular plus random elements, and where the surface fitted to the data is sufficiently flexible to remove the regular elements, the multiple correlation technique yields results which are identical with those obtained by correlating the trend residuals. It follows that the partial regression of x on y obtained by multiple correlation will approximate the elasticity of demand under the same circumstances as those outlined in the previous section. In other words, the "shift conditions" necessary for the success of the multiple correlation method are the same as those required for the method of correlating trend residuals.

The Method of Trend Ratios

Let

$$(31) \qquad X_i = \frac{x_i}{T_{x_i}}$$

and

$$Y_i = \frac{y_i}{T_{y_i}}.$$

Substituting the values of Eqs. (11) and (12) for x_i, y_i, T_{x_i}, and T_{y_i}, we find

$$(32) \qquad X_i = 1 + b_1 \eta_i - b_2 \xi_i$$

and

$$Y_i = 1 + \zeta_i - v_i,$$

where

$$(33) \qquad \eta_i = \frac{\varepsilon_{2i}}{b_1 a_{2i} - b_2 a_{1i}}, \qquad \zeta_i = \frac{\varepsilon_{2i}}{a_{2i} - a_{1i}},$$

$$\xi_i = \frac{\varepsilon_{1i}}{b_1 a_{2i} - b_2 a_{1i}}, \quad \text{and} \quad v_i = \frac{\varepsilon_{1i}}{a_{2i} - a_{1i}}.$$

From Eqs. (32) we have

$$(34) \qquad B_{XY} = \frac{b_1(\mu_{\eta\zeta} - \mu_{\eta v}) - b_2(\mu_{\zeta\xi} - \mu_{v\xi})}{\mu_{\zeta\zeta} - 2\mu_{\zeta v} + \mu_{vv}}$$

and

$$B_{YX} = \frac{b_1{}^2\mu_{\eta\eta} - 2b_1 b_2 \mu_{\eta\xi} + b_2{}^2 \mu_{\xi\xi}}{b_1(\mu_{\eta\zeta} - \mu_{\eta v}) - b_2(\mu_{\zeta\xi} - \mu_{v\xi})},$$

where $\mu_{\eta\zeta}$ is the product-moment about the means of η and ζ, and so on.

We shall consider now the special case in which our earlier method yielded an exact elasticity of demand, namely, the case where there are random fluctuations in supply but only regular ones in demand. In this case $\varepsilon_{2i} = 0$, so that η_i and ζ_i are both zero. Hence Eqs. (34) reduce to

(35)
$$B_{XY} = b_2 \cdot \frac{\mu_{v\xi}}{\mu_{vv}}$$

and
$$B_{YX} = b_2 \cdot \frac{\mu_{\xi\xi}}{\mu_{v\xi}}.$$

In a similar manner, it may be shown that, where there are random fluctuations in demand but only regular fluctuations in supply,

(36)
$$B_{XY} = b_1 \cdot \frac{\mu_{\eta\zeta}}{\mu_{\zeta\zeta}}$$

and
$$B_{YX} = b_1 \cdot \frac{\mu_{\eta\eta}}{\mu_{\eta\zeta}}.$$

Something must be known about the moments, $\mu_{v\xi}$, μ_{vv}, and so forth, before the results of Eqs. (35) and (36) may be evaluated. To simplify the discussion, let us assume that there is no "trend movement" in either supply or demand so that both a_1 and a_2 are constants. In this case it is easily verified that

(37)
$$\frac{\mu_{v\xi}}{\mu_{vv}} = \frac{\mu_{\xi\xi}}{\mu_{v\xi}} = \frac{\mu_{\eta\zeta}}{\mu_{\zeta\zeta}} = \frac{\mu_{\eta\eta}}{\mu_{\eta\zeta}} = \frac{m_y}{m_x},$$

where m_y is the mean of the y's, and so on. Thus for the case of demand stability with random supply fluctuations, we have

(38)
$$B_{XY} = B_{YX} = b_2 \cdot \frac{m_y}{m_x}$$

and for the case of supply stability with random demand fluctuations

(39)
$$B_{XY} = B_{YX} = b_1 \cdot \frac{m_y}{m_x}.$$

The interpretation of Eqs. (38) and (39) depends upon what assumptions have been made regarding the nature of the original supply and demand curves. If the curves were assumed to be constant elasticity curves, so that all calculations have been carried through in logarithms, then Eqs. (38) and (39) will not yield the true elasticities. To correct them, we must multiply by the quotient of the average quantity logarithm by the average price logarithm. On the other hand, we might have carried through our calculations with actual prices and actual quantities (presumably on the assumption that the demand curves and supply curves could be represented by a series of parallel straight lines). In this case, $b_2 . m_y/m_x$ and $b_1 . m_y/m_x$ represent, in a sense, "average elasticities" and no corrections need be made.

The cases considered in this section thus far are trivial, however, since the desired information could have been obtained directly from the price-quantity scatter. We learned earlier that the important cases, from the point of view of demand analysis, are those in which there are trend movements in both supply and demand, with an additional random element in the supply shifts. In such cases, no simple values may be substituted for the moments of (35) and (36). It may be demonstrated, however, that the quotients approach the value m_y/m_x whenever the trends in prices and quantities are not too steep, so that $T_{x_i}/m_x = 1$ and $T_{y_i}/m_y = 1$. In this instance, the bias introduced by the use of trend ratios will not be large. On the other hand, if the slopes of the trend lines are large as compared with the mean quantities, the bias may be of considerable magnitude. Its origin may be found in the unequal weights given to equal deviations from the trend lines where the deviations appear at different parts of the trends.[21] Such bias will occur in all situations where there is a large upward or downward trend of prices or quantities except in the special case where the random fluctuations, while uncorrelated with the price and quantity trends, are nevertheless of such a character that the absolute value of the fluctuations are proportional to the values of the trend. For this reason, the method of correlating residuals seems preferable to the trend ratio procedure, although in many cases the trend movements are small enough that the results will not differ materially between the two methods.

Conclusion

We have seen that the trend residual, multiple correlation, and trend ratio techniques all yield substantially the same results in attempts to estimate demand and supply elasticities from market data. What practical consequences arise from this fact?

21. For an analysis of this problem in a slightly different connection, see W. L. Crum, A. C. Patton, and A. R. Tebbutt, *Introduction to Economic Statistics* (New York, McGraw-Hill, 1938), p. 351.

In the first place, similarity of results obtained by different methods provides no verification of derived elasticities. If one of the methods secures an incorrect elasticity, the other methods will err in the same direction *and for the same reasons.* Inaccurate elasticities do not arise primarily from a failure to adopt the correct method, but from the fact that the underlying demand and supply shifts do not correspond to those implied in the analysis. Thus we have found that none of the methods yields significant elasticities when both the supply and demand shifts are erratic and of comparable magnitude. Likewise, we have found that the most accurate approximation to the demand elasticity was obtained where the supply shifts were erratic and large, while the demand shifts were "regular." This probably accounts for the comparative success of demand studies with staple agricultural commodities where demand shifts occur slowly with changes in population and other factors, while supply is subject to large and erratic fluctuations from weather conditions. Similarly, we found that the methods yield accurate supply elasticities where supply shifts are regular while demand shifts are random.

Unfortunately, no general criteria exist for testing the reliability of results. In some cases, where there is little possibility that the random supply and demand shifts can be correlated, the size of the coefficient of partial correlation between price residuals and quantity residuals may give some indication of reliability. But if correlation does exist between the supply and demand shifts which are random with respect to time, then a high partial correlation coefficient does not indicate proximity to a demand or supply elasticity. The "bunch map" technique is also inadequate for this case, since no "exploding" of the regression coefficients will be apparent. However, in the situation where random demand and supply shifts are small or entirely absent, so that the partial correlation coefficient would be indeterminate except for the presence of errors of observation, the "bunch map" analysis will show clearly the danger of relying on the derived elasticity. In all cases it probably will be necessary to depend upon a knowledge of the industry under consideration as a test of the "reasonableness" of the shift assumptions implied in the study.

Finally, it should be borne in mind that the validity of our results is limited by the restrictive assumptions made in the introduction regarding the nature of the demand and supply curves themselves. For those to whom these restrictive assumptions are repugnant, a further line of approach may perhaps be suggested. A similar analysis might be carried through, permitting the slopes (b_1 and b_2) to vary at the same time that the curves shift horizontally or vertically. Were this to be done however, it would no longer be possible to speak of "the" elasticity of demand or supply, and any derived elasticity could only be a sort of average elasticity whose significance would depend upon the degree of dispersion of the slopes of the individual curves.